# PROGRAMMING LOGIC AND DESIGN INTRODUCTORY

**FOURTH EDITION**

Joyce Farrell

**Programming Logic and Design, Introductory, Fourth Edition**

by Joyce Farrell


**Managing Editor:**
William Pitkin III

**Senior Acquisitions Editor:**
Drew Strawbridge

**Senior Product Manager:**
Tricia Boyle

**Development Editor:**
Dan Seiter

**Marketing Manager:**
Brian Berkeley

**Associate Product Manager:**
Sarah Santoro

**Editorial Assistant:**
Jennifer Smith

**Production Editor:**
Jennifer Goguen

**Cover Designer:**
Steve Deschene

**Interior Designer:**
Betsy Young

**Compositor:**
GEX Publishing Services

**Manufacturing Coordinator:**
Justin Palmeiro





Printed in the United States of America

1 2 3 4 5 6 7 8 9 BU 08 07 06 05

For more information, contact Course Technology, 25 Thomson Place, Boston, Massachusetts, 02210.

Or find us on the World Wide Web at: www.course.com





ISBN 1-4188-3634-6

# BRIEF CONTENTS

# TABLE OF CONTENTS

# PREFACE

*Programming Logic and Design, Introductory, Fourth Edition* provides the beginning programmer with a guide to developing structured program logic. This textbook assumes no programming language experience. The writing is nontechnical and emphasizes good programming practices. The examples are business examples; they do not assume mathematical background beyond high school business math. Additionally, the examples illustrate one or two major points; they do not contain so many features that students become lost following irrelevant and extraneous details.

The examples in *Programming Logic and Design* have been created to provide students with a sound background in logic, no matter what programming languages they eventually use to write programs. This book can be used in a stand-alone logic course that students take as a prerequisite to a programming course, or as a companion book to an introductory programming text using any programming language.

## Organization and Coverage

*Programming Logic and Design, Introductory, Fourth Edition* introduces students to programming concepts and enforces good style and logical thinking. General programming concepts are introduced in Chapter 1. Chapter 2 discusses the key concepts of structure, including what structure is, how to recognize it, and, most importantly, the advantages to writing structured programs. Chapter 3 extends the information on structured programming to the area of modules. By Chapter 4 students can develop complete, structured business programs. Chapters 5 and 6 explore the intricacies of decision making and looping. Students learn to develop sophisticated programs that use control breaks and arrays in Chapters 7 and 8. Three appendices allow students to gain extra experience with structuring large unstructured programs, using the binary numbering system, and working with large decision tables.

*Programming Logic and Design* combines text explanation with flowcharts and pseudocode examples to provide students with alternative means of expressing structured logic. Numerous detailed, full-program exercises at the end of each chapter illustrate the concepts explained within the chapter, and reinforce understanding and retention of the material presented.

*Programming Logic and Design* distinguishes itself from other programming logic books in the following ways:

- It is written and designed to be non-language specific. The logic used in this book can be applied to any programming language.
- The examples are everyday business examples; no special knowledge of mathematics, accounting, or other disciplines is assumed.
- The concept of structure is covered earlier than in many other texts. Students are exposed to structure naturally, so they will automatically create properly designed programs.
- Text explanation is interspersed with both flowcharts and pseudocode so students can become comfortable with both logic development tools and understand their interrelationship.
- Complex programs are built through the use of complete business examples. Students see how an application is built from start to finish instead of studying only segments of programs.

## Features of the Text

This edition of the text includes several new features to help students become better programmers and understand the big picture in program development. Because examining programs critically and closely is a crucial programming skill, each chapter includes a "Find the Bugs" section in which programming examples are presented that contain syntax errors and logical errors for the student to find and correct. Each chapter contains a new "Detective Work" section that presents programming-related topics for the student to research. Each chapter also contains a new section called "Up For Discussion," in which questions present personal and ethical issues that programmers must consider. These questions can be used for written assignments or as a starting point for classroom discussions.

To improve students' comprehension of arrays as they are used in most modern programming languages, arrays are now covered as zero-based arrays. Learning about arrays in this way will help students make the transition to using arrays effectively in languages such as C++, Java, and C#.

Each chapter lists key terms and their definitions; the list appears in the order the terms are encountered in the chapter. Along with the chapter summary, the list of key terms provides a snapshot overview of a chapter's main ideas. A glossary at the end of the book lists all the key terms in alphabetical order, along with working definitions.

Multiple-choice review questions appear at the end of every chapter to allow students to test their comprehension of the major ideas and techniques presented. Additionally, multiple end-of-chapter flowcharting and pseudocoding exercises are included so students have more opportunities to practice concepts as they learn them.

*Programming Logic and Design* is a superior textbook because it includes the following features:

*New!*

- Microsoft® Office Visio® Professional 2003, 60-day version: This text includes Visio 2003, a diagramming program that helps users create flowcharts and diagrams easily while working through the text, enabling them to visualize concepts and learn more effectively.

*New!*

- Visual Logic™, version 2.0: Visual Logic™ is a simple but powerful tool for teaching programming logic and design without traditional high-level programming language syntax. Visual Logic uses flowcharts to explain essential programming concepts, including variables, input, assignment, output, conditions, loops, procedures, graphics, arrays, and files. It also has the ability to interpret and execute flowcharts, providing students with immediate and accurate feedback about their solutions. By executing student solutions, Visual Logic combines the power of a high-level language with the ease and simplicity of flowcharts.

  You have the option to bundle this software with your text! Please contact your Course Technology sales representative for more information.

- Interior design: A highly visual, full-color interior presents material in a way that is engaging and appealing to the reader.
- Objectives: Each chapter begins with a list of objectives so the student knows the topics that will be presented in the chapter. In addition to providing a quick reference to topics covered, this feature provides a useful study aid.

- Flowcharts: This book has plenty of figures and illustrations, including flowcharts, which provide the reader with a visual learning experience, rather than one that involves simply studying text. You can see an example of a flowchart in the sample page shown in this Preface.
- Pseudocode: This book also includes numerous examples of pseudocode, which illustrate correct usage of the programming logic and design concepts being taught. You can see an example of pseudocode in the sample page shown in this Preface.
- Tips: These notes provide additional information—for example, another location in the book that expands on a topic, or a common error to watch out for. You can see an example of a tip in the sample page shown in this Preface.
- Chapter summaries: Following each chapter is a summary that recaps the programming concepts and techniques covered in the chapter. This feature provides a concise means for students to review and check their understanding of the main points in each chapter.
- Key terms: Chapters end with a collection of all the key terms found throughout the chapter, as shown in the following sample. Definitions are included in sentence format and in the order in which they appear in the chapter.

SAMPLE LIST OF END-OF-CHAPTER KEY TERMS

## KEY TERMS

The **mainline logic** of a program is the overall logic of the main program from beginning to end.

A **housekeeping** module includes steps you must perform at the beginning of a program, to get ready for the rest of the program.

The **main loop** of a program contains the steps that are repeated for every record.

- Review questions: Review questions at the end of each chapter reinforce the main ideas introduced in the chapter, as shown in the following sample. Successfully answering these questions demonstrates mastery of the concepts and information presented.

SAMPLE REVIEW QUESTIONS

REVIEW QUESTIONS

**1. Input records usually contain ________.**

a. less data than an application needs
b. more data than an application needs
c. exactly the amount of data an application needs
d. none of the data an application needs

**2. A program in which one operation follows another from the beginning until the end is a ________ program.**

a. modular
b. functional
c. procedural
d. object-oriented

- Exercises: Each chapter concludes with meaningful programming exercises that provide students with additional practice of the skills and concepts they have learned. These exercises increase in difficulty and are designed to allow students to explore logical programming concepts. Each exercise can be completed using flowcharts, pseudocode, or both. In addition, instructors can choose to assign the exercises as programming problems to be coded and executed in a programming language.

The following figure shows an example of our highly visual design, including an example of the numbered lists, tips, flowcharts, and pseudocode seen throughout the text.

SAMPLE PAGE SHOWING KEY ELEMENTS FOUND IN THE TEXT



follows another from the beginning until the end. You write the entire set of instructions for a procedural program, and when the program executes, instructions take place one at a time, following your program's logic. The overall logic, or **mainline logic**, of almost every procedural computer program can follow a general structure that consists of three distinct parts:

1. Performing housekeeping, or initialization tasks. **Housekeeping** includes steps you must perform at the beginning of a program to get ready for the rest of the program.
2. Performing the main loop repeatedly within the program. The **main loop** contains the instructions that are executed for every record until you reach the end of the input of records, or `eof`.
3. Performing the end-of-job routine. The **end-of-job routine** holds the steps you take at the end of the program to finish the application.

TIP Not all programs are procedural; some are object-oriented. A distinguishing feature of many (but not all) object-oriented programs is that they are event-driven; often the user determines the timing of events in the main loop of the program by using an input device such as a mouse. As you advance in your knowledge of programming, you will learn more about object-oriented techniques.

You can write any procedural program as one long series of programming language statements, but most programmers prefer to break their programs into at least three parts. The main program can call the three major modules, as shown in the flowchart and pseudocode in Figure 4-6. The module or subroutine names, of course, are entirely up to the programmer.

TIP Reducing a large program into more manageable modules is sometimes called **functional decomposition**.

**FIGURE 4-6:** FLOWCHART AND PSEUDOCODE OF MAINLINE LOGIC

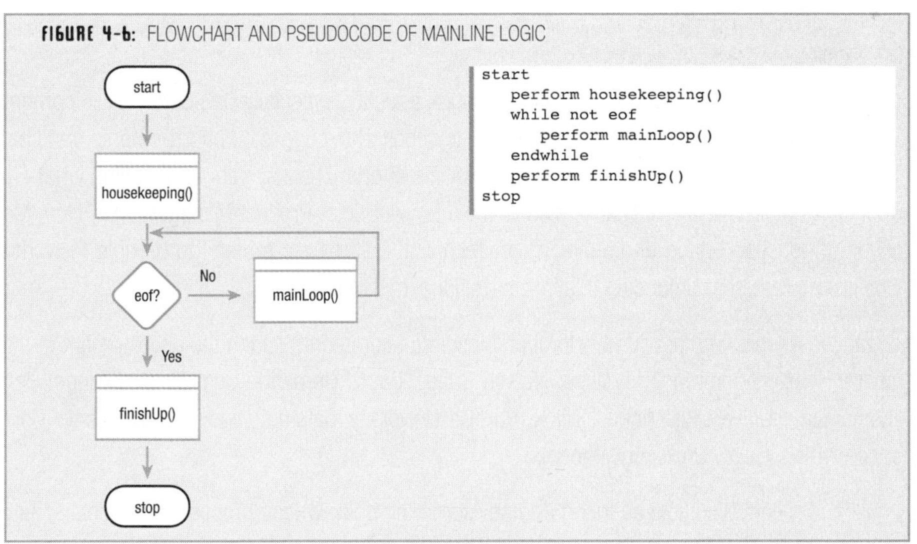


```
start
   perform housekeeping()
   while not eof
      perform mainLoop()
   endwhile
   perform finishUp()
stop
```

## Teaching Tools

The following supplemental materials are available when this book is used in a classroom setting. All of the teaching tools available with this book are provided to the instructor on a single CD-ROM.

**Electronic Instructor's Manual**. The Instructor's Manual that accompanies this textbook provides additional instructional material to assist in class preparation, including items such as Sample Syllabi, Chapter Outlines, Technical Notes, Lecture Notes, Quick Quizzes, Teaching Tips, Discussion Topics, and Key Terms.

**ExamView®**. This textbook is accompanied by ExamView, a powerful testing software package that allows instructors to create and administer printed, computer (LAN-based), and Internet exams. ExamView includes hundreds of questions that correspond to the topics covered in this text, enabling students to generate detailed study guides that include page references for further review. The computer-based and Internet testing components allow students to take exams at their computers, and save the instructor time by grading each exam automatically.

**PowerPoint Presentations**. This book comes with Microsoft PowerPoint slides for each chapter. These are included as a teaching aid for classroom presentation, to make available to students on the network for chapter review, or to be printed for classroom distribution. Instructors can add their own slides for additional topics they introduce to the class.

**Solutions**. Solutions to Review Questions and Exercises are provided on the Teaching Tools CD-ROM and may also be found on the Course Technology Web site at *www.course.com*. The solutions are password protected.

**Distance Learning**. Course Technology is proud to present online test banks in WebCT and Blackboard to provide the most complete and dynamic learning experience possible. Instructors are encouraged to make the most of the course, both online and offline. For more information on how to access the online test bank, contact your local Course Technology sales representative.

## Acknowledgments

I would like to thank all of the people who helped to make this book a reality, especially Dan Seiter, Development Editor, whose hard work and attention to detail have made this a quality textbook. Dan suggested improvements that I had never considered in the first three editions, and this is a better book for his efforts. Thanks, Dan, for knowing what changes I meant to make even if I forgot to make them. Thanks also to Tricia Boyle, Senior Product Manager; Will Pitkin, Managing Editor; Jennifer Goguen, Production Editor; and John Bosco, Technical Editor. I am grateful to be able to work with so many fine people who are dedicated to producing quality instructional materials.

I am grateful to the many reviewers who provided helpful and insightful comments during the development of this book, including Reni Abraham, Houston Community College; Nelson Capaz, Pasco Hernando Community College; Betty Clay, Southeastern Oklahoma State University; Michael Mick, Purdue University Calumet; Judy Scholl, Austin Community College; and Catherine Wyman, DeVry University, Phoenix.

Thanks, too, to my husband, Geoff, who acts as friend and advisor in the book-writing process. This book is, as were its previous editions, dedicated to him and to my daughters, Andrea and Audrey.

–Joyce Farrell

# 1 AN OVERVIEW OF COMPUTERS AND LOGIC

## After studying Chapter 1, you should be able to:

- Understand computer components and operations
- Describe the steps involved in the programming process
- Describe the data hierarchy
- Understand how to use flowchart symbols and pseudocode statements
- Use and name variables
- Use a sentinel, or dummy value, to end a program
- Use a connector symbol
- Assign values to variables
- Recognize the proper format of assignment statements
- Describe data types
- Understand the evolution of programming techniques

## UNDERSTANDING COMPUTER COMPONENTS AND OPERATIONS

Hardware and software are the two major components of any computer system. **Hardware** is the equipment, or the devices, associated with a computer. For a computer to be useful, however, it needs more than equipment; a computer needs to be given instructions. The instructions that tell the computer what to do are called **software**, or programs, and are written by programmers. This book focuses on the process of writing these instructions.

TIP □□□□ Software can be classified as application software or system software. Application software comprises all the programs you apply to a task—word-processing programs, spreadsheets, payroll and inventory programs, and even games. System software comprises the programs that you use to manage your computer—operating systems, such as Windows, Linux, or UNIX. This book focuses on the logic used to write application software programs, although many of the concepts apply to both types of software.

Together, computer hardware and software accomplish four major operations:

1. Input
2. Processing
3. Output
4. Storage

Hardware devices that perform **input** include keyboards and mice. Through these devices, **data**, or facts, enter the computer system. **Processing** data items may involve organizing them, checking them for accuracy, or performing mathematical operations on them. The piece of hardware that performs these sorts of tasks is the **central processing unit**, or **CPU**. After data items have been processed, the resulting information is sent to a printer, monitor, or some other **output** device so people can view, interpret, and use the results. Often, you also want to store the output information on storage hardware, such as magnetic disks, tapes, compact discs, or flash media. Computer software consists of all the instructions that control how and when the data items are input, how they are processed, and the form in which they are output or stored.

TIP □□□□ Data includes all the text, numbers, and other information that are processed by a computer. However, many computer professionals reserve the term "information" for data that has been processed. For example, your name, Social Security number, and hourly pay rate are data items, but your paycheck holds information.

Computer hardware by itself is useless without a programmer's instructions, or software, just as your stereo equipment doesn't do much until you provide music on a CD or tape. You can buy prewritten software that is stored on a disk or that you download from the Internet, or you can write your own software instructions. You can enter instructions into a computer system through any of the hardware devices you use for data; most often, you type your instructions using a keyboard and store them on a device such as a disk or CD.

You write computer instructions in a computer **programming language**, such as Visual Basic, C#, C++, Java, or COBOL. Just as some people speak English and others speak Japanese, programmers also write programs in different languages. Some programmers work exclusively in one language, whereas others know several and use the one that seems most appropriate for the task at hand.

No matter which programming language a computer programmer uses, the language has rules governing its word usage and punctuation. These rules are called the language's **syntax**. If you ask, "How the get to store do I?" in English, most people can figure out what you probably mean, even though you have not used proper English syntax. However, computers are not nearly as smart as most people; with a computer, you might as well have asked, "Xpu mxv ot dodnm cadf B?" Unless the syntax is perfect, the computer cannot interpret the programming language instruction at all.

Every computer operates on circuitry that consists of millions of on/off switches. Each programming language uses a piece of software to translate the specific programming language into the computer's on/off circuitry language, or **machine language**. The language translation software is called a **compiler** or **interpreter**, and it tells you if you have used a programming language incorrectly. Therefore, syntax errors are relatively easy to locate and correct—the compiler or interpreter you use highlights every syntax error. If you write a computer program using a language such as C++ but spell one of its words incorrectly or reverse the proper order of two words, the translator lets you know that it found a mistake by displaying an error message as soon as you try to translate the program.

**TIP** Although there are differences in how compilers and interpreters work, their basic function is the same—to translate your programming statements into code the computer can use. When you use a compiler, an entire program is translated before it can execute; when you use an interpreter, each instruction is translated just prior to execution. Usually, you do not choose which type of translation to use—it depends on the programming language. However, there are some languages for which both compilers and interpreters are available.

A program without syntax errors can be executed on a computer, but it might not produce correct results. For a program to work properly, you must give the instructions to the computer in a specific sequence, you must not leave any instructions out, and you must not add extraneous instructions. By doing this, you are developing the **logic** of the computer program. Suppose you instruct someone to make a cake as follows:

```
Stir
Add two eggs
Add a gallon of gasoline
Bake at 350 degrees for 45 minutes
Add three cups of flour
```

Even though you have used the English language syntax correctly, the instructions are out of sequence, some instructions are missing, and some instructions belong to procedures other than baking a cake. If you follow these instructions, you are not going to end up with an edible cake, and you may end up with a disaster. Logical errors are much more difficult to locate than syntax errors; it is easier for you to determine whether "eggs" is spelled incorrectly in a recipe than it is for you to tell if there are too many eggs or if they are added too soon.

**TIP** Programmers often call logical errors semantic errors. For example, if you misspell a programming language word, you commit a syntax error, but if you use an otherwise correct word that does not make any sense in the current context, you commit a **semantic error**.

Just as baking directions can be given correctly in French, German, or Spanish, the same logic of a program can be expressed in any number of programming languages. This book is almost exclusively concerned with the logic development process. Because this book is not concerned with any specific language, the programming examples could have been written in Japanese, C++, or Java. The logic is the same in any language. For convenience, the book uses English!

Once instructions have been input to the computer and translated into machine language, a program can be **run**, or **executed**. You can write a program that takes a number (an input step), doubles it (processing), and tells you the answer (output) in a programming language such as Java or C++, but if you were to write it using English-like statements, it would look like this:

```
Get inputNumber.
Compute calculatedAnswer as inputNumber times 2.
Print calculatedAnswer.
```

TIP

You will learn about the odd elimination of the space between words like "input" and "Number" and "calculated" and "Answer" in the next few pages.

The instruction to `Get inputNumber` is an example of an input operation. When the computer interprets this instruction, it knows to look to an input device to obtain a number. Computers often have several input devices, perhaps a keyboard, a mouse, a CD drive, and two or more disk drives. When you learn a specific programming language, you learn how to tell the computer which of those input devices to access for input. Logically, however, it doesn't really matter which hardware device is used, as long as the computer knows to look for a number. The logic of the input operation—that the computer must obtain a number for input, and that the computer must obtain it before multiplying it by two—remains the same regardless of any specific input hardware device. The same is true in your daily life. If you follow the instruction "Get eggs from store," it does not really matter if you are following a handwritten instruction from a list or a voice-mail instruction left on your cell phone—the process of getting the eggs, and the result of doing so, are the same.

TIP

Many computer professionals categorize disk drives and CD drives as storage devices rather than input devices. Such devices actually can be used for input, storage, and output.

Processing is the step that occurs when the arithmetic is performed to double the `inputNumber`; the statement `Compute calculatedAnswer as inputNumber times 2` represents processing. Mathematical operations are not the only kind of processing, but they are very typical. After you write a program, the program can be used on computers of different brand names, sizes, and speeds. Whether you use an IBM, Macintosh, Linux, or UNIX operating system, and whether you use a personal computer that sits on your desk or a mainframe that costs hundreds of thousands of dollars and resides in a special building in a university, multiplying by 2 is the same process. The hardware is not important; the processing will be the same.

In the number-doubling program, the `Print calculatedAnswer` statement represents output. Within a particular program, this statement could cause the output to appear on the monitor (which might be a flat panel screen or a cathode-ray tube), or the output could go to a printer (which could be laser or ink-jet), or the output could be written to a disk or CD. The logic of the process called "Print" is the same no matter what hardware device you use.

Besides input, processing, and output, the fourth operation in any computer system is storage. When computers produce output, it is for human consumption. For example, output might be displayed on a monitor or sent to a printer. Storage, on the other hand, is meant for future computer use (for example, when data items are saved on a disk).

Computer storage comes in two broad categories. All computers have **internal storage**, often referred to as **memory**, **main memory**, **primary memory**, or **random access memory (RAM)**. This storage is located inside the system unit of the machine. (For example, if you own a microcomputer, the system unit is the large case that holds your CD or other disk drives. On a laptop computer, the system unit is located beneath the keyboard.) Internal storage is the type of storage most often discussed in this book.

Computers also use **external storage**, which is **persistent** (relatively permanent) storage on a device such as a floppy disk, hard disk, flash media, or magnetic tape. In other words, external storage is outside the main memory, not necessarily outside the computer. Both programs and data sometimes are stored on each of these kinds of media.

To use computer programs, you must first load them into memory. You might type a program into memory from the keyboard, or you might use a program that has already been written and stored on a disk. Either way, a copy of the instructions must be placed in memory before the program can be run.

A computer system needs both internal memory and external storage. Internal memory is needed to run the programs, but internal memory is **volatile**—that is, its contents are lost every time the computer loses power. Therefore, if you are going to use a program more than once, you must store it, or **save** it, on some nonvolatile medium. Otherwise, the program in main memory is lost forever when the computer is turned off. External storage (usually disks or tape) provides a nonvolatile (or persistent) medium.

**TIP**

Even though a hard disk drive is located inside your computer, the hard disk is not main, internal memory. Internal memory is temporary and volatile; a hard drive is permanent, nonvolatile storage. After one or two "tragedies" of losing several pages of a typed computer program due to a power failure or other hardware problem, most programmers learn to periodically save the programs they are in the process of writing, using a nonvolatile medium such as a disk.

Once you have a copy of a program in main memory, you want to execute, or run, the program. To do so, you must also place any data that the program requires into memory. For example, after you place the following program into memory and start to run it, you need to provide an actual `inputNumber`—for example, 8—that you also place in main memory.

```
Get inputNumber.
Compute calculatedAnswer as inputNumber times 2.
Print calculatedAnswer.
```

The `inputNumber` is placed in memory at a specific memory location that the program will call `inputNumber`. Then, and only then, can the `calculatedAnswer`, in this case 16, be calculated and printed.

Computer memory consists of millions of numbered locations where data can be stored. The memory location of `inputNumber` has a specific numeric address, for example, 48604. Your program associates `inputNumber` with that address. Every time you refer to `inputNumber` within a program, the computer retrieves the value at the associated memory location. When you write programs, you seldom need to be concerned with the value of the memory address; instead, you simply use the easy-to-remember name you created.

Computer programmers often refer to memory addresses using hexadecimal notation, or base 16. Using this system, they might use a value like 42FF01A to refer to a memory address. Despite the use of letters, such an address is still a number. When you use the hexadecimal numbering system, the letters A through F stand for the values 10 through 15.

## UNDERSTANDING THE PROGRAMMING PROCESS

A programmer's job involves writing instructions (such as the three instructions in the doubling program in the preceding section), but a professional programmer usually does not just sit down at a computer keyboard and start typing. The programmer's job can be broken down into six programming steps:

1. Understanding the problem
2. Planning the logic
3. Coding the program
4. Using software to translate the program into machine language
5. Testing the program
6. Putting the program into production

### UNDERSTANDING THE PROBLEM

Professional computer programmers write programs to satisfy the needs of others. Examples could include a Human Resources Department that needs a printed list of all employees, a Billing Department that wants a list of clients who are 30 or more days overdue on their payments, and an office manager who wants to be notified when specific supplies reach the reorder point. Because programmers are providing a service to these users, programmers must first understand what it is the users want.

Suppose the director of human resources says to a programmer, "Our department needs a list of all employees who have been here over five years, because we want to invite them to a special thank-you dinner." On the surface, this seems like a simple enough request. An experienced programmer, however, will know that he or she may not yet understand the whole problem. Does the director want a list of full-time employees only, or a list of full- and part-time employees together? Does she want people who have worked for the company on a month-to-month contractual basis over the past five years, or only regular, permanent employees? Do the listed employees need to have worked for the organization for five years as of today, as of the date of the dinner, or as of some other cutoff date? What about an employee who worked three years, took a two-year leave of absence, and has been back for three years? Does he or she qualify? The programmer cannot make any of these decisions; the user is the one who must address these questions.

More decisions still might be required. For example, what does the user want the report of five-year employees to look like? Should it contain both first and last names? Social Security numbers? Phone numbers? Addresses? Is all this data available? Several pieces of documentation are often provided to help the programmer understand the problem. This documentation includes print layout charts and file specifications, which you will learn about in Chapter 3.

Really understanding the problem may be one of the most difficult aspects of programming. On any job, the description of what the user needs may be vague—worse yet, the user may not even really know what he or she wants, and users who think they know what they want frequently change their minds after seeing sample output. A good programmer is often part counselor, part detective!

## PLANNING THE LOGIC

The heart of the programming process lies in planning the program's logic. During this phase of the programming process, the programmer plans the steps of the program, deciding what steps to include and how to order them. You can plan the solution to a problem in many ways. The two most common planning tools are flowcharts and pseudocode. Both tools involve writing the steps of the program in English, much as you would plan a trip on paper before getting into the car, or plan a party theme before going shopping for food and favors.

**TIP** You may hear programmers refer to planning a program as "developing an algorithm." An **algorithm** is the sequence of steps necessary to solve any problem. You will learn more about flowcharts and pseudocode later in this chapter.

The programmer doesn't worry about the syntax of any particular language at this point, just about figuring out what sequence of events will lead from the available input to the desired output. Planning the logic includes thinking carefully about all the possible data values a program might encounter and how you want the program to handle each scenario. The process of walking through a program's logic on paper before you actually write the program is called **desk-checking**. You will learn more about planning the logic later; in fact, this book focuses on this crucial step almost exclusively.

## CODING THE PROGRAM

Once the programmer has developed the logic of a program, only then can he or she write the program in one of more than 400 programming languages. Programmers choose a particular language because some languages have built-in capabilities that make them more efficient than others at handling certain types of operations. Despite their differences, programming languages are quite alike—each can handle input operations, arithmetic processing, output operations, and other standard functions. The logic developed to solve a programming problem can be executed using any number of languages. It is only after a language is chosen that the programmer must worry about each command being spelled correctly and all of the punctuation getting into the right spots—in other words, using the correct *syntax*.

Some very experienced programmers can successfully combine the logic planning and the actual instruction writing, or **coding**, of the program in one step. This may work for planning and writing a very simple program, just as you can plan and write a postcard to a friend using one step. A good term paper or a Hollywood screenplay, however, needs planning before writing, and so do most programs.

Which step is harder, planning the logic or coding the program? Right now, it may seem to you that writing in a programming language is a very difficult task, considering all the spelling and grammar rules you must learn. However, the planning step is actually more difficult. Which is more difficult: thinking up the twists and turns to the plot of a best-selling mystery novel, or writing a translation of an already written novel from English to Spanish? And who do you think gets paid more, the writer who creates the plot or the translator? (Try asking friends to name any famous translator!)

## USING SOFTWARE TO TRANSLATE THE PROGRAM INTO MACHINE LANGUAGE

Even though there are many programming languages, each computer knows only one language, its machine language, which consists of many 1s and 0s. Computers understand machine language because computers themselves are made up of thousands of tiny electrical switches, each of which can be set in either the on or off state, which is represented by a 1 or 0, respectively.

Languages like Java or Visual Basic are available for programmers to use because someone has written a translator program (a compiler or interpreter) that changes the English-like **high-level programming language** in which the programmer writes into the **low-level machine language** that the computer understands. If you write a programming language statement incorrectly (for example, by misspelling a word, using a word that doesn't exist in the language, or using "illegal" grammar), the translator program doesn't know what to do and issues an error message identifying a **syntax error**, or misuse of a language's grammar rules. You receive the same response when you speak nonsense to a human-language translator. Imagine trying to look up a list of words in a Spanish-English dictionary if some of the listed words are misspelled—you can't complete the task until the words are spelled correctly. Although making errors is never desirable, syntax errors are not a major concern to programmers, because the compiler or interpreter catches every syntax error, and the computer will not execute a program that contains them.

A computer program must be free of syntax errors before you can execute it. Typically, a programmer develops a program's logic, writes the code, and then compiles the program, receiving a list of syntax errors. The programmer then corrects the syntax errors, and compiles the program again. Correcting the first set of errors frequently reveals a new set of errors that originally were not apparent to the compiler. For example, if you could use an English compiler and submit the sentence `The grl go to school`, the compiler at first would point out only one syntax error to you. The second word, `grl`, is illegal because it is not part of the English language. Only after you corrected the word `girl` would the compiler find another syntax error on the third word, `go`, because it is the wrong verb form for the subject `girl`. This doesn't mean `go` is necessarily the wrong word. Maybe `girl` is wrong; perhaps the subject should be `girls`, in which case `go` is right. Compilers don't always know exactly what you mean, nor do they know what the proper correction should be, but they do know when something is wrong with your syntax.

When writing a program, a programmer might need to recompile the code several times. An executable program is created only when the code is free of syntax errors. When you run an executable program, it typically also might require input data. Figure 1-1 shows a diagram of this entire process.

**FIGURE 1-1:** CREATING AN EXECUTABLE PROGRAM

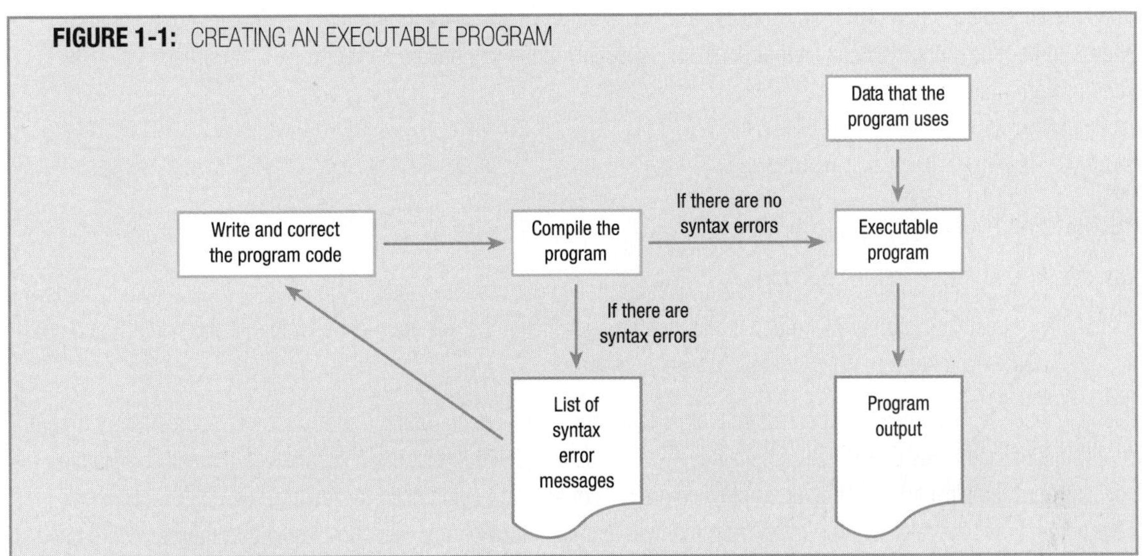


## TESTING THE PROGRAM

A program that is free of syntax errors is not necessarily free of **logical errors**. For example, the sentence `The girl goes to school`, although syntactically perfect, is not logically correct if the girl is a baby or a dropout.

Once a program is free from syntax errors, the programmer can test it—that is, execute it with some sample data to see whether the results are logically correct. Recall the number-doubling program:

```
Get inputNumber.
Compute calculatedAnswer as inputNumber times 2.
Print calculatedAnswer.
```

If you provide the value 2 as input to the program and the answer 4 prints, you have executed one successful test run of the program.

However, if the answer 40 prints, maybe it's because the program contains a logical error. Maybe the second line of code was mistyped with an extra zero, so that the program reads:

```
Get inputNumber.
Compute calculatedAnswer as inputNumber times 20.
Print calculatedAnswer.
```

The error of placing 20 instead of 2 in the multiplication statement caused a logical error. Notice that nothing is syntactically wrong with this second program—it is just as reasonable to multiply a number by 20 as by 2—but if the programmer intends only to double the `inputNumber`, then a logical error has occurred.

Programs should be tested with many sets of data. For example, if you write the program to double a number and enter 2 and get an output value of 4, that doesn't necessarily mean you have a correct program. Perhaps you have typed this program by mistake:

```
Get inputNumber.
Compute calculatedAnswer as inputNumber plus 2.
Print calculatedAnswer.
```

An input of 2 results in an answer of 4, but that doesn't mean your program doubles numbers—it actually only adds 2 to them. If you test your program with additional data and get the wrong answer—for example, if you use a 3 and get an answer of 5—you know there is a problem with your code.

Selecting test data is somewhat of an art in itself, and it should be done carefully. If the Human Resources Department wants a list of the names of five-year employees, it would be a mistake to test the program with a small sample file of only long-term employees. If no newer employees are part of the data being used for testing, you don't really know if the program would have eliminated them from the five-year list. Many companies don't know that their software has a problem until an unusual circumstance occurs—for example, the first time an employee has more than nine dependents, the first time a customer orders more than 999 items at a time, or when (in an example that was well-documented in the popular press) a new century begins.

## PUTTING THE PROGRAM INTO PRODUCTION

Once the program is tested adequately, it is ready for the organization to use. Putting the program into production might mean simply running the program once, if it was written to satisfy a user's request for a special list. However, the process might take months if the program will be run on a regular basis, or if it is one of a large system of programs being developed. Perhaps data-entry people must be trained to prepare the input for the new program, users must be trained to understand the output, or existing data in the company must be changed to an entirely new format to accommodate this program. **Conversion**, the entire set of actions an organization must take to switch over to using a new program or set of programs, can sometimes take months or years to accomplish.

**TIP**

You might consider maintaining programs as a seventh step in the programming process. After programs are put into production, making required changes is called maintenance. Maintenance is necessary for many reasons: for example, new tax rates are legislated, the format of an input file is altered, or the end user requires additional information not included in the original output specifications. Frequently, your first programming job will require maintaining previously written programs. When you maintain the programs others have written, you will appreciate the effort the original programmer put into writing clear code, using reasonable variable names, and documenting his or her work.

You might consider retiring the program as the eighth and final step in the programming process. A program is retired when it is no longer needed by an organization—usually when a new program is in the process of being put into production.

## UNDERSTANDING THE DATA HIERARCHY

Some very simple programs require very simple data. For example, the number-doubling program requires just one value as input. Most business programs, however, use much more data—inventory files list thousands of items, personnel and customer files list thousands of people. When data items are stored for use on computer systems, they are often stored in what is known as a **data hierarchy**, where the smallest usable unit of data is the character. **Characters** are letters, numbers, and special symbols, such as "A", "7", and "$". Anything you can type from the keyboard in one keystroke (including a space or a tab) is a character. Characters are made up of smaller elements called bits, but just as most human beings can use a pencil without caring whether atoms are flying around inside it, most computer users can store characters without caring about these bits.

**TIP** Computers also recognize characters you cannot enter from the keyboard, such as foreign alphabet characters like φ or Σ.

Characters are grouped together to form a field. A **field** is a single data item, such as `lastName`, `streetAddress`, or `annualSalary`. For most of us, an "S", an "m", an "i", a "t", and an "h" don't have much meaning individually, but if the combination of characters makes up your last name, "Smith", then as a group, the characters have useful meaning.

Related fields are often grouped together to form a record. **Records** are groups of fields that go together for some logical reason. A random name, address, and salary aren't very useful, but if they're your name, your address, and your salary, then that's your record. An inventory record might contain fields for item number, color, size, and price; a student record might contain ID number, grade point average, and major.

Related records, in turn, are grouped together to form a file. **Files** are groups of records that go together for some logical reason. The individual records of each student in your class might go together in a file called STUDENTS. Records of each person at your company might be in a file called PERSONNEL. Items you sell might be in an INVENTORY file.

Some files can have just a few records; others, such as the file of credit-card holders for a major department-store chain or policyholders of an insurance company, can contain thousands or even millions of records.

Finally, many organizations use database software to organize many files. A **database** holds a group of files, often called **tables**, that together serve the information needs of an organization. Database software establishes and maintains relationships between fields in these tables, so that users can write questions called **queries**. Queries pull related data items together in a format that allows businesspeople to make managerial decisions efficiently. Chapter 16 of the Comprehensive version of this text covers database creation.

In summary, you can picture the data hierarchy, as shown in Figure 1-2.

**FIGURE 1-2:** THE DATA HIERARCHY

```
Database
   File
      Record
         Field
            Character
```

A database contains many files. A file contains many records. Each record in a file has the same fields. Each record's fields contain different data items that consist of one or more stored characters in each field.

As an example, you can picture a file as a set of index cards, as shown in Figure 1-3. The stack of cards is the EMPLOYEE file, in which each card represents one employee record. On each card, each line holds one field—`name`, `address`, or `salary`. Almost all the program examples in this book use files that are organized in this way.

**FIGURE 1-3:** EMPLOYEE FILE REPRESENTED AS A STACK OF INDEX CARDS

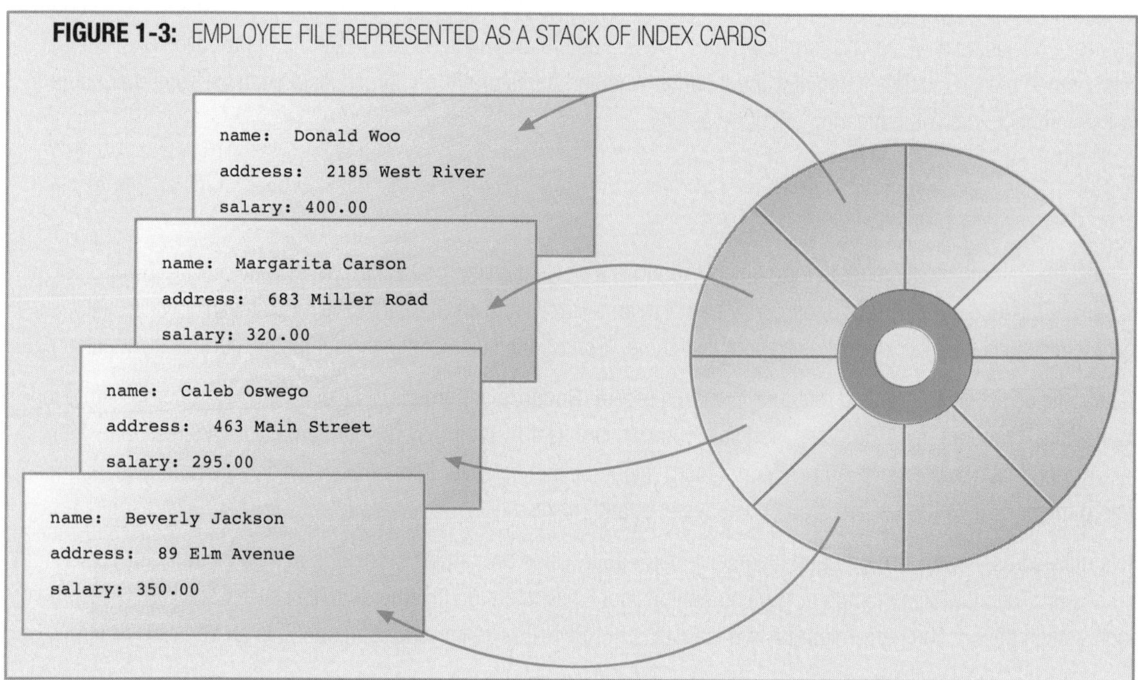


## USING FLOWCHART SYMBOLS AND PSEUDOCODE STATEMENTS

When programmers plan the logic for a solution to a programming problem, they often use one of two tools, **flowcharts** or **pseudocode** (pronounced "sue-doe-code"). A flowchart is a pictorial representation of the logical steps it takes to solve a problem. **Pseudocode** is an English-like representation of the same thing. *Pseudo* is a prefix that means "false," and to *code* a program means to put it in a programming language; therefore, *pseudocode* simply means "false code," or sentences that appear to have been written in a computer programming language but don't necessarily follow all the syntax rules of any specific language.

You have already seen examples of statements that represent pseudocode earlier in this chapter, and there is nothing mysterious about them. The following five statements constitute a pseudocode representation of a number-doubling problem:

```
start
  get inputNumber
  compute calculatedAnswer as inputNumber times 2
  print calculatedAnswer
stop
```

Using pseudocode involves writing down all the steps you will use in a program. Usually, programmers preface their pseudocode statements with a beginning statement like "start" and end them with a terminating statement like "stop". The statements between "start" and "stop" look like English and are indented slightly so that "start" and "stop" stand out. Most programmers do not bother with punctuation such as periods at the end of pseudocode statements, although it would not be wrong to use them if you prefer that style. Similarly, there is no need to capitalize the first word in a sentence, although you might choose to do so. This book follows the conventions of using lowercase letters for verbs that begin pseudocode statements and omitting periods at the end of statements.

Some professional programmers prefer writing pseudocode to drawing flowcharts, because using pseudocode is more similar to writing the final statements in the programming language. Others prefer drawing flowcharts to represent the logical flow, because flowcharts allow programmers to visualize more easily how the program statements will connect. Especially for beginning programmers, flowcharts are an excellent tool to help visualize how the statements in a program are interrelated.

Almost every program involves the steps of input, processing, and output. Therefore, most flowcharts need some graphical way to separate these three steps. When you create a flowchart, you draw geometric shapes around the individual statements and connect them with arrows.

When you draw a flowchart, you use a parallelogram to represent an **input symbol**, which indicates an input operation. You write an input statement, in English, inside the parallelogram, as shown in Figure 1-4.

**FIGURE 1-4:** INPUT SYMBOL

get
inputNumber

**TIP**

When you want to represent entering two or more values in a program, you can use one or multiple flowchart symbols or pseudocode statements—whichever seems more reasonable and clear to you. For example, the pseudocode to input a user's name and address might be written as:

```
get inputName
get inputAddress
```

or as:

```
get inputName,inputAddress
```

The first version implies two separate input operations, whereas the second implies a single input operation retrieving two data items. If your application will accept user input from a keyboard, using two separate input statements might make sense, because the user will type one item at a time. If your application will accept data from a storage device, obtaining all the data at once is more common. Logically, either format represents the retrieval of two data items. The end result is the same in both cases—after the statements have executed, `inputName` and `inputAddress` will have received values from an input device.

Arithmetic operation statements are examples of processing. In a flowchart, you use a rectangle as the **processing symbol** that contains a processing statement, as shown in Figure 1-5.

**FIGURE 1-5:** PROCESSING SYMBOL

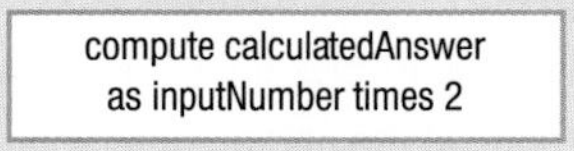

compute calculatedAnswer
as inputNumber times 2

To represent an output statement, you use the same symbol as for input statements—the **output symbol** is a parallelogram, as shown in Figure 1-6.

**FIGURE 1-6:** OUTPUT SYMBOL

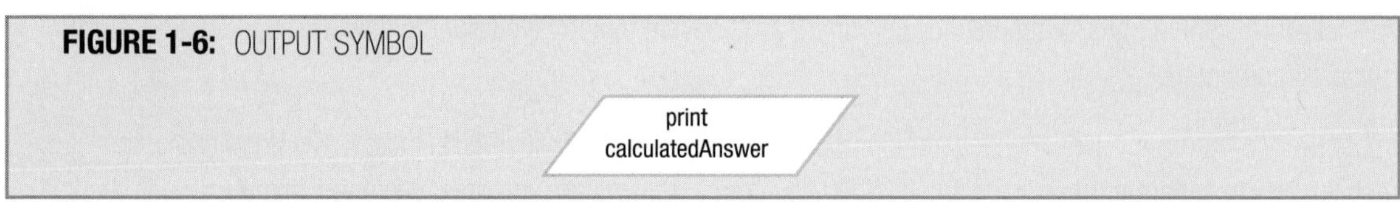
print
calculatedAnswer

**TIP**

As with input, output statements can be organized in whatever way seems most reasonable. A program that prints the length and width of a room might use the statement:

```
print length
print width
```

or:

```
print length, width
```

In some programming languages, using two print statements places the output values on two separate lines on the monitor or printer, whereas using a single print statement places the values next to each other on the same line. This book follows the convention of using one print statement per line of output.

To show the correct sequence of these statements, you use arrows, or **flowlines**, to connect the steps. Whenever possible, most of a flowchart should read from top to bottom or from left to right on a page. That's the way we read English, so when flowcharts follow this convention, they are easier for us to understand.

To be complete, a flowchart should include two more elements: a **terminal symbol**, or start/stop symbol, at each end. Often, you place a word like "start" or "begin" in the first terminal symbol and a word like "end" or "stop" in the other. The standard terminal symbol is shaped like a racetrack; many programmers refer to this shape as a **lozenge**, because it resembles the shape of a medicated candy lozenge you might use to soothe a sore throat. Figure 1-7 shows a complete flowchart for the program that doubles a number, and the pseudocode for the same problem.

**FIGURE 1-7:** FLOWCHART AND PSEUDOCODE OF PROGRAM THAT DOUBLES A NUMBER

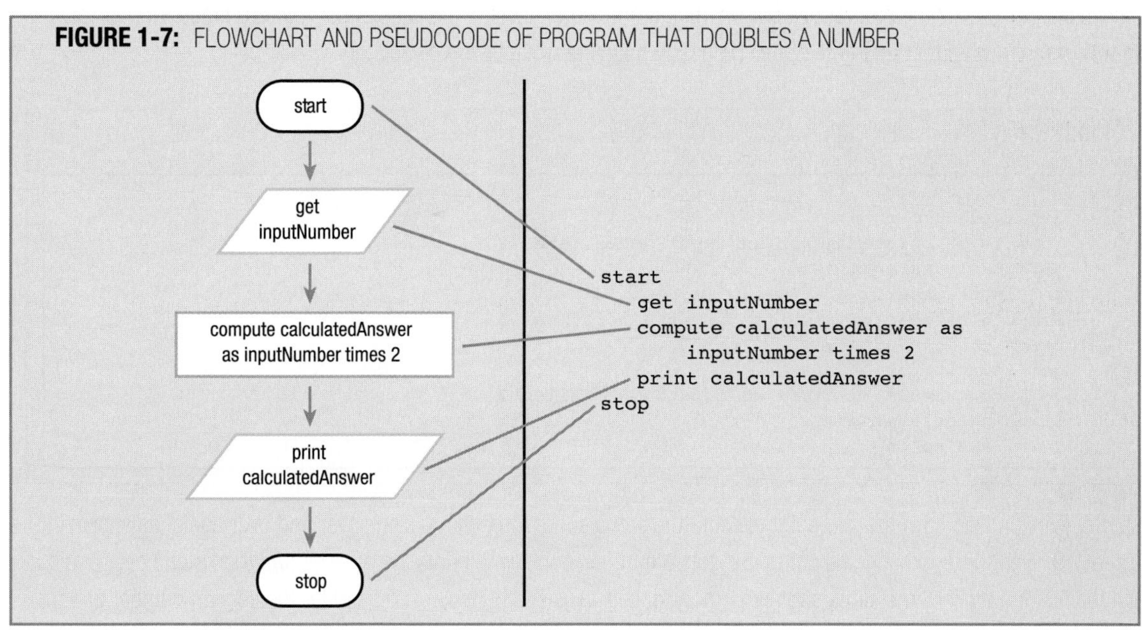


```
start
   get inputNumber
   compute calculatedAnswer as
        inputNumber times 2
   print calculatedAnswer
stop
```

**TIP** Programmers seldom create both pseudocode and a flowchart for the same problem. You usually use one or the other.

The logic for the program represented by the flowchart and pseudocode in Figure 1-7 is correct no matter what programming language the programmer eventually uses to write the corresponding code. Just as the same statements could be translated into Italian or Chinese without losing their meaning, they also can be coded in C#, Java, or any other programming language.

After the flowchart or pseudocode has been developed, the programmer only needs to: (1) buy a computer, (2) buy a language compiler, (3) learn a programming language, (4) code the program, (5) attempt to compile it, (6) fix the syntax errors, (7) compile it again, (8) test it with several sets of data, and (9) put it into production.

"Whoa!" you are probably saying to yourself. "This is simply not worth it! All that work to create a flowchart or pseudocode, and *then* all those other steps? For five dollars, I can buy a pocket calculator that will double any number for me instantly!" You are absolutely right. If this were a real computer program, and all it did was double the value of a number, it simply would not be worth all the effort. Writing a computer program would be worth the effort only if you had many—let's say 10,000—numbers to double in a limited amount of time—let's say the next two minutes. Then, it would be worth your while to create a computer program.

Unfortunately, the number-doubling program represented in Figure 1-7 does not double 10,000 numbers; it doubles only one. You could execute the program 10,000 times, of course, but that would require you to sit at the computer telling it to run the program over and over again. You would be better off with a program that could process 10,000 numbers, one after the other.

One solution is to write the program as shown in Figure 1-8 and execute the same steps 10,000 times. Of course, writing this program would be very time-consuming; you might as well buy the calculator.

**FIGURE 1-8:** INEFFICIENT PSEUDOCODE FOR PROGRAM THAT DOUBLES 10,000 NUMBERS

```
start
     get inputNumber
     compute calculatedAnswer as inputNumber times 2
     print calculatedAnswer
     get inputNumber
     compute calculatedAnswer as inputNumber times 2
     print calculatedAnswer
     get inputNumber
     compute calculatedAnswer as inputNumber times 2
     print calculatedAnswer
     . . . and so on
```

A better solution is to have the computer execute the same set of three instructions over and over again, as shown in Figure 1-9. With this approach, the computer gets a number, doubles it, prints the answer, and then starts over again with the first instruction. The same spot in memory, called `inputNumber`, is reused for the second number and for any subsequent numbers. The spot in memory named `calculatedAnswer` is reused each time to store the result of the multiplication operation. The logic illustrated in the flowchart shown in Figure 1-9 contains a major problem—the sequence of instructions never ends. You will learn to handle this problem later in this chapter.

**FIGURE 1-9:** FLOWCHART OF INFINITE NUMBER-DOUBLING PROGRAM

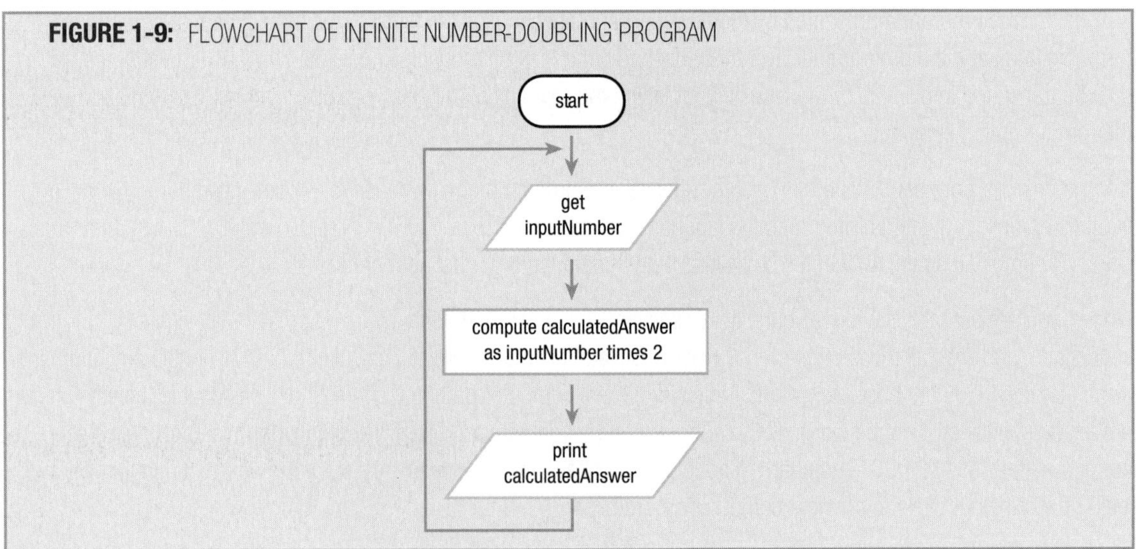

## USING AND NAMING VARIABLES

Programmers commonly refer to the locations in memory called `inputNumber` and `calculatedAnswer` as variables. **Variables** are memory locations, whose contents can vary or differ over time. Sometimes, `inputNumber` can hold a 2 and `calculatedAnswer` will hold a 4; at other times, `inputNumber` can hold a 6 and `calculatedAnswer` will hold a 12. It is the ability of memory variables to change in value that makes computers and programming worthwhile. Because one memory location can be used over and over again with different values, you can write program instructions once and then use them for thousands of separate calculations. *One* set of payroll instructions at your company produces each individual's paycheck, and *one* set of instructions at your electric company produces each household's bill.

The number-doubling example requires two variables, `inputNumber` and `calculatedAnswer`. These can just as well be named `userEntry` and `programSolution`, or `inputValue` and `twiceTheValue`. As a programmer, you choose reasonable names for your variables. The language interpreter then associates the names you choose with specific memory addresses.

A variable name is also called an **identifier**. Every computer programming language has its own set of rules for naming identifiers. Most languages allow both letters and digits within variable names. Some languages allow hyphens in variable names—for example, `hourly-wage`. Others allow underscores, as in `hourly_wage`. Still others allow neither. Some languages allow dollar signs or other special characters in variable names (for example, `hourly$`); others allow foreign alphabet characters, such as π or Ω.

**TIP**

You also can refer to a variable name as a **mnemonic**. In everyday language, a mnemonic is a memory device, like the sentence "Every good boy does fine," which makes it easier to remember the notes that occupy the lines on the staff in sheet music. In programming, a variable name is a device that makes it easier to reference a memory address.

**TIP**

Different languages put different limits on the length of variable names, although in general, newer languages allow longer names. For example, in some very old versions of BASIC, a variable name could consist of only one or two letters and one or two digits. You could have some cryptic variable names like `hw` or `a3` or `re02`. Fortunately, most modern languages allow variable names to be much longer; in the newest versions of C++, C#, and Java, the length of identifiers is virtually unlimited. Variable names in these languages usually consist of lowercase letters, don't allow hyphens, but do allow underscores, so you can use a name like `price_of_item`. These languages are case sensitive, so `HOURLYWAGE`, `hourlywage`, and `hourlyWage` are considered three separate variable names, although the last example, in which the new word begins with an uppercase letter, is easiest to read. Most programmers who use the more modern languages employ the format in which multiple-word variable names are run together, and each new word within the variable name begins with an uppercase letter. This format is called **camel casing**, because such variable names, like `hourlyWage`, have a "hump" in the middle. The variable names in this text are shown using camel casing.

Even though every language has its own rules for naming variables, when designing the logic of a computer program, you should not concern yourself with the specific syntax of any particular computer language. The logic, after all, works with any language. The variable names used throughout this book follow only two rules:

1. *Variable names must be one word.* The name can contain letters, digits, hyphens, underscores, or any other characters you choose, with the exception of *spaces*. Therefore, `r` is a legal variable name, as is `rate`, as is `interestRate`. The variable name `interest rate` is not allowed because of the space. No programming language allows spaces within a variable name. If you see a name such as `interest rate` in a flowchart or pseudocode, you should assume that the programmer is discussing two variables, `interest` and `rate`, each of which individually would be a fine variable name.

TIP As a convention, this book begins variable names with a lowercase letter. You might find programming texts in languages such as Visual Basic and C++ in which the author has chosen to begin variable names with an uppercase letter. As long as you adopt a convention and use it consistently, your programs will be easier to read and understand.

TIP When you write a program using an editor that is packaged with a compiler, the compiler may display variable names in a different color from the rest of the program. This visual aid helps your variable names stand out from words that are part of the programming language.

2. *Variable names should have some appropriate meaning.* This is not a rule of any programming language. When computing an interest rate in a program, the computer does not care if you call the variable `g`, `u84`, or `fred`. As long as the correct numeric result is placed in the variable, its actual name doesn't really matter. However, it's much easier to follow the logic of a program with a statement in it like `compute finalBalance as equal to initialInvestment times interestRate` than one with a statement in it like `compute someBanana as equal to j89 times myFriendLinda`. You might think you will remember how you intended to use a cryptic variable name within a program, but several months or years later when a program requires changes, you, and other programmers working with you, will appreciate clear, descriptive variable names.

Notice that the flowchart in Figure 1-9 follows these two rules for variables: both variable names, `inputNumber` and `calculatedAnswer`, are one word, and they have appropriate meanings. Some programmers have fun with their variable names by naming them after friends or creating puns with them, but such behavior is unprofessional and marks those programmers as amateurs. Table 1-1 lists some possible variable names that might be used to hold an employee's last name and provides a rationale for the appropriateness of each one.

TIP Another general rule in all programming languages is that variable names may not begin with a digit, although usually they may contain digits. Thus, in most languages `budget2013` is a legal variable name, but `2013Budget` is not.

**TABLE 1-1:** VALID AND INVALID VARIABLE NAMES FOR AN EMPLOYEE'S LAST NAME

| Suggested variable names for employee's last name | Comments |
|---|---|
| `employeeLastName` | Good |
| `employeeLast` | Good—most people would interpret `Last` as meaning `Last Name` |
| `empLast` | Good—`emp` is short for employee |
| `emlstnam` | Legal—but cryptic |
| `lastNameOfTheEmployeeInQuestion` | Legal—but awkward |
| `last name` | Not legal—embedded space |
| `employeelastname` | Legal—but hard to read without camel casing |

## ENDING A PROGRAM BY USING SENTINEL VALUES

Recall that the logic in the flowchart for doubling numbers, shown in Figure 1-9, has a major flaw—the program never ends. This programming situation is known as an **infinite loop**—a repeating flow of logic with no end. If, for example, the input numbers are being entered at the keyboard, the program will keep accepting numbers and printing doubles forever. Of course, the user could refuse to type in any more numbers. But the computer is very patient, and if you refuse to give it any more numbers, it will sit and wait forever. When you finally type in a number, the program will double it, print the result, and wait for another. The program cannot progress any further while it is waiting for input; meanwhile, the program is occupying computer memory and tying up operating system resources. Refusing to enter any more numbers is not a practical solution. Another way to end the program is simply to turn the computer off. But again, that's neither the best nor an elegant way to bring the program to an end.

A superior way to end the program is to set a predetermined value for `inputNumber` that means "Stop the program!" For example, the programmer and the user could agree that the user will never need to know the double of 0 (zero), so the user could enter a 0 when he or she wants to stop. The program could then test any incoming value contained in `inputNumber` and, if it is a 0, stop the program. Testing a value is also called making a **decision**.

You represent a decision in a flowchart by drawing a **decision symbol**, which is shaped like a diamond. The diamond usually contains a question, the answer to which is one of two mutually exclusive options—often yes or no. All good computer questions have only two mutually exclusive answers, such as yes and no or true and false. For example, "What day of the year is your birthday?" is not a good computer question because there are 366 possible answers. But "Is your birthday June 24?" is a good computer question because, for everyone in the world, the answer is either yes or no.

**TIP** A yes-or-no decision is called a **binary decision**, because there are two possible outcomes.

The question to stop the doubling program should be "Is the `inputNumber` just entered equal to 0?" or "`inputNumber = 0`?" for short. The complete flowchart will now look like the one shown in Figure 1-10.

**FIGURE 1-10:** FLOWCHART FOR NUMBER-DOUBLING PROGRAM WITH SENTINEL VALUE OF 0

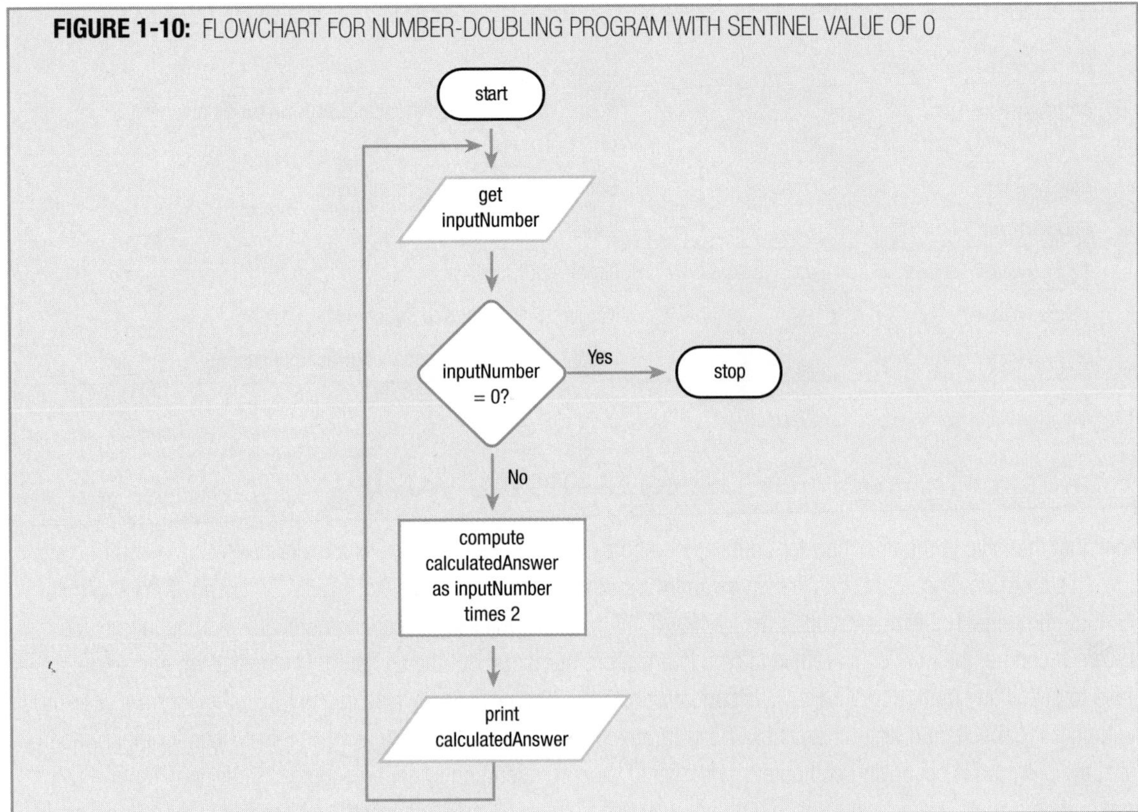


One drawback to using 0 to stop a program, of course, is that it won't work if the user does need to find the double of 0. In that case, some other data-entry value that the user never will need, such as 999 or –1, could be selected to signal that the program should end. A preselected value that stops the execution of a program is often called a **dummy value** because it does not represent real data, but just a signal to stop. Sometimes, such a value is called a **sentinel value** because it represents an entry or exit point, like a sentinel who guards a fortress.

Not all programs rely on user data entry from a keyboard; many read data from an input device, such as a disk or tape drive. When organizations store data on a disk or other storage device, they do not commonly use a dummy value to signal the end of the file. For one thing, an input record might have hundreds of fields, and if you store a dummy record in every file, you are wasting a large quantity of storage on "non-data." Additionally, it is often difficult to choose sentinel values for fields in a company's data files. Any `balanceDue`, even a zero or a negative number, can be a legitimate value, and any `customerName`, even "ZZ", could be someone's name. Fortunately, programming languages can recognize the end of data in a file automatically, through a code that is stored at the end of the data. Many programming languages use the term **eof** (for "end of file") to talk about this marker that automatically acts as a sentinel. This book, therefore, uses **eof** to indicate the end of data, regardless of whether the code is a special disk marker or a dummy value such as 0 that comes from the keyboard. Therefore, the flowchart and pseudocode can look like the examples shown in Figure 1-11.

**FIGURE 1-11:** FLOWCHART USING **eof**

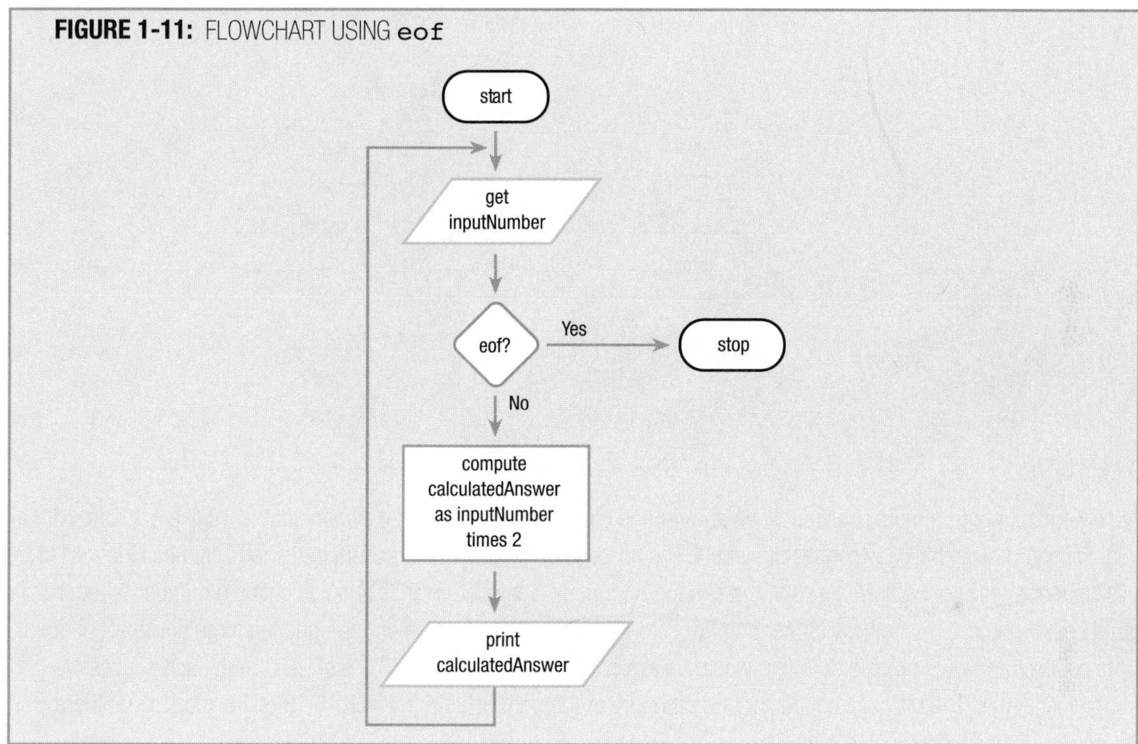


## USING THE CONNECTOR

By using just the input, processing, output, decision, and terminal symbols, you can represent the flowcharting logic for many diverse applications. When drawing a flowchart segment, you might use another symbol, the **connector**. You can use a connector when limited page size forces you to continue a flowchart in an unconnected location or on another page. If a flowchart has six processing steps and a page provides room for only three, you might represent the logic as shown in Figure 1-12.

**FIGURE 1-12:** FLOWCHART USING THE CONNECTOR

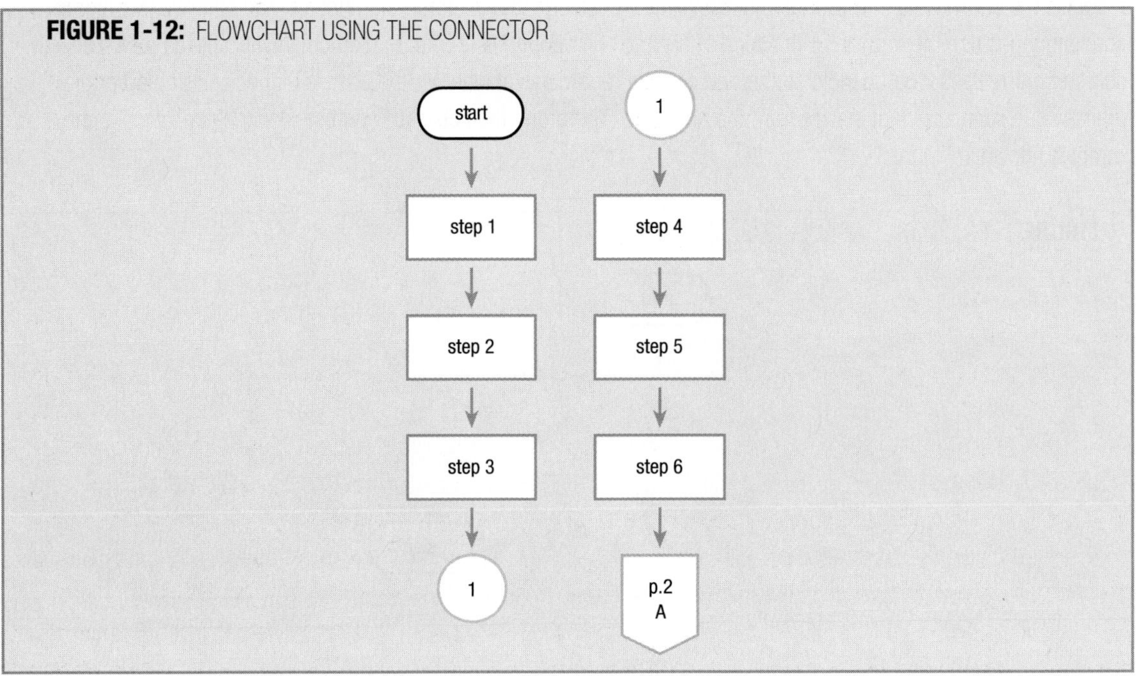


By convention, programmers use a circle as an on-page connector symbol, and a symbol that looks like a square with a pointed bottom as an off-page connector symbol. The on-page connector at the bottom of the left column in Figure 1-12 tells someone reading the flowchart that there is more to the flowchart. The circle should contain a number or letter that can then be matched to another number or letter somewhere else, in this case on the right. If a large flowchart needed more connectors, new numbers or letters would be assigned in sequence (1, 2, 3... or A, B, C...) to each successive pair of connectors. The off-page connector at the bottom of the right column in Figure 1-12 tells a reader that there is more to the flowchart on another page.

When you are creating your own flowcharts, you should avoid using any connectors, if at all possible; flowcharts are more difficult to follow when their segments do not fit together on a page. Some programmers would even say that if a flowchart must connect to another page, it is a sign of poor design. Your instructor or future programming supervisor may require that long flowcharts be redrawn so you don't need to use the connector symbol. However, when continuing to a new location or page is unavoidable, the connector provides the means.

## ASSIGNING VALUES TO VARIABLES

When you create a flowchart or pseudocode for a program that doubles numbers, you can include the statement `compute calculatedAnswer as inputNumber times 2`. This statement incorporates two actions. First, the computer calculates the arithmetic value of `inputNumber times 2`. Second, the computed value is stored in the `calculatedAnswer` memory location. Most programming languages allow a shorthand expression for **assignment statements** such as `compute calculatedAnswer as inputNumber times 2`. The shorthand takes the form `calculatedAnswer = inputNumber * 2`. The equal sign is the **assignment operator**; it always requires the name of a memory location on its left side—the name of the location where the result will be stored.

TIP

When they write pseudocode or draw a flowchart, most programmers use the asterisk (*) to represent multiplication. When you write pseudocode, you can use an X or a dot for multiplication (as most mathematicians do), but you will be using an unconventional format. This book will always use an asterisk to represent multiplication.

According to the rules of algebra, a statement like `calculatedAnswer = inputNumber * 2` should be exactly equivalent to the statement `inputNumber * 2 = calculatedAnswer`. That's because in algebra, the equal sign always represents equivalency. In most programming languages, however, the equal sign represents assignment, and `calculatedAnswer = inputNumber * 2` means "multiply `inputNumber` by 2 and store the result in the variable called `calculatedAnswer`." Whatever operation is performed to the right of the equal sign results in a value that is placed in the memory location to the left of the equal sign. Therefore, the incorrect statement `inputNumber * 2 = calculatedAnswer` means to attempt to take the value of `calculatedAnswer` and store it in a location called `inputNumber * 2`, but there can't be a location called `inputNumber * 2`. For one thing, you should recognize that the expression `inputNumber * 2` can't be a variable because it has spaces in it. For another, a location can't be multiplied. Its contents can be multiplied, but the location itself cannot be. The backward statement `inputNumber * 2 = calculatedAnswer` contains a syntax error, no matter what programming language you use; a program with such a statement will not execute.

TIP

When you create an assignment statement, it may help to imagine the word "let" in front of the statement. Thus, you can read the statement `calculatedAnswer = inputNumber * 2` as "Let `calculatedAnswer` equal `inputNumber` times two." The BASIC programming language allows you to use the word "let" in such statements. You might also imagine the word "gets" or "receives" in place of the assignment operator. In other words, `calculatedAnswer = inputNumber * 2` means both `calculatedAnswer gets inputNumber * 2` and `calculatedAnswer receives inputNumber * 2`.

Computer memory is made up of millions of distinct locations, each of which has an address. Fifty or sixty years ago, programmers had to deal with these addresses and had to remember, for instance, that they had stored a salary in location 6428 of their computer. Today, we are very fortunate that high-level computer languages allow us to pick a reasonable "English" name for a memory address and let the computer keep track of where it is. Just as it is easier for you to remember that the president lives in the White House than at 1600 Pennsylvania Avenue, Washington, D.C., it is also easier for you to remember that your salary is in a variable called `mySalary` than at memory location 6428104.

Similarly, it does not usually make sense to perform mathematical operations on names given to memory addresses, but it does make sense to perform mathematical operations on the *contents* of memory addresses. If you live in `blueSplitLevelOnTheCorner`, adding 1 to that would be meaningless, but you certainly can add 1 person to the number of people already in that house. For our purposes, then, the statement `calculatedAnswer = inputNumber * 2` means exactly the same thing as the statement `calculate inputNumber * 2` (that is, double the contents in the memory location named `inputNumber`) `and store the result in the memory location named calculatedAnswer.`

TIP

Many programming languages allow you to create named constants. A named constant is a named memory location, similar to a variable, except its value never changes during the execution of a program. If you are working with a programming language that allows it, you might create a constant for a value such as `PI = 3.14` or `COUNTY_SALES_TAX_RATE = .06`. Many programmers follow the convention of using camel casing for variable identifiers but all capital letters for constant identifiers.

## UNDERSTANDING DATA TYPES

Computers deal with two basic types of data—text and numeric. When you use a specific numeric value, such as 43, within a program, you write it using the digits and no quotation marks. A specific numeric value is often called a **numeric constant**, because it does not change—a 43 always has the value 43. When you use a specific text value, or string of characters, such as "Amanda", you enclose the **string constant**, or **character constant**, within quotation marks.

TIP

Some languages require single quotation marks surrounding character constants, whereas others require double quotation marks. Many languages, including C++, C#, and Java, reserve single quotes for a single character such as 'A', and double quotes for a character string such as "Amanda".

Similarly, most computer languages allow at least two distinct types of variables. A variable's **data type** describes the kind of values the variable can hold and the types of operations that can be performed with it. One type of variable can hold a number, and is often called a **numeric variable**. A numeric variable is one that can have mathematical operations performed on it; it can hold digits, and usually can hold a decimal point and a sign indicating positive or negative if you want. In the statement `calculatedAnswer = inputNumber * 2`, both `calculatedAnswer` and `inputNumber` are numeric variables; that is, their intended contents are numeric values, such as 6 and 3, 150 and 75, or –18 and –9.

Most programming languages have a separate type of variable that can hold letters of the alphabet and other special characters such as punctuation marks. Depending on the language, these variables are called **character**, **text**, or **string variables**. If a working program contains the statement `lastName = "Lincoln"`, then `lastName` is a character or string variable.

Programmers must distinguish between numeric and character variables, because computers handle the two types of data differently. Therefore, means are provided within the syntax rules of computer programming languages to tell the computer which type of data to expect. How this is done is different in every language; some languages have different rules for naming the variables, but with others you must include a simple statement (called a **declaration**) telling the computer which type of data to expect.

Some languages allow for several types of numeric data. Languages such as C++, C#, Visual Basic, and Java distinguish between **integer** (whole number) numeric variables and **floating-point** (fractional) numeric variables that contain a decimal point. Thus, in some languages, the values 4 and 4.3 would be stored in different types of numeric variables.

Some programming languages allow even more specific variable types, but the character versus numeric distinction is universal. For the programs you develop in this book, assume that each variable is one of the two broad types. If a variable called `taxRate` is supposed to hold a value of 2.5, assume that it is a numeric variable. If a variable called `inventoryItem` is supposed to hold a value of "monitor", assume that it is a character variable.

**TIP** Values such as "monitor" and 2.5 are called constants or literal constants because they never change. A variable value *can* change. Thus, `inventoryItem` can hold "monitor" at one moment during the execution of a program, and later you can change its value to "modem".

**TIP** Some languages allow you to invent your own data type. In Chapter 12 of the Comprehensive version of this book, you will learn that object-oriented programming languages allow you to create new data types called classes.

By convention, this book encloses character data like "monitor" within quotation marks to distinguish the characters from yet another variable name. Also by convention, numeric data values are not enclosed within quotation marks. According to these conventions, then, `taxRate = 2.5` and `inventoryItem = "monitor"` are both valid statements. The statement `inventoryItem = monitor` is a valid statement only if `monitor` is also a character variable. In other words, if `monitor = "color"`, and subsequently `inventoryItem = monitor`, then the end result is that the memory address named `inventoryItem` contains the string of characters "color".

Every computer handles text or character data differently from the way it handles numeric data. You may have experienced these differences if you have used application software such as spreadsheets or database programs. For example, in a spreadsheet, you cannot sum a column of words. Similarly, every programming language requires that you distinguish variables as to their correct type, and that you use each type of variable appropriately. Identifying your variables correctly as numeric or character is one of the first steps you have to take when writing programs in any programming language. Table 1-2 provides you with a few examples of legal and illegal variable assignment statements.

**TIP** The process of naming program variables and assigning a type to them is called **making declarations**, or **declaring variables**. You will learn how to declare variables in Chapter 4.

**TABLE 1-2:** SOME EXAMPLES OF LEGAL AND ILLEGAL ASSIGNMENTS

*Assume* `lastName` *and* `firstName` *are character variables.*

*Assume* `quizScore` *and* `homeworkScore` *are numeric variables.*

| Examples of valid assignments | Examples of invalid assignments | Explanation of invalid examples |
|---|---|---|
| `lastName = "Parker"` | `lastName = Parker` | If `Parker` is the last name, it requires quotes. If `Parker` is a named string variable, this assignment would be allowed. |
| `firstName = "Laura"` | `"Parker" = lastName` | Value on left must be a variable name, not a constant |
| `lastName = firstName` | `lastName = quizScore` | The data types do not match |
| `quizScore = 86` | `homeworkScore = firstName` | The data types do not match |
| `homeworkScore = quizScore` | `homeworkScore = "92"` | The data types do not match |
| `homeworkScore = 92` | `quizScore = "zero"` | The data types do not match |
| `quizScore = homeworkScore + 25` | `firstName = 23` | The data types do not match |
| `homeworkScore = 3 * 10` | `100 = homeworkScore` | Value on left must be a variable name, not a constant |

## UNDERSTANDING THE EVOLUTION OF PROGRAMMING TECHNIQUES

People have been writing computer programs since the 1940s. The oldest programming languages required programmers to work with memory addresses and to memorize awkward codes associated with machine languages. Newer programming languages look much more like natural language and are easier for programmers to use. Part of the reason it is easier to use newer programming languages is that they allow programmers to name variables instead of using awkward memory addresses. Another reason is that newer programming languages provide programmers with the means to create self-contained modules or program segments that can be pieced together in a variety of ways. The oldest computer programs were written in one piece, from start to finish; modern programs are rarely written that way—they are created by teams of programmers, each developing his or her own reusable and connectable program procedures. Writing several small modules is easier than writing one large program, and most large tasks are easier when you break the work into units and get other workers to help with some of the units.

**TIP** You will learn to create program modules in Chapter 3.

Currently, there are two major techniques used to develop programs and their procedures. One technique, called **procedural programming**, focuses on the procedures that programmers create. That is, procedural programmers focus on the actions that are carried out—for example, getting input data for an employee and writing the calculations needed to produce a paycheck from the data. Procedural programmers would approach the job of producing a paycheck by breaking down the paycheck-producing process into manageable subtasks.

The other popular programming technique, called **object-oriented programming**, focuses on objects, or "things," and describes their features, or attributes, and their behaviors. For example, object-oriented programmers might design a payroll application by thinking about employees and paychecks, and describing their attributes (such as last name or check amount) and behaviors (such as the calculations that result in the check amount).

With either approach, procedural or object-oriented, you can produce a correct paycheck, and both techniques employ reusable program modules. The major difference lies in the focus the programmer takes during the earliest planning stages of a project. Object-oriented programming employs a large vocabulary; you can learn this terminology in Chapter 13 of the Comprehensive version of this book. For now, this book focuses on procedural programming techniques. The skills you gain in programming procedurally—declaring variables, accepting input, making decisions, producing output, and so on—will serve you well whether you eventually write programs in a procedural or object-oriented fashion, or in both.

## CHAPTER SUMMARY

- Together, computer hardware (equipment) and software (instructions) accomplish four major operations: input, processing, output, and storage. You write computer instructions in a computer programming language that requires specific syntax; the instructions are translated into machine language by a compiler or interpreter. When both the syntax and logic of a program are correct, you can run, or execute, the program to produce the desired results.
- A programmer's job involves understanding the problem, planning the logic, coding the program, translating the program into machine language, testing the program, and putting the program into production.
- When data items are stored for use on computer systems, they are stored in a data hierarchy of character, field, record, file, and database.
- When programmers plan the logic for a solution to a programming problem, they often use flowcharts or pseudocode. When you draw a flowchart, you use parallelograms to represent input and output operations, and rectangles to represent processing.
- Variables are named memory locations, the contents of which can vary. As a programmer, you choose reasonable names for your variables. Every computer programming language has its own set of rules for naming variables; however, all variable names must be written as one word without embedded spaces, and should have appropriate meaning.
- Testing a value involves making a decision. You represent a decision in a flowchart by drawing a diamond-shaped decision symbol containing a question, the answer to which is either yes or no. You can stop a program's execution by using a decision to test for a sentinel value.
- A connector symbol is used to continue a flowchart that does not fit together on a page, or must continue on an additional page.
- Most programming languages use the equal sign to assign values to variables. Assignment always takes place from right to left.
- Programmers must distinguish between numeric and character variables, because computers handle the two types of data differently. A variable declaration tells the computer which type of data to expect. By convention, character data values are included within quotation marks.
- Procedural and object-oriented programmers approach program problems differently. Procedural programmers concentrate on the actions performed with data. Object-oriented programmers focus on objects and their behaviors and attributes.

## KEY TERMS

**Hardware** is the equipment of a computer system.

**Software** consists of the programs that tell the computer what to do.

**Input** devices include keyboards and mice; through these devices, data items enter the computer system. Data can also enter a system from storage devices such as magnetic disks and CDs.

**Data** includes all the text, numbers, and other information that are processed by a computer.

**Processing** data items may involve organizing them, checking them for accuracy, or performing mathematical operations on them.

The **central processing unit**, or **CPU**, is the piece of hardware that processes data.

Information is sent to a printer, monitor, or some other **output** device so people can view, interpret, and work with the results.

**Programming languages**, such as Visual Basic, C#, C++, Java, or COBOL, are used to write programs.

The **syntax** of a language consists of its rules.

**Machine language** is a computer's on/off circuitry language.

A **compiler** or **interpreter** translates a high-level language into machine language and tells you if you have used a programming language incorrectly.

You develop the **logic** of the computer program when you give instructions to the computer in a specific sequence, without leaving any instructions out or adding extraneous instructions.

A **semantic error** occurs when a correct word is used in an incorrect context.

The **running**, or **executing**, of a program occurs when the computer actually uses the written and compiled program.

**Internal storage** is called **memory**, **main memory**, **primary memory**, or **random access memory (RAM)**.

**External storage** is **persistent** (relatively permanent) storage outside the main memory of the machine, on a device such as a floppy disk, hard disk, or magnetic tape.

Internal memory is **volatile**—that is, its contents are lost every time the computer loses power.

You **save** a program on some nonvolatile medium.

An **algorithm** is the sequence of steps necessary to solve any problem.

**Desk-checking** is the process of walking through a program solution on paper.

**Coding** a program means writing the statements in a programming language.

**High-level programming languages** are English-like.

**Machine language** is the **low-level** language made up of 1s and 0s that the computer understands.

A **syntax error** is an error in language or grammar.

**Logical errors** occur when incorrect instructions are performed, or when instructions are performed in the wrong order.

**Conversion** is the entire set of actions an organization must take to switch over to using a new program or set of programs.

The **data hierarchy** represents the relationship of databases, files, records, fields, and characters.

**Characters** are letters, numbers, and special symbols such as "A", "7", and "$".

A **field** is a single data item, such as `lastName`, `streetAddress`, or `annualSalary`.

**Records** are groups of fields that go together for some logical reason.

**Files** are groups of records that go together for some logical reason.

A **database** holds a group of files, often called **tables**, that together serve the information needs of an organization.

**Queries** are questions that pull related data items together from a database in a format that enhances efficient management decision making.

A **flowchart** is a pictorial representation of the logical steps it takes to solve a problem.

**Pseudocode** is an English-like representation of the logical steps it takes to solve a problem.

**Input symbols**, which indicate input operations, are represented as parallelograms in flowcharts.

**Processing symbols** are represented as rectangles in flowcharts.

**Output symbols**, which indicate output operations, are represented as parallelograms in flowcharts.

**Flowlines**, or arrows, connect the steps in a flowchart.

A **terminal symbol**, or start/stop symbol, is used at each end of a flowchart. Its shape is a **lozenge**.

**Variables** are memory locations, whose contents can vary or differ over time.

A variable name is also called an **identifier**.

A **mnemonic** is a memory device; variable identifiers act as mnemonics for hard-to-remember memory addresses.

**Camel casing** is the format for naming variables in which multiple-word variable names are run together, and each new word within the variable name begins with an uppercase letter.

An **infinite loop** is a repeating flow of logic without an ending.

Testing a value is also called making a **decision**.

You represent a decision in a flowchart by drawing a **decision symbol**, which is shaped like a diamond.

A yes-or-no decision is called a **binary decision**, because there are two possible outcomes.

A **dummy value** is a preselected value that stops the execution of a program. Such a value is sometimes called a **sentinel value** because it represents an entry or exit point, like a sentinel who guards a fortress.

Many programming languages use the term **eof** (for "end of file") to talk about an end-of-data file marker.

A **connector** is a flowchart symbol used when limited page size forces you to continue the flowchart elsewhere on the same page or on the following page.

An **assignment statement** stores the result of any calculation performed on its right side to the named location on its left side.

The equal sign is the **assignment operator**; it always requires the name of a memory location on its left side.

A **numeric constant** is a specific numeric value.

A **string constant**, or **character constant**, is enclosed within quotation marks.

A variable's data type describes the kind of values the variable can hold and the types of operations that can be performed with it.

Numeric variables hold numeric values.

Character, text, or string variables hold character values. If a working program contains the statement `lastName = "Lincoln"`, then `lastName` is a character or string variable.

A declaration is a statement that names a variable and tells the computer which type of data to expect.

Integer values are whole-number, numeric variables.

Floating-point values are fractional, numeric variables that contain a decimal point.

The process of naming program variables and assigning a type to them is called making declarations, or declaring variables.

The technique known as procedural programming focuses on the procedures that programmers create.

The technique known as object-oriented programming focuses on objects, or "things," and describes their features, or attributes, and their behaviors.

## REVIEW QUESTIONS

**1. The two major components of any computer system are its __________.**

a. input and output
b. data and programs
c. hardware and software
d. memory and disk drives

**2. The major computer operations include __________.**

a. hardware and software
b. input, processing, output, and storage
c. sequence and looping
d. spreadsheets, word processing, and data communications

**3. Another term meaning "computer instructions" is __________.**

a. hardware
b. software
c. queries
d. data

**4. Visual Basic, C++, and Java are all examples of computer __________.**

a. operating systems
b. hardware
c. machine languages
d. programming languages

5. **A programming language's rules are its ________.**
   a. syntax
   b. logic
   c. format
   d. options

6. **The most important task of a compiler or interpreter is to ________.**
   a. create the rules for a programming language
   b. translate English statements into a language such as Java
   c. translate programming language statements into machine language
   d. execute machine language programs to perform useful tasks

7. **Which of the following is a typical input instruction?**
   a. `get accountNumber`
   b. `calculate balanceDue`
   c. `print customerIdentificationNumber`
   d. `total = janPurchase + febPurchase`

8. **Which of the following is a typical processing instruction?**
   a. `print answer`
   b. `get userName`
   c. `pctCorrect = rightAnswers / allAnswers`
   d. `print calculatedPercentage`

9. **Which of the following is not associated with internal storage?**
   a. main memory
   b. hard disk
   c. primary memory
   d. volatile

10. **Which of the following pairs of steps in the programming process is in the correct order?**
    a. code the program, plan the logic
    b. test the program, translate it into machine language
    c. put the program into production, understand the problem
    d. code the program, translate it into machine language

11. **The two most commonly used tools for planning a program's logic are ________.**
    a. flowcharts and pseudocode
    b. ASCII and EBCDIC
    c. Java and Visual Basic
    d. word processors and spreadsheets

**12. The most important thing a programmer must do before planning the logic to a program is ________.**

a. decide which programming language to use
b. code the problem
c. train the users of the program
d. understand the problem

**13. Writing a program in a language such as C++ or Java is known as ________ the program.**

a. translating
b. coding
c. interpreting
d. compiling

**14. A compiler would find all of the following programming errors except ________.**

a. the misspelled word "prrint" in a language that includes the word "print"
b. the use of an "X" for multiplication in a language that requires an asterisk
c. a `newBalanceDue` calculated by adding a `customerPayment` to an `oldBalanceDue` instead of subtracting it
d. an arithmetic statement written as `regularSales + discountedSales = totalSales`

**15. Which of the following is true regarding the data hierarchy?**

a. files contain records
b. characters contain fields
c. fields contain files
d. fields contain records

**16. The parallelogram is the flowchart symbol representing ________.**

a. input
b. output
c. both a and b
d. none of the above

**17. Which of the following is not a legal variable name in any programming language?**

a. `semester grade`
b. `fall2005_grade`
c. `GradeInCIS100`
d. `MY_GRADE`

**18. In flowcharts, the decision symbol is a ________.**

a. parallelogram
b. rectangle
c. lozenge
d. diamond

**19. The term "`eof`" represents ________.**

a. a standard input device
b. a generic sentinel value
c. a condition in which no more memory is available for storage
d. the logical flow in a program

**20. The two broadest types of data are ________.**

a. internal and external
b. volatile and constant
c. character and numeric
d. permanent and temporary

## FIND THE BUGS

Since the early days of computer programming, program errors have been called "bugs." The term is often said to have originated from an actual moth that was discovered trapped in the circuitry of a computer at Harvard University in 1945. Actually, the term "bug" was in use prior to 1945 to mean trouble with any electrical apparatus; even during Thomas Edison's life, it meant an "industrial defect." However, the process of finding and correcting program errors has come to be known as debugging.

Each of the following pseudocode segments contains one or more bugs that you must find and correct.

**1. This pseudocode segment is intended to describe computing your average score of two classroom tests.**

```
input midtermGrade
input finalGrade
average = (inputGrade + final) / 3
print average
```

**2. This pseudocode segment is intended to describe computing the number of miles per gallon you get with your automobile.**

```
input milesTraveled
input gallonsOfGasUsed
gallonsOfGasUsed / milesTravelled = milesPerGallon
print milesPerGal
```

**3. This pseudocode segment is intended to describe computing the cost per day and the cost per week for a vacation.**

```
input totalDollarsSpent
input daysOnTrip
costPerDay = totalMoneySpent * daysOnTrip
weeks = daysOnTrip / 7
costPerWeek = daysOnTrip / numberOfWeeks
print costPerDay, week
```

## EXERCISES

1. **Match the definition with the appropriate term.**

| | |
|---|---|
| 1. Computer system equipment | a. compiler |
| 2. Another word for programs | b. syntax |
| 3. Language rules | c. logic |
| 4. Order of instructions | d. hardware |
| 5. Language translator | e. software |

2. **In your own words, describe the steps to writing a computer program.**

3. **Consider a student file that contains the following data:**

| LAST NAME | FIRST NAME | MAJOR | GRADE POINT AVERAGE |
|---|---|---|---|
| Andrews | David | Psychology | 3.4 |
| Broederdorf | Melissa | Computer Science | 4.0 |
| Brogan | Lindsey | Biology | 3.8 |
| Carson | Joshua | Computer Science | 2.8 |
| Eisfelder | Katie | Mathematics | 3.5 |
| Faris | Natalie | Biology | 2.8 |
| Fredricks | Zachary | Psychology | 2.0 |
| Gonzales | Eduardo | Biology | 3.1 |

**Would this set of data be suitable and sufficient to use to test each of the following programs? Explain why or why not.**

a. a program that prints a list of Psychology majors
b. a program that prints a list of Art majors
c. a program that prints a list of students on academic probation—those with a grade point average under 2.0
d. a program that prints a list of students on the dean's list
e. a program that prints a list of students from Wisconsin
f. a program that prints a list of female students

4. **Suggest a good set of test data to use for a program that gives an employee a $50 bonus check if the employee has produced more than 1,000 items in a week.**

5. **Suggest a good set of test data for a program that computes gross paychecks (that is, before any taxes or other deductions) based on hours worked and rate of pay. The program computes gross as hours times rate, unless hours are over 40. If so, the program computes gross as regular rate of pay for 40 hours, plus one and a half times the rate of pay for the hours over 40.**

6. **Suggest a good set of test data for a program that is intended to output a student's grade point average based on letter grades (A, B, C, D, or F) in five courses.**

7. **Suggest a good set of test data for a program for an automobile insurance company that wants to increase its premiums by $50 per month for every ticket a driver receives in a three-year period.**

8. **Assume that a grocery store keeps a file for inventory, where each grocery item has its own record. Two fields within each record are the name of the manufacturer and the weight of the item. Name at least six more fields that might be stored for each record. Provide an example of the data for one record. For example, for one product the manufacturer is DelMonte, and the weight is 12 ounces.**

9. **Assume that a library keeps a file with data about its collection, one record for each item the library lends out. Name at least eight fields that might be stored for each record. Provide an example of the data for one record.**

10. **Match the term with the appropriate shape.**

| | | |
|---|---|---|
| 1. Input | A. | (diamond) |
| 2. Processing | B. | (rounded rectangle) |
| 3. Decision | C. | (parallelogram) |
| 4. Terminal | D. | (rectangle) |
| 5. Connector | E. | (circle) |

11. **Which of the following names seem like good variable names to you? If a name doesn't seem like a good variable name, explain why not.**

    a. `c`
    b. `cost`
    c. `costAmount`
    d. `cost amount`

e. `cstofdngbsns`
f. `costOfDoingBusinessThisFiscalYear`
g. `cost2004`

**12. If `myAge` and `yourRate` are numeric variables, and `departmentCode` is a character variable, which of the following statements are valid assignments? If a statement is not valid, explain why not.**

a. `myAge = 23`
b. `myAge = yourRate`
c. `myAge = departmentCode`
d. `myAge = "departmentCode"`
e. `42 = myAge`
f. `yourRate = 3.5`
g. `yourRate = myAge`
h. `yourRate = departmentCode`
i. `6.91 = yourRate`
j. `departmentCode = Personnel`
k. `departmentCode = "Personnel"`
l. `departmentCode = 413`
m. `departmentCode = "413"`
n. `departmentCode = myAge`
o. `departmentCode = yourRate`
p. `413 = departmentCode`
q. `"413" = departmentCode`

**13. Complete the following tasks:**

a. Draw a flowchart to represent the logic of a program that allows the user to enter a value. The program multiplies the value by 10 and prints the result.
b. Write pseudocode for the same problem.

**14. Complete the following tasks:**

a. Draw a flowchart to represent the logic of a program that allows the user to enter a value that represents the radius of a circle. The program calculates the diameter (by multiplying the radius by 2), and then calculates the circumference (by multiplying the diameter by 3.14). The program prints both the diameter and the circumference.
b. Write pseudocode for the same problem.

**15. Complete the following tasks:**

a. Draw a flowchart to represent the logic of a program that allows the user to enter two values. The program prints the sum of the two values.
b. Write pseudocode for the same problem.

16. **Complete the following tasks:**
    a. Draw a flowchart to represent the logic of a program that allows the user to enter three values. The first value represents hourly pay rate, the second represents the number of hours worked this pay period, and the third represents the percentage of gross salary that is withheld. The program multiplies the hourly pay rate by the number of hours worked, giving the gross pay; then, it multiplies the gross pay by the withholding percentage, giving the withholding amount. Finally, it subtracts the withholding amount from the gross pay, giving the net pay after taxes. The program prints the net pay.
    b. Write pseudocode for the same problem.

## DETECTIVE WORK

1. **Even Shakespeare referred to a "bug" as a negative occurrence. Name the work in which he wrote, "Warwick was a bug that fear'd us all."**
2. **What are the distinguishing features of the programming language called Short Code? When was it invented?**
3. **What is the difference between a compiler and an interpreter? Under what conditions would you prefer to use one over the other?**

## UP FOR DISCUSSION

1. **Which is the better tool for learning programming—flowcharts or pseudocode? Cite any educational research you can find.**
2. **What is the image of the computer programmer in popular culture? Is the image different in books than in TV shows and movies? Would you like that image for yourself?**

# 2 UNDERSTANDING STRUCTURE

## After studying Chapter 2, you should be able to:

- Describe the features of unstructured spaghetti code
- Describe the three basic structures—sequence, selection, and loop
- Use a priming read
- Appreciate the need for structure
- Recognize structure
- Describe three special structures—case, do-while, and do-until

## UNDERSTANDING UNSTRUCTURED SPAGHETTI CODE

Professional computer programs usually get far more complicated than the number-doubling program from Chapter 1, shown in Figure 2-1.

**FIGURE 2-1:** NUMBER-DOUBLING PROGRAM

```
get inputNumber
calculatedAnswer = inputNumber * 2
print calculatedAnswer
```

Imagine the number of instructions in the computer program that NASA uses to calculate the launch angle of a space shuttle, or in the program the IRS uses to audit your income tax return. Even the program that produces a paycheck for you on your job contains many, many instructions. Designing the logic for such a program can be a time-consuming task. When you add several thousand instructions to a program, including several hundred decisions, it is easy to create a complicated mess. The popular name for logically snarled program statements is **spaghetti code**. The reason for the name should be obvious—the code is as confusing to read as following one noodle through a plate of spaghetti.

For example, suppose you are in charge of admissions at a college, and you've decided you will admit prospective students based on the following criteria:

- You will admit students who score 90 or better on the admissions test your college gives, as long as they are in the upper 75 percent of their high-school graduating class. (These are smart students who score well on the admissions test. Maybe they didn't do so well in high school because it was a tough school, or maybe they have matured.)
- You will admit students who score at least 80 on the admissions test if they are in the upper 50 percent of their high-school graduating class. (These students score fairly well on the test, and do fairly well in school.)
- You will admit students who score as low as 70 on your test if they are in the top 25 percent of their class. (Maybe these students don't take tests well, but obviously they are achievers.)

Table 2-1 summarizes the admission requirements.

**TABLE 2-1:** ADMISSION REQUIREMENTS

| Test score | High-school rank |
|---|---|
| 90–100 | Upper 75 percent (from 25th to 100th percentile) |
| 80–89 | Upper half (from 50th to 100th percentile) |
| 70–79 | Upper 25 percent (from 75th to 100th percentile) |

The flowchart for this program could look like the one in Figure 2-2. This kind of flowchart is an example of spaghetti code. Many computer programs (especially older computer programs) bear a striking resemblance to the flowchart in Figure 2-2. Such programs might "work"—that is, they might produce correct results—but they are very difficult to read and maintain, and their logic is difficult to follow.

**FIGURE 2-2:** SPAGHETTI CODE EXAMPLE

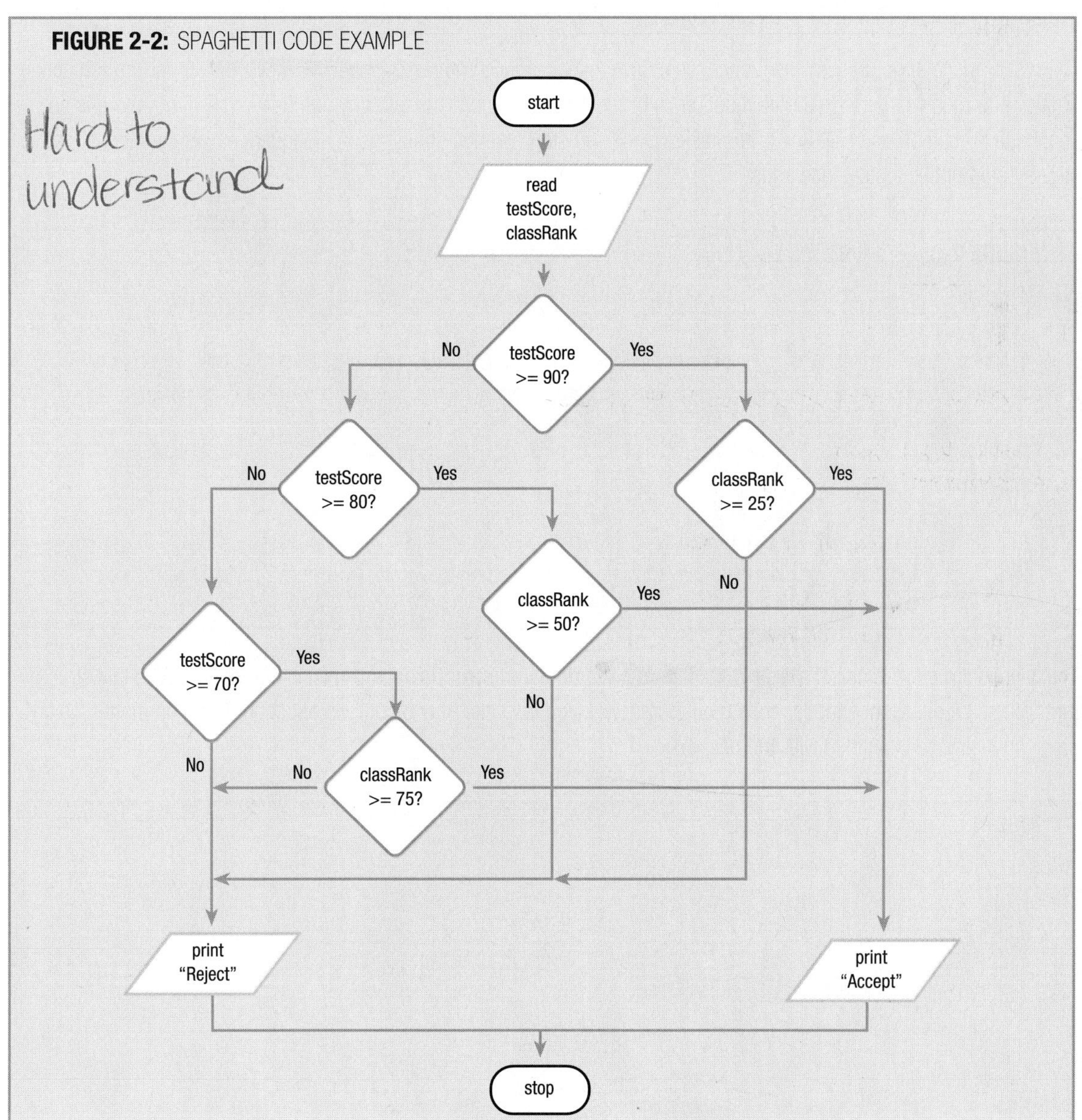

## UNDERSTANDING THE THREE BASIC STRUCTURES

In the mid-1960s, mathematicians proved that any program, no matter how complicated, can be constructed using one or more of only three structures. A **structure** is a basic unit of programming logic; each structure is a sequence, selection, or loop. With these three structures alone, you can diagram any task, from doubling a number to performing brain surgery. You can diagram each structure with a specific configuration of flowchart symbols.

The first of these structures is a sequence, as shown in Figure 2-3. With a **sequence structure**, you perform an action or task, and then you perform the next action, in order. A sequence can contain any number of tasks, but there is no chance to branch off and skip any of the tasks. Once you start a series of actions in a sequence, you must continue step-by-step until the sequence ends.

**FIGURE 2-3:** SEQUENCE STRUCTURE

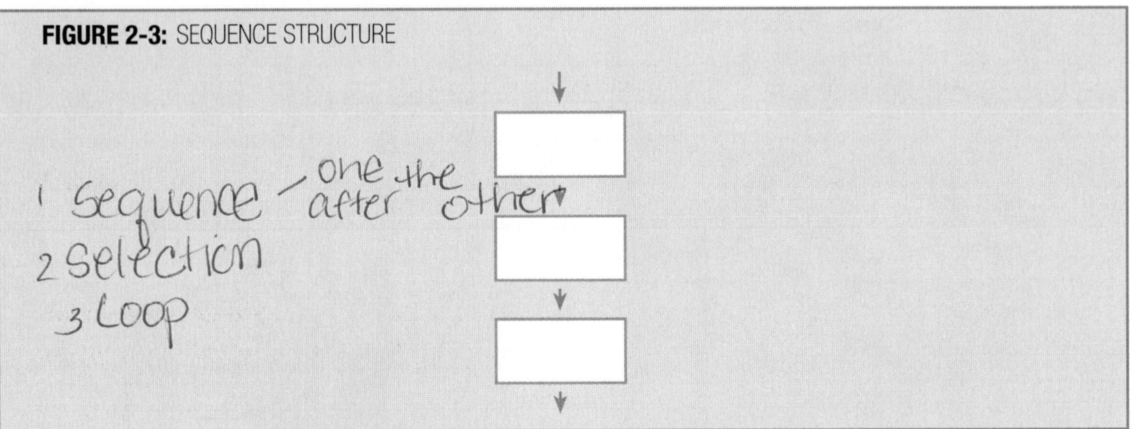

The second structure is called a **selection structure** or **decision structure**, as shown in Figure 2-4. With this structure, you ask a question, and, depending on the answer, you take one of two courses of action. Then, no matter which path you follow, you continue with the next task.

**FIGURE 2-4:** SELECTION STRUCTURE

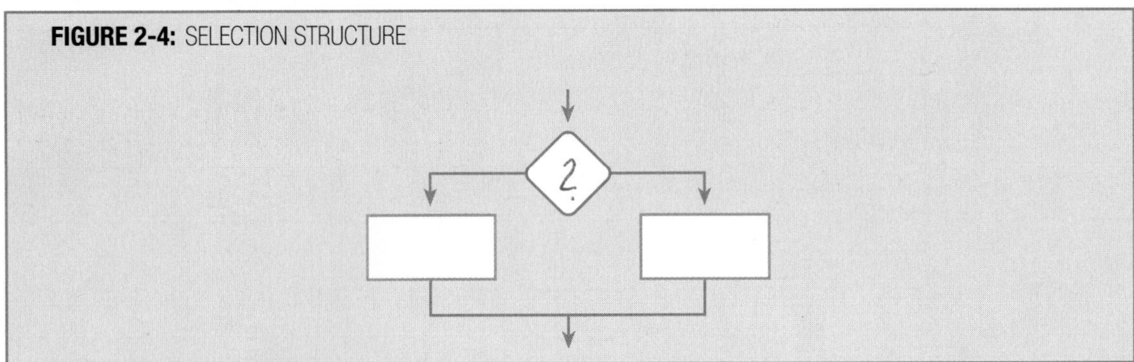

Some people call the selection structure an **if-then-else** because it fits the following statement:

```
if someCondition is true then
   do oneProcess
else
   do theOtherProcess
```

For example, while cooking you may decide the following:

```
if we have brownSugar then
   use brownSugar
else
   use whiteSugar
```

Similarly, a payroll program might include a statement such as:

```
if hoursWorked is more than 40 then
   calculate regularPay and overtimePay
else
   calculate regularPay
```

The previous examples can also be called **dual-alternative ifs**, because they contain two alternatives—the action taken when the tested condition is true and the action taken when it is false. Note that it is perfectly correct for one branch of the selection to be a "do nothing" branch. For example:

```
if it is raining then
   take anUmbrella
```

or

```
if employee belongs to dentalPlan then
   deduct $40 from employeeGrossPay
```

The previous examples are **single-alternative ifs**, and a diagram of their structure is shown in Figure 2-5. In these cases, you don't take any special action if it is not raining or if the employee does not belong to the dental plan. The case where nothing is done is often called the **null case**.

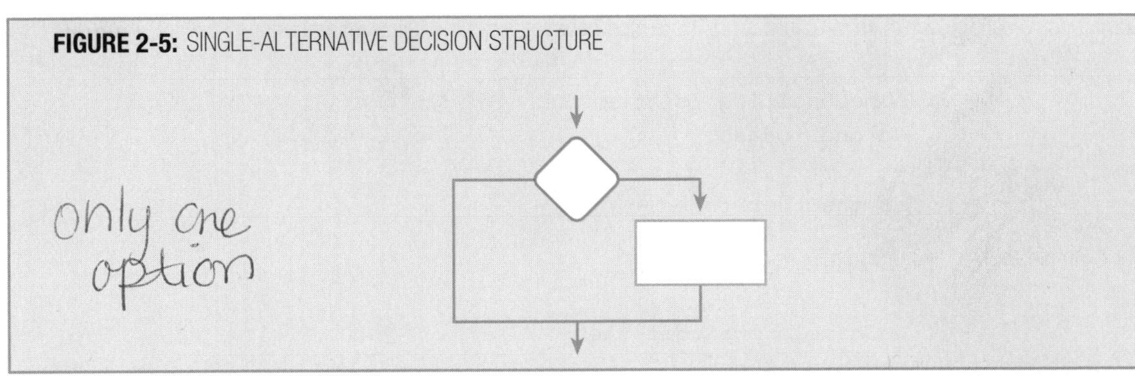

**FIGURE 2-5:** SINGLE-ALTERNATIVE DECISION STRUCTURE

The third structure, shown in Figure 2-6, is a loop. In a **loop structure**, you continue to repeat actions based on the answer to a question. In the most common type of loop, you first ask a question; if the answer requires an action, you perform the action and ask the original question again. If the answer requires that the action be taken again, you take the action and then ask the original question again. This continues until the answer to the question is such that the action is no longer required; then you exit the structure. You may hear programmers refer to looping as **repetition** or **iteration**.

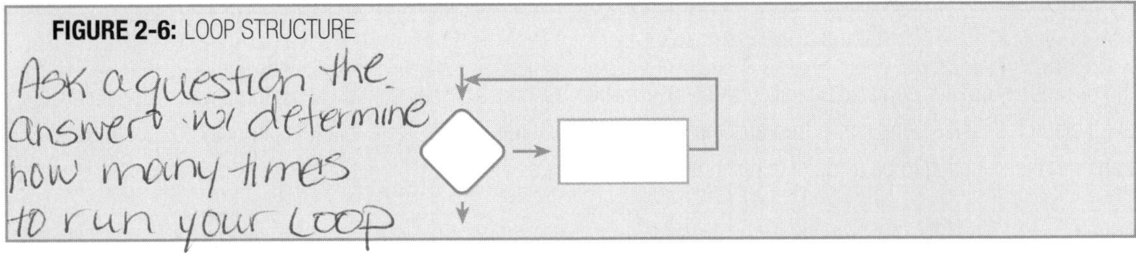

**FIGURE 2-6:** LOOP STRUCTURE

Some programmers call this structure a **while...do**, or more simply, a **while** loop, because it fits the following statement:

```
while testCondition continues to be true
   do someProcess
```

You encounter examples of looping every day, as in:

```
while you continue to beHungry
   take anotherBiteOfFood
```

or

```
while unreadPages remain in the readingAssignment
   read another unreadPage
```

In a business program, you might write:

```
while quantityInInventory remains low
   continue to orderItems
```

or

```
while there are more retailPrices to be discounted
   compute a discount
```

All logic problems can be solved using only these three structures—sequence, selection, and loop. The three structures, of course, can be combined in an infinite number of ways. For example, you can have a sequence of tasks followed by a selection, or a loop followed by a sequence. Attaching structures end-to-end is called **stacking** structures. For example, Figure 2-7 shows a structured flowchart achieved by stacking structures, and shows pseudocode that might follow that flowchart logic.

**FIGURE 2-7:** STRUCTURED FLOWCHART AND PSEUDOCODE

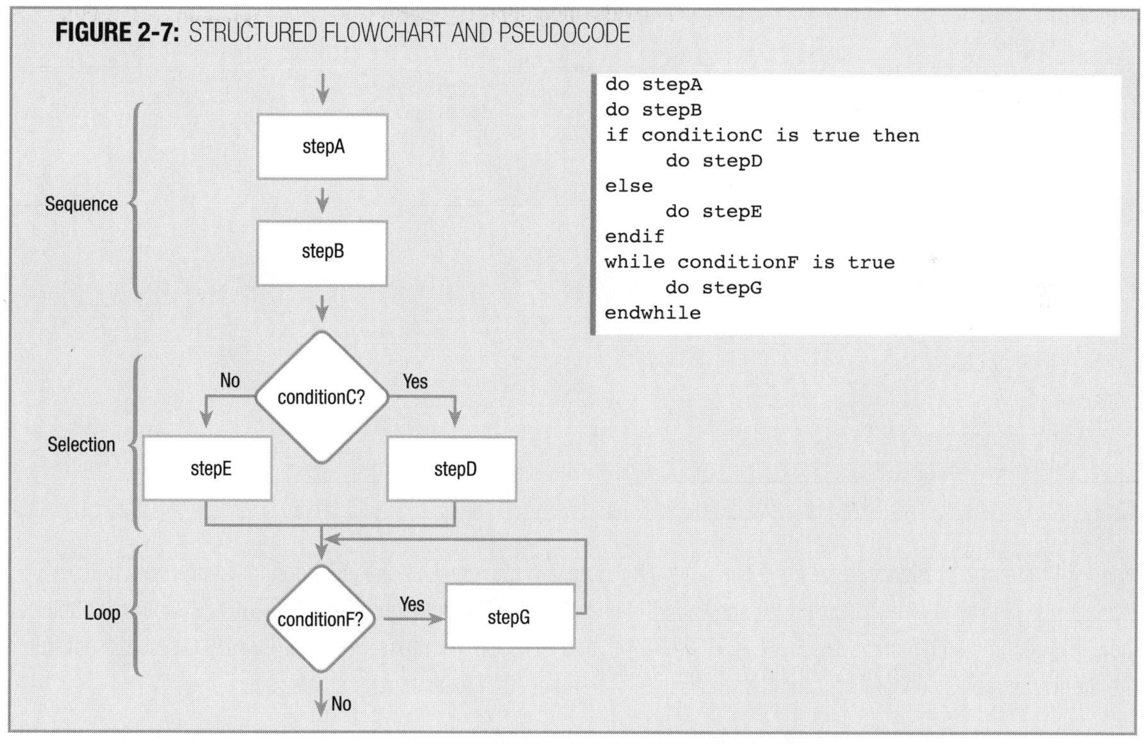


```
do stepA
do stepB
if conditionC is true then
     do stepD
else
     do stepE
endif
while conditionF is true
     do stepG
endwhile
```

The pseudocode in Figure 2-7 shows two end-structure statements—`endif` and `endwhile`. You can use an `endif` statement to clearly show where the actions that depend on a decision end. The instruction that follows `if` occurs when its tested condition is true, the instruction that follows `else` occurs when the tested condition is false, and the instruction that follows `endif` occurs in either case—it is not dependent on the `if` statement at all. In other words, statements beyond the `endif` statement are "outside" the decision structure. Similarly, you use an `endwhile` statement to show where a loop structure ends. In Figure 2-7, while `conditionF` continues to be true, `stepG` continues to execute. If any statements followed the `endwhile` statement, they would be outside of, and not a part of, the loop.

**TIP** Whether you are drawing a flowchart or writing pseudocode, you can use either of the following pairs to represent decision outcomes: yes and no or true and false. This book follows the convention of using yes and no in flowchart diagrams and true and false in pseudocode.

Besides stacking structures, you can replace any individual tasks or steps in a structured flowchart diagram or pseudocode segment with additional structures. In other words, any sequence, selection, or loop can contain other sequences, selections, or loops. For example, you can have a sequence of three tasks on one side of a selection, as shown in Figure 2-8. Placing a structure within another structure is called **nesting** the structures.

**FIGURE 2-8:** FLOWCHART AND PSEUDOCODE SHOWING A SEQUENCE NESTED WITHIN A SELECTION

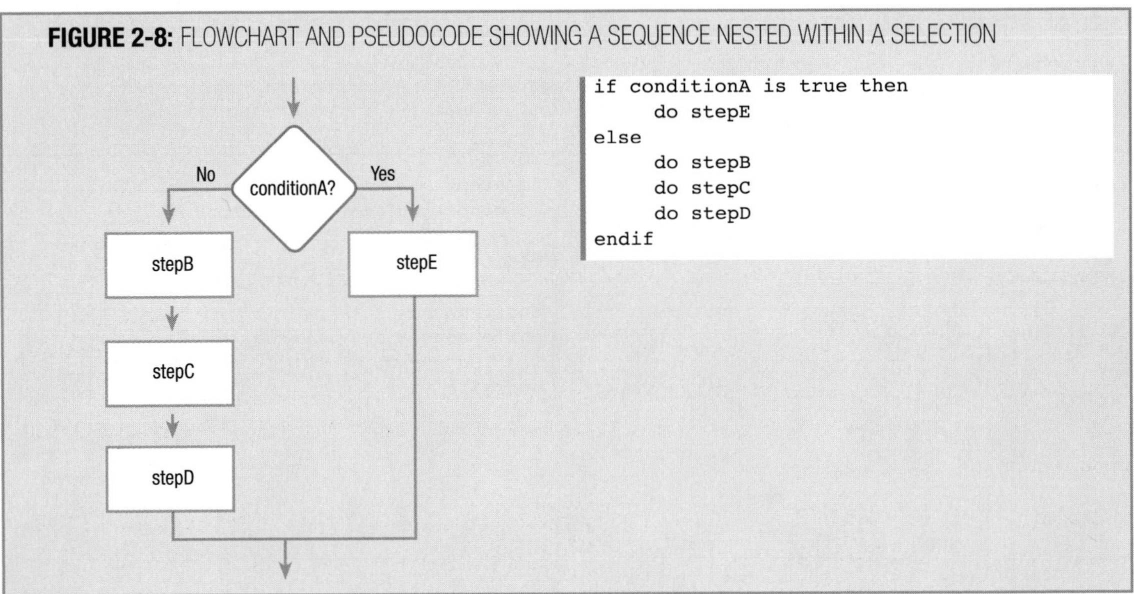


```
if conditionA is true then
     do stepE
else
     do stepB
     do stepC
     do stepD
endif
```

When you write the pseudocode for the logic shown in Figure 2-8, the convention is to indent all statements that depend on one branch of the decision, as shown in the pseudocode. The indentation and the `endif` statement both show that all three statements (`do stepB`, `do stepC`, and `do stepD`) must execute if `conditionA` is not true. The three statements constitute a **block**, or a group of statements that execute as a single unit.

In place of one of the steps in the sequence in Figure 2-8, you can insert a selection. In Figure 2-9, the process named `stepC` has been replaced with a selection structure that begins with a test of the condition named `conditionF`.

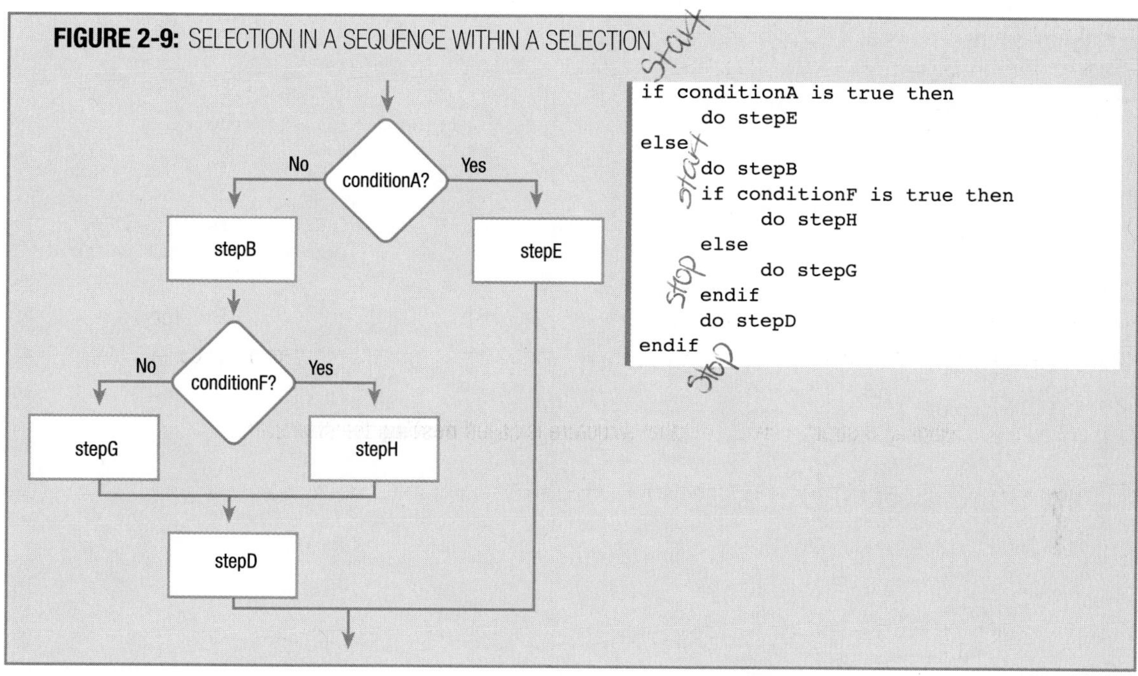


```
if conditionA is true then
    do stepE
else
    do stepB
    if conditionF is true then
        do stepH
    else
        do stepG
    endif
    do stepD
endif
```

**FIGURE 2-9:** SELECTION IN A SEQUENCE WITHIN A SELECTION

In the pseudocode shown in Figure 2-9, notice that `do stepB`, `if conditionF is true then`, `else`, `endif`, and `do stepD` all align vertically with each other. This shows that they are all "on the same level." If you look at the same problem flowcharted in Figure 2-9, you see that you could draw a vertical line through the symbols containing `stepB`, `conditionF`, and `stepD`. The flowchart and the pseudocode represent exactly the same logic. The `stepH` and `stepG` processes, on the other hand, are one level "down"; they are dependent on the answer to the `conditionF` question. Therefore, the `do stepH` and `do stepG` statements are indented one additional level in the pseudocode.

Also notice that the pseudocode in Figure 2-9 has two `endif` statements. Each is aligned to correspond to an `if`. An `endif` always partners with the most recent `if` that does not already have an `endif` partner, and an `endif` should always align vertically with its `if` partner.

In place of `do stepH` on one side of the new selection in Figure 2-9, you can insert a loop. This loop, based on `conditionI`, appears inside the selection that is within the sequence that constitutes the "No" side of the original `conditionA` selection. In the pseudocode in Figure 2-10, notice that the `while` aligns with the `endwhile`, and that the entire `while` structure is indented within the true ("Yes") half of the `if` structure that begins with the decision based on `conditionF`. The indentation used in the pseudocode reflects the logic you can see laid out graphically in the flowchart.

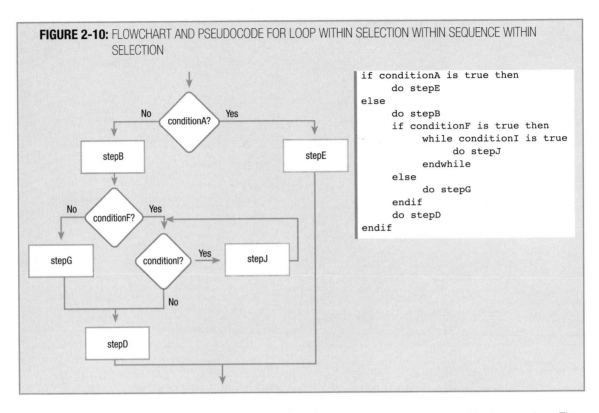

**FIGURE 2-10:** FLOWCHART AND PSEUDOCODE FOR LOOP WITHIN SELECTION WITHIN SEQUENCE WITHIN SELECTION

```
if conditionA is true then
     do stepE
else
     do stepB
     if conditionF is true then
          while conditionI is true
               do stepJ
          endwhile
     else
          do stepG
     endif
     do stepD
endif
```

The combinations are endless, but each of a structured program's segments is a sequence, a selection, or a loop. The three structures are shown together in Figure 2-11. Notice that each structure has one entry and one exit point. One structure can attach to another only at one of these points.

**FIGURE 2-11:** THE THREE STRUCTURES

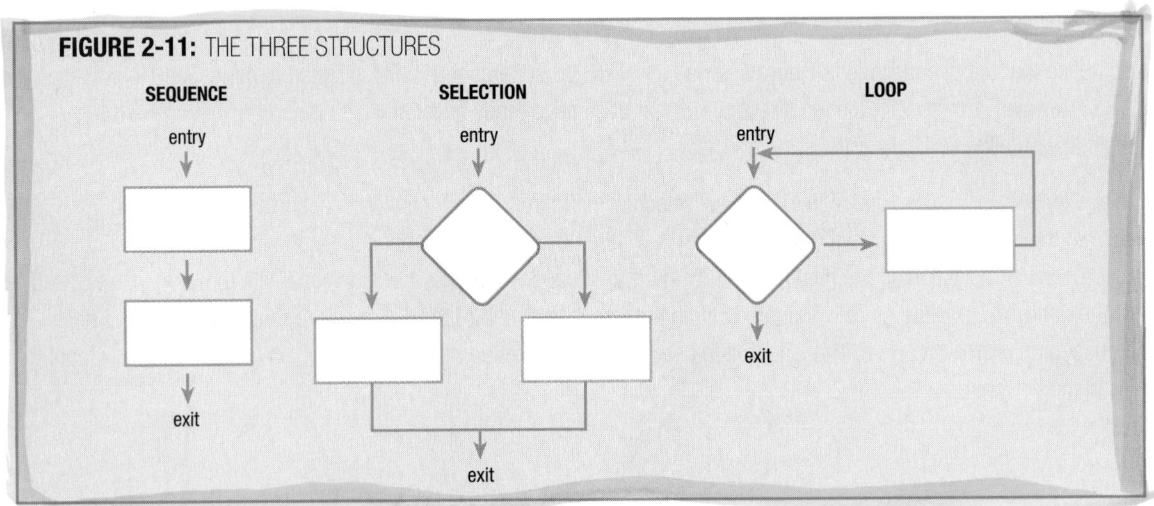

Try to imagine physically picking up any of the three structures using the "handles" marked entry and exit. These are the spots at which you could connect a structure to any of the others. Similarly, any complete structure, from its entry point to its exit point, can be inserted within the process symbol of any other structure.

In summary, a structured program has the following characteristics:

- A structured program includes only combinations of the three basic structures—sequence, selection, and loop. Any structured program might contain one, two, or all three types of structures.
- Structures can be stacked or connected to one another only at their entry or exit points.
- Any structure can be nested within another structure.

TIP

A structured program is never required to contain examples of all three structures; a structured program might contain only one or two of them. For example, many simple programs contain only a sequence of several tasks that execute from start to finish without any needed selections or loops. As another example, a program might display a series of numbers, looping to do so, but never making any decisions about the numbers.

## USING THE PRIMING READ

For a program to be structured and work the way you want it to, sometimes you need to add extra steps. The priming read is one kind of added step. A **priming read** or **priming input** is the statement that reads the first input data record. If a program will read 100 data records, you read the first data record in a statement that is separate from the other 99. You must do this to keep the program structured.

At the end of Chapter 1, you read about a program like the one in Figure 2-12. The program gets a number and checks for the end-of-file condition. If it is not the end of file, then the number is doubled, the answer is printed, and the next number is input.

1 Reads the first input data Record -(File)
2 Assign variables to values.

**FIGURE 2-12:** UNSTRUCTURED FLOWCHART OF A NUMBER-DOUBLING PROGRAM

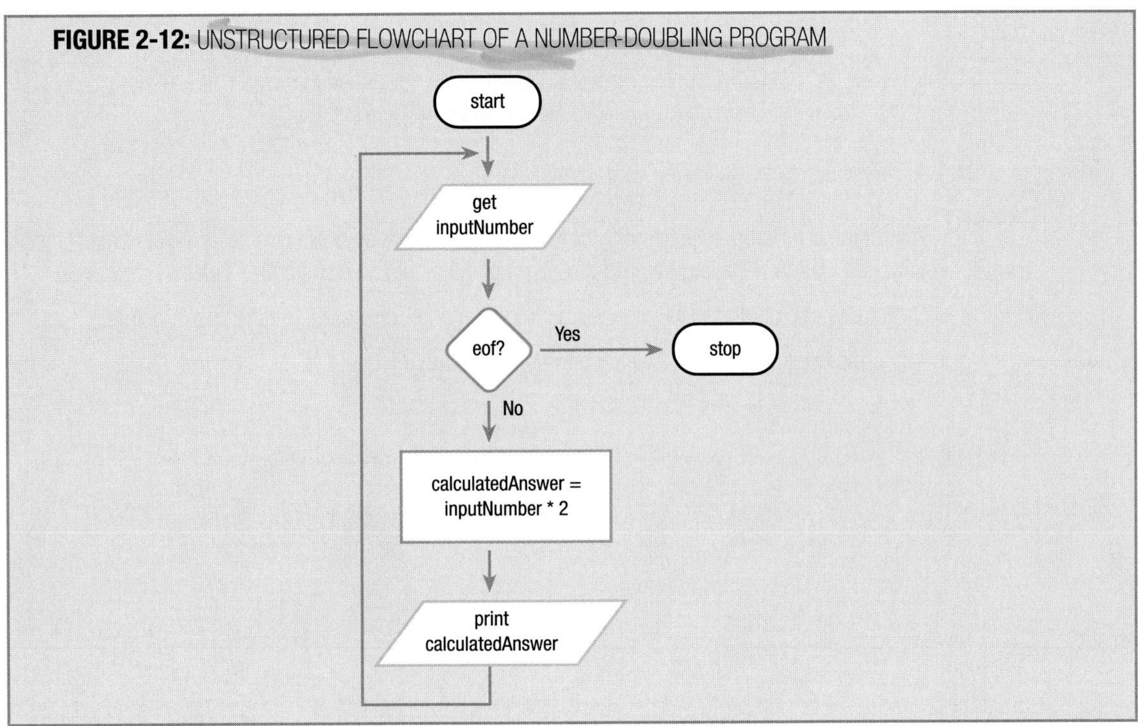


Is the program represented by Figure 2-12 structured? At first, it might be hard to tell. The three allowed structures were illustrated in Figure 2-11.

The flowchart in Figure 2-12 does not look exactly like any of the three shapes shown in Figure 2-11. However, because you may stack and nest structures while retaining overall structure, it might be difficult to determine whether a flowchart as a whole is structured. It's easiest to analyze the flowchart in Figure 2-12 one step at a time. The beginning of the flowchart looks like Figure 2-13.

**FIGURE 2-13:** BEGINNING OF A NUMBER-DOUBLING FLOWCHART

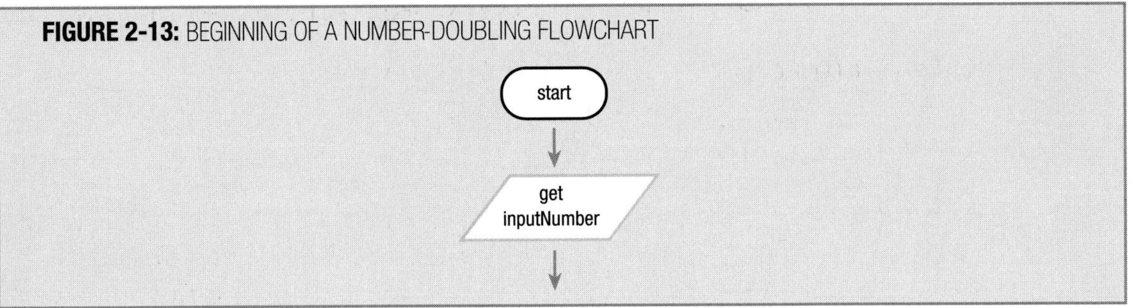


Is this portion of the flowchart structured? Yes, it's a sequence. (Even a single task can be a sequence—it's just a brief sequence.) Adding the next piece of the flowchart looks like Figure 2-14.

FIGURE 2-14: NUMBER-DOUBLING FLOWCHART

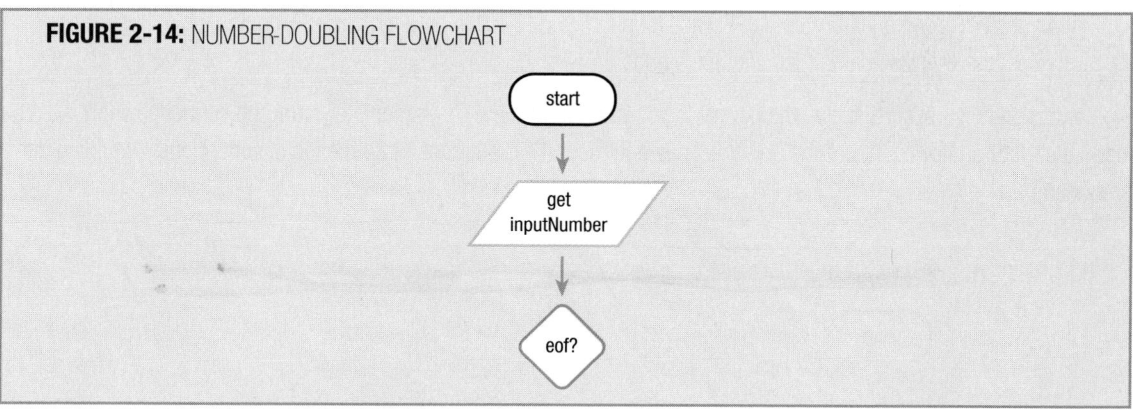


The sequence is finished; either a selection or a loop is starting. You might not know which one, but you do know the sequence is not continuing, because sequences can't contain questions. With a sequence, each task or step must follow without any opportunity to branch off. Therefore, which type of structure starts with the question in Figure 2-14? Is it a selection or a loop?

With a selection structure, the logic goes in one of two directions after the question, and then the flow comes back together; the question is not asked a second time. However, in a loop, if the answer to the question results in the loop being entered and the loop statements executing, then the logic returns to the question that started the loop; when the body of a loop executes, the question that controls the loop is always asked again.

In the number-doubling problem in the original Figure 2-12, if it is not `eof` (that is, if the end-of-file condition is not met), then some math is done, an answer is printed, a new number is obtained, and the `eof` question is asked again. In other words, while the answer to the `eof` question continues to be *no*, eventually the logic will return to the `eof` question. (Another way to phrase this is that while it continues to be true that `eof` has not yet been reached, the logic keeps returning to the same question.) Therefore, the number-doubling problem contains a structure beginning with the `eof` question that is more like the beginning of a loop than it is like a selection.

The number-doubling problem *does* contain a loop, but it's not a structured loop. In a structured loop, the rules are:

1. You ask a question.
2. If the answer indicates you should take some action or perform a procedure, then you do so.
3. If you perform the procedure, then you must go right back to repeat the question.

The flowchart in Figure 2-12 asks a question; if the answer is *no* (that is, while it is true that the `eof` condition has not been met), then the program performs two tasks: it does the arithmetic and it prints the results. Doing two things is acceptable because two tasks with no possible branching constitute a sequence, and it is fine to nest a structure within another structure. However, when the sequence ends, the logic doesn't flow right back to the question. Instead, it goes *above* the question to get another number. For the loop in Figure 2-12 to be a structured loop, the logic must return to the `eof` question when the embedded sequence ends.

The flowchart in Figure 2-15 shows the flow of logic returning to the `eof` immediately after the sequence. Figure 2-15 shows a structured flowchart, but the flowchart has one major flaw—it doesn't do the job of continuously doubling different numbers.

**FIGURE 2-15:** STRUCTURED, BUT NONFUNCTIONAL, FLOWCHART OF NUMBER-DOUBLING PROBLEM

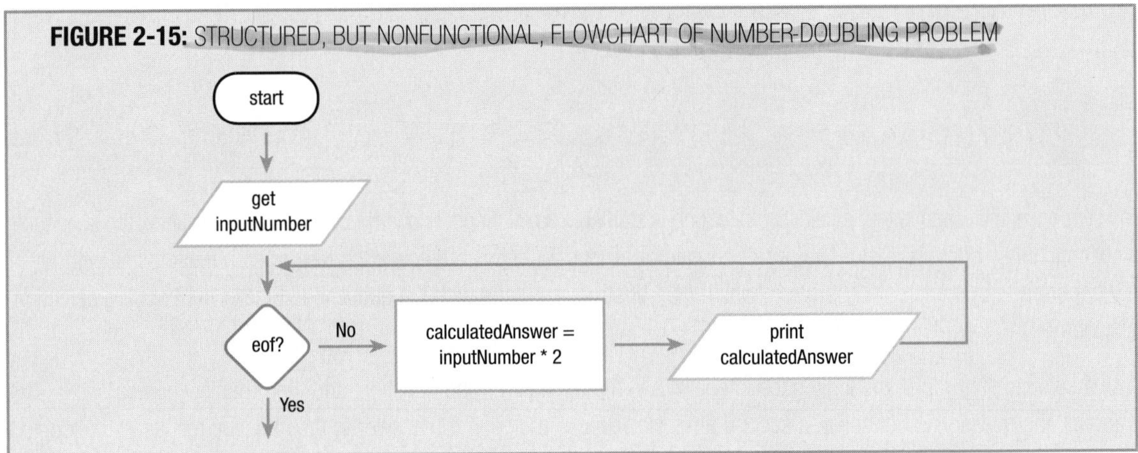


Follow the flowchart in Figure 2-15 through a typical program run. Suppose when the program starts, the user enters a 9 for the value of `inputNumber`. That's not `eof`, so the number doubles, and 18 prints out as the `calculatedAnswer`. Then the question `eof?` is asked again. It can't be `eof` because a new value representing the sentinel (ending) value can't be entered. The logic never returns to the `get inputNumber` task, so the value of `inputNumber` never changes. Therefore, 9 doubles again and the answer 18 prints again. It's still not `eof`, so the same steps are repeated. This goes on *forever*, with the answer 18 printing repeatedly. The program logic shown in Figure 2-15 is structured, but it doesn't work as intended; the program in Figure 2-16 works, but it isn't structured!

**FIGURE 2-16:** FUNCTIONAL BUT NONSTRUCTURED FLOWCHART

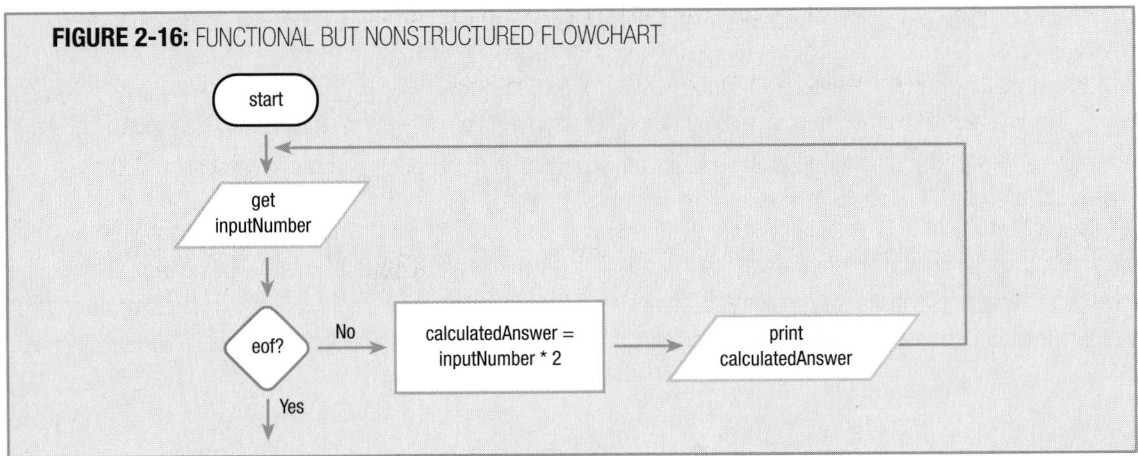

**TIP** □□□□ The loop in Figure 2-16 is not structured because in a structured loop, after the tasks execute within the loop, the flow of logic must return directly to the loop-controlling question. In Figure 2-16, the logic does not return to the loop-controlling question; instead, it goes "too high" outside the loop to repeat the `get inputNumber` task.

How can the number-doubling problem be both structured and work as intended? Often, for a program to be structured, you must add something extra. In this case, it's an extra `get inputNumber` step. Consider the solution in Figure 2-17; it's structured *and* it does what it's supposed to do. The program logic illustrated in Figure 2-17 contains a sequence and a loop. The loop contains another sequence.

**FIGURE 2-17:** FUNCTIONAL, STRUCTURED FLOWCHART AND PSEUDOCODE FOR THE NUMBER-DOUBLING PROBLEM

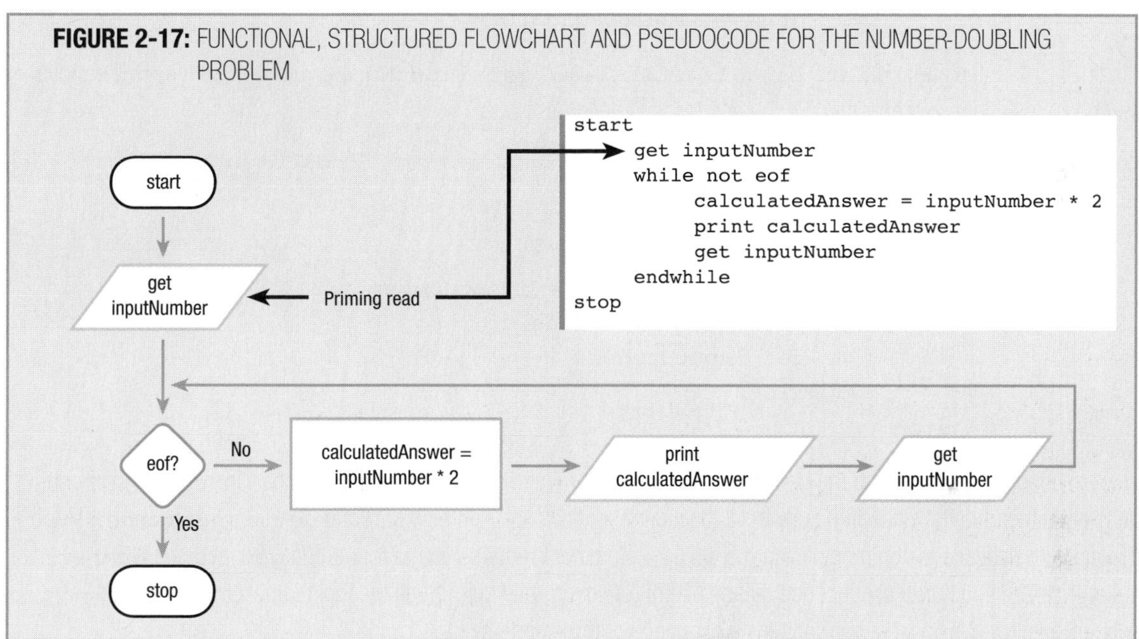


The additional `get inputNumber` step is typical in structured programs. The first of the two input steps is the priming input, or priming read. The term *priming* comes from the fact that the read is first, or *primary* (what gets the process going, as in "priming the pump"). The purpose of the priming read step is to control the upcoming loop that begins with the `eof` question. The last element within the structured loop gets the next, and all subsequent, input values. This is also typical in structured loops—the last step executed within the loop alters the condition tested in the question that begins the loop, which in this case is the `eof` question.

As an additional way to determine whether a flowchart segment is structured, you can try to write pseudocode for it. Examine the unstructured flowchart in Figure 2-12 again. To write pseudocode for it, you would begin with the following:

```
start
     get inputNumber
```

eof (end of file)

When you encounter the `eof` question in the flowchart, you know that either a selection or loop structure should begin. Because you return to a location higher in the flowchart when the answer to the `eof` question is *no* (that is, while the `not eof` condition continues to be *true*), you know that a loop is beginning. So you continue to write the pseudocode as follows:

```
start
     get inputNumber
     while not eof
          calculatedAnswer = inputNumber * 2
          print calculatedAnswer
```

Continuing, the step after `print calculatedAnswer` is `get inputNumber`. This ends the `while` loop that began with the `eof` question. So the pseudocode becomes:

```
start
     get inputNumber
     while not eof
          calculatedAnswer = inputNumber * 2
          print calculatedAnswer
          get inputNumber
     endwhile
stop
```

This pseudocode is identical to the pseudocode in Figure 2-17 and now matches the flowchart in the same figure. It does not match the flowchart in Figure 2-12, because that flowchart contains only one `get inputNumber` step. Creating the pseudocode correctly using the `while` statement requires you to repeat the `get inputNumber` statement. The structured pseudocode makes use of a priming read and forces the logic to become structured—a sequence followed by a loop that contains a sequence of three statements.

**TIP**

Years ago, programmers could avoid using structure by inserting a "go to" statement into their pseudocode. A "go to" statement would say something like "after print answer, go to the first get number box", and would be the equivalent of drawing an arrow starting after "print answer" and pointing directly to the first "get number" box in the flowchart. Because "go to" statements cause spaghetti code, they are not allowed in structured programming. Some programmers call structured programming "goto-less" programming.

Figure 2-18 shows another way you might attempt to draw the logic for the number-doubling program. At first glance, the figure might seem to show an acceptable solution to the problem—it is structured, containing a single loop with a sequence of three steps within it, and it appears to eliminate the need for the priming input statement. When the program starts, the `eof` question is asked. The answer is *no*, so the program gets an input number, doubles it, and prints it. Then, if it is still not `eof`, the program gets another number, doubles it, and prints it. The program continues until `eof` is encountered when getting input. The last time the `get inputNumber` statement executes, it encounters `eof`, but the program does not stop—instead, it calculates and prints one last time. This last output is extraneous—the `eof` value should not be doubled and printed. As a general rule, an `eof` question should always come immediately after an input statement. Therefore, the best solution to the number-doubling problem remains the one shown in Figure 2-17—the solution containing the priming input statement.

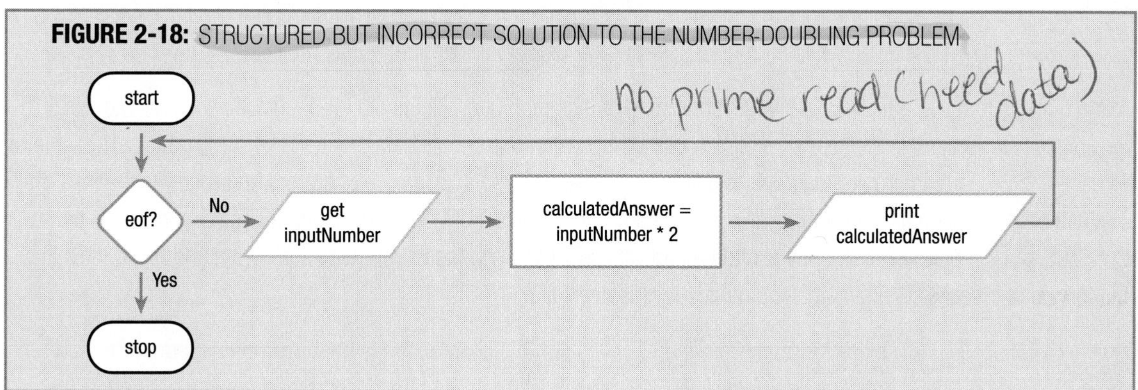


**FIGURE 2-18:** STRUCTURED BUT INCORRECT SOLUTION TO THE NUMBER-DOUBLING PROBLEM

**TIP** A few languages do not require the priming read. For example, programs written using the Visual Basic programming language can "look ahead" to determine whether the end of file will be reached on the next input record. However, most programming languages cannot predict the end of file until an actual read operation is performed, and they require a priming read to properly handle file data.

## UNDERSTANDING THE REASONS FOR STRUCTURE

At this point, you may very well be saying, "I liked the original number-doubling program just fine. I could follow it. Also, the first program had one less step in it, so it was less work. Who cares if a program is structured?"

Until you have some programming experience, it is difficult to appreciate the reasons for using only the three structures—sequence, selection, and loop. However, staying with these three structures is better for the following reasons:

- *Clarity*—The number-doubling program is a small program. As programs get bigger, they get more confusing if they're not structured.
- *Professionalism*—All other programmers (and programming teachers you might encounter) expect your programs to be structured. It's the way things are done professionally.
- *Efficiency*—Most newer computer languages are structured languages with syntax that lets you deal efficiently with sequence, selection, and looping. Older languages, such as assembly languages, COBOL, and RPG, were developed before the principles of structured programming were discovered. However, even programs that use those older languages can be written in a structured form, and structured programming is expected on the job today. Newer languages such as C#, C++, and Java enforce structure by their syntax.

- *Maintenance*—You, as well as other programmers, will find it easier to modify and maintain structured programs as changes are required in the future.
- *Modularity*—Structured programs can be easily broken down into routines or modules that can be assigned to any number of programmers. The routines are then pieced back together like modular furniture at each routine's single entry or exit point. Additionally, often a module can be used in multiple programs, saving development time in the new project.

Most programs that you purchase are huge, consisting of thousands or millions of statements. If you've worked with a word-processing program or spreadsheet, think of the number of menu options and keystroke combinations available to the user. Such programs are not the work of one programmer. The modular nature of structured programs means that work can be divided among many programmers; then the modules can be connected, and a large program can be developed much more quickly. Money is often a motivating factor—the faster you write a program and make it available for use, the sooner it begins making money for the developer.

Consider the college admissions program from the beginning of this chapter. It has been rewritten in structured form in Figure 2-19 and is easier to follow now. Figure 2-19 also shows structured pseudocode for the same problem.

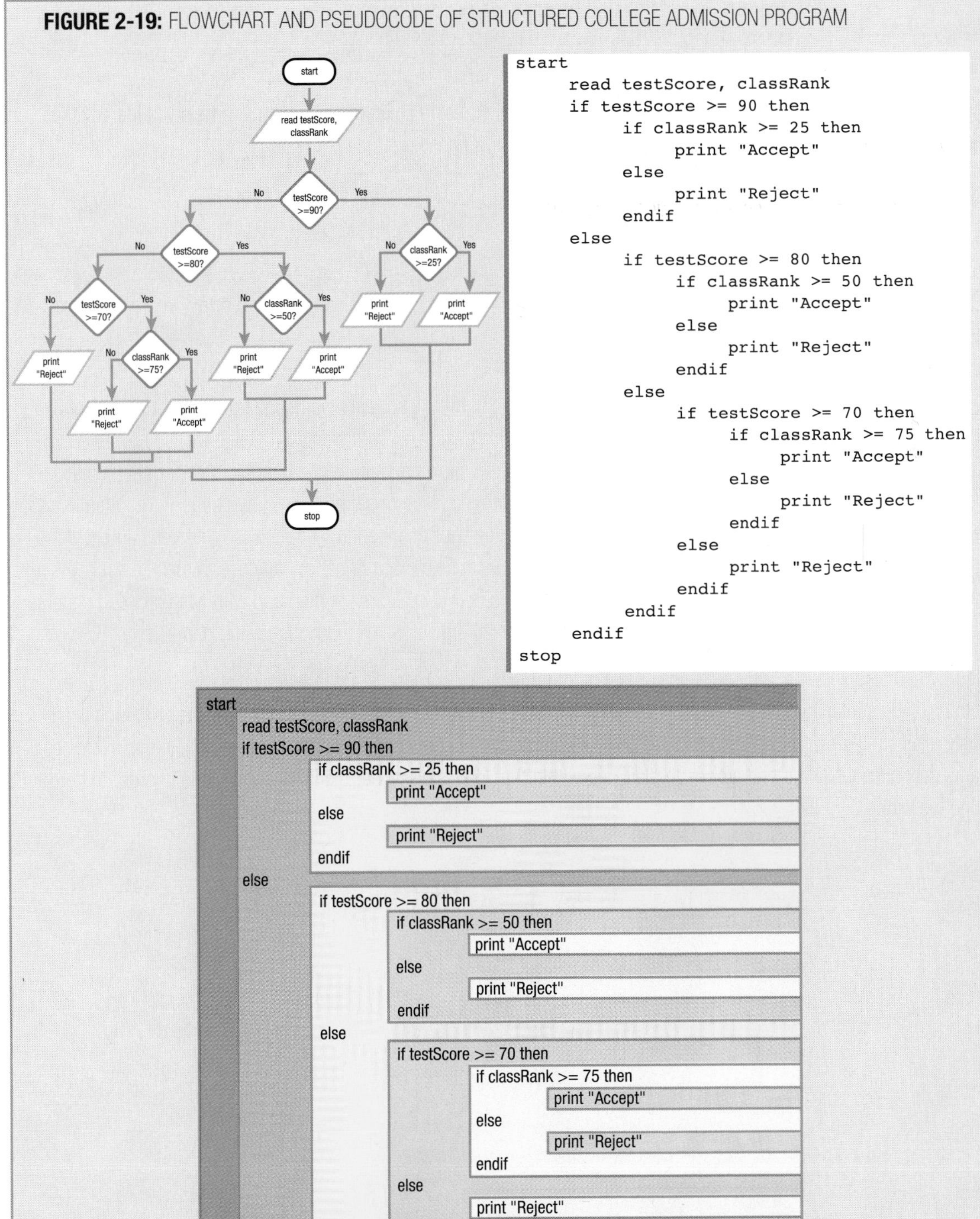


```
start
     read testScore, classRank
     if testScore >= 90 then
          if classRank >= 25 then
               print "Accept"
          else
               print "Reject"
          endif
     else
          if testScore >= 80 then
               if classRank >= 50 then
                    print "Accept"
               else
                    print "Reject"
               endif
          else
               if testScore >= 70 then
                    if classRank >= 75 then
                         print "Accept"
                    else
                         print "Reject"
                    endif
               else
                    print "Reject"
               endif
          endif
     endif
stop
```

**FIGURE 2-19:** FLOWCHART AND PSEUDOCODE OF STRUCTURED COLLEGE ADMISSION PROGRAM

**TIP**

Don't be alarmed if it is difficult for you to follow the many nested `ifs` within the pseudocode in Figure 2-19. After you study the selection process in more detail, reading this type of pseudocode will become much easier for you.

In the lower portion of Figure 2-19, the pseudocode is repeated using colored backgrounds to help you identify the indentations that match, distinguishing the different levels of the nested structures.

**TIP**

As you examine Figure 2-19, notice that the bottoms of the three `testScore` decision structures join at the bottom of the diagram. These three joinings correspond to the last three `endif` statements in the pseudocode.

## RECOGNIZING STRUCTURE

Any set of instructions can be expressed in a structured format. If you can teach someone how to perform any ordinary activity, then you can express it in a structured way. For example, suppose you wanted to teach a child how to play Rock, Paper, Scissors. In this game, two players simultaneously show each other one hand, in one of three positions—clenched in a fist, representing a rock; opened flat, representing a piece of paper; or with two fingers extended in a V, representing scissors. The goal is to guess which hand position your opponent might show, so that you can show the one that beats it. The rules are that a flat hand beats a fist (because a piece of paper can cover a rock), a fist beats a hand with two extended fingers (because a rock can smash a pair of scissors), and a hand with two extended fingers beats a flat hand (because scissors can cut paper). Figure 2-20 shows the pseudocode for the game.

Figure 2-20 also shows a fairly complicated set of statements. Its purpose is not to teach you how to play a game (although you could learn how to play by following the logic), but rather to convince you that any task to which you can apply rules can be expressed logically using only combinations of sequence, selection, and looping. In this example, a game continues while a friend agrees to play, and within that loop, several decisions must be made in order to determine the winner.

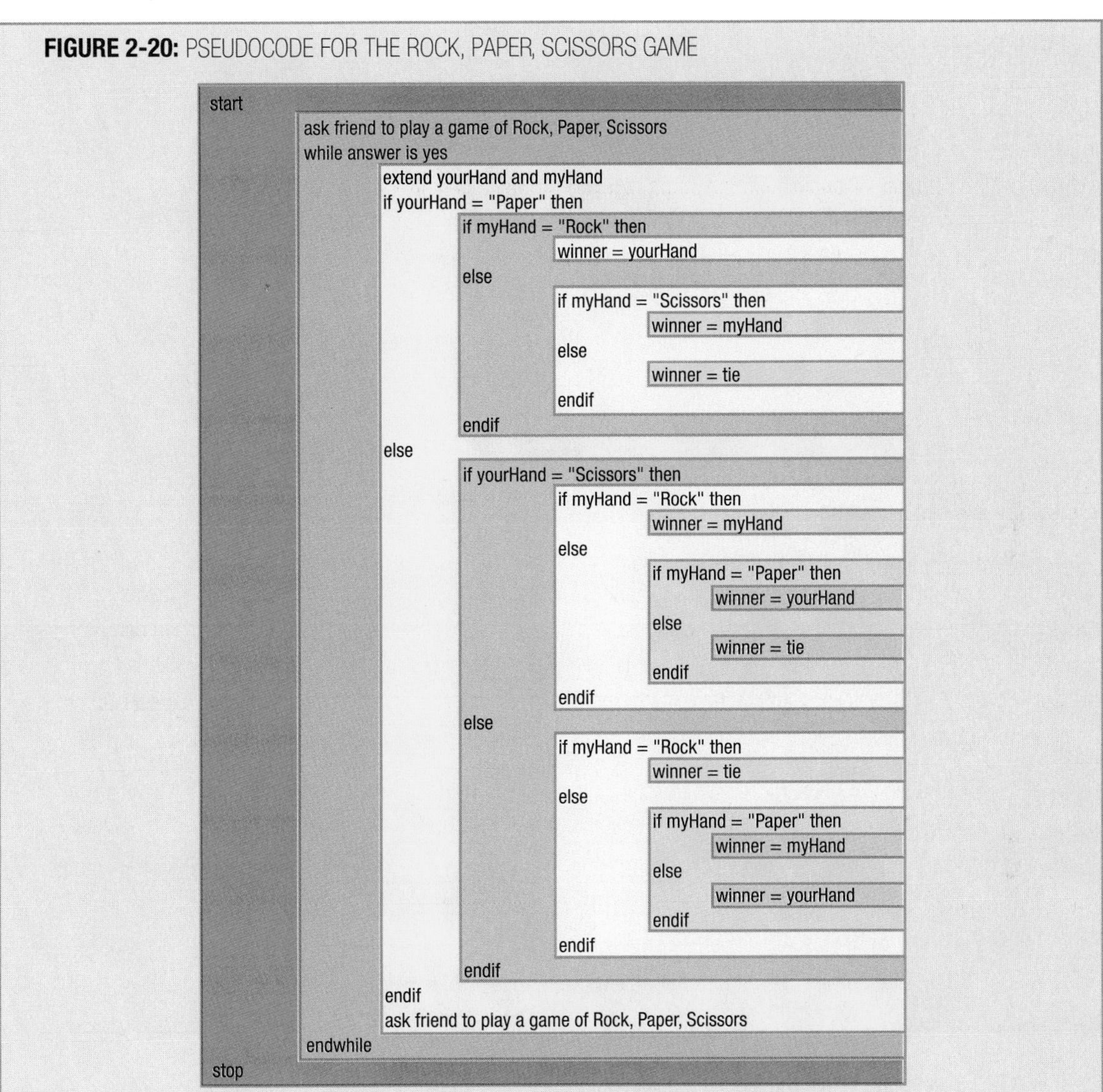

**FIGURE 2-20:** PSEUDOCODE FOR THE ROCK, PAPER, SCISSORS GAME

```
start
    ask friend to play a game of Rock, Paper, Scissors
    while answer is yes
        extend yourHand and myHand
        if yourHand = "Paper" then
            if myHand = "Rock" then
                winner = yourHand
            else
                if myHand = "Scissors" then
                    winner = myHand
                else
                    winner = tie
                endif
            endif
        else
            if yourHand = "Scissors" then
                if myHand = "Rock" then
                    winner = myHand
                else
                    if myHand = "Paper" then
                        winner = yourHand
                    else
                        winner = tie
                    endif
                endif
            else
                if myHand = "Rock" then
                    winner = tie
                else
                    if myHand = "Paper" then
                        winner = myHand
                    else
                        winner = yourHand
                    endif
                endif
            endif
        endif
        ask friend to play a game of Rock, Paper, Scissors
    endwhile
stop
```

When you are just learning about structured program design, it is difficult to detect whether a flowchart of a program's logic is structured. For example, is the flowchart segment in Figure 2-21 structured?

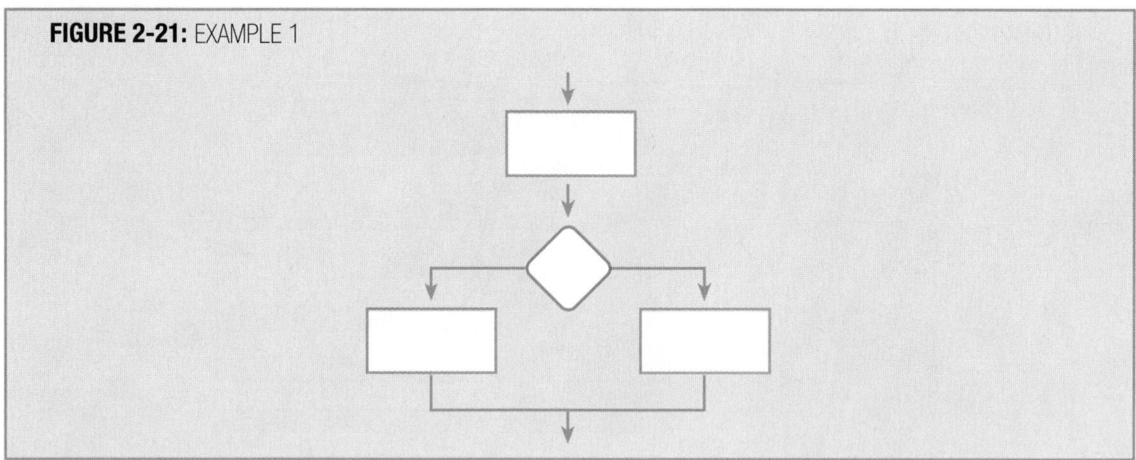

**FIGURE 2-21:** EXAMPLE 1

Yes, it is. It has a sequence and a selection structure.

Is the flowchart segment in Figure 2-22 structured?

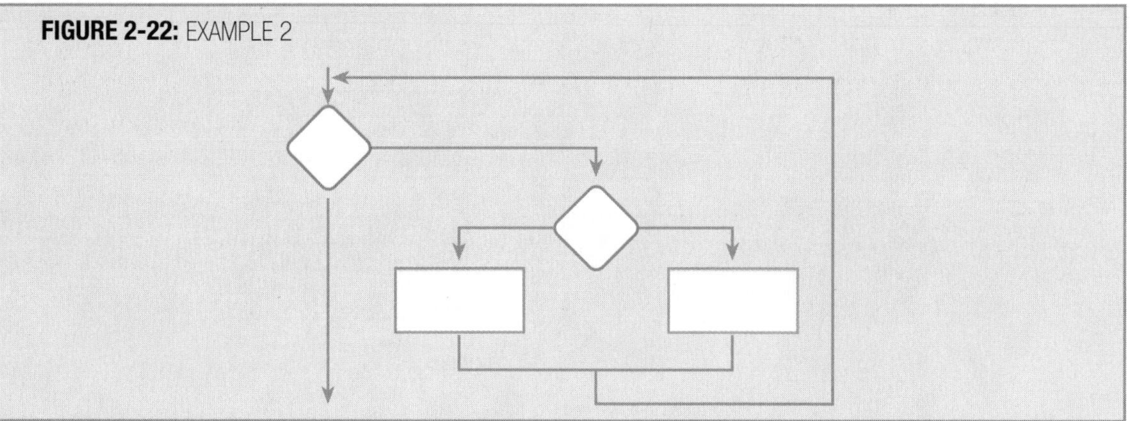

**FIGURE 2-22:** EXAMPLE 2

Yes, it is. It has a loop, and within the loop is a selection.

Is the flowchart segment in Figure 2-23 structured? (The symbols are lettered so you can better follow the discussion.)

**FIGURE 2-23:** EXAMPLE 3

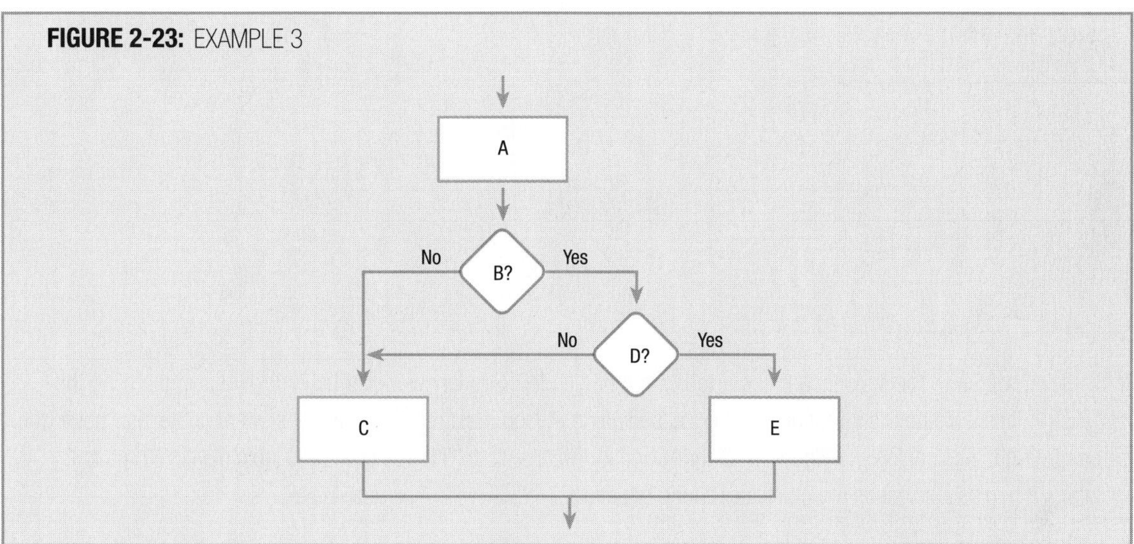


No, it isn't; it is not constructed from the three basic structures. One way to straighten out a flowchart segment that isn't structured is to use what you can call the "spaghetti bowl" method; that is, picture the flowchart as a bowl of spaghetti that you must untangle. Imagine you can grab one piece of pasta at the top of the bowl, and start pulling. As you "pull" each symbol out of the tangled mess, you can untangle the separate paths until the entire segment is structured. For example, with the diagram in Figure 2-23, if you start pulling at the top, you encounter a procedure box, labeled A. (See Figure 2-24.)

**FIGURE 2-24:** UNTANGLING EXAMPLE 3, FIRST STEP

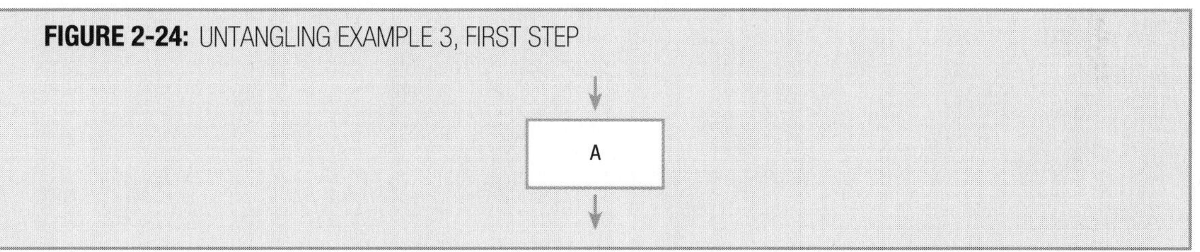


A single process like A is part of an acceptable structure—it constitutes at least the beginning of a sequence structure. Imagine you continue pulling symbols from the tangled segment. The next item in the flowchart is a question that tests a condition labeled B, as you can see in Figure 2-25.

**FIGURE 2-25:** UNTANGLING EXAMPLE 3, SECOND STEP

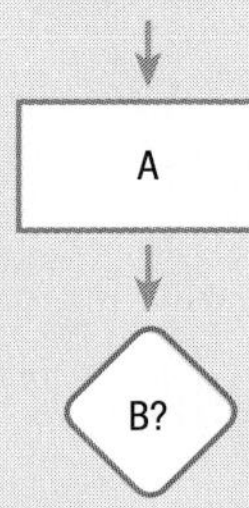

A

B?

At this point, you know the sequence that started with A has ended. Sequences never have decisions in them, so the sequence is finished; either a selection or a loop is beginning. A loop must return to the question at some later point. You can see from the original logic in Figure 2-23 that whether the answer to B is yes or no, the logic never returns to B. Therefore, B begins a selection structure, not a loop structure.

To continue detangling the logic, you (imaginarily) pull up on the flowline that emerges from the left side (the "No" side) of Question B. You encounter C, as shown in Figure 2-26. When you continue beyond C, you reach the end of the flowchart.

**FIGURE 2-26:** UNTANGLING EXAMPLE 3, THIRD STEP

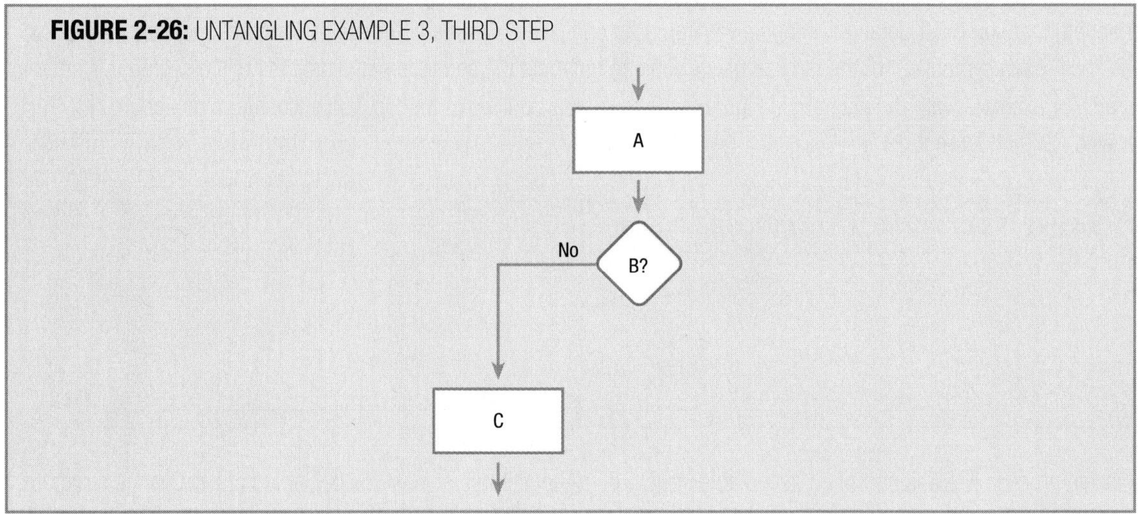


Now you can turn your attention to the "Yes" side (the right side) of the condition tested in B. When you pull up on the right side, you encounter Question D. (See Figure 2-27.)

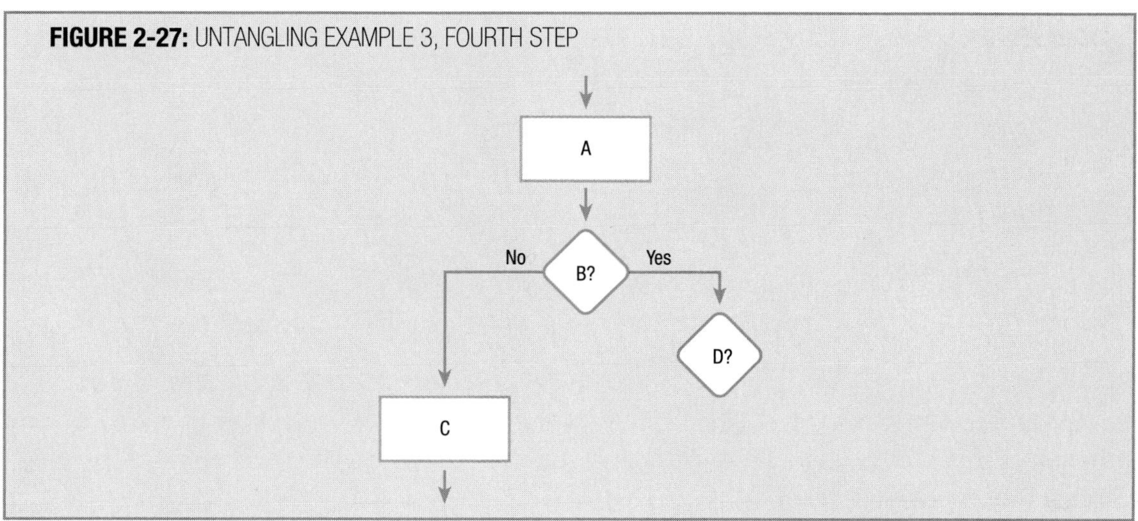

**FIGURE 2-27:** UNTANGLING EXAMPLE 3, FOURTH STEP

In Figure 2-23, follow the line on the left side of Question D. The line extending from the selection is attached to a task outside the selection. The line emerging from the left side of selection D is attached to Step C. You might say the D selection is becoming entangled with the B selection, so you must untangle the structures by repeating the step that is causing the tangle. (In this example, you repeat Step C to untangle it from the other usage of C.) Continue pulling on the flowline that emerges from Step C until you reach the end of the program segment, as shown in Figure 2-28.

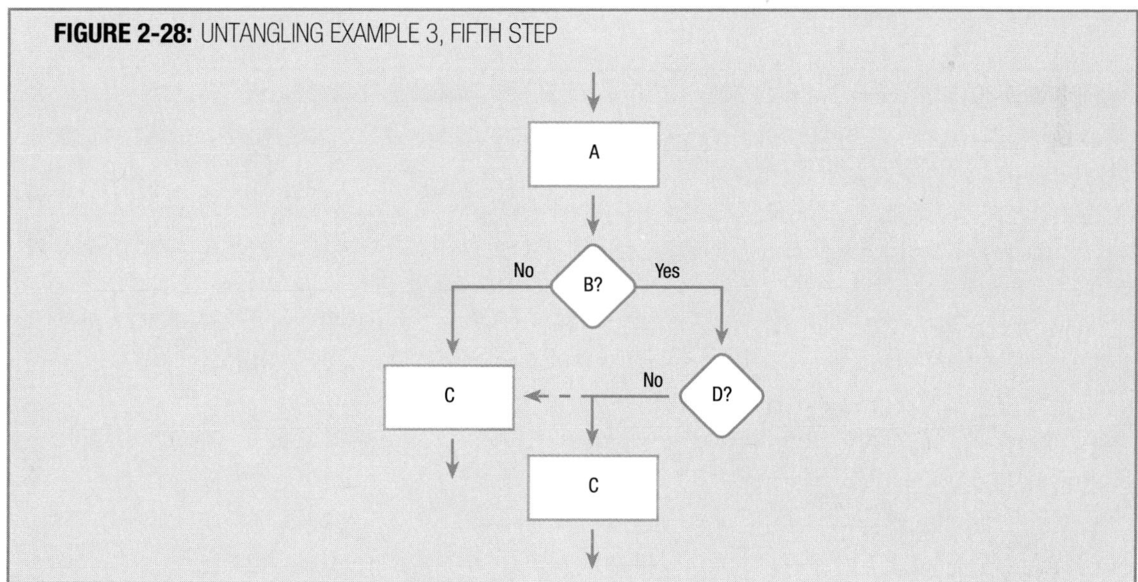

**FIGURE 2-28:** UNTANGLING EXAMPLE 3, FIFTH STEP

Now pull on the right side of Question D. Process E pops up, as shown in Figure 2-29; then you reach the end.

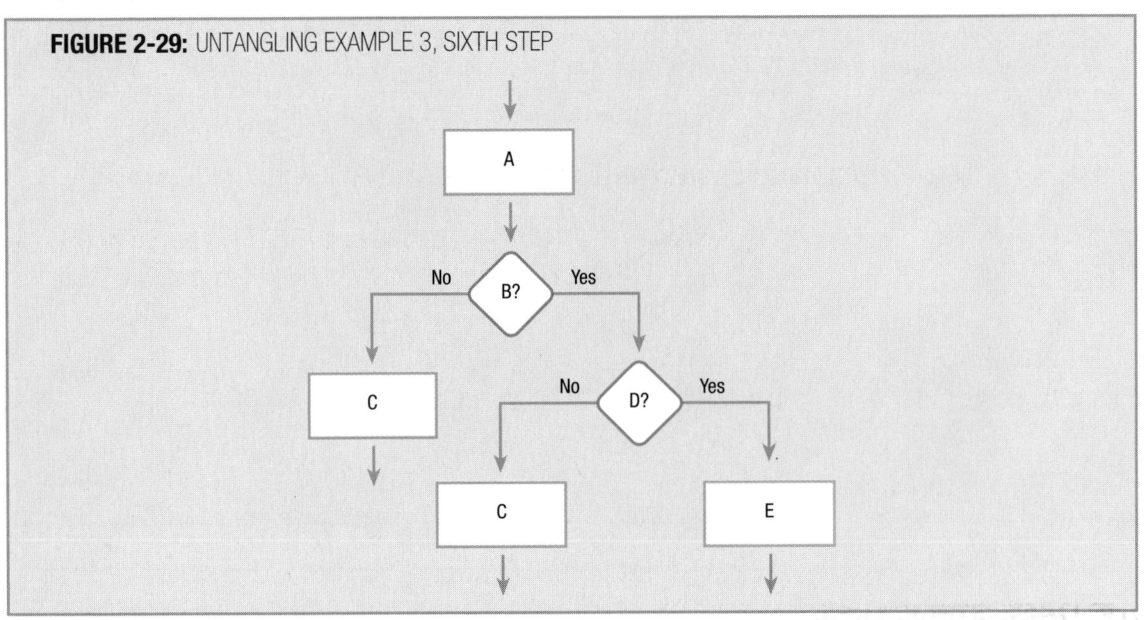

**FIGURE 2-29:** UNTANGLING EXAMPLE 3, SIXTH STEP

At this point, the untangled flowchart has three loose ends. The loose ends of Question D can be brought together to form a selection structure; then the loose ends of Question B can be brought together to form another selection structure. The result is the flowchart shown in Figure 2-30. The entire flowchart segment is structured—it has a sequence (A) followed by a selection inside a selection.

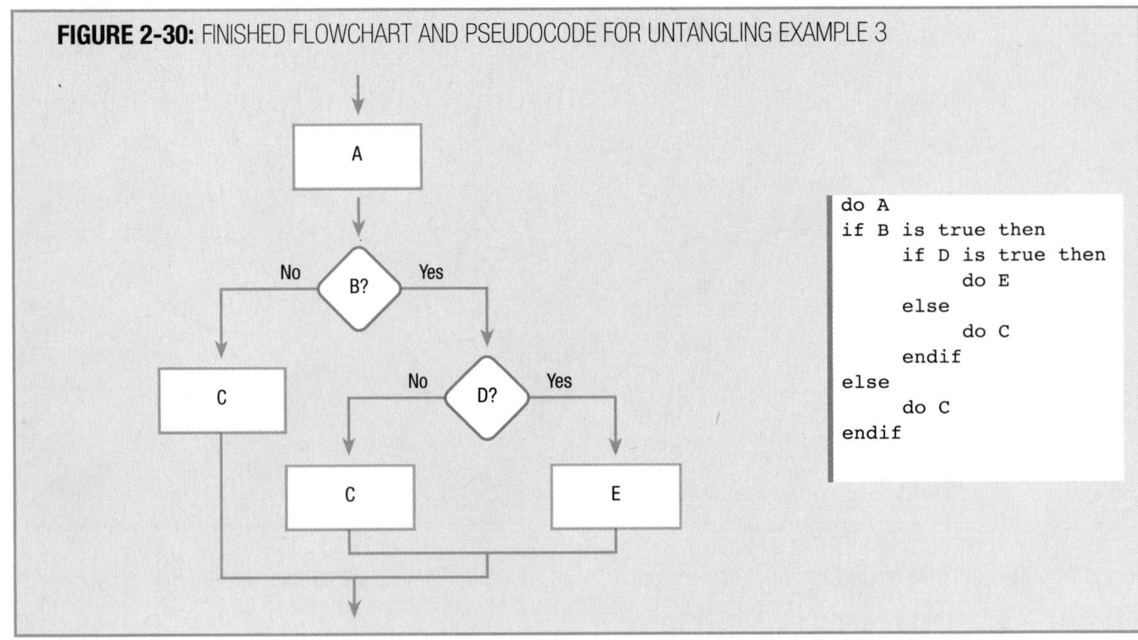


```
do A
if B is true then
     if D is true then
          do E
     else
          do C
     endif
else
     do C
endif
```

**FIGURE 2-30:** FINISHED FLOWCHART AND PSEUDOCODE FOR UNTANGLING EXAMPLE 3

**TIP** □□□□ If you want to try structuring a very difficult example of an unstructured program, see Appendix A.

## THREE SPECIAL STRUCTURES—CASE, DO WHILE, AND DO UNTIL

**TIP** □□□□ You can skip this section for now without any loss in continuity. Your instructor may prefer to discuss the case structure with the Decision chapter (Chapter 5), and the do-while and do-until loops with the Looping chapter (Chapter 6).

You can solve any logic problem you might encounter using only the three structures: sequence, selection, and loop. However, many programming languages allow three more structures: the case structure and the do-while and do-until loops. These structures are never *needed* to solve any problem—you can always use a series of selections instead of the case structure, and you can always use a sequence plus a while loop in place of the do-while or do-until loops. However, sometimes these additional structures are convenient. Programmers consider them all to be acceptable, legal structures.

### THE CASE STRUCTURE

You can use the **case structure** when there are several distinct possible values for a single variable you are testing, and each value requires a different course of action. Suppose you administer a school at which tuition is $75, $50, $30, or $10 per credit hour, depending on whether a student is a freshman, sophomore, junior, or senior. The structured flowchart and pseudocode in Figure 2-31 show a series of decisions that assigns the correct tuition to a student.

**FIGURE 2-31:** FLOWCHART AND PSEUDOCODE OF TUITION DECISIONS

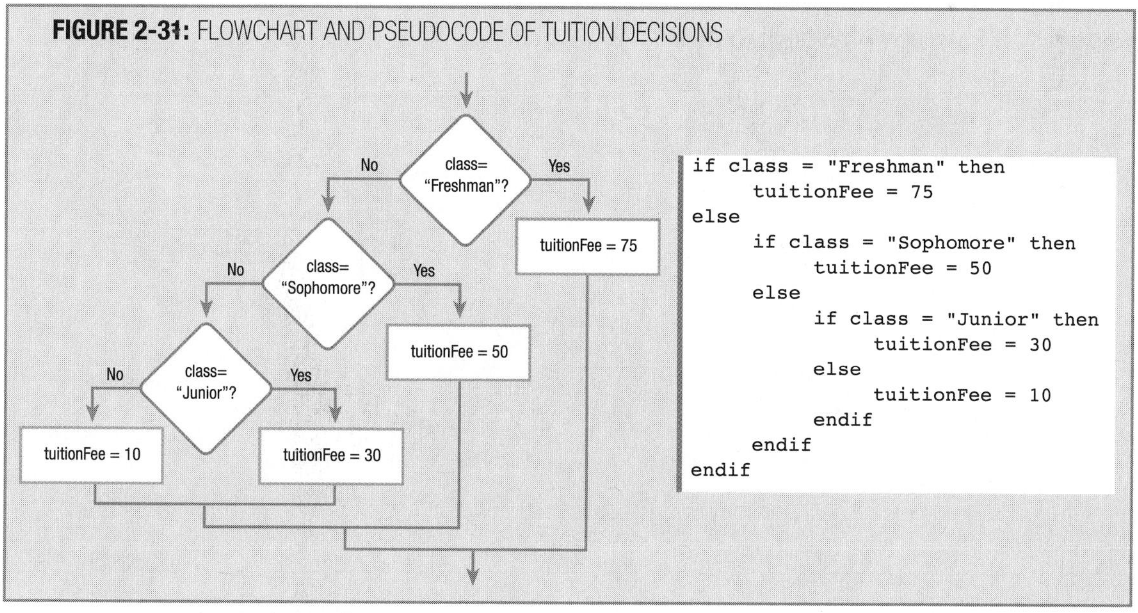


```
if class = "Freshman" then
     tuitionFee = 75
else
     if class = "Sophomore" then
          tuitionFee = 50
     else
          if class = "Junior" then
               tuitionFee = 30
          else
               tuitionFee = 10
          endif
     endif
endif
```

TIP

The indentation in the pseudocode in Figure 2-31 reflects the nested nature of the decisions, as illustrated in the flowchart. For clarity, some programmers might prefer to write the pseudocode as follows:

```
if class = "Freshman" then
   tuitionFee = 75
else if class = "Sophomore" then
   tuitionFee = 50
else if class = "Junior" then
   tuitionFee = 30
endif
```

This style, with `else` and the next `if` on the same line and a single `endif` at the end, is often preferred by Visual Basic programmers because it resembles a style they use in their programs. However, this book will use the style shown in Figure 2-31, with each `endif` aligned with its corresponding `if` statement.

The logic shown in Figure 2-31 is absolutely correct and completely structured. The `class="Junior"` selection structure is contained within the `class="Sophomore"` structure, which is contained within the `class="Freshman"` structure. Note that there is no need to ask if a student is a senior, because if a student is not a freshman, sophomore, or junior, it is assumed the student is a senior.

Even though the program segments in Figure 2-31 are correct and structured, many programming languages permit using a case structure, as shown in Figure 2-32. When using the case structure, you test a variable against a series of values, taking appropriate action based on the variable's value. To many, such programs seem easier to read, and the case structure is allowed because the same results *could* be achieved with a series of structured selections (thus making the program structured). That is, if the first program is structured and the second one reflects the first one point by point, then the second one must be structured also.

**FIGURE 2-32:** FLOWCHART AND PSEUDOCODE OF CASE STRUCTURE

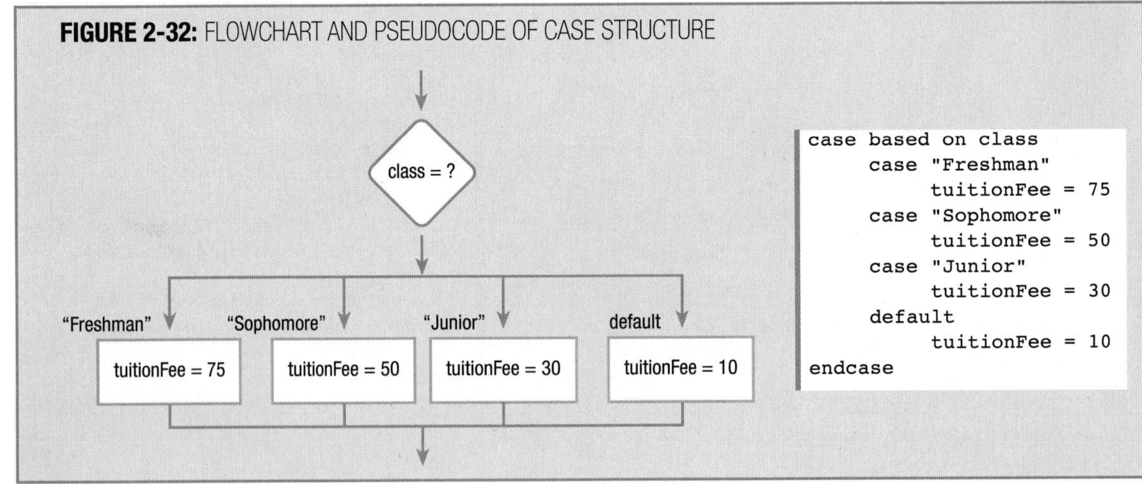


```
case based on class
     case "Freshman"
          tuitionFee = 75
     case "Sophomore"
          tuitionFee = 50
     case "Junior"
          tuitionFee = 30
     default
          tuitionFee = 10
endcase
```

**TIP** The term "default" used in Figure 2-32 means "if none of the other cases were true." Each programming language you learn may use a different syntax for the default case.

Even though a programming language permits you to use the case structure, you should understand that the case structure is just a convenience that might make a flowchart, pseudocode, or actual program code easier to understand at first glance. When you write a series of decisions using the case structure, the computer still makes a series of individual decisions, just as though you had used many if-then-else combinations. In other words, you might prefer looking at the diagram in Figure 2-32 to understand the tuition fees charged by a school, but a computer actually makes the decisions as shown in Figure 2-31—one at a time. When you write your own programs, it is always acceptable to express a complicated decision-making process as a series of individual selections.

**TIP** You usually use the case structure only when a series of decisions is based on different values stored in a single variable. If multiple variables are tested, then most programmers use a series of decisions.

## THE DO-WHILE AND DO-UNTIL LOOPS

Recall that a structured loop (often called a while loop) looks like Figure 2-33. A special-case loop called a do-while or do-until loop looks like Figure 2-34.

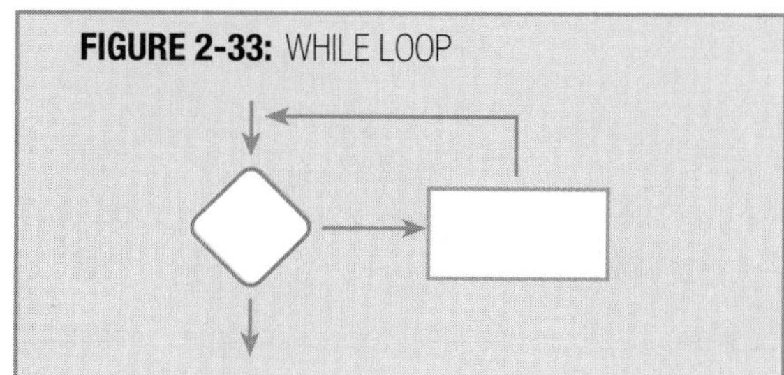

**FIGURE 2-33:** WHILE LOOP

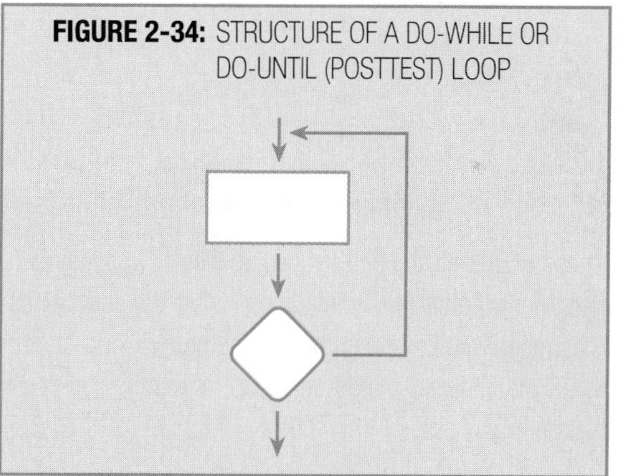

**FIGURE 2-34:** STRUCTURE OF A DO-WHILE OR DO-UNTIL (POSTTEST) LOOP

An important difference exists between these two structures. In a while loop, you ask a question and, depending on the answer, you might or might not enter the loop to execute the loop's procedure. Conversely, in **do-while** and **do-until loops**, you ensure that the procedure executes at least once; then, depending on the answer to the controlling question, the loop may or may not execute additional times. In a do-while loop, the loop body continues to execute as long as the answer to the controlling question is yes, or true. In a do-until loop, the loop body continues to execute as long as the answer to the controlling question is no, or false; that is, the body executes *until* the controlling question is yes or true.

**TIP** Notice that the word "do" begins the names of both the do-while and do-until loops. This should remind you that the action you "do" precedes testing the condition.

In a while loop, the question that controls a loop comes at the beginning, or "top," of the loop body. A while loop is also called a **pretest loop** because a condition is tested before entering the loop even once. In a do-while or do-until loop, the question that controls the loop comes at the end, or "bottom," of the loop body. Do-while and do-until loops are also called **posttest loops** because a condition is tested after the loop body has executed.

You encounter examples of do-until looping every day. For example:

```
do
     pay bills
until all bills are paid
```

and

```
do
     wash dishes
until all dishes are washed
```

Similarly, you encounter examples of do-while looping every day. For example:

```
do
     pay bills
while more bills remain to be paid
```

and

```
do
     wash dishes
while more dishes remain to be washed
```

In these examples, the activity (paying bills or washing dishes) must occur at least one time. You ask the question that determines whether you continue only after the activity has been executed at least once. The only difference in these structures is whether the answer to the bottom loop-controlling question must be false for the loop to continue (as in all bills are paid), which is a do-until loop, or true for the loop to continue (as in more bills remain to be paid), which is a do-while loop.

You are never required to use a posttest loop. You can duplicate the same series of actions generated by any posttest loop by creating a sequence followed by a standard, pretest while loop. For example, the following code performs the bill-paying task once, then asks the loop-controlling question at the top of a while loop, in which the action might be performed again:

```
pay bills
while there are more bills to pay
     pay bills
endwhile
```

Consider the flowcharts and pseudocode in Figures 2-35 and 2-36.

In Figure 2-35, A is done, and then B is asked. If B is yes, then A is done and B is asked again. In Figure 2-36, A is done, and then B is asked. If B is yes, then A is done and B is asked again. In other words, both flowcharts and pseudocode segments do exactly the same thing.

**FIGURE 2-35:** FLOWCHART AND PSEUDOCODE FOR DO-WHILE LOOP

```
do
     A
while B is true
```

**FIGURE 2-36:** FLOWCHART AND PSEUDOCODE FOR SEQUENCE FOLLOWED BY WHILE LOOP

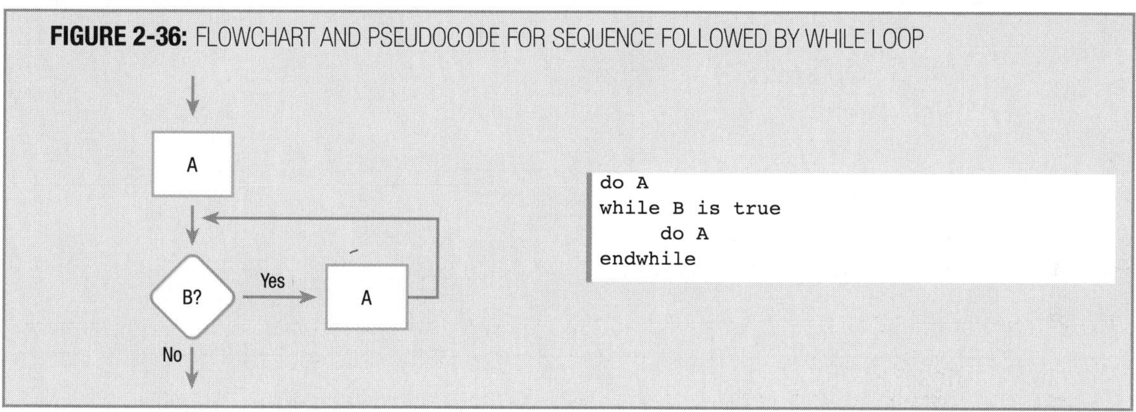


```
do A
while B is true
     do A
endwhile
```

Because programmers understand that any posttest loop (do-while or do-until) can be expressed with a sequence followed by a while loop, most languages allow the posttest loop. (Frequently, languages allow one type of posttest loop or the other.) Again, you are never required to use a posttest loop; you can always accomplish the same tasks with a sequence followed by a pretest while loop.

Figure 2-37 shows an unstructured loop. It is neither a while loop (which begins with a decision and, after an action, returns to the decision) nor a do-while or do-until loop (which begins with an action and ends with a decision that might repeat the action). Instead, it begins like a posttest loop (a do-while or a do-until loop), with a process followed by a decision, but one branch of the decision does not repeat the initial process; instead, it performs an additional new action before repeating the initial process. If you need to use the logic shown in Figure 2-37—performing a task, asking a question, and perhaps performing an additional task before looping back to the first process—then the way to make the logic structured is to repeat the initial process within the loop, at the end of the loop. Figure 2-38 shows the same logic as Figure 2-37, but now it is structured logic, with a sequence of two actions occurring within the loop.

Does this diagram look familiar to you? It uses the same technique of repeating a needed step that you saw earlier in this chapter, when you learned the rationale for the priming read.

**FIGURE 2-37:** UNSTRUCTURED LOOP

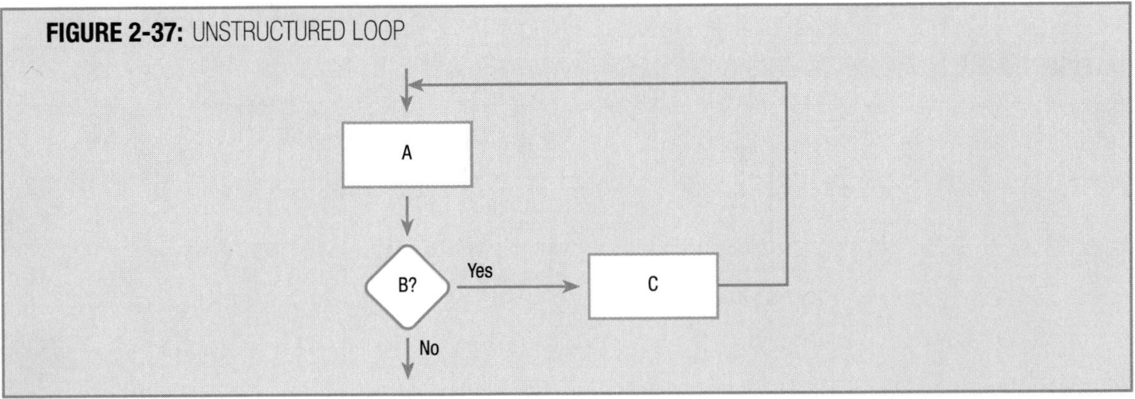


**FIGURE 2-38:** SEQUENCE AND STRUCTURED LOOP THAT ACCOMPLISH THE SAME TASKS AS FIGURE 2-37

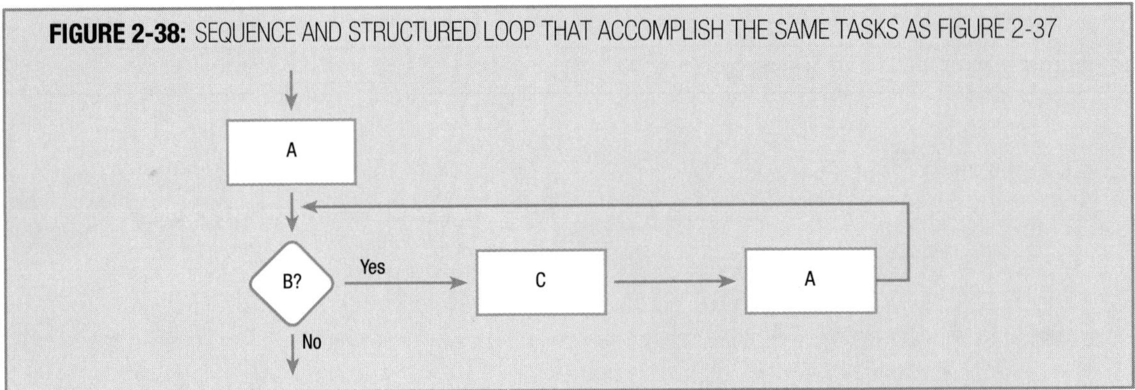


It is difficult for beginning programmers to distinguish among while, do-while, and do-until loops. A while loop asks the question first—for example, while you are hungry, eat. The answer to the question might never be true and the loop body might never execute. A while loop is the only type of loop you ever need in order to solve a problem. You can think of a do-while loop as one that continues to execute while a condition remains true—for example, process records while not end of file is true, or eat food while hungry is true. On the other hand, a do-until loop continues while a condition is false, or, in other words, until the condition becomes true—for example, address envelopes until there are no more envelopes, or eat food until you are full. When you use a do-while or a do-until loop, at least one performance of the action always occurs.

**TIP**

Especially when you are first mastering structured logic, you might prefer to only use the three basic structures—sequence, selection, and while loop. Every logical problem can be solved using only these three structures, and you can understand all of the examples in the rest of this book using only these three.

## CHAPTER SUMMARY

- The popular name for snarled program statements is spaghetti code.
- Clearer programs can be constructed using only three basic structures: sequence, selection, and loop. These three structures can be combined in an infinite number of ways by stacking and nesting them. Each structure has one entry and one exit point; one structure can attach to another only at one of these points.
- A priming read or priming input is the statement that reads the first input data record prior to starting a structured loop. The last step within the loop gets the next, and all subsequent, input values.
- You use structured techniques to promote clarity, professionalism, efficiency, and modularity.
- One way to straighten a flowchart segment that isn't structured is to imagine the flowchart as a bowl of spaghetti that you must untangle.
- You can use a case structure when there are several distinct possible values for a variable you are testing. When you write a series of decisions using the case structure, the computer still makes a series of individual decisions.
- In a pretest while loop, you ask a question and, depending on the answer, you might never enter the loop to execute the loop's body. In a posttest do-while loop (which executes as long as the answer to the controlling question is true) or a posttest do-until loop (which executes as long as the answer to the controlling question is false), you ensure that the loop body executes at least once. You can duplicate the same series of actions generated by any posttest loop by creating a sequence followed by a while loop.

## KEY TERMS

**Spaghetti code** is snarled, unstructured program logic.

A **structure** is a basic unit of programming logic; each structure is a sequence, selection, or loop.

With a **sequence structure**, you perform an action or task, and then you perform the next action, in order. A sequence can contain any number of tasks, but there is no chance to branch off and skip any of the tasks.

With a **selection**, or **decision**, **structure**, you ask a question, and, depending on the answer, you take one of two courses of action. Then, no matter which path you follow, you continue with the next task.

An **if-then-else** is another name for a selection structure.

**Dual-alternative ifs** define one action to be taken when the tested condition is true, and another action to be taken when it is false.

**Single-alternative ifs** take action on just one branch of the decision.

The **null case** is the branch of a decision in which no action is taken.

With a **loop structure**, you continue to repeat actions based on the answer to a question.

**Repetition** and **iteration** are alternate names for a loop structure.

A **while...do**, or more simply, a **while** loop, is a loop in which a process continues while some condition continues to be true.

Attaching structures end-to-end is called **stacking** structures.

Placing a structure within another structure is called **nesting** the structures.

A **block** is a group of statements that execute as a single unit.

A **priming read** or **priming input** is the statement that reads the first input data record prior to starting a structured loop.

You can use the **case structure** when there are several distinct possible values for a single variable you are testing, and each requires a different course of action.

In **do-while** and **do-until loops**, you ensure that a procedure executes at least once; then, depending on the answer to the controlling question, the loop may or may not execute additional times.

A while loop is also called a **pretest loop** because a condition is tested before entering the loop even once.

Do-while and do-until loops are also called **posttest loops** because a condition is tested after the loop body has executed.

## REVIEW QUESTIONS

1. **Snarled program logic is called ______________ code.**
   a. snake
   b. spaghetti
   c. string
   d. gnarly

2. **A sequence structure can contain ______________.**
   a. only one task
   b. exactly three tasks
   c. no more than three tasks
   d. any number of tasks

3. **Which of the following is not another term for a selection structure?**
   a. decision structure
   b. if-then-else structure
   c. loop structure
   d. dual-alternative if structure

4. **The structure in which you ask a question, and, depending on the answer, take some action and then ask the question again, can be called all of the following except ______________.**
   a. if-then-else
   b. loop
   c. repetition
   d. iteration

5. **Placing a structure within another structure is called ______________ the structures.**
   a. stacking
   b. nesting
   c. building
   d. untangling

6. **Attaching structures end-to-end is called ______________.**
   a. stacking
   b. nesting
   c. building
   d. untangling

7. **The statement** `if age >= 65 then seniorDiscount = "yes"` **is an example of a ______________.**
   a. single-alternative if
   b. loop
   c. dual-alternative if
   d. sequence

8. **The statement** `while temperature remains below 60, leave the furnace on` **is an example of a ______________.**
   a. single-alternative if
   b. loop
   c. dual-alternative if
   d. sequence

9. **The statement** `if age < 13 then movieTicket = 4.00 else movieTicket = 8.50` **is an example of a ______________.**
   a. single-alternative if
   b. loop
   c. dual-alternative if
   d. sequence

10. **Which of the following attributes do all three basic structures share?**
    a. Their flowcharts all contain exactly three processing symbols.
    b. They all contain a decision.
    c. They all begin with a process.
    d. They all have one entry and one exit point.

11. **When you read input data in a loop within a program, the input statement that precedes the loop ______________.**
    a. is called a priming input
    b. cannot result in `eof`
    c. is the only part of a program allowed to be unstructured
    d. executes hundreds or even thousands of times in most business programs

**12. A group of statements that execute as a unit is a ____________.**

a. cohort
b. family
c. chunk
d. block

**13. Which of the following is acceptable in a structured program?**

a. placing a sequence within the true half of a dual-alternative decision
b. placing a decision within a loop
c. placing a loop within one of the steps in a sequence
d. All of these are acceptable.

**14. Which of the following is not a reason for enforcing structure rules in computer programs?**

a. Structured programs are clearer to understand than unstructured ones.
b. Other professional programmers will expect programs to be structured.
c. Structured programs can be broken down into modules easily.
d. Structured programs usually are shorter than unstructured ones.

**15. Which of the following is not a benefit of modularizing programs?**

a. Modular programs are easier to read and understand than nonmodular ones.
b. Modular components are reusable in other programs.
c. If you use modules, you can ignore the rules of structure.
d. Multiple programmers can work on different modules at the same time.

**16. Which of the following is true of structured logic?**

a. Any task can be described using some combination of the three structures.
b. You can use structured logic with newer programming languages, such as Java and C#, but not with older ones.
c. Structured programs require that you break the code into easy-to-handle modules that each contain no more than five actions.
d. All of these are true.

**17. The structure that you can use when you must make a decision with several possible outcomes, depending on the value of a single variable, is the ____________.**

a. multiple-alternative if structure
b. case structure
c. do-while structure
d. do-until structure

**18. Which type of loop ensures that an action will take place at least one time?**

a. a do-until loop
b. a while loop
c. a do-over loop
d. any structured loop

**19. A do-until loop can always be converted to ______________.**

a. a while followed by a sequence
b. a sequence followed by a while
c. a case structure
d. a selection followed by a while

**20. Which of the following structures is never required by any program?**

a. a while
b. a do-until
c. a selection
d. a sequence

## FIND THE BUGS

As you learned in Chapter 1, program errors have been called "bugs" since the early days of computer programming. The term is often said to have originated from an actual moth that was discovered trapped in the circuitry of a computer at Harvard University in 1945. Actually, the term "bug" was in use prior to 1945 to mean trouble with any electrical apparatus; even during Thomas Edison's life, it meant an "industrial defect." However, the process of finding and correcting program errors has come to be known as debugging.

Each of the following pseudocode segments contains one or more bugs that you must find and correct.

1. **This pseudocode segment is intended to describe determining whether you have passed or failed a course based on the average score of two classroom tests.**

```
input midtermGrade
input finalGrade
average = (midGrade + finalGrade) / 2
print avg
if average >= 60 then
   print "Pass"
endif
else
   print "Fail"
```

2. **This pseudocode segment is intended to describe computing the number of miles per gallon you get with your automobile. The program segment should continue as long as the user enters a positive value for miles traveled.**

```
input gallonsOfGasUsed
input milesTraveled
while milesTraveled > 0
       milesPerGallon = gallonsOfGasUsed / milesTraveled
        print milesPerGal
endwhile
```

3. **This pseudocode segment is intended to describe computing the cost per day for a vacation. The user enters a value for total dollars available to spend and can continue to enter new dollar amounts while the amount entered is not 0. For each new amount entered, if the amount of money available to spend per day is below $100, a message displays.**

```
input totalDollarsAvailable
while totalDollarsAvailable not = 0
   dollarsPerDay = totalMoneyAvailable / 7
   print dollarsPerDay
endwhile
input totalDollarsAvailable
if dollarsPerDay > 100 then
   print "You better search for a bargain vacation"
endwhile
```

## EXERCISES

1. **Match the term with the structure diagram. (Because the structures go by more than one name, there are more terms than diagrams.)**

   1. sequence
   2. selection
   3. loop
   4. do-while
   5. decision
   6. if-then-else
   7. iteration

a.

b.

c.

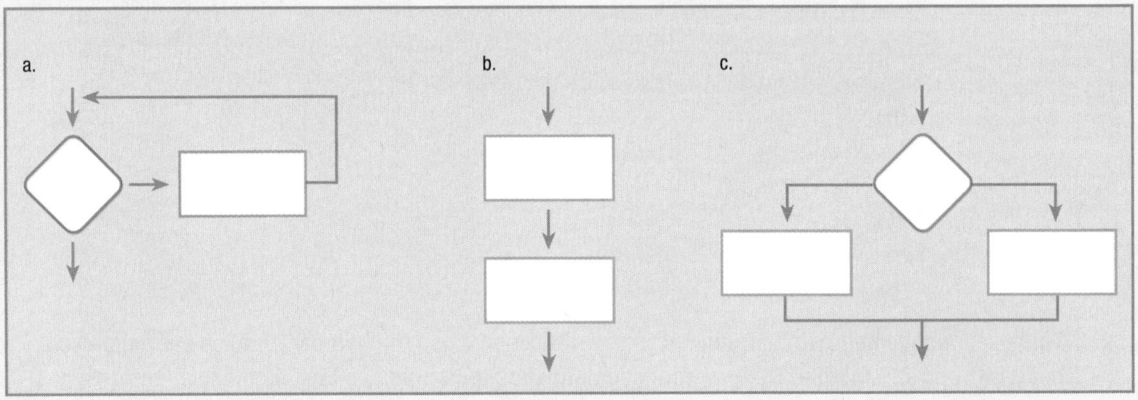

2. **Match the term with the pseudocode segment. (Because the structures go by more than one name, there are more terms than pseudocode segments.)**

1. sequence
2. selection
3. loop
4. decision
5. if-then-else
6. iteration

a.
```
while not eof
     print theAnswer
endwhile
```
b.
```
if inventoryQuantity  >  0 then
     do fillOrderProcess
else
     do backOrderNotification
endif
```
c.
```
do localTaxCalculation
do stateTaxCalculation
do federalTaxCalculation
```

3. **Is each of the following segments structured, or unstructured? If unstructured, redraw it so that it does the same thing but is structured.**

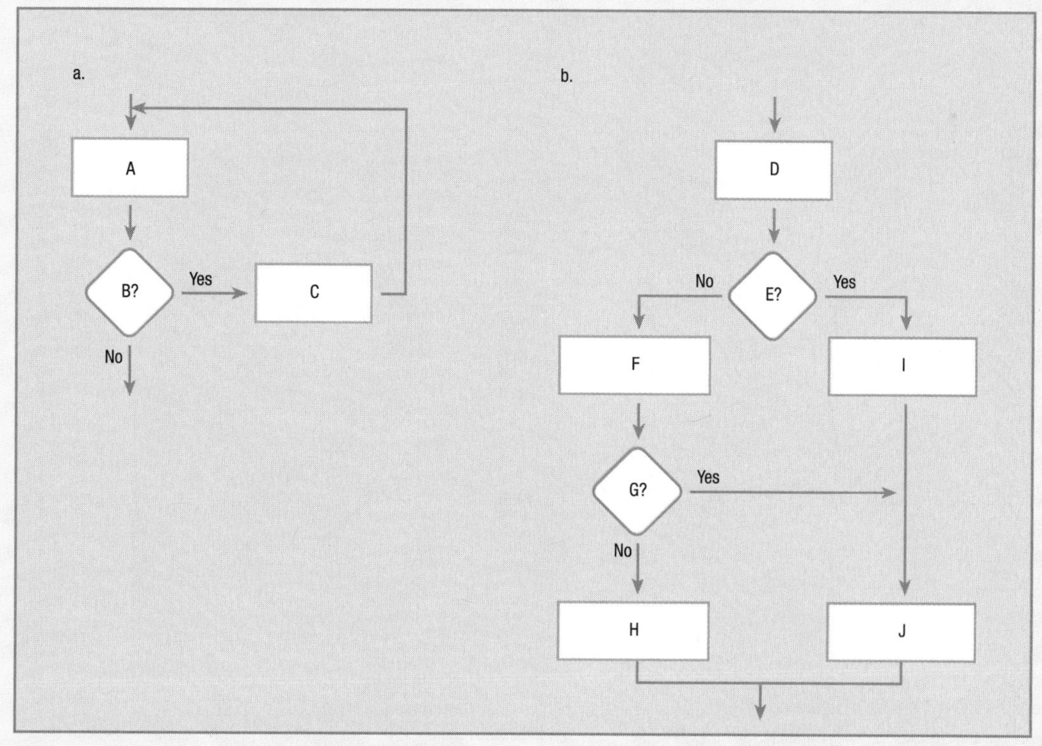

c.
K?
No
Yes
L
M?
No
Yes
N
O
P?
Yes
Q
No

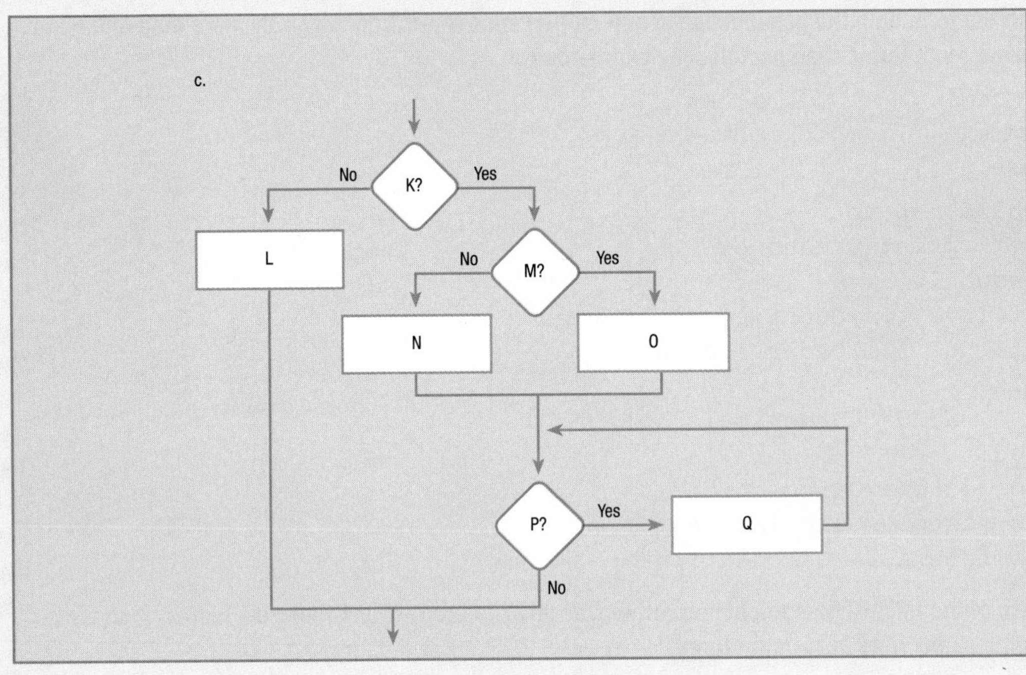

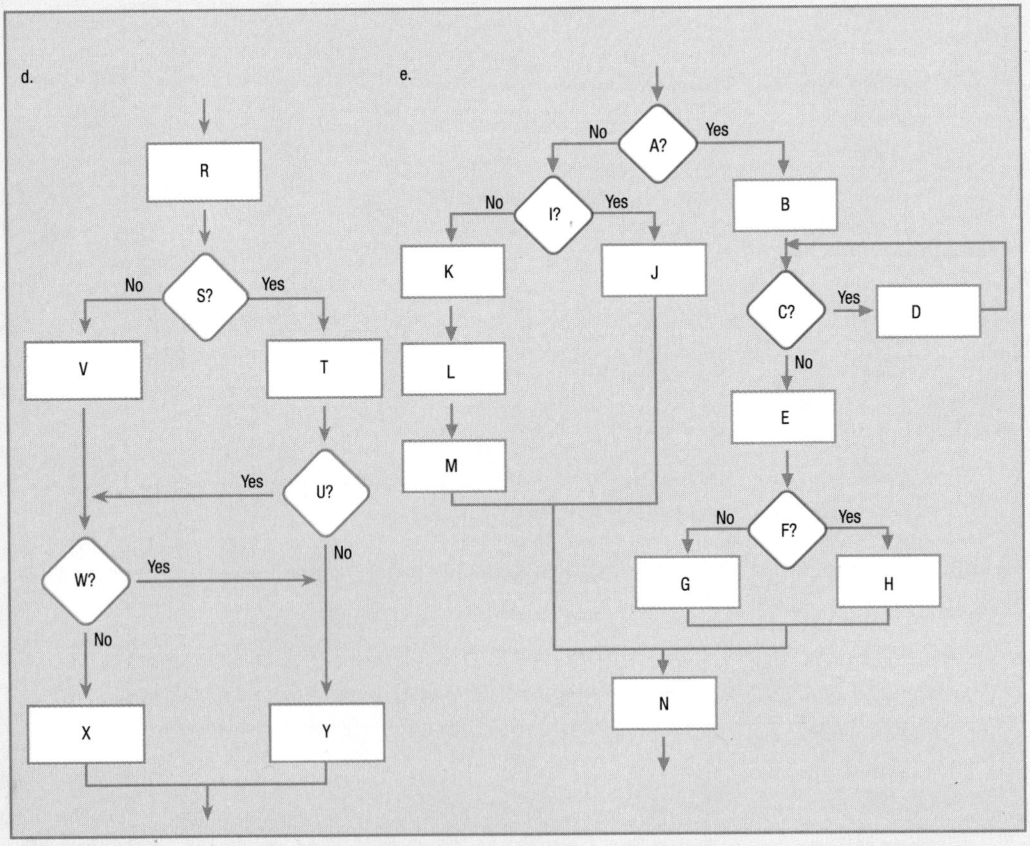

d.
R
S?
No
Yes
V
T
U?
Yes
No
W?
Yes
No
X
Y
e.
A?
No
Yes
I?
No
Yes
B
K
J
C?
Yes
D
L
No
E
M
F?
No
Yes
G
H
N

4. **Write pseudocode for each example (a through e) in Exercise 3.**

5. **Assume you have created a mechanical arm that can hold a pen. The arm can perform the following tasks:**
   - ☐ Lower the pen to a piece of paper.
   - ☐ Raise the pen from the paper.
   - ☐ Move the pen one inch along a straight line. (If the pen is lowered, this action draws a one-inch line from left to right; if the pen is raised, this action just repositions the pen one inch to the right.)
   - ☐ Turn 90 degrees to the right.
   - ☐ Draw a circle that is one inch in diameter.

   **Draw a structured flowchart or write pseudocode describing the logic that would cause the arm to draw the following:**

   a. a one-inch square
   b. a two-inch by one-inch rectangle
   c. a string of three beads

   **Have a fellow student act as the mechanical arm and carry out your instructions.**

6. **Assume you have created a mechanical robot that can perform the following tasks:**
   - ☐ Stand up.
   - ☐ Sit down.
   - ☐ Turn left 90 degrees.
   - ☐ Turn right 90 degrees.
   - ☐ Take a step.

   **Additionally, the robot can determine the answer to one test condition:**
   - ☐ Am I touching something?

   **Place two chairs 20 feet apart, directly facing each other. Draw a structured flowchart or write pseudocode describing the logic that would allow the robot to start from a sitting position in one chair, cross the room, and end up sitting in the other chair.**

   **Have a fellow student act as the robot and carry out your instructions.**

7. **Draw a structured flowchart or write structured pseudocode describing your preparation to go to work or school in the morning. Include at least two decisions and two loops.**

8. **Draw a structured flowchart or write structured pseudocode describing your preparation to go to bed at night. Include at least two decisions and two loops.**

9. **Choose a very simple children's game and describe its logic, using a structured flowchart or pseudocode. For example, you might try to explain Musical Chairs; Duck, Duck, Goose; the card game War; or the elimination game Eenie, Meenie, Minie, Moe.**

10. **Draw a structured flowchart or write structured pseudocode describing how your paycheck is calculated. Include at least two decisions.**

11. **Draw a structured flowchart or write structured pseudocode describing the steps a retail store employee should follow to process a customer purchase. Include at least two decisions.**

## DETECTIVE WORK

1. **In this chapter, you learned what spaghetti code is. What is "ravioli code"?**

2. **Who was Edsger Dijkstra? What programming statement did he want to eliminate?**

3. **Who were Bohm and Jacopini? What contribution did they make to programming?**

## UP FOR DISCUSSION

1. **Just because every logical program can be solved using only three structures (sequence, selection, and loop) does not mean there cannot be other useful structures. For example, the case, do-while, and do-until structures are never required, but they exist in many programming languages and can be quite useful. Try to design a new structure of your own and explain situations in which it would be useful.**

# 3 MODULES, HIERARCHY CHARTS, AND DOCUMENTATION

## After studying Chapter 3, you should be able to:

- Describe the advantages of modularization
- Modularize a program
- Understand how a module can call another module
- Explain how to declare variables
- Create hierarchy charts
- Understand documentation
- Design output
- Interpret file descriptions
- Understand the attributes of complete documentation

## MODULES, SUBROUTINES, PROCEDURES, FUNCTIONS, OR METHODS

Programmers seldom write programs as one long series of steps. Instead, they break down the programming problem into reasonable units, and tackle one small task at a time. These reasonable units are called **modules**. Programmers also refer to them as **subroutines**, **procedures**, **functions**, or **methods**.

The name that programmers use for their modules usually reflects the programming language they use. For example, Visual Basic programmers use "procedure" (or "subprocedure"). C and C++ programmers call their modules "functions," whereas C#, Java, and other object-oriented language programmers are more likely to use "method." Programmers in COBOL, RPG, and BASIC (all older languages) are most likely to use "subroutine."

The process of breaking down a large program into modules is called **modularization**. You are never required to break down a large program into modules, but there are at least four reasons for doing so:

- Modularization provides abstraction.
- Modularization allows multiple programmers to work on a problem.
- Modularization allows you to reuse your work.
- Modularization makes it easier to identify structures.

### MODULARIZATION PROVIDES ABSTRACTION

One reason modularized programs are easier to understand is that they enable a programmer to see the big picture. **Abstraction** is the process of paying attention to important properties while ignoring nonessential details. Abstraction is selective ignorance. Life would be tedious without abstraction. For example, you can create a list of things to accomplish today:

```
Do laundry
Call Aunt Nan
Start term paper
```

Without abstraction, the list of chores would begin:

```
Pick up laundry basket
Put laundry basket in car
Drive to laundromat
Get out of car with basket
Walk into laundromat
Set basket down
Find quarters for washing machine
. . . and so on.
```

You might list a dozen more steps before you finish the laundry and move on to the second chore on your original list. If you had to consider every small, **low-level** detail of every task in your day, you would probably never make it out of bed in the morning. Using a higher-level, more abstract list makes your day manageable. Abstraction makes complex tasks look simple.

**TIP** Abstract artists create paintings in which they see only the "big picture"—color and form—and ignore the details. Abstraction has a similar meaning among programmers.

Likewise, some level of abstraction occurs in every computer program. Fifty years ago, a programmer had to understand the low-level circuitry instructions the computer used. But now, newer **high-level** programming languages allow you to use English-like vocabulary in which one broad statement corresponds to dozens of machine instructions. No matter which high-level programming language you use, if you display a message on the monitor, you are never required to understand how a monitor works to create each pixel on the screen. You write an instruction like `print message` and the details of the hardware operations are handled for you.

Modules or subroutines provide another way to achieve abstraction. For example, a payroll program can call a module named `computeFederalWithholdingTax.` You can write the mathematical details of the function later, someone else can write them, or you can purchase them from an outside source. When you plan your main payroll program, your only concern is that a federal withholding tax will have to be calculated; you save the details for later.

## MODULARIZATION ALLOWS MULTIPLE PROGRAMMERS TO WORK ON A PROBLEM

When you dissect any large task into modules, you gain the ability to divide the task among various people. Rarely does a single programmer write a commercial program that you buy. Consider any word-processing, spreadsheet, or database program you have used. Each program has so many options, and responds to user selections in so many possible ways, that it would take years for a single programmer to write all the instructions. Professional software developers can write new programs in weeks or months, instead of years, by dividing large programs into modules and assigning each module to an individual programmer or programming team.

## MODULARIZATION ALLOWS YOU TO REUSE YOUR WORK

If a subroutine or function is useful and well-written, you may want to use it more than once within a program or in other programs. For example, a routine that checks the current date to make sure it is valid (the month is not lower than 1 or higher than 12, the day is not lower than 1 or higher than 31 if the month is 1, and so on) is useful in many programs written for a business. A program that uses a personnel file containing each employee's birth date, hire date, last promotion date, and termination date can use the date-validation module four times with each employee record. Other programs in an organization can also use the module; these include programs that ship customer orders, plan employees' birthday parties, and calculate when loan payments should be made. If you write the date-checking instructions so they are entangled with other statements in a program, they are difficult to extract and reuse. On the other hand, if you place the instructions in their own module, the unit is easy to use and portable to other applications. The feature of modular programs that allows individual modules to be used in a variety of applications is known as **reusability**.

You can find many real-world examples of reusability. When you build a house, you don't invent plumbing and heating systems; you incorporate systems with proven designs. This certainly reduces the time and effort it takes to build a house. Assuming the plumbing and electrical systems you choose are also in service in other houses, they also improve the reliability of your house's systems—they have been tested under a variety of circumstances and have been proven to function correctly. Similarly, software that is reusable is more reliable. **Reliability** is the feature of programs that assures you a module has been tested and proven to function correctly. Reliable software saves time and money. If you create the functional components of your programs as stand-alone modules and test them in your current programs, much of the work will already be done when you use the modules in future applications.

## MODULARIZATION MAKES IT EASIER TO IDENTIFY STRUCTURES

When you combine several programming tasks into modules, it may be easier for you to identify structures. For example, you learned in Chapter 2 that the selection structure looks like Figure 3-1.

When you work with a program segment that looks like Figure 3-2, you may question whether it is structured. If you can modularize some of the statements and give them a more abstract group name, as in Figure 3-3, it is easier to see that the program involves a major selection (whether the hours value is greater than 40) that determines the type of pay (regular or overtime). In Figure 3-3, it is also easier to see that the program segment is structured.

**FIGURE 3-1:** SELECTION STRUCTURE

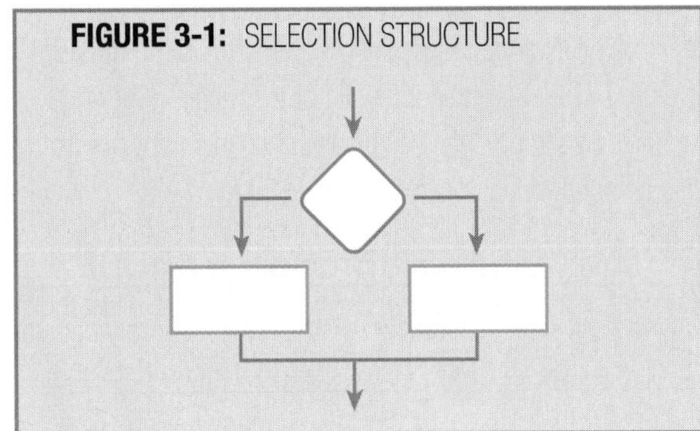

**FIGURE 3-2:** SECTION OF LOGIC FROM A PAYROLL PROGRAM

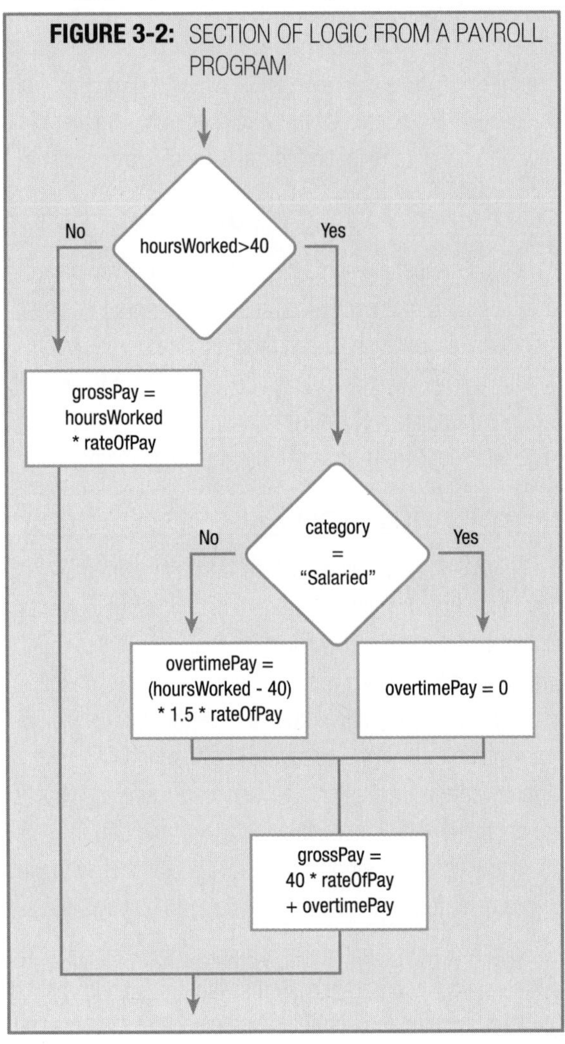

**FIGURE 3-3:** MODULARIZED LOGIC FROM A PAYROLL PROGRAM

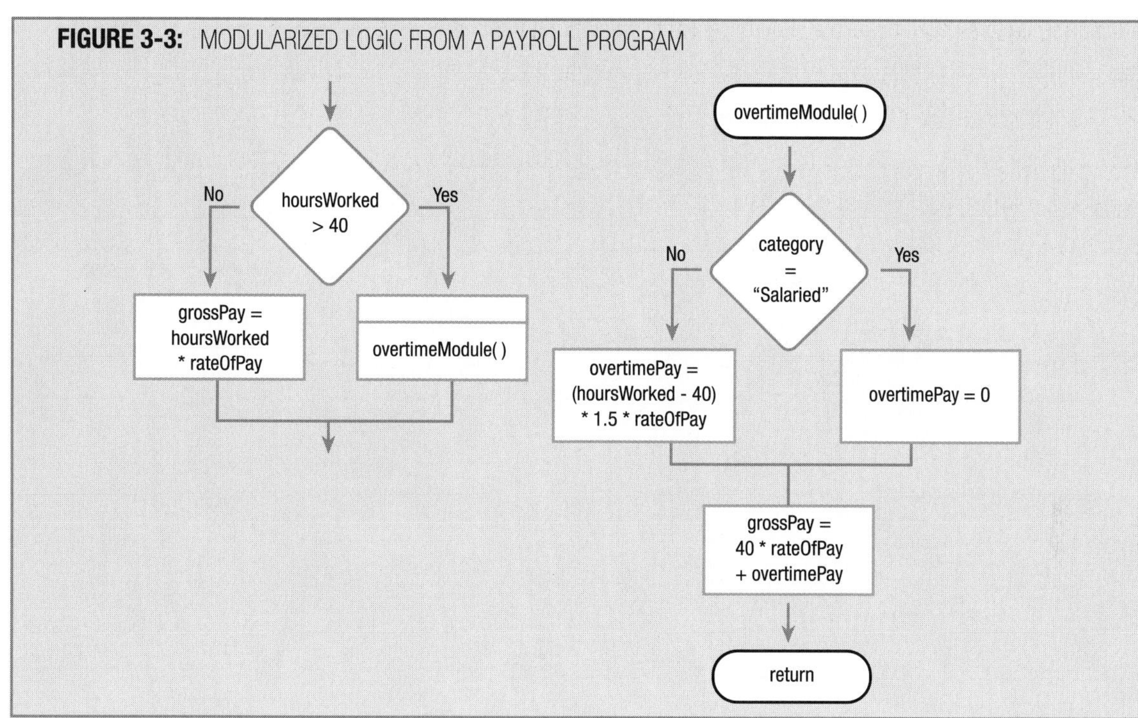


The single program segment shown in Figure 3-2 accomplishes the same steps as the two program segments shown together in Figure 3-3; both program segments are structured. The structure may be more obvious in the program segments in Figure 3-3 because you can see two distinct parts—a decision structure calls a subroutine named `overtimeModule()`, and that module contains another decision structure, which is followed by a sequence. Neither of the program segments shown in Figures 3-2 and 3-3 is superior to the other in terms of functionality, but you may prefer to modularize to help you identify structures.

> **TIP** A professional programmer will never modularize simply to *identify* whether a program is structured—he or she modularizes for reasons of abstraction, ease of dividing the work, and reusability. However, for a beginning programmer, being able to see and identify structure is important.

## MODULARIZING A PROGRAM

Most programs contain a main module which contains the **mainline logic**; this module then accesses other modules or subroutines. When you create a module or subroutine, you give it a name. The rules for naming modules are different in every programming language, but they often are similar to the language's rules for variable names. In this text, module names follow the same two rules used for variable names:

- Module names must be one word.
- Module names should have some meaning.

Additionally, in this text, module names are followed by a set of parentheses. This will help you distinguish module names from variable names. This style corresponds to the way modules are named in many programming languages, such as Java, C++, and C#.

Table 3-1 lists some possible module names for a module that calculates an employee's gross pay, and provides a rationale for the appropriateness of each one.

**TABLE 3-1:** VALID AND INVALID MODULE NAMES FOR A MODULE THAT CALCULATES AN EMPLOYEE'S GROSS PAY

| Suggested module names for a module that calculates an employee's gross pay | Comments |
|---|---|
| `calculateGrossPay()` | Good |
| `calculateGross()` | Good—most people would interpret "Gross" to be short for "Gross pay" |
| `calGrPy()` | Legal, but cryptic |
| `calculateGrossPayForOneEmployee()` | Legal, but awkward |
| `calculate gross()` | Not legal—embedded space |
| `calculategrosspay()` | Legal, but hard to read without camel casing |

**TIP** As you learn more about modules in specific programming languages, you will find that you sometimes place variable names within the parentheses of module names. Any variables enclosed in the parentheses contain information you want to send to the module. For now, the parentheses we use at the end of module names will be empty.

**TIP** Most programming languages require that module names begin with an alphabetic character. This text follows that convention.

**TIP** Although it is not a requirement of any programming language, it frequently makes sense to use a verb as all or part of a module's name, because modules perform some action. Typical module names begin with words such as `get`, `compute`, and `print`. When you program in visual languages that use screen components such as buttons and text boxes, the module names frequently contain verbs representing user actions, such as `click` and `drag`.

When a program or module uses another module, you can refer to the main program as the **calling program** (or **calling module**), because it "calls" the module's name when it wants to use the module. The flowchart symbol used to call a module is a rectangle with a bar across the top. You place the name of the module you are calling inside the rectangle.

**TIP** When one module calls another, the called module is a **submodule**.

Instead of placing only the name of the module they are calling in the flowchart, many programmers insert an appropriate verb, such as "perform" or "do," before the module name. These verbs help clarify that the module represents an action to be carried out.

TIP

A module can call another module, and the called module can call another. The number of chained calls is limited only by the amount of memory available on your computer.

You draw each module separately with its own sentinel symbols. The symbol that is the equivalent of the `start` symbol in a program contains the name of the module. This name must be identical to the name used in the calling program. The symbol that is the equivalent of the `stop` symbol in a program does not contain "stop"; after all, the program is not ending. Instead, the module ends with a "gentler," less final term, such as `exit` or `return`. These words correctly indicate that when the module ends, the logical progression of statements will return to the calling program.

A flowchart and pseudocode for a program that calculates the arithmetic average of two numbers a user enters can look like Figure 3-4. Here the **main program**, or program that runs from start to stop and calls other modules, calls three modules: `getInput()`, `calculateAverage()`, and `printResult()`.

The logic of the program in Figure 3-4 proceeds as follows:

1. The main program starts.
2. The main program calls the `getInput()` module.
3. Within the `getInput()` module, the prompt "Enter a number" appears. A **prompt** is a message that is displayed on a monitor, asking the user for a response.
4. Within the `getInput()` module, the program accepts a value into the `firstNumber` variable.
5. Within the `getInput()` module, the prompt "Enter another number" appears.
6. Within the `getInput()` module, the program accepts a value into the `secondNumber` variable.
7. The `getInput()` module ends, and control returns to the main calling program.
8. The main program calls the `calculateAverage()` module.
9. Within the `calculateAverage()` module, a value for the variable `average` is calculated.
10. The `calculateAverage()` module ends, and control returns to the main calling program.
11. The main program calls the `printResult()` module.
12. Within the `printResult()` module, the value of `average` is displayed.
13. Within the `printResult()` module, a thank-you message is displayed.
14. The `printResult()` module ends, and control returns to the main calling program.
15. The main program ends.

**FIGURE 3-4:** FLOWCHART AND PSEUDOCODE FOR AVERAGING PROGRAM WITH MODULES

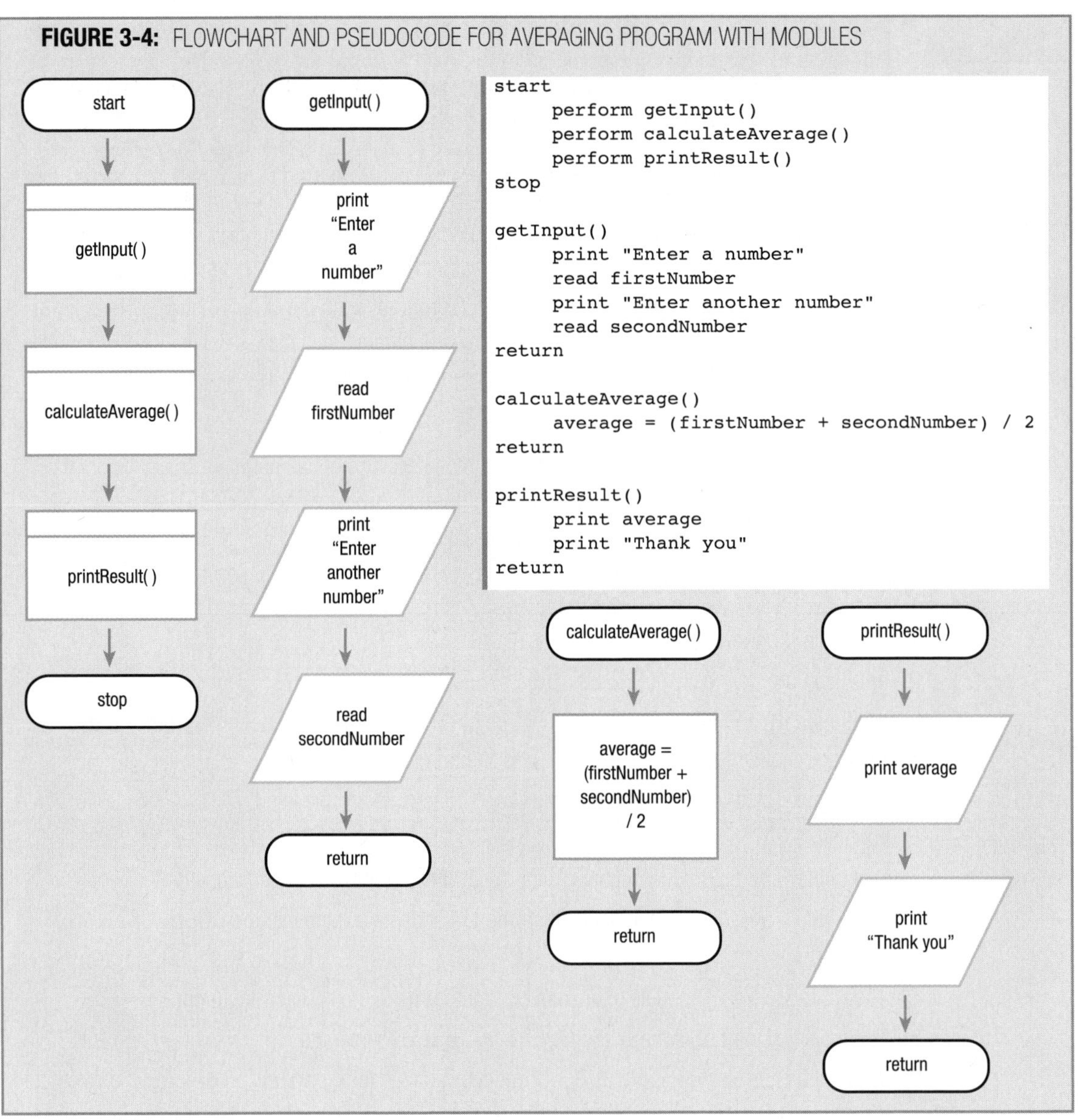


```
start
     perform getInput()
     perform calculateAverage()
     perform printResult()
stop

getInput()
     print "Enter a number"
     read firstNumber
     print "Enter another number"
     read secondNumber
return

calculateAverage()
     average = (firstNumber + secondNumber) / 2
return

printResult()
     print average
     print "Thank you"
return
```

Whenever a main program calls a module, the logic transfers to the module. When the module ends, the logical flow transfers back to the main calling program and resumes where it left off.

**TIP** The computer keeps track of the correct memory address to which it should return after executing a module by recording the memory address in a location known as the *stack*.

## MODULES CALLING OTHER MODULES

Just as a program can call a module or subroutine, any module can call another module. For example, the program illustrated in Figure 3-4 can be broken down further, as shown in Figure 3-5.

**FIGURE 3-5:** FLOWCHART AND PSEUDOCODE FOR AVERAGING PROGRAM WITH SUBMODULES

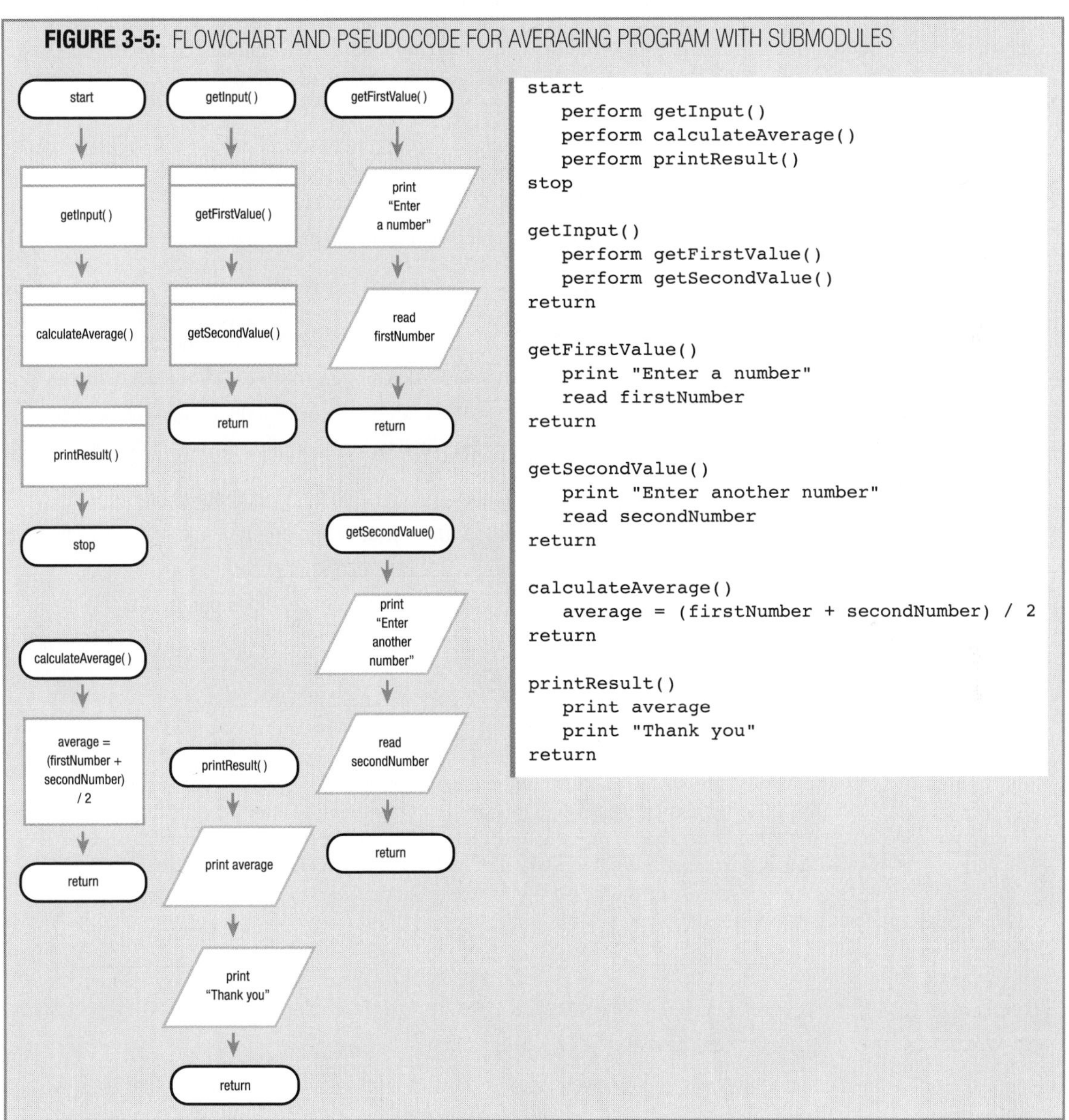


```
start
   perform getInput()
   perform calculateAverage()
   perform printResult()
stop

getInput()
   perform getFirstValue()
   perform getSecondValue()
return

getFirstValue()
   print "Enter a number"
   read firstNumber
return

getSecondValue()
   print "Enter another number"
   read secondNumber
return

calculateAverage()
   average = (firstNumber + secondNumber) / 2
return

printResult()
   print average
   print "Thank you"
return
```

After the program in Figure 3-5 begins:

1. The main program calls the `getInput()` module, and the logical flow transfers to that module.
2. From there, the `getInput()` module calls the `getFirstValue()` module, and the logical flow immediately transfers to the `getFirstValue()` module.
3. The `getFirstValue()` module displays a prompt and reads a number. When `getFirstValue()` ends, control passes back to `getInput()`, where `getSecondValue()` is called.
4. Control passes to `getSecondValue()`, which displays a prompt and retrieves a second value from the user. When this module ends, control passes back to the `getInput()` module.
5. When the `getInput()` module ends, control returns to the main program.
6. Then, `calculateAverage()` and `printResult()` execute as before.

Determining when to break down any particular module into its own subroutines or submodules is an art. Programmers do follow some guidelines when deciding how far to break down subroutines, or how much to put in each of them. Some companies may have arbitrary rules, such as "a subroutine should never take more than a page," or "a module should never have more than 30 statements in it," or "never have a method or function with only one statement in it."

Rather than use such arbitrary rules, a better policy is to place together statements that contribute to one specific task. The more the statements contribute to the same job, the greater the **functional cohesion** of the module. A routine that checks the validity of a `date` variable's value, or one that prompts a user and allows the user to type in a value, is considered cohesive. A routine that checks date validity, deducts insurance premiums, and computes federal withholding tax for an employee would be less cohesive.

**TIP** □□□□ Date-checking is an example of a commonly used module in business programs, and one that is quite functionally cohesive. In business programs, many dates are represented using six or eight digits in month-day-year format. For example, January 21, 2007 might be stored as 012107 or 01212007. However, you might also see day-month-year format, as in 21012007. The current International Organization for Standardization (ISO) standard for representing dates is to use eight digits, with the year first, followed by the month and day. For example, January 21, 2007 is 20070121 and would be displayed as 2007-01-21. The ISO creates standards for businesses that make products more reliable and trade between countries easier and fairer.

## DECLARING VARIABLES

The primary work of most modules in most programs you write is to manipulate data—for example, to calculate the figures needed for a paycheck, customer bill, or sales report. You store your program data in variables.

Many program languages require you to declare all variables before you use them. **Declaring a variable** involves providing a name for the memory location where the computer will store the variable value, and notifying the computer of what type of data to expect. Every programming language requires that you follow specific rules when declaring variables, but all the rules involve identifying at least two attributes for every variable:

- You must declare a data type.
- You must give the variable a name.

You learned in Chapter 1 that different programming languages provide different variable types, but that all allow at least the distinction between character and numeric data. The rest of this book uses just two data types—`num`, which holds number values, and `char`, which holds all other values, including those that contain letters and combinations of letters and numbers.

Remember, you also learned in Chapter 1 that variable names must not contain spaces, so this book uses statements such as `char lastName` and `num weeklySalary` to declare two variables of different types.

**TIP** Although it is not a requirement of any programming language, it usually makes sense to give a variable a name that is a noun, because it represents a thing.

Some programming languages, such as Visual Basic and BASIC, do not require you to name any variable until the first time you use it. However, other languages, including COBOL, C++, C#, and Java, require that you declare variables with a name and a data type. Some languages require that you declare all variables at the beginning of a program, before you write any executable statements; others allow you to declare variables at any point, but require the declaration before you can use the variable. For our purposes, this book follows the convention of declaring all variables at the beginning of a program.

In many modern programming languages, variables typically are declared within each module that uses them. Such variables are known as **local variables**. As you continue your study of programming logic, you will learn how to use local variables and understand their advantages. For now, this text will use **global variables**—variables that are given a type and name once, and then used in all modules of the program.

For example, to complete the averaging program shown in Figure 3-5 so that its variables are properly declared, you can redraw the main program flowchart to look like the one shown in Figure 3-6. Three variables are required: `firstNumber`, `secondNumber`, and `average`. The variables are declared as the first step in the program, before you use any of them, and each is correctly identified as numeric. They appear to the side of the "declare variables" step in an **annotation symbol** or **annotation box**, which is simply an attached box containing notes. You can use an annotation symbol any time you have more to write than you can conveniently fit within a flowchart symbol, or any time you want to add an explanatory comment to a flowchart.

**FIGURE 3-6:** FLOWCHART AND PSEUDOCODE FOR MAINLINE LOGIC FOR AVERAGING PROGRAM SHOWING DECLARED VARIABLES

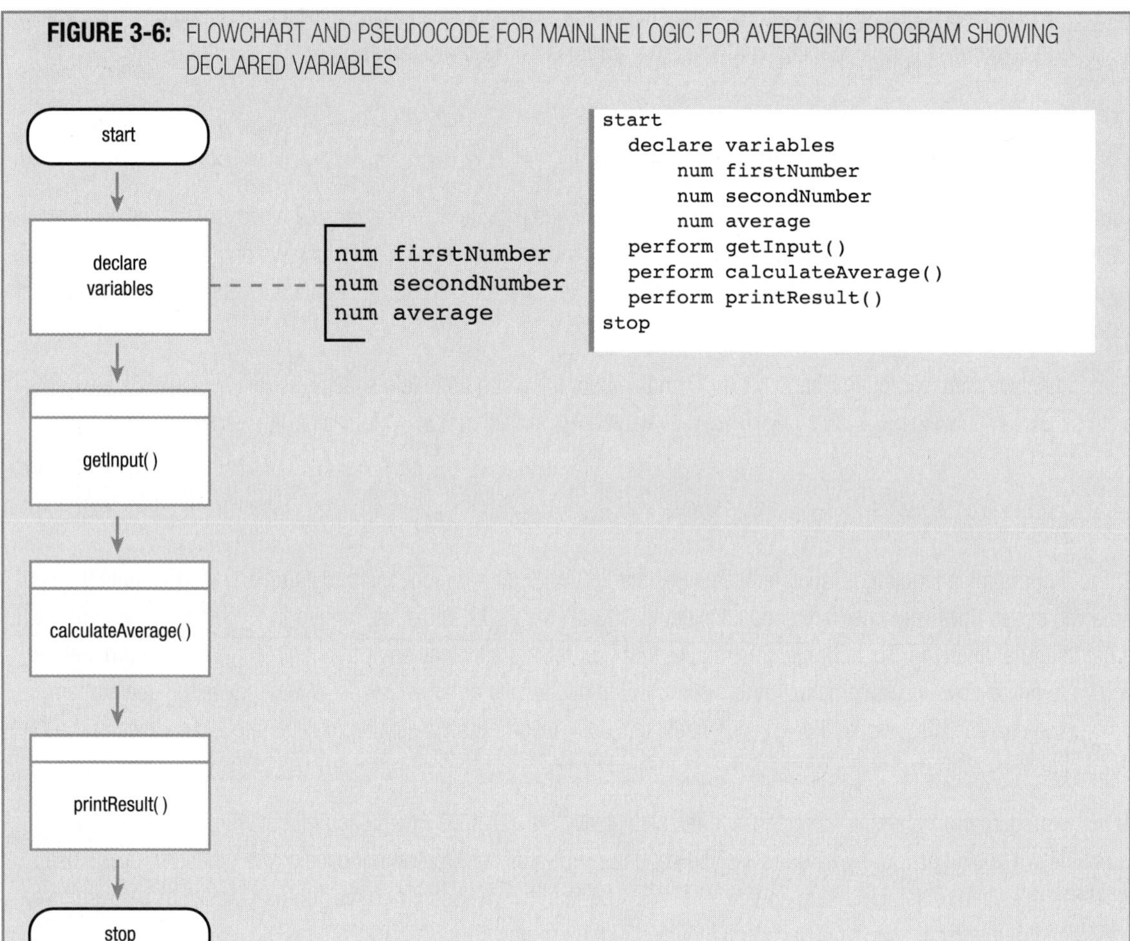
start
declare variables
num firstNumber
num secondNumber
num average
getInput( )
calculateAverage( )
printResult( )
stop

```
start
  declare variables
      num firstNumber
      num secondNumber
      num average
  perform getInput()
  perform calculateAverage()
  perform printResult()
stop
```

**TIP**

Many programming languages support more specific numeric types with names like int (for integers or whole numbers), float or single (for single-precision, floating-point values; that is, values that contain one or more decimal-place digits), and double (for double-precision, floating-point values, which means more memory space is reserved). Many languages distinguish even more precisely. For example, in addition to whole-number integers, C++, C#, and Java allow short integers and long integers, which require less and more memory, respectively.

**TIP**

Many programming languages support more specific character types. Often, programming languages provide a distinction between single-character variables (such as an initial or a grade in a class) and string variables (such as a last name), which hold multiple characters.

Figure 3-6 also shows pseudocode for the same program. Because pseudocode is written and not drawn, you might choose to list the variable names below the `declare variables` statement, as shown.

Programmers sometimes create a **data dictionary**, which is a list of every variable name used in a program, along with its type, size, and description. When a data dictionary is created, it becomes part of the program documentation.

**TIP** After you name a variable, you must use that exact name every time you refer to the variable within your program. In many programming languages, even the case matters, so a variable name like `firstNumber` represents a different memory location than `firstnumber` or `FirstNumber`.

## CREATING HIERARCHY CHARTS

Besides describing program logic with a flowchart or pseudocode, when a program has several modules calling other modules, programmers often use a tool to show the overall picture of how these modules are related to one another. You can use a **hierarchy chart** to illustrate modules' relationships. A hierarchy chart does not tell you what tasks are to be performed within a module; it doesn't tell you *when* or *how* a module executes. It tells you only which routines exist within a program and which routines call which other routines.

The hierarchy chart for the last version of the number-averaging program looks like Figure 3-7, and shows which modules call which others. You don't know *when* the modules are called or *why* they are called; that information is in the flowchart or pseudocode. A hierarchy chart just tells you *which* modules are called by other modules.

**FIGURE 3-7:** HIERARCHY CHART FOR NUMBER-AVERAGING PROGRAM IN FIGURE 3-6

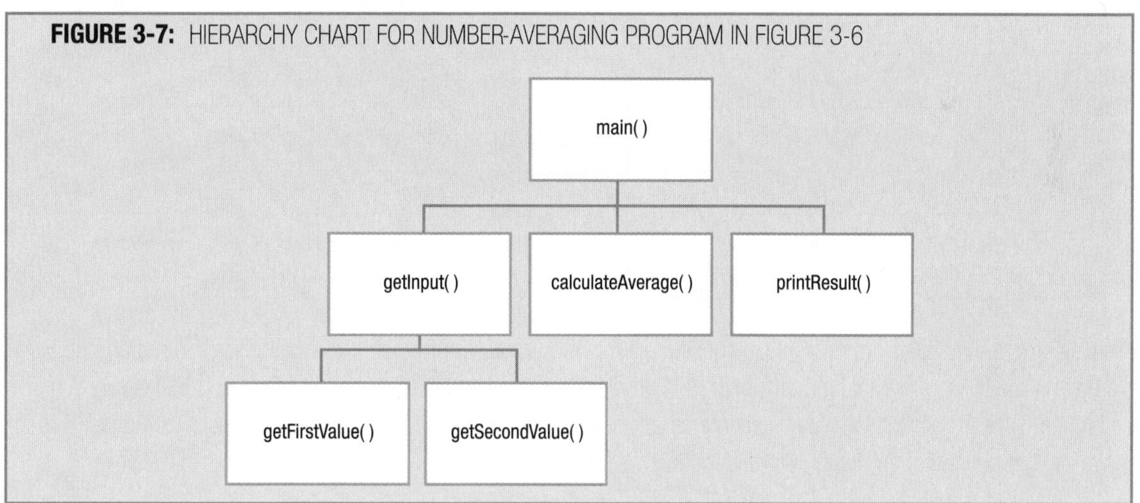


You may have seen hierarchy charts for organizations, such as the one in Figure 3-8. The chart shows who reports to whom, not when or how often they report. Program hierarchy charts operate in an identical manner.

Figure 3-9 shows an example of a hierarchy chart for the billing program of a mail-order company. The hierarchy chart supplies module names only; it provides a general overview of the tasks to be performed, without specifying any details.

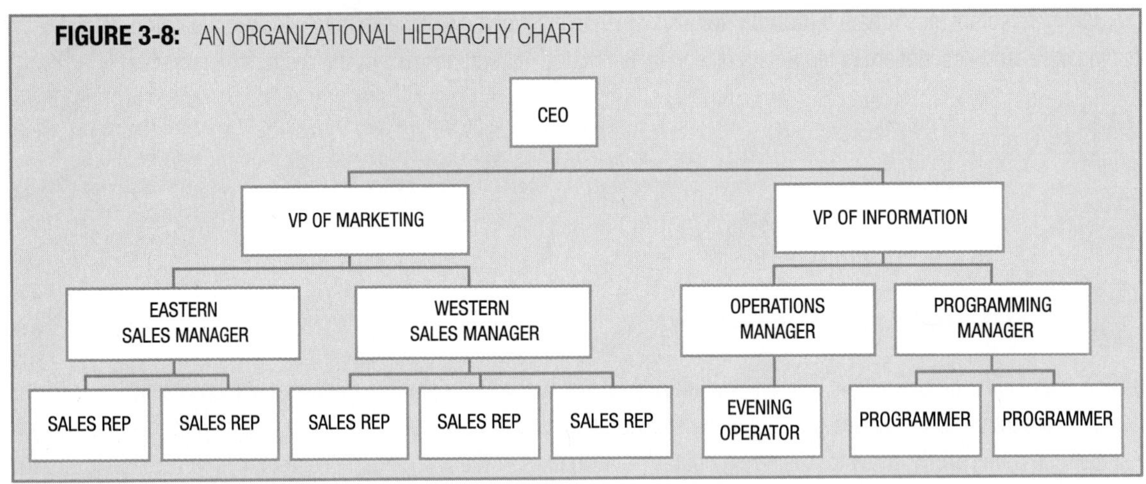


**FIGURE 3-8:** AN ORGANIZATIONAL HIERARCHY CHART

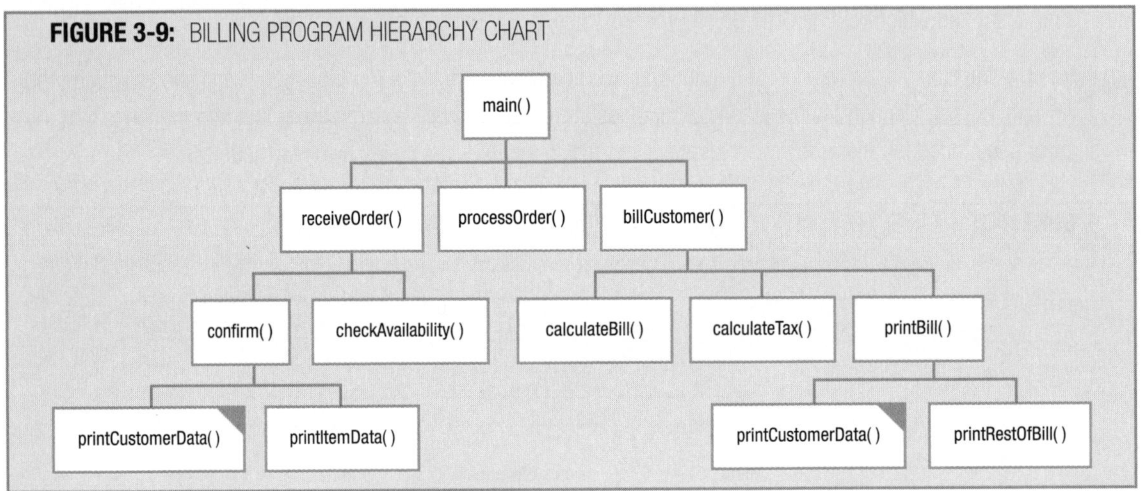


**FIGURE 3-9:** BILLING PROGRAM HIERARCHY CHART

Because program modules are reusable, a specific module may be called from several locations within a program. For example, in the billing program hierarchy chart in Figure 3-9, you can see that the `printCustomerData()` module is used twice. By convention, you blacken a corner of each box representing a module used more than once. This action alerts readers that any change to this module will affect more than one location.

The hierarchy chart can be a useful tool when a program must be modified months or years after the original writing. For example, if a tax law changes, a programmer might be asked to rewrite the `calculateTax()` module in the billing program diagrammed in Figure 3-9. As the programmer changes the `calculateTax()` routine, the hierarchy chart shows what other dependent routines might be affected. If a change is made to `printCustomerData()`, the programmer is alerted that changes will occur in multiple locations. A hierarchy chart is useful for "getting the big picture" in a complex program.

Hierarchy charts are used in procedural programming, but they are infrequently used in object-oriented programming. Other types of diagrams frequently are used in object-oriented environments. In Chapter 15 of the Comprehensive edition of this book, you learn about the Unified Modeling Language, which is a set of diagrams you use to describe a system.

## UNDERSTANDING DOCUMENTATION

**Documentation** refers to all of the supporting material that goes with a program. Two broad categories of documentation are the documentation intended for users and the documentation intended for programmers. People who use computer programs are called **end users**, or **users** for short. Most likely, you have been the end user of an application such as a word-processing program or a game. When you purchase software that other programmers have written, you appreciate clearly written instructions on how to install and use the software. These instructions constitute user documentation. In a small organization, programmers may write user documentation, but in most organizations, systems analysts or technical writers produce end-user instructions. These instructions may take the form of a printed manual, or may be presented online through a Web site or on a compact disc.

When programmers begin to plan the logic of a computer program, they require instructions known as **program documentation**. End users never see program documentation; rather, programmers use it when planning or modifying programs.

Program documentation falls into two categories: internal and external. **Internal program documentation** consists of program **comments**, or nonexecuting statements that programmers place within their code to explain program statements in English. Comments serve only to clarify code; they do not affect the running of a program. Because methods for inserting comments vary, you will learn how to insert comments when you learn a specific programming language.

In Visual Basic, program comments begin with the letters REM (for REMark) or with a single apostrophe. In C++, C#, and Java, comments can begin with two forward slashes (//). Some newer programming languages such as C# and Java provide a tool that automatically converts the programmer's internal comments to external documentation.

**External program documentation** includes all the supporting paperwork that programmers develop before they write a program. Because most programs have input, processing, and output, usually there is documentation for each of these functions.

## OUTPUT DOCUMENTATION

Output documentation is usually the first to be written. This may seem backwards, but if you're planning a trip, which do you decide first: how to get to your destination or where you're going?

Most requests for programs arise because a user needs particular information to be output, so the planning of program output is usually done in consultation with the person or persons who will be using it. Only after the desired output is known can the programmer hope to plan the processes needed to produce the output.

Often the programmer does not design the output. Instead, the user who requests the output presents the programmer (or programming team) with an example or sketch of the desired result. Then the programmer might work with the user to refine the request, suggest improvements in the design, or clarify the user's needs. If you don't determine precisely what the user wants or needs at this point, you will write a program that the user soon wants redesigned and rewritten.

A very common type of output is a printed report. You can design a printed report on a **printer spacing chart**, which is also referred to as a **print chart** or a **print layout**. Figure 3-10 shows a printer spacing chart, which basically looks like graph paper. The chart has many boxes, and in each box the designer places one character that will be printed.

For example, suppose you want to create a printed report with the following features:

- A printed title, INVENTORY REPORT, that begins 11 spaces over from the left of the page and one line down
- Column headings for ITEM NAME, PRICE, and QUANTITY IN STOCK two lines below the title and centered over the actual data items that display
- Variable data appearing below each of the column headings

With these features, the print chart you create would resemble the one in Figure 3-10.

**FIGURE 3-10:** PLANNED PRINT CHART

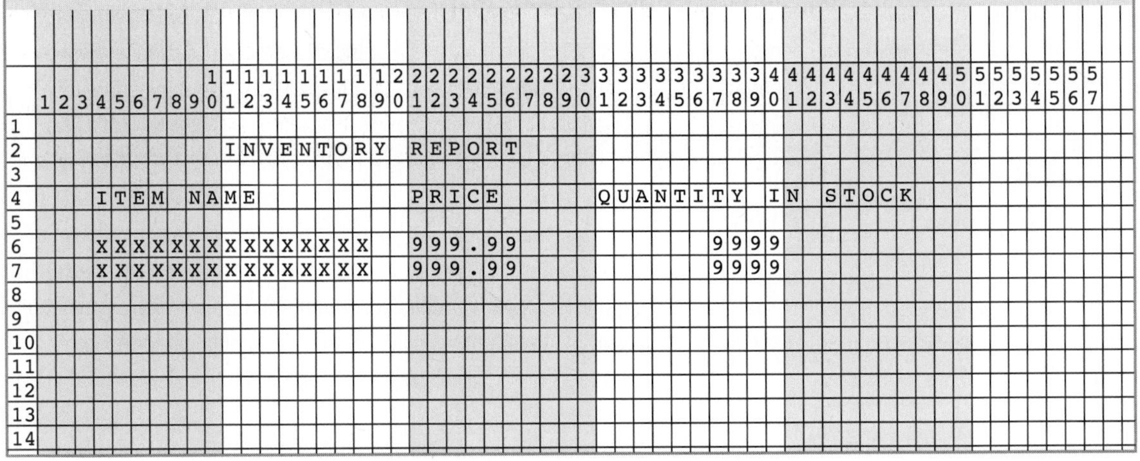

```
            1111111111222222222233333333334444444444555555555
   123456789012345678901234567890123456789012345678901234567
1
2            INVENTORY REPORT
3
4     ITEM NAME        PRICE     QUANTITY IN STOCK
5
6     XXXXXXXXXXXXXXX  999.99          9999
7     XXXXXXXXXXXXXXX  999.99          9999
8
9
10
11
12
13
14
```

The exact spacing and the use of uppercase or lowercase characters in the print chart make a difference. Notice that the constant data in the output, the items that do not vary but remain the same in every execution of the report, do not need to follow the same rules as variable names in the program. Within a report, constants like INVENTORY REPORT and ITEM NAME can contain spaces. These headings exist to help readers understand the information presented in the report—not for a computer to interpret; there is no need to run the names together, as you do when choosing identifiers for variables.

A print layout typically shows how the variable data will appear on the report. Of course, the data will probably be different every time the report is run. Thus, instead of writing in actual item names and prices, the users and programmers usually use Xs to represent generic variable character data and 9s to represent generic variable numeric data. (Some programmers use Xs for both character and numeric data.) Each line containing Xs and 9s representing data is a **detail line**, or a line that displays the data details. Detail lines typically appear many times per page, as opposed to **heading lines**, which contain the title and any column headings, and usually appear only once per page.

Even though an actual inventory report might eventually go on for hundreds or thousands of detail lines, writing two or three rows of Xs and 9s is sufficient to show how the data will appear. For example, if a report contains employee names and salaries, those data items will occupy the same print positions on output for line after line, whether the output eventually contains 10 employees or 10,000. A few rows of identically positioned Xs and 9s are sufficient to establish the pattern.

In any report layout, then, you write in constant data (such as headings) that will be the same on every run of the report. You write Xs and 9s to represent the variable data (such as the items, their prices, and their quantities) that will change from run to run.

Besides header lines and detail lines, reports often include special lines at the end of a report. These may contain a message that indicates the report is done (so that users do not worry there might be additional pages they are missing), or numeric statistics such as totals or averages. Even though lines at the end of a report don't always contain numeric totals, they are usually referred to generically as **total lines** or **summary lines**.

Printed reports do not necessarily contain detail lines. A report might contain only headers and summary lines. For example, a payroll report might contain only a heading and a total gross payroll figure for each department in the company, or a college might print a report showing how many students have declared each available major. These reports contain no detail—no information about individual employees or students—but they do contain summaries. Instead of creating a print chart, you might choose to create a less formal plan for output. For example, you might just sketch a plan using paper and pencil. Many programmers never use formal print charts, but they are discussed here so you will be familiar with them if you encounter them on the job. Besides using handwritten print charts, you also can design report layouts on a computer using a word-processing program or design software.

Not all program output takes the form of printed reports. If your program's output will appear on a monitor screen, particularly if you are working in a **GUI** (graphical user interface) environment like Windows, your design issues will differ. In a GUI program, the user sees a screen and can typically make selections using a mouse or other pointing device. Instead of a print chart, your output design might resemble a sketch of a screen. Figure 3-11 shows a hand-drawn sketch of a window that displays inventory records in a graphical environment. On a monitor, you might choose to allow the user to see only one or a few records at a time, so one concern is providing a means for users to scroll through displayed records. In Figure 3-11, records are accessed using a single button that the user can click to read the next record; in a more sophisticated design, the user might be able to "jump" to the first or last record, or look up a specific record.

**FIGURE 3-11:** INVENTORY RECORDS DISPLAYED IN A GUI ENVIRONMENT

**TIP** A printed report is also called a **hard copy**, whereas screen output is referred to as a **soft copy**.

**TIP** Achieving good screen design is an art that requires much study and thought to master. Besides being visually pleasing, good screen design also requires ease of use and accessibility.

**TIP** GUI programs often include several different screen formats that a user will see while running a program. In such cases, you would design several screens.

## INPUT DOCUMENTATION

Once you have planned the design of the output, you need to know what input is available to produce this output. If you are producing a report from stored data, you frequently will be provided with a **file description** that describes the data contained in a file. You usually find a file's description as part of an organization's information systems documentation; physically, the description might be on paper in a binder in the Information Systems department, or it might be stored on a disk. If the file you will use comes from an outside source, the person requesting the report will have to provide you with a description of the data stored on the file. Figure 3-12 shows an example of an inventory file description.

**FIGURE 3-12:** INVENTORY FILE DESCRIPTION

```
INVENTORY FILE DESCRIPTION
File name: INVENTORY
FIELD DESCRIPTION      DATA TYPE    COMMENTS
Name of item           Character    15 bytes
Price of item          Numeric      2 decimal places
Quantity in stock      Numeric      0 decimal places
```

TIP

Not all programs use previously stored input files. Some use interactive input data supplied by a user during the execution of a program. In the next chapter, you will see that whether input comes from a file or from user input, the process is very similar.

TIP

Some programs do not produce a printed report or screen display, but instead produce an output file that is stored directly on a storage device, such as a disk. If your program produces file output, you will create a file description for your output. Other programs then may use your output file description as an input description.

The inventory file description in Figure 3-12 shows that each item's name is character data that occupies the first 15 bytes of each record in the file. A **byte** is a unit of computer storage that can contain any of 256 combinations of 0s and 1s that often represent a character. The code of 0s and 1s depends on the type of computer system you are using. Popular coding schemes include ASCII (American Standard Code for Information Interchange), EBCDIC (Extended Binary Coded Decimal Interchange Code), and Unicode. Each of these codes uses a different combination of 1s and 0s to represent characters—you can see a listing of each code's values in Appendix B. For example, in ASCII, an uppercase "A" is represented by 01000001. Programmers seldom care about the code used; for example, if an "A" is stored as part of a person's name, the programmer's only concern is that the "A" in the name appears correctly on output—not the combination of 0s and 1s that represents it. This book assumes that one stored character occupies one byte in an input file.

Some item names may require all 15 positions allowed for the name in the input file—for example, "12 by 16 carpet", which contains exactly 15 characters, including spaces. Other item names require fewer than the allotted 15 positions—for example, "door mat". In such cases, the remaining allotted positions might remain blank, or the short description might be followed by a string-terminating character. (For example, in some systems, a string is followed by a special character in which all the bits are 0s.) On the other hand, when only 15 storage positions are allowed for a name, some names might be too long and have to be truncated or abbreviated. For example, "hand woven carpet" might be stored as "hand woven carp". Whether the item name requires all 15 positions or not, you can see from the input file description in Figure 3-12 that the price for each item begins after the description name, in position 16 of each input record.

The price of any item in the inventory file is numeric. In different storage systems, a number might occupy a different number of physical file positions. Additionally, numbers with decimal places frequently are stored using more bytes than integer numbers, even when the integer number is a "bigger" number. For example, in many systems, 5678 might be stored in a four-byte numeric integer field, while 2.2 might be stored in an eight-byte floating-point numeric field. When thinking logically about numeric fields, you do not care how many bytes of storage they occupy; what's important is that they hold numbers. For convenience, this book will simply designate numeric values as such, and let you know whether decimal places are included.

TIP

Repeated characters whose position is assumed frequently are not stored in data files. For example, dashes in Social Security numbers or telephone numbers, dollar signs on money amounts, or a period after a middle initial are seldom stored in data files. These symbols are used on printed reports, where it is important for the reader to be able to easily interpret these values.

Typically, programmers create one program variable for each field that is part of the input file. In addition to the field descriptions contained in the input documentation, the programmer might be given specific variable names to use for each field, particularly if such variable names must agree with the ones that other programmers working on the project are using. In many cases, however, programmers are allowed to choose their own variable names. Therefore, you can choose `itemName`, `nameOfItem`, `itemDescription`, or any other reasonable one-word variable name when you refer to the inventory item name within your program. The variable names you use within your program need not match constants, such as column headings, that might be printed on a hard copy report. Thus, the variable `itemName` might hold the characters that will print under the column heading NAME OF ITEM.

For example, examine the input file description in Figure 3-12. When this file is used for a project in which the programmer can choose variable names, he or she might choose the following variable declaration list:

```
char itemName
num itemPrice
num itemQuantity
```

Each data field in the list is declared using the data type that corresponds to the data type indicated in the file description, and has an appropriate, easy-to-read, single-word variable name.

**TIP** Some programmers argue that starting each field with a prefix indicating the file name (for example, "item" in `itemName` and `itemPrice`), helps to identify those variables as "belonging together." Others argue that repeating the "item" prefix is redundant and requires unnecessary typing by the programmer; these programmers would argue that "name", "price", and "quantity" are descriptive enough.

**TIP** When a programmer uses an identifier like `itemName`, that variable identifier exists in computer memory only for the duration of the program in which the variable is declared. Another program can use the same input file and refer to the same field as `nameOfItem`. Variable names exist in memory during the run of a program—they are not stored in the data file. Variable names simply represent memory addresses at which pieces of data are stored while a program executes.

Recall the data hierarchy relationship introduced in Chapter 1:

- Database
- File
- Record
- Field
- Character

Whether the inventory file is part of a database or not, it will contain many records; each record will contain an item name, price, and quantity, which are fields. In turn, the field that holds the name of an item might contain up to 15 characters—for example, "12 by 16 carpet", "blue miniblinds", or "diskette holder".

Organizations may use different forms to relay the information about records and fields, but the very least the programmer needs to know is:

- What is the name of the file?
- What data fields does it contain, and in what order?
- What type of data can be stored in each field—character or numeric?

Notice that a data field's position on the input file never has to correspond with the same item's position in an output file or in a print chart. For example, you can use the data file described in Figure 3-12 to produce the report shown in Figure 3-10. In the input data file, the item name appears in positions 1 through 15. However, on the printed report, the same information appears in columns 4 through 18. In an input file, data are "squeezed" together—no human being will read this file, and there is no need for it to be attractively spaced. However, on printed output, you typically include spaces between data items so they are legible as well as attractive. Figure 3-13 illustrates how input fields are read by the program and converted to output fields.

**FIGURE 3-13:** STORAGE OF INPUT AND DISPLAY OF OUTPUT

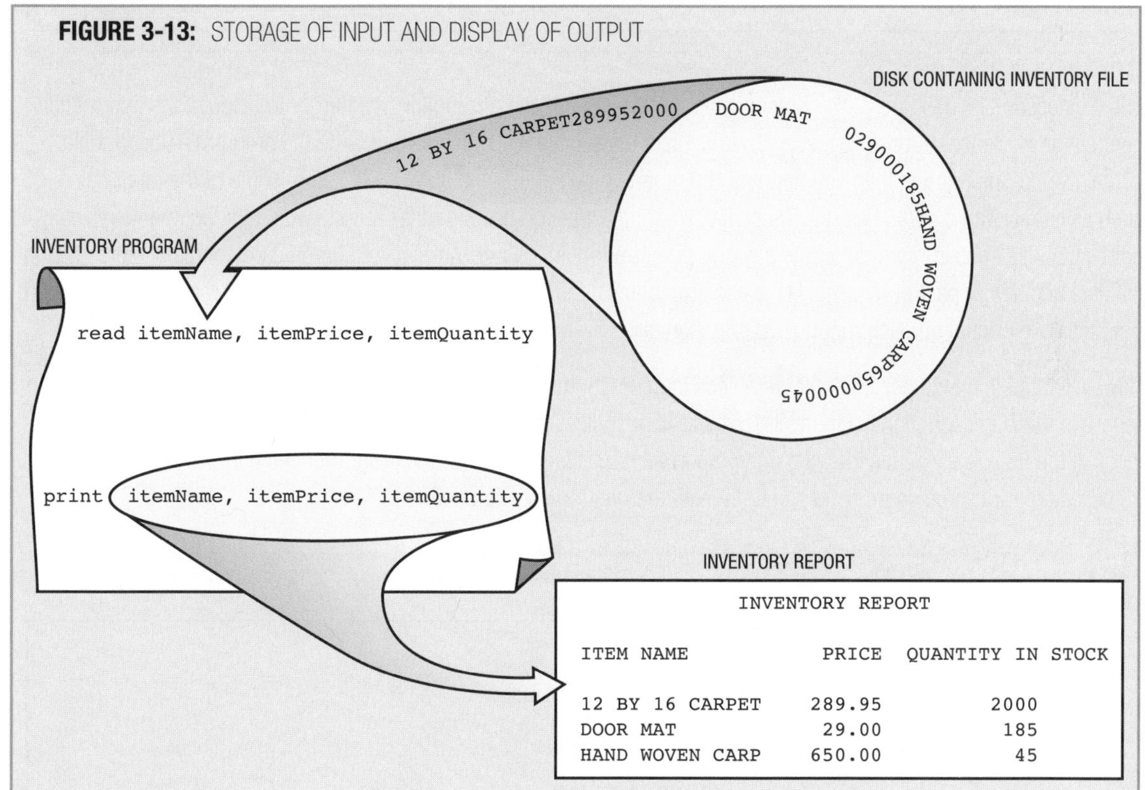


**TIP**

You are never required to output all the available characters that exist in a field in an input record. For example, even though the item name in the input file description in Figure 3-12 shows that each item contains 15 stored characters, you might decide to display only 10 of them on output, especially if your output report contained many columns and you were "crunched" for space.

The inventory file description in Figure 3-12 contains all the data the programmer needs to create the output requested in Figure 3-10—the output lists each item's name, price, and quantity, and the input records clearly contain that data. Often, however, a file description more closely resembles the description in Figure 3-14.

**FIGURE 3-14:** EXPANDED INVENTORY FILE DESCRIPTION

```
INVENTORY FILE DESCRIPTION
File name: INVENTORY
FIELD DESCRIPTION            DATA TYPE    COMMENTS
Item Number                  Numeric      0 decimal places
Name of item                 Character    15 bytes
Size                         Numeric      0 decimal places
Manufacturing cost of item   Numeric      2 decimal places
Retail price of item         Numeric      2 decimal places
Quantity in stock            Numeric      0 decimal places
Reorder point                Numeric      0 decimal places
Sales rep                    Character    10 bytes
Sales last year              Numeric      2 decimal places
```

The file description in Figure 3-14 contains nine fields. With this file description, it's harder to pinpoint the information needed for the report, but the necessary data fields are available, and you still can write the program. The input file contains more information than you need for the report you want to print, so you will ignore some of the input fields, such as Item Number and Sales rep. These fields certainly may be used in other reports within the company. Typically, data input files contain more data than any one program requires. For example, your credit card company stores historical data about your past purchases, but these are not included on every bill. Similarly, your school records contain more data than are printed on each report card or tuition bill.

However, if the input file description resembles Figure 3-15, there are not enough data items to produce the requested report. In the file description in Figure 3-15, there is no indication that the input file contains a value for quantity in stock. If the user really needs (or wants) the report as requested, it's out of the programmer's hands until the data can be collected from some source and stored in a file the programmer can use.

**FIGURE 3-15:** INSUFFICIENT INVENTORY FILE DESCRIPTION IF QUANTITY IN STOCK IS NEEDED FOR OUTPUT

```
INVENTORY FILE DESCRIPTION
File name: INVENTORY
FIELD DESCRIPTION            DATA TYPE    COMMENTS
Item Number                  Numeric      0 decimal places
Name of item                 Character    15 bytes
Size                         Numeric      0 decimal places
Manufacturing cost of item   Numeric      2 decimal places
Retail price of item         Numeric      2 decimal places
Reorder point                Numeric      0 decimal places
Sales rep                    Character    10 bytes
Sales last year              Numeric      2 decimal places
```

Each field printed on a report does not need to exist on the input file. Assume that a user requests a report in the format shown in the example in Figure 3-16, which includes a column labeled "Profit", and that the input file description is the one in Figure 3-14. In this case, it's difficult to determine whether you can create the requested report, because the input file does not contain a `profit` field. However, because the input data include the company's cost and selling price for each item, you can (after consulting with the user to make sure you agree on the definition of "profit") calculate the `profit` within your program by subtracting the cost from the price, and then produce the desired output.

**FIGURE 3-16:** SAMPLE PROFIT REPORT

```
          Profit Report

Item Number       Price     Cost    Profit

  1265             9.99     8.50     1.49
  1288            15.00    12.62     2.38
  1376            18.89    16.00     2.89
  1644            21.99    14.50     7.49
```

## COMPLETING THE DOCUMENTATION

When you have designed the output and confirmed that it is possible to produce it from the input, then you can plan the logic of the program, code the program, and test the program. The original output design, input description, flowchart or pseudocode, and program code all become part of the program documentation. These pieces of documentation are typically stored together in a binder within the programming department of an organization, where they can be studied later when program changes become necessary.

In addition to this program documentation, you typically must create user documentation. **User documentation** includes all the manuals or other instructional materials that nontechnical people use, as well as the operating instructions that computer operators and data-entry personnel need. It needs to be written clearly, in plain language, with reasonable expectations of the users' expertise. Within a small organization, the programmer may prepare the user documentation. In a large organization, user documentation is usually prepared by technical writers or systems analysts, who oversee programmers' work and coordinate programmers' efforts. These professionals consult with the programmer to ensure that the user documentation is complete and accurate.

The areas addressed in user documentation may include:

- How to prepare input for the program
- To whom the output should be distributed
- How to interpret the normal output
- How to interpret and react to any error message generated by the program
- How frequently the program needs to run

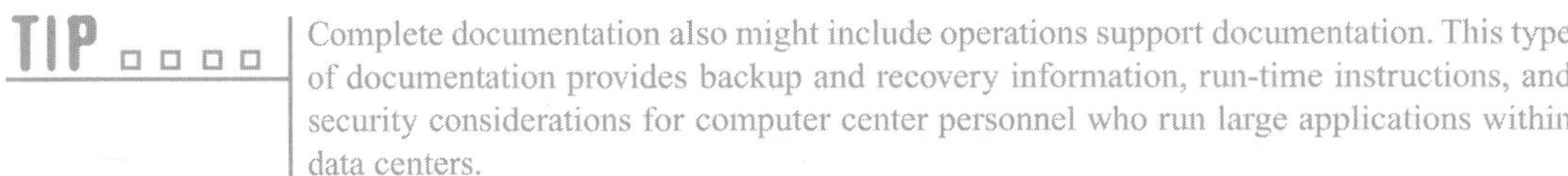

TIP

Complete documentation also might include operations support documentation. This type of documentation provides backup and recovery information, run-time instructions, and security considerations for computer center personnel who run large applications within data centers.

All these issues must be addressed before a program can be fully functional in an organization. When users throughout an organization can supply input data to computer programs and obtain the information they need in order to do their jobs well, then a skilled programmer has provided a complete piece of work.

## CHAPTER SUMMARY

- Programmers break down programming problems into smaller, reasonable units called modules, subroutines, procedures, functions, or methods. Modularization provides abstraction, allows multiple programmers to work on a problem, makes it easy to reuse your work, and allows you to identify structures more easily.
- When you create a module or subroutine, you give the module a name that a calling program uses when the module is about to execute. The flowchart symbol used to call a subroutine is a rectangle with a bar across the top; the name of the module that you are calling is inside the rectangle. You draw a flowchart for each module separately, with its own sentinel symbols.
- A module can call other modules.
- Declaring a variable involves providing a name for the memory location where the computer will store the variable value, and notifying the computer of what type of data to expect.
- You can use a hierarchy chart to illustrate modules' relationships.
- Documentation refers to all of the supporting material that goes with a program.
- Output documentation is usually written first. You can design a printed report on a printer spacing chart to represent both constant and variable data. You also can design report layouts on a computer using a word-processing program or design software, or draw diagrams of planned screen output.
- A file description lists the data contained in a file, including a description, data type, and any other necessary information, such as number of decimal places in numeric data.
- In addition to program documentation, you typically must create user documentation, which includes the manuals or other instructional materials that nontechnical people use, as well as the operating instructions that computer operators and data-entry personnel may need.

## KEY TERMS

**Modules** are small program units that you can use together to make a program. Programmers also refer to modules as **subroutines**, **procedures**, **functions**, or **methods**.

The process of breaking down a program into modules is called **modularization**.

**Abstraction** is the process of paying attention to important properties while ignoring nonessential details.

**Low-level** details are small, nonabstract steps.

**High-level** programming languages allow you to use English-like vocabulary in which one broad statement corresponds to dozens of machine instructions.

**Reusability** is the feature of modular programs that allows individual modules to be used in a variety of applications.

**Reliability** is the feature of modular programs that assures you that a module has been tested and proven to function correctly.

The **mainline logic** is the logic used in the main module that calls other program modules.

A **calling program** or **calling module** is one that calls a module.

A module that is called by another is a **submodule**.

A **main program** runs from start to stop and calls other modules.

A **prompt** is a message that is displayed on a monitor, asking the user for a response.

The **functional cohesion** of a module is a measure of the degree to which all the module statements contribute to the same task.

**Declaring a variable** involves providing a name for the memory location where the computer will store the variable value, and notifying the computer of what type of data to expect.

**Local variables** are declared within each module that uses them.

**Global variables** are given a type and name once, and then are used in all modules of the program.

An **annotation symbol** or **annotation box** is a flowchart symbol that represents an attached box containing notes.

A **data dictionary** is a list of every variable name used in a program, along with its type, size, and description.

A **hierarchy chart** is a diagram that illustrates modules' relationships to each other.

**Documentation** refers to all of the supporting material that goes with a program.

**End users**, or **users**, are people who use computer programs.

**Program documentation** is the set of instructions that programmers use when they begin to plan the logic of a program.

**Internal program documentation** is documentation within a program.

Program **comments** are nonexecuting statements that programmers place within their code to explain program statements in English.

**External program documentation** includes all the supporting paperwork that programmers develop before they write a program.

A **printer spacing chart**, which is also referred to as a **print chart** or a **print layout**, is a tool for planning program output.

A **detail line** on a report is a line that contains data details. Most reports contain many detail lines.

**Heading lines** on a report contain the title and any column headings, and usually appear only once per page.

**Total lines** or **summary lines** contain end-of-report information.

A **GUI**, or graphical user interface, environment uses screens to display program output. Users interact with GUI programs with a device such as a mouse.

A **hard copy** is a printed copy.

A **soft copy** is a screen copy.

A **file description** is a document that describes the data contained in a file.

A **byte** is a unit of computer storage that can contain any of 256 combinations of 0s and 1s that often represent a character.

**User documentation** includes all the manuals or other instructional materials that nontechnical people use, as well as the operating instructions that computer operators and data-entry personnel need.

## REVIEW QUESTIONS

1. **Which of the following is *not* a term used as a synonym for "module" in any programming language?**
   a. structure
   b. procedure
   c. method
   d. function

2. **Which of the following is *not* a reason to use modularization?**
   a. Modularization provides abstraction.
   b. Modularization allows multiple programmers to work on a problem.
   c. Modularization allows you to reuse your work.
   d. Modularization eliminates the need for structure.

3. **What is the name for the process of paying attention to important properties while ignoring nonessential details?**
   a. structure
   b. iteration
   c. abstraction
   d. modularization

4. **All modern programming languages that use English-like vocabulary to create statements that correspond to dozens of machine instructions are referred to as ________.**
   a. high-level
   b. object-oriented
   c. modular
   d. obtuse

5. **Modularizing a program makes it ________ to identify structures.**
   a. unnecessary
   b. easier
   c. more difficult
   d. impossible

6. **Programmers say that one module can ________ another, meaning that the first module causes the second module to execute.**
   a. declare
   b. define
   c. enact
   d. call

7. **A message that appears on a monitor, asking the user for a response, is a ________.**
   a. call
   b. prompt
   c. command
   d. declaration

8. **The more that a module's statements contribute to the same job, the greater the _______ of the module.**
   a. structure
   b. modularity
   c. functional cohesion
   d. size

9. **When you declare a variable, you must provide _______.**
   a. a name
   b. a name and a type
   c. a name, a type, and a value
   d. a name, a type, a value, and a purpose

10. **A _______ is a list of every variable name used in a program, along with its type, size, and description.**
   a. flowchart
   b. hierarchy chart
   c. data dictionary
   d. variable map

11. **A hierarchy chart tells you _______.**
   a. what tasks are to be performed within each program module
   b. when a module executes
   c. which routines call which other routines
   d. all of the above

12. **Two broad categories of documentation are the documentation intended for _______.**
   a. management and workers
   b. end users and programmers
   c. people and the computer
   d. defining variables and defining actions

13. **Nonexecuting statements that programmers place within their code to explain program statements in English are called _______.**
   a. comments
   b. pseudocode
   c. trivia
   d. user documentation

14. **The first type of documentation usually created when writing a program pertains to _______.**
   a. end users
   b. input
   c. output
   d. data

**15. Lines of output that never change, no matter what data values are input, are referred to as _______.**

a. detail lines
b. headers
c. rigid
d. constant

**16. Report lines that contain the information stored in individual data records are known as _______.**

a. headers
b. footers
c. detail lines
d. X-lines

**17. Summary lines appear _______.**

a. at the end of every printed report
b. at the end of some printed reports
c. in printed reports, but never in screen output
d. only when detail lines also appear

**18. If an input file description stores a first name followed by a last name, then _______.**

a. the first name must appear first on any output
b. the first name must not appear first on any output
c. the first and last names must both appear on output
d. None of the above are true.

**19. Of the following items, which does a programmer usually not need to know about an input file?**

a. the name of the file
b. the number of records in the file
c. the order of the data fields in the file
d. whether each field in each record is numeric or character

**20. A field holding a student's last name is stored in bytes 10 through 29 of each student record. Therefore, when you design a print chart for a report that contains each student's last name, _______.**

a. the name must print in positions 10 through 29 of the print chart
b. the name must occupy exactly 20 positions on the print chart
c. Both of these are true.
d. Neither of these is true.

## FIND THE BUGS

Each of the following pseudocode segments contains one or more bugs that you must find and correct.

1. **This pseudocode is intended to describe determining whether you have passed or failed a course based on the average score of two classroom tests. The main program calls three modules—one that gets the input values, one that performs the average calculation, and another that displays the results.**

```
start
   declare variables
      num test1Score
      num test2Score
      char letterGrade
   perform getInputValues()
   perform computeAvg()
   perform displayResults()
stop
getInput()
   input test1Score
   input test2Score
return
computeAverage()
   average = (test1Score + test2Score) / 2
   if average >= 60 then
      letterGrade = "P"
   else
      average = "F"
   endif
return
displayResults()
   print average
   print letter
return
```

2. **This pseudocode is intended to describe computing the number of miles per gallon you get with your automobile as well as the cost of gasoline per mile. The main program calls modules that allow the user to enter data, compute statistics, and display results.**

```
start
   declare variables
      num gallonsOfGasUsed
      num milesTraveled
      num pricePerGallon
      num milesPerGallon
      num costPerMile
   perform inputData()
   perform computeStatistics()
   perform displayResults()
inputData()
   input gallonsOfGasUsed
   input milesTravelled
   input pricePerGallonOfGas
return
computeStatistics()
   milesPerGallon = gallonsOfGasUsed / milesTraveled
   costPerMile = pricePerGallon - milesPerGallon
return
displayResults()
   print milesPerGal
   print costPerMile
return
stop
```

3. **This pseudocode segment is intended to describe computing the cost per day for a vacation. The user enters a value for total dollars available to spend and can continue to enter new dollar amounts while the amount entered is not 0. For each new amount entered, a module is called that calculates the amount of money available to spend per day.**

```
start
   declare variables
      num totalDollars
      num costPerDay
   input totalDollarsSpent
   while totalDollarsSpent = 0
      perform caclulateCost()
   endwhile
end
calculateCost()
   costPerDay = totalMoneySpent / 7
   print costPerDay
endwhile
```

## EXERCISES

1. **Redraw the following flowchart so that the decisions and compensation calculations are in a module.**

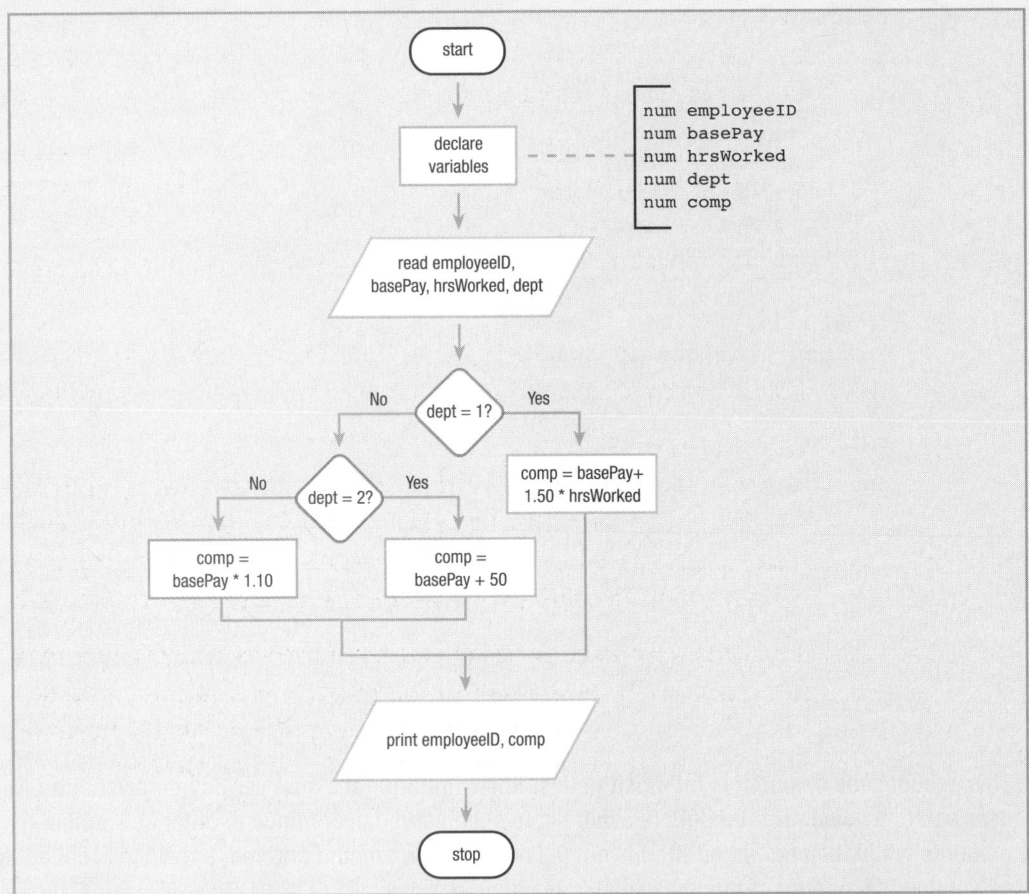


2. **Rewrite the following pseudocode so the discount decisions and calculations are in a module.**

```
start
   read customerRecord
   if quantityOrdered > 100 then
       discount = .20
   else
       if quantityOrdered > 12 then
           discount = .10
       endif
   endif
   total = priceEach * quantityOrdered
   total = total - discount * total
   print total
stop
```

3. **What are the final values of variables a, b, and c after the following program runs?**

```
start
          a = 2
          b = 4
          c = 10
          while c > 6
                    perform changeBAndC()
          endwhile
          if a = 2 then
                    perform changeAAndB()
          endif
          if c = 10 then
                    perform changeAAndB()
          else
                    perform changeBAndC()
          endif
          print a, b, c
stop
changeBAndC()
          b = b + 1
          c = c - 1
return
changeAAndB()
          a = a + 1
          b = b - 1
return
```

4. **What are the final values of variables d, e, and f after the following program runs?**

```
start
          d = 1
          e = 3
          f = 100
          while e > d
                    perform module1()
          endwhile
          if f > 0 then
                    perform module2()
          else
                    d = d + 5
          endif
          print d, e, f
stop
module1()
          f = f - 50
          e = e + 1
          d = d + 3
return

module2()
          f = f + 13
          d = d * 10
return
```

5. **Draw a typical hierarchy chart for a paycheck-producing program. Try to think of at least 10 separate modules that might be included. For example, one module might calculate an employee's dental insurance premium.**

6. **a.** Design a print chart for a payroll roster that is intended to list the following items for every employee: employee's first name, last name, and salary.
   **b.** Design sample output for the same report, including at least three lines of data.

7. **a.** Design a print chart for a payroll roster that is intended to list the following items for every employee: employee's first name, last name, hours worked, rate per hour, gross pay, federal withholding tax, state withholding tax, union dues, and net pay.
   **b.** Design sample output for the same report, including at least three lines of data.

8. **Given the following input file description, determine whether there is enough information provided to produce each of the requested reports:**

```
INSURANCE PREMIUM LIST
File name: INSPREM
FIELD DESCRIPTION               DATA TYPE    COMMENTS
Name of insured driver          Character    40 bytes
Birth date                      Numeric      8 digits (for example, 19820624)
Gender                          Numeric      1 or 2 for male or female
Make of car                     Character    10 bytes
Year of car                     Numeric      4 digits
Miles driven per year           Numeric      0 decimal places
Number of traffic tickets       Numeric      0 decimal places
Balance owed                    Numeric      2 decimal places
```

   a. a list of the names of all insured drivers
   b. a list of very high-risk insured drivers, defined as male, under 25 years old, with more than two tickets
   c. a list of low-risk insured drivers, defined as those with no tickets in the last three years, and over 30 years old
   d. a list of insured drivers to contact about a special premium offer for those with a passenger car who drive under 10,000 miles per year
   e. a list of the names of female drivers whose balance owed is more than $99.99

9. **Given the INSPREM file description in Exercise 8, design a print chart or sample report to satisfy each of the following requests:**
   a. a list of every driver's name and make of car
   b. a list of the names of all insured drivers who drive more than 20,000 miles per year
   c. a list of the name, gender, make of car, and year of car for all drivers who have more than two tickets
   d. a report that summarizes the number of tickets held by drivers who were born in 1940 or before, from 1941–1960, from 1961–1980, and from 1981 on
   e. a report that summarizes the number of tickets held by drivers in the four birth-date categories listed in part d, grouped by gender

10. A program calculates the gown size that a student needs for a graduation ceremony. The program accepts as input a student's height in feet and inches and weight in pounds. It converts the student's height to centimeters and weight to grams. Then, it calculates the graduation gown size needed by adding ⅓ of the weight in grams to the value of the height in centimeters. Finally, the program prints the results. There are 2.54 centimeters in an inch and 453.59 grams in a pound. Write the pseudocode that matches the following flowchart.

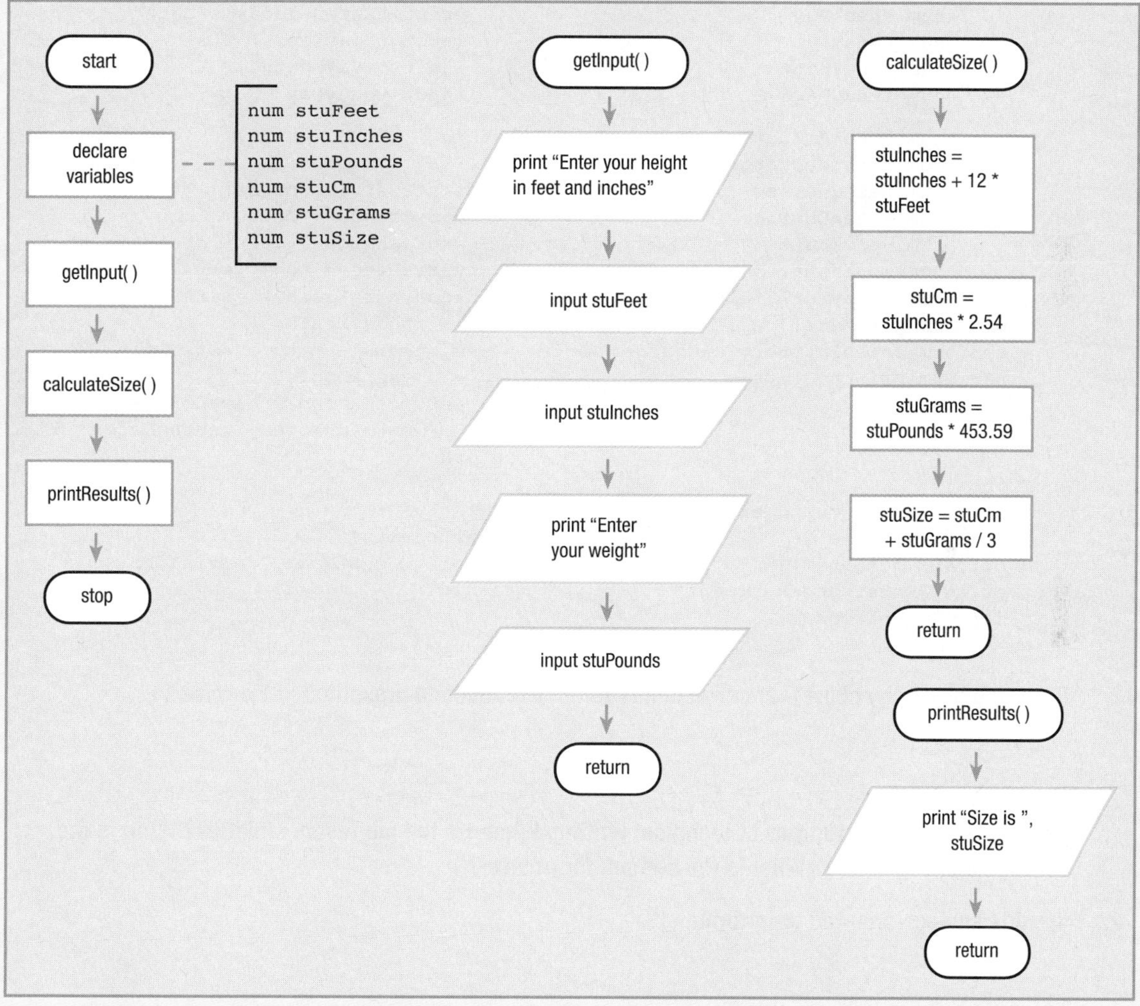


11. A program calculates the service charge a customer owes for writing a bad check. The program accepts a customer's name, the date the check was written (year, month, and day), the current date (year, month, and day), and the amount of the check in dollars and cents. The service charge is $20 plus 2 percent of the amount of the check, plus $5 for every month that has passed since the check was written. Draw the flowchart that matches the pseudocode.

**(This pseudocode assumes that all checks entered are already written—that is, their dates are prior to today's date. Additionally, a check is one month late as soon as a new month starts—so a bad check written on September 30 is one month overdue on October 1.)**

```
start
     declare variables
          char custName
          num checkYear
          num checkMonth
          num checkDay
          num todayYear
          num todayMonth
          num todayDay

          num checkAmount
          num serviceCharge
          num baseCharge
          num extraCharge
          num yearsLate
          num monthsLate
          num todayWorkField
     perform getInput()
     perform calculateServiceCharge()
     perform printResults()

stop

getInput()
     print "Enter customer name"
     input custName
     perform getDates()
     print "Enter check amount"
     input checkAmount
return

getDates()
     print "Enter the date of the check"
     input checkYear
     input checkMonth
     input checkDay
     print "Enter today's date"
     input todayYear
     input todayMonth
     input todayDay

return

calculateServiceCharge()
     baseCharge = 20.00
     extraCharge = .02 * checkAmount
     yearsLate = todayYear - checkYear
     todayWorkField = yearsLate * 12 +
          todayMonth
     monthsLate = todayWorkField -
          checkMonth
     serviceCharge = baseCharge +
          extraCharge + monthsLate * 5
return

printResults()
     print custName, serviceCharge
return
```

12. **Draw the hierarchy chart that corresponds to the pseudocode presented in Exercise 11.**

## DETECTIVE WORK

1. **Explore the job opportunities in technical writing. What are the job responsibilities? What is the average starting salary? What is the outlook for growth?**

2. **What is subject-oriented programming?**

## UP FOR DISCUSSION

1. **Would you prefer to be a programmer, write documentation, or both? Why?**

2. **Would you prefer to write a large program by yourself, or work on a team in which each programmer produces one or more modules? Why?**

3. **Can you think of any disadvantages to providing program documentation for other programmers or for the user?**

# 4 DESIGNING AND WRITING A COMPLETE PROGRAM

## After studying Chapter 4, you should be able to:

- Plan the mainline logic for a complete program
- Describe typical housekeeping tasks
- Describe tasks typically performed in the main loop of a program
- Describe tasks performed in the end-of-job module
- Understand the need for good program design
- Appreciate the advantages of storing program components in separate files
- Select superior variable and module names
- Design clear module statements
- Understand the need for maintaining good programming habits

## UNDERSTANDING THE MAINLINE LOGICAL FLOW THROUGH A PROGRAM

In the first chapters of this book, you gained an understanding of programming structures, and learned about the documentation needed for program input, processing, and output. Now, you're ready to plan the logic for your first complete computer program. The output is an inventory report; a print chart is shown in Figure 4-1. The report lists inventory items along with the price, cost, and profit of each item.

**FIGURE 4-1:** PRINT CHART FOR INVENTORY REPORT

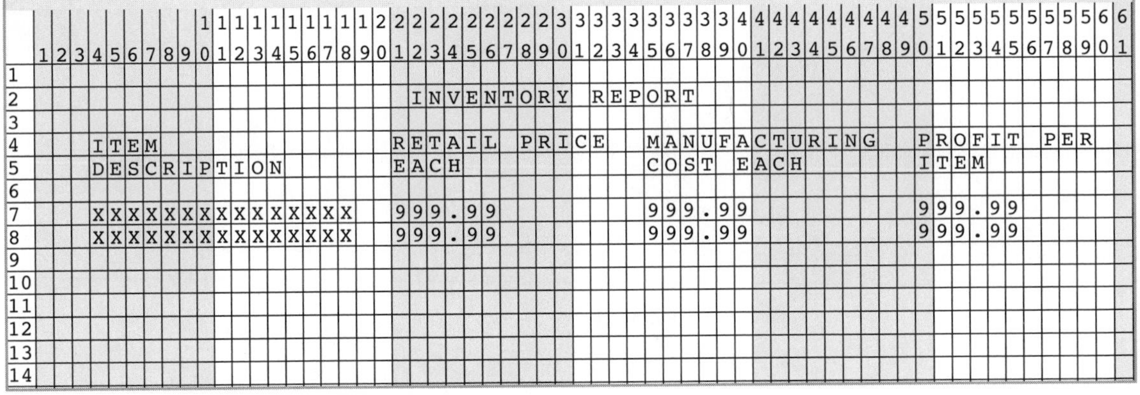

```
            1111111111222222222233333333334444444444555555555566
   1234567890123456789012345678901234567890123456789012345678901
1
2                        INVENTORY REPORT
3
4      ITEM            RETAIL PRICE   MANUFACTURING  PROFIT PER
5      DESCRIPTION     EACH           COST EACH      ITEM
6
7      XXXXXXXXXXXXXXX 999.99         999.99         999.99
8      XXXXXXXXXXXXXXX 999.99         999.99         999.99
9
10
11
12
13
14
```

Figure 4-2 shows the input INVENTORY file description, Figure 4-3 shows some typical data that might exist in the input file, and Figure 4-4 shows how the output would actually look if the input file in Figure 4-3 were used.

**FIGURE 4-2:** INVENTORY FILE DESCRIPTION

```
INVENTORY FILE DESCRIPTION
File name: INVENTORY
FIELD DESCRIPTION       DATA TYPE    COMMENTS
Item name               Character    15 bytes
Price                   Numeric      2 decimal places
Cost                    Numeric      2 decimal places
Quantity in stock       Numeric      0 decimal places
```

**FIGURE 4-3:** TYPICAL DATA THAT MIGHT BE STORED IN INVENTORY FILE

```
cotton shirt      01995     01457     2500
wool scarf        01450     01125     0060
silk blouse       16500     04850     0525
cotton shorts     01750     01420     1500
```

**FIGURE 4-4:** TYPICAL OUTPUT FOR INVENTORY REPORT PROGRAM

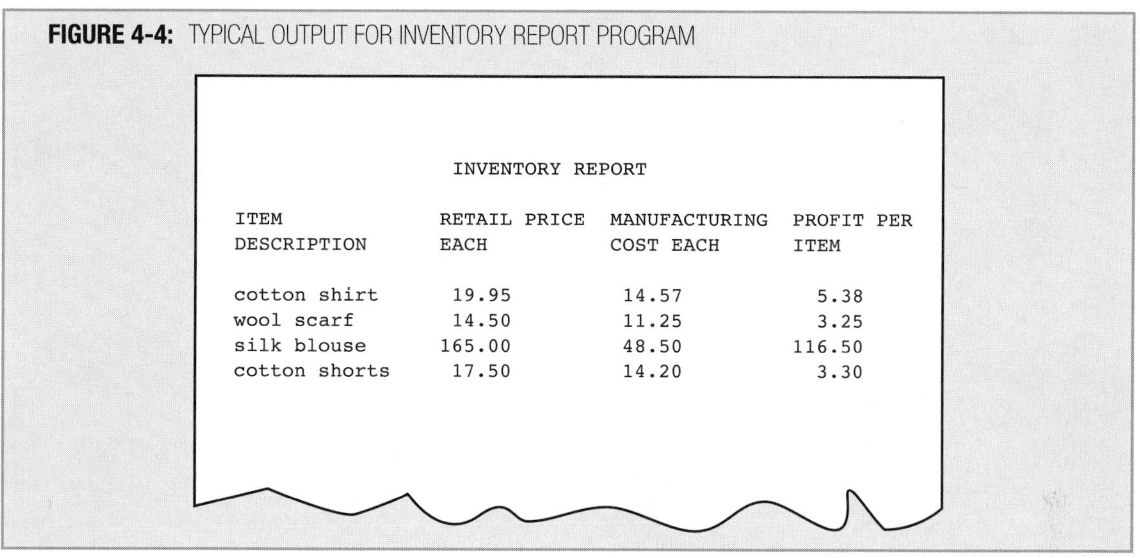

```
                    INVENTORY REPORT

ITEM              RETAIL PRICE  MANUFACTURING  PROFIT PER
DESCRIPTION       EACH          COST EACH      ITEM

cotton shirt       19.95         14.57            5.38
wool scarf         14.50         11.25            3.25
silk blouse       165.00         48.50          116.50
cotton shorts      17.50         14.20            3.30
```

**TIP** In some older operating systems, file names are limited to eight characters, in which case INVENTORY might be an unacceptable file name.

Examine the print chart and the input file description. Your first task is to make sure you understand what the report requires; your next job is to determine whether you have all the data you need to produce the report. (Figure 4-5 shows this process.) The output requires the item name, price, and cost, and you can see that all three are data items in the input file. The output also requires a profit figure for each item; you need to understand how profit is calculated—which could be done differently in various companies. If there is any doubt as to what a term used in the output means or how a value is calculated, you must ask the **user**, or your **client**—the person who has requested the program and who will read and use the report to make management decisions. In this case, suppose you are told you can determine the profit by subtracting an item's cost from its selling price. The input record contains an additional field, "Quantity in stock". Input records often contain more data than an application needs; in this example, you will not use the quantity field. You have all the necessary data, so you can begin to plan the program.

FIGURE 4-5: STEPS TO CREATING A PROGRAM

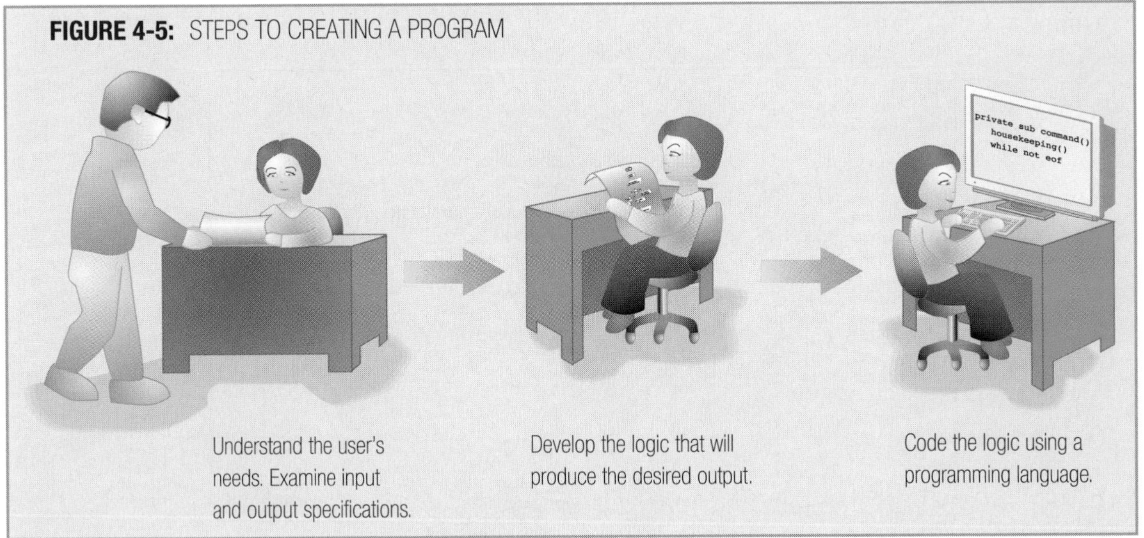

private sub command()
housekeeping()
while not eof
Understand the user's needs. Examine input and output specifications.
Develop the logic that will produce the desired output.
Code the logic using a programming language.


**TIP** It is very common for input records to contain more data than an application uses. For example, although your doctor stores your blood pressure in your patient record, that field does not appear on your bill, and although your school stores your grades from your first semester, they do not appear on your report card for your second semester.

Where should you begin? It's wise to try to understand the big picture first. You can write a program that reads records from an input file and produces a printed report as a **procedural program**—that is, a program in which one procedure follows another from the beginning until the end. You write the entire set of instructions for a procedural program, and when the program executes, instructions take place one at a time, following your program's logic. The overall logic, or **mainline logic**, of almost every procedural computer program can follow a general structure that consists of three distinct parts:

1. Performing housekeeping, or initialization tasks. **Housekeeping** includes steps you must perform at the beginning of a program to get ready for the rest of the program.
2. Performing the main loop repeatedly within the program. The **main loop** contains the instructions that are executed for every record until you reach the end of the input of records, or `eof`.
3. Performing the end-of-job routine. The **end-of-job routine** holds the steps you take at the end of the program to finish the application.

**TIP** Not all programs are procedural; some are object-oriented. A distinguishing feature of many (but not all) object-oriented programs is that they are event-driven; often the user determines the timing of events in the main loop of the program by using an input device such as a mouse. As you advance in your knowledge of programming, you will learn more about object-oriented techniques.

You can write any procedural program as one long series of programming language statements, but programs are easier to understand if you break their logic down into at least three parts, or modules. The main program can call the three major modules, as shown in the flowchart and pseudocode in Figure 4-6. Of course, the names of the modules, or subroutines, are entirely up to the programmer.

**FIGURE 4-6:** FLOWCHART AND PSEUDOCODE OF MAINLINE LOGIC

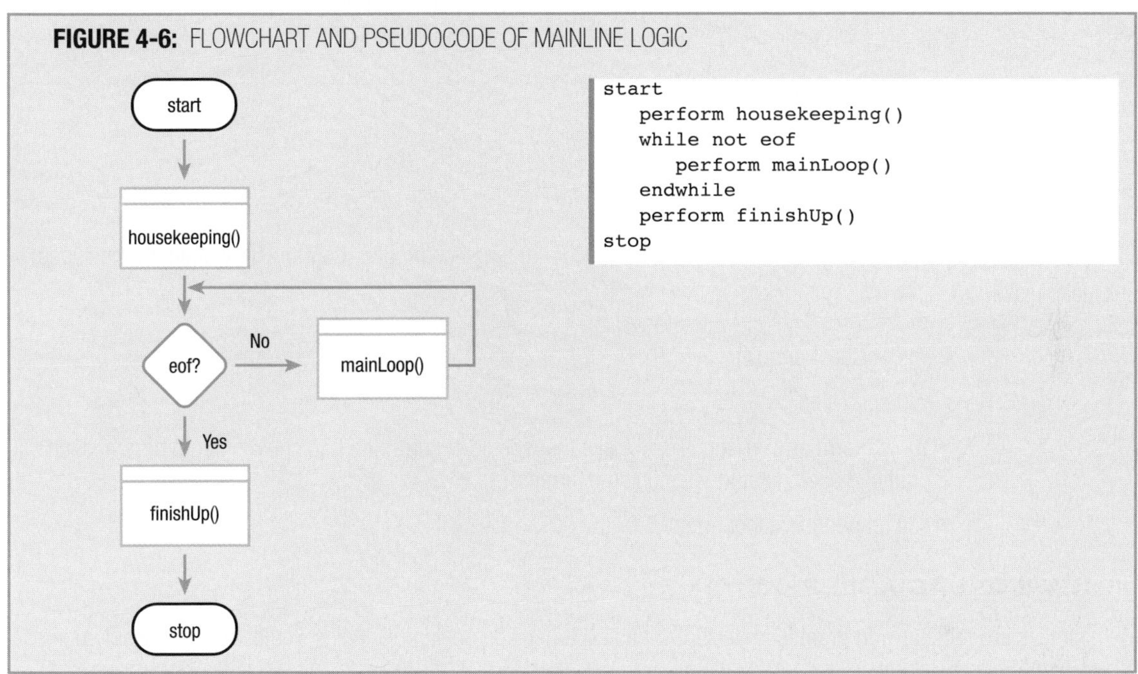


```
start
   perform housekeeping()
   while not eof
      perform mainLoop()
   endwhile
   perform finishUp()
stop
```

**TIP** Reducing a large program into more manageable modules is sometimes called **functional decomposition**.

**TIP** In later examples, this book will use more descriptive names for the `mainLoop()` module. For example, in this program, appropriate names for the `mainLoop()` might be `processRecord()` or `createInventoryReport()`.

Figure 4-7 shows the hierarchy chart for this program.

In summary, breaking down a big program into three basic procedures, or modularizing the program, helps keep the job manageable, allowing you to tackle a large job one step at a time. Dividing the work into routines also might allow you to assign the three major procedures to three different programmers, if you choose. It also helps you keep the program structured.

**FIGURE 4-7:** HIERARCHY CHART FOR INVENTORY REPORT PROGRAM

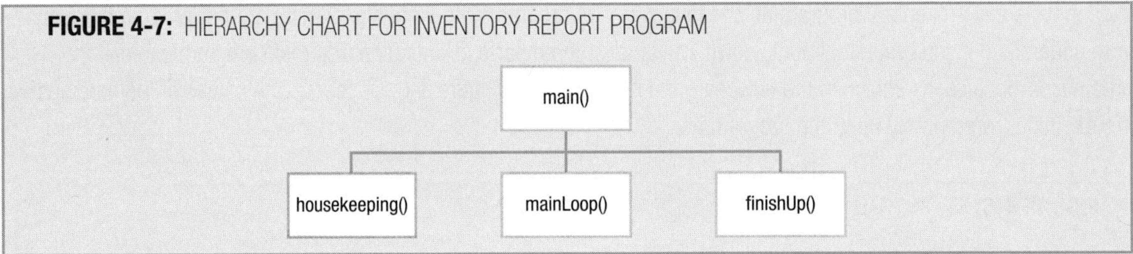


## HOUSEKEEPING TASKS

Housekeeping tasks include all the steps that must take place at the beginning of a program. Very often, this includes four major tasks:

- You declare variables.
- You open files.
- You perform any one-time-only tasks that should occur at the beginning of the program, such as printing headings at the beginning of a report.
- You read the first input record.

### DECLARING VARIABLES

Your first task in writing any program is to declare variables. When you declare variables, you assign reasonable names (identifiers) to memory locations, so you can store and retrieve data there. Declaring a variable involves selecting a name and a type. When you declare a variable in program code, the operating system reserves space in memory to hold the contents of the variable. It uses the type (`num` or `char`) to determine how to store the information; it stores numeric and character values in different formats.

For example, within the inventory report program, you need to supply variable names for the data fields that appear in each input record. You might decide on the variable names and types shown in Figure 4-8.

**FIGURE 4-8:** VARIABLE DECLARATIONS FOR THE INVENTORY FILE

```
char  invItemName
num   invPrice
num   invCost
num   invQuantity
```

Some languages require that you provide storage size, in addition to a type and name, for each variable. Other languages provide a predetermined amount of storage based on the variable type: for example, four bytes for an integer or one byte for a character. Also, many languages require you to provide a length for strings of characters. For simplicity, this book just declares variables as either character or numeric.

You can provide any names you choose for your variables. When you write another program that uses the same input file, you are free to choose completely new variable names. Similarly, other programmers can write programs that use the same file and choose their own variable names. The variable names just represent memory positions, and are internal to your program. The files do not contain any variable names; files contain only data. When you read the characters "cotton shirt" from an input file, it doesn't matter whether you store those characters at a memory location named `invItemName`, `nameOfItem`, `productDescription`, or any other one-word variable name. The variable name is simply an easy-to-remember name for a specific memory address where those characters are stored.

TIP □□□□ Programmers always must decide between descriptive, but long, variable names and cryptic, but short, variable names. In general, more descriptive names are better, but certain abbreviations are almost always acceptable in the business world. For example, SSN is commonly used as an abbreviation for Social Security number, and if you use it as a variable name, it will be interpreted correctly by most of your associates who read your program.

Each of the four variable declarations in Figure 4-8 contains a type (character or numeric) and an identifier. You can choose any one-word name to identify the variable, but a typical practice involves beginning similar variables with a common **prefix**—for example, `inv`. In a large program in which you eventually declare dozens of variables, the `inv` prefix will help you immediately identify a variable as part of the inventory file.

TIP □□□□ Organizations sometimes enforce different rules for programmers to follow when naming variables. Some use a variable-naming convention called **Hungarian notation**, in which a variable's data type or other information is stored as part of the name. For example, a numeric field might always start with the prefix num.

Creating the inventory report as planned in Figure 4-1 involves using the `invItemName`, `invPrice`, and `invCost` fields, but you do not need to use the `invQuantity` field in this program. However, the information regarding quantity does take room in the input file, so you typically declare the variable to allocate space for it when it is read into memory. If you imagine the surface of a disk as pictured in Figure 4-9, you can envision how the data fields follow one another in the file.

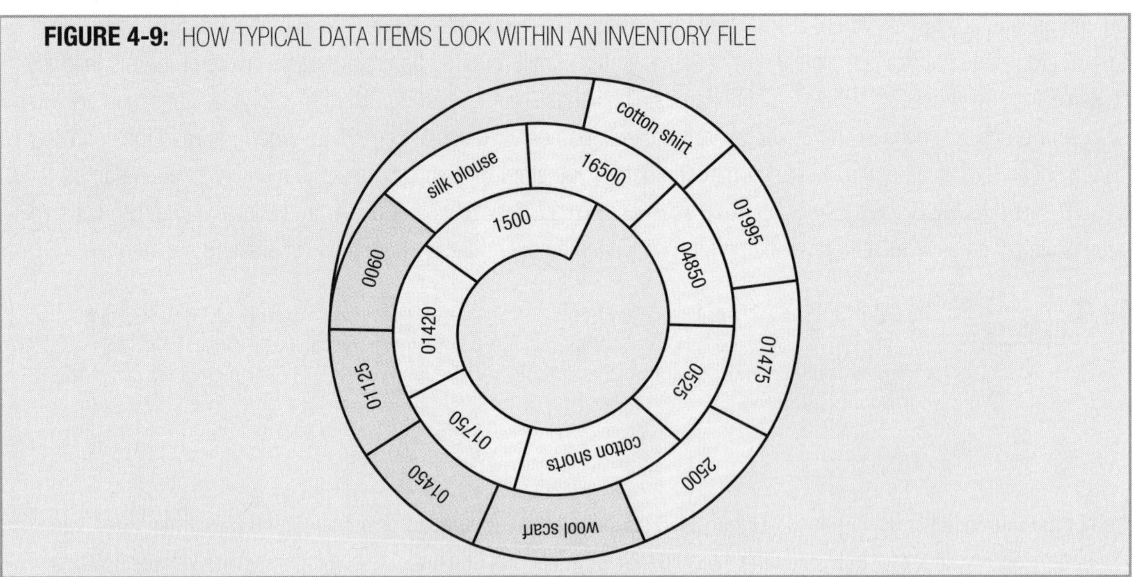


**FIGURE 4-9:** HOW TYPICAL DATA ITEMS LOOK WITHIN AN INVENTORY FILE

When you ask the program to read an inventory record, four "chunks" of data will be transferred from the input device to the computer's main memory: name, price, cost, and quantity. When you declare the variables that represent the input data, you must provide a memory position for each of the four pieces of data, whether or not they all are used within this program.

**TIP**

Some languages do not require you to use a unique name for each data field in an input record. For example, in COBOL, you can use the generic name FILLER for all unused data positions. This frees you from the task of creating variable names for items you do not intend to use. Because it is common to do so using newer languages, the examples in this book always provide a unique identifier for each variable in a file.

**TIP**

Considering that dozens of programs within the organization might access the INVENTORY file, some organizations create the data file descriptions for you. This system is efficient because the description of variable names and types is stored in one location, and each programmer who uses the file simply imports the data file description into his or her own program. Of course, the organization must provide the programmer with documentation specifying and describing the chosen names.

In most programming languages, you can give a group of associated variables a **group name**. This allows you to handle several associated variables using a single instruction. Just as it is easier to refer to "The Andersons" than it is to list "Nancy, Bud, Jim, Tom, Julie, Jane, Kate, and John," the benefit of using a group name is the ability to reference several variables with one all-encompassing name. For example, if you group four fields together and call them `invRecord`, then you can write a statement such as `read invRecord`. This is simpler than writing `read invItemName`, `invPrice`, `invCost`, and `invQuantity`. The way you assign a group name to several variables differs in each programming language. This book follows the convention of underlining any group name and indenting the group members beneath, as shown in Figure 4-10.

**FIGURE 4-10:** VARIABLE DECLARATIONS FOR THE INVENTORY FILE INCLUDING A GROUP NAME

```
invRecord
   char   invItemName
   num    invPrice
   num    invCost
   num    invQuantity
```

**TIP**

A group of variables is often called a *data structure*, or more simply, a *structure*. Some object-oriented languages refer to a group as a *class*, although a class often contains method definitions as well as variables.

**TIP**

In many programming languages, you can use the group name along with the field name, separated by a dot. For example, you might refer to `invRecord.invItemName`. This book will use the field name only, for simplicity.

**TIP**

The ability to group variable names does not automatically provide you with the ability to perform every sort of operation with a group. For example, you cannot multiply or divide one `invRecord` by another (unless, with some languages, you write special code to do so). In this book, assume that you can use one input or output statement on a set of fields that constitute a record.

In addition to declaring variables, sometimes you want to provide a variable with an initial value. Providing a variable with a value when you create it is known as **initializing**, or **defining**, **the variable**. For example, for the inventory report print chart shown in Figure 4-1, you might want to create a variable named `mainHeading` and store the value "INVENTORY REPORT" in that variable. The declaration is `char mainHeading = "INVENTORY REPORT"`. This indicates that `mainHeading` is a character variable, and that the character contents are the words "INVENTORY REPORT".

**TIP**

*Declaring* a variable provides it with a name and type. *Defining*, or declaring and initializing, a variable also provides it with a value. If you declare a variable, but do not provide a value, you can always initialize it later.

**TIP**

In some programming languages, you can declare a variable such as `mainHeading` to be constant, or never changing. Even though `invItemName`, `invPrice`, and the other fields in the input file will hold a variety of values when a program executes, the `mainHeading` value will never change.

In many programming languages, if you do not provide an initial value when declaring a variable, then the value is unknown, or **garbage**. Some programming languages do provide you with an automatic starting value; for example, in Java, Visual Basic, BASIC, or RPG, all numeric variables automatically begin with the value zero. However, in C++, C#, Pascal, and COBOL, variables generally do not receive any initial value unless you provide one. No matter which programming language you use, it is always clearest to provide a value for those variables that require them.

**TIP**

Be especially careful to make sure all variables you use in calculations have initial values. If you attempt to perform arithmetic with garbage values, either the program will fail to execute, or worse, the result will also contain garbage.

When you declare the variables `invItemName`, `invPrice`, `invCost`, and `invQuantity`, you do not provide them with any initial value. The values for these variables will be assigned when the first file record is read into memory. It would be *legal* to assign a value to input file record variables—for example, `invItemName = "cotton shirt"`—but it would be a waste of time and might mislead others who read your program. The first `invItemName` will come from an input device, and may or may not be "cotton shirt".

The report illustrated in Figure 4-1 contains three individual heading lines. The most common practice is to declare one variable or constant for each of these lines. The three declarations are as follows:

```
char mainHeading = "INVENTORY REPORT"
char columnHead1 = "ITEM         RETAIL PRICE
    MANUFACTURING        PROFIT PER"
char columnHead2 = "DESCRIPTION  EACH
    COST EACH            ITEM"
```

Within the program, when it is time to write the heading lines to an output device, you will code:

```
print mainHeading
print columnHead1
print columnHead2
```

You are not required to create variables for your headings. Your program can contain the following statements, in which you use literal strings of characters instead of variable names. The printed results are the same either way.

```
print "INVENTORY REPORT"
print "ITEM          RETAIL PRICE   MANUFACTURING    PROFIT PER"
print "DESCRIPTION   EACH           COST EACH        ITEM"
```

Using variable names, as in `print mainHeading`, is usually more convenient than spelling out the heading's contents within the statement that prints, especially if you will use the headings in multiple locations within your program. Additionally, if the contents of all of a program's heading lines can be found in one location at the start of the program, it is easier to locate them all if changes need to be made in the future.

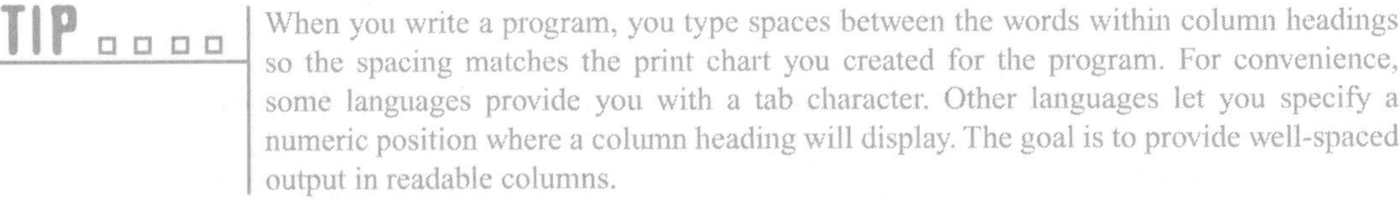


When you write a program, you type spaces between the words within column headings so the spacing matches the print chart you created for the program. For convenience, some languages provide you with a tab character. Other languages let you specify a numeric position where a column heading will display. The goal is to provide well-spaced output in readable columns.

Dividing the headings into three lines is not required either, but it is a common practice. In most programming languages, you could write all the headings in one statement, using a code that indicates a new line at every appropriate position. Alternatively, most programming languages let you produce a character for output without advancing to a new line. You could write out the headings using separate print statements to display one character at a time, advancing to a new line only after all the line's characters were individually printed, although this approach seems painstakingly detailed. Storing and writing one complete line at a time is a reasonable compromise.

Every programming language provides you with a means to physically advance printer paper to the top of a page when you print the first heading. Similarly, every language provides you with a means to produce double- and triple-spaced lines of text by sending specific codes to the printer or monitor. Because the methods and codes differ from language to language, examples in this book assume that if a print chart or sample output shows a heading that prints at the top of the page and then skips a line, any corresponding variable you create, such as `mainHeading`, will also print in this manner. You can add the appropriate language-specific codes to implement the `mainHeading` spacing when you write the actual computer program. Similarly, if you create a print chart that shows detail lines as double-spaced, assume your detail lines will double-space when you execute the step to write them.

Often, you must create dozens of variables when you write a computer program. If you are using a flowchart to diagram the logic, it is physically impossible to fit the variables in one flowchart box. Therefore, you might want to use an annotation symbol. The beginning of a flowchart for the `housekeeping()` module of the inventory report program is shown in Figure 4-11.

**FIGURE 4-11:** BEGINNING OF FLOWCHART FOR `housekeeping()` MODULE FOR THE INVENTORY REPORT PROGRAM

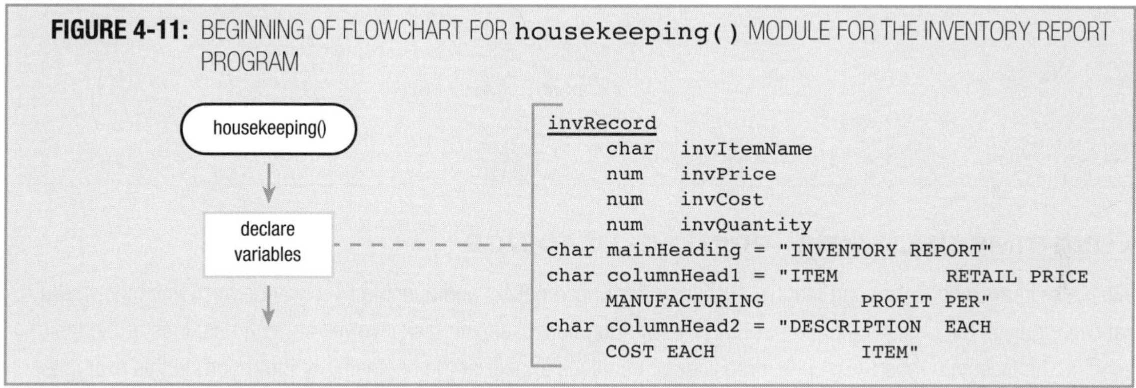
housekeeping()
declare variables
invRecord
char invItemName
num invPrice
num invCost
num invQuantity
char mainHeading = "INVENTORY REPORT"
char columnHead1 = "ITEM RETAIL PRICE MANUFACTURING PROFIT PER"
char columnHead2 = "DESCRIPTION EACH COST EACH ITEM"

**TIP** You learned about the annotation symbol in Chapter 3.

Notice that the three heading variables defined in Figure 4-11 are not indented under `invRecord` as the `invRecord` fields are. This shows that although `invItemName`, `invPrice`, `invCost`, and `invQuantity` are part of the `invRecord` group, `mainHeading`, `columnHead1`, and `columnHead2` are not.

In Figure 4-11, notice that `columnHead1` contains only the words that appear in the first line of column headings, in row 4 of the print chart in Figure 4-1: "ITEM RETAIL PRICE MANUFACTURING PROFIT PER". Similarly, `columnHead2` contains only the words that appear in the second row of column headings.

## OPENING FILES

If a program will use input files, you must tell the computer where the input is coming from—for example, a specific disk drive, CD, or tape drive. You also must indicate the name (and possibly the path, the list of folders or directories in which the file resides) for the file. Then you must issue a command to **open the file**, or prepare it for reading. In many languages, if no input file is opened, input is accepted from a default or **standard input device**, most often the keyboard.

If a program will have output, you must also open a file for output. Perhaps the output file will be sent to a disk or tape. Although you might not think of a printed report as a file, computers treat a printer as just another output device, and if output will go to a printer, then you must open the printer output device as well. Again, if no file is opened, a default or **standard output device**, usually the monitor, is used.

When you create a flowchart, you usually write the command to open the files within a parallelogram. You use the parallelogram because it is the input/output symbol, and you are opening the input and output devices. You can use an annotation box to list the files that you open, as shown in Figure 4-12.

**FIGURE 4-12:** SPECIFYING FILES THAT YOU OPEN

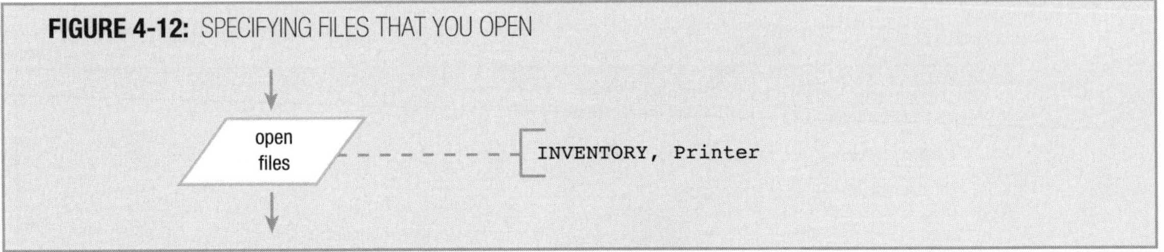


## A ONE-TIME-ONLY TASK—PRINTING HEADINGS

Within a program's housekeeping module, besides declaring variables and opening files, you perform any other tasks that occur only at the beginning of the program. A common housekeeping task involves printing headings at the top of a report. In the inventory report example, three lines of headings appear at the beginning of the report. In this example, printing the heading lines is straightforward:

```
print mainHeading
print columnHead1
print columnHead2
```

## READING THE FIRST INPUT RECORD

The last task you execute in the housekeeping module of most computer programs is to read the first data record into memory. In this example, the input data is read from a stored file. Other applications might be **interactive applications**—that is, applications that interact with a user who types data at a keyboard. When you write your first computer programs, you probably will use interactive input so that you don't have to complicate the programs by including the statements necessary to locate and open an input file. To read the necessary data interactively from the user, you could issue a statement such as the following:

```
read invItemName, invPrice, invCost, invQuantity
```

The statement would pause program execution until the user typed four values from the keyboard, typically separating them with a **delimiter**, or character produced by a keystroke that separates data items. Depending on the programming language, the delimiter might be the Enter key, the tab character, or a comma.

Requiring a user to type four values in the proper order is asking a lot. More frequently, the read statement would be separated into four distinct read statements, each preceded by an output statement called a **prompt** that asks the user for a specific item. For example, the following set of statements prompts the user for and accepts each of the necessary data items for the inventory program:

```
print "Please enter the inventory item name"
read invItemName
print "Enter the price"
read invPrice
print "Enter the cost of the item"
read invCost
print "Enter the quantity in stock"
read invQuantity
```

If the four data fields have already been stored and are input from a data file instead of interactively, then no prompts are needed, and you can write the following:

```
read invItemName, invPrice, invCost, invQuantity
```

In most programming languages, if you have declared a group name such as `invRecord`, it is simpler to obtain values for all the data fields by writing the following:

```
read invRecord
```

This statement fills the entire group item with values from the input file. Using the group name is a shortcut for writing each field name. When you write your first programs, you might get your data interactively, in which case you will write prompts and separate input statements, or you might obtain input from a data file, but delay studying how to create group items, so you might list each field separately. For simplicity, most of the input statements in this book will assume the data comes from files and is grouped; this assumption will allow the book to use the shortest version of the statement that simply means "obtain all the data fields this application needs."

## CHECKING FOR THE END OF THE FILE

The last task within the `housekeeping()` module is to read the first `invRecord`; the first task following `housekeeping()` is to check for `eof` on the file that contains the inventory records. If the program is an interactive one, the user might indicate that input is complete by typing a predetermined value from the keyboard, or using a mouse to select a screen option indicating completion of data entry. If the program reads data from an input file stored on a disk, tape, or other storage device, the input device recognizes that it has reached the end of a file when it attempts to read a record and finds no records available. Recall the mainline logic of the inventory report program from Figure 4-6—`eof` is tested immediately after `housekeeping()` ends.

If the input file has no records, when you read the first record the computer recognizes the end-of-file condition and proceeds to the `finishUp()` module, never executing `mainLoop()`. More commonly, an input file does have records, and after the first `read` the computer determines that the `eof` condition is false, and the logic proceeds to `mainLoop()`.

Immediately after reading from a file, the next step always should determine whether `eof` was encountered. Notice in Figure 4-6 that the `eof` question always follows both the `housekeeping()` module and the `mainLoop()` module. When the last instruction in each of these modules reads a record, then the `eof` question correctly follows each `read` instruction immediately.

Not reading the first record within the `housekeeping()` module is a mistake. If `housekeeping()` does not include a step to read a record from the input file, you must read a record as the first step in `mainLoop()`, as shown on the left side of Figure 4-13. In this program, a record is read, a profit is calculated, and a line is printed. Then, if it is not `eof`, another record is read, a profit calculated, and a line printed. The program works well, reading records, calculating profits, and printing information until reaching a `read` command in which the computer encounters the `eof` condition. When this last read occurs, the next steps involve computing a profit and writing a line—but there isn't any data to process. Depending on the programming language you use, either garbage data will calculate and print, or a repeat of the data from the last record before `eof` will print.

**FIGURE 4-13:** COMPARING FAULTY AND CORRECT RECORD-READING LOGIC

FAULTY RECORD-READING LOGIC

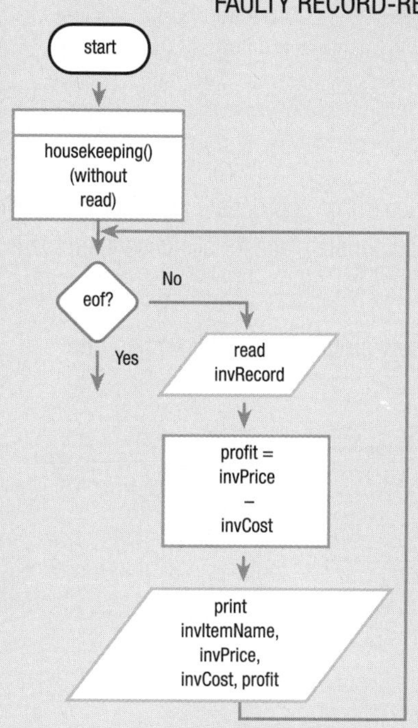


```
start
     perform housekeeping() (without read)
     while not eof
          read invRecord
          profit = invPrice - invCost
          print invItemName, invPrice, invCost, profit
     endwhile
```

CORRECT RECORD-READING LOGIC

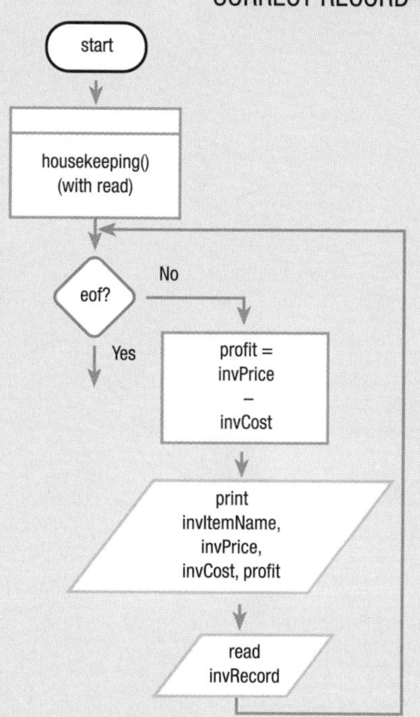


```
start
     perform housekeeping() (with read)
     while not eof
          profit = invPrice - invCost
          print invItemName, invPrice, invCost, profit
          read invRecord
     endwhile
```

**TIP** Reading an input record in the `housekeeping()` module is an example of a priming read. You learned about the priming read in Chapter 2.

**TIP** In some modern programming languages, such as Visual Basic, file read commands can look ahead to determine if the *next* record is empty. With these languages, the priming read is no longer necessary. Because most languages do not currently have this type of read statement, and because the priming read is always necessary when input is based on user response rather than reading from a file, this book uses the conventional priming read.

The flowchart in the lower part of Figure 4-13 shows correct record-reading logic. The appropriate place for the priming record `read` is at the end of the preliminary housekeeping steps, and the appropriate place for all subsequent reads is at the end of the main processing loop.

Figure 4-14 shows a completed `housekeeping()` routine for the inventory program in both flowchart and pseudocode versions.

**FIGURE 4-14:** FLOWCHART AND PSEUDOCODE FOR `housekeeping()` ROUTINE IN INVENTORY REPORT PROGRAM

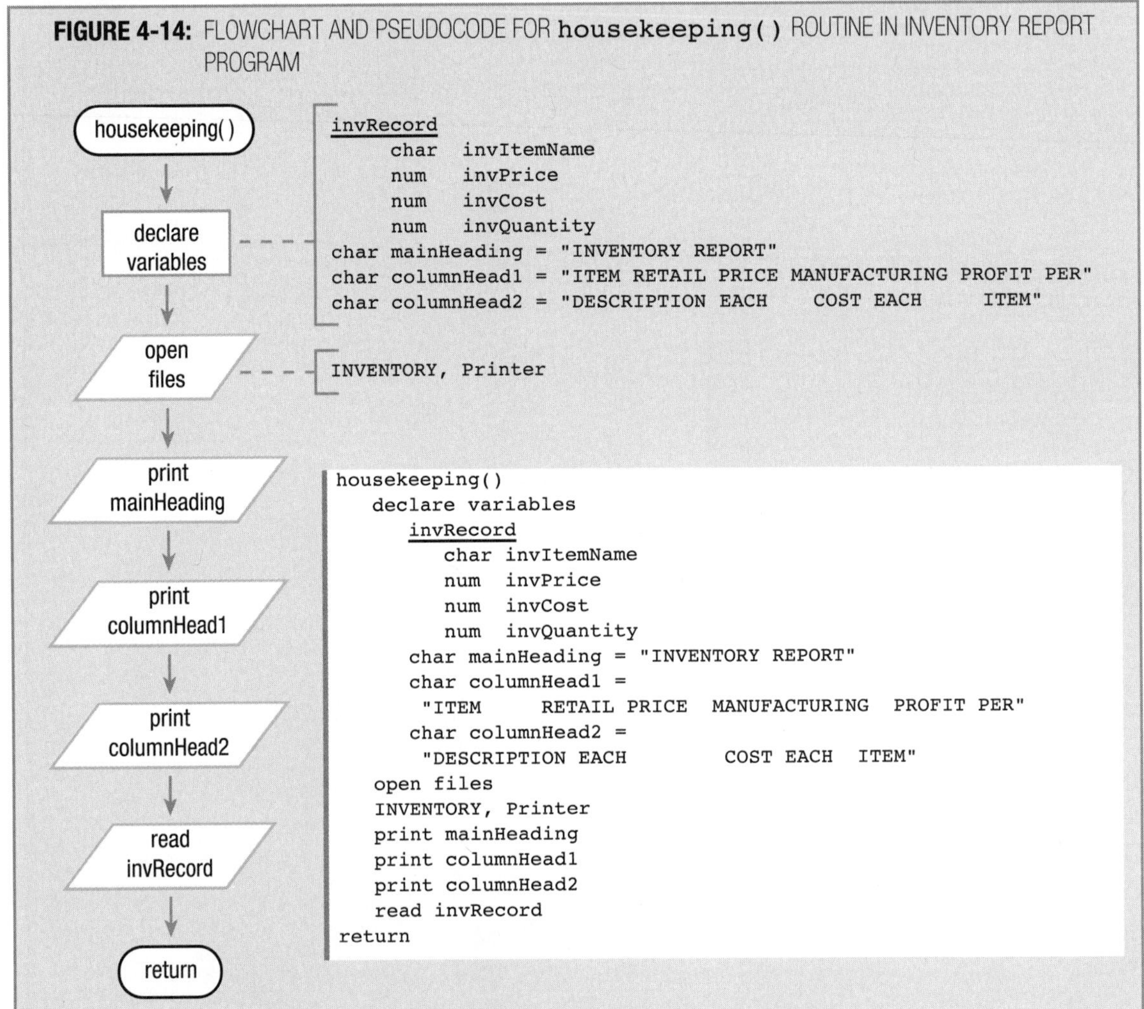
housekeeping()
declare variables
open files
print mainHeading
print columnHead1
print columnHead2
read invRecord
return
invRecord
char invItemName
num invPrice
num invCost
num invQuantity
char mainHeading = "INVENTORY REPORT"
char columnHead1 = "ITEM RETAIL PRICE MANUFACTURING PROFIT PER"
char columnHead2 = "DESCRIPTION EACH COST EACH ITEM"
INVENTORY, Printer

```
housekeeping()
   declare variables
      invRecord
         char invItemName
         num  invPrice
         num  invCost
         num  invQuantity
      char mainHeading = "INVENTORY REPORT"
      char columnHead1 =
       "ITEM     RETAIL PRICE  MANUFACTURING  PROFIT PER"
      char columnHead2 =
       "DESCRIPTION EACH        COST EACH   ITEM"
   open files
   INVENTORY, Printer
   print mainHeading
   print columnHead1
   print columnHead2
   read invRecord
return
```

As an alternative to including `print mainHeading`, `print columnHead1`, and `print columnHead2` within the `housekeeping()` module, you can place the three heading line statements in their own module. In this case, the flowchart and pseudocode for `housekeeping()` will look like Figure 4-15, with the steps in the newly created `headings()` module appearing in Figure 4-16. Either approach is fine; the logic of the program is the same whether or not the heading line statements are segregated into their own routine. The programmer can decide on the program organization that makes the most sense.

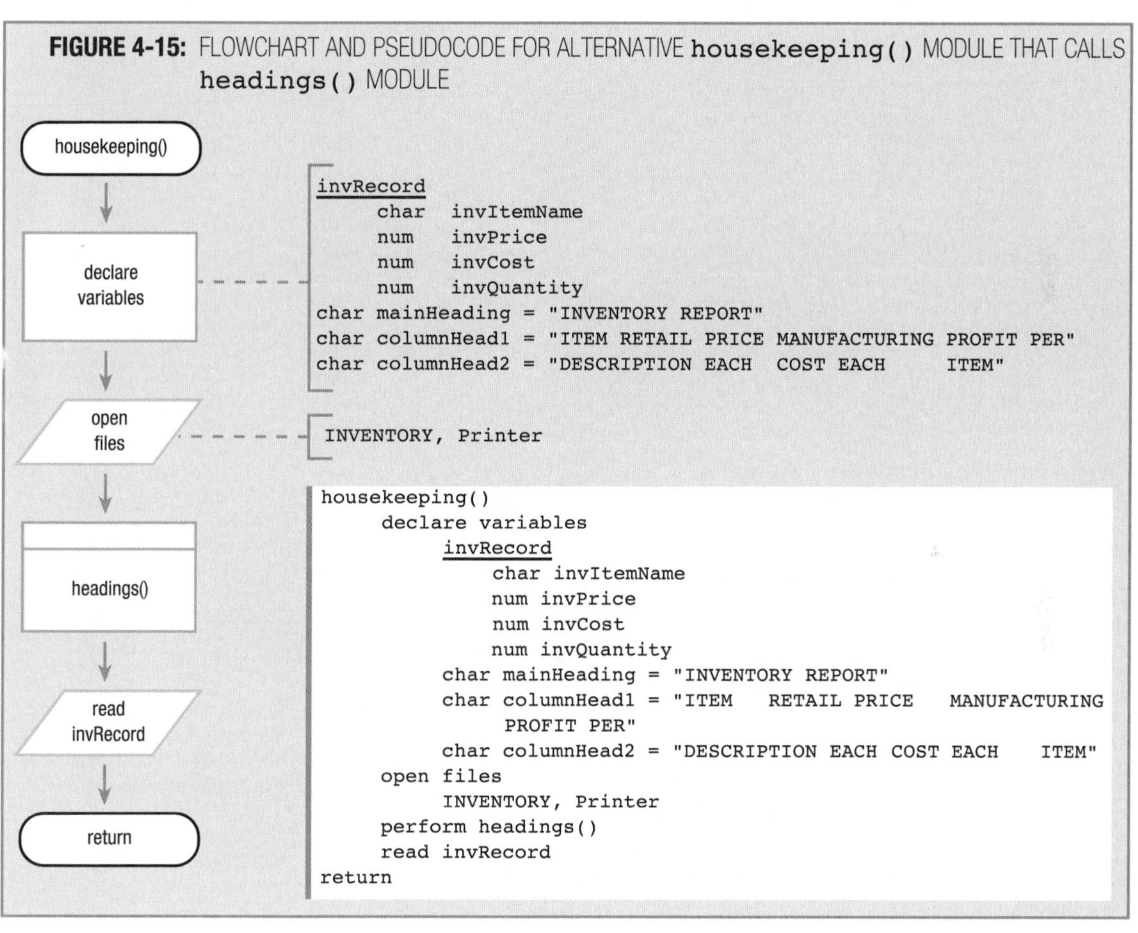

housekeeping()
declare variables
open files
headings()
read invRecord
return
invRecord
char invItemName
num invPrice
num invCost
num invQuantity
char mainHeading = "INVENTORY REPORT"
char columnHead1 = "ITEM RETAIL PRICE MANUFACTURING PROFIT PER"
char columnHead2 = "DESCRIPTION EACH COST EACH ITEM"
INVENTORY, Printer
housekeeping()
declare variables
invRecord
char invItemName
num invPrice
num invCost
num invQuantity
char mainHeading = "INVENTORY REPORT"
char columnHead1 = "ITEM RETAIL PRICE MANUFACTURING PROFIT PER"
char columnHead2 = "DESCRIPTION EACH COST EACH ITEM"
open files
INVENTORY, Printer
perform headings()
read invRecord
return

**FIGURE 4-15:** FLOWCHART AND PSEUDOCODE FOR ALTERNATIVE `housekeeping()` MODULE THAT CALLS `headings()` MODULE

**FIGURE 4-16:** FLOWCHART AND PSEUDOCODE FOR `headings()` MODULE CALLED BY MAINLINE IN FIGURE 4-15

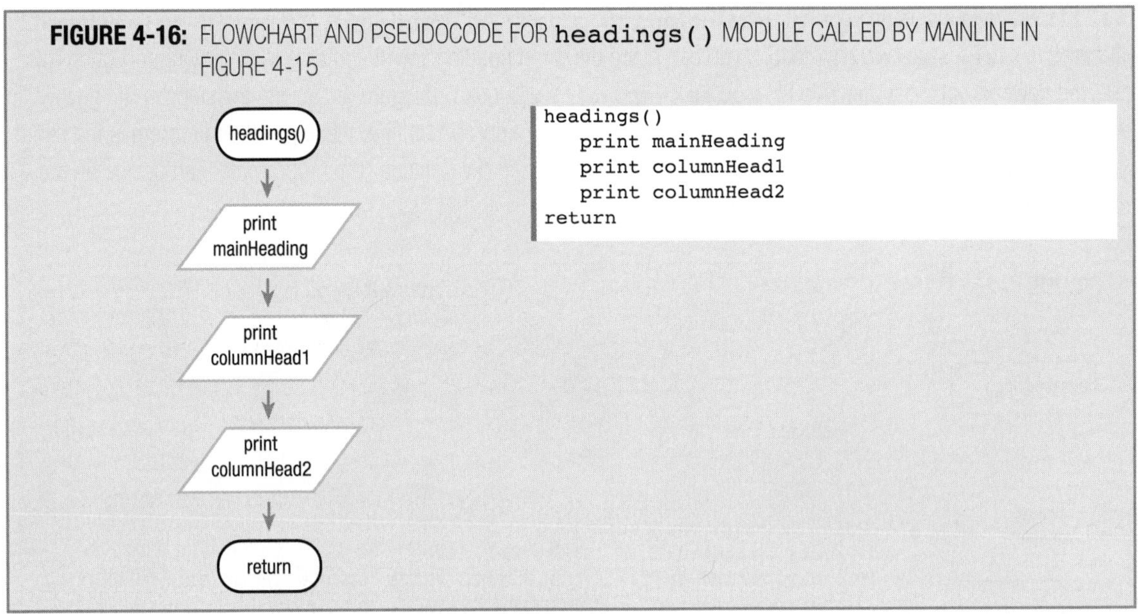


```
headings()
   print mainHeading
   print columnHead1
   print columnHead2
return
```

## WRITING THE MAIN LOOP

After you declare the variables for a program and perform the housekeeping tasks, the "real work" of the program begins. The inventory report described at the beginning of this chapter and depicted in Figure 4-1 needs just one set of variables and one set of headings, yet there might be hundreds or thousands of inventory items to process. The main loop of a program, controlled by the **eof** decision, is the program's "workhorse." Each data record will pass once through the main loop, where calculations are performed with the data and the results printed.

**TIP** If the inventory report contains more records than will fit on a page of output, you probably will want to print a new set of headings at the top of each page. You will learn how to do this in Chapter 7.

For the inventory report program to work, the **mainLoop()** module must include three steps:

1. Calculate the profit for an item.
2. Print the item information on the report.
3. Read the next inventory record.

At the end of **housekeeping()**, you read one data record into the computer's memory. As the first step in **mainLoop()**, you can calculate an item's profit by subtracting its manufacturing cost from its retail price: **profit = invPrice - invCost**. The name **profit** is the programmer-created variable name for a new spot in computer memory where the value of the profit is stored. Although it is legal to use any variable name to represent profit, naming it **invProfit** would be misleading. Using the **inv** prefix would lead those who read your program to believe that profit was part of the input record, like the other variable names that start with `inv`. The profit value is not part of the input record, however; it represents a memory location used to store the arithmetic difference between two other variables.

**TIP** Recall that the standard way to express mathematical statements is to assign values from the right side of an assignment operator to the left. That is, `profit = invPrice - invCost` assigns a value to `profit`. The statement `invPrice - invCost = profit` is an illegal statement.

Because you have a new variable, you must add **`profit`** to the list of declared variables at the beginning of the program. Programmers often work back and forth between the variable list and the logical steps during the creation of a program, listing some of the variables they will need as soon as they start to plan, and adding others later as they think of them. Because **`profit`** will hold the result of a mathematical calculation, you should declare it as a numeric variable when you add it to the variable list, as shown in Figure 4-17. Notice that, like the headings, **`profit`** is not indented under **`invRecord`**. You want to show that **`profit`** is not part of the **`invRecord`** group; instead, it is a separate variable that you are declaring to store a calculated value.

**FIGURE 4-17:** VARIABLE LIST FOR INVENTORY REPORT PROGRAM, INCLUDING PROFIT

```
invRecord
   char  invItemName
   num   invPrice
   num   invCost
   num   invQuantity
char mainHeading = "INVENTORY REPORT"
char columnHead1 = "ITEM            RETAIL PRICE     MANUFACTURING     PROFIT PER"
char columnHead2 = "DESCRIPTION     EACH             COST EACH         ITEM"
num profit
```

**TIP** You can declare `mainHeading`, `columnHead1`, `columnHead2`, and `profit` in any order. The important point is that none of these four variables is part of the `invRecord` group.

After you determine an item's profit, you can write a detail line of information on the inventory report: **`print invItemName, invPrice, invCost, profit`**. Notice that in the flowchart and pseudocode for the **`mainLoop()`** routine in Figure 4-18, the output statement is not **`print invRecord`**. For one thing, the entire **`invRecord`** is not printed—the quantity is not part of the report. Also, the calculated profit is included in the detail line—it does not appear on the input record. Even if the report detail lines listed each of the **`invRecord`** fields in the exact same order as on the input file, the print statement still would most often be written listing the individual fields to be printed. Usually, you would include a formatting statement with each printed field to control the spacing within the detail line. Because the way you space fields on detail lines differs greatly in programming languages, discussion of the syntax to space fields is not included in this book. However, the fields that are printed are listed separately, as you would usually do when coding in a specific programming language.

The last step in the `mainLoop()` module of the inventory report program involves reading the next `invRecord`. Figure 4-18 shows the flowchart and pseudocode for `mainLoop()`.

**FIGURE 4-18:** FLOWCHART AND PSEUDOCODE FOR `mainLoop()` OF INVENTORY REPORT PROGRAM

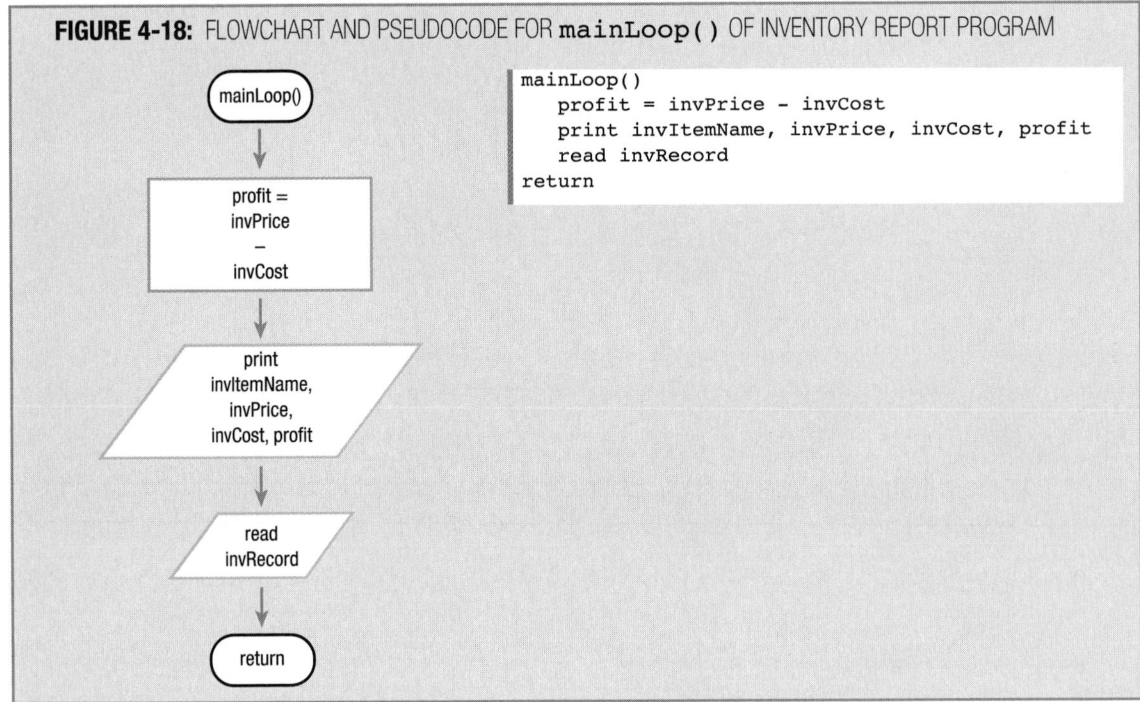


```
mainLoop()
   profit = invPrice - invCost
   print invItemName, invPrice, invCost, profit
   read invRecord
return
```

Just as headings are printed one full line at a time, detail lines are also printed one line at a time. You can print each field separately, as in the following code, but it is clearer and more efficient to write one full line at a time, as shown in Figure 4-18.

```
print invItemName
print invPrice
print invCost
print profit
```

In most programming languages, you also have the option of calculating the profit and printing it in one statement, as in the following:

```
print invItemName, invPrice, invCost, invPrice - invCost
```

If the language you use allows this type of statement, in which a calculation takes place within the output statement, it is up to you to decide which format to use. Performing the arithmetic as part of the `print` statement allows you to avoid declaring a `profit` variable. However, if you need the `profit` figure for further calculations, then it makes sense to compute the profit and store it in a `profit` field. Using a separate **work variable**, or **work field**, such as `profit` to temporarily hold a calculation is never wrong, and often it's the clearest course of action.

TIP ▫▫▫▫ As with performing arithmetic within a print statement, different languages often provide multiple ways to combine several steps into one. For example, many languages allow you to print multiple lines of output or read a record and check for the end of the file using one statement. This book uses only the most common combinations, such as performing arithmetic within a print statement.

Although a language may allow you to combine actions into a single statement, you are never required to do so. If the program is clearer using separate statements, then that is what you should do.

After the detail line containing the item name, price, cost, and profit has been written, the last step you take before leaving the `mainLoop()` module is to read the next record from the input file into memory. When you exit `mainLoop()`, the logic flows back to the `eof` question in the mainline logic. If it is not `eof`—that is, if an additional data record exists—then you enter `mainLoop()` again, compute profit on the second record, print the detail line, and read the third record.

Eventually, during an execution of `mainLoop()`, the program will read a new record and encounter the end of the file. Then, when you ask the `eof` question in the mainline of the program, the answer will be *yes*, and the program will not enter `mainLoop()` again. Instead, the program logic will enter the `finishUp()` routine.

## PERFORMING END-OF-JOB TASKS

Within any program, the end-of-job routine holds the steps you must take at the end of the program, after all input records are processed. Some end-of-job modules print summaries or grand totals at the end of a report. Others might print a message such as "End of Report", so readers can be confident that they have received all the information that should be included. Such end-of-job message lines often are called **footer lines**, or **footers** for short. Very often, end-of-job modules must close any open files.

The end-of-job module for the inventory report program is very simple. The print chart does not indicate that any special messages, such as "Thank you for reading this report", print after the detail lines end. Likewise, there are no required summary or total lines; nothing special happens. Only one task needs to be performed in the end-of-job routine that this program calls `finishUp()`. In `housekeeping()`, you opened files; in `finishUp()`, you close them. The complete `finishUp()` module is flowcharted and written in pseudocode in Figure 4-19.

**FIGURE 4-19:** FLOWCHART AND PSEUDOCODE OF `finishUp()` MODULE

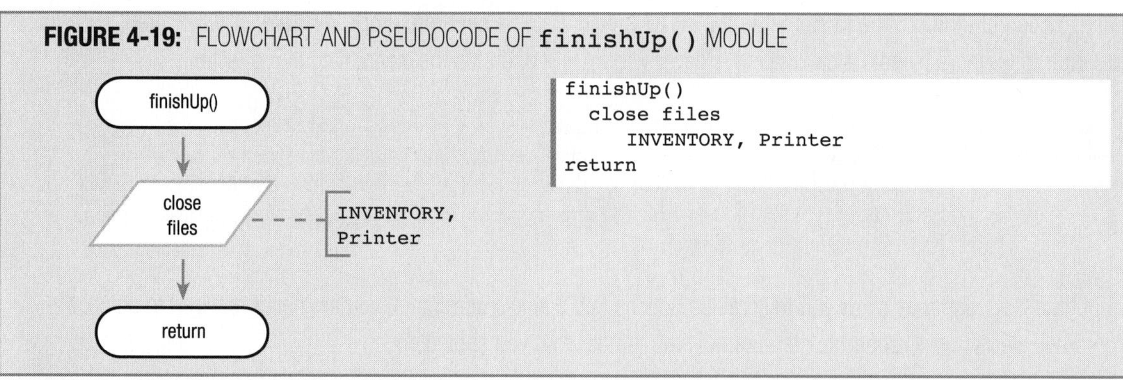
finishUp()
close files
INVENTORY, Printer
return
finishUp()
close files
INVENTORY, Printer
return

Many programmers wouldn't bother with a subroutine for just one statement, but as you create more complicated programs, your end-of-job routines will get bigger, and it will make more sense to see the necessary job-finishing tasks together in a module.

For your convenience, Figure 4-20 shows the flowchart and pseudocode for the entire inventory report program. Make sure you understand the importance of each flowchart symbol and each pseudocode line. There is nothing superfluous—each is included to accomplish a specific part of the program that creates the completed inventory report.

**FIGURE 4-20:** FLOWCHART AND PSEUDOCODE FOR INVENTORY REPORT PROGRAM

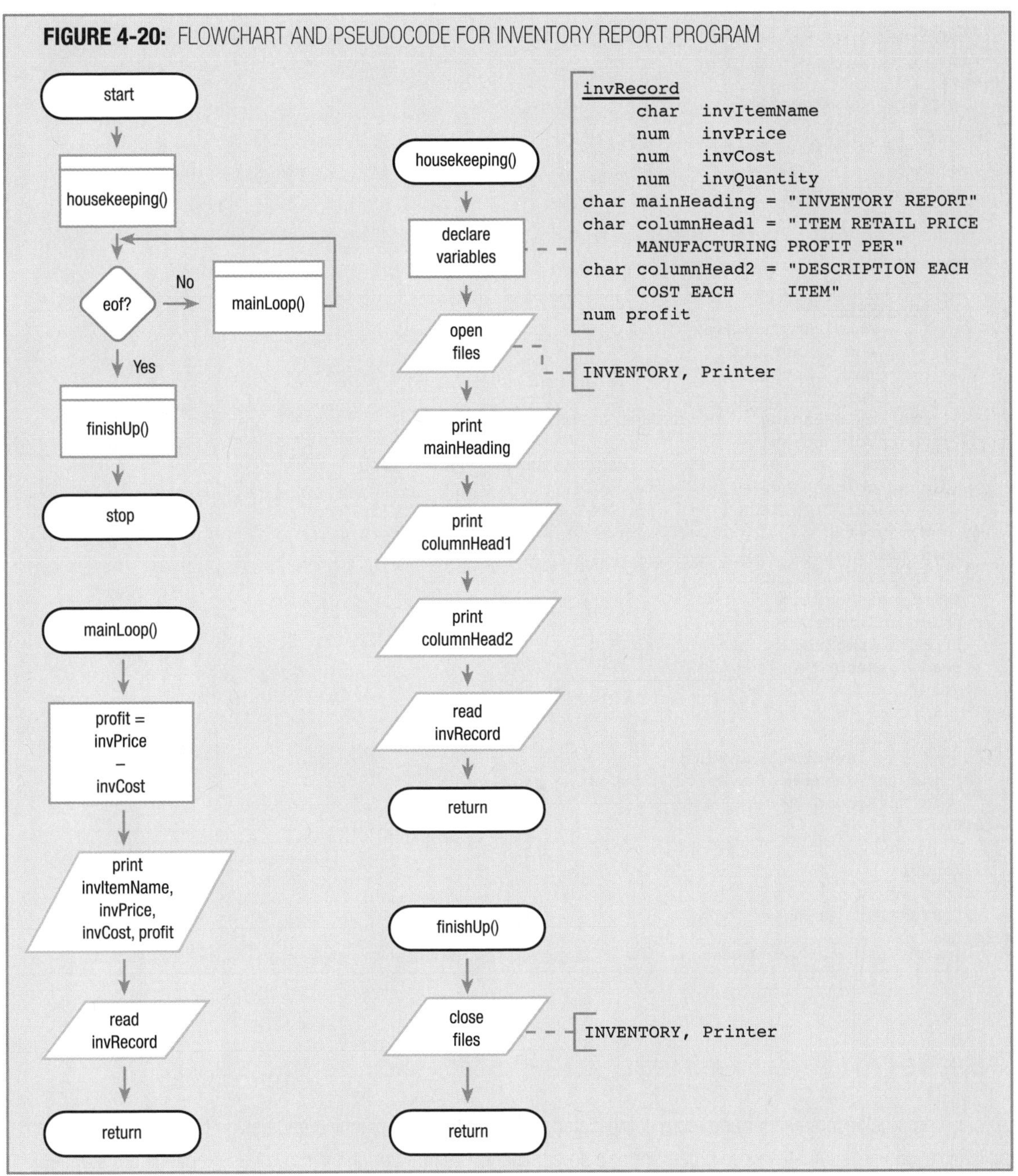

**FIGURE 4-20:** FLOWCHART AND PSEUDOCODE FOR INVENTORY REPORT PROGRAM (CONTINUED)

```
start
   perform housekeeping()
   while not eof
        perform mainLoop()
   endwhile
   perform finishUp()
stop

housekeeping()
   declare variables
      invRecord
           char  invItemName
           num   invPrice
           num   invCost
           num   invQuantity
      char mainHeading = "INVENTORY REPORT"
      char columnHead1 =
       "ITEM        RETAIL PRICE  MANUFACTURING  PROFIT PER"
      char columnHead2 =
       "DESCRIPTION EACH           COST EACH      ITEM"
      num profit
   open files
      INVENTORY, Printer
   print mainHeading
   print columnHead1
   print columnHead2
   read invRecord
return

mainLoop()
   profit = invPrice - invCost
   print invItemName, invPrice, invCost,  profit
   read invRecord
return

finishUp()
  close files
    INVENTORY, Printer
return
```

## UNDERSTANDING THE NEED FOR GOOD PROGRAM DESIGN

As your programs become larger and more complicated, the need for good planning and design increases. Think of an application you use, such as a word processor or a spreadsheet. The number and variety of user options are staggering. Not only would it be impossible for a single programmer to write such an application, but without thorough planning and design, the components would never work together properly. Ideally, each program module you design needs to work well as a stand-alone module and as an element of larger systems. Just as a house with poor plumbing or a car with bad brakes is fatally flawed, a computer-based application can be great only if each component is designed well.

## STORING PROGRAM COMPONENTS IN SEPARATE FILES

When you start to work on professional programs, you will see that many of them are quite lengthy, with some containing hundreds of variables and thousands of lines of code. Earlier in this chapter, you learned you can manage lengthy procedural programs by breaking them down into modules. Although modularization helps you to organize your programs, sometimes it is still difficult to manage all of a program's components.

Most modern programming languages allow you to store program components in separate files. If you write a module and store it in the same file as the program that uses it, your program files become large and hard to work with, whether you are trying to read them on a screen or on multiple printed pages. In addition, when you define a useful module, you might want to use it in many programs. Of course, you can copy module definitions from one file to another, but this method is time-consuming as well as prone to error. A better solution (if you are using a language that allows it) is to store your modules in individual files and use an instruction to include them in any program that uses them. The statement needed to access modules from separate files varies from language to language, but it usually involves using a verb such as *include*, *import*, or *copy*, followed by the name of the file that contains the module.

For example, suppose your company has a standard employee record definition, part of which is shown in Figure 4-21. Files with the same format are used in many applications within the organization—personnel reports, production reports, payroll, and so on. It would be a tremendous waste of resources if every programmer rewrote this file definition in multiple applications. Instead, once a programmer writes the statements that constitute the file definition, those statements should be imported in their entirety into any program that uses a record with the same structure. For example, Figure 4-22 shows how the data fields in Figure 4-21 would be defined in the C++ programming language. If the statements in Figure 4-22 are saved in a file named Employees, then any C++ program can contain the statement `#include Employees` and all the data fields are automatically declared.

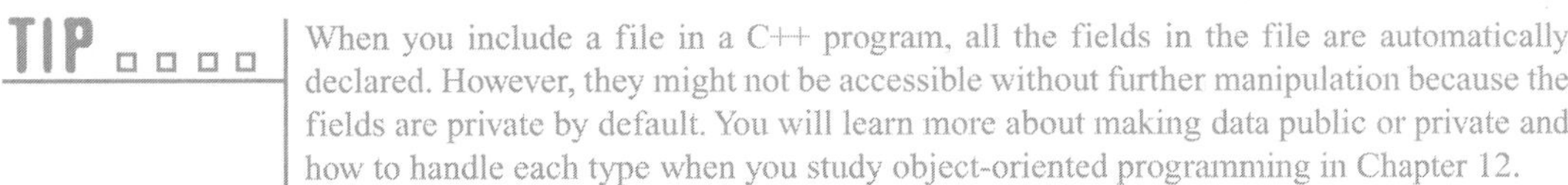

**TIP** When you include a file in a C++ program, all the fields in the file are automatically declared. However, they might not be accessible without further manipulation because the fields are private by default. You will learn more about making data public or private and how to handle each type when you study object-oriented programming in Chapter 12.

**TIP** The pound sign (#) is used with the `include` statement in C++ to notify the compiler that it is part of a special type of statement called a *`pre-processor directive`*.

**FIGURE 4-21:** PARTIAL EMPLOYEES FILE DESCRIPTION

```
EMPLOYEES FILE DESCRIPTION
File name: EMPLOYEES
FIELD DESCRIPTION       DATA TYPE     COMMENTS
Employee ID             Character     5 bytes
Last Name               Character     20 bytes
First Name              Character     15 bytes
Hire Date               Numeric       8 digits yyyymmdd
Hourly Wage             Numeric       2 decimal places
Birth Date              Numeric       8 digits yyyymmdd
Termination Date        Numeric       8 digits yyyymmdd
```

**FIGURE 4-22:** DATA FIELDS IN FIGURE 4-21 DEFINED IN THE C++ LANGUAGE

```
class Employee
{
      int employeeID;
      string lastName;
      string firstName;
      long hireDate;
      double hourlyWage;
      long birthDate;
      long terminationDate;
};
```

**TIP** Don't be concerned with the syntax used in the file description in Figure 4-22. The words `class`, `int`, `string`, `long`, and `double` are all part of the C++ programming language and are not important to you now. Simply concentrate on how the variable names reflect the field descriptions in Figure 4-21.

Suppose you write a useful module that checks dates to guarantee their validity. For example, the two digits that represent a month can be neither less than 01 nor greater than 12, and the two digits that represent the day can contain different possible values, depending on the month. Any program that uses the employee file description shown in Figure 4-21 might want to call the date-validating module several times in order to validate any employee's hire date, birth date, and termination date. Not only do you want to call this module from several locations within any one program, you want to call it from many programs. For example, programs used for company ordering and billing would each contain several dates. If the date-validating module is useful and well-written, you might even want to market it to other companies. By storing the module in its own file, you enable its use to be flexible. When you write a program of any length, you should consider storing each of its components in its own file.

Storing components in separate files can provide an advantage beyond ease of reuse. When you let others use your programs or modules, you often provide them with only the compiled (that is, machine-language) version of your code, not the **source code**, which is composed of readable statements. Storing your program statements in a separate, non-readable, compiled file is an example of **implementation hiding**, or hiding the details of how the program or module works. Other programmers can use your code, but cannot see the statements you used to create it. A programmer who cannot see your well-designed modules is more likely to use them simply as they were intended; the programmer also will not be able to attempt to make adjustments to your code, thereby introducing error. Of course, in order to work with your modules or data definitions, a programmer must know the names and types of data you are using. Typically, you provide programmers who use your definitions with written documentation of the data names and purposes.

TIP Recall from Chapter 1 that when you write a program in a programming language, you must compile or interpret it into machine language before the computer can actually carry out your instructions.

## SELECTING VARIABLE AND MODULE NAMES

An often-overlooked element in program design is the selection of good data and module names (sometimes generically called **identifiers**). In Chapter 1, you learned that every programming language has specific rules for the construction of names—some languages limit the number of characters, some allow dashes, and so on—but there are other general guidelines:

- Use meaningful names. Creating a data field named `someData` or a module named `firstModule()` makes a program cryptic. Not only will others find it hard to read your programs, but you will forget the purpose of these identifiers even within your own programs. All programmers occasionally use short, nondescriptive names such as `x` or `temp` in a quick program written to test a procedure; however, in most cases, data and module names should be meaningful. Programmers refer to programs that contain meaningful names as **self-documenting**. This means that even without further documentation, the program code explains itself to readers.
- Usually, you should use pronounceable names. A variable name like `pzf` is neither pronounceable nor meaningful. A name that looks meaningful when you write it might not be as meaningful when someone else reads it; for instance, `preparead()` might mean "Prepare ad" to you, but "Prep a read" to others. Look at your names critically to make sure they are pronounceable. Very standard abbreviations do not have to be pronounceable. For example, most business people would interpret `ssn` as Social Security number.

TIP Don't forget that not all programmers share your culture. An abbreviation whose meaning seems obvious to you might be cryptic to someone in a different part of the world.

- Be judicious in your use of abbreviations. You can save a few keystrokes when creating a module called `getStat()`, but is its purpose to find the state in which a city is located, output some statistics, or determine the status of some variables? Similarly, is a variable named `fn` meant to hold a first name, file number, or something else?

**TIP**

To save typing time when you develop a program, you can use a short name like `efn`. After the program operates correctly, you can use an editor's Search and Replace feature to replace your coded name with a more meaningful name such as `employeeFirstName`. Some newer compilers support an automatic statement completion feature that saves typing time. After the first time you use a name like `employeeFirstName`, you need to type only the first few letters before the compiler editor offers a list of available names from which to choose. The list is constructed from all the names you have used in the file that begin with the same characters.

- Usually, avoid digits in a name. Zeroes get confused with the letter "O", and lowercase "l"s are misread as the numeral 1. Of course, use your judgment: `budgetFor2007` is probably not going to be misinterpreted.
- Use the system your language allows to separate words in long, multiword variable names. For example, if the programming language you use allows dashes or underscores, then use a method name like `initialize-data()` or `initialize_data()`, which is easier to read than `initializedata()`. If you use a language that allows camel casing, then use `initializeData()`. If you use a language that is case sensitive, it is legal but confusing to use variable names that differ only in case—for example, `empName`, `EmpName`, and `Empname`.
- Consider including a form of the verb *to be*, such as *is* or *are*, in names for variables that are intended to hold a status. For example, use `isFinished` as a flag variable that holds a "Y" or "N" to indicate whether a file is exhausted. The shorter name `finished` is more likely to be confused with a module that executes when a program is done.

When you begin to write programs, the process of determining what data variables and modules you will need and what to name them all might seem overwhelming. The design process is crucial, however. When you acquire your first professional programming assignment, the design process might very well be completed already. Most likely, your first assignment will be to write or make modifications to one small member module of a much larger application. The more the original programmers stuck to these guidelines, the better the original design was, and the easier your job of modification will be.

## DESIGNING CLEAR MODULE STATEMENTS

In addition to selecting good identifiers, you can use the following tactics to contribute to the clarity of the statements within your program modules:

- Avoid confusing line breaks.
- Use temporary variables to clarify long statements.
- Use constants where appropriate.

## AVOIDING CONFUSING LINE BREAKS

Some older programming languages require that program statements be placed in specific columns. Most modern programming languages are free-form; you can arrange your lines of code any way you see fit. As in real life, with freedom comes responsibility; when you have flexibility in arranging your lines of code, you must take care to make sure your meaning is clear. With free-form code, programmers often do not provide enough line breaks, or they provide inappropriate ones.

Figure 4-23 shows an example of code (part of the `housekeeping()` module from Figure 4-14) that does not provide enough line breaks for clarity. If you have been following the examples used throughout this book, the code in Figure 4-24 looks clearer to you; it will also look clearer to most other programmers.

**FIGURE 4-23:** PART OF A `housekeeping()` MODULE WITH INSUFFICIENT LINE BREAKS

```
open files  print mainHeading  print columnHead1
 print columnHead2  read invRecord
```

**FIGURE 4-24:** PART OF A `housekeeping()` MODULE WITH APPROPRIATE LINE BREAKS

```
open files
print mainHeading
print columnHead1
print columnHead2
read invRecord
```

Figure 4-24 shows that more, but shorter, lines usually improve your ability to understand a program's logic; appropriately breaking lines will become even more important as you introduce decisions and loops into your programs in the next chapters.

## USING TEMPORARY VARIABLES TO CLARIFY LONG STATEMENTS

When you need several mathematical operations to determine a result, consider using a series of temporary variables to hold intermediate results. For example, Figure 4-25 shows two ways to calculate a value for a real estate `salespersonCommission` variable. Each method achieves the same result—the salesperson's commission is based on the square feet multiplied by the price per square foot, plus any premium for a lot with special features, such as a wooded or waterfront lot. However, the second example uses two temporary variables, `sqFootPrice` and `totalPrice`. When the computation is broken down into less complicated, individual steps, it is easier to see how the total price is calculated. In calculations with even more computation steps, performing the arithmetic in stages would become increasingly helpful.

**FIGURE 4-25:** TWO WAYS OF ACHIEVING THE SAME `salespersonCommission` RESULT

```
salespersonCommission = (sqFeet * pricePerSquareFoot + lotPremium) * commissionRate
```

```
sqFootPrice = sqFeet * pricePerSquareFoot
totalPrice = sqFootPrice + lotPremium
salespersonCommission = totalPrice * commissionRate
```

**TIP** A statement, or part of a statement, that performs arithmetic and has a resulting value is called an **arithmetic expression**. For example, 2 + 3 is an arithmetic expression with the value 5.

**TIP** Programmers might say using temporary variables, like the example in Figure 4-25, is *cheap*. When executing a lengthy arithmetic statement, even if you don't explicitly name temporary variables, the programming language compiler creates them behind the scenes, so declaring them yourself does not cost much in terms of program execution time.

## USING CONSTANTS WHERE APPROPRIATE

Whenever possible, use named values in your programs. If your program contains a statement like `salesTax = price * taxRate` instead of `salesTax = price * .06`, you gain two benefits:

- It is easier for readers to know that the price is being multiplied by a tax rate instead of a discount, commission, or some other rate represented by .06.
- When the tax rate changes, you make one change to the value where `taxRate` is defined, rather than searching through a program for every instance of .06.

Named values can be variables or constants. For example, if a `taxRate` is one value when a price is over $100 and a different value when the price is not over $100, then you can store the appropriate value in a variable named `taxRate`, and use it when computing the sales tax. A named value also can be declared to be a **named constant**, meaning its value will never change during the execution of the program. For example, the program segment in Figure 4-26 uses the constants TUITION_PER_CREDIT_HOUR and ATHLETIC_FEE. Because the fields are declared to be constant, using the modifier `const`, you know that their values will not change during the execution of the program. If the values of either of these should change in the future, then the values assigned to the constants can be made in the declaration list, the code can be recompiled, and the actual program statements that perform the arithmetic with the values do not have to be disturbed. By convention, many programmers use all capital letters in constant names, so they stand out as distinct from variables.

**FIGURE 4-26:** PROGRAM SEGMENT THAT CALCULATES STUDENT BALANCE DUE USING DEFINED CONSTANTS

```
declare variables
   studentRecord
      num studentId
      num creditsEnrolled
   num tuitionDue
   num totalDue
   const num TUITION_PER_CREDIT_HOUR = 74.50
   const num ATHLETIC_FEE = 25.00
read studentRecord
tuitionDue = creditsEnrolled * TUITION_PER_CREDIT_HOUR
totalDue = tuitionDue + ATHLETIC_FEE
```

**TIP** Some programmers refer to unnamed numeric constants as "magic numbers." They feel that using magic numbers should always be avoided, and that you should provide a descriptive name for every numeric constant you use.

## MAINTAINING GOOD PROGRAMMING HABITS

When you learn a programming language and begin to write lines of program code, it is easy to forget the principles you have learned in this text. Having some programming knowledge and a keyboard at your fingertips can lure you into typing lines of code before you think things through. But every program you write will be better if you plan before you code. If you maintain the habits of first drawing flowcharts or writing pseudocode, as you have learned here, your future programming projects will go more smoothly. If you walk through your program logic on paper (called **desk-checking**) before starting to type statements in C++, COBOL, Visual Basic, or Java, your programs will run correctly sooner. If you think carefully about the variable and module names you use, and design your program statements so they are easy for others to read, you will be rewarded with programs that are easier to get up and running, and are easier to maintain as well.

## CHAPTER SUMMARY

- When you write a complete program, you first determine whether you have all the necessary data to produce the output. Then, you plan the mainline logic, which usually includes modules to perform housekeeping, a main loop that contains the steps that repeat for every record, and an end-of-job routine.
- Housekeeping tasks include all steps that must take place at the beginning of a program. These tasks include declaring variables, opening files, performing any one-time-only tasks—such as printing headings at the beginning of a report—and reading the first input record.
- The main loop of a program is controlled by the `eof` decision. Each data record passes once through the main loop, where calculations are performed with the data and results are printed.
- Within any program, the end-of-job module holds the steps you must take at the end of the program, after all the input records have been processed. Typical tasks include printing summaries, grand totals, or final messages at the end of a report, and closing all open files.
- As your programs become larger and more complicated, the need for good planning and design increases.
- Most modern programming languages allow you to store program components in separate files and use instructions to include them in any program that uses them. Storing components in separate files can provide the advantages of easy reuse and implementation hiding.
- When selecting data and module names, use meaningful, pronounceable names. Be judicious in your use of abbreviations, avoid digits in a name, and visually separate words in multiword names. Consider including a form of the verb *to be*, such as *is* or *are*, in names for variables that are intended to hold a status.
- When writing program statements, you should avoid confusing line breaks, use temporary variables to clarify long statements, and use constants where appropriate.

## KEY TERMS

A **user**, or **client**, is a person who requests a program, and who will actually use the output of the program.

A **procedural program** is a program in which one procedure follows another from the beginning until the end.

The **mainline logic** of a program is the overall logic of the main program from beginning to end.

A **housekeeping** module includes steps you must perform at the beginning of a program to get ready for the rest of the program.

The **main loop** of a program contains the steps that are repeated for every record.

The **end-of-job routine** holds the steps you take at the end of the program to finish the application.

**Functional decomposition** is the act of reducing a large program into more manageable modules.

A prefix is a set of characters used at the beginning of related variable names.

Hungarian notation is a variable-naming convention in which a variable's data type or other information is stored as part of its name.

A group name is a name for a group of associated variables.

Initializing, or defining, a variable is the process of providing a variable with a value, as well as a name and a type, when you create it.

Garbage is the unknown value of an undefined variable.

Opening a file is the process of telling the computer where the input is coming from, the name of the file (and possibly the folder), and preparing the file for reading.

The standard input device is the default device from which input comes, most often the keyboard.

The standard output device is the default device to which output is sent, usually the monitor.

Interactive applications are applications that interact with a user who types data at a keyboard.

A delimiter is a keystroke that separates data items.

An output statement called a prompt asks the user for a specific item.

A work variable, or work field, is a variable you use to temporarily hold a calculation.

Footer lines, or footers, are end-of-job message lines.

Source code is the readable statements of a program, written in a programming language.

Implementation hiding is hiding the details of the way a program or module works.

Identifiers are the names of variables and modules.

Self-documenting programs are those that contain meaningful data and module names that describe the programs' purpose.

An arithmetic expression is a statement, or part of a statement, that performs arithmetic and has a value.

A named constant holds a value that never changes during the execution of a program.

Desk-checking is the process of walking through a program's logic on paper.

## REVIEW QUESTIONS

**1. Input records usually contain ___________.**

a. less data than an application needs
b. more data than an application needs
c. exactly the amount of data an application needs
d. none of the data an application needs

2. **A program in which one operation follows another from the beginning until the end is a ________ program.**
   a. modular
   b. functional
   c. procedural
   d. object-oriented

3. **The mainline logic of many computer programs contains ________.**
   a. calls to housekeeping, record processing, and finishing routines
   b. steps to declare variables, open files, and read the first record
   c. arithmetic instructions that are performed for each record in the input file
   d. steps to print totals and close files

4. **Modularizing a program ________.**
   a. keeps large jobs manageable
   b. allows work to be divided easily
   c. helps keep a program structured
   d. all of the above

5. **Which of the following is not a typical housekeeping module task?**
   a. declaring variables
   b. printing summaries
   c. opening files
   d. performing a priming read

6. **When a programmer uses a data file and names the first field stored in each record `idNumber`, then other programmers who use the same file ________ in their programs.**
   a. must also name the field `idNumber`
   b. might name the field `idNumber`
   c. cannot name the field `idNumber`
   d. cannot name the field

7. **If you use a data file containing student records, and the first field is the student's last name, then you can name the field ________.**
   a. `stuLastName`
   b. `studentLastName`
   c. `lastName`
   d. any of the above

8. **If a field in a data file used for program input contains "Johnson", then the best choice among the following names for a programmer to use when declaring a memory location for the data is ________.**
   a. Johnson
   b. n
   c. `lastName`
   d. A programmer cannot declare a variable name for this field; it is already called Johnson.

9. **The purpose of using a group name is ________.**
   a. to be able to handle several variables with a single instruction
   b. to eliminate the need for machine-level instructions
   c. to be able to use both character and numeric values within the same program
   d. to be able to use multiple input files concurrently

10. **Defining a variable means the same as ________ it and providing a starting value for it.**
   a. declaring
   b. initializing
   c. deleting
   d. assigning

11. **In most programming languages, the initial value of unassigned variables is ________.**
   a. 0
   b. spaces
   c. 0 or spaces, depending on whether the variable is numeric or character
   d. unknown

12. **The types of variables you usually do not initialize are ________.**
   a. those that will never change value during a program
   b. those representing fields in an input file
   c. those that will be used in mathematical statements
   d. those that will not be used in mathematical statements

13. **The name programmers use for unknown variable values is ________.**
   a. default
   b. trash
   c. naive
   d. garbage

14. **Preparing an input device to deliver data records to a program is called ________ a file.**
   a. prompting
   b. opening
   c. refreshing
   d. initializing

**15. A computer system's standard input device is most often a ________.**

a. mouse
b. floppy disk
c. keyboard
d. compact disc

**16. The last task performed in a housekeeping module is most often to ________.**

a. open files
b. close files
c. check for `eof`
d. read an input record

**17. Most business programs contain a ________ that executes once for each record in an input file.**

a. housekeeping module
b. main loop
c. finish routine
d. terminal symbol

**18. Which of the following pseudocode statements is equivalent to this pseudocode:**

```
salePrice = salePrice - discount
finalPrice = salePrice + tax
print finalPrice
```

a. `print salePrice + tax`
b. `print salePrice - discount`
c. `print salePrice - discount + tax`
d. `print discount + tax - salePrice`

**19. Common end-of-job module tasks in programs include all of the following except ________.**

a. opening files
b. printing totals
c. printing end-of-job messages
d. closing files

**20. Which of the following is least likely to be performed in an end-of-job module?**

a. closing files
b. checking for `eof`
c. printing the message "End of report"
d. adding two values

## FIND THE BUGS

Each of the following pseudocode segments contains one or more bugs that you must find and correct.

1. **This pseudocode should create a report containing first-quarter profit statistics for a retail store. Input records contain a department name (for example, "Cosmetics"), expenses for each of the months January, February, and March, and sales for each of the same three months. Profit is determined by subtracting total expenses from total sales. The main program calls three modules—`housekeeping()`, `mainLoop()`, and `finishUp()`. The `housekeeping()` module calls `printHeadings()`.**

```
start
   perform housekeeping()
   while eof
      perform mainLoop()
   perform finishUp()
stop

housekeeping()
   declare variables
         profitRec
            char department
            num janExpenses
            num febExpenses
            num marExpenses
            num janSales
            num febSales
            num marSales
        char mainHeader = "First Quarter Profit Report"
        char columnHeaders = "Department       Profit"
   open files
   perform headings()
   read profitRec
stop

printHeadings()
   print mainHeader
   print columnHeaders
return

mainLoop()
   totalSales = janSales + febSales + febSales
   totalExpenses = janExpenses + marExpenses + marExpenses
   profit = totalSales - totalExpenses
   print department, totalProfit
return

finishUp()
   close files
return
```

2. **This pseudocode should create a report containing rental agents' commissions at an apartment complex. Input records contain each salesperson's ID number and name, as well as number of three-bedroom, two-bedroom, one-bedroom, and studio apartments rented during the month. The commission for each apartment rented is $50 times the number of bedrooms, except for studio apartments, for which the commission is $35. The main program calls three modules—** `housekeeping()`, `calculateCommission()`, **and** `finishUp()`**. The** `housekeeping()` **module calls** `displayHeaders()`**.**

```
start
   perform housekeeping()
   while not eof
      perform calcCommission()
   perform finishUp()
stop

housekeeping()
   declare variables
        rentalRecord
            num salesPersonID
            char salesPersonName
            num numThreeBedroomAptsRented
            num numTwoBedroomApts
            num numOneBedroomAptsRented
            num numStudioAptsRented
        char mainHeader = "Commission Report"
        char columnHeaders =
            "Salesperson ID        Name       Commission Earned"
        num commissionEarned
        num regRate = 50.00
        char studioRate = 35.00
   open files
   perform displayHeaders()
stop

displayHeader()
   print mainHeader
   print columnHeaders
return

calculateCommission()
   commissionEarned = (numThreeBedroomAptsRented * 2 +
      numTwoBedroomAptsRented
  * 3 + numOneBedroomAptsRented) * regRate +
      (numStudioAptsRented * studioRate)
   print salespersonID, salespersonName, commissionEarned
return

finishUp()
   close files
return
```

## EXERCISES

1. **A pet store owner needs a weekly sales report. The output consists of a printed report titled PET SALES, with column headings TYPE OF ANIMAL and PRICE. Fields printed on output are: type of animal and price. After all records print, a footer line END OF REPORT prints. The input file description is shown below.**

```
File name: PETS
FIELD DESCRIPTION      DATA TYPE      COMMENTS
Type of Animal         Character      20 characters
Price of Animal        Numeric        2 decimal places
```

   a. Design the output for this program; create either sample output or a print chart.
   b. Draw the hierarchy chart for this program.
   c. Draw the flowchart for this program.
   d. Write the pseudocode for this program.

2. **An employer wants to produce a personnel report. The output consists of a printed report titled ACTIVE PERSONNEL. Fields printed on output are: last name of employee, first name of employee, and current weekly salary. Include appropriate column headings and a footer. The input file description is shown below.**

```
File name: PERSONNEL
FIELD DESCRIPTION      DATA TYPE      COMMENTS
Last Name              Character      15 characters
First Name             Character      15 characters
Soc. Sec. Number       Numeric        9 digits, 0 decimal places
Department             Numeric        2 digits, 0 decimal places
Current Salary         Numeric        2 decimal places
```

   a. Design the output for this program; create either sample output or a print chart.
   b. Draw the hierarchy chart for this program.
   c. Draw the flowchart for this program.
   d. Write the pseudocode for this program.

3. **An employer wants to produce a personnel report that shows the end result if she gives everyone a 10 percent raise in salary. The output consists of a printed report entitled PROJECTED RAISES. Fields printed on output are: last name of employee, first name of employee, current weekly salary, and projected weekly salary. The input file description is shown below.**

```
File name: PERSONNEL
FIELD DESCRIPTION      DATA TYPE      COMMENTS
Last Name              Character      15 characters
First Name             Character      15 characters
Soc. Sec. Number       Numeric        9 digits, 0 decimal places
Department             Numeric        2 digits, 0 decimal places
Current Salary         Numeric        2 decimal places
```

   a. Design the output for this program; create either sample output or a print chart.
   b. Draw the hierarchy chart for this program.
   c. Draw the flowchart for this program.
   d. Write the pseudocode for this program.

4. **A furniture store maintains an inventory file that includes data about every item it sells. The manager wants a report that lists each stock number, description, and profit, which is the retail price minus the wholesale price. The fields include a stock number, description, wholesale price, and retail price. The input file description is shown below.**

```
File name: FURNITURE
FIELD DESCRIPTION      DATA TYPE      COMMENTS
Stock Number           Numeric        4 digits, 0 decimal places
Description            Character      25 characters
Wholesale Price        Numeric        2 decimal places
Retail Price           Numeric        2 decimal places
```

a. Design the output for this program; create either sample output or a print chart.
b. Draw the hierarchy chart for this program.
c. Draw the flowchart for this program.
d. Write the pseudocode for this program.

5. **A summer camp keeps a record for every camper, including first name, last name, birth date, and skill scores that range from 1 to 10 in four areas: swimming, tennis, horsemanship, and crafts. (The birth date is stored in the format YYYYMMDD without any punctuation. For example, January 21, 1991 is 19910121.) The camp wants a printed report listing each camper's data, plus a total score that is the sum of the camper's four skill scores. The input file description is shown below.**

```
File name: CAMPERS
FIELD DESCRIPTION      DATA TYPE      COMMENTS
First Name             Character      15 characters
Last Name              Character      15 characters
Birth Date             Numeric        8 digits, 0 decimals
Swimming Skill         Numeric        0 decimals
Tennis Skill           Numeric        0 decimals
Horsemanship Skill     Numeric        0 decimals
Crafts Skill           Numeric        0 decimals
```

a. Design the output for this program; create either sample output or a print chart.
b. Draw the hierarchy chart for this program.
c. Draw the flowchart for this program.
d. Write the pseudocode for this program.

6. **An employer needs to determine how much tax to withhold for each employee. This withholding amount computes as 20 percent of each employee's weekly pay. The output consists of a printed report titled WITHHOLDING FOR EACH EMPLOYEE. Fields printed on output are: last name of employee, first name of employee, hourly pay, weekly pay based on a 40-hour workweek, and withholding amount per week. The input file description is shown below.**

```
File name: EMPLOYEES
FIELD DESCRIPTION      DATA TYPE      COMMENTS
Company ID             Numeric        5 digits, 0 decimals
First Name             Character      12 characters
Last Name              Character      12 characters
Hourly Rate            Numeric        2 decimal places
```

a. Design the output for this program; create either sample output or a print chart.
b. Draw the hierarchy chart for this program.
c. Draw the flowchart for this program.
d. Write the pseudocode for this program.

7. **A baseball team manager wants a report showing her players' batting statistics. A batting average is computed as hits divided by at-bats, and it is usually expressed to three decimal positions (for example, .235). The output consists of a printed report titled TEAM STATISTICS. Fields printed on output are: player number, first name, last name, and batting average. The input file description is shown below.**

```
File name: BASEBALL
FIELD DESCRIPTION      DATA TYPE      COMMENTS
Player Number          Numeric        2 digits, 0 decimals
First Name             Character      16 characters
Last Name              Character      17 characters
At-bats                Numeric        never more than 999, 0 decimals
Hits                   Numeric        never more than 999, 0 decimals
```

a. Design the output for this program; create either sample output or a print chart.
b. Draw the hierarchy chart for this program.
c. Draw the flowchart for this program.
d. Write the pseudocode for this program.

8. **A car rental company manager wants a report showing the revenue earned per mile on vehicles rented each week. An automobile's miles traveled are computed by subtracting the odometer reading when the car is rented from the odometer reading when the car is returned. The amount earned per mile is computed by dividing the rental fee by the miles traveled. The output consists of a printed report titled CAR RENTAL REVENUE STATISTICS. Fields printed on output are: vehicle identification number, odometer reading out, odometer reading in, miles traveled, rental fee, and amount earned per mile. The input file description is shown below.**

File name: AUTORENTALS

| FIELD DESCRIPTION | DATA TYPE | COMMENTS |
|---|---|---|
| Vehicle Identification Number | Numeric | 12 digits |
| Odometer Reading Out | Numeric | 0 decimals |
| Odometer Reading In | Numeric | 0 decimals |
| Rental fee | Numeric | 2 decimals |

a. Design the output for this program; create either sample output or a print chart.
b. Draw the hierarchy chart for this program.
c. Draw the flowchart for this program.
d. Write the pseudocode for this program.

9. **Professor Smith provides her programming logic students with a final grade that is based on their performance in attendance (a percentage based on 16 class meetings), homework (a percentage based on 10 assignments that might total up to 100 points), and exams (a percentage based on two 100-point exams). A student's final percentage for the course is determined using a weighted average of these figures, with exams counting twice as much as attendance or homework. For example, a student who attended 12 class meetings (75%), achieved 90 points on homework assignments (90%), and scored an average of 60% on tests would have a final average of 71.25% (75 + 90 + 2 * 60) / 4. Professor Smith wants a report that shows each student's ID number and his or her final percentage score.**

File name: STUDENTSCORES

| FIELD DESCRIPTION | DATA TYPE | COMMENTS |
|---|---|---|
| Student ID Number | Numeric | 6 digits, 0 decimal places |
| Classes attended | Numeric | a value of 16 or lower, 0 decimals |
| Homework 1 | Numeric | a value of 10 or lower, 0 decimals |
| Homework 2 | Numeric | a value of 10 or lower, 0 decimals |
| Homework 3 | Numeric | a value of 10 or lower, 0 decimals |
| Homework 4 | Numeric | a value of 10 or lower, 0 decimals |
| Homework 5 | Numeric | a value of 10 or lower, 0 decimals |
| Homework 6 | Numeric | a value of 10 or lower, 0 decimals |
| Homework 7 | Numeric | a value of 10 or lower, 0 decimals |
| Homework 8 | Numeric | a value of 10 or lower, 0 decimals |
| Homework 9 | Numeric | a value of 10 or lower, 0 decimals |
| Homework 10 | Numeric | a value of 10 or lower, 0 decimals |
| Test 1 | Numeric | a value of 100 or lower, 2 decimals |
| Test 2 | Numeric | a value of 100 or lower, 2 decimals |

a. Design the output for this program; create either sample output or a print chart.
b. Draw the hierarchy chart for this program.
c. Draw the flowchart for this program.
d. Write the pseudocode for this program.

## DETECTIVE WORK

1. **Explore the job opportunities in programming. What are the job responsibilities? What is the average starting salary? What is the outlook for growth?**

2. **Many style guides are published on the Web. These guides suggest good identifiers, standard indentation rules, and similar issues in specific programming languages. Find style guides for at least two languages (for example, C++, Java, Visual Basic, C#, COBOL, RPG, or Pascal) and list any differences you notice.**

## UP FOR DISCUSSION

1. **When you write computer programs, you will generate errors. Syntax errors are errors in the language—for example, misspellings. Logical errors are caused by statements with correct syntax but that perform an incorrect task, or a correct task at the wrong time. Which is more dangerous? How could the number of occurrences of both types of errors be reduced?**

2. **Extreme programming is a system for rapidly developing software. One of its tenets is that all production code is written by two programmers sitting at one machine. Is this a good idea? Does working this way as a programmer appeal to you?**

# 5 MAKING DECISIONS

## After studying Chapter 5, you should be able to:

- Evaluate Boolean expressions to make comparisons
- Use the relational comparison operators
- Understand AND logic
- Understand OR logic
- Use selections within ranges
- Understand precedence when combining AND and OR selections
- Understand the case structure
- Use decision tables

## EVALUATING BOOLEAN EXPRESSIONS TO MAKE COMPARISONS

One reason people think computers are smart lies in a computer program's ability to make decisions. For example, a medical diagnosis program that can decide if your symptoms fit various disease profiles seems quite intelligent, as does a program that can offer you potential vacation routes based on your destination.

The selection structure (also called the decision structure) involved in such programs is not new to you—it's one of the basic structures of structured programming. See Figures 5-1 and 5-2.

**FIGURE 5-1:** THE DUAL-ALTERNATIVE SELECTION STRUCTURE

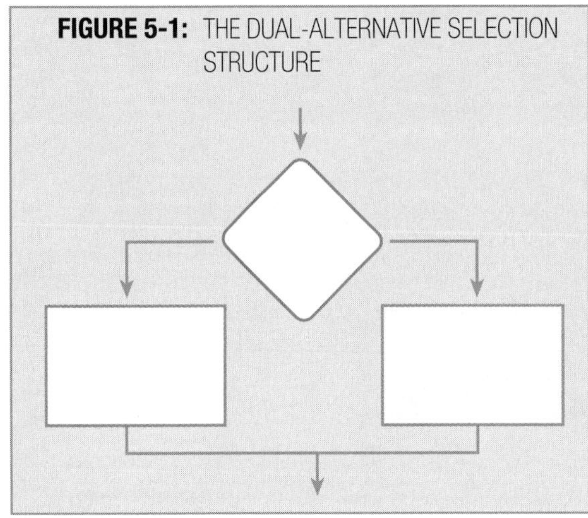

**FIGURE 5-2:** THE SINGLE-ALTERNATIVE SELECTION STRUCTURE

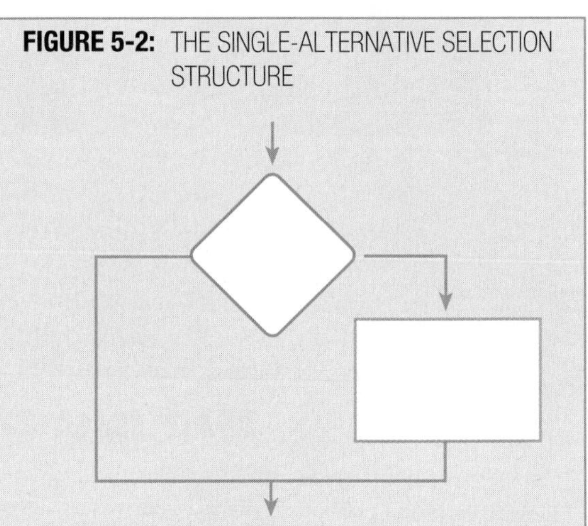

You can refer to the structure in Figure 5-1 as a **dual-alternative**, or **binary**, selection because there is an action associated with each of two possible outcomes. Depending on the answer to the question represented by the diamond, the logical flow proceeds either to the left branch of the structure or to the right. The choices are mutually exclusive; that is, the logic can flow only to one of the two alternatives, never to both. This selection structure is also called an **if-then-else** structure because it fits the statement:

```
if the answer to the question is yes, then
    do something
else
    do somethingElse
endif
```

The flowchart segment in Figure 5-2 represents a **single-alternative**, or **unary**, selection where action is required for only one outcome of the question. You call this form of the if-then-else structure an **if-then**, because no alternative or "else" action is included or necessary.

**TIP** You can call a single-alternative decision (or selection) a *single-sided decision*. Similarly, a dual-alternative decision (or selection) is a *double-sided decision*.

For example, Figure 5-3 shows the flowchart and pseudocode for a typical if-then-else decision in a business program. Many organizations pay employees time and a half (one and one-half times their usual hourly rate) for hours in excess of 40 per week. The logic segments in the figure show this decision.

**FIGURE 5-3:** FLOWCHART AND PSEUDOCODE FOR OVERTIME PAY DECISION

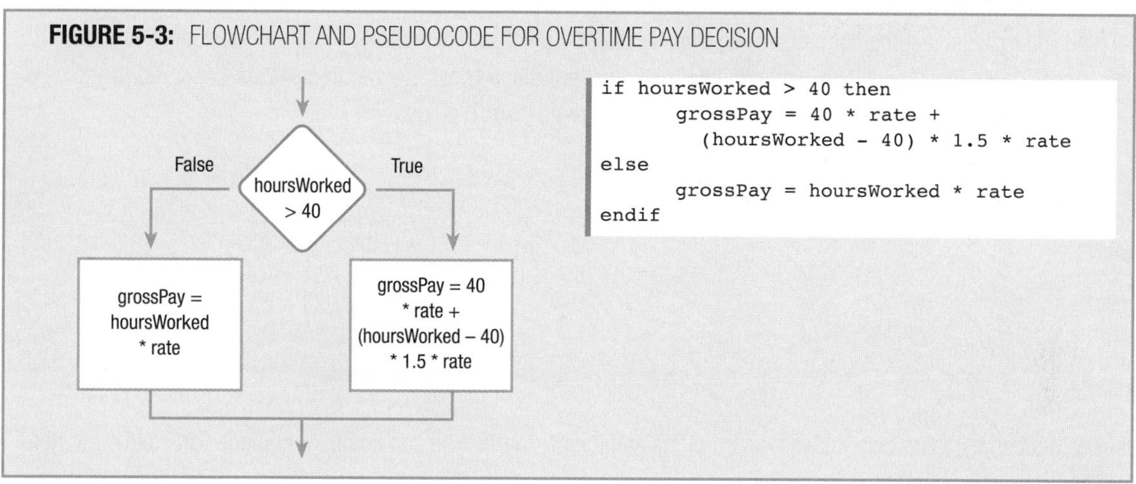


```
if hoursWorked > 40 then
      grossPay = 40 * rate +
        (hoursWorked - 40) * 1.5 * rate
else
      grossPay = hoursWorked * rate
endif
```

In the example in Figure 5-3, the longer calculation that adds a time-and-a-half factor to an employee's gross pay executes only when the expression `hoursWorked > 40` is true. The overtime calculation exists in the **if clause** of the decision—the part of the decision that holds the action or actions that execute when the tested condition in the decision is true. The shorter, regular pay calculation, which produces `grossPay` by multiplying `hoursWorked` by `rate`, constitutes the **else clause** of the decision—the part that executes only when the tested condition in the decision is false.

The typical if-then decision in Figure 5-4 shows an employee's paycheck being reduced if the employee participates in the dental plan. No action is taken if the employee is not a dental plan participant.

**FIGURE 5-4:** FLOWCHART AND PSEUDOCODE FOR DENTAL PLAN DECISION

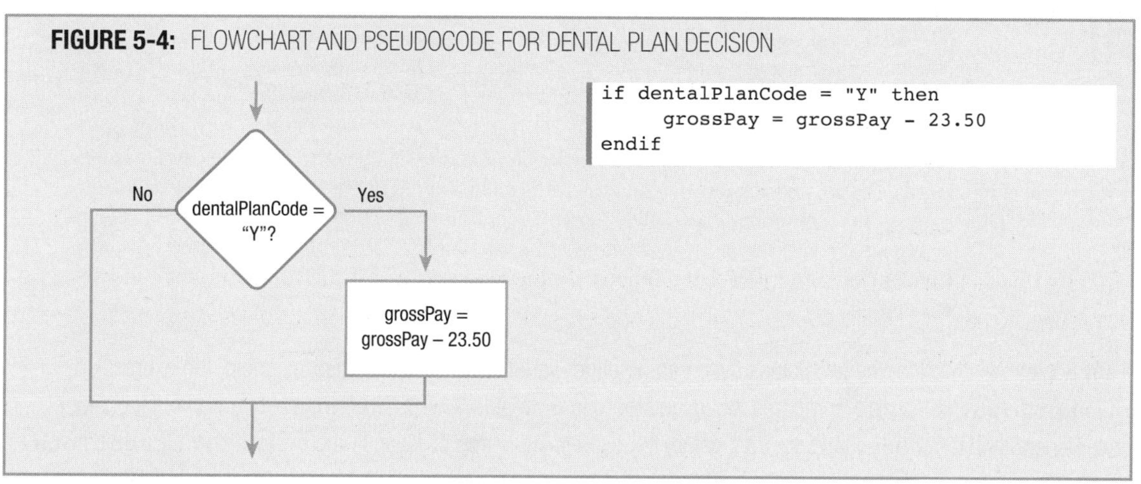


```
if dentalPlanCode = "Y" then
     grossPay = grossPay - 23.50
endif
```

The expressions `hoursWorked > 40` and `dentalPlanCode = "Y"` that appear in Figures 5-3 and 5-4, respectively, are Boolean expressions. In Chapter 4, you learned that in programming, an expression is a statement, or part of a statement, that has a value. For example, an arithmetic expression is one that performs arithmetic, resulting in a value. A **Boolean expression** is one that represents only one of two states, usually expressed as true or false. Every decision you make in a computer program involves evaluating a Boolean expression. True/false evaluation is "natural" from a computer's standpoint, because computer circuitry consists of two-state, on-off switches, often represented by 1 or 0. Every computer decision yields a true-or-false, yes-or-no, 1-or-0 result.

TIP George Boole was a mathematician who lived from 1815 to 1864. He approached logic more simply than his predecessors did, by expressing logical selections with common algebraic symbols. He is considered a pioneer in mathematical logic, and Boolean (true/false) expressions are named for him.

## USING THE RELATIONAL COMPARISON OPERATORS

Usually, you can compare only values that are of the same type; that is, you can compare numeric values to other numbers and character values to other characters. You can ask every programming question by using one of only six types of comparison operators in a Boolean expression. For any two values that are the same type, you can decide whether:

- The two values are equal.
- The first value is greater than the second value.
- The first value is less than the second value.
- The first value is greater than or equal to the second value.
- The first value is less than or equal to the second value.
- The two values are not equal.

TIP Usually, character variables are not considered to be equal unless they are identical, including the spacing and whether they appear in uppercase or lowercase. For example, "black pen" is *not* equal to "blackpen", "BLACK PEN", or "Black Pen".

TIP Some programming languages allow you to compare a character to a number. If this is the case, then a single character's numeric code value is used in the comparison. For example, most microcomputers use either the ASCII or Unicode coding system. In both of these systems, an uppercase "A" is represented numerically as a 65, an uppercase "B" is a 66, and so on. See Appendix B for more information on ASCII code and how numbers are used to store data.

In any Boolean expression, the two values used can be either variables or constants. For example, the expression `currentTotal = 100?` compares the value stored in a variable, `currentTotal`, to a numeric constant, `100`. Depending on the `currentTotal` value, the expression is true or false. In the expression `currentTotal = previousTotal?` both values are variables, and the result is also true or false depending on the values stored in each of the two variables. Although it's legal to do so, you would never use expressions in which you compare two unnamed constants—for example, `20 = 20?` or `30 = 40?`. Such expressions are considered **trivial** because each will always evaluate to the same result: true for the first expression and false for the second.

Each programming language supports its own set of **relational comparison operators**, or comparison symbols, that express these Boolean tests. For example, many languages such as Visual Basic and Pascal use the equal sign (=) to express testing for equivalency, so `balanceDue = 0` compares `balanceDue` to zero. COBOL programmers can use the equal sign, but they also can spell out the expression, as in `balanceDue equal to 0`. RPG programmers use the two-letter operator `EQ` in place of a symbol. C#, C++, and Java programmers use two equal signs to test for equivalency, so they write `balanceDue == 0` to compare the two values. Although each programming language supports its own syntax for comparing values' equivalency, all languages provide for the same logical concept of equivalency.

TIP

Visual Basic uses the single equal sign both for assignment and when testing for equivalency; the interpretation of the operator depends on the context. The reason some languages use two equal signs for comparisons is to avoid confusion with assignment statements such as `balanceDue = 0`. In C++, C#, or Java, this statement only assigns the value 0 to `balanceDue`; it does not compare `balanceDue` to zero.

TIP

Whenever you use a comparison operator, you must provide a value on each side of the operator. Comparison operators are sometimes called ***binary operators*** because of this requirement. Some programmers use the terms "comparison operator," "relational operator," and "**logical operator**" interchangeably. However, many prefer to reserve the term "logical operator" for manipulations on single bits.

Most languages allow you to use the algebraic signs for greater than (>) and less than (<) to make the corresponding comparisons. Additionally, COBOL, which is very similar to English, allows you to spell out the comparisons in expressions such as `daysPastDue is greater than 30` or `packageWeight is less than maximumWeightAllowed`. RPG uses the two-letter abbreviations `GT` and `LT` to represent greater than or less than. When you create a flowchart or pseudocode, you can use any form of notation you want to express "greater than" and "less than." It's simplest to use the symbols > and < if you are comfortable with their meaning. As with equivalency, the syntax changes when you change languages, but the concepts of greater than and less than exist in all programming languages.

Most programming languages allow you to express "greater than or equal to" by typing a greater-than sign immediately followed by an equal sign (>=). When you are drawing a flowchart or writing pseudocode, you might prefer a greater-than sign with a line under it (≥) because mathematicians use that symbol to mean "greater than or equal to." However, when you write a program, you type >= as two separate characters, because no single key on the keyboard expresses this concept. Similarly, "less than or equal to" is written with two symbols, < immediately followed by =.

TIP

The operators >= and <= are always treated as a single unit; no spaces separate the two parts of the operator. Also, the equal sign always appears second. No programming language allows => or =< as a comparison operator.

Any logical situation can be expressed using just three types of comparisons: equal, greater than, and less than. You never need the three additional comparisons (greater than or equal to, less than or equal to, or not equal to), but using them often makes decisions more convenient. For example, assume you need to issue a 10 percent discount to any customer whose age is 65 or greater, and charge full price to other customers. You can use the greater-than-or-equal-to symbol to write the logic as follows:

```
if customerAge >= 65 then
    discount = 0.10
else
    discount = 0
endif
```

As an alternative, if you want to use only one of the three basic comparisons (=, >, and <), you can express the same logic by writing:

```
if customerAge < 65 then
    discount = 0
else
    discount = 0.10
endif
```

In any decision for which `a >= b` is true, then `a < b` is false. Conversely, if `a >= b` is false, then `a < b` is true. By rephrasing the question and swapping the actions taken based on the outcome, you can make the same decision in multiple ways. The clearest route is often to ask a question so the positive or true outcome results in the unusual action. For example, assume that charging a customer full price is the ordinary course, and that providing a discount is the unusual occurrence. When your company policy is to "provide a discount for those who are 65 and older," the phrase "greater than or equal to" comes to mind, so it is the most natural to use. Conversely, if your policy is to "provide no discount for those under 65," then it is more natural to use the "less than" syntax. Either way, the same people receive a discount.

Comparing two amounts to decide if they are *not* equal to each other is the most confusing of all the comparisons. Using "not equal to" in decisions involves thinking in double negatives, which makes you prone to include logical errors in your programs. For example, consider the flowchart segment in Figure 5-5.

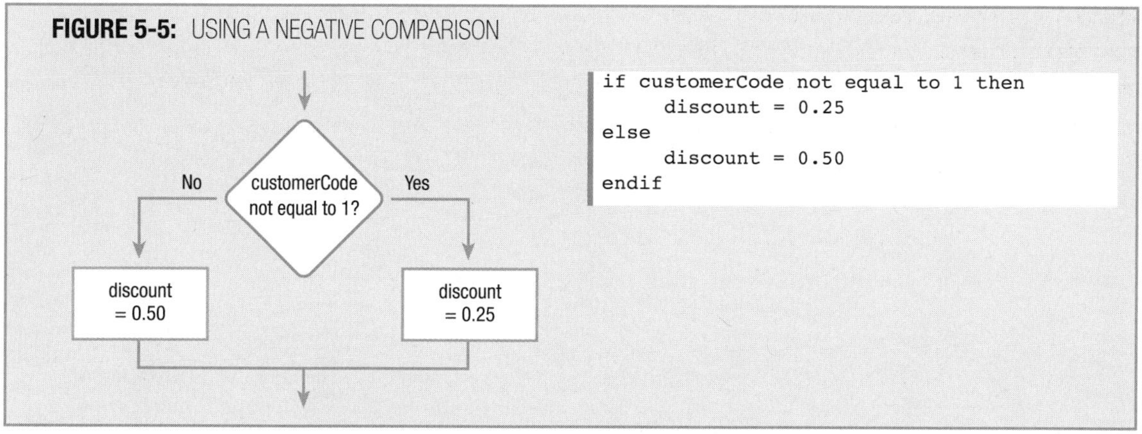


```
if customerCode not equal to 1 then
     discount = 0.25
else
     discount = 0.50
endif
```

**FIGURE 5-5:** USING A NEGATIVE COMPARISON

In Figure 5-5, if the value of `customerCode` *is* equal to 1, the logical flow follows the false branch of the selection. If `customerCode not equal to 1` is true, the `discount` is 0.25; if `customerCode not equal to 1` is not true, it means the `customerCode` *is* 1, and the `discount` is 0.50. Even using the phrase "`customerCode not equal to 1 is not true`" is awkward.

Figure 5-6 shows the same decision, this time asked in the positive. Making the decision `if customerCode` *is* `1 then discount = 0.50` is clearer than trying to determine what `customerCode` is *not*.

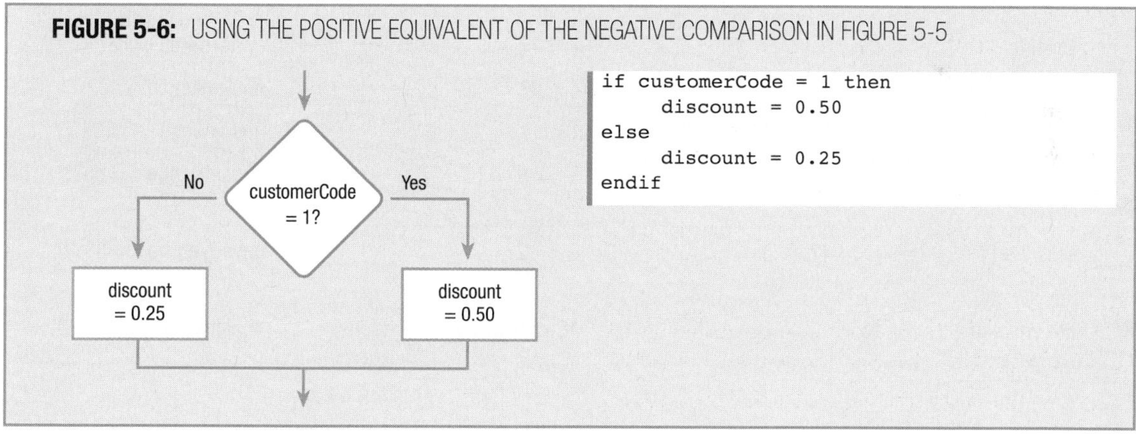


```
if customerCode = 1 then
     discount = 0.50
else
     discount = 0.25
endif
```

**FIGURE 5-6:** USING THE POSITIVE EQUIVALENT OF THE NEGATIVE COMPARISON IN FIGURE 5-5

Besides being awkward to use, the "not equal to" comparison operator is the one most likely to be different in the various programming languages you may use. COBOL allows you to write "not equal to"; Visual Basic and Pascal use a less-than sign followed immediately by a greater-than sign (<>); C#, C++, C, and Java use an exclamation point followed by an equal sign (!=). In a flowchart or in pseudocode, you can use the symbol that mathematicians use to mean "not equal," an equal sign with a slash through it (≠). When you program, you will not be able to use this symbol, because no single key on the keyboard produces it.

**TIP**

Although NOT comparisons can be awkward to use, there are times when your meaning is clearest if you use one. Frequently, this occurs when you take action only when some comparison is expressed negatively–for example, when one value is not equal to another value. Examples of situations in which a negative comparison makes sense include the following:

```
if customerZipCode is not equal to localZipCode then
    add DELIVERY_CHARGE to total
endif

if creditCardBalance is not 0 then
     financeCharge = balance * INTEREST_RATE
endif
```

In these cases, action is taken when two values are not equal. The mainline logic of many programs, including those you have worked with in this book, includes a negative comparison that controls a loop. The pseudocode you have seen for almost every program includes a statement similar to: `while not eof, perform mainLoop()`.

Figure 5-7 summarizes the six comparison operators and contrasts trivial (both true and false) examples with typical examples of their use.

**FIGURE 5-7:** RELATIONAL COMPARISONS

| Comparison | Trivial true example | Trivial false example | Typical example |
|---|---|---|---|
| Equal to | 7 = 7? | 7 = 4? | amtOrdered = 12? |
| Greater than | 12 > 3? | 4 > 9? | hoursWorked > 40? |
| Less than | 1 < 8? | 13 < 10? | hourlyWage < 5.65? |
| Greater than or equal to | 5 >= 5? | 3 >= 9? | customerAge >= 65? |
| Less than or equal to | 4 <= 4? | 8 <= 2? | daysOverdue <= 60? |
| Not equal to | 16 <> 3? | 18 <> 18? | customerBalance <> 0? |

## UNDERSTANDING AND LOGIC

Often, you need more than one selection structure to determine whether an action should take place. For example, suppose that your employer wants a report that lists workers who have registered for both insurance plans offered by the company: the medical plan and the dental plan. This type of situation is known as an **AND decision** because the employee's record must pass two tests—participation in the medical plan *and* participation in the dental plan—before you write that employee's information on the report. A compound, or AND, decision requires a **nested decision**, or a **nested if**. A nested decision is a decision "inside of" another decision. The logic looks like Figure 5-8.

**FIGURE 5-8:** FLOWCHART AND PSEUDOCODE OF AN AND DECISION

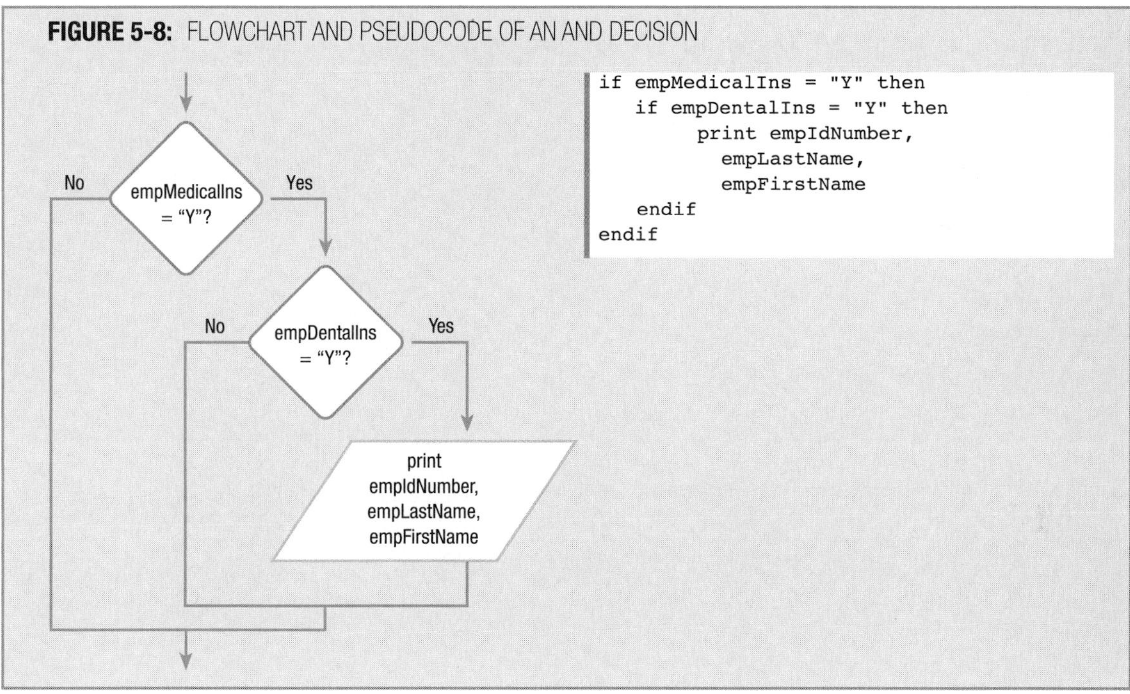


```
if empMedicalIns = "Y" then
   if empDentalIns = "Y" then
         print empIdNumber,
           empLastName,
           empFirstName
   endif
endif
```

TIP You first learned about nesting structures in Chapter 2.

TIP A series of nested `if` statements can also be called a **cascading if statement**.

The AND decision shown in Figure 5-8 is part of a much larger program. To help you develop this program, suppose your employer provides you with the employee data file description shown in Figure 5-9, and you learn that the medical and dental insurance fields contain a single character, "Y" or "N", indicating each employee's participation status. With your employer's approval, you develop the sample output shown in Figure 5-10.

**FIGURE 5-9:** EMPLOYEE FILE DESCRIPTION

**EMPLOYEE FILE DESCRIPTION**
**File Name: EMPFILE**

| FIELD DESCRIPTION | DATA TYPE | COMMENTS |
|---|---|---|
| ID Number | Numeric | 4 digits, 0 decimal places |
| Last Name | Character | 15 characters |
| First Name | Character | 15 characters |
| Department | Numeric | 1 digit |
| Hourly Rate | Numeric | 2 decimal places |
| Medical Plan | Character | 1 character, Y or N |
| Dental Plan | Character | 1 character, Y or N |
| Number of Dependents | Numeric | 0 decimal places |

**FIGURE 5-10:** SAMPLE REPORT LISTING EMPLOYEES PARTICIPATING IN BOTH INSURANCE PLANS

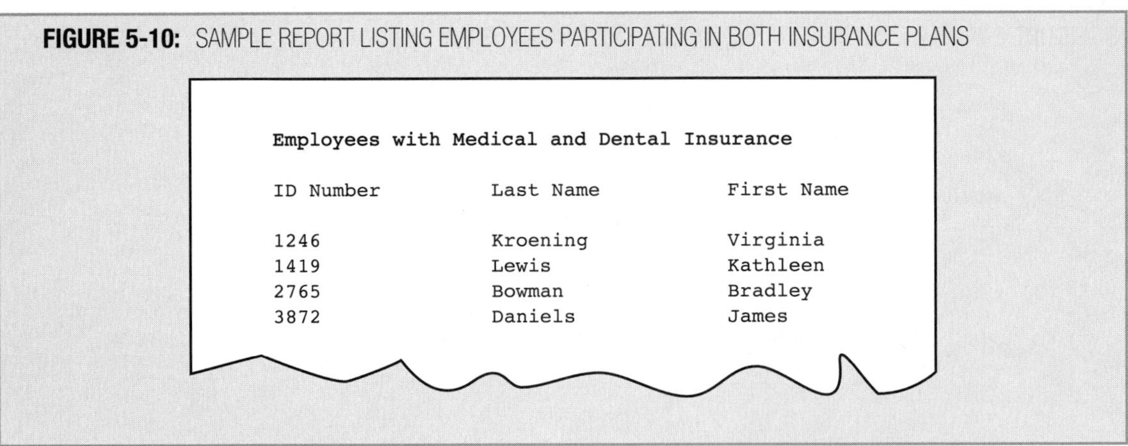

**Employees with Medical and Dental Insurance**

| ID Number | Last Name | First Name |
|---|---|---|
| 1246 | Kroening | Virginia |
| 1419 | Lewis | Kathleen |
| 2765 | Bowman | Bradley |
| 3872 | Daniels | James |

The mainline logic and `housekeeping()` routines for this program are diagrammed in Figures 5-11 and 5-12.

**FIGURE 5-11:** FLOWCHART AND PSEUDOCODE OF MAINLINE LOGIC FOR MEDICAL AND DENTAL PARTICIPANT REPORT

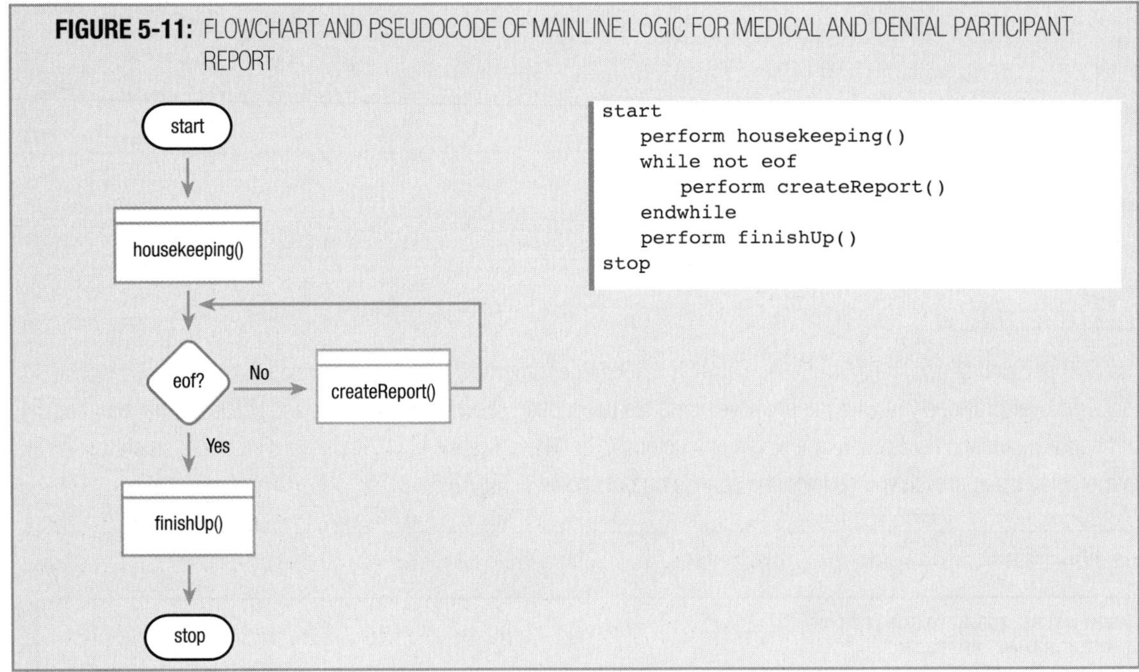


```
start
   perform housekeeping()
   while not eof
      perform createReport()
   endwhile
   perform finishUp()
stop
```

**FIGURE 5-12:** FLOWCHART AND PSEUDOCODE OF `housekeeping()` MODULE FOR MEDICAL AND DENTAL PARTICIPANT REPORT

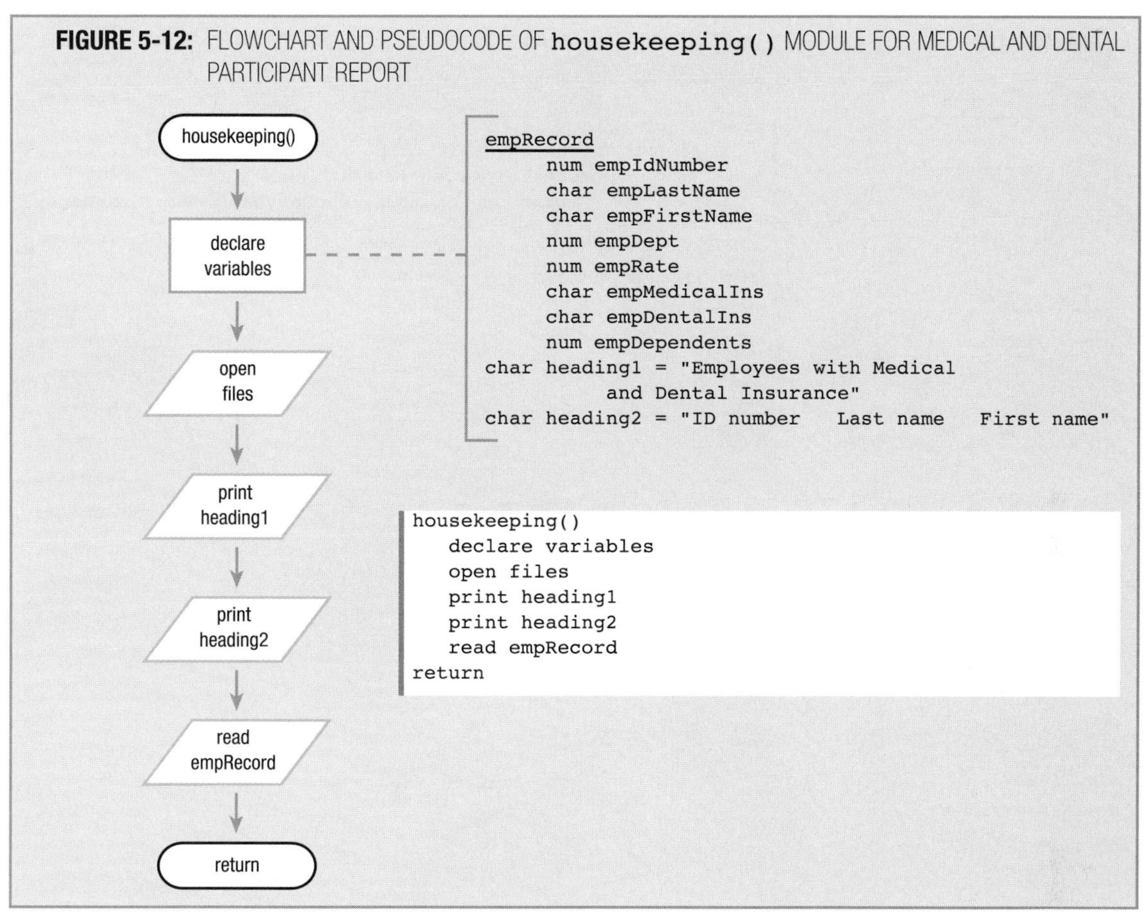


```
empRecord
     num empIdNumber
     char empLastName
     char empFirstName
     num empDept
     num empRate
     char empMedicalIns
     char empDentalIns
     num empDependents
char heading1 = "Employees with Medical
          and Dental Insurance"
char heading2 = "ID number   Last name   First name"
```

```
housekeeping()
   declare variables
   open files
   print heading1
   print heading2
   read empRecord
return
```

At the end of the `housekeeping()` module, the first employee record is read into computer memory. Assuming that the `eof` condition is not yet met, the logical flow proceeds to the `createReport()` method. If the program required data for all employees to be printed, this method would simply print the information from the current record and get the next record. However, in this case, the output should contain only the names of those employees who participate in both the medical and dental insurance plans. Therefore, within the `createReport()` module of this program, you ask the questions that determine whether the current employee's record will print; if the employee's data meet the medical and dental insurance requirements, then you print the record. Whether or not you take the path that prints the record, the last thing you do in the `createReport()` method is to read the next input record. Figure 5-13 shows the `createReport()` module.

**FIGURE 5-13:** THE `createReport()` MODULE OF A PROGRAM THAT LISTS EMPLOYEES WHO ARE BOTH MEDICAL AND DENTAL INSURANCE PROGRAM PARTICIPANTS

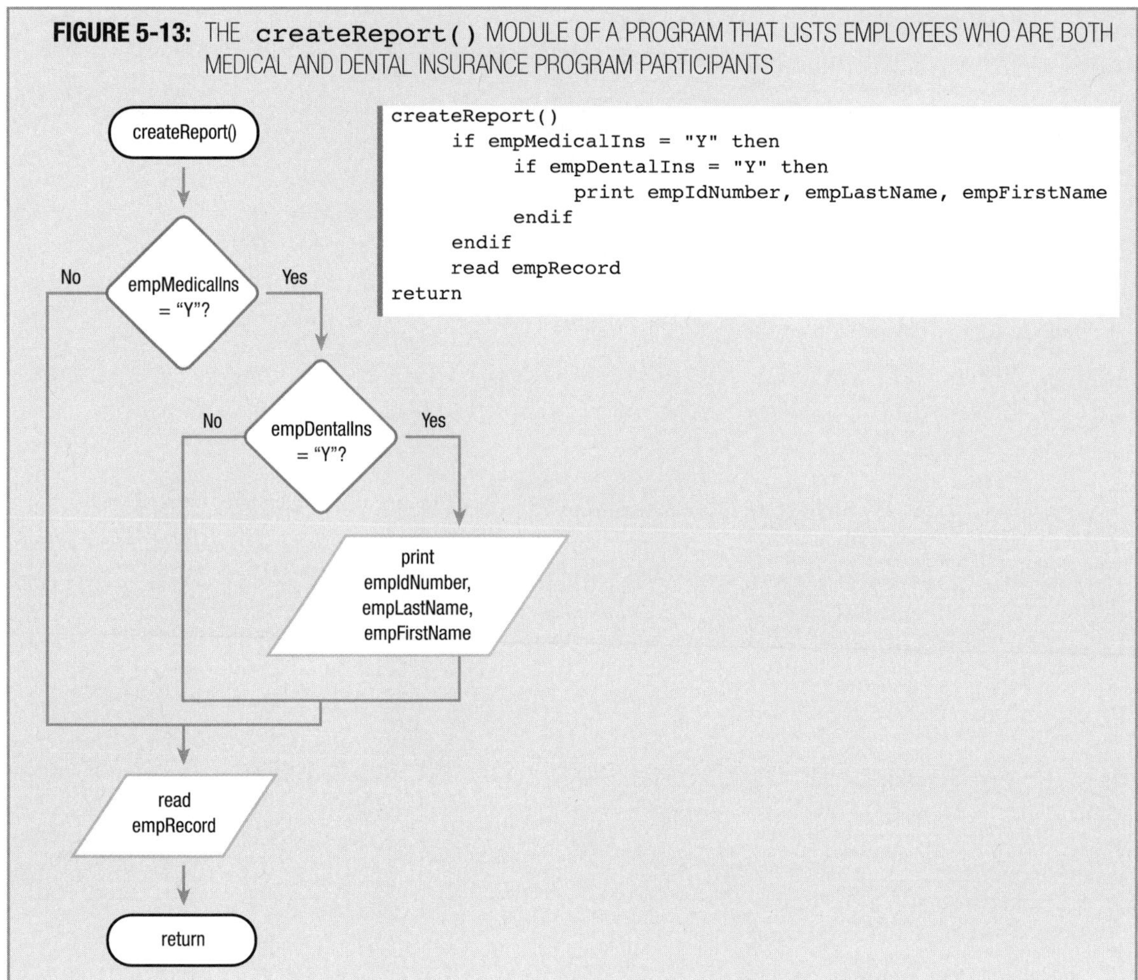


```
createReport()
     if empMedicalIns = "Y" then
          if empDentalIns = "Y" then
               print empIdNumber, empLastName, empFirstName
          endif
     endif
     read empRecord
return
```

**TIP**

At the end of the `housekeeping()` module in Figure 5-12, instead of the statement `read empRecord`, an interactive program might prompt the user for values for each of the eight data fields. Instead of the single read statement, you might choose to call a method containing eight pairs of statements, such as `print "Please enter employee ID number"` and `read empIdNumber`. The programs in this chapter read data from a file to keep them simpler.

The `createReport()` module works like this: If the employee has medical insurance, *then* and *only then* test to see if the employee has dental insurance. If so, *then* and *only then* print the employee's data. The dental insurance question is nested entirely within half of the medical insurance question structure. If an employee does not carry medical insurance, there is no need to ask about the dental insurance; the employee is already disqualified from the report. Pseudocode for the entire program is shown in Figure 5-14. Notice how the second (dental insurance) decision within the `createReport()` method is indented within the first (medical insurance) decision. This technique shows that the second question is asked only when the result of the first comparison is true.

**FIGURE 5-14:** PSEUDOCODE OF PROGRAM THAT PRINTS RECORDS OF EMPLOYEES WHO PARTICIPATE IN BOTH THE MEDICAL AND DENTAL INSURANCE PLANS

```
start
    perform housekeeping()
    while not eof
      perform createReport()
    endwhile
    perform finishUp()
stop

housekeeping()
    declare variables
    open files
    print heading1
    print heading2
    read empRecord
return

createReport()
    if empMedicalIns = "Y" then
         if empDentalIns = "Y" then
            print empIdNumber, empLastName, empFirstName
         endif
    endif
    read empRecord
return

finishUp()
    close files
return
```

```
empRecord
     num empIdNumber
     char empLastName
     char empFirstName
     num empDept
     num empRate
     char empMedicalIns
     char empDentalIns
     num empDependents
char heading1 = "Employees with Medical
           and Dental Insurance"
char heading2 = "ID number   Last name   First name"
```

## WRITING NESTED AND DECISIONS FOR EFFICIENCY

When you nest decisions because the resulting action requires that two conditions be true, you must decide which of the two decisions to make first. Logically, either selection in an AND decision can come first. However, when there are two selections, you often can improve your program's performance by making an appropriate choice as to which selection to make first.

For example, Figure 5-15 shows the nested decision structure in the `createReport()` method logic of the program that produces a report of employees who participate in both the medical and dental insurance plans. Alternatively, you can write the decision as in Figure 5-16.

**FIGURE 5-15:** FINDING MEDICAL AND DENTAL PLAN PARTICIPANTS, CHECKING MEDICAL FIRST

```
if empMedicalIns = "Y" then
     if empDentalIns = "Y" then
          print empIdNumber, empLastName, empFirstName
     endif
endif
```

**FIGURE 5-16:** FINDING DENTAL AND MEDICAL PLAN PARTICIPANTS, CHECKING DENTAL FIRST

```
if empDentalIns = "Y" then
     if empMedicalIns = "Y" then
           print empIdNumber, empLastName, empFirstName
     endif
endif
```

Examine the decision statements in Figures 5-15 and 5-16. If you want to print employees who participate in the medical AND dental plans, you can ask about the medical plan first, eliminate those employees who do not participate, and ask about the dental plan only for those employees who "pass" the medical insurance test. Or, you could ask about the dental plan first, eliminate those who do not participate, and ask about the medical plan only for those employees who "pass" the dental insurance test. Either way, the final list contains only those employees who have both kinds of insurance.

Does it make a difference which question is asked first? As far as the output goes, no. Either way, the same employee names appear on the report—those with both types of insurance. As far as program efficiency goes, however, it *might* make a difference which question is asked first.

Assume you know that out of 1,000 employees in your company, about 90 percent, or 900, participate in the medical insurance plan. Assume you also know that out of 1,000 employees, only about half, or 500, participate in the dental plan.

The medical and dental insurance program will ask the first question in the `createReport()` method 1,000 times during its execution—once for each employee record contained in the input file. If the program uses the logic in Figure 5-15, it asks the first question `empMedicalIns = "Y"?` 1,000 times. For approximately 90 percent of the employees, or 900 of the records, the answer is true, meaning the `empMedicalIns` field contains the character "Y". So 100 employees are eliminated, and 900 proceed to the next question about dental insurance. Only about half of the employees participate in the dental plan, so 450 out of the 900 will appear on the printed report.

Using the alternate logic in Figure 5-16, the program asks the first question `empDentalIns = "Y"?` 1,000 times. Because only about half of the company's employees participate, only 500 will "pass" this test and proceed to the medical insurance question. Then about 90 percent of the 500, or 450 employees, will appear on the printed report. Whether you use the logic in Figure 5-15 or 5-16, the same 450 employees who have both types of insurance appear on the report.

The difference lies in the fact that when you use the logic in Figure 5-15, the program must ask 1,900 questions to produce the report—the medical insurance question tests all 1,000 employee records, and 900 continue to the dental insurance question. If you use the logic in Figure 5-16 to produce the report, the program asks only 1,500 questions—all 1,000 records are tested for dental insurance, but only 500 proceed to the medical insurance question. By asking about the dental insurance first, you "save" 400 decisions.

The 400-question difference between the first set of decisions and the second set really doesn't take much time on most computers. But it will take *some* time, and if there are hundreds of thousands of employees instead of only 1,000, or if many such decisions have to be made within a program, performance time can be significantly improved by asking questions in the proper order.

In many AND decisions, you have no idea which of two events is more likely to occur; in that case, you can legitimately ask either question first. In addition, even though you know the probability of each of two conditions, the two events might not be mutually exclusive; that is, one might depend on the other. For example, if employees with dental insurance are significantly more likely to carry medical insurance than those who don't carry dental insurance, the order in which to ask the questions might matter less or not matter at all. However, if you do know the probabilities of the conditions, or can make a reasonable guess, the general rule is: *In an AND decision, first ask the question that is less likely to be true.* This eliminates as many records as possible from having to go through the second decision, which speeds up processing time.

## COMBINING DECISIONS IN AN AND SELECTION

Most programming languages allow you to ask two or more questions in a single comparison by using a **logical AND operator**. For example, if you want to select employees who carry both medical and dental insurance, you can use nested `if`s, or you can include both decisions in a single statement by writing `empDentalIns = "Y" AND empMedicalIns = "Y"?`. When you use one or more AND operators to combine two or more Boolean expressions, each Boolean expression must be true in order for the entire expression to be evaluated as true. For example, if you ask, "Are you at least 18, and are you a registered voter, and did you vote in the last election?", the answer to all three parts of the question must be "yes" before the response can be a single, summarizing "yes". If any part of the question is false, then the entire question is false.

**TIP** You can think of an AND expression in an algebraic way if you consider 0 to be false and any nonzero value to be true. The AND operator works like multiplication (not addition, as you might suspect). A true expression AND a true expression yields a true result because 1 * 1 is 1. Any other combination yields a false result because 1 * 0, 0 * 1, and 0 * 0 all result in 0.

If the programming language you use allows an AND operator (and almost all do), you still must realize that the question you place first is the question that will be asked first, and cases that are eliminated based on the first question will not proceed to the second question. The computer can ask only one question at a time; even when your logic follows the flowchart segment in Figure 5-17, the computer will execute the logic in the flowchart in Figure 5-18.

**FIGURE 5-17:** FLOWCHART AND PSEUDOCODE OF AN AND DECISION USING AN AND OPERATOR

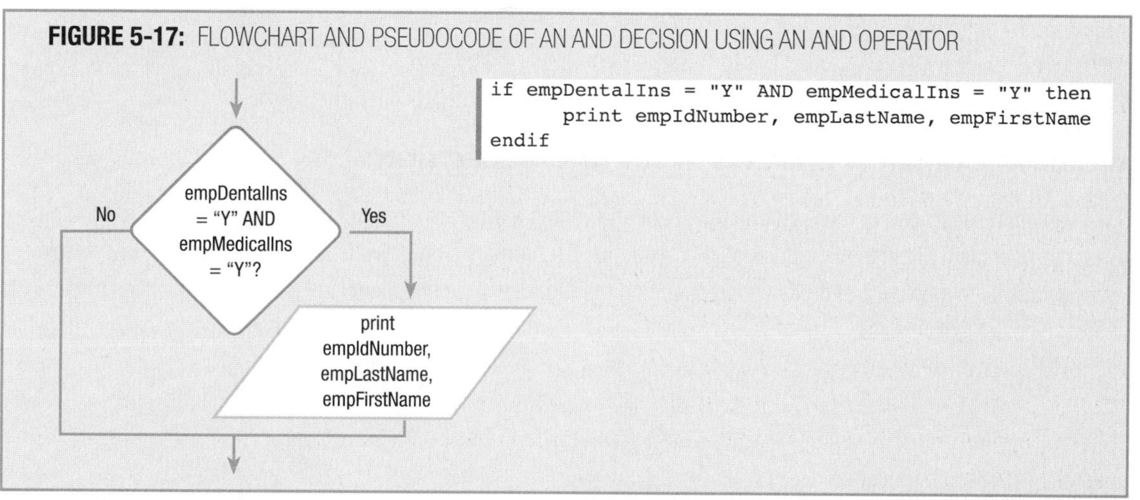
empDentalIns = "Y" AND empMedicalIns = "Y"?
No
Yes
print empIdNumber, empLastName, empFirstName

```
if empDentalIns = "Y" AND empMedicalIns = "Y" then
      print empIdNumber, empLastName, empFirstName
endif
```

FIGURE 5-18: FLOWCHART AND PSEUDOCODE OF COMPUTER LOGIC OF PROGRAM CONTAINING AN AND OPERATOR IN THE DECISION (THE COMPUTER STILL MAKES TWO SEPARATE DECISIONS, EVEN THOUGH AN AND OPERATOR IS USED)

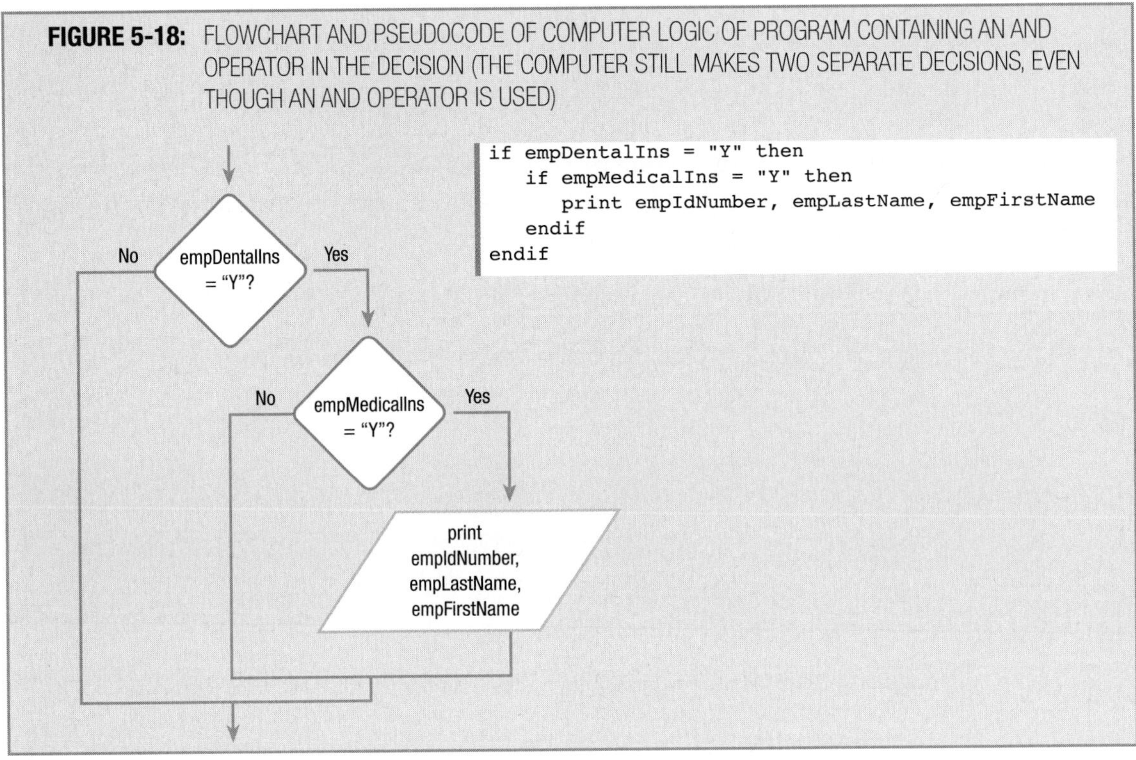


```
if empDentalIns = "Y" then
   if empMedicalIns = "Y" then
      print empIdNumber, empLastName, empFirstName
   endif
endif
```

**TIP** The AND operator in Java, C++, and C# consists of two ampersands, with no spaces between them (&&).

**TIP** Using an AND operator in a decision that involves multiple conditions does not eliminate your responsibility for determining which of the conditions to test first. Even when you use an AND operator, the computer makes decisions one at a time, and makes them in the order you ask them. If the first question in an AND expression evaluates to false, then the entire expression is false, and the second question will not even be tested. Not bothering to test the second expression when it would make no difference in the ultimate result is called **short-circuiting**. (Some languages—for example, VB .NET—provide special non-short-circuiting operators. However, the standard AND operator is short-circuiting.)

## AVOIDING COMMON ERRORS IN AN AND SELECTION

When you must satisfy two or more criteria to initiate an event in a program, you must make sure that the second decision is made entirely within the first decision. For example, if a program's objective is to print a report of those employees who carry both medical and dental insurance, then the program segment shown in Figure 5-19 contains three different types of logic errors.

**FIGURE 5-19:** INCORRECT LOGIC TO PRODUCE REPORT CONTAINING EMPLOYEES WHO PARTICIPATE IN BOTH MEDICAL AND DENTAL INSURANCE PLANS

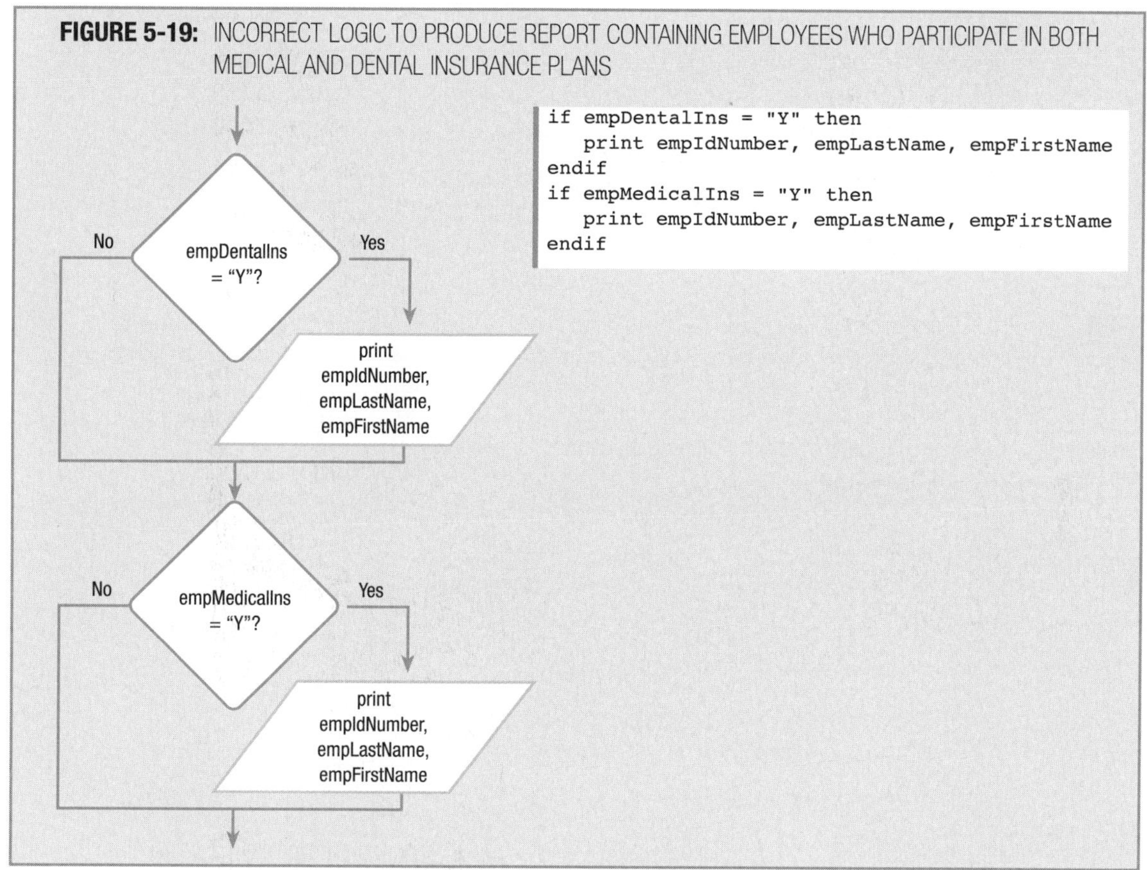

No
empDentalIns = "Y"?
Yes
print empIdNumber, empLastName, empFirstName
No
empMedicalIns = "Y"?
Yes
print empIdNumber, empLastName, empFirstName

```
if empDentalIns = "Y" then
   print empIdNumber, empLastName, empFirstName
endif
if empMedicalIns = "Y" then
   print empIdNumber, empLastName, empFirstName
endif
```

The diagram shows that the program asks the dental insurance question first. However, if an employee participates in the dental program, the employee's record prints immediately. The employee record should not print, because the employee might not have the medical insurance. In addition, the program should eliminate an employee without dental insurance from the next selection, but every employee's record proceeds to the medical insurance question, where it might print, whether the employee has dental insurance or not. Additionally, any employee who has both medical and dental insurance, having passed each test successfully, will appear twice on this report. For many reasons, the logic shown in Figure 5-19 is *not* correct for this problem.

Beginning programmers often make another type of error when they must make two comparisons on the same field when using a logical AND operator. For example, suppose you want to list employees who make between $10.00 and $11.99 per hour, inclusive. When you make this type of decision, you are basing it on a **range** of values—every value between low and high limits. For example, you want to select employees whose `empRate` is greater than or equal to

10.00 AND whose `empRate` is less than 12.00; therefore, you need to make two comparisons on the same field. Without the logical AND operator, the comparison is:

```
if empRate >= 10.00 then
     if empRate < 12.00 then
          print empIdNumber, empLastName, empFirstName
     endif
endif
```

**TIP** To check for `empRate` values that are 10.00 or greater, you can use either `empRate > 9.99?` or `empRate >= 10.00?`. To check for `empRate` values under 12.00, you can write `empRate <= 11.99?` or `empRate < 12.00?`.

The correct way to make this comparison with the AND operator is as follows:

```
if empRate >= 10.00 AND empRate < 12.00 then
     print empIdNumber, empLastName, empFirstName
endif
```

You substitute the AND operator for the phrase `then if`. However, some programmers might try to make the comparison as follows:

```
if empRate >= 10.00 AND < 12.00 then
     print empIdNumber, empLastName, empFirstName
endif
```

In most languages, the phrase `empRate >= 10.00 AND < 12.00` is incorrect. The logical AND is usually a binary operator that requires a complete Boolean expression on each side. The expression to the right of the AND, `< 12.00`, is not a complete Boolean expression; you must indicate *what* is being compared to 12.00.

**TIP** In some programming languages, such as COBOL and RPG, you can write the equivalent of `empRate >= 10.00 AND < 12.00?` and the `empRate` variable is implied for both comparisons. Still, it is clearer, and therefore preferable, to use the two full expressions, `empRate >= 10.00 AND empRate < 12.00?`.

## UNDERSTANDING OR LOGIC

Sometimes, you want to take action when one *or* the other of two conditions is true. This is called an **OR decision** because either a first condition must be met *or* a second condition must be met for an event to take place. If someone asks you, "Are you free Friday or Saturday?", only one of the two conditions has to be true in order for the answer to the whole question to be "yes"; only if the answers to both halves of the question are false is the value of the entire expression false.

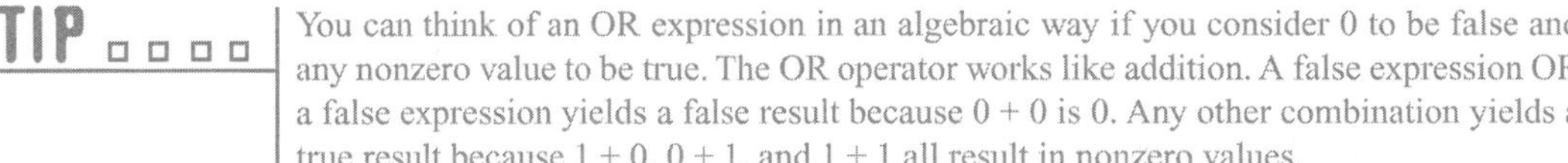

**TIP** You can think of an OR expression in an algebraic way if you consider 0 to be false and any nonzero value to be true. The OR operator works like addition. A false expression OR a false expression yields a false result because 0 + 0 is 0. Any other combination yields a true result because 1 + 0, 0 + 1, and 1 + 1 all result in nonzero values.

For example, suppose your employer wants a list of all employees who participate in either the medical or dental plan. Assuming you are using the same input file described in Figure 5-9, the mainline logic and `housekeeping()` module for this program are identical to those used in Figures 5-11 and 5-12. You only need to change the heading on the sample output (Figure 5-10) and change the `heading1` variable in Figure 5-12 from `heading1 = "Employees with Medical and Dental Insurance"` to `heading1 = "Employees with Medical or Dental Insurance"`. The only substantial changes to the program occur in the `createReport()` module.

Figure 5-20 shows the possible logic for the `createReport()` method in this OR selection. As each record enters the `createReport()` method, you ask the question `empMedicalIns = "Y"?`, and if the result is true, you print the employee data. Because the employee needs to participate in only one of the two insurance plans to be selected for printing, there is no need for further questioning after you have determined that an employee has medical insurance. If the employee does not participate in the medical insurance plan, only then do you need to ask if `empDentalIns = "Y"?`. If the employee does not have medical insurance, but does have dental, you want this employee information to print on the report.

**FIGURE 5-20:** FLOWCHART AND PSEUDOCODE FOR `createReport()` MODULE OF PROGRAM THAT PRINTS RECORDS OF EMPLOYEES WHO PARTICIPATE IN EITHER THE MEDICAL OR DENTAL INSURANCE PLAN

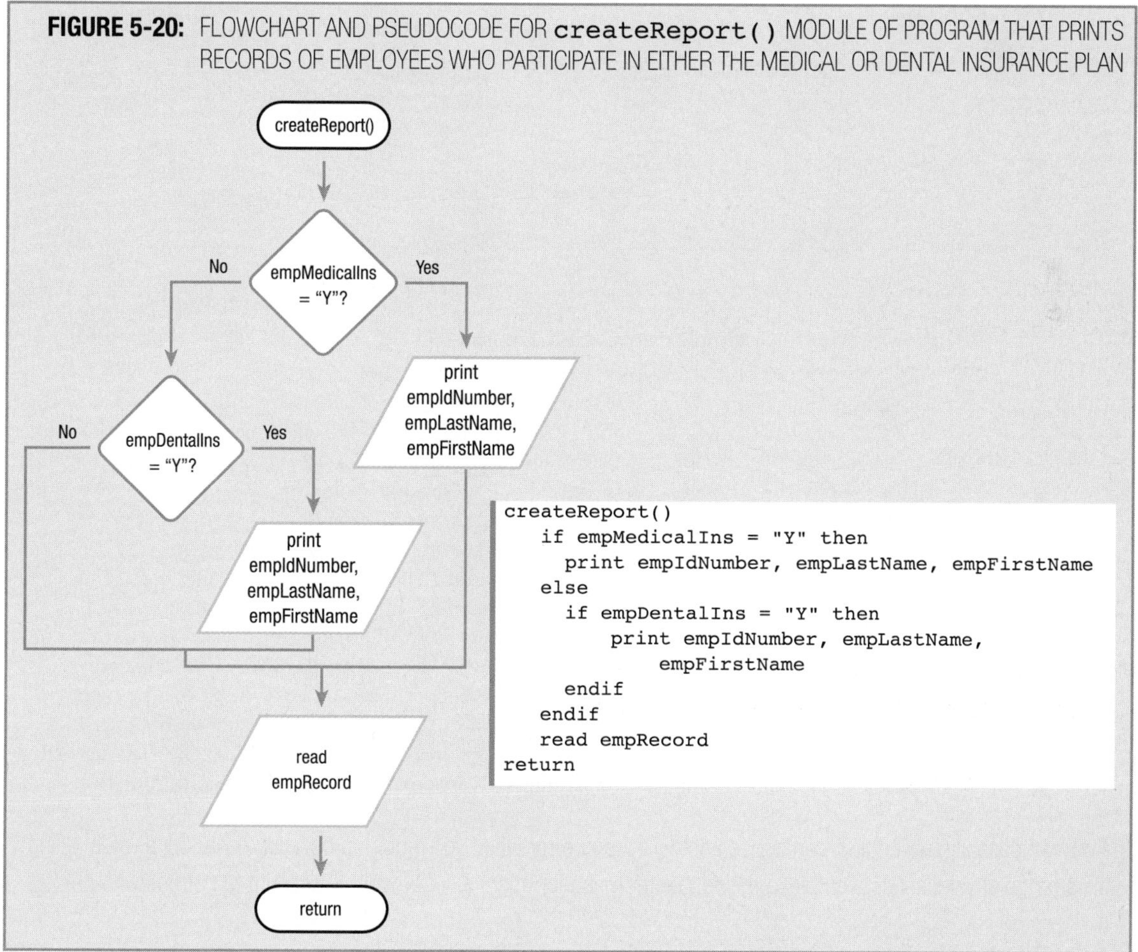


```
createReport()
   if empMedicalIns = "Y" then
     print empIdNumber, empLastName, empFirstName
   else
     if empDentalIns = "Y" then
         print empIdNumber, empLastName,
             empFirstName
     endif
   endif
   read empRecord
return
```

## AVOIDING COMMON ERRORS IN AN OR SELECTION

You might have noticed that the statement `print empIdNumber, empLastName, empFirstName` appears twice in the flowchart and in the pseudocode shown in Figure 5-20. The temptation is to redraw the flowchart in Figure 5-20 to look like Figure 5-21. Logically, you can argue that the flowchart in Figure 5-21 is correct because the correct employee records print. However, this flowchart is not allowed because it is not structured.

**FIGURE 5-21:** INCORRECT FLOWCHART FOR `createReport()` MODULE

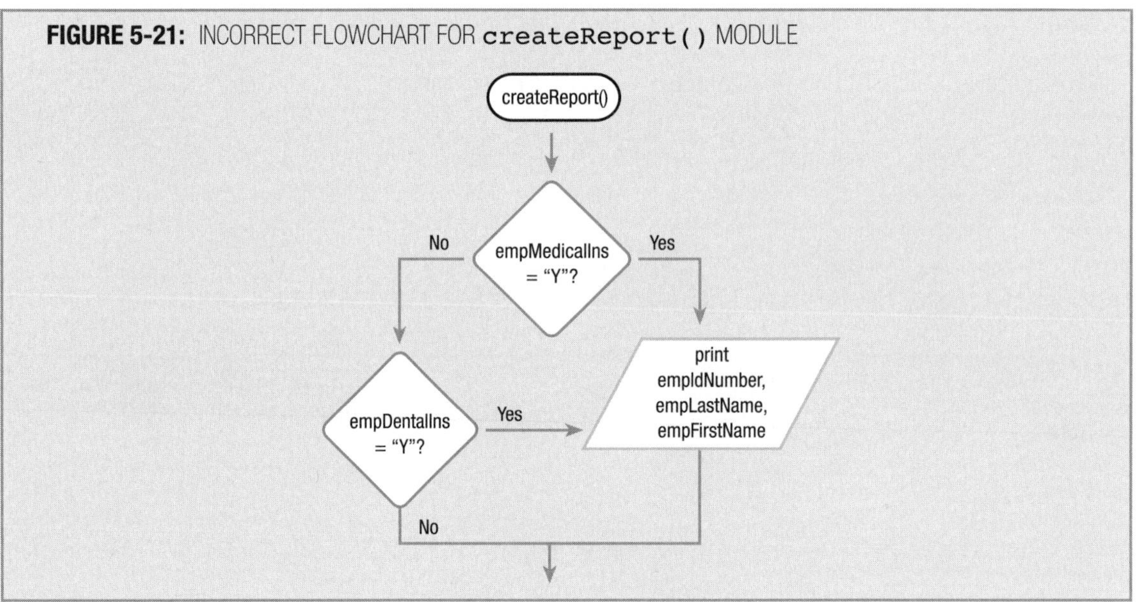


**TIP** If you do not see that Figure 5-21 is not structured, go back and review Chapter 2. In particular, review the example that begins at Figure 2-21.

**TIP** An additional source of error that is specific to the OR selection stems from a problem with language and the way people use it too casually. When your boss needs a report of all employees who carry medical or dental insurance, she is likely to say, "I need a report of all the people who have medical insurance and all those who have dental insurance." The request contains the word "and," and the report contains people who have one type of insurance "and" people who have another. However, the records you want to print are those from employees who have medical insurance OR dental insurance OR both. The logical situation requires an OR decision. Instead of saying "people who have medical insurance and people who have dental insurance," it would be clearer if your boss asked for "people who have medical or dental insurance." In other words, it would be more correct to put the question-joining "or" conjunction between the insurance types held by each person than between the people, but bosses and other human beings often do not speak like computers. As a programmer, you have the job of clarifying what really is being requested, and determining that often a request for A *and* B means a request for A *or* B.

The way we casually use English can cause another type of error when you require a decision based on a value falling within a range of values. For example, a movie theater manager might say, "Provide a discount to patrons who are under 13 years old and those who are over 64 years old; otherwise, charge the full price." Because the manager has used the word "and" in the request, you might be tempted to create the decision shown in Figure 5-22; however, this logic will not provide a discounted price for any movie patron. You must remember that every time the decision in Figure 5-22 is made, it is made using a single data record. If the age field in that record contains an age lower than 13, then it cannot possibly contain an age over 64. Similarly, if it contains an age over 64, then there is no way it can contain an age under that. Therefore, there is no value that could be stored in the age field of a movie patron record for which both parts of the AND question are true—and the price will never be set to the `discountPrice` for any record. Figure 5-23 shows the correct logic.

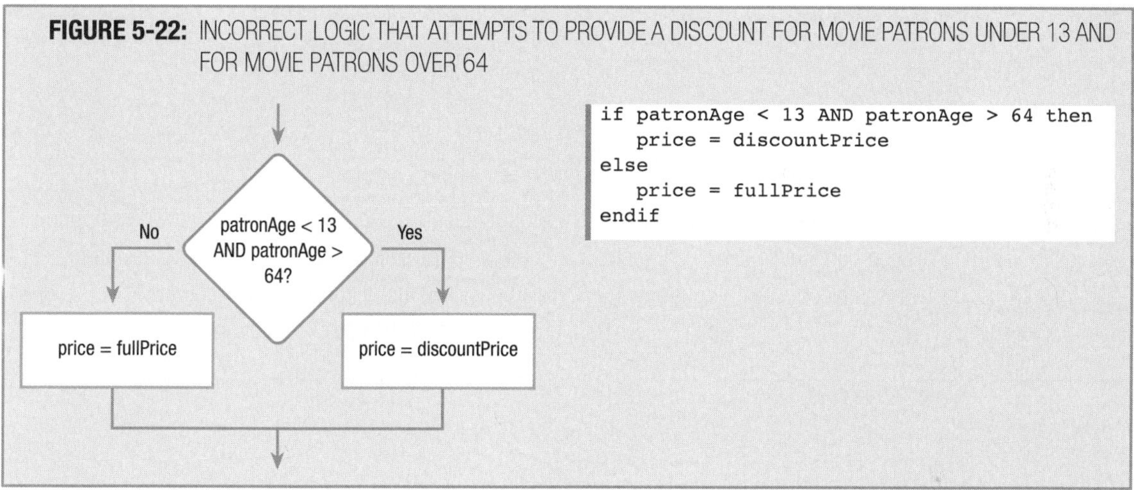
No
patronAge < 13
AND patronAge >
64?
Yes
price = fullPrice
price = discountPrice
if patronAge < 13 AND patronAge > 64 then
price = discountPrice
else
price = fullPrice
endif

**FIGURE 5-22:** INCORRECT LOGIC THAT ATTEMPTS TO PROVIDE A DISCOUNT FOR MOVIE PATRONS UNDER 13 AND FOR MOVIE PATRONS OVER 64

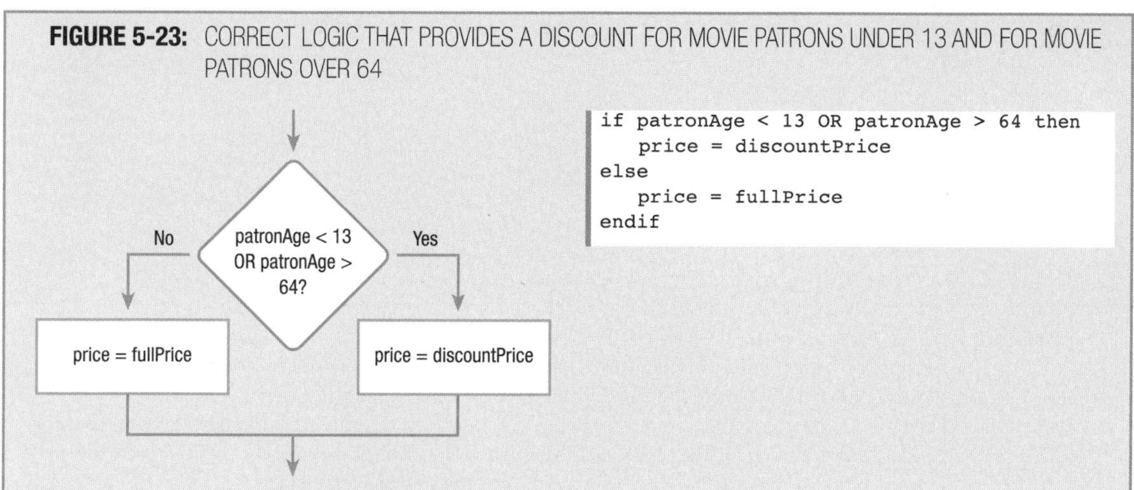
No
patronAge < 13
OR patronAge >
64?
Yes
price = fullPrice
price = discountPrice
if patronAge < 13 OR patronAge > 64 then
price = discountPrice
else
price = fullPrice
endif

**FIGURE 5-23:** CORRECT LOGIC THAT PROVIDES A DISCOUNT FOR MOVIE PATRONS UNDER 13 AND FOR MOVIE PATRONS OVER 64

A similar error can occur in your logic if the theater manager says something like, "Don't give a discount—that is, charge full price—if a patron is over 12 or under 65." Because the word "or" appears in the request, you might plan your logic like that shown in Figure 5-24.

**FIGURE 5-24:** INCORRECT LOGIC THAT ATTEMPTS TO CHARGE FULL PRICE FOR MOVIE PATRONS OVER 12 AND UNDER 65

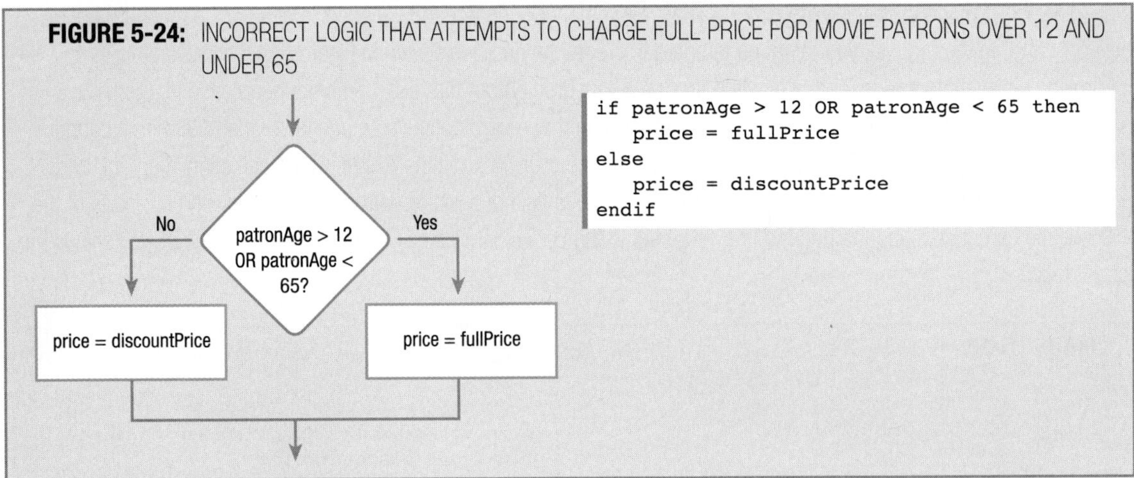
No
patronAge > 12
OR patronAge <
65?
Yes
price = discountPrice
price = fullPrice
if patronAge > 12 OR patronAge < 65 then
price = fullPrice
else
price = discountPrice
endif

As in Figure 5-22, in Figure 5-24, no patron ever receives a discount, because every patron is either over 12 or under 65. Remember, in an OR decision, only one of the conditions needs to be true in order for the entire expression to be evaluated as true. So, for example, because a patron who is 10 is under 65, the full price is charged, and because a patron who is 70 is over 12, the full price also is charged. Figure 5-25 shows the correct logic for this decision.

**FIGURE 5-25:** CORRECT LOGIC THAT CHARGES FULL PRICE FOR MOVIE PATRONS OVER 12 AND UNDER 65

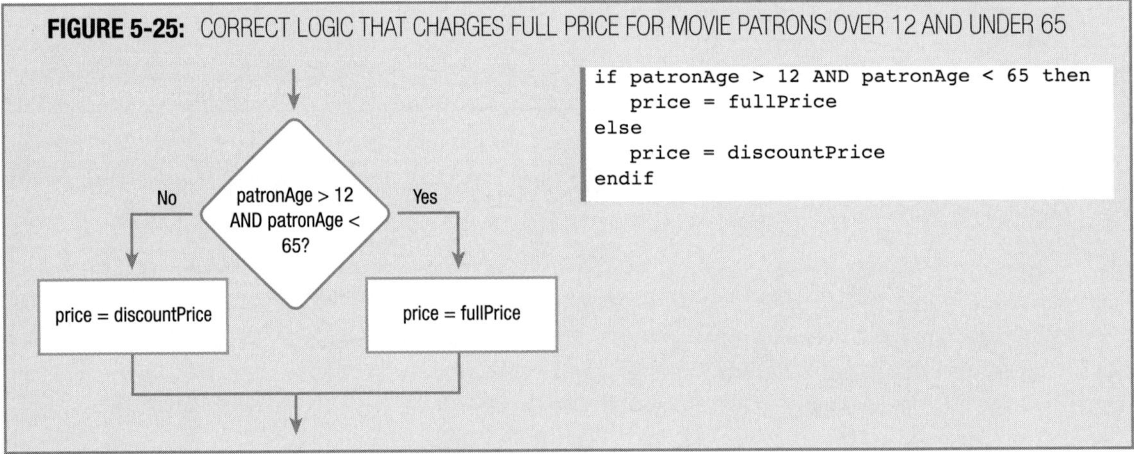
No
patronAge > 12
AND patronAge <
65?
Yes
price = discountPrice
price = fullPrice
if patronAge > 12 AND patronAge < 65 then
price = fullPrice
else
price = discountPrice
endif

**TIP**

Using an OR operator in a decision that involves multiple conditions does not eliminate your responsibility for determining which of the conditions to test first. Even when you use an OR operator, the computer makes decisions one at a time, and makes them in the order you ask them. If the first question in an OR expression evaluates to true, then the entire expression is true, and the second question will not even be tested.

## WRITING OR DECISIONS FOR EFFICIENCY

You can write a program that creates a report containing all employees who have either medical or dental insurance by using the `createReport()` method in either Figure 5-26 or Figure 5-27.

**FIGURE 5-26:** THE `createReport()` MODULE TO SELECT EMPLOYEES WITH MEDICAL OR DENTAL INSURANCE, USING MEDICAL DECISION FIRST

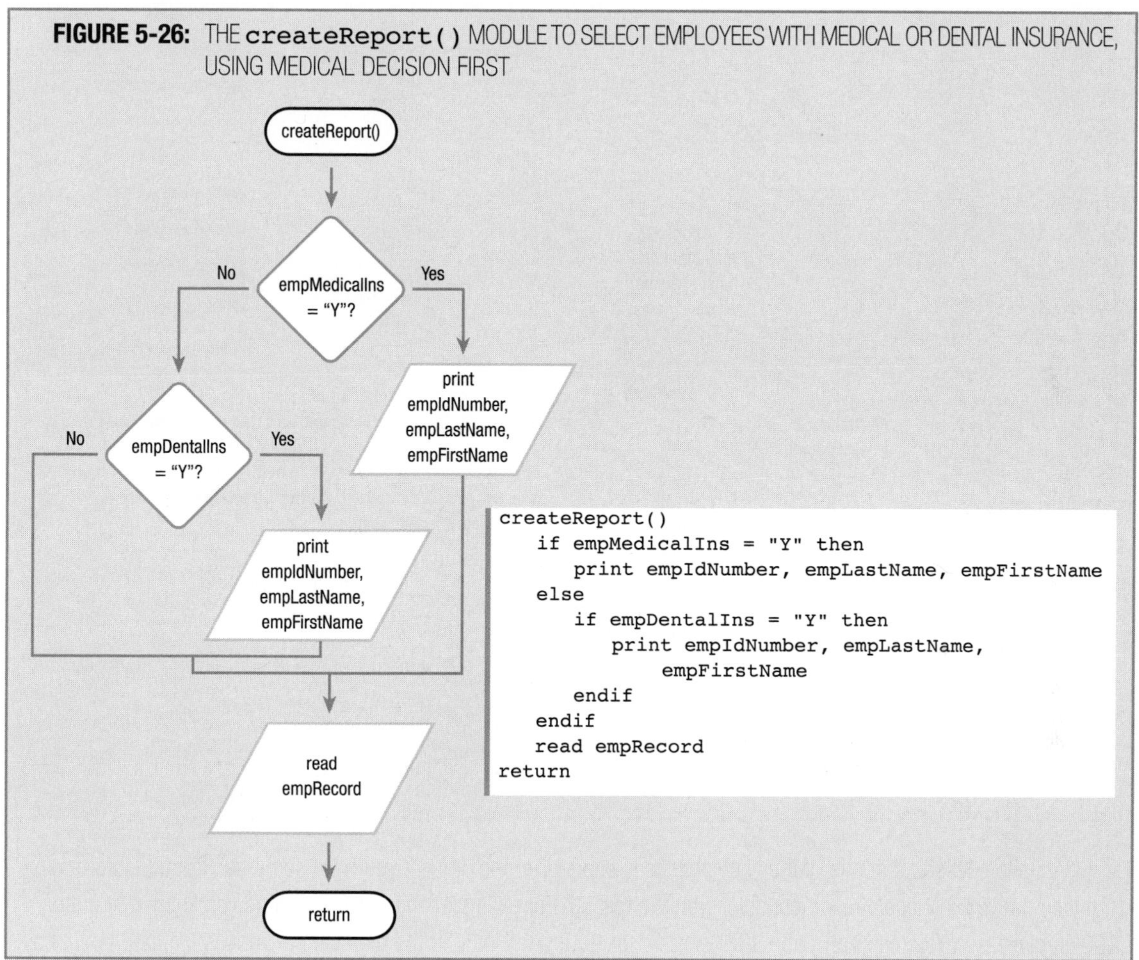


```
createReport()
   if empMedicalIns = "Y" then
      print empIdNumber, empLastName, empFirstName
   else
      if empDentalIns = "Y" then
         print empIdNumber, empLastName,
             empFirstName
      endif
   endif
   read empRecord
return
```

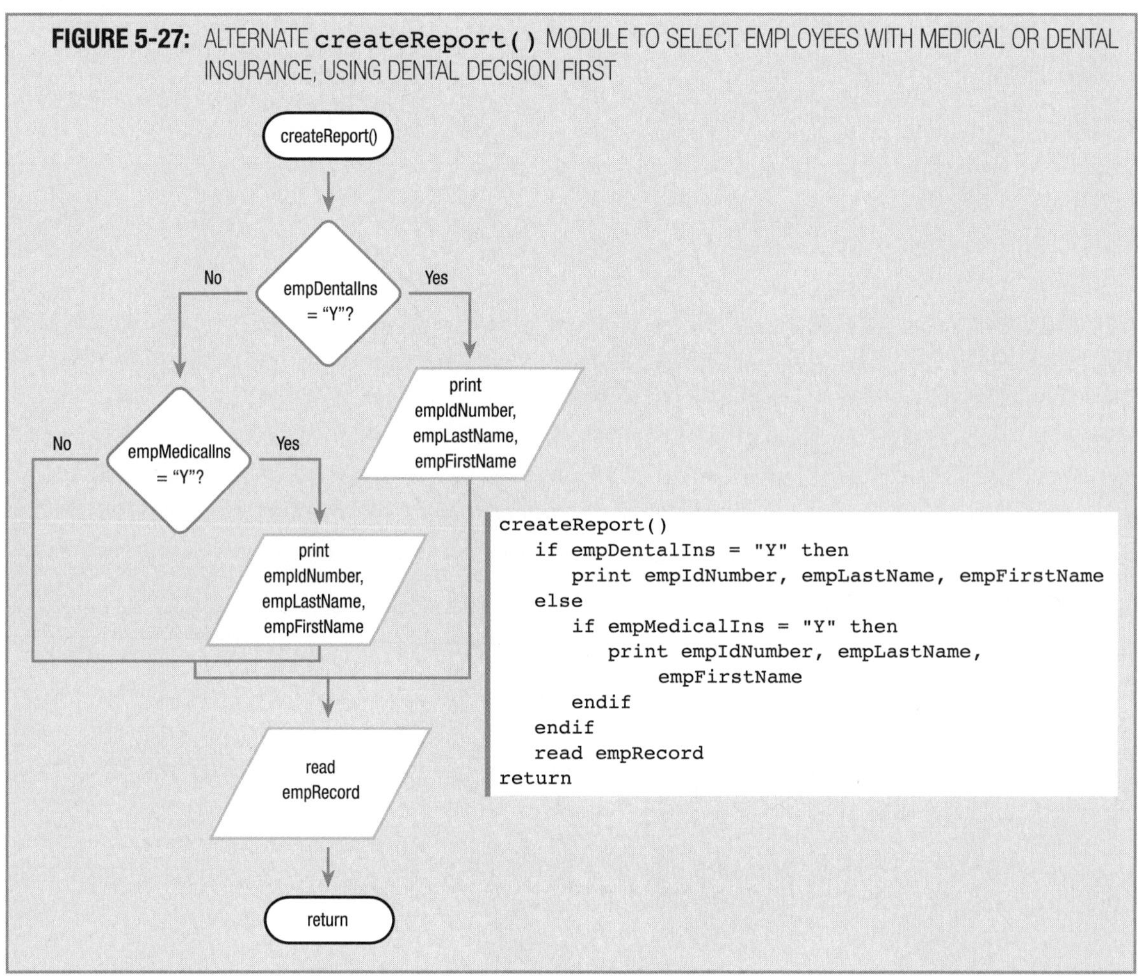


**FIGURE 5-27:** ALTERNATE `createReport()` MODULE TO SELECT EMPLOYEES WITH MEDICAL OR DENTAL INSURANCE, USING DENTAL DECISION FIRST

```
createReport()
   if empDentalIns = "Y" then
      print empIdNumber, empLastName, empFirstName
   else
      if empMedicalIns = "Y" then
         print empIdNumber, empLastName,
             empFirstName
      endif
   endif
   read empRecord
return
```

You might have guessed that one of these selections is superior to the other, if you have some background information about the relative likelihood of each condition you are testing. For example, once again assume you know that out of 1,000 employees in your company, about 90 percent, or 900, participate in the medical insurance plan, and about half, or 500, participate in the dental plan.

When you use the logic shown in Figure 5-26 to select employees who participate in either insurance plan, you first ask about medical insurance. For 900 employees, the answer is true; you print these employee records. Only about 100 records continue to the next question regarding dental insurance, where about half, or 50, fulfill the requirements to print. In the end, you print about 950 employees.

If you use Figure 5-27, you ask `empDentalIns = "Y"?` first. The result is true for 50 percent, or 500 employees, whose names then print. Five hundred employee records then progress to the medical insurance question, after which 90 percent, or 450, of them print.

Using either scenario, 950 employee records appear on the list, but the logic used in Figure 5-26 requires 1,100 decisions, whereas the logic used in Figure 5-27 requires 1,500 decisions. The general rule is: *In an OR decision, first ask the question that is more likely to be true.* Because a record qualifies for printing as soon as it passes one test, asking the more likely question first eliminates as many records as possible from having to go through the second decision. The time it takes to execute the program is decreased.

## COMBINING DECISIONS IN AN OR SELECTION

When you need to take action when either one or the other of two conditions is met, you can use two separate, nested selection structures, as in the previous examples. However, most programming languages allow you to ask two or more questions in a single comparison by using a **logical OR operator**—for example, `empDentalIns = "Y" OR empMedicalIns = "Y"`. When you use the logical OR operator, only one of the listed conditions must be met for the resulting action to take place. If the programming language you use allows this construct, you still must realize that the question you place first is the question that will be asked first, and cases eliminated by the first question will not proceed to the second question. The computer can ask only one question at a time; even when you draw the flowchart in Figure 5-28, the computer will execute the logic in the flowchart in Figure 5-29.

**TIP** C#, C++, C, and Java use the symbol || to represent the logical OR.

**FIGURE 5-28:** FLOWCHART AND PSEUDOCODE OF AN OR DECISION USING AN OR OPERATOR

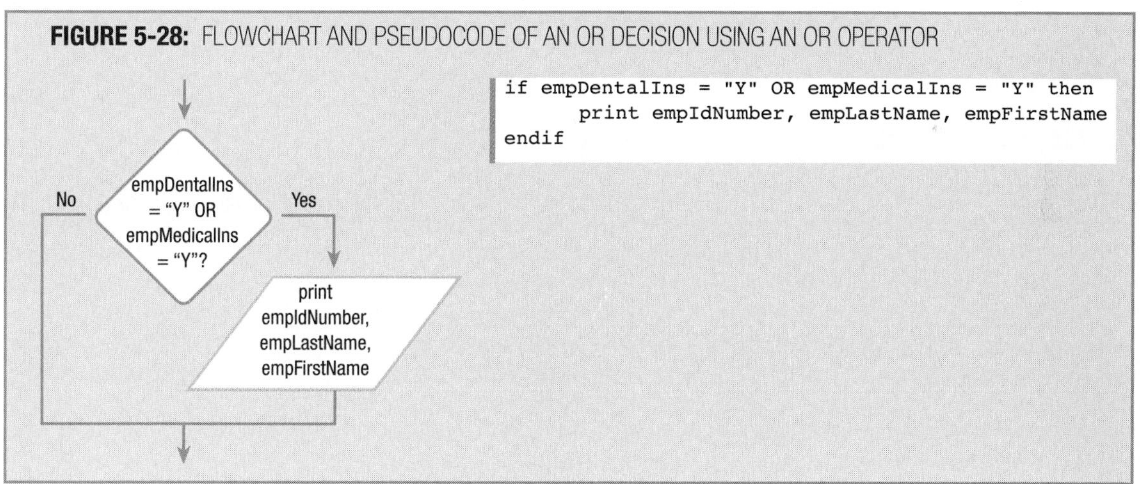


```
if empDentalIns = "Y" OR empMedicalIns = "Y" then
      print empIdNumber, empLastName, empFirstName
endif
```

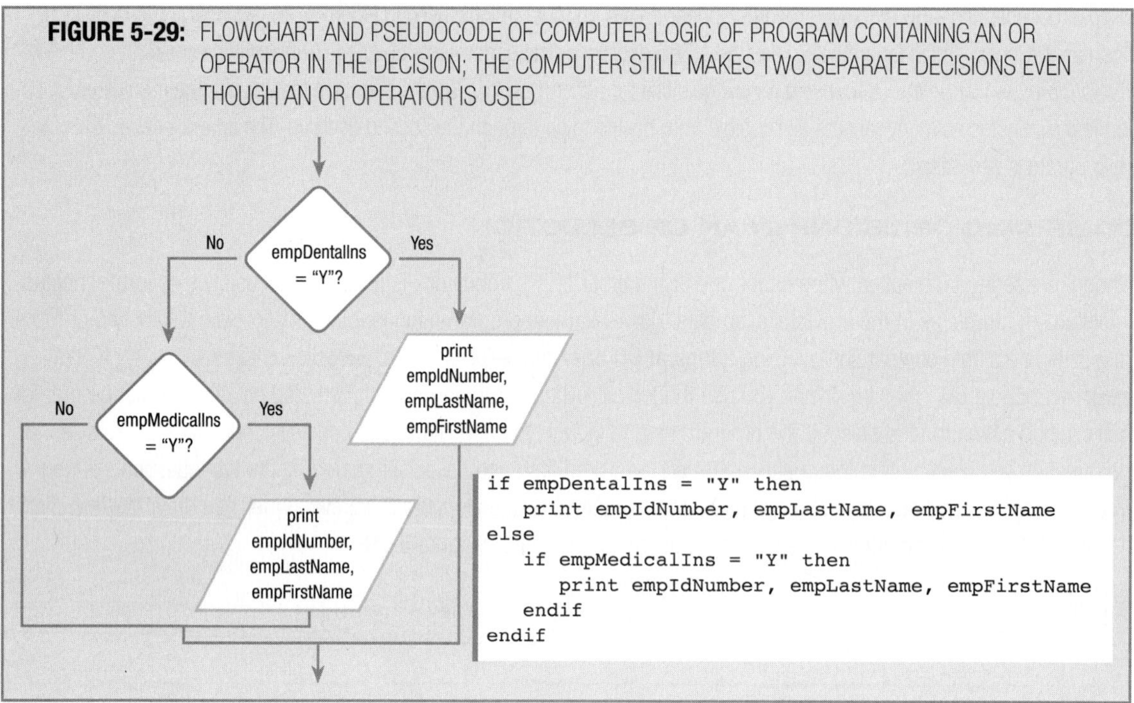
empDentalIns = "Y"?
No
Yes
print empIdNumber, empLastName, empFirstName
empMedicalIns = "Y"?
No
Yes
print empIdNumber, empLastName, empFirstName
if empDentalIns = "Y" then
   print empIdNumber, empLastName, empFirstName
else
   if empMedicalIns = "Y" then
      print empIdNumber, empLastName, empFirstName
   endif
endif

**FIGURE 5-29:** FLOWCHART AND PSEUDOCODE OF COMPUTER LOGIC OF PROGRAM CONTAINING AN OR OPERATOR IN THE DECISION; THE COMPUTER STILL MAKES TWO SEPARATE DECISIONS EVEN THOUGH AN OR OPERATOR IS USED

## USING SELECTIONS WITHIN RANGES

Business programs often need to make selections based on a variable falling within a range of values. For example, suppose you want to print a list of all employees and the names of their supervisors. An employee's supervisor is assigned according to the employee's department number, as shown in Figure 5-30.

**FIGURE 5-30:** SUPERVISORS BY DEPARTMENT

| DEPARTMENT NUMBER | SUPERVISOR |
|---|---|
| 1-3 | Dillon |
| 4–7 | Escher |
| 8–9 | Fontana |

When you write the program that reads each employee's record, you could make nine decisions before printing the supervisor's name, such as `empDept = 1?`, `empDept = 2?`, and so on. However, it is more convenient to find the supervisor by using a range check.

When you use a **range check**, you compare a variable to a series of values between limits. To perform a range check, make comparisons using either the lowest or highest value in each range of values you are using. For example, to find each employee's supervisor as listed in Figure 5-30, either use the values 1, 4, and 8, which represent the low ends of each supervisor's department range, or use the values 3, 7, and 9, which represent the high ends.

Figure 5-31 shows the flowchart and pseudocode that represent the logic for choosing a supervisor name by using the high-end range values. You test the `empDept` value for less than or equal to the high end of the lowest range group. If the comparison evaluates as true, you know the intended value of `supervisorName`. If not, you continue checking.

**FIGURE 5-31:** USING HIGH-END VALUES FOR A RANGE CHECK

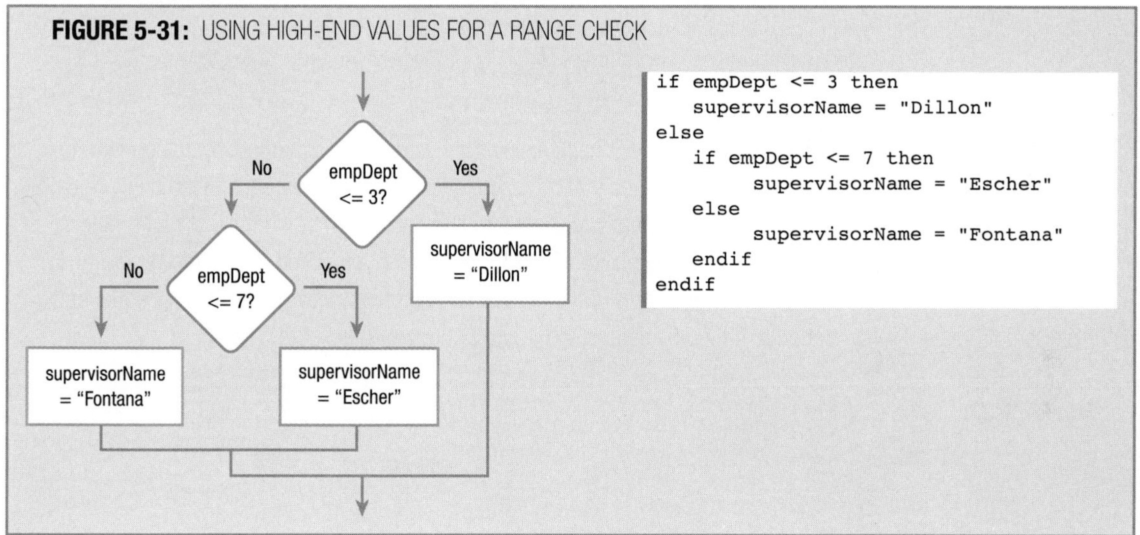


```
if empDept <= 3 then
   supervisorName = "Dillon"
else
   if empDept <= 7 then
        supervisorName = "Escher"
   else
        supervisorName = "Fontana"
   endif
endif
```

**TIP** In Figure 5-31, notice how each `else` aligns vertically with its corresponding `if`.

For example, consider records containing three different values for `empDept`, and compare how they would be handled by the set of decisions in Figure 5-31.

- First, assume that the value of `empDept` for a record is 2. Using the logic in Figure 5-31, the value of the Boolean expression `empDept <= 3` is true, `supervisorName` is set to "Dillon", and the `if` structure ends. In this case, the second decision, `empDept <= 7`, is never made, because the `else` half of `empDept <= 3` never executes.
- Next, assume that for another record, the value of `empDept` is 7. Then, `empDept <= 3` evaluates as false, so the `else` clause of the decision executes. There, `empDept <= 7` is evaluated, and found to be true, so `supervisorName` becomes "Escher".
- Finally, assume that the value of `empDept` is 9. In this case, the first decision, `empDept <= 3`, is false, so the `else` clause executes. Then, the second decision, `empDept <=7`, also evaluates as false, so the `else` clause of the second decision executes, and `supervisorName` is set to "Fontana". In this example, "Fontana" can be called a **default value**, because if neither of the two decision expressions is true, `supervisorName` becomes "Fontana" by default. A default value is the value assigned after a series of selections are all false.

TIP

Using the logic in Figure 5-31, `supervisorName` becomes "Fontana" even if `empDept` is a high, invalid value such as 10, 12, or even 300. The example is intended to be simple, using only two decisions. However, in a business application, you might consider amending the logic so an additional, third decision is made that compares `empDept` less than or equal to 9. Then, you could assign "Fontana" as the supervisor name if `empDept` is less than or equal to 9, and issue an error message if `empDept` is not. You might also want to insert a similar decision at the beginning of the program segment to make sure `empDept` is not less than 1.

The flowchart and pseudocode for choosing a supervisor name using the reverse of this method, by comparing the employee department to the low end of the range values that represent each supervisor's area, appear in Figure 5-32. Using the technique shown in Figure 5-32, you compare **`empDept`** to the low end (8) of the highest range (8 to 9) first; if **`empDept`** falls in the range, **`supervisorName`** is known; otherwise, you check the next lower group. In this example, "Dillon" becomes the default value. That is, if the department number is not greater than or equal to 8, and it is also not greater than or equal to 4, then by default, **`supervisorName`** is set to "Dillon".

**FIGURE 5-32:** USING LOW-END VALUES OF RANGES TO DETERMINE EMPLOYEE'S SUPERVISOR

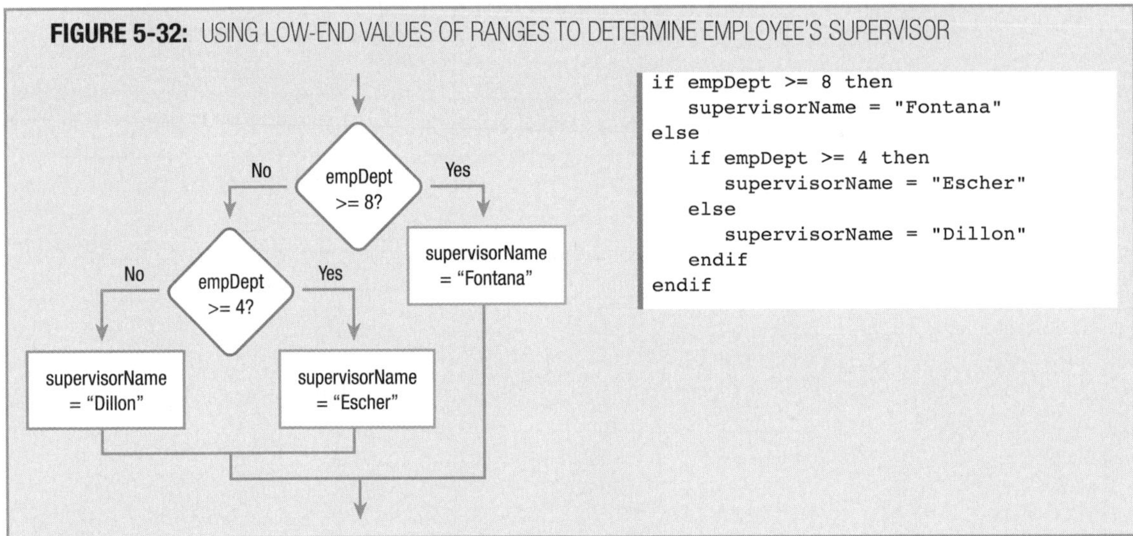


```
if empDept >= 8 then
   supervisorName = "Fontana"
else
   if empDept >= 4 then
      supervisorName = "Escher"
   else
      supervisorName = "Dillon"
   endif
endif
```

## COMMON ERRORS USING RANGE CHECKS

Two common errors that occur when programmers perform range checks both entail doing more work than is necessary. Figure 5-33 shows a range check in which the programmer has asked one question too many. If you know that all **`empDept`** values are positive numbers, then if **`empDept`** is not greater than or equal to 8, and it is also not greater than or equal to 4, then by default it must be greater than or equal to 1. Asking whether **`empDept`** is greater than or equal to 1 is a waste of time; no employee record can ever travel the logical path on the far left. You might say that the path that can never be traveled is a **dead** or **unreachable path**, and that the statements written there constitute dead or unreachable code. Providing such a path is always a logical error.

**FIGURE 5-33:** INEFFICIENT RANGE SELECTION INCLUDING UNREACHABLE PATH

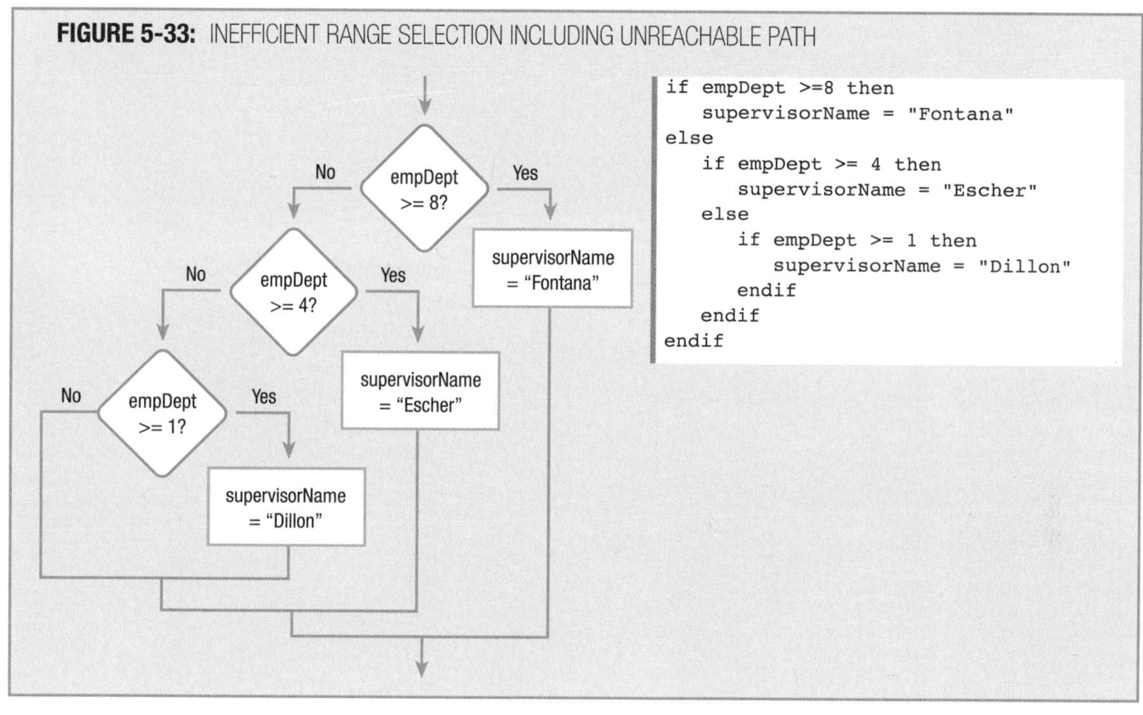


```
if empDept >=8 then
   supervisorName = "Fontana"
else
   if empDept >= 4 then
      supervisorName = "Escher"
   else
      if empDept >= 1 then
         supervisorName = "Dillon"
      endif
   endif
endif
```

**TIP** When you ask questions of human beings, you sometimes ask a question to which you already know the answer. For example, in court, a good trial lawyer seldom asks a question if the answer will be a surprise. With computer logic, however, such questions are an inefficient waste of time.

Another error that programmers make when writing the logic to perform a range check also involves asking unnecessary questions. You should never ask a question if there is only one possible answer or outcome. Figure 5-34 shows an inefficient range selection that asks two unneeded questions. In the figure, if `empDept` is greater than or equal to 8, "Fontana" is the supervisor. If `empDept` is not greater than or equal to 8, then it must be less than 8, so the next question does not have to check for less than 8. The computer logic will never execute the second decision unless `empDept` is already less than 8—that is, unless it follows the false branch of the first selection. If you use the logic in Figure 5-34, you are wasting computer time asking a question that has previously been answered. Similarly, if `empDept` is not greater than or equal to 8 and it is also not greater than or equal to 4, then it must be less than 4. Therefore, there is no reason to compare `empDept` to 4 to determine whether "Dillon" is the supervisor. If the logic makes it past the first two `if` statements in Figure 5-34, then the supervisor must be "Dillon".

**FIGURE 5-34:** INEFFICIENT RANGE SELECTION INCLUDING UNNECESSARY QUESTION

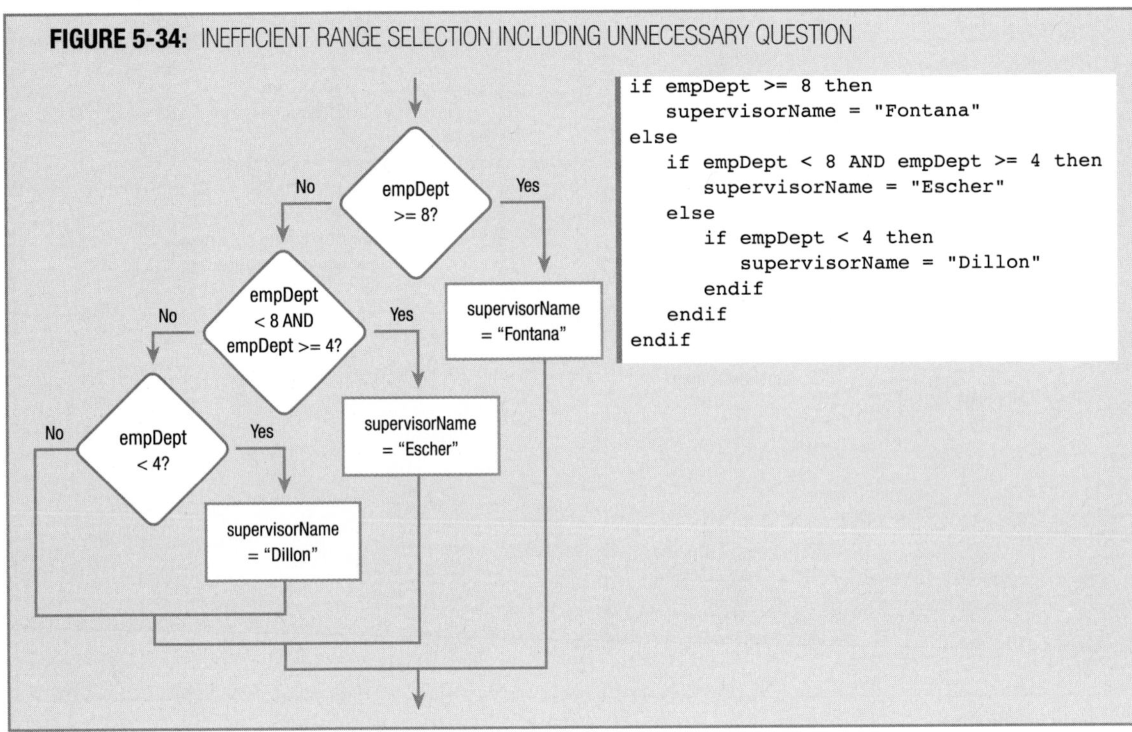


```
if empDept >= 8 then
   supervisorName = "Fontana"
else
   if empDept < 8 AND empDept >= 4 then
      supervisorName = "Escher"
   else
      if empDept < 4 then
         supervisorName = "Dillon"
      endif
   endif
endif
```

**TIP** Beginning programmers sometimes justify their use of unnecessary questions as "just making really sure." Such caution is unnecessary when writing computer logic.

## UNDERSTANDING PRECEDENCE WHEN COMBINING AND AND OR SELECTIONS

Most programming languages allow you to combine as many AND and OR operators in an expression as you need. For example, assume you need to achieve a score of at least 75 on each of three tests in order to pass a course. When multiple conditions must be true before performing an action, you can use an expression like the following:

```
if score1 >= 75 AND score2 >= 75 AND score3 >= 75 then
   classGrade = "Pass"
else
   classGrade = "Fail"
endif
```

On the other hand, if you need to pass only one test in order to pass the course, then the logic is as follows:

```
if score1 >= 75 OR score2 >= 75 OR score3 >= 75 then
   classGrade = "Pass"
else
   classGrade = "Fail"
endif
```

The logic becomes more complicated when you combine AND and OR operators within the same statement. When you combine AND and OR operators, the AND operators take **precedence**, meaning their Boolean values are evaluated first.

For example, consider a program that determines whether a movie theater patron can purchase a discounted ticket. Assume discounts are allowed for children (age 12 and under) and senior citizens (age 65 and older) who attend "G"-rated movies. The following code looks reasonable, but produces incorrect results, because the AND operator evaluates before the OR.

```
if age <= 12 OR age >= 65 AND rating = "G" then
  print "Discount applies"
```

For example, assume a movie patron is 10 years old and the movie rating is "R". The patron should not receive a discount—or be allowed to see the movie! However, within the previous `if` statement, the part of the expression containing the AND, `age >= 65 AND rating = "G"`, evaluates first. For a 10-year-old and an "R"-rated movie, the question is false (on both counts), so the entire `if` statement becomes the equivalent of the following:

```
if age <= 12 OR aFalseExpression
```

Because the patron is 10, `age <= 12` is true, so the original `if` statement becomes the equivalent of:

```
if aTrueExpression OR aFalseExpression
```

which evaluates as true. Therefore, the statement "Discount applies" prints when it should not.

Many programming languages allow you to use parentheses to correct the logic and force the expression `age <= 12 OR age >= 65` to evaluate first, as shown in the following pseudocode:

```
if (age <= 12 OR age >= 65) AND rating = "G" then
   print "Discount applies"
```

With the added parentheses, if the patron's age is 12 or under OR 65 or over, the expression is evaluated as:

```
if aTrueExpression AND rating = "G"
```

When the age value qualifies a patron for a discount, then the rating value must also be acceptable before the discount applies. This was the original intention of the statement.

You always can avoid the confusion of mixing AND and OR decisions by nesting `if` statements instead of using ANDs and ORs. With the flowchart and pseudocode shown in Figure 5-35, it is clear which movie patrons receive the discount. In the flowchart in the figure, you can see that the OR is nested entirely within the Yes branch of the `rating = "G"?` selection. Similarly, by examining the pseudocode in Figure 5-35, you can see by the alignment that if the rating is not "G", the logic proceeds directly to the last `endif` statement, bypassing any checking of the age at all.

**FIGURE 5-35:** NESTED `if` LOGIC THAT DETERMINES MOVIE PATRON DISCOUNTS

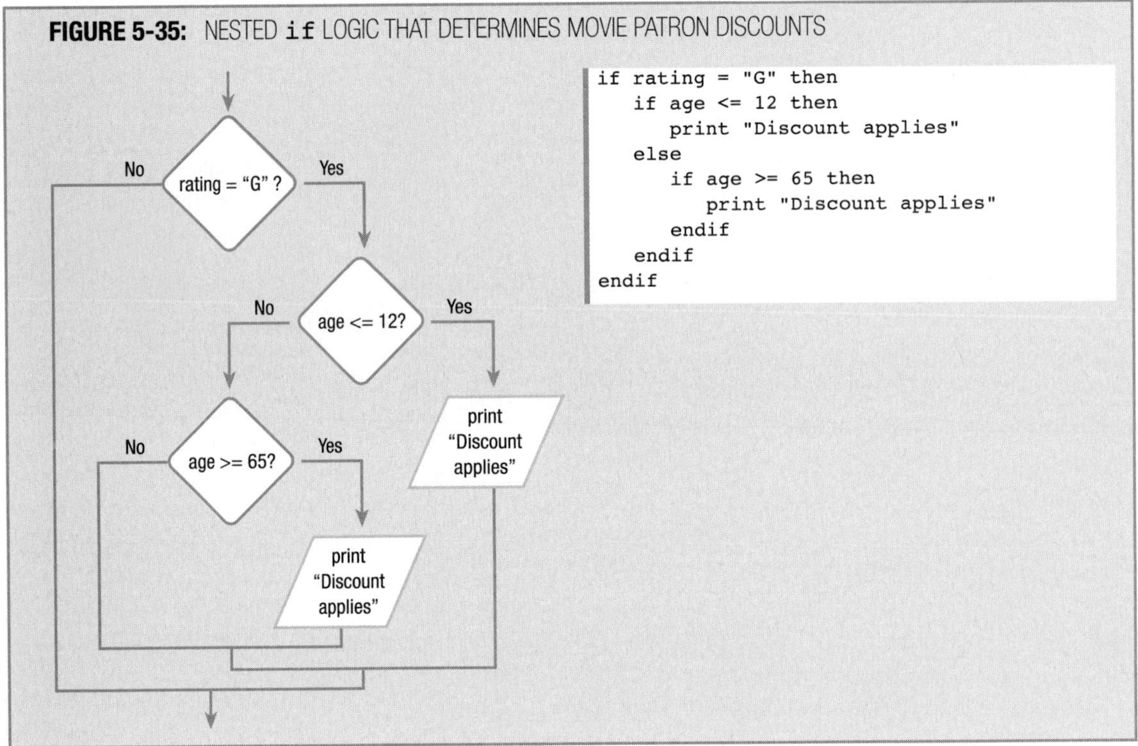


```
if rating = "G" then
   if age <= 12 then
      print "Discount applies"
   else
      if age >= 65 then
         print "Discount applies"
      endif
   endif
endif
```

**TIP**

In every programming language, multiplication has precedence over addition in an arithmetic statement. That is, the value of 2 + 3 * 4 is 14 because the multiplication occurs before the addition. Similarly, in every programming language, AND has precedence over OR. That's because computer circuitry treats the AND operator as multiplication and the OR operator as addition. In every programming language, 1 represents true and 0 represents false. So, for example, `aTrueExpression` AND `aTrueExpression` results in true, because 1 * 1 is 1, and `aTrueExpression` AND `aFalseExpression` is false, because 1 * 0 is 0. Similarly, `aFalseExpression` OR `aFalseExpression` AND `aTrueExpression` evaluates to `aFalseExpression` because 0 + 0 * 1 is 0, whereas `aFalseExpression` AND `aFalseExpression` OR `aTrueExpression` evaluates to `aTrueExpression` because 0 * 0 + 1 is 1.

## UNDERSTANDING THE CASE STRUCTURE

When you have a series of decisions based on the value stored in a single variable, most languages allow you to use a case structure. You first learned about the case structure in Chapter 2. There, you learned that you can solve any programming problem using only the three basic structures—sequence, selection, and loop. You are never required to use a case structure—you can always substitute a series of nested selections. The **case structure** simply provides a convenient alternative to using a series of decisions when you must make choices based on the value stored in a single variable.

**TIP** In some languages, the case structure is called the switch statement.

For example, suppose you work for a real estate developer who is selling houses that have one of three different floor plans. The logic segment of a program that determines the base price of the house might look like the logic shown in Figure 5-36.

**FIGURE 5-36:** FLOWCHART AND PSEUDOCODE DETERMINING HOUSE MODEL PRICE USING `if`S

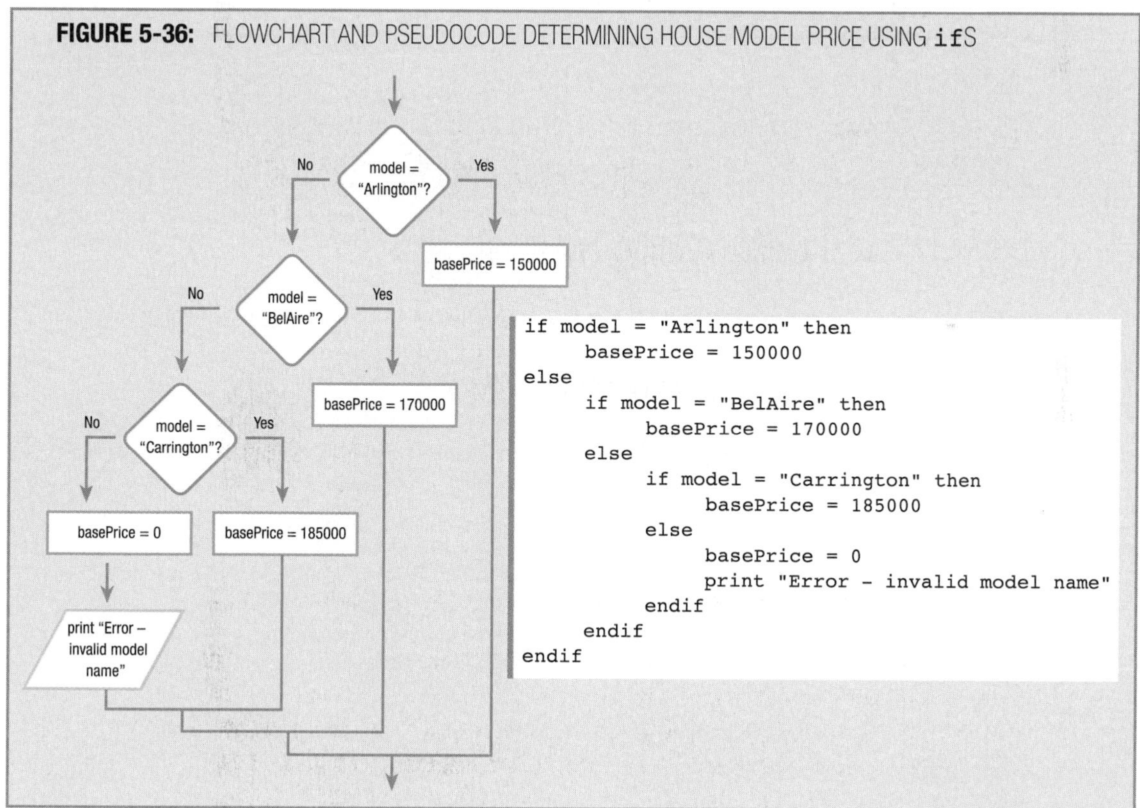


```
if model = "Arlington" then
     basePrice = 150000
else
     if model = "BelAire" then
          basePrice = 170000
     else
          if model = "Carrington" then
               basePrice = 185000
          else
               basePrice = 0
               print "Error - invalid model name"
          endif
     endif
endif
```

The logic shown in Figure 5-36 is completely structured. However, rewriting the logic using a case structure, as shown in Figure 5-37, might make it easier to understand. When using the case structure, you test a variable against a series of values, taking appropriate action based on the variable's value.

**FIGURE 5-37:** FLOWCHART AND PSEUDOCODE DETERMINING HOUSE MODEL PRICE USING THE CASE STRUCTURE

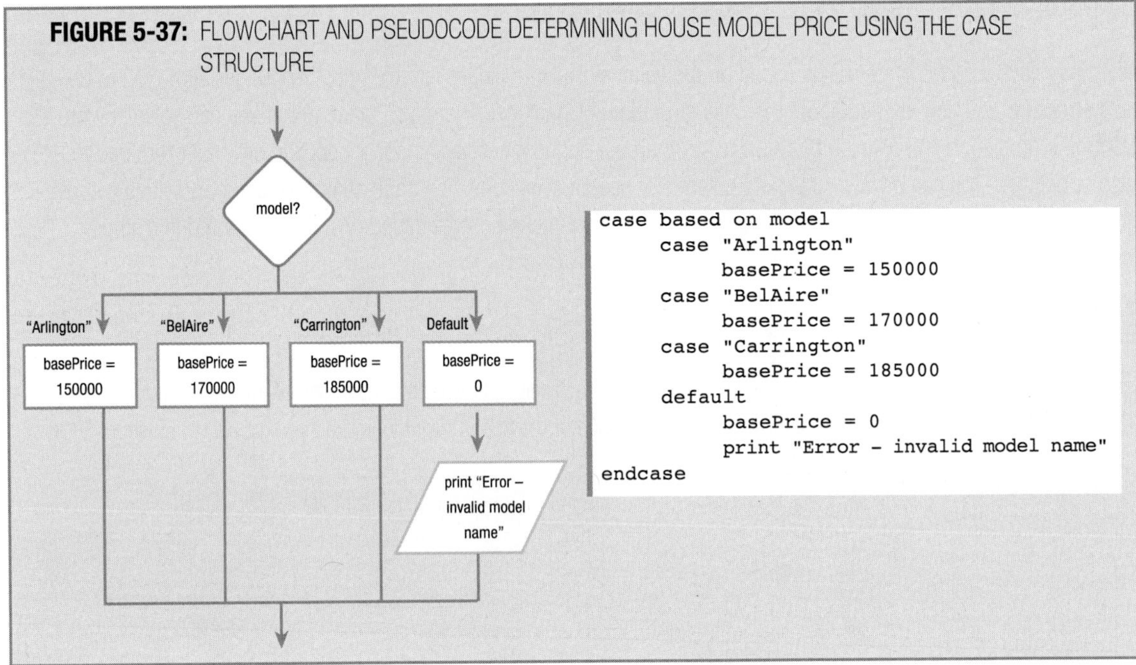


```
case based on model
     case "Arlington"
          basePrice = 150000
     case "BelAire"
          basePrice = 170000
     case "Carrington"
          basePrice = 185000
     default
          basePrice = 0
          print "Error - invalid model name"
endcase
```

In Figure 5-37, the `model` variable is compared in turn with "Arlington", "BelAire", and "Carrington", and an appropriate `basePrice` value is set. The default case is the case that executes in the event no other cases execute. The logic shown in Figure 5-36 is identical to that shown in Figure 5-37; your choice of method to set the housing model prices is entirely a matter of preference.

**TIP** When you look at a nested if-else structure containing an outer and inner selection, if the inner nested `if` is within the `if` portion of the outer `if`, the program segment is a candidate for AND logic. On the other hand, if the inner `if` is within the `else` portion of the outer `if`, the program segment might be a candidate for the case structure.

**TIP** Some languages require a break statement at the end of each case selection segment. In those languages, once a case is true, all the following cases execute until a break statement is encountered. When you study a specific programming language, you will learn how to use break statements if they are required in that language.

## USING DECISION TABLES

Some programs require multiple decisions to produce the correct output. Managing all possible outcomes of multiple decisions can be a difficult task, so programmers sometimes use a tool called a decision table to help organize the possible decision outcome combinations.

A **decision table** is a problem-analysis tool that consists of four parts:

- Conditions
- Possible combinations of Boolean values for the conditions
- Possible actions based on the conditions
- The specific action that corresponds to each Boolean value of each condition

For example, suppose a college collects input data like that shown in Figure 5-38. Each student's data record includes the student's age and a variable that indicates whether the student has requested a residence hall that enforces quiet study hours.

**FIGURE 5-38:** STUDENT RESIDENCE FILE DESCRIPTION

```
STUDENT RESIDENCE FILE DESCRIPTION
File Name: STURESFILE
FIELD DESCRIPTION        DATA TYPE     COMMENTS
ID Number                Numeric       4 digits, 0 decimal places
Last Name                Character     15 characters
First Name               Character     15 characters
Age                      Numeric       0 decimal places
Request for Hall         Character     1 character, Y or N
  with Quiet Hours
```

Assume that the residence hall director makes residence hall assignments based on the following rules:

- Students who are under 21 years old and who request a residence hall with quiet study hours are assigned to Addams Hall.
- Students who are under 21 years old and who do not request a residence hall with quiet study hours are assigned to Grant Hall.
- Students who are 21 years old and over and who request a residence hall with quiet study hours are assigned to Lincoln Hall.
- Students who are 21 years old and over and who do not request a residence hall with quiet study hours are also assigned to Lincoln Hall.

You can create a program that assigns each student to the appropriate residence hall and prints a list of students along with each student's hall assignment. A sample report is shown in Figure 5-39. The mainline logic for this program appears in Figure 5-40. Most programs you write will contain the same basic mainline logic: Each performs start-up or housekeeping tasks, a main loop that acts repeatedly—once for each input record—and a finishing module that performs any necessary program-ending tasks, including closing the open files.

FIGURE 5-39: SAMPLE REPORT LISTING STUDENT RESIDENCE HALL ASSIGNMENTS

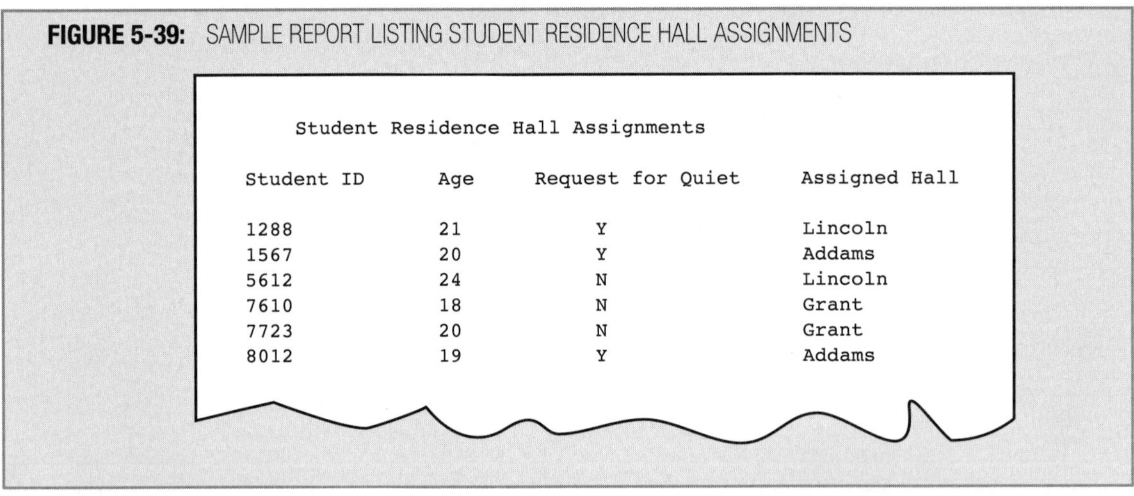

Student Residence Hall Assignments

| Student ID | Age | Request for Quiet | Assigned Hall |
|---|---|---|---|
| 1288 | 21 | Y | Lincoln |
| 1567 | 20 | Y | Addams |
| 5612 | 24 | N | Lincoln |
| 7610 | 18 | N | Grant |
| 7723 | 20 | N | Grant |
| 8012 | 19 | Y | Addams |

FIGURE 5-40: FLOWCHART AND PSEUDOCODE OF MAINLINE LOGIC FOR STUDENT RESIDENCE HALL ASSIGNMENTS REPORT

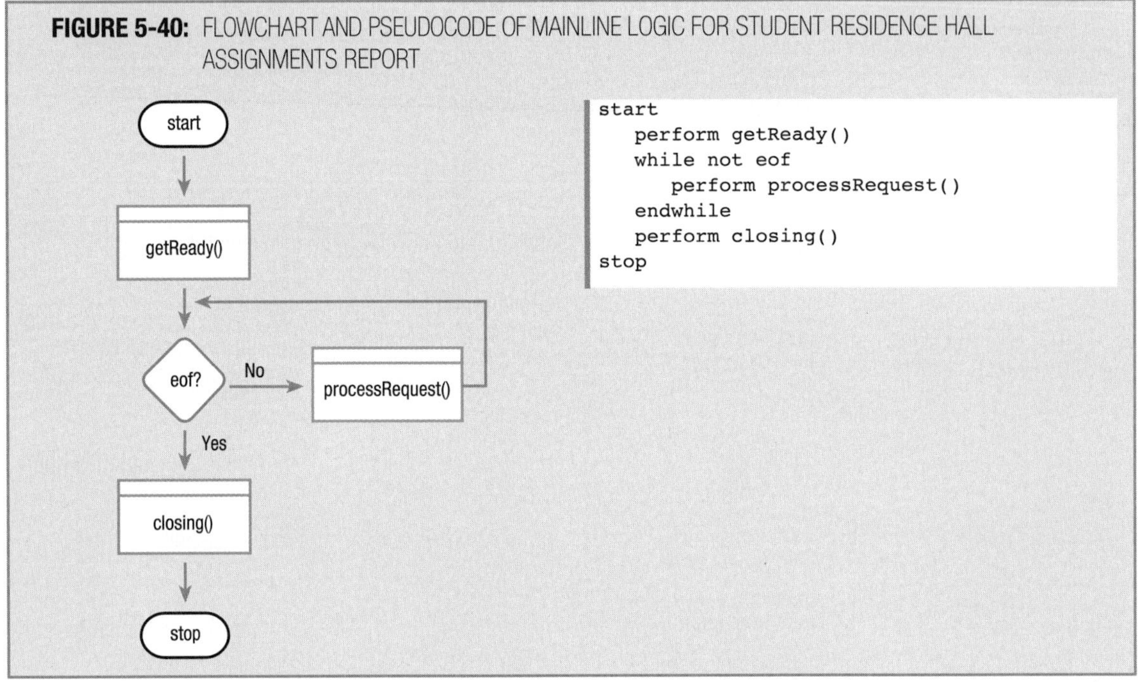


```
start
   perform getReady()
   while not eof
      perform processRequest()
   endwhile
   perform closing()
stop
```

The `getReady()` module for the program that produces the residence hall report is shown in Figure 5-41. It declares variables, opens the files, prints the report headings, and reads the first data record into memory.

**FIGURE 5-41:** FLOWCHART AND PSEUDOCODE OF **`getReady()`** MODULE FOR STUDENT RESIDENCE HALL ASSIGNMENTS REPORT

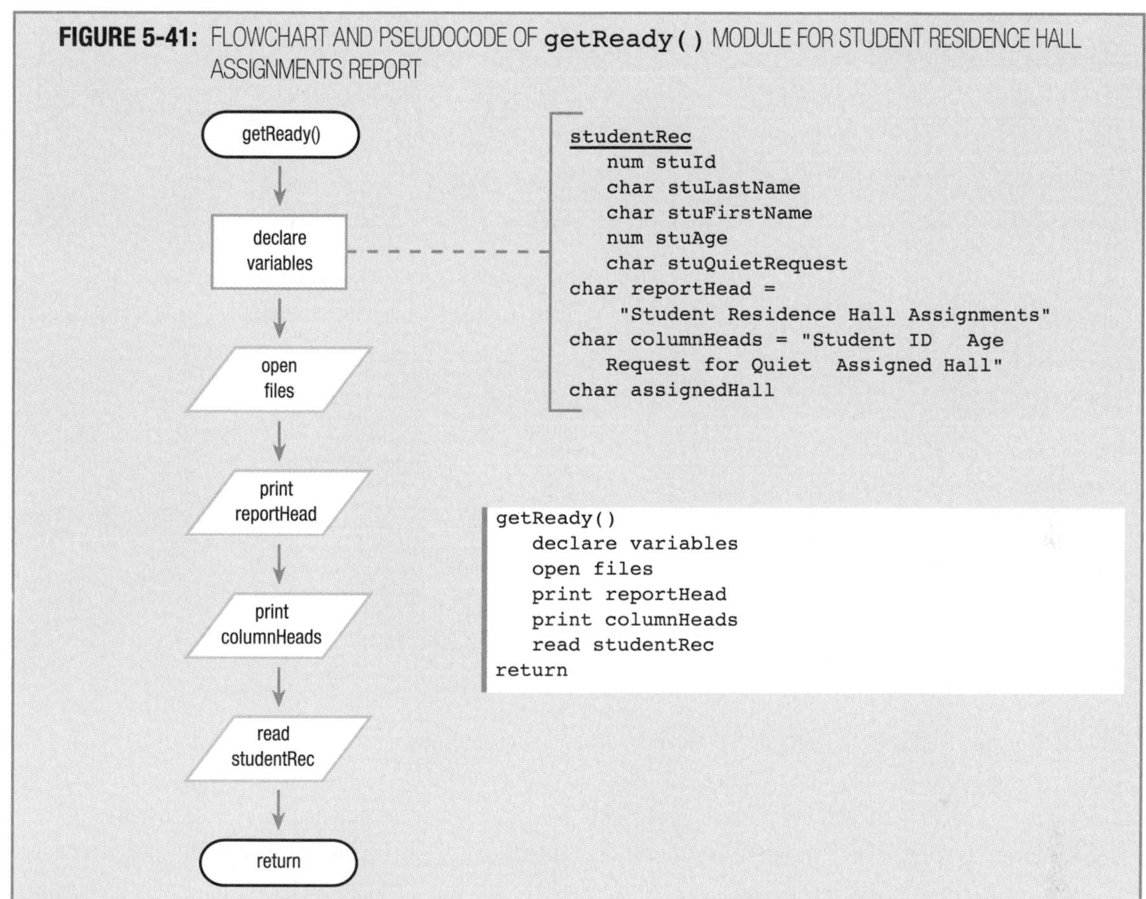


```
studentRec
   num stuId
   char stuLastName
   char stuFirstName
   num stuAge
   char stuQuietRequest
char reportHead =
    "Student Residence Hall Assignments"
char columnHeads = "Student ID   Age
   Request for Quiet  Assigned Hall"
char assignedHall
```

```
getReady()
   declare variables
   open files
   print reportHead
   print columnHeads
   read studentRec
return
```

Before you draw a flowchart or write the pseudocode for the `processRequest()` module, you can create a decision table to help you manage all the decisions. You can begin to create a decision table by listing all possible conditions. They are:

- `stuAge < 21`, or not
- `stuQuietRequest = "Y"`, or not

Next, determine how many possible Boolean value combinations exist for the conditions. In this case, there are four possible combinations, shown in Figure 5-42. A student can be under 21, request a residence hall with quiet hours, both, or neither. Because each condition has two outcomes and there are two conditions, there are 2 * 2, or four, possibilities. Three conditions would produce eight possible outcome combinations (2 * 2 * 2); four conditions would produce 16 possible outcome combinations (2 * 2 * 2 * 2), and so on.

**FIGURE 5-42:** POSSIBLE OUTCOMES OF RESIDENCE HALL REQUEST CONDITIONS

| Condition | Outcome | | | |
|---|---|---|---|---|
| stuAge < 21 | T | T | F | F |
| stuQuietRequest = "Y" | T | F | T | F |

Next, add rows to the decision table to list the possible outcome actions. A student might be assigned to Addams, Grant, or Lincoln Hall. Figure 5-43 shows an expanded decision table that includes these three possible outcomes.

**FIGURE 5-43:** DECISION TABLE INCLUDING POSSIBLE OUTCOMES OF RESIDENCE HALL DECISIONS

| Condition | Outcome | | | |
|---|---|---|---|---|
| stuAge < 21 | T | T | F | F |
| stuQuietRequest = "Y" | T | F | T | F |
| assignedHall = "Addams" | | | | |
| assignedHall = "Grant" | | | | |
| assignedHall = "Lincoln" | | | | |

You choose one required outcome for each possible combination of conditions. As shown in Figure 5-44, you place an X in the Addams Hall row when **stuAge** is less than 21 and the student requests a residence hall with quiet study hours. You place an X in the Grant Hall row when a student is under 21 but does not request a residence hall with quiet hours. Finally, you place Xs in the Lincoln Hall row for both **stuQuietRequest** values when a student is not under 21 years old—only one residence hall is available for students 21 and over, whether they have requested a hall with quiet hours or not.

**FIGURE 5-44:** COMPLETED DECISION TABLE FOR RESIDENCE HALL SELECTION

| Condition | Outcome | | | |
|---|---|---|---|---|
| stuAge < 21 | T | T | F | F |
| stuQuietRequest = "Y" | T | F | T | F |
| assignedHall = "Addams" | X | | | |
| assignedHall = "Grant" | | X | | |
| assignedHall = "Lincoln" | | | X | X |

The decision table is complete (count the Xs—there are four possible outcomes). Take a moment and confirm that each residence hall selection is the appropriate value based on the original specifications. Now that the decision table is complete, you can start to plan the logic.

If you choose to use a flowchart to express the logic, you start by drawing a path to the outcome shown in the first column. This result (which occurs when `stuAge < 21` and `stuQuietRequest = "Y"`) sets the residence hall to "Addams". Next, add the resulting action shown in the second column of the decision table, which occurs when `stuAge < 21` is true and `stuQuietRequest = "Y"` is false. In those cases, the residence hall becomes "Grant". See Figure 5-45.

**FIGURE 5-45:** PARTIALLY COMPLETED FLOWCHART SEGMENT FOR RESIDENCE HALL SELECTION

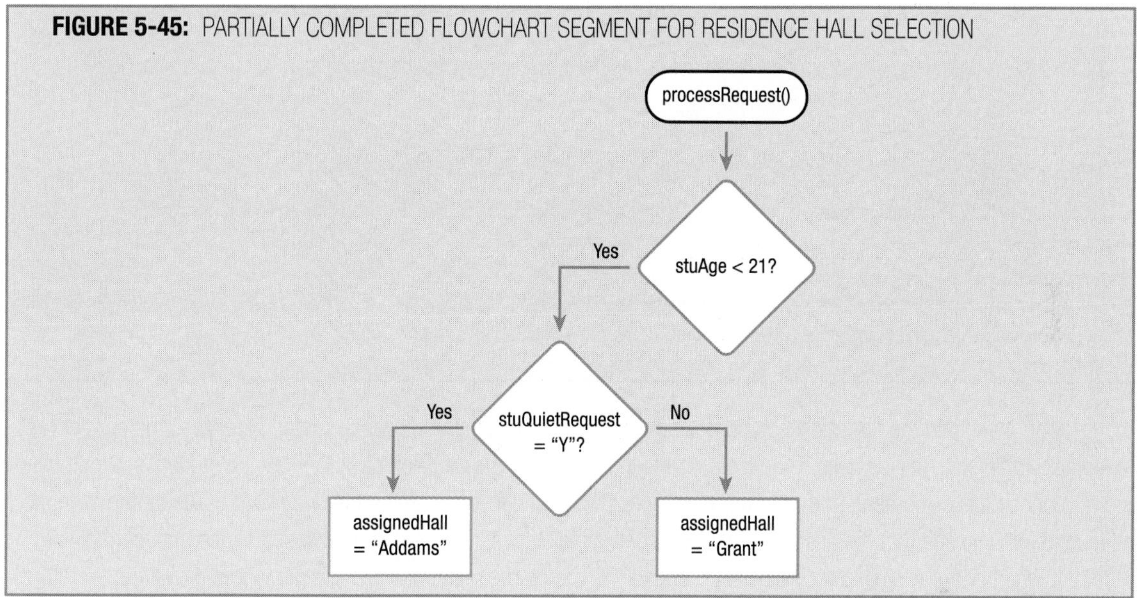


Next, on the false outcome side of the `stuAge < 21` question, you add the resulting action shown in the third column of the decision table—set the residence hall to "Lincoln". This action occurs when `stuAge < 21` is false and `stuQuietRequest = "Y"` is true. Finally, add the resulting action shown in the fourth column of the decision table, which occurs when both conditions are false. When a student is not under 21 and does not request a hall with quiet study hours, then the assigned hall is "Lincoln". See Figure 5-46.

**FIGURE 5-46:** MOSTLY COMPLETED FLOWCHART SEGMENT FOR RESIDENCE HALL SELECTION

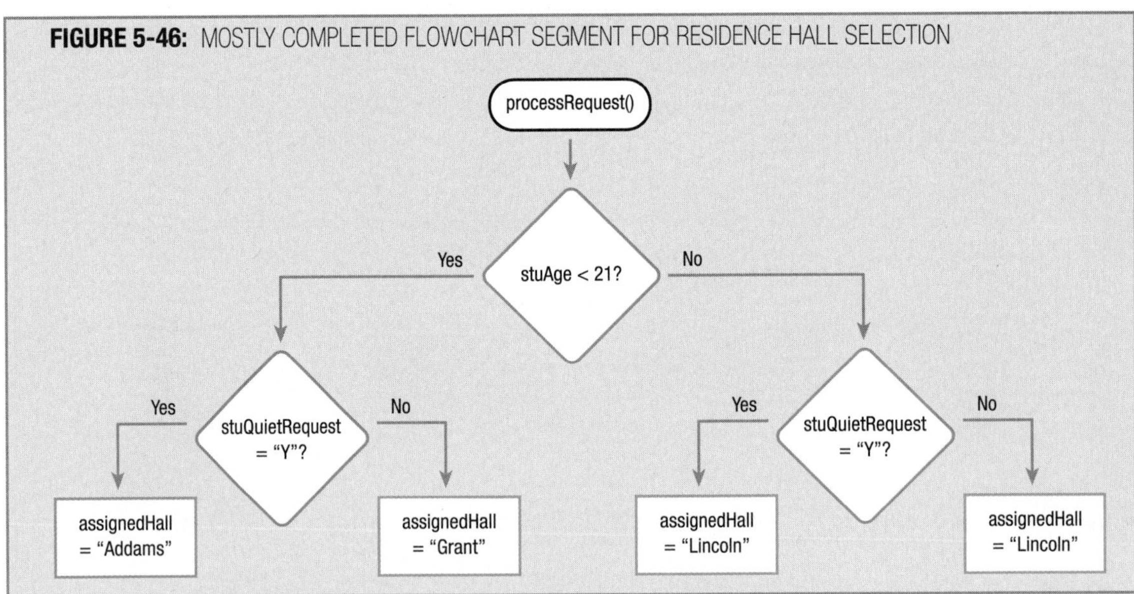


The decision making in the flowchart segment is now complete and accurately assigns each student to the correct residence hall. To finish it, all you need to do is tie up the loose ends of the decision structure, print a student's ID number and residence hall assignment, and read the next record. However, if you examine the two result boxes on the far right in Figure 5-46, you see that the assigned residence hall is identical—"Lincoln" in both cases. When a student is not under 21, whether the `stuQuietRequest` equals "Y" or not, the residence hall assignment is the same; therefore, there is no point in asking the `stuQuietRequest` question. Additionally, many programmers prefer that the True or Yes side of a flowchart decision always appears on the right side of a flowchart. Figure 5-47 shows the complete residence hall assignment program, including the redrawn `processRequest()` module, which has only one "Lincoln" assignment statement and True results to the right of each selection. Figure 5-47 also shows the pseudocode for the same problem.

Perhaps you could have created the final decision-making `processRequest()` module without creating the decision table first. If so, you need not use the table. Decision tables are more useful to the programmer when the decision-making process becomes more complicated. Additionally, they serve as a useful graphic tool when you want to explain the decision-making process of a program to a user who is not familiar with flowcharting symbols.

**TIP** In Appendix C, you can walk through the process used to create a larger decision table.

**FIGURE 5-47:** COMPLETE FLOWCHART AND PSEUDOCODE FOR RESIDENCE HALL SELECTION PROBLEM

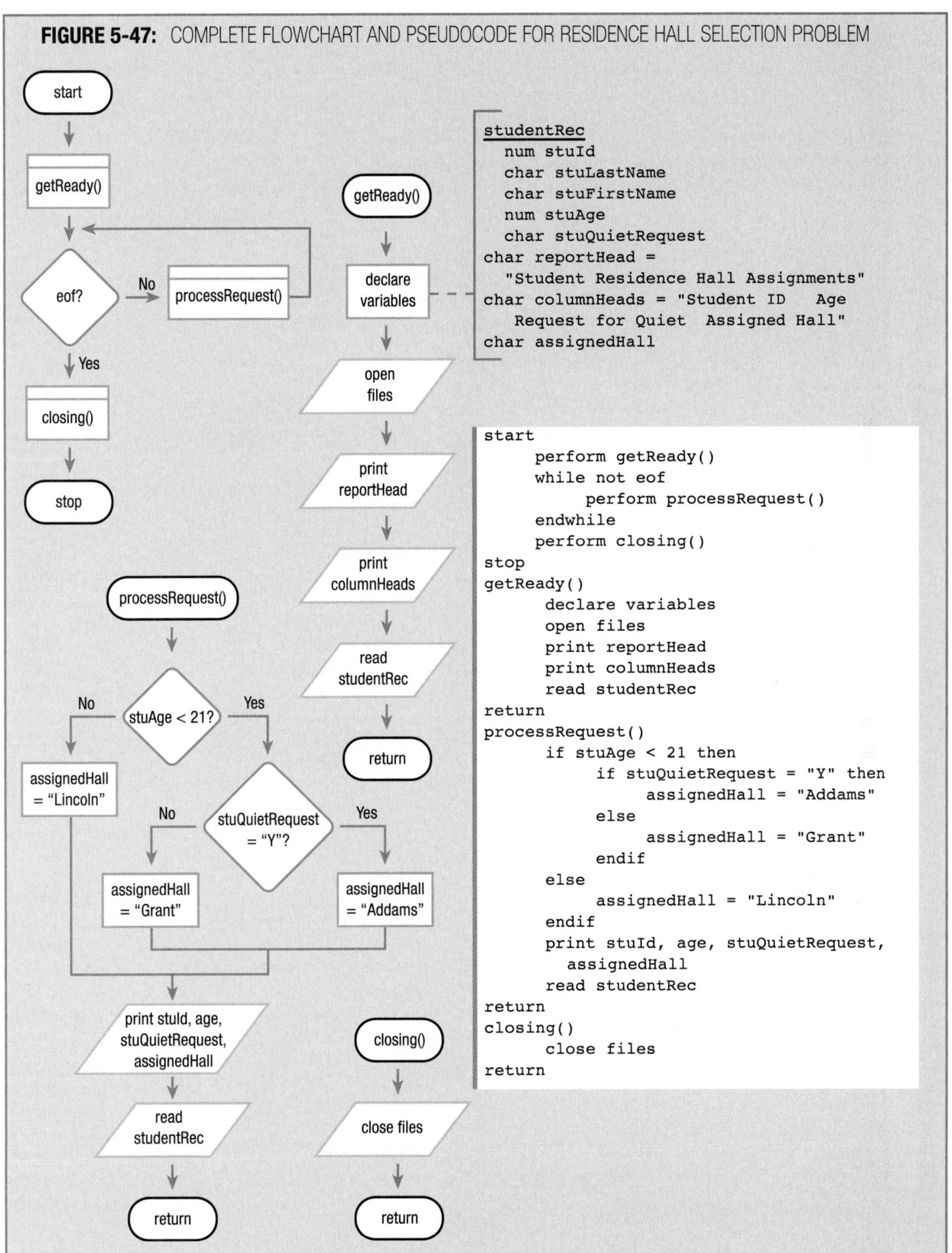


```
studentRec
  num stuId
  char stuLastName
  char stuFirstName
  num stuAge
  char stuQuietRequest
char reportHead =
  "Student Residence Hall Assignments"
char columnHeads = "Student ID   Age
   Request for Quiet  Assigned Hall"
char assignedHall
```

```
start
     perform getReady()
     while not eof
          perform processRequest()
     endwhile
     perform closing()
stop
getReady()
      declare variables
      open files
      print reportHead
      print columnHeads
      read studentRec
return
processRequest()
      if stuAge < 21 then
           if stuQuietRequest = "Y" then
                assignedHall = "Addams"
           else
                assignedHall = "Grant"
           endif
      else
           assignedHall = "Lincoln"
      endif
      print stuId, age, stuQuietRequest,
        assignedHall
      read studentRec
return
closing()
      close files
return
```

## CHAPTER SUMMARY

- Every decision you make in a computer program involves evaluating a Boolean expression. You can use dual-alternative, or binary, selections or if-then-else structures to choose between two possible outcomes. You also can use single-alternative, or unary, selections or if-then structures when there is only one outcome for the question where an action is required.
- For any two values that are the same type, you can use relational comparison operators to decide whether the two values are equal, the first value is greater than the second value, or the first value is less than the second value. The two values used in a Boolean expression can be either variables or constants.
- An AND decision occurs when two conditions must be true in order for a resulting action to take place. An AND decision requires a nested decision, or a nested `if`.
- In an AND decision, first ask the question that is less likely to be true. This eliminates as many records as possible from having to go through the second decision, which speeds up processing time.
- Most programming languages allow you to ask two or more questions in a single comparison by using a logical AND operator.
- When you must satisfy two or more criteria to initiate an event in a program, you must make sure that the second decision is made entirely within the first decision, and that you use a complete Boolean expression on both sides of the AND.
- An OR decision occurs when you want to take action when one or the other of two conditions is true.
- Errors occur in OR decisions when programmers do not maintain structure. An additional source of errors that are particular to the OR selection stems from people using the word AND to express OR requirements.
- In an OR decision, first ask the question that is more likely to be true.
- Most programming languages allow you to ask two or more questions in a single comparison by using a logical OR operator.
- To perform a range check, make comparisons with either the lowest or highest value in each range of values you are using.
- Common errors that occur when programmers perform range checks include asking unnecessary and previously answered questions.
- The case structure provides a convenient alternative to using a series of decisions when you must make choices based on the value stored in a single variable.
- A decision table is a problem-analysis tool that consists of conditions, possible combinations of Boolean values for the conditions, possible actions based on the conditions, and the action that corresponds to each Boolean value of each condition.

## KEY TERMS

A **dual-alternative**, or **binary**, selection structure offers two actions, each associated with one of two possible outcomes. It is also called an **if-then-else** structure.

In a **single-alternative**, or **unary**, selection structure, an action is required for only one outcome of the question. You call this form of the selection structure an **if-then**, because no "else" action is necessary.

The **if clause** of a decision holds the action or actions that execute when a Boolean expression in a decision is true.

The **else clause** of a decision holds the action or actions that execute when the Boolean expression in a decision is false.

A **Boolean expression** is one that represents only one of two states, usually expressed as true or false.

A **trivial** Boolean expression is one that always evaluates to the same result.

**Relational comparison operators** are the symbols that express Boolean comparisons. Examples include =, >, <, >=, <=, and <>.

A **logical operator** (as the term is most often used) compares single bits. However, some programmers use the term synonymously with "relational comparison operator."

With an **AND decision**, two conditions must both be true for an action to take place. An AND decision requires a **nested decision**, or a **nested if**—that is, a decision "inside of" another decision. A series of nested `if` statements can also be called a **cascading if statement**.

A **logical AND operator** is a symbol that you use to combine decisions so that two (or more) conditions must be true for an action to occur.

**Short-circuiting** is the compiler technique of not evaluating an expression when the outcome makes no difference.

A **range** of values encompasses every value between a high and low limit.

An **OR decision** contains two (or more) decisions; if at least one condition is met, the resulting action takes place.

A **logical OR operator** is a symbol that you use to combine decisions when any one condition can be true for an action to occur.

When you use a **range check**, you compare a variable to a series of values between limits.

A **default value** is one that is assigned after all test conditions are found to be false.

A **dead** or **unreachable path** is a logical path that can never be traveled.

When an operator has **precedence**, it is evaluated before others.

The **case structure** provides a convenient alternative to using a series of decisions when you must make choices based on the value stored in a single variable.

A **decision table** is a problem-analysis tool that consists of four parts: conditions, possible combinations of Boolean values for the conditions, possible actions based on the conditions, and the specific action that corresponds to each Boolean value of each condition.

## REVIEW QUESTIONS

1. **The selection statement** `if quantity > 100 then discountRate = 0.20` **is an example of a ________.**
    a. single-alternative selection
    b. dual-alternative selection
    c. binary selection
    d. all of the above

2. **The selection statement** `if dayOfWeek = "S" then price = 5.00 else price = 6.00` **is an example of a ________.**
    a. unary selection
    b. single-alternative selection
    c. binary selection
    d. all of the above

3. **All selection statements must have ________.**
    a. an `if` clause
    b. an `else` clause
    c. both of these
    d. neither a nor b

4. **An expression like** `amount < 10` **is a ________ expression.**
    a. Gregorian
    b. Boolean
    c. unary
    d. binary

5. **Usually, you compare only variables that have the same ________.**
    a. value
    b. size
    c. name
    d. type

6. **Symbols like > and < are known as ________ operators.**
    a. arithmetic
    b. relational comparison
    c. sequential
    d. scripting accuracy

7. **If you could use only three relational comparison operators, you could get by with ________.**
    a. greater than, less than, and greater than or equal to
    b. less than, less than or equal to, and not equal to
    c. equal to, less than, and greater than
    d. equal to, not equal to, and less than

8. **If `a > b` is false, then which of the following is always true?**
   a. `a < b`
   b. `a <= b`
   c. `a = b`
   d. `a >= b`

9. **Usually, the most difficult comparison operator to work with is ________.**
   a. equal to
   b. greater than
   c. less than
   d. not equal to

10. **Which of the lettered choices is equivalent to the following decision?**

```
if x > 10 then
   if y > 10 then
      print "X"
   endif
endif
```

   a. `if x > 10 AND y > 10 then print "X"`
   b. `if x > 10 OR y > 10 then print "X"`
   c. `if x > 10 AND x > y then print "X"`
   d. `if y > x then print "X"`

11. **The Midwest Sales region of Acme Computer Company consists of five states—Illinois, Indiana, Iowa, Missouri, and Wisconsin. Suppose you have input records containing Acme customer data, including state of residence. To most efficiently select and display all customers who live in the Midwest Sales region, you would use ________.**
   a. five completely separate unnested `if` statements
   b. nested `if` statements using AND logic
   c. nested `if` statements using OR logic
   d. Not enough information is given.

12. **The Midwest Sales region of Acme Computer Company consists of five states—Illinois, Indiana, Iowa, Missouri, and Wisconsin. About 50 percent of the regional customers reside in Illinois, 20 percent in Indiana, and 10 percent in each of the other three states. Suppose you have input records containing Acme customer data, including state of residence. To most efficiently select and display all customers who live in the Midwest Sales region, you would ask first about residency in ________.**
   a. Illinois
   b. Indiana
   c. Wisconsin
   d. either Iowa, Missouri, or Wisconsin—it does not matter which one is first

13. **The Boffo Balloon Company makes helium balloons. Large balloons cost $13 a dozen, medium-sized balloons cost $11 a dozen, and small balloons cost $8.60 a dozen. About 60 percent of the company's sales are the smallest balloons, 30 percent are the medium, and large balloons constitute only 10 percent of sales. Customer order records include customer information, quantity ordered, and size. When you write a program to determine price based on size, for the most efficient decision, you should ask first whether the size is ________.**
    a. large
    b. medium
    c. small
    d. It does not matter.

14. **The Boffo Balloon Company makes helium balloons in three sizes, 12 colors, and with a choice of 40 imprinted sayings. As a promotion, the company is offering a 25 percent discount on orders of large, red "Happy Valentine's Day" balloons. To most efficiently select the orders to which a discount applies, you would use ________.**
    a. three completely separate unnested `if` statements
    b. nested `if` statements using AND logic
    c. nested `if` statements using OR logic
    d. Not enough information is given.

15. **Radio station FM-99 keeps a record of every song played on the air in a week. Each record contains the day, hour, and minute the song started, and the title and artist of the song. The station manager wants a list of every title played during the important 8 a.m. commute hour on the two busiest traffic days, Monday and Friday. Which logic would select the correct titles?**

a.
```
if day = "Monday" OR day = "Friday" OR hour = 8 then
   print title
endif
```
b.
```
if day = "Monday" then
   if hour = 8 then
      print title
   else
      if day = "Friday" then
         print title
      endif
   endif
endif
```
c.
```
if hour = 8 AND day = "Monday" OR day = "Friday" then
   print title
endif
```
d.
```
if hour = 8 then
   if day = "Monday" OR day = "Friday" then
      print title
   endif
endif
```

**16. In the following pseudocode, what percentage raise will an employee in Department 5 receive?**

```
if department < 3 then
   raise = 25
else
   if department < 5 then
     raise = 50
   else
     raise = 75
   endif
endif
```

a. 25
b. 50
c. 75
d. impossible to tell

**17. In the following pseudocode, what percentage raise will an employee in Department 8 receive?**

```
if department < 5 then
   raise = 100
else
   if department < 9 then
     raise = 250
   else
      if department < 14 then
        raise = 375
      endif
   endif
endif
```

a. 100
b. 250
c. 375
d. impossible to tell

**18. In the following pseudocode, what percentage raise will an employee in Department 10 receive?**

```
if department < 2 then
   raise = 1000
else
   if department < 6 then
     raise = 2500
   else
      if department < 10 then
        raise = 3000
      endif
   endif
endif
```

a. 1000
b. 2500
c. 3000
d. impossible to tell

**19. When you use a range check, you compare a variable to the ________ value in the range.**

a. lowest
b. middle
c. highest
d. lowest or highest

**20. Which of the following is not a part of a decision table?**

a. conditions
b. declarations
c. possible actions
d. specific actions that will take place under given conditions

## FIND THE BUGS

Each of the following pseudocode segments contains one or more bugs that you must find and correct.

1. **This pseudocode should create a report containing annual profit statistics for a retail store. Input records contain a department name (for example, "Cosmetics") and profits for each quarter for the last two years. For each quarter, the program should determine whether the profit is higher, lower, or the same as in the same quarter of the previous year. Additionally, the program should determine whether the annual profit is higher, lower, or the same as in the previous year. For example, the line that displays the Cosmetics Department statistics might read "Cosmetics Same Lower Lower Higher Higher" if profits were the same in the first quarter as last year, lower in the second and third quarters, but higher in the fourth quarter and for the year as a whole.**

```
start
   perform housekeeping()
   while not eof
      perform detrmineProfitStatistics()
   perform finalTasks()
stop

housekeeping()
   declare variables
        profitRec
             char department
             num salesQuarter1ThisYear
             num salesQuarter2ThisYear
             num salesQuarter2ThisYear
             num salesQuarter4ThisYear
             num salesQuarter1LastYear
             num salesQuarter2LastYear
             num salesQuarter3ThisYear
             num salesQuarter4LastYear
             char mainHead = "Profit Report"
             char columnHeaders = "Department     Quarter 1
Quarter 2      Quarter 3      Quarter 4      Over All"
        num totalThisYear
        num totalLastYear
        char word1
        char word2
        char word3
        char word4
        char word5
   open files
   perform printHeadings()
   read profitRec
return

printHeadings()
   print mainHeader
   print columnHeaders
return
```

```
determineProfitStatistics()
   if salesQuarter1ThisYear > salesQuarter1LastYear then
      word1 = "Higher"
   else
      if salesQuarter1ThisYear < salesQuarter2LastYear then
            word1 = "Lower"
      else
            word1 = "Same"
      endif
   endif
   if salesQuarter2ThisYear > salesQuarter3LastYear then
      word2 = "Higher"
   else
      if salesQuarter2LastYear < salesQuarter2LastYear then
            word2 = "Lower"
      else
            word2 = "Equal"
      endif
   endif
   if salesQuarter3ThisYear > salesQuarter3LastYear then
      word3 = "Higher"
   else
      if salesQuarter3ThisYear < salesQuarter3LastYear then
            word2 = "Lower"
      else
            word3 = "Same"
      endif
   endif
   if salesQuarter4ThisYear > salesQuarter4LastYear then
      word4 = "Higher"
   else
      if salesQuarter4LastYear < salesQuarter4LastYear then
            word4 = "Lower"
      else
            word4 = "Same"
      endif
   endif
```

```
        totalThisYear = salesQuarter1ThisYear + salesQuarter1ThisYear +
            salesQuarter3LastYear + salesQuarter4ThisYear
        totalLastYear = salesQuarter1LastYear + salesQuarter1LastYear +
            salesQuarter3LastYear + salesQuarter4LastYear
        if totalThisYear > totalLastYear then
            word5 = "Higher"
        else
            if totalThisYear > totalLastYear then
                  word5 = "Lower"
            else
                  word5 = "Same"
          endif
        endif
        print department, word1, word2, word3, word4, word5
        read profitRec
    return

    finalTasks()
        close files
    return
```

2. **This pseudocode should create a report containing rental agents' commissions at an apartment complex. Input records contain an apartment number, the ID number and name of the agent who rented the apartment, and the number of bedrooms in the apartment. The commission is $100 for renting a three-bedroom apartment, $75 for renting a two-bedroom apartment, $55 for renting a one-bedroom apartment, and $30 for renting a studio (zero-bedroom) apartment. Each report line should list the apartment number, the salesperson's name and ID number, and the commission earned on the rental.**

```
start
    perform housekeeping()
    while not eof
        perform calculateCommission()
    perform finishUp()
stop
```

```
housekeeping()
   declare variables
      rentalRecord
         num apartmentNum
         num salesPersonID
         char salesPersonName
         num numBedrooms
     char mainHeader = "Commission Report"
     char columnHeaders = "Apartment number     Salesperson ID
        Name    Commission Earned"
     num comm3Bedroom = 100.00
     num comm2Bedroom = 75.00
     num comm1Bedroom = 55.00
     num commStudio = 30.00
   open files
   perform displayHeaders()
   read rentalRecord
stop

displayHeader()
   print mainHeader
   print columnHeaders
return

calculateCommission()
   if numBedrooms = 3 then
      commissionEarned = comm3Bedroom
   else
      if numBedrooms = 3 then
         commissionEarned = comm3Bedroom
      else
         if numBedrooms = 3 then
              commission = comm3Bedroom
         else
             commissionEarned = comStudio
         endif
   endif
   print apartmentNum, salesPersonID, salesPersonName,
      commissionEarned
   read rentalRecord
return

finishUp()
   close files
return
```

## EXERCISES

1. **Assume that the following variables contain the values shown:**

```
numberRed = 100        numberBlue = 200      numberGreen = 300
wordRed = "Wagon"      wordBlue = "Sky"      wordGreen = "Grass"
```

**For each of the following Boolean expressions, decide whether the statement is true, false, or illegal.**

   a. `numberRed = numberBlue?`
   b. `numberBlue > numberGreen?`
   c. `numberGreen < numberRed?`
   d. `numberBlue = wordBlue?`
   e. `numberGreen = "Green"?`
   f. `wordRed = "Red"?`
   g. `wordBlue = "Blue"?`
   h. `numberRed <= numberGreen?`
   i. `numberBlue >= 200?`
   j. `numberGreen >= numberRed + numberBlue?`

2. **A candy company wants a list of its best-selling items, including the item number and the name of candy. Best-selling items are those that sell over 2,000 pounds per month. Input records contain fields for the item number (three digits), the name of the candy (20 characters), the price per pound (four digits, two assumed decimal places), and the quantity in pounds sold last month (four digits, no decimals).**
   a. Design the output for this program; create either sample output or a print chart.
   b. Draw the hierarchy chart for this program.
   c. Draw the flowchart for this program.
   d. Write the pseudocode for this program.

3. **The same candy company described in Exercise 2 wants a list of its high-priced, best-selling items. Best-selling items are those that sell over 2,000 pounds per month. High-priced items are those that sell for $10 per pound or more.**
   a. Design the output for this program; create either sample output or a print chart.
   b. Draw the hierarchy chart for this program.
   c. Draw the flowchart for this program.
   d. Write the pseudocode for this program.

4. **The Literary Honor Society needs a list of English majors who have a grade point average of 3.5 or higher. The student record file includes students' last names and first names, major (for example, "History" or "English"), and grade point average (for example, 3.9 or 2.0).**
   a. Design the output for this program; create either sample output or a print chart.
   b. Draw the hierarchy chart for this program.
   c. Draw the flowchart for this program.
   d. Write the pseudocode for this program.

5. **A telephone company charges 10 cents per minute for all calls outside the customer's area code that last over 20 minutes. All other calls are 13 cents per minute. The phone company has a file with one record for every call made in one day. (In other words, a single customer might have many such records on file.) Fields for each call include customer area code (three digits), customer phone number (seven digits), called area code (three digits), called number (seven digits), and call time in minutes (never more than four digits). The company wants a report listing one detail line for each call, including the customer area code and number, the called area code and number, the minutes, and the total charge.**
   a. Design the output for this program; create either sample output or a print chart.
   b. Draw the hierarchy chart for this program.
   c. Create a decision table to use while planning the logic for this program.
   d. Draw the flowchart for this program.
   e. Write the pseudocode for this program.

6. **A nursery maintains a file of all plants in stock. Each record contains the name of a plant, its price, and fields that indicate the plant's light and soil requirements. The light field contains either "sunny", "partial sun", or "shady". The soil field contains either "clay" or "sandy". Only 20 percent of the nursery stock does well in shade, and 50 percent does well in sandy soil. Customers have requested a report that lists the name and price of each plant that would be appropriate in a shady, sandy yard. Consider program efficiency when designing your solution.**
   a. Design the output for this program; create either sample output or a print chart.
   b. Draw the hierarchy chart for this program.
   c. Create a decision table to use while planning the logic for this program.
   d. Draw the flowchart for this program.
   e. Write the pseudocode for this program.

7. **You have declared variables for an insurance company program as follows:**

| FIELD | EXAMPLE |
|---|---|
| `num custPolicyNumber` | `223356` |
| `char custLastName` | `Salvatore` |
| `num custAge` | `25` |
| `num custDueMonth` | `06` |
| `num custDueDay` | `24` |
| `num custDueYear` | `2007` |
| `num custAccidents` | `2` |

   **Draw the flowchart or write the pseudocode for the selection structures that print the `custPolicyNumber` and `custLastName` for customers whose data satisfy the following requests for lists of policyholders:**
   a. over 35 years old
   b. at least 21 years old
   c. no more than 30 years old
   d. due no later than March 15 any year

e. due up to and including January 1, 2007
f. due by April 27, 2010
g. due as early as December 1, 2006
h. fewer than 11 accidents
i. no more than five accidents
j. no accidents

**8. Student files contain an ID number (four digits), last and first names (15 characters each), and major field of study (10 characters). Plan a program that lists ID numbers and names for all French or Spanish majors.**

a. Design the output for this program; create either sample output or a print chart.
b. Draw the hierarchy chart for this program.
c. Create a decision table to use while planning the logic for this program.
d. Draw the flowchart for this program.
e. Write the pseudocode for this program.

**9. A florist wants to send coupons to her best customers, so she needs a list of names and addresses for customers who placed orders more than three times last year or spent more than $200 last year. Consider program efficiency when designing your solution. The input file description follows:**

```
File name: FLORISTCUSTS
FIELD DESCRIPTION      DATA TYPE        COMMENTS
Customer ID            Numeric          4 digits, 0 decimals
First Name             Character        15 characters
Last Name              Character        15 characters
Street Address         Character        20 characters
Orders Last Year       Numeric          0 decimals
Amount Spent           Numeric          2 decimals
  Last Year
```

**(Note: To save room, the record does not include a city or state. Assume that all the florist's best customers are in town.)**

a. Design the output for this program; create either sample output or a print chart.
b. Draw the hierarchy chart for this program.
c. Create a decision table to use while planning the logic for this program.
d. Draw the flowchart for this program.
e. Write the pseudocode for this program.

**10. A carpenter needs a program that computes the price of any desk a customer orders, based on the following input fields: order number, desk length and width in inches (three digits each, no decimals), type of wood (20 characters), and number of drawers (two digits). The price is computed as follows:**

- The charge for all desks is a minimum $200.
- If the surface (length * width) is over 750 square inches, add $50.
- If the wood is "mahogany", add $150; for "oak", add $125. No charge is added for "pine".
- For every drawer in the desk, there is an additional $30 charge.

a. Design the output for this program; create either sample output or a print chart.
b. Draw the hierarchy chart for this program.
c. Create a decision table to use while planning the logic for this program.
d. Draw the flowchart for this program.
e. Write the pseudocode for this program.

**11. A company is attempting to organize carpools to save energy. Each input record contains an employee's name and town of residence. Ten percent of the company's employees live in Wonder Lake. Thirty percent of the employees live in Woodstock. Because these towns are both north of the company, the company wants a list of employees who live in either town, so it can recommend that these employees drive to work together.**

a. Design the output for this program; create either sample output or a print chart.
b. Draw the hierarchy chart for this program.
c. Create a decision table to use while planning the logic for this program.
d. Draw the flowchart for this program.
e. Write the pseudocode for this program.

**12. A supervisor in a manufacturing company wants to produce a report showing which employees have increased their production this year over last year, so that she can issue them a certificate of commendation. She wants to have a report with three columns: last name, first name, and either the word "UP" or blanks printed under the column heading PRODUCTION. "UP" is printed when this year's production is a greater number than last year's production. Input exists as follows:**

```
PRODUCTION FILE DESCRIPTION
File name: PRODUCTION
FIELD DESCRIPTION          DATA TYPE      COMMENTS
Last Name                  Character      15 characters
First Name                 Character      15 characters
Last Year's Production     Numeric        0 decimals
This Year's Production     Numeric        0 decimals
```

a. Design the output for this program; create either sample output or a print chart.
b. Draw the hierarchy chart for this program.
c. Create a decision table to use while planning the logic for this program.
d. Draw the flowchart for this program.
e. Write the pseudocode for this program.

13. **A supervisor in the same manufacturing company as described in Exercise 12 wants to produce a report from the PRODUCTION input file showing bonuses she is planning to give based on this year's production. She wants to have a report with three columns: last name, first name, and bonus. The bonuses will be distributed as follows.**

**If this year's production is:**

- 1,000 units or fewer, the bonus is $25
- 1,001 to 3,000 units, the bonus is $50
- 3,001 to 6,000 units, the bonus is $100
- 6,001 units and up, the bonus is $200

a. Design the output for this program; create either sample output or a print chart.
b. Draw the hierarchy chart for this program.
c. Create a decision table to use while planning the logic for this program.
d. Draw the flowchart for this program.
e. Write the pseudocode for this program.

14. **Modify Exercise 13 to reflect the following new facts, and have the program execute as efficiently as possible:**

- Only employees whose production this year is higher than it was last year will receive bonuses. This is true for approximately 30 percent of the employees.
- Sixty percent of employees produce over 6,000 units per year; 20 percent produce 3,001 to 6,000; 15 percent produce 1,001 to 3,000 units; and only 5 percent produce fewer than 1,001.

a. Design the output for this program; create either sample output or a print chart.
b. Draw the hierarchy chart for this program.
c. Create a decision table to use while planning the logic for this program.
d. Draw the flowchart for this program.
e. Write the pseudocode for this program.

15. **The Richmond Riding Club wants to assign the title of Master or Novice to each of its members. A member earns the title of Master by accomplishing two or more of the following:**

- Participating in at least eight horse shows
- Winning a first-place or second-place ribbon in at least two horse shows, no matter how many shows the member has participated in
- Winning a first-place, second-place, third-place, or fourth-place ribbon in at least four horse shows, no matter how many shows the member has participated in

**Create a report that prints each club member's name along with the designation "Master" or "Novice". Input exists as follows:**

```
RIDING FILE DESCRIPTION
File name: RIDING
FIELD DESCRIPTION        DATA TYPE     COMMENTS
Last Name                Character     15 characters
First Name               Character     15 characters
Number of Shows          Numeric       0 decimals
First-Place Ribbons      Numeric       0 decimals
Second-Place Ribbons     Numeric       0 decimals
Third-Place Ribbons      Numeric       0 decimals
Fourth-Place Ribbons     Numeric       0 decimals
```

a. Design the output for this program; create either sample output or a print chart.
b. Draw the hierarchy chart for this program.
c. Create a decision table to use while planning the logic for this program.
d. Draw the flowchart for this program.
e. Write the pseudocode for this program.

**16. Freeport Financial Services manages clients' investment portfolios. The company charges for its services based on each client's annual income, net worth, and length of time as a client, as follows:**

- Clients with an annual income over $100,000 and a net worth over $1 million are charged 1.5 percent of their net worth.
- Clients with an annual income over $100,000 and a net worth between $500,000 and $1 million inclusive are charged $8,000.
- Clients with an annual income over $100,000 and a net worth of less than $500,000 are charged $6,000.
- Clients with an annual income from $75,000 up to and including $100,000 are charged 1 percent of their net worth.
- Clients with an income of $75,000 or less are charged $4,000, unless their net worth is over $1 million, in which case they are charged $4,500.
- Any client for over four years gets a 10 percent discount; any client for over seven years gets a 15 percent discount.

**Create a report that prints each client's name and the client's annual fee. Input records contain the following data:**

```
FINANCIAL SERVICE CLIENTS' FILE DESCRIPTION
File name: CLIENTS
FIELD DESCRIPTION        DATA TYPE     COMMENTS
Last Name                Character     15 characters
First Name               Character     15 characters
Annual Income            Numeric       0 decimals
Portfolio Value          Numeric       0 decimals
Years as Client          Numeric       0 decimals
```

a. Design the output for this program; create either sample output or a print chart.
b. Draw the hierarchy chart for this program.
c. Create a decision table to use while planning the logic for this program.
d. Draw the flowchart for this program.
e. Write the pseudocode for this program.

## DETECTIVE WORK

1. **Computers are expert chess players because they can make many good decisions very rapidly. Explore the history of computer chess playing.**

2. **George Boole is considered the father of symbolic logic. Find out about his life.**

## UP FOR DISCUSSION

1. **Computer programs can be used to make decisions about your insurability as well as the rates you will be charged for health and life insurance policies. For example, certain preexisting conditions may raise your insurance premiums considerably. Is it ethical for insurance companies to access your health records and then make insurance decisions about you?**

2. **Job applications are sometimes screened by software that makes decisions about a candidate's suitability based on keywords in the applications. Is such screening fair to applicants?**

3. **Medical facilities often have more patients waiting for organ transplants than there are available organs. Suppose you have been asked to write a computer program that selects which of several candidates should receive an available organ. What data would you want on file to be able to use in your program, and what decisions would you make based on the data? What data do you think others might use that you would choose not to use?**

# 6 LOOPING

## After studying Chapter 6, you should be able to:

- Understand the advantages of looping
- Control a **while** loop using a loop control variable
- Increment a counter to control a loop
- Loop with a variable sentinel value
- Control a loop by decrementing a loop control variable
- Avoid common loop mistakes
- Use a **for** statement
- Use **do while** and **do until** loops
- Recognize the characteristics shared by all loops
- Nest loops
- Use a loop to accumulate totals

## UNDERSTANDING THE ADVANTAGES OF LOOPING

If making decisions is what makes computers seem intelligent, it's looping that makes computer programming worthwhile. When you use a loop within a computer program, you can write one set of instructions that operates on multiple, unique sets of data. Consider the following set of tasks required for each employee in a typical payroll program:

- Determine regular pay.
- Determine overtime pay, if any.
- Determine federal withholding tax based on gross wages and number of dependents.
- Determine state withholding tax based on gross wages, number of dependents, and state of residence.
- Determine insurance deduction based on insurance code.
- Determine Social Security deduction based on gross pay.
- Subtract federal tax, state tax, Social Security, and insurance from gross pay.

In reality, this list is too short—companies deduct stock option plans, charitable contributions, union dues, and other items from checks in addition to the items mentioned in this list. Also, they might pay bonuses and commissions and provide sick days and vacation days that must be taken into account and handled appropriately. As you can see, payroll programs are complicated.

The advantage of having a computer perform payroll calculations is that all of the deduction instructions need to be written *only once* and can be repeated over and over again for each paycheck using a **loop**, the structure that repeats actions while some condition continues.

## USING A WHILE LOOP WITH A LOOP CONTROL VARIABLE

Recall the loop, or `while` structure, that you learned about in Chapter 2. (See Figure 6-1.) In Chapter 4, you learned that almost every program has a **main loop**, or a basic set of instructions that is repeated for every record. The main loop is a typical loop—within it, you write one set of instructions that executes repeatedly while records continue to be read from an input file. Several housekeeping tasks execute at the start of most programs, and a few cleanup tasks execute at the end. However, most of a program's tasks are located in a main loop; these tasks repeat over and over for many records (sometimes hundreds, thousands, or millions).

**FIGURE 6-1:** THE `while` LOOP

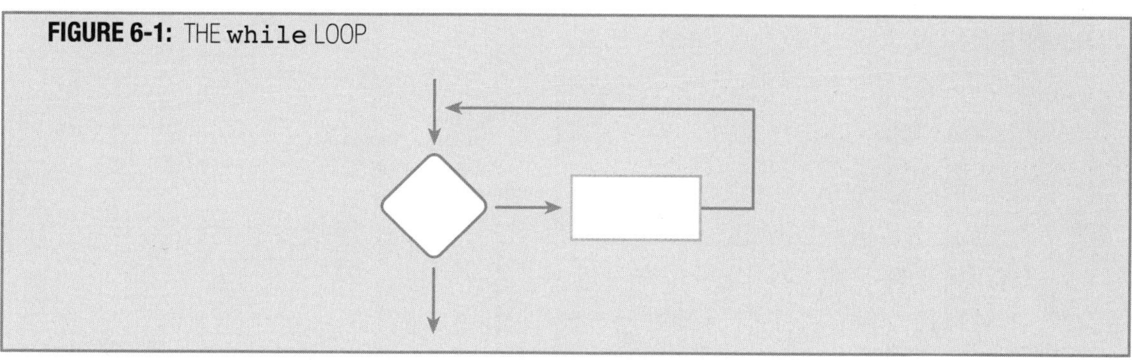

In addition to this main loop, loops also appear within a program's modules. They are used any time you need to perform a task several times and don't want to write identical or similar instructions over and over. Suppose, for example, as part of a much larger program, you want to print a warning message on the computer screen when the user has made a potentially dangerous menu selection (for example, "Delete all files"). To get the user's attention, you want to print the message four times. You can write this program segment as a sequence of four steps, as shown in Figure 6-2, but you can also use a loop, as shown in Figure 6-3.

**FIGURE 6-2:** PRINTING FOUR WARNING MESSAGES IN SEQUENCE

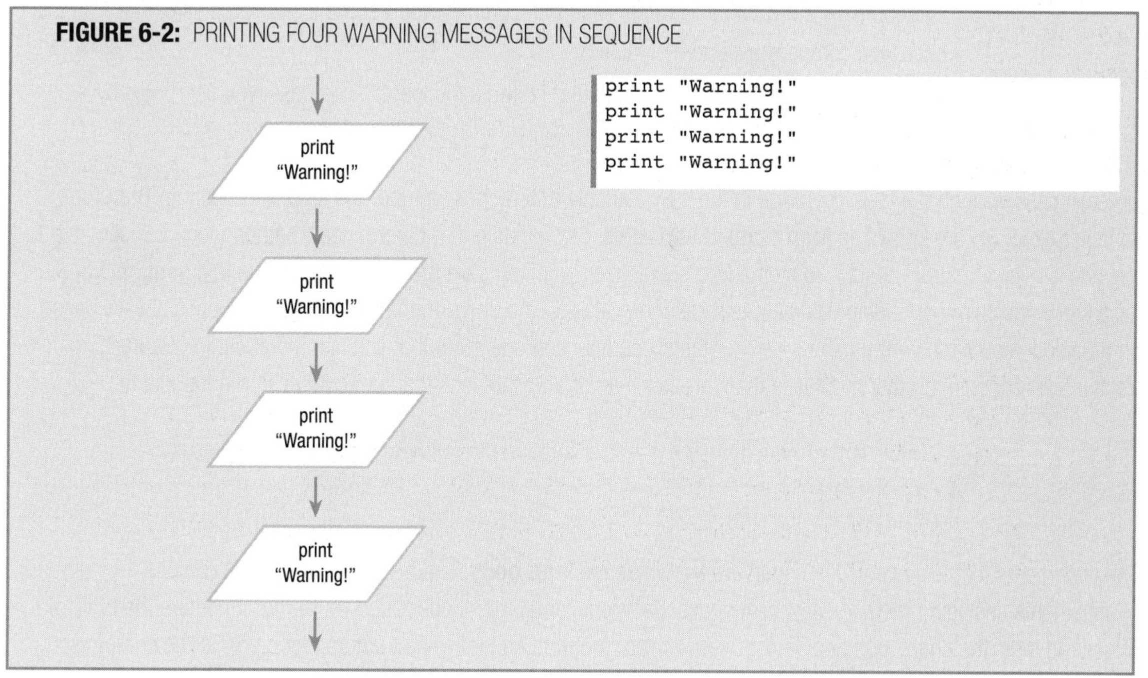


```
print "Warning!"
print "Warning!"
print "Warning!"
print "Warning!"
```

**FIGURE 6-3:** PRINTING FOUR WARNING MESSAGES IN A LOOP

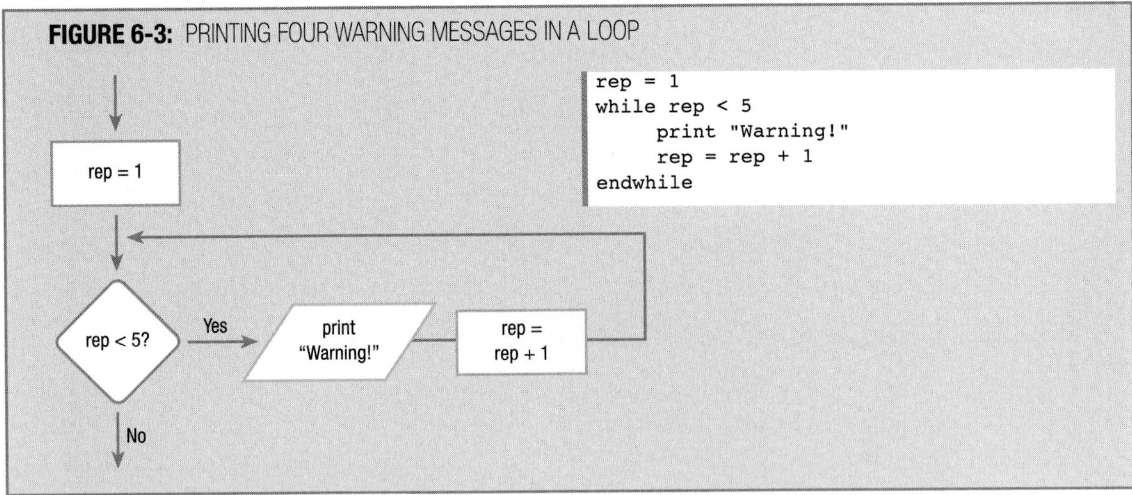


```
rep = 1
while rep < 5
     print "Warning!"
     rep = rep + 1
endwhile
```

The flowchart and pseudocode segments in Figure 6-3 show three steps that should occur in every loop:

1. You initialize a variable that will control the loop. The variable in this case is named `rep`.
2. You compare the variable to some value that controls whether the loop continues or stops. In this case, you compare `rep` to the value 5.
3. Within the loop, you alter the variable that controls the loop. In this case, you alter `rep` by adding 1 to it.

On each pass through the loop, the value in the `rep` variable determines whether the loop will continue. Therefore, variables like `rep` are known as **loop control variables**. Any variable that determines whether a loop will continue to execute is a loop control variable. To stop a loop's execution, you compare the loop control value to a **sentinel value** (also known as a limit or ending value), in this case the value 5. The decision that controls every loop is always based on a Boolean comparison. You can use any of the six comparison operators that you learned about in Chapter 5 to control a loop—equal to, greater than, less than, greater than or equal to, less than or equal to, and not equal to.

**TIP** Just as with a selection, the Boolean comparison that controls a `while` loop must compare same-type values: numeric values are compared to other numeric values, and character values to other character values.

The statements that execute within a loop are known as the **loop body**. The body of a loop might contain any number of statements, including method calls, sequences, decisions, and other loops. Once your program enters the body of a structured loop, the entire loop body must execute. Your program can leave a structured loop only at the comparison that tests the loop control variable.

## USING A COUNTER TO CONTROL LOOPING

Suppose you own a factory and have decided to place a label on every product you manufacture. The label contains the words "Made for you personally by " followed by the first name of one of your employees. For one week's production, suppose you need 100 personalized labels for each employee.

Assume you already have a personnel file that can be used for input. This file has more information than you'll need for this program: an employee last name, first name, Social Security number, address, date hired, and salary. The important feature of the file is that it does contain each employee's name stored in a separate record. The input file description appears in Figure 6-4.

**FIGURE 6-4:** EMPLOYEE FILE DESCRIPTION

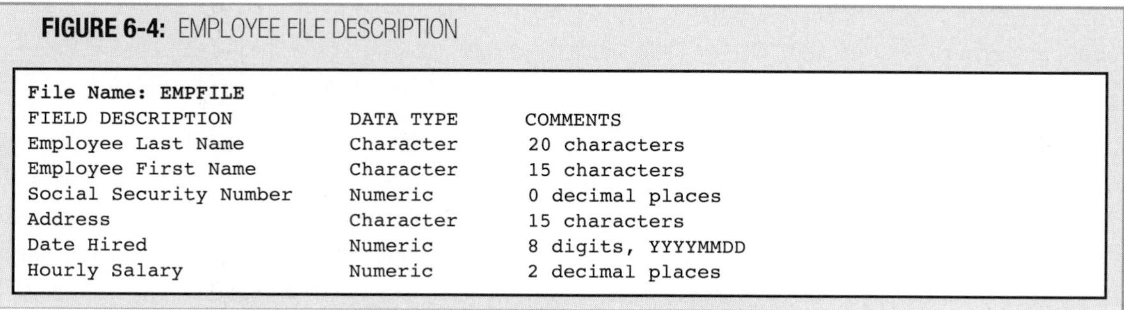

```
File Name: EMPFILE
FIELD DESCRIPTION          DATA TYPE      COMMENTS
Employee Last Name         Character      20 characters
Employee First Name        Character      15 characters
Social Security Number     Numeric        0 decimal places
Address                    Character      15 characters
Date Hired                 Numeric        8 digits, YYYYMMDD
Hourly Salary              Numeric        2 decimal places
```

In the mainline logic of this program, you call three modules: a housekeeping module (`housekeep()`), a main loop module (`createLabels()`), and a finish routine (`finishUp()`). See Figure 6-5.

**FIGURE 6-5:** MAINLINE LOGIC FOR LABEL-MAKING PROGRAM

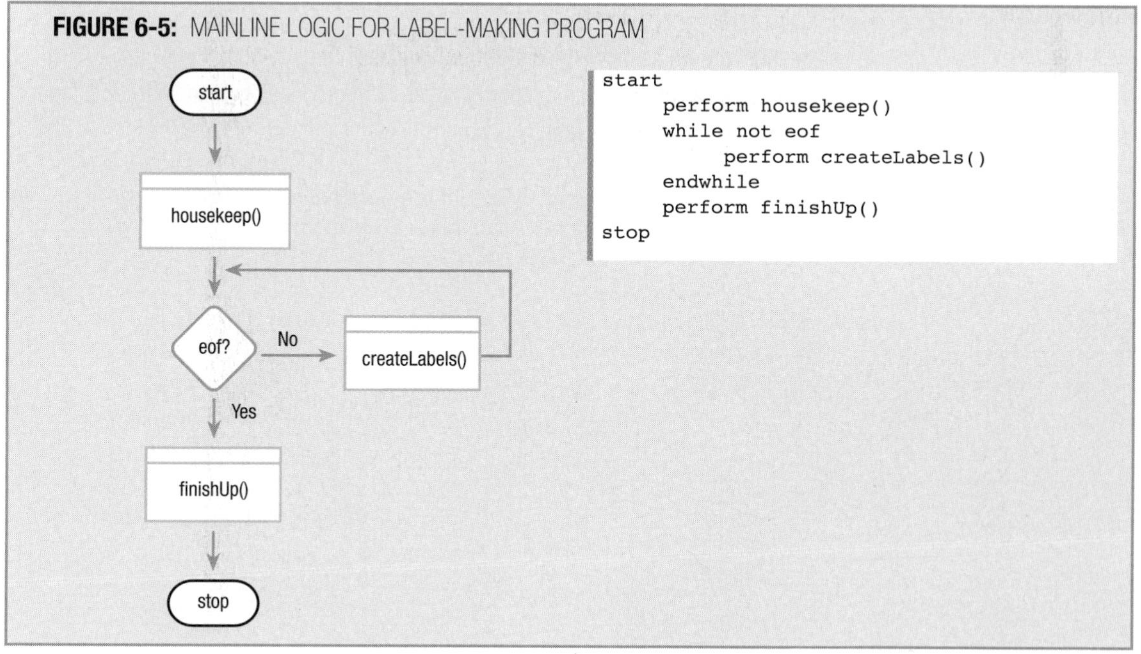


```
start
     perform housekeep()
     while not eof
          perform createLabels()
     endwhile
     perform finishUp()
stop
```

The first task for the label-making program is to name the fields in the input record so you can refer to them within the program. As a programmer, you can choose any variable names you like, for example: `inLastName`, `inFirstName`, `inSSN`, `inAddress`, `inDate`, and `inSalary`.

TIP

In Chapter 4 you learned that starting all field names in the input record with the same prefix, such as `in`, is a common programming technique to help identify these fields in a large program and differentiate them from work areas and output areas that will have other names. Another benefit to using a prefix like `in` is that some language compilers produce a dictionary of variable names when you compile your program. These dictionaries show at which lines in the program each data name is referenced. If all your input field names start with the same prefix, they will be together alphabetically in the dictionary, and perhaps be easier to find and work with.

You also can set up a variable to hold the characters "Made for you personally by " and name it `labelLine`. You eventually will print this `labelLine` variable followed by the employee's first name (`inFirstName`).

You will need one more variable: a location to be used as a counter. A **counter** is any numeric variable you use to count the number of times an event has occurred; in this example, you need a counter to keep track of how many labels have been printed at any point. Each time you read an employee record, the counter variable is set to 0. Then every time a label is printed, you add 1 to the counter. Adding to a variable is called **incrementing** the variable; programmers often use the term "incrementing" specifically to mean "increasing by one." Before the next employee label is printed, the program checks the variable to see if it has reached 100 yet. When it has, that means 100 labels have been printed, and the job is done for that employee. While the counter remains below 100, you continue to print labels. As with all variables, the programmer can choose any name for a counter; this program uses `labelCounter`. In this example, `labelCounter` is the loop control variable.

The `housekeep()` module for the label program, shown in Figure 6-6, includes a step to open the files: the employee file and the printer. Unlike a program that produces a report, this program produces no headings, so the next and last task performed in `housekeep()` is to read the first input record.

Remember, you can give any name to modules within your programs. This program uses `housekeep()` for its first routine, but `housekeeping()`, `startUp()`, `prep()`, or any other name with the same general meaning could be used.

TIP

If you don't know why the first record is read in the `housekeep()` module, go back and review the concept of the priming read, presented in Chapter 2.

**FIGURE 6-6:** THE `housekeep()` MODULE FOR THE LABEL PROGRAM

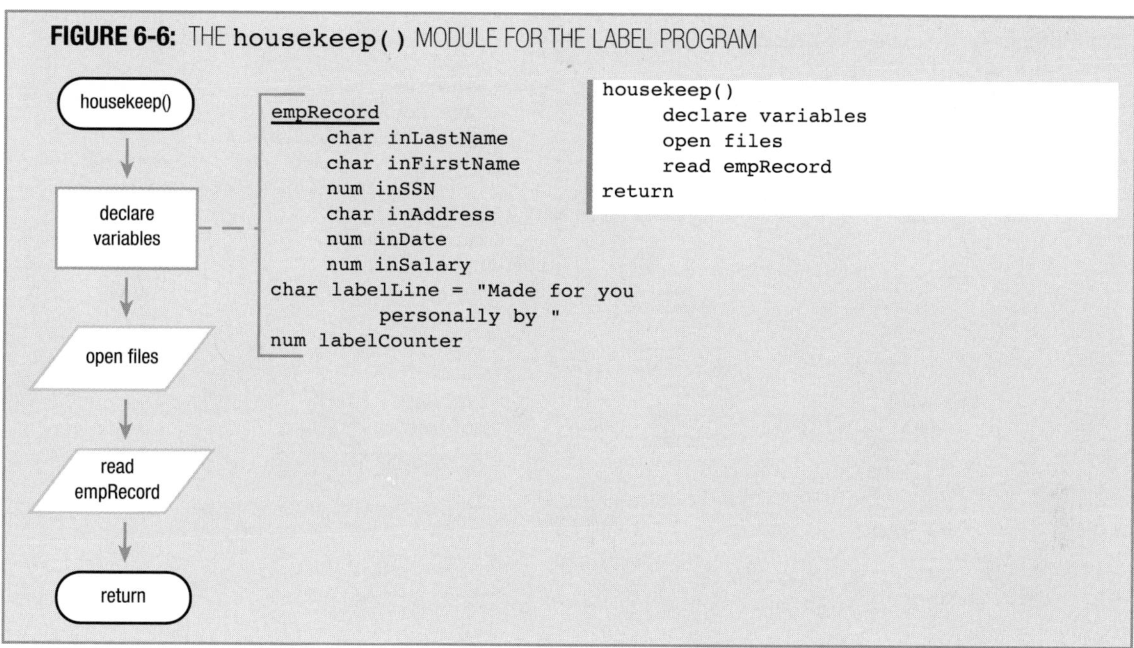


```
housekeep()
     declare variables
     open files
     read empRecord
return
```

**TIP** The label-making program could be interactive instead of reading data from a file. An easy way to make the program interactive would be to replace the `read empRecord` statement with a series of statements or a call to a module that provides a prompt and a read statement for each of the six data fields needed for each employee. A user could then enter these values from the keyboard. (If this were an interactive program, the programmer would likely require the user to enter data only in the field that is necessary for output—the employee's name.) Also, if this were an interactive program, the user might be asked to type a sentinel value, such as "XXX", when finished. This program is discussed as one that reads from a file to reduce the number of statements you must view to understand the logical process.

**TIP** In previous chapters, the list of declared variables was shown with both the flowchart and the pseudocode. To save space in the rest of the chapters in this book, the variable list will be shown only with the flowchart.

When the `housekeep()` module is done, the logical flow returns to the `eof` question in the mainline logic. If you attempt to read the first record at the end of `housekeep()` and for some reason there is no record, the answer to `eof?` is Yes, so the `createLabels()` module is never entered; instead, the logic of the program flows directly to the `finishUp()` module.

Usually, however, employee records will exist and the program will enter the `createLabels()` module, which is shown in Figure 6-7. When this happens, the first employee record is sitting in memory waiting to be processed. During one execution of the `createLabels()` module, 100 labels will be printed for one employee. As the last event within the `createLabels()` module, the program reads the next employee record. Control of the program then returns to the `eof` question. If the new read process has not resulted in the `eof` condition, control reenters the `createLabels()` module, where 100 more labels print for the new employee.

FIGURE 6-7: THE `createLabels()` MODULE FOR THE LABEL PROGRAM

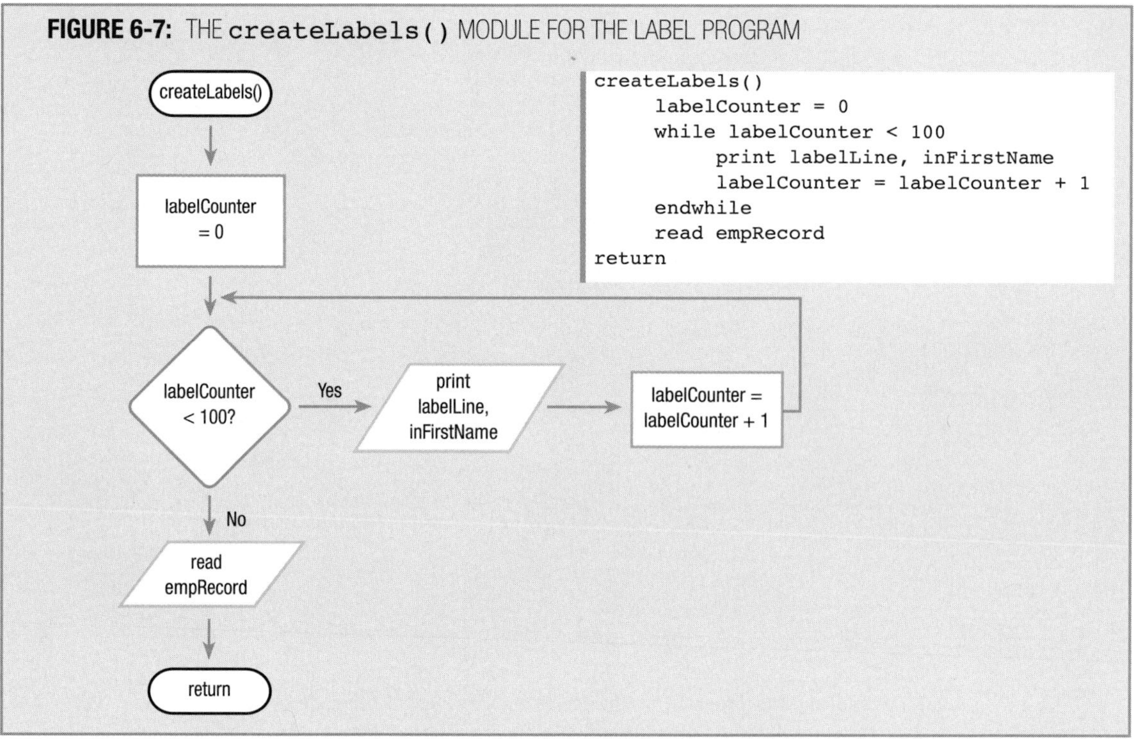


```
createLabels()
     labelCounter = 0
     while labelCounter < 100
          print labelLine, inFirstName
          labelCounter = labelCounter + 1
     endwhile
     read empRecord
return
```

The `createLabels()` method of this label-making program contains three parts:

- Set `labelCounter` to 0.
- Compare `labelCounter` to 100.
- While `labelCounter` is less than 100, print `labelLine` and `inFirstName`, and add 1 to `labelCounter`.

When the first employee record enters the `createLabels()` module, `labelCounter` is set to 0. The `labelCounter` value is less than 100, so the record enters the label-making loop. One label prints for the first employee, `labelCounter` increases by one, and the logical flow returns to the question `labelCounter < 100?`. After the first label is printed, `labelCounter` holds a value of only 1. It is nowhere near 100 yet, so the value of the Boolean expression is true, and the loop is entered for a second time, thus printing a second label.

After the second printing, `labelCounter` holds a value of 2. After the third printing, it holds a value of 3. Finally, after the 100th label prints, `labelCounter` has a value of 100. When the question `labelCounter < 100?` is asked, the answer will finally be No, and the loop will exit.

Before leaving the `createLabels()` method, and after the program prints 100 labels for an employee, there is one final step: the next input record is read from the EMPLOYEES file. When the `createLabels()` method is over, control returns to the `eof` question in the main line of the logic. If it is not `eof` (if another employee record is present), the program enters the `createLabels()` method again, resets `labelCounter` to 0, and prints 100 new labels with the next employee's name.

**TIP** Setting `labelCounter` to 0 when the `createLabels()` module is entered is important. With each new record, `labelCounter` must begin at 0 if 100 labels are to print. When the first employee's set of labels is complete, `labelCounter` holds the value 100. If it is not reset to 0 for the second employee, then no labels will ever print for that employee.

**TIP** In this example, the label-making loop executes as `labelCounter` varies from 0 to 100. The program would work just as well if you decided to vary the counter from 1 to 101 or use any other pair of values that differs by 100.

At some point while attempting to read a new record, the program encounters the end of the file, the `createLabels()` module is not entered again, and control passes to the `finishUp()` module. In this program, the `finishUp()` module simply closes the files. See Figure 6-8.

**FIGURE 6-8:** THE `finishUp()` MODULE FOR THE LABEL PROGRAM

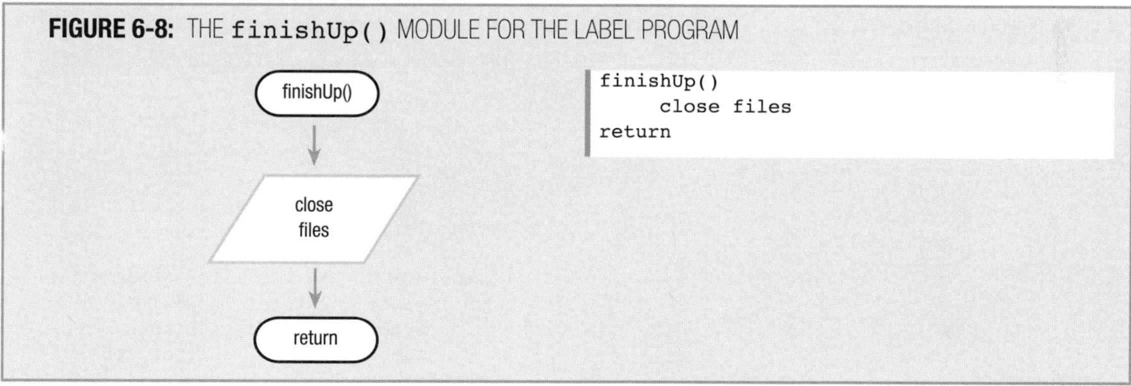


```
finishUp()
     close files
return
```

## LOOPING WITH A VARIABLE SENTINEL VALUE

Sometimes you don't want to be forced to repeat every pass through a loop the same number of times. For example, instead of printing 100 labels for each employee, you might want to vary the number of labels based on how many items a worker actually produces. That way, high-achieving workers won't run out of labels, and less productive workers won't have too many. Instead of printing the same number of labels for every employee, a more sophisticated program prints a different number for each employee, depending on that employee's production the previous week. For example, you might decide to print enough labels to cover 110 percent of each employee's production rate from the previous week; this ensures that the employee will have enough labels for the week, even if his or her production level improves.

For example, assume that employee production data exists in an input file called EMPPRODUCTION in the format shown in Figure 6-9.

A real-life production file would undoubtedly have more fields in each record, but these fields supply more than enough information to produce the labels. You need the first name to print on the label, and you need the field that holds production for the last week in order to calculate the number of labels to print for each employee. Assume this field can contain any number from 0 through 999.

**FIGURE 6-9:** EMPLOYEE PRODUCTION FILE DESCRIPTION

```
File Name: EMPPRODUCTION
FIELD DESCRIPTION          DATA TYPE     COMMENTS
Last Name                  Character     20 characters
First Name                 Character     15 characters
Production Last Week       Numeric       0 decimal places
```

To write a program that produces an appropriate number of labels for each employee, you can make some minor modifications to the original label-making program. For example, the input file variables have changed; you must declare a variable for an `inLastProduction` field. Additionally, you might want to create a numeric field named `labelsToPrint` that can hold a value equal to 110 percent of a worker's `inLastProduction`.

The major modification to the original label-making program is in the question that controls the label-producing loop. Instead of asking if `labelCounter < 100`, you now can ask if `labelCounter < labelsToPrint`. The sentinel, or limit, value can be a variable like `labelsToPrint` just as easily as it can be a constant like 100. See Figure 6-10 for the flowchart as well as the pseudocode.

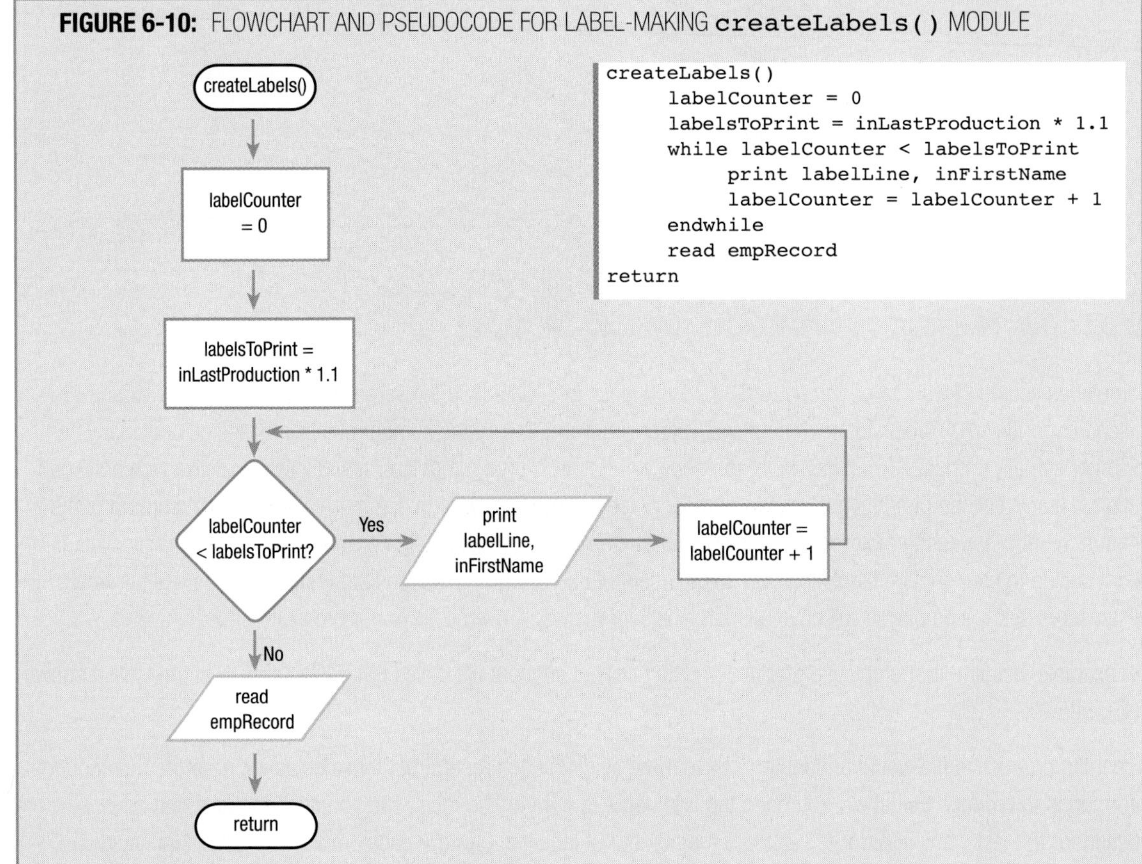


```
createLabels()
     labelCounter = 0
     labelsToPrint = inLastProduction * 1.1
     while labelCounter < labelsToPrint
          print labelLine, inFirstName
          labelCounter = labelCounter + 1
     endwhile
     read empRecord
return
```

**FIGURE 6-10:** FLOWCHART AND PSEUDOCODE FOR LABEL-MAKING `createLabels()` MODULE

TIP

The statement `labelsToPrint = inLastProduction * 1.1` calculates `labelsToPrint` as 110 percent of `inLastProduction`. Alternatively, you can perform the calculation as `labelsToPrint = inLastProduction + 0.10 * inLastProduction`. The mathematical result is the same.

## LOOPING BY DECREMENTING

Rather than increasing a loop control variable until it passes some sentinel value, sometimes it is more convenient to reduce a loop control variable on every cycle through a loop. For example, again assume you want to print enough labels for every worker to cover 110 percent production. As an alternative to setting a `labelCounter` variable to 0 and increasing it after each label prints, you initially can set `labelCounter` equal to the number of labels to print (`inLastProduction * 1.1`), and subsequently reduce the `labelCounter` value every time a label prints. You continue printing labels and reducing `labelCounter` until you have counted down to zero. Decreasing a variable is called **decrementing** the variable; programmers most often use the term to mean a decrease by one.

For example, when you write the following, you produce enough labels to equal 110 percent of `inLastProduction`:

```
labelCounter = inLastProduction * 1.1
while labelCounter > 0
     print labelLine, inFirstName
     labelCounter = labelCounter - 1
endwhile
```

TIP

Many languages provide separate numeric data types for whole number (integer) values and floating-point values (those with decimal places). Depending on the data type you choose for `labelCounter`, you might end up calculating a fraction of a label to print. For example, if `inLastProduction` is 5, then the number of labels to produce is 5.5. The logic shown here would print the additional label.

When you decrement, you can avoid declaring a special variable for `labelsToPrint`. The `labelCounter` variable starts with a value that represents the labels to print, and works its way down to zero.

Yet another alternative allows you to eliminate the `labelCounter` variable. You could use the `inLastProduction` variable itself to keep track of the labels. For example, the following pseudocode segment also produces a number of labels equal to 110 percent of each worker's `inLastProduction` value:

```
inLastProduction = inLastProduction * 1.1
while inLastProduction > 0
     print labelLine, inFirstName
     inLastProduction = inLastProduction - 1
endwhile
```

In this example, `inLastProduction` is first increased by 10 percent. Then, while it remains above 0, there are more labels to print; when it is eventually reduced to hold the value 0, all the needed labels will have been printed. With this method, you do not need to create any new counter variables such as `labelCounter`, because `inLastProduction` itself acts as a counter. However, you can't use this method if you need to use the value of `inLastProduction` for this record later in the program. By decrementing the variable, you are changing its value on every cycle through the loop; when you have finished, the original value in `inLastProduction` has been lost.

**TIP** Do not think the value of `inLastProduction` is gone forever when you alter it. If the data is being read from a file, then the original value still exists within the data file. It is the main memory location called `inLastProduction` that is being reduced.

## AVOIDING COMMON LOOP MISTAKES

The mistakes that programmers make most often with loops are:

- Neglecting to initialize the loop control variable
- Neglecting to alter the loop control variable
- Using the wrong comparison with the loop control variable
- Including statements inside the loop that belong outside the loop
- Initializing a variable that does not require initialization

### NEGLECTING TO INITIALIZE THE LOOP CONTROL VARIABLE

It is always a mistake to fail to initialize a loop's control variable. For example, assume you remove the statement `labelCounter = 0` from the program illustrated in Figure 6-10. When `labelCounter` is compared to `labelsToPrint` at the start of the `while` loop, it is impossible to predict whether any labels will print. Because uninitialized values contain unknown, unpredictable garbage, comparing such a variable to another value is meaningless. Even if you initialize `labelCounter` to 0 in the `housekeep()` module of the program, you must reset `labelCounter` to 0 for each new record that is processed within the `while` loop. If you fail to reset `labelCounter`, it never surpasses 100 because after it reaches 100, the answer to the question `labelCounter < 100` is always No, and the logic never enters the loop where a label can be printed.

### NEGLECTING TO ALTER THE LOOP CONTROL VARIABLE

A different sort of error occurs if you remove the statement that adds 1 to `labelCounter` from the program in Figure 6-10. This error results in the following code:

```
while labelCounter < labelsToPrint
     print labelLine, inFirstName
endwhile
```

Following this logic, if `labelCounter` is 0 and `labelsToPrint` is, for example, 110, then `labelCounter` will be less than `labelsToPrint` forever. Nothing in the loop changes either variable, so when `labelCounter` is less than `labelsToPrint` once, then `labelCounter` is less than `labelsToPrint` forever, and labels will continue to print. A loop that never stops executing is called an **infinite loop**. It is unstructured and incorrect to create a loop that cannot terminate on its own.

**TIP** □□□□ Although most programmers advise that infinite loops must be avoided, some programmers argue that there are legitimate uses for them. Intentional uses for infinite loops include programs that are supposed to run continuously, such as product demonstrations, or in programming for embedded systems.

## USING THE WRONG COMPARISON WITH THE LOOP CONTROL VARIABLE

Programmers must be careful to use the correct comparison in the statement that controls a loop. Although there is only a one-keystroke difference between the following two code segments, one performs the loop 10 times and the other performs the loop 11 times.

```
counter = 0
while counter < 10
     perform someModule()
     counter = counter + 1
endwhile
```

and

```
counter = 0
while counter <= 10
     perform someModule()
     counter = counter + 1
endwhile
```

The seriousness of the error of using <= or >= when only < or > is needed depends on the actions performed within the loop. For example, if such an error occurred in a loan company program, each customer might be charged a month's additional interest; if the error occurred in an airline's program, it might overbook a flight; and if it occurred in a pharmacy's drug-dispensing program, each patient might receive one extra (and possibly harmful) unit of medication.

## INCLUDING STATEMENTS INSIDE THE LOOP THAT BELONG OUTSIDE THE LOOP

When you run a computer program that uses the loop in Figure 6-10, hundreds or thousands of employee records might pass through the `createLabels()` method. If there are 100 employee records, then `labelCounter` is set to 0 exactly 100 times; it must be reset to 0 once for each employee, in order to count each employee's labels correctly. Similarly, `labelsToPrint` is reset (to 1.1 times the current `inLastProduction` value) once for each employee.

If the average employee produces 100 items during a week, then the loop within the `createLabels()` method, the one controlled by the statement `while labelCounter < labelsToPrint`, executes 11,000 times—110 times each for 100 employees. This number of repetitions is necessary in order to print the correct number of labels.

A repetition that is *not* necessary would be to execute 11,000 separate multiplication statements to recalculate the value to compare to `labelCounter`. See Figure 6-11.

**FIGURE 6-11:** INEFFICIENT PSEUDOCODE FOR LABEL-MAKING `createLabels()` MODULE

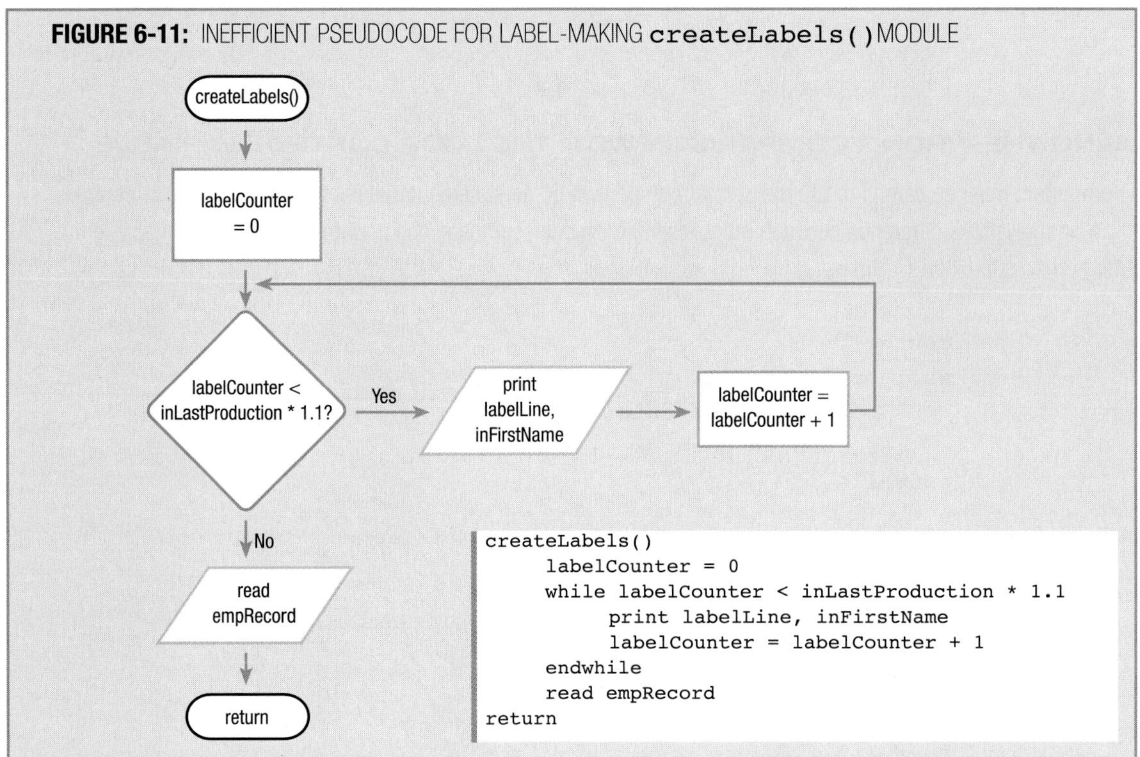


```
createLabels()
     labelCounter = 0
     while labelCounter < inLastProduction * 1.1
          print labelLine, inFirstName
          labelCounter = labelCounter + 1
     endwhile
     read empRecord
return
```

Although the logic shown in Figure 6-11 will produce the correct number of labels for every employee, the statement `while labelCounter < inLastProduction * 1.1` executes an average of 110 times for each employee. That means the arithmetic operation that is part of the question—multiplying `inLastProduction` by 1.1—occurs 110 separate times for each employee. Performing the same calculation that results in the same mathematical answer 110 times in a row is inefficient. Instead, it is superior to perform the multiplication just once for each employee and use the result 110 times, as shown in the original version of the program in Figure 6-10. In the pseudocode in Figure 6-10, you still must recalculate `labelsToPrint` once for each record, but not once for each label, so you have improved the program's efficiency.

The modules illustrated in Figures 6-10 and 6-11 do the same thing: print enough labels for every employee to cover 110 percent of production. As you become more proficient at programming, you will recognize many opportunities to perform the same tasks in alternative, more elegant, and more efficient ways.

## INITIALIZING A VARIABLE THAT DOES NOT REQUIRE INITIALIZATION

Another common error made by beginning programmers involves initializing a variable that does not require initialization. When declaring variables for the label-making program, you might be tempted to declare `num labelsToPrint = inLastProduction * 1.1`. It seems as though this declaration statement indicates that the value of `labelsToPrint` will always be 110 percent of the `inLastProduction` figure. However, this approach is incorrect for two reasons. First, at the time `labelsToPrint` is declared, the first employee record has not yet been read into memory, so the value of `inLastProduction` is garbage; therefore, the result in `labelsToPrint` after multiplication will also be garbage. Second, even if you read the first `empRecord` into memory before declaring the `labelsToPrint` variable, the mathematical calculation of `labelsToPrint` within the `housekeep()` module would be valid for the first record only. The value of `labelsToPrint` must be recalculated for each employee record in the input file. Therefore, calculation of `labelsToPrint` correctly belongs within the `createLabels()` module, as shown in Figure 6-10.

## USING THE FOR STATEMENT

The label-making programs discussed in this chapter each contain two loops. For example, Figures 6-12 and 6-13 show the loop within the mainline program as well as the loop within the `createLabels()` module for a program that produces exactly 100 labels for each employee. (These flowcharts were shown earlier in this chapter.)

**FIGURE 6-12:** MAINLINE LOGIC FOR LABEL-MAKING PROGRAM

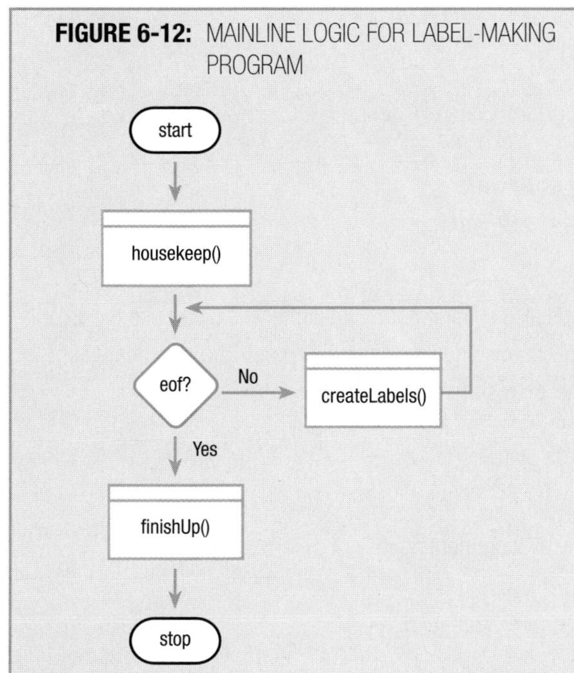


**FIGURE 6-13:** THE `createLabels()` LOGIC FOR LABEL-MAKING PROGRAM

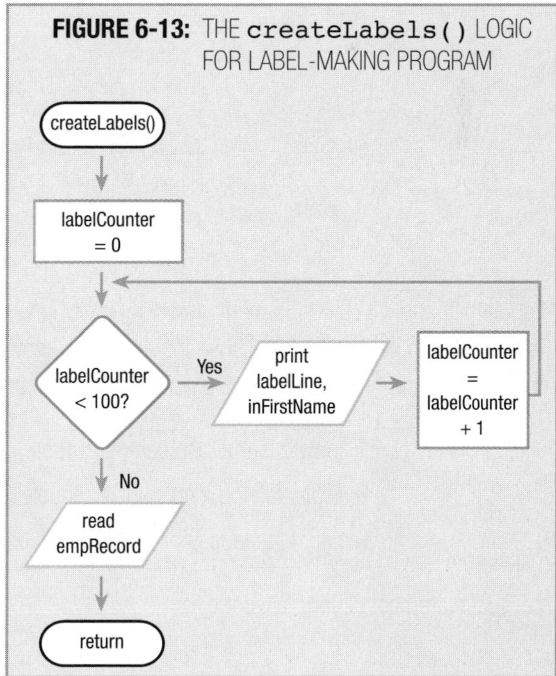

Entry to the `createLabels()` module in the mainline logic of the label-making program is controlled by the `eof` decision. Within the `createLabels()` method, the loop that produces labels is controlled by the `labelCounter` decision. When you execute the mainline logic, you cannot predict how many times the `createLabels()` module will execute. Depending on the size of the input file (that is, depending on the number of employees who require labels), any number of records might be processed; while the program runs, you don't know what the total number of records finally will be. Until you attempt to read a record and encounter the end of the file, you don't know if more records are going to become available. Of course, not being able to predict the number of input records is valuable—it allows the program to function correctly no matter how many employees exist from week to week or year to year. Because you can't determine ahead of time how many records there might be and, therefore, how many times the loop might execute, the mainline loop in the label-making program is called an **indeterminate**, or **indefinite**, **loop**.

With some loops, you know exactly how many times they will execute. If every employee needs 100 printed labels, then the loop within the `createLabels()` module executes exactly 100 times for each employee. This kind of loop, in which you definitely know the repetition factor, is a **definite loop**.

Every high-level computer programming language contains a **`while` statement** that you can use to code any loop, including indefinite loops (like the mainline loop) and definite loops (like the label-printing loop). You can write statements like the following:

```
while not eof
     perform createLabels()
endwhile
```

and

```
while labelCounter < 100
     print labelLine, inFirstName
     labelCounter = labelCounter + 1
endwhile
```

In addition to the `while` statement, most computer languages also support a `for` statement. You can use the **`for` statement** with definite loops—those for which you know how many times the loop will repeat. The `for` statement provides you with three actions in one compact statement. The `for` statement:

- initializes the loop control variable
- evaluates the loop control variable
- alters the loop control variable (typically by incrementing it)

The `for` statement usually takes the form:

```
for initialValue to finalValue
     do something
endfor
```

For example, to print 100 labels you can write:

```
for labelCounter = 0 to 99
     print labelLine, inFirstName
endfor
```

This `for` statement accomplishes several tasks at once in a compact form:

- The `for` statement initializes `labelCounter` to 0.
- The `for` statement checks `labelCounter` against the limit value 99 and makes sure that `labelCounter` is less than or equal to that value.
- If the evaluation is true, the `for` statement body that prints the label executes.
- After the `for` statement body executes, `labelCounter` increases by 1 and the comparison to the limit value is made again.

**TIP** As an alternative to using the loop `for labelCounter = 0 to 99`, you can use `for labelCounter = 1 to 100`. You can use any combination of values, as long as there are 100 whole number values between (and including) the two limits.

The `for` statement does not represent a new structure; it simply provides a compact way to write a pretest loop. You are never required to use a `for` statement; the label loop executes correctly using a `while` statement with `labelCounter` as a loop control variable. However, when a loop is based on a loop control variable progressing from a known starting value to a known ending value in equal increments, the `for` statement presents you with a convenient shorthand.

**TIP** The programmer needs to know neither the starting nor the ending value for the loop control variable; only the program must know those values. For example, you don't know the value of a worker's `inLastProduction`, but when you tell the program to read a record, the program knows. To use this value as a limit value, you can write a `for` statement that begins `for labelCounter = 1 to inLastProduction`.

**TIP** In most programming languages, you can provide a `for` statement with a step value. A step value is a number you use to increase (or decrease) a loop control variable on each pass through a loop. In most programming languages, the default loop step value is 1. You specify a step value when you want each pass through the loop to change the loop control variable by a value other than 1.

**TIP** In Java, C++, C#, and other modern languages, the `for` statement is written using the keyword `for` followed by parentheses that contain the increment test, which alters portions of the loop. For example, the following `for` statement could be used in several languages:

```
for(labelCounter = 0; labelCounter < 100; labelCounter = labelCounter + 1)
   print labelLine, inFirstName
```

In this example, the first section within the parentheses initializes the loop control variable, the middle section tests it, and the last section alters it. In languages that use this format, you can use the `for` statement for indefinite loops as well as definite loops.

## USING THE DO WHILE AND DO UNTIL LOOPS

When you use either a `while` loop or a `for` statement, the body of the loop may never execute. For example, in the mainline logic in Figure 6-5, the last action in the `housekeep()` module is to read an input record. If the input file contains no records, the result of the `eof` decision is true, and the program executes the `finishUp()` module without ever entering the `createLabels()` module.

Similarly, when you produce labels within the `createLabels()` module shown in Figure 6-10, labels are produced `while labelCounter < labelsToPrint`. Suppose an employee record contains a 0 in the `inLastProduction` field—for example, in the case of a new employee or an employee who was on vacation during the previous week. In such a case, the value of `labelsToPrint` would be 0, and the label-producing body of the loop would never execute. With a `while` loop, you evaluate the loop control variable prior to executing the loop body, and the evaluation might indicate that you can't enter the loop.

With a `while` loop, the loop body might not execute. When you want to ensure that a loop's body executes at least one time, you can use either a `do while` or a `do until` loop. In both types of loops, the loop control variable is evaluated after the loop body executes, instead of before. Therefore, the body always executes at least one time. Although the loops have similarities, as explained above, they are different in that the `do while` loop continues when the result of the test of the loop control variable is true, but the `do until` loop continues when the result of the test of the loop control variable is false. In other words, the difference between the two loops is simply in how the question at the bottom of the loop is phrased.

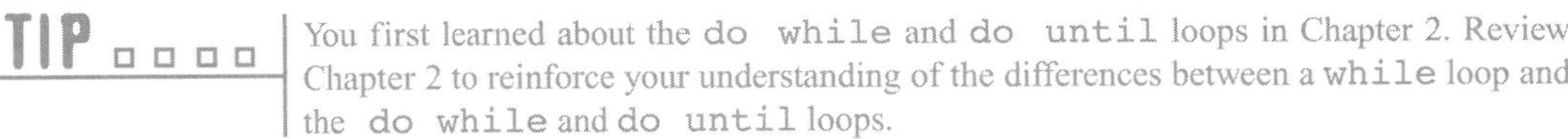

TIP You first learned about the `do while` and `do until` loops in Chapter 2. Review Chapter 2 to reinforce your understanding of the differences between a `while` loop and the `do while` and `do until` loops.

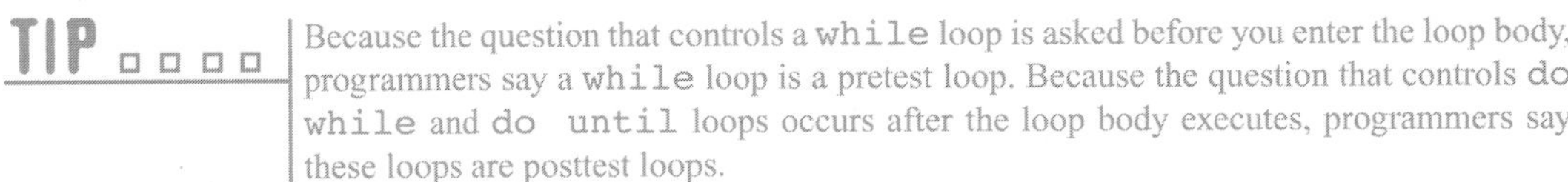

TIP Because the question that controls a `while` loop is asked before you enter the loop body, programmers say a `while` loop is a pretest loop. Because the question that controls `do while` and `do until` loops occurs after the loop body executes, programmers say these loops are posttest loops.

For example, suppose you want to produce one label for each employee to wear as identification, before you produce enough labels to cover 110 percent of last week's production. You can write the `do until` loop that appears in Figure 6-14.

**FIGURE 6-14:** USING A `do until` LOOP TO PRINT ONE IDENTIFICATION LABEL, THEN PRINT ENOUGH TO COVER PRODUCTION REQUIREMENTS

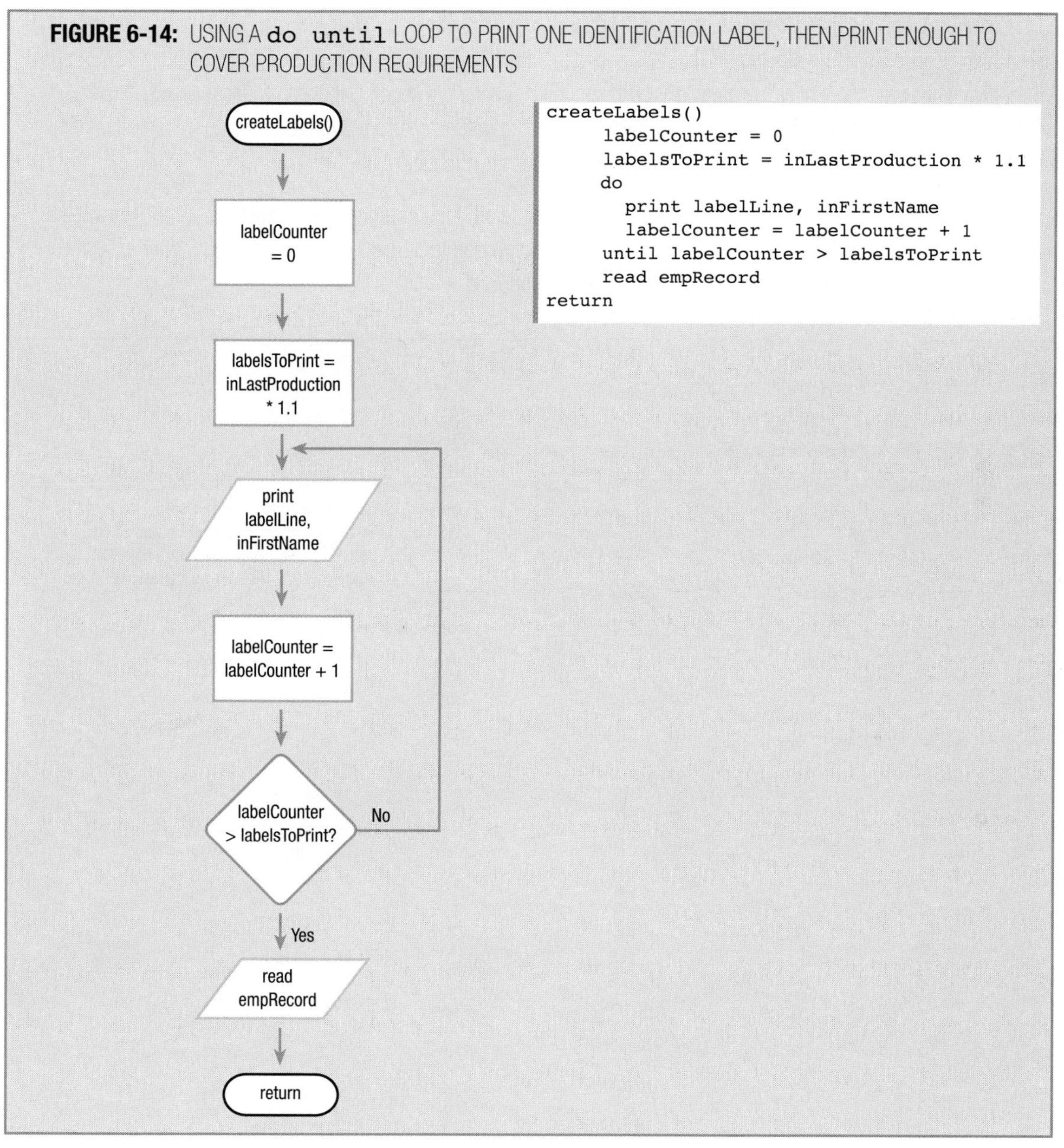


```
createLabels()
     labelCounter = 0
     labelsToPrint = inLastProduction * 1.1
     do
       print labelLine, inFirstName
       labelCounter = labelCounter + 1
     until labelCounter > labelsToPrint
     read empRecord
return
```

In Figure 6-14, the `labelCounter` variable is set to 0 and `labelsToPrint` is calculated. Suppose `labelsToPrint` is computed to be 0. The `do until` loop will be entered, a label will print, 1 will be added to `labelCounter`, and then and only then will `labelCounter` be compared to `labelsToPrint`. Because `labelCounter` is now 1 and `labelsToPrint` is only 0, the loop is exited, having printed a single identification label and no product labels.

As a different example using the logic in Figure 6-14, suppose that for a worker `labelsToPrint` is calculated to be 1. In this case, the loop is entered, a label prints, and 1 is added to `labelCounter`. Now, the value of `labelCounter` is not yet greater than the value of `labelsToPrint`, so the loop repeats, a second label prints, and `labelCounter` is incremented again. This time `labelCounter` (with a value of 2) does exceed `labelsToPrint` (with a value of 1), so the loop ends. This employee gets an identification label as well as one product label.

Of course, you could achieve the same results by printing one label, then entering a `while` loop, as in Figure 6-15. In this example, one label prints before `labelCounter` is compared to `labelsToPrint`. No matter what the value of `labelsToPrint` is, one identification label is produced.

**FIGURE 6-15:** USING A `while` LOOP TO PRINT ONE IDENTIFICATION LABEL, THEN PRINT ENOUGH TO COVER PRODUCTION REQUIREMENTS

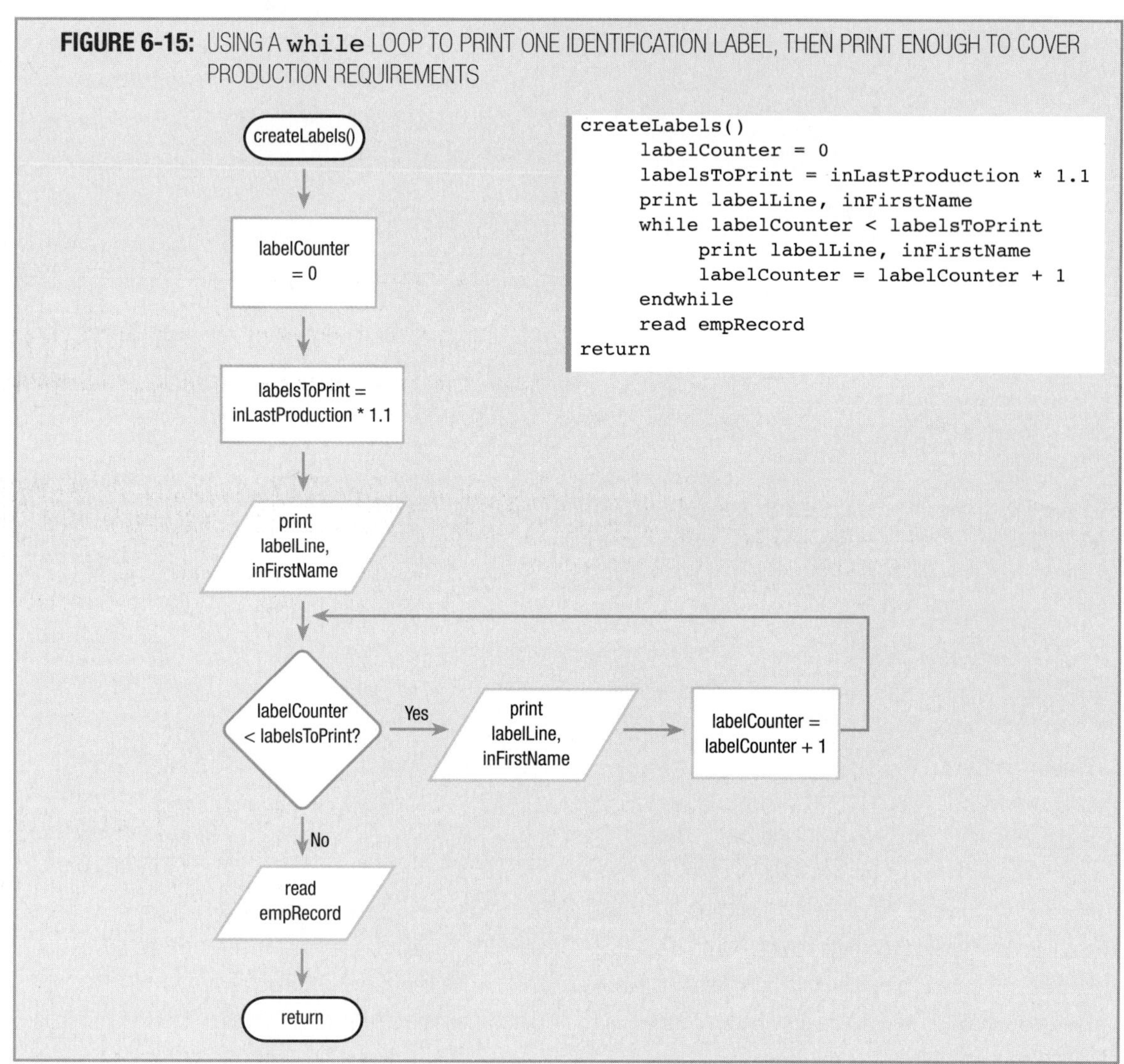


```
createLabels()
     labelCounter = 0
     labelsToPrint = inLastProduction * 1.1
     print labelLine, inFirstName
     while labelCounter < labelsToPrint
          print labelLine, inFirstName
          labelCounter = labelCounter + 1
     endwhile
     read empRecord
return
```

**TIP** The logic in Figure 6-15, in which you print one label and then test a value to determine whether you will print more, takes the same form as the mainline logic in most of the programs you have worked with so far. When you read records from a file, you read one record (the priming read) and then test for `eof` before continuing. In effect, the first label printed in Figure 6-15 is a "priming label."

The results of the programs shown in Figures 6-14 and 6-15 are the same. Using either, every employee will receive an identification label and enough labels to cover production. Each module works correctly, and neither is logically superior to the other. There is almost always more than one way to solve the same programming problem. As you learned in Chapter 2, a posttest loop (`do while` or `do until`) can always be replaced by pairing a sequence and a pretest `while` loop. Which method you choose depends on your (or your instructor's or supervisor's) preference.

**TIP** There are several additional ways to approach the logic shown in the programs in Figures 6-14 and 6-15. For example, after calculating `labelsToPrint`, you could immediately add 1 to the value. Then, you could use the logic in Figure 6-14, as long as you change the loop-ending question to `labelCounter >= labelsToPrint` (instead of only >). Alternatively, using the logic in Figure 6-15, after adding 1 to `labelsToPrint`, you could remove the lone first label-printing instruction; that way, one identification label would always be printed, even if the last production figure was 0.

## RECOGNIZING THE CHARACTERISTICS SHARED BY ALL LOOPS

You can see from Figure 6-15 that you are never required to use posttest loops (either a `do while` loop or a `do until` loop). The same results always can be achieved by performing the loop body steps once before entering a `while` loop. If you follow the logic of either of the loops shown in Figures 6-14 and 6-15, you will discover that when an employee has an `inLastProduction` value of 3, then exactly four labels print. Likewise, when an employee has an `inLastProduction` value of 0, then exactly one label prints. You can accomplish the same results with either type of loop; the posttest `do while` and `do until` loops simply are a convenience when you need a loop's statements to execute at least one time.

**TIP** In some languages, the `do until` loop is called a `repeat until` loop.

If you can express the logic you want to perform by saying "while a is true, keep doing b," you probably want to use a `while` loop. If what you want to accomplish seems to fit the statement "do a until b is true," you can probably use a `do until` loop. If the statement "do a while b is true" makes more sense, then you might choose to use a `do while` loop.

As you examine Figures 6-14 and 6-15, notice that with the `do until` loop in Figure 6-14, the loop-controlling question is placed at the *end* of the sequence of the steps that repeat. With the `while` loop, the loop-controlling question is placed at the *beginning* of the steps that repeat. All structured loops (whether they are `while` loops, `do while` loops, or `do until` loops) share these characteristics:

- The loop-controlling question provides either entry to or exit from the repeating structure.
- The loop-controlling question provides the *only* entry to or exit from the repeating structure.

You should also notice the difference between *unstructured* loops and the structured `do until` and `while` loops. Figure 6-16 diagrams the outline of two unstructured loops. In each case, the decision labeled X breaks out of the loop prematurely. In each case, the loop control variable (labeled `LC`) does not provide the only entry to or exit from the loop.

**FIGURE 6-16:** EXAMPLES OF UNSTRUCTURED LOOPS

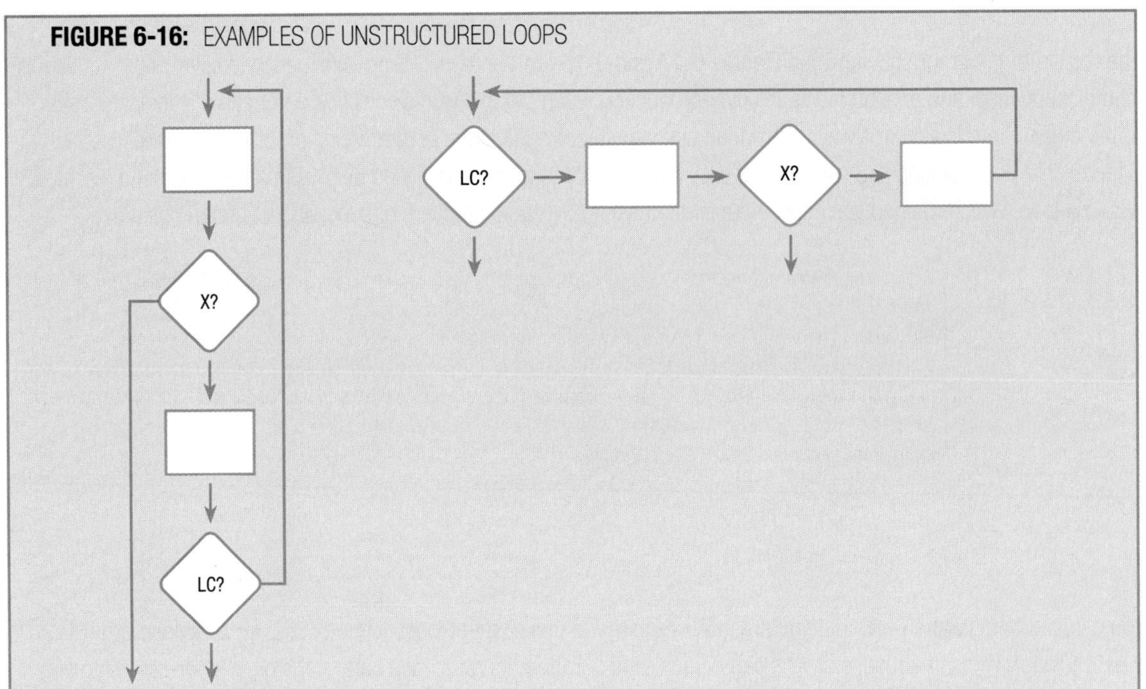


## NESTING LOOPS

Program logic gets more complicated when you must use loops within loops, or **nesting loops**. When one loop appears inside another, the loop that contains the other loop is called the **outer loop**, and the loop that is contained is called the **inner loop**. For example, suppose you work for a company that pays workers twice per month. The company has decided on an incentive plan to provide each employee with a one-fourth of one percent raise for each pay period during the coming year, and it wants a report for each employee like that shown in Figure 6-17. A list will be printed for each employee showing the exact paycheck amounts for each of the next 24 pay periods—two per month for 12 months. A description of the employee input record is shown in Figure 6-18.

**FIGURE 6-17:** SAMPLE PROJECTED PAYROLL REPORT FOR ONE EMPLOYEE

```
        Projected Payroll for
          Roberto Martinez
   Month      Check        Amount

     1          1          501.25
     1          2          502.50
     2          1          503.76
     2          2          505.02
     3          1          506.28
```

**FIGURE 6-18:** EMPLOYEE PAYROLL RECORD DATA FILE DESCRIPTION

```
File Name: EMPPAY
FIELD DESCRIPTION         DATA TYPE        COMMENTS
Employee Last Name        Character        12 characters
Employee First Name       Character        8 characters
Weekly salary at          Numeric          2 decimal places
   start of year
```

To produce the Projected Payroll report, you need to maintain two separate counters to control two separate loops. One counter will keep track of the month (1 through 12), and another will keep track of the pay period within the month (1 through 2). When nesting loops, you must maintain individual loop control variables—one for each loop—and alter each at the appropriate time.

Figure 6-19 shows the mainline, `housekeeping()`, and `finish()` logic for the program. These modules are standard. Besides the input file variables and the headers that print for each employee, the list of declared variables includes two counters. One, named `monthCounter`, keeps track of the month that is currently printing. The other, named `checkCounter`, keeps track of which check within the month is currently printing. Three additional declarations hold the number of months in a year (12), the number of checks in a month (2), and the rate of increase (0.0025). Declaring these constants is not required; the program could just use the numeric constants 12, 2, and 0.0025 within its statements, but providing those values with names serves two purposes. First, the program becomes more self-documenting—that is, it describes itself to the reader because the choice of variable names is clear. When other programmers read a program and encounter a number like 2, they might wonder about the meaning. Instead, if the value is named `CHECKS_IN_A_MONTH`, the meaning of the value is much clearer. Second, after the program is in production, the company might choose to change one of the values—for example, by going to an 11-month year, producing more or fewer paychecks in a month, or changing the raise rate. In those cases, the person who modifies the program would not have to search for appropriate spots to make those changes, but would simply redefine the values assigned to the appropriate named constants.

**FIGURE 6-19:** MAINLINE LOGIC, `housekeeping()`, AND `finish()` MODULES FOR PROJECTED PAYROLL REPORT PROGRAM

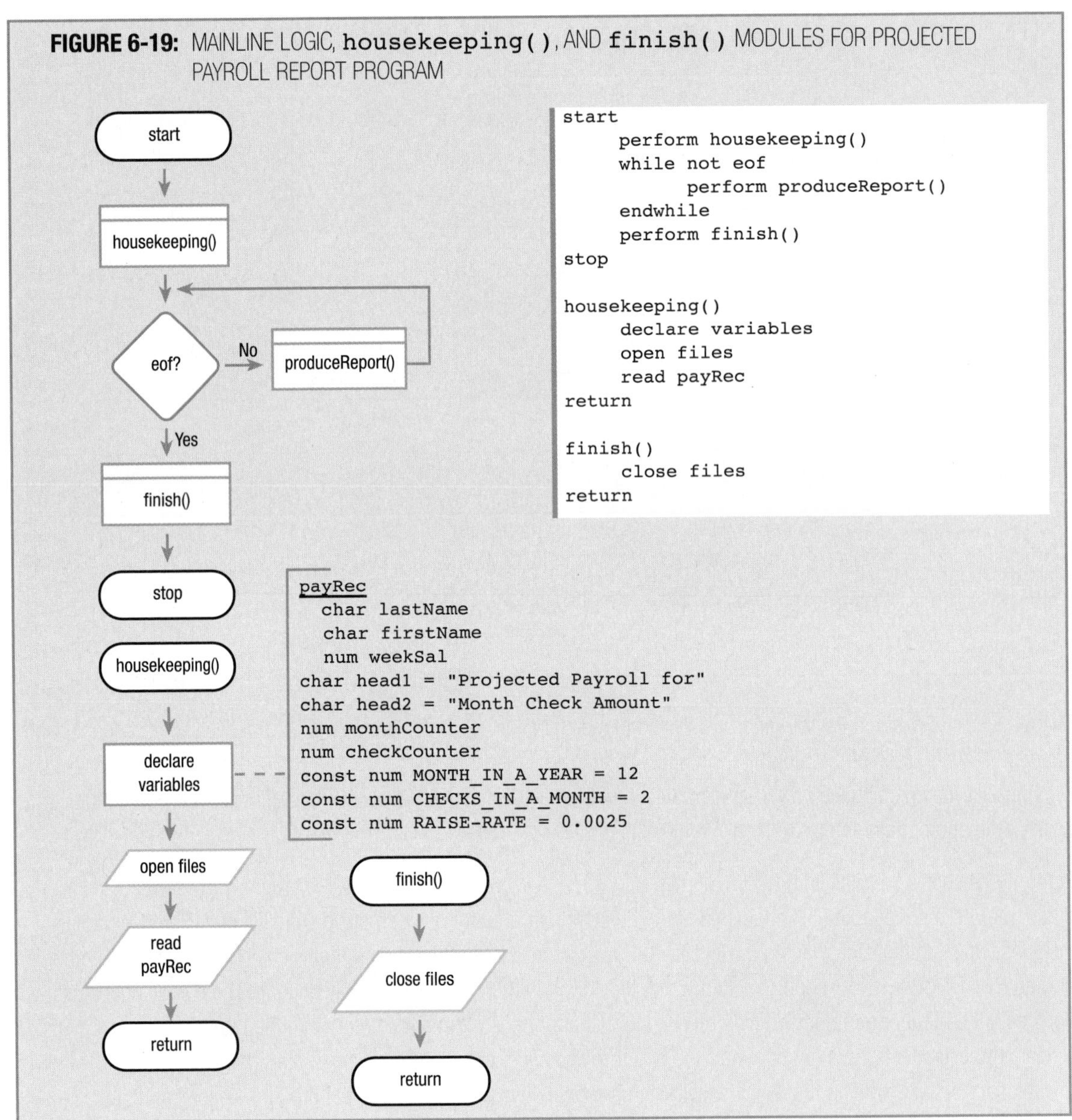
start
housekeeping()
eof?
No
produceReport()
Yes
finish()
stop
housekeeping()
declare variables
open files
read payRec
return
finish()
close files
return
payRec
char lastName
char firstName
num weekSal
char head1 = "Projected Payroll for"
char head2 = "Month Check Amount"
num monthCounter
num checkCounter
const num MONTH_IN_A_YEAR = 12
const num CHECKS_IN_A_MONTH = 2
const num RAISE-RATE = 0.0025

```
start
     perform housekeeping()
     while not eof
           perform produceReport()
     endwhile
     perform finish()
stop

housekeeping()
     declare variables
     open files
     read payRec
return

finish()
     close files
return
```

**TIP** In Chapter 1 you learned that by convention, many programmers use all uppercase letters when naming constants.

At the end of the `housekeeping()` module in Figure 6-19, the first employee record is read into main memory. Figure 6-20 shows how the record is processed in the `produceReport()` module. The program proceeds as follows:

1. The first heading prints, followed by the employee name and the column headings.
2. The `monthCounter` variable is set to 1; `monthCounter` is the loop control variable for the outer loop, and this step provides it with its initial value.
3. The `monthCounter` variable is compared to the number of months in a year, and because the comparison evaluates as true, the outer loop is entered. Within this loop, the `checkCounter` variable is used as a loop control variable for an inner loop.
4. The `checkCounter` variable is initialized to 1, and then compared to the number of checks in a month. Because this comparison evaluates as true, the inner loop is entered.
5. Within this inner loop, the employee's weekly salary is increased by one-fourth of one percent (the old salary plus 0.0025 of the old salary).
6. The month number (currently 1), check number (also currently 1), and newly calculated salary are printed.
7. The check number is increased (to 2), and the inner loop reaches its end; this causes the logical control to return to the top of the inner loop, where the `while` condition is tested again. Because the check number (2) is still less than or equal to the number of checks in a month, the inner loop is entered again.
8. The pay amount increases, and the month (still 1), check number (2), and new salary are printed.
9. Then, the check number becomes 3. Now, when the loop condition is tested for the third time, the check number is no longer less than or equal to the number of checks in a month, so the inner loop ends.
10. As the last step in the outer loop, `monthCounter` becomes 2.
11. After `monthCounter` increases to 2, control returns to the entry point of the outer loop.
12. The `while` condition is tested, and because 2 is not greater than the number of months in a year, the outer loop is entered for a second time.
13. The `checkCounter` variable is reset to 1 so that it will correctly count two checks for this month.
14. Because the newly reset `checkCounter` is not more than the number of checks in a month, the salary is increased, and the amount prints for month 2, check 1.
15. The `checkCounter` variable increases to 2 and another value is printed for month 2, check 2 before the inner loop ends and `monthCounter` is increased to 3.
16. Then, month 3, check 1 prints, followed by month 3, check 2. The inner loop is evaluated again. The `checkCounter` value is 3, so the evaluation result is false.
17. The `produceReport()` module continues printing two check amounts for each of 12 months before the outer loop is finished, when `monthCounter` eventually exceeds 12. Only then is the next employee record read into memory, and control leaves the `produceReport()` module and returns to the mainline logic, where the end of file is tested. If a new record exists, control returns to the `produceReport()` module for the new employee, for whom headings are printed, and `monthCounter` is set to 1 to start the set of 24 calculations for this employee.

**FIGURE 6-20:** THE `produceReport()` MODULE FOR THE PROJECTED PAYROLL REPORT PROGRAM

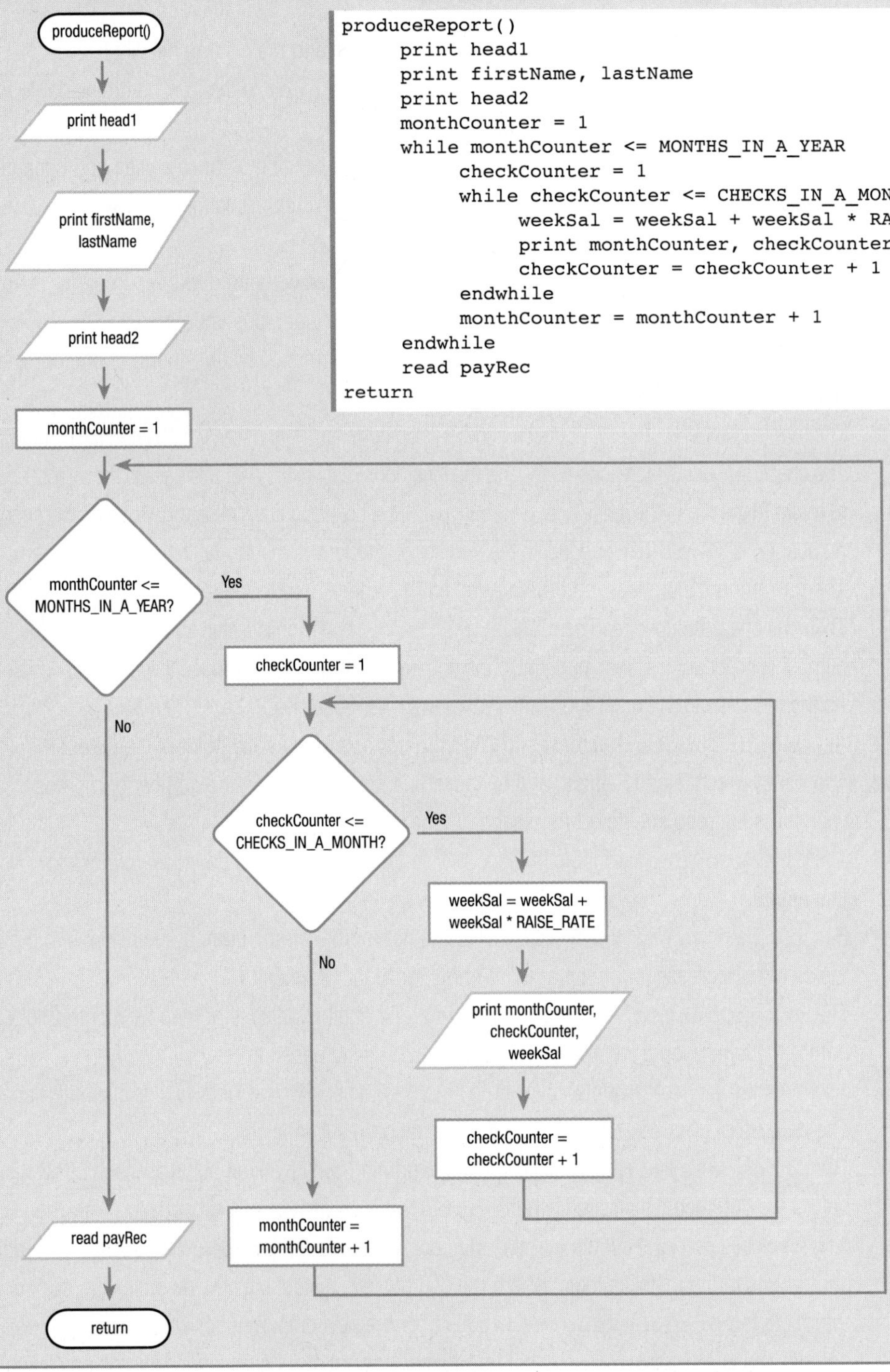

```
produceReport()
     print head1
     print firstName, lastName
     print head2
     monthCounter = 1
     while monthCounter <= MONTHS_IN_A_YEAR
          checkCounter = 1
          while checkCounter <= CHECKS_IN_A_MONTH
               weekSal = weekSal + weekSal * RAISE_RATE
               print monthCounter, checkCounter, weekSal
               checkCounter = checkCounter + 1
          endwhile
          monthCounter = monthCounter + 1
     endwhile
     read payRec
return
```

**TIP** If you have trouble seeing that the flowchart in Figure 6-20 is structured, consider moving the `checkCounter` loop and its three resulting actions to its own module. Then you should see that the `monthCounter` loop contains a sequence of three steps and that the middle step is a loop.

There is no limit to the number of loop-nesting levels a program can contain. For instance, suppose that in the projected payroll example, the company wanted to provide a slight raise each hour or each day of each pay period in each month for each of several years. No matter how many levels deep the nesting goes, each loop must still contain a loop control variable that is initialized, tested, and altered.

## USING A LOOP TO ACCUMULATE TOTALS

Business reports often include totals. The supervisor requesting a list of employees who participate in the company dental plan is often as much interested in *how many* such employees there are as in *who* they are. When you receive your telephone bill at the end of the month, you are usually more interested in the total than in the charges for the individual calls. Some business reports list no individual detail records, just totals or other overall statistics such as averages. Such reports are called **summary reports**. Many business reports list both the details of individual records and totals at the end.

For example, a real estate broker might maintain a file of company real estate listings. Each record in the file contains the street address and the asking price of a property for sale. The broker wants a listing of all the properties for sale; she also wants a total value for all the company's listings. A typical report appears in Figure 6-21.

**FIGURE 6-21:** TYPICAL REAL ESTATE REPORT

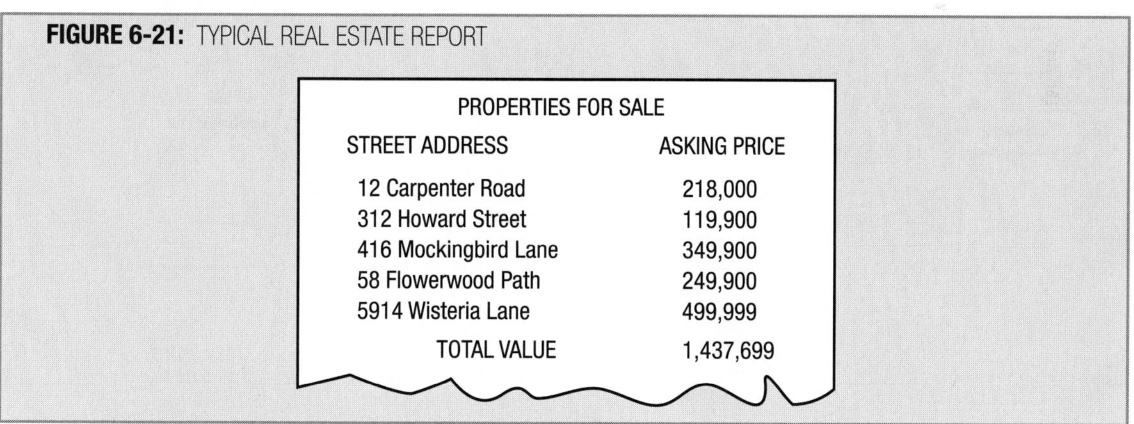

PROPERTIES FOR SALE

| STREET ADDRESS | ASKING PRICE |
|---|---|
| 12 Carpenter Road | 218,000 |
| 312 Howard Street | 119,900 |
| 416 Mockingbird Lane | 349,900 |
| 58 Flowerwood Path | 249,900 |
| 5914 Wisteria Lane | 499,999 |
| TOTAL VALUE | 1,437,699 |

When you read a real estate listing record, besides printing it you must add its value to an accumulator. An **accumulator** is a variable that you use to gather, or accumulate, values. An accumulator is very similar to a counter. The difference lies in the value that you add to the variable; usually, you add just 1 to a counter, whereas you add some other value to an accumulator. If the real estate broker wants to know how many listings the company holds, you count them. When she wants to know total real estate value, you accumulate it.

In order to accumulate total real estate prices, you declare a numeric variable at the beginning of the program, as shown in the `housekeep()` module in Figure 6-22. You must initialize the accumulator, `accumValue`, to 0. In

Chapter 4, you learned that when using most programming languages, declared variables do not automatically assume any particular value; the unknown value is called garbage. When you read the first real estate record, you will add its value to the accumulator. If the accumulator contains garbage, the addition will not work. Some programming languages issue an error message if you don't initialize a variable you use for accumulating; others let you accumulate, but the results are worthless because you start with garbage.

**FIGURE 6-22:** THE REAL ESTATE PROGRAM

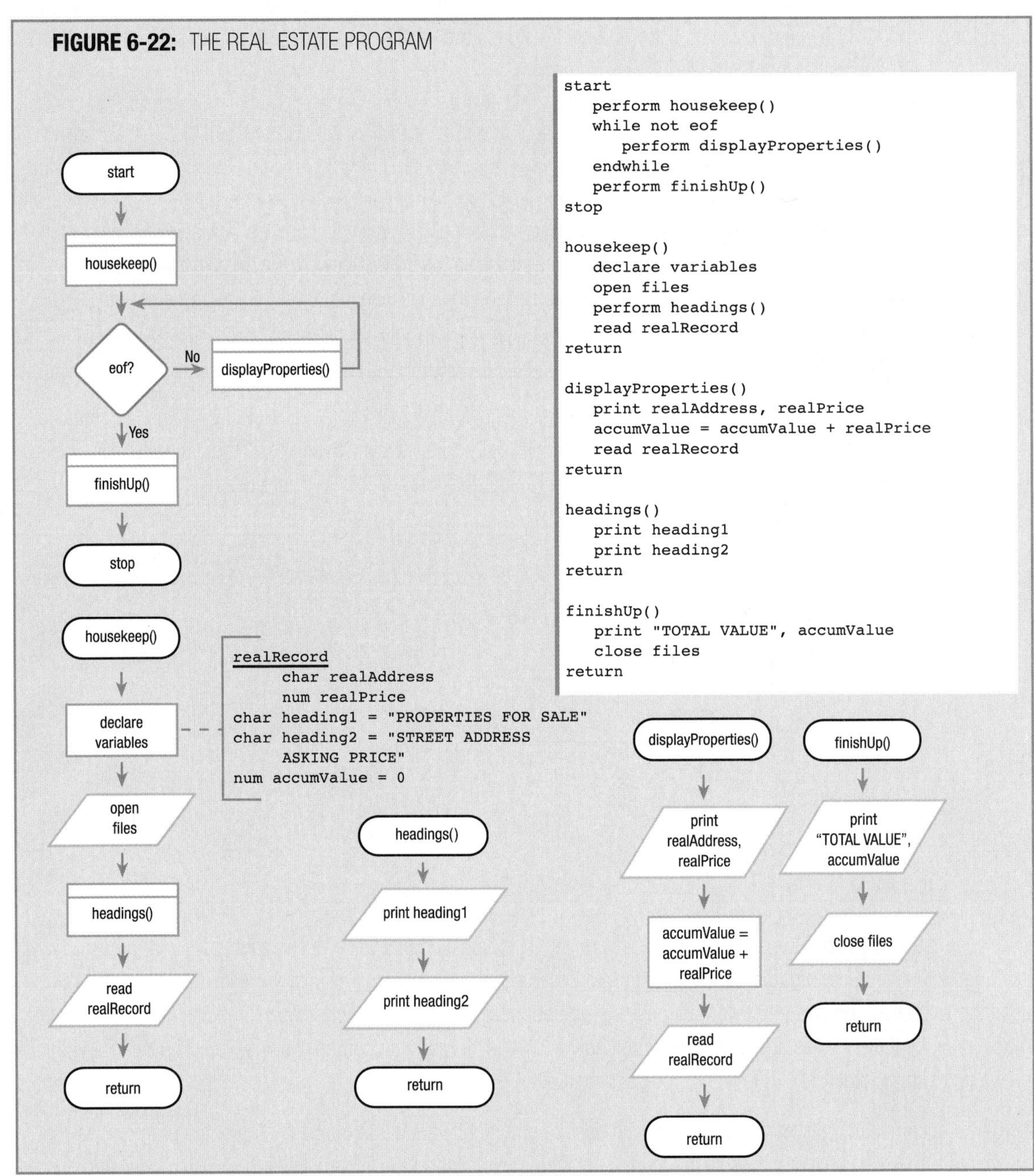


```
start
   perform housekeep()
   while not eof
      perform displayProperties()
   endwhile
   perform finishUp()
stop

housekeep()
   declare variables
   open files
   perform headings()
   read realRecord
return

displayProperties()
   print realAddress, realPrice
   accumValue = accumValue + realPrice
   read realRecord
return

headings()
   print heading1
   print heading2
return

finishUp()
   print "TOTAL VALUE", accumValue
   close files
return
```

If you name the input record fields `realAddress` and `realPrice`, then the `displayProperties()` module of the real estate listing program can be written as shown in Figure 6-22. For each real estate record, you print it and add its value to the accumulator `accumValue`. Then you can read the next record.

After the program reaches the end of the file, the accumulator will hold the grand total of all the real estate values. When you reach the end of the file, the `finishUp()` module executes, and it is within the `finishUp()` module that you print the accumulated value, `accumValue`. After printing the total, you can close both the input and the output files and return to the mainline logic, where the program ends.

New programmers often want to reset the `accumValue` to 0 after printing it. Although you *can* take this step without harming the execution of the program, it does not serve any useful purpose. You cannot set `accumValue` to 0 in anticipation of having it ready for the next program, or even for the next time you execute this program. Program variables exist only for the life of the program, and even if a future program happens to contain a variable named `accumValue`, the variable will not necessarily occupy the same memory location as this one. Even if you run the program a second time, the variables might occupy physical memory locations different from those they occupied during the first run. At the beginning of the program, it is the programmer's responsibility to initialize all variables that must start with a specific value. There is no benefit to changing a variable's value when it will never be used again during the current execution of the program.

**TIP** It is especially important to avoid changing the value of a variable unnecessarily when the change occurs within a loop. One extra, unnecessary statement in a loop that executes hundreds of thousands of times can significantly slow a program's performance speed.

## CHAPTER SUMMARY

- When you use a loop within a computer program, you can write one set of instructions that operates on multiple, separate sets of data.
- Three steps must occur in every loop: You must initialize a loop control variable, compare the variable to some value that controls whether the loop continues or stops, and alter the variable that controls the loop.
- A counter is a numeric variable you use to count the number of times an event has occurred. You can count occurrences by incrementing or decrementing a variable.
- You can use a variable sentinel value to control a loop.
- Sometimes it is convenient to reduce, or decrement, a loop control variable on every cycle through a loop.
- Mistakes that programmers often make with loops include neglecting to initialize the loop control variable and neglecting to alter the loop control variable. Other mistakes include using the wrong comparison with the loop control variable, including statements inside the loop that belong outside the loop, and initializing a variable that does not require initialization.
- Most computer languages support a **`for`** statement that you can use with definite loops when you know how many times a loop will repeat. The **`for`** statement uses a loop control variable that it automatically initializes, evaluates, and increments.
- When you want to ensure that a loop's body executes at least one time, you can use a **`do while`** loop or a **`do until`** loop, in which the loop control variable is evaluated after the loop body executes.
- All structured loops share these characteristics: The loop-controlling question provides either entry to or exit from the repeating structure, and the loop-controlling question provides the *only* entry to or exit from the repeating structure.
- When you must use loops within loops, you are using nested loops. When you create nested loops, you must maintain two individual loop control variables and alter each at the appropriate time.
- Business reports often include totals. Summary reports list no detail records—only totals. An accumulator is a variable that you use to gather or accumulate values.

## KEY TERMS

A **loop** is a structure that repeats actions while some condition continues.

A **main loop** is a basic set of instructions that is repeated for every record.

A **loop control variable** is a variable that determines whether a loop will continue.

A **sentinel value** is a limit or ending value.

A **loop body** is the set of statements that executes within a loop.

A **counter** is any numeric variable you use to count the number of times an event has occurred.

Adding to a variable (often, adding one) is called **incrementing** the variable.

Decreasing a variable (often by one) is called **decrementing** the variable.

A loop that never stops executing is called an **infinite loop**.

An **indeterminate**, or **indefinite**, **loop** is one for which you cannot predetermine the number of executions.

A loop for which you definitely know the repetition factor is a **definite loop**.

A `while` **statement** can be used to code any loop.

A `for` **statement** frequently is used to code a definite loop. Most often, it contains a loop control variable that it initializes, evaluates, and increments.

**Nesting loops** are loops within loops.

When one loop appears inside another, the loop that contains the other loop is called the **outer loop**, and the loop that is contained is called the **inner loop**.

A **summary report** lists only totals and other statistics, without individual detail records.

An **accumulator** is a variable that you use to gather, or accumulate, values.

## REVIEW QUESTIONS

1. **The structure that allows you to write one set of instructions that operates on multiple, separate sets of data is the ________.**
   a. sequence
   b. selection
   c. loop
   d. case

2. **Which of the following is not a step that must occur in every loop?**
   a. Initialize a loop control variable.
   b. Compare the loop control value to a sentinel.
   c. Set the loop control value equal to a sentinel.
   d. Alter the loop control variable.

3. **The statements executed within a loop are known collectively as the ________.**
   a. sentinels
   b. loop controls
   c. sequences
   d. loop body

4. **A counter keeps track of ________.**
   a. the number of times an event has occurred
   b. the number of modules in a program
   c. the number of loop structures within a program
   d. a total that prints at the end of a summary report

5. **Adding 1 to a variable is also called ________.**
   a. digesting
   b. incrementing
   c. decrementing
   d. resetting

6. **In the following pseudocode, what is printed?**

```
a = 1
b = 2
c = 5
while a < c
     a = a + 1
     b = b + c
endwhile
print a, b, c
```

   a. 1 2 5
   b. 5 22 5
   c. 5 6 5
   d. 6 22 9

7. **In the following pseudocode, what is printed?**

```
d = 4
e = 6
f = 7
while d > f
     d = d + 1
     e = e - 1
endwhile
print d, e, f
```

   a. 7 3 7
   b. 8 2 8
   c. 4 6 7
   d. 5 5 7

8. **When you decrement a variable, most frequently you ________.**
   a. set it to 0
   b. reduce it by one-tenth
   c. subtract 1 from it
   d. remove it from a program

9. **In the following pseudocode, what is printed?**

```
g = 4
h = 6
while g < h
     g = g + 1
endwhile
print g, h
```

   a. nothing
   b. 4 6
   c. 5 6
   d. 6 6

10. **Most programmers use a `for` statement ________.**
    a. for every loop they write
    b. as a compact version of the `while` statement
    c. when they do not know the exact number of times a loop will repeat
    d. when a loop will not repeat

11. **Unlike a `while` loop, you use a `do until` loop when ________.**
    a. you can predict the exact number of loop repetitions
    b. the loop body might never execute
    c. the loop body must execute exactly one time
    d. the loop body must execute at least one time

12. **Which of the following is a characteristic shared by all loops—`while`, `do while`, and `do until` loops?**
    a. They all have one entry and one exit.
    b. They all have a body that executes at least once.
    c. They all compare a loop control variable at the top of the loop.
    d. All of these are true.

13. **A comparison with a loop control variable provides ________.**
    a. the only entry to a `while` loop
    b. the only exit from a `do until` loop
    c. both of the above
    d. none of the above

**14. When two loops are nested, the loop that is contained by the other is the ________ loop.**

a. inner
b. outer
c. unstructured
d. captive

**15. In the following pseudocode, how many times is "Hello" printed?**

```
j = 2
k = 5
m = 6
n = 9
while j < k
    while m < n
        print "Hello"
        m = m + 1
    endwhile
    j = j + 1
endwhile
```

a. zero
b. three
c. six
d. nine

**16. In the following pseudocode, how many times is "Hello" printed?**

```
j = 2
k = 5
n = 9
while j < k
    m = 6
    while m < n
        print "Hello"
        m = m + 1
    endwhile
    j = j + 1
endwhile
```

a. zero
b. three
c. six
d. nine

**17. In the following pseudocode, how many times is "Hello" printed?**

```
p = 2
q = 4
while p < q
    print "Hello"
    r = 1
    while r < q
        print "Hello"
        r = r + 1
    endwhile
    p = p + 1
endwhile
```

a. zero
b. four
c. six
d. eight

**18. A report that lists no details about individual records, but totals only, is a(n) ________ report.**

a. accumulator
b. final
c. summary
d. detailless

**19. Typically, the value added to a counter variable is ________.**

a. 0
b. 1
c. 10
d. 100

**20. Typically, the value added to an accumulator variable is ________.**

a. 0
b. 1
c. at least 1000
d. Any value might be added to an accumulator variable.

## FIND THE BUGS

Each of the following pseudocode segments contains one or more bugs that you must find and correct.

1. **This method is supposed to print every fifth year starting with 2005; that is, 2005, 2010, 2015, and so on, for 30 years.**

```
printEveryFifthYear()
   const num YEAR = 2005
   num factor = 5
   const num END_YEAR = 2035
   while year > END_YEAR
      print year
      year = year + 1
   endwhile
return
```

2. **A standard mortgage is paid monthly over 30 years. This method is intended to print 360 payment coupons for a new borrower. Each coupon lists the month number, year number, and a friendly reminder.**

```
printCoupons()
   const num MONTHS = 12
   const num YEARS = 30
   num monthCounter
   num yearCounter
   while yearCounter <= YEARS
      while monthCounter <= 12
         print month, year, "Remember to send your payment by the 10th"
         yearCounter = yearCounter + 1
      endwhile
   endwhile
return
```

3. **This application is intended to print estimated monthly payment amounts for customers of the EZ Credit Loan Company. The application reads customer records, each containing an account number, name and address, requested original loan amount, term in months, and annual interest rate. The interest rate per month is calculated by dividing the annual interest rate by 12. The customer's total payback amount is calculated by charging the monthly interest rate on the original balance every month for the term of the loan. The customer's monthly payment is then calculated by dividing the total payback amount by the number of months in the loan. The application produces a notice containing the customer's name, address, and estimated monthly payment amount.**

```
start
   perform getReady()
   while not eof
      perform produceEstimate()
   perform ending()
stop
startUp()
   declare variables
   custRecord
      num acctNumber
      char name
      char address
      num originalLoanAmount
      num termInMonths
      num annualRate
   const num MONTHS_IN_YEAR = 12
   const num totalPayback
   num monthlyRate
   num count
   open files
   read custRecord
return

produceEstimate()
   count = 1
   monthlyRate = annualRate / monthsInYear
   while count = termInMonths
      totalPayback = totalPayback + monthlyRate * originalLoanAmount
      count = count + 1
   endwhile
   monthlyPayment = totalPayback / MONTHS_IN_YEAR
   print "Loan Payment Estimate for:"
   print name
   print address
   print "$", monthPayment
return

ending()
   close files
return
```

## EXERCISES

1. **Design the logic for a module that would print every number from 1 through 10.**
   a. Draw the flowchart.
   b. Design the pseudocode.

2. **Design the logic for a module that would print every number from 1 through 10 along with its square and cube.**
   a. Draw the flowchart.
   b. Design the pseudocode.

3. **Design a program that reads credit card account records and prints payoff schedules for customers. Input records contain an account number, customer name, and balance due. For each customer, print the account number and name; then print the customer's projected balance each month for the next 10 months. Assume that there is no finance charge on this account, that the customer makes no new purchases, and that the customer pays off the balance with equal monthly payments, which are 10 percent of the original bill.**
   a. Design the output for this program; create either sample output or a print chart.
   b. Design the hierarchy chart for this program.
   c. Design the flowchart for this program.
   d. Write pseudocode for this program.

4. **Design a program that reads credit card account records and prints payoff schedules for customers. Input records contain an account number, customer name, and balance due. For each customer, print the account number and name; then print the customer's payment amount and new balance each month until the card is paid off. Assume that when the balance reaches $10 or less, the customer can pay off the account. At the beginning of every month, 1.5 percent interest is added to the balance, and then the customer makes a payment equal to 5 percent of the current balance. Assume the customer makes no new purchases.**
   a. Design the output for this program; create either sample output or a print chart.
   b. Design the hierarchy chart for this program.
   c. Design the flowchart for this program.
   d. Write pseudocode for this program.

5. **Assume you have a bank account that compounds interest on a yearly basis. In other words, if you deposit $100 for two years at 4 percent interest, at the end of one year you will have $104. At the end of two years, you will have the $104 plus 4 percent of that, or $108.16. Create the logic for a program that would (1) read in records containing a deposit amount, a term in years, and an interest rate, and (2) for each record, print the running total balance for each year of the term.**
   a. Design the output for this program; create either sample output or a print chart.
   b. Design the hierarchy chart for this program.
   c. Design the flowchart for this program.
   d. Write pseudocode for this program.

6. **A school maintains class records in the following format:**

```
CLASS FILE DESCRIPTION
File name: CLASS
FIELD DESCRIPTION      DATA TYPE      EXAMPLE
Class Code             Character      CIS111
Section No.            Numeric        101
Teacher Name           Character      Gable
Enrollment             Numeric        24
Room                   Character      A213
```

**There is one record for each class section offered in the college. Design the program that would print as many stickers as a class needs to provide one for each enrolled student, plus one for the teacher. Each sticker would leave a blank for the student's (or teacher's) name, like this:**

Hello!

My name is ____________________

Class: XXXXXX Section: 999

**The border is preprinted, but you must design the program to print all the text you see on the sticker. (You do not need to worry about the differing font sizes of the sticker text. You do not need to design a print chart or sample output—the image of the sticker serves as a print chart.)**

a. Design the hierarchy chart for this program.
b. Design the flowchart for this program.
c. Write pseudocode for this program.

7. **A mail-order company often sends multiple packages per order. For each customer order, print enough mailing labels to use on each of the separate boxes that will be mailed. The mailing labels contain the customer's complete name and address, along with a box number in the form "Box 9 of 9". For example, an order that requires three boxes produces three labels: Box 1 of 3, Box 2 of 3, and Box 3 of 3. The file description is as follows:**

```
SHIPPING FILE DESCRIPTION
File name: ORDERS
FIELD DESCRIPTION      DATA TYPE      EXAMPLE
Title                  Character      Ms
First Name             Character      Kathy
Last Name              Character      Lewis
Street                 Character      847 Pine
```

| | | |
|---|---|---|
| City | Character | Aurora |
| State | Character | IL |
| Boxes | Numeric | 3 |
| Balance Due | Numeric | 129.95 |

a. Design the output for this program; create either sample output or a print chart.
b. Design the hierarchy chart for this program.
c. Design the flowchart for this program.
d. Write pseudocode for this program.

**8. A secondhand store is having a seven-day sale during which the price of any unsold item drops 10 percent each day. The inventory file includes an item number, description, and original price on day one. For example, an item that costs $10.00 on the first day costs 10 percent less, or $9.00, on the second day. On the third day, the same item is 10 percent less than $9.00, or $8.10. Produce a report that shows the price of the item on each day, one through seven.**

a. Design the output for this program; create either sample output or a print chart.
b. Design the hierarchy chart for this program.
c. Design the flowchart for this program.
d. Write pseudocode for this program.

**9. The state of Florida maintains a census file in which each record contains the name of a county, the current population, and a number representing the rate at which the population is increasing per year. The governor wants a report listing each county and the number of years it will take for the population of the county to double, assuming the present rate of growth remains constant.**

CENSUS FILE DESCRIPTION
File name: CENSUS

| FIELD DESCRIPTION | DATA TYPE | EXAMPLE |
|---|---|---|
| County Name | Character | Dade |
| Current Population | Numeric | 525000 |
| Rate of Growth | Numeric | 0.07 |

a. Design the output for this program; create either sample output or a print chart.
b. Design the hierarchy chart for this program.
c. Design the flowchart for this program.
d. Write pseudocode for this program.

**10. A Human Resources Department wants a report that shows its employees the benefits of saving for retirement. Produce a report that shows 12 predicted retirement account values for each employee—the values if the employee saves 5, 10, or 15 percent of his or her annual salary for 10, 20, 30, or 40 years. The department maintains a file in which each record contains the name of an employee and the employee's current annual salary. Assume that savings grow at a rate of 8 percent per year.**

a. Design the output for this program; create either sample output or a print chart.
b. Design the hierarchy chart for this program.
c. Design the flowchart for this program.
d. Write pseudocode for this program.

11. **Randy's Recreational Vehicles pays its salespeople once every three months. Salespeople receive one-quarter of their annual base salary plus 7 percent of all sales made in the last three-month period. Randy creates an input file with four records for each salesperson. The first of the four records contains the salesperson's name and annual base salary, while each of the three records that follow contains the name of a month and the monthly sales figure. For example, the first eight records in the file might contain the following data:**

| | |
|---|---|
| **Kimball** | **20000** |
| **April** | **30000** |
| **May** | **40000** |
| **June** | **60000** |
| **Johnson** | **15000** |
| **April** | **65000** |
| **May** | **78000** |
| **June** | **135500** |

**Because the two types of records contain data in the same format—a character field followed by a numeric field—you can define one input record format containing two variables that you use with either type of record. Design the logic for the program that reads a salesperson's record, and if not at `eof`, reads the next three records in a loop, accumulating sales and computing commissions. For each salesperson, print the quarterly base salary, the three commission amounts, and the total salary, which is the quarterly base plus the three commission amounts.**

a. Design the output for this program; create either sample output or a print chart.
b. Design the hierarchy chart for this program.
c. Design the flowchart for this program.
d. Write pseudocode for this program.

12. **Mr. Furly owns 20 apartment buildings. Each building contains 15 units that he rents for $800 per month each. Design the logic for the program that would print 12 payment coupons for each of the 15 apartments in each of the 20 buildings. Each coupon should contain the building number (1 through 20), the apartment number (1 through 15), the month (1 through 12), and the amount of rent due.**

a. Design the output for this program; create either sample output or a print chart.
b. Design the hierarchy chart for this program.
c. Design the flowchart for this program.
d. Write pseudocode for this program.

13. **Mr. Furly owns 20 apartment buildings. Each building contains 15 units that he rents. The usual monthly rent for apartments numbered 1 through 9 in each building is $700; the monthly rent is $850 for apartments numbered 10 through 15. The usual rent is due every month except July and December; in those months Mr. Furly gives his renters a 50 percent credit, so they owe only half the usual amount. Design the logic for the program that would print 12 payment coupons for each of the 15 apartments in each of the 20 buildings. Each coupon should contain the building number (1 through 20), the apartment number (1 through 15), the month (1 through 12), and the amount of rent due.**
    a. Design the output for this program; create either sample output or a print chart.
    b. Design the hierarchy chart for this program.
    c. Design the flowchart for this program.
    d. Write pseudocode for this program.

## DETECTIVE WORK

1. **What company's address is at One Infinite Loop, Cupertino, California?**
2. **What are fractals? How do they use loops? Find some examples of fractal art on the Web.**

## UP FOR DISCUSSION

1. **If programs could only make decisions or loops, but not both, which structure would you prefer to retain?**
2. **Suppose you wrote a program that you suspect is in an infinite loop because it just keeps running for several minutes with no output and without ending. What would you add to your program to help you discover the origin of the problem?**
3. **Suppose you know that every employee in your organization has a seven-digit ID number used for logging on to the computer system to retrieve sensitive information about their own customers. A loop would be useful to guess every combination of seven digits in an ID. Are there any circumstances in which you should try to guess another employee's ID number?**

# 7 CONTROL BREAKS

## After studying Chapter 7, you should be able to:

- Understand control break logic
- Perform single-level control breaks
- Use control data within a heading in a control break module
- Use control data within a footer in a control break module
- Perform control breaks with totals
- Perform multiple-level control breaks
- Perform page breaks

## UNDERSTANDING CONTROL BREAK LOGIC

A **control break** is a temporary detour in the logic of a program. In particular, programmers refer to a program as a **control break program** when a change in the value of a variable initiates special actions or causes special or unusual processing to occur. You usually write control break programs to organize output for programs that handle data records that are organized logically in groups based on the value in a field. As you read records, you examine the same field in each record, and when you encounter a record that contains a different value from the ones that preceded it, you perform a special action. If you have ever read a report that lists items in groups, with each group followed by a subtotal, then you have read a type of **control break report**. For example, you might generate a report that lists all company clients in order by state of residence, with a count of clients after each state's client list. See Figure 7-1 for an example of a report that breaks after each change in state.

**FIGURE 7-1:** A CONTROL BREAK REPORT WITH TOTALS AFTER EACH STATE

```
Company Clients by State of Residence

Name                City                State

Albertson           Birmingham          Alabama
Davis               Birmingham          Alabama
Lawrence            Montgomery          Alabama
                                        Count for Alabama    3

Smith               Anchorage           Alaska
Young               Anchorage           Alaska
Davis               Fairbanks           Alaska
Mitchell            Juneau              Alaska
Zimmer              Juneau              Alaska
                                        Count for Alaska     5

Edwards             Phoenix             Arizona
                                        Count for Arizona    1
```

Some other examples of control break reports produced by control break programs include:

- All employees listed in order by department number, with a new page started for each department
- All books for sale in a bookstore in order by category (such as reference or self-help), with a count following each category of book
- All items sold in order by date of sale, with a different ink color for each new month

Each of these reports shares two traits:

- The records used in each report are listed in order by a specific variable: department, state, category, or date.
- When that variable changes, the program takes special action: starts a new page, prints a count or total, or switches ink color.

To generate a control break report, your input records must be organized in sequential order based on the field that will cause the breaks. In other words, if you are going to write a program that produces a report that lists customers by state, like the one in Figure 7-1, then the records must be grouped by state before you begin processing. Frequently, grouping by state will mean placing the records in alphabetical order by state, although they could just as easily be placed in order by population, governor's last name, or any other factor as long as all of one state's records are together. As you grow more proficient in programming logic, you will learn techniques for writing programs that sort records before you proceed with creating a program that contains control break logic. Programs that **sort** records take records that are not in order and rearrange them to be in order, according to the data in some field. For now, assume that a sorting program has already been used to presort your records before you begin the part of a program that determines control breaks.

**TIP**

To use control break logic, either the records must arrive already in order in the input file or you must sort the records yourself. You will learn techniques for processing unsorted records in Chapter 8. In Chapter 9, you will learn to sort records. It is easier to work with sorted records than unsorted ones, so you are learning the easier techniques first.

## PERFORMING A SINGLE-LEVEL CONTROL BREAK TO START A NEW PAGE

Suppose you want to print a list of employees, advancing to a new page for each department. Figure 7-2 shows the input file description, from which you can see that the employee department is a numeric field, and that the file has been presorted so that the records will arrive in a program in department-number order. Figure 7-3 shows a sample report with the desired output—a simple list of employee names, with one department per page.

**FIGURE 7-2:** EMPLOYEE FILE DESCRIPTION

```
File name: EMPSBYDEPT
Sorted by: Department
FIELD DESCRIPTION        DATA TYPE     COMMENTS
Department               Numeric       0 decimals
Last Name                Character     15 characters
First Name               Character     15 characters
```

**FIGURE 7-3:** SAMPLE CONTROL BREAK REPORT LISTING EMPLOYEES, WITH EACH DEPARTMENT ON A NEW PAGE

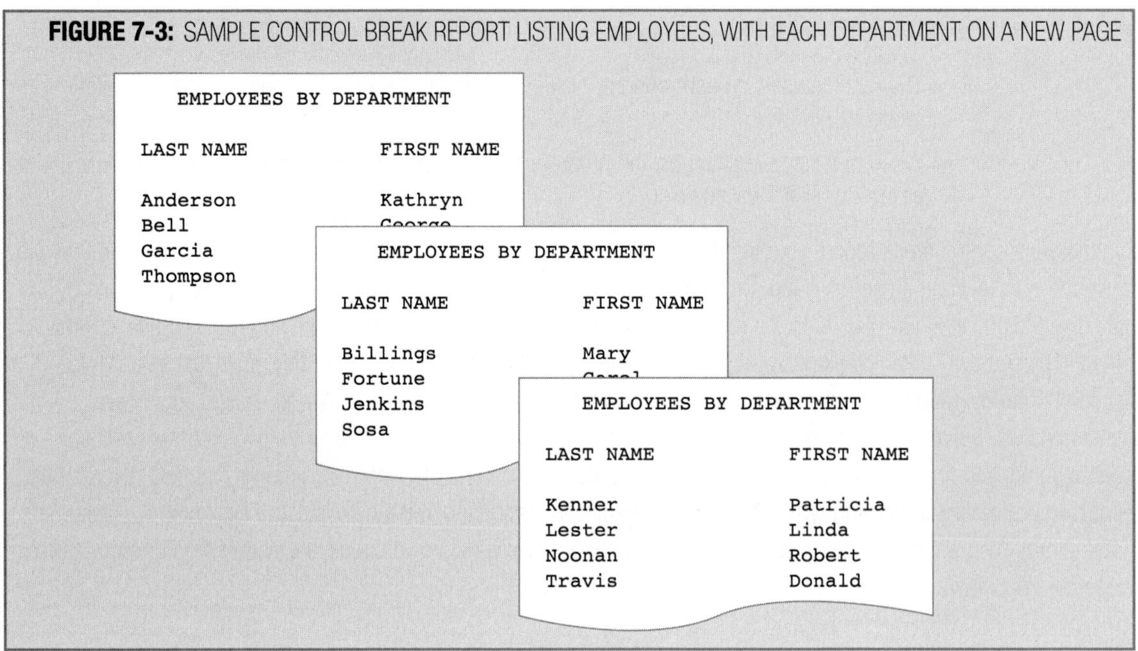


**TIP** In the report in Figure 7-3, each new page contains employees from a new department. Later in this chapter, department numbers will be added to the headings, making this point clearer to those who read the report.

The basic logic of the program works like this: Each time you read an employee record from the input file, you will determine whether the employee belongs to the same department as the previous employee. If so, you simply print the employee record and read another record, without any special processing. If there are 20 employees in a department, these steps are repeated 20 times in a row—read an employee record and print the employee record. However, eventually you will read an employee record that does not belong to the same department. At that point, before you print the employee record from the new department, you must print headings at the top of a new page. Then, you can proceed to read and print employee records that belong to the new department, and you continue to do so until the next time you encounter an employee in a different department. This type of program contains a **single-level control break**, a break in the logic of the program (pausing or detouring to print new headings) that is based on the value of a single variable (the department number).

However, there is a slight problem you must solve before you can determine whether a new input record contains the same department number as the previous input record. When you read a record from an input file, you copy the data from storage locations (for example, from a disk) to temporary computer memory locations. After they are read, the data items that represent department, last name, and first name occupy specific physical locations in computer memory. For each new record that is read from storage, new data must occupy the same positions in memory as the previous record occupied, and the previous set of data is lost. For example, if you read a record containing data for Donald Travis in Department 1, when you read the next record for Mary Billings in Department 2, "Mary" replaces "Donald", "Billings" replaces "Travis", and 2 replaces 1. After you read a new record into memory, there is no way to look back at the previous record to determine whether that record had a different department number. The previous record's data has been replaced in memory by the new record's data.

The technique you must use to "remember" the old department number is to create a special variable, called a **control break field**, to hold the previous department number. With a control break field, every time you read a record and print it, you also can save the crucial part of the record that will signal the change or control the program break. In this case, you want to store the department number in this specially created variable. Comparing the new and old department-number values will determine when it is time to print headings at the top of a new page.

The mainline logic for the Employees by Department report is the same as the mainline logic for all the other programs you've analyzed so far. It performs a `housekeeping()` module, after which an `eof` question controls execution of a `mainLoop()` module. At `eof`, a `finish()` module executes. See Figure 7-4.

**FIGURE 7-4:** MAINLINE LOGIC FOR EMPLOYEES BY DEPARTMENT REPORT PROGRAM

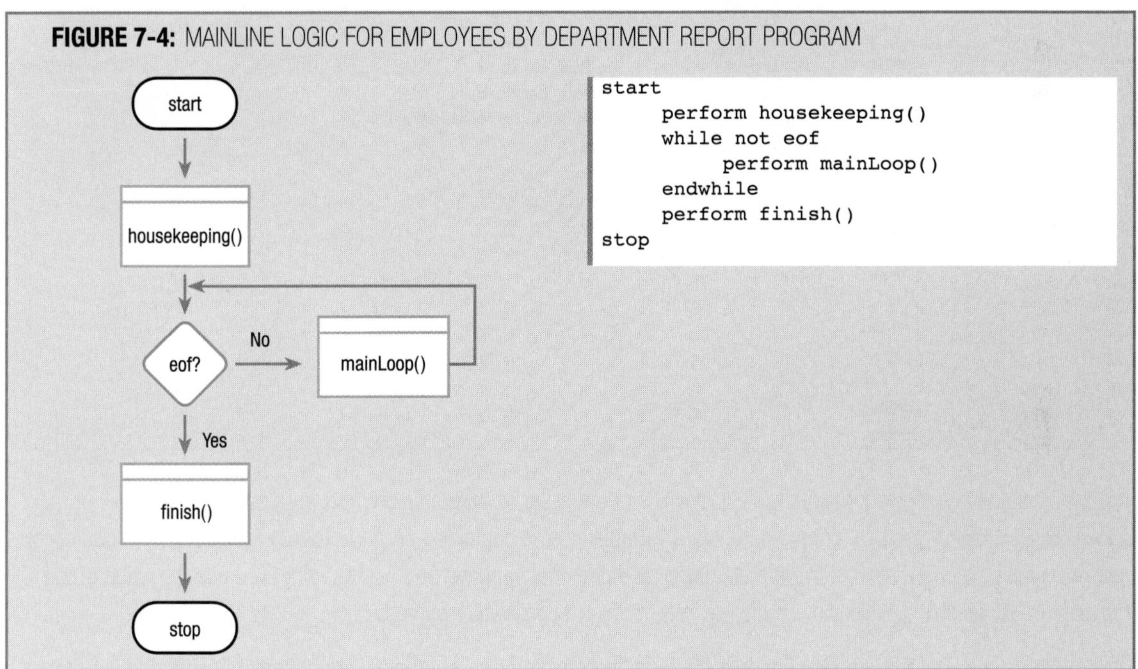


```
start
     perform housekeeping()
     while not eof
          perform mainLoop()
     endwhile
     perform finish()
stop
```

The `housekeeping()` module for this program begins like others you have seen. You declare variables as shown in Figure 7-5, including those you will use for the input data: `empDept`, `empLast`, and `empFirst`. You can also declare variables to hold the headings, and an additional variable that is named `oldDept` in this example. The purpose of `oldDept` is to serve as the control break field. Every time you read a record from a new department, you can save its department number in `oldDept` before you read the next record. The `oldDept` field provides you with a comparison for each new department so you can determine whether there has been a change in value.

**FIGURE 7-5:** THE `housekeeping()` MODULE FOR EMPLOYEES BY DEPARTMENT REPORT PROGRAM

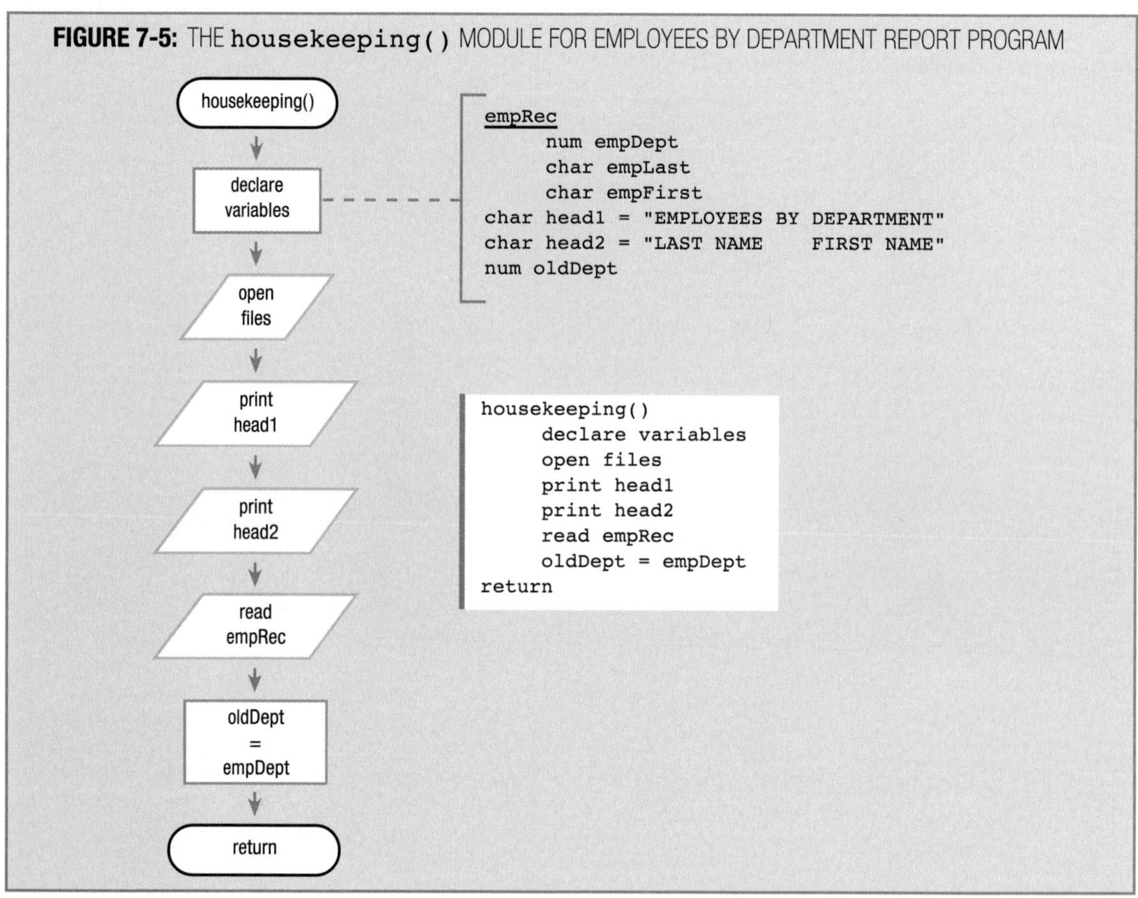
housekeeping()
declare variables
open files
print head1
print head2
read empRec
oldDept = empDept
return
empRec
num empDept
char empLast
char empFirst
char head1 = "EMPLOYEES BY DEPARTMENT"
char head2 = "LAST NAME FIRST NAME"
num oldDept
housekeeping()
declare variables
open files
print head1
print head2
read empRec
oldDept = empDept
return

Note that it would be incorrect to initialize `oldDept` to the value of `empDept` when you declare `oldDept` in the `housekeeping()` module. When you declare variables at the beginning of the `housekeeping()` module, you have not yet read the first record; therefore, `empDept` does not yet have any usable value. You use the value of the first `empDept` variable at the end of the module, only after you read the first input record.

In the `housekeeping()` module, after declaring variables, you also open files, print headings, and read the first input record. Before you leave the `housekeeping()` module, you can set the `oldDept` variable to equal the `empDept` value in the first input record. You will write the `mainLoop()` module of the program to check for any change in department number; that's the signal to print headings at the top of a new page. Because you just printed headings and read the first record, you do not want to print headings again for this first record, so you want to ensure that `empDept` and `oldDept` are equal when you enter `mainLoop()`.

**TIP**

As an alternative to the `housekeeping()` logic shown here, you can remove printing headings from the `housekeeping()` module and set `oldDept` to any impossible value—for example, –1. Then, in `mainLoop()`, the first record will force the control break, and the headings will print in the `newPage()` control break routine.

The first task within the `mainLoop()` module is to check whether `empDept` holds the same value as `oldDept`. For the first record, on the first pass through `mainLoop()`, the values are equal; you set them to be equal in the `housekeeping()` module. Therefore, you proceed without performing the `newPage()` module, printing the first employee's record and reading a second record. At the end of the `mainLoop()` module, shown in Figure 7-6, the logical flow returns to the mainline logic, shown in Figure 7-4. If it is not `eof`, the flow travels back into the `mainLoop()` module. There, you compare the second record's `empDept` to `oldDept`. If the second record holds an employee from the same department as the first employee, then you simply print that second employee's record and read a third record into memory. As long as each new record holds the same `empDept` value, you continue reading and printing, never pausing to perform the `newPage()` module.

**FIGURE 7-6:** THE `mainLoop()` MODULE FOR EMPLOYEES BY DEPARTMENT REPORT PROGRAM

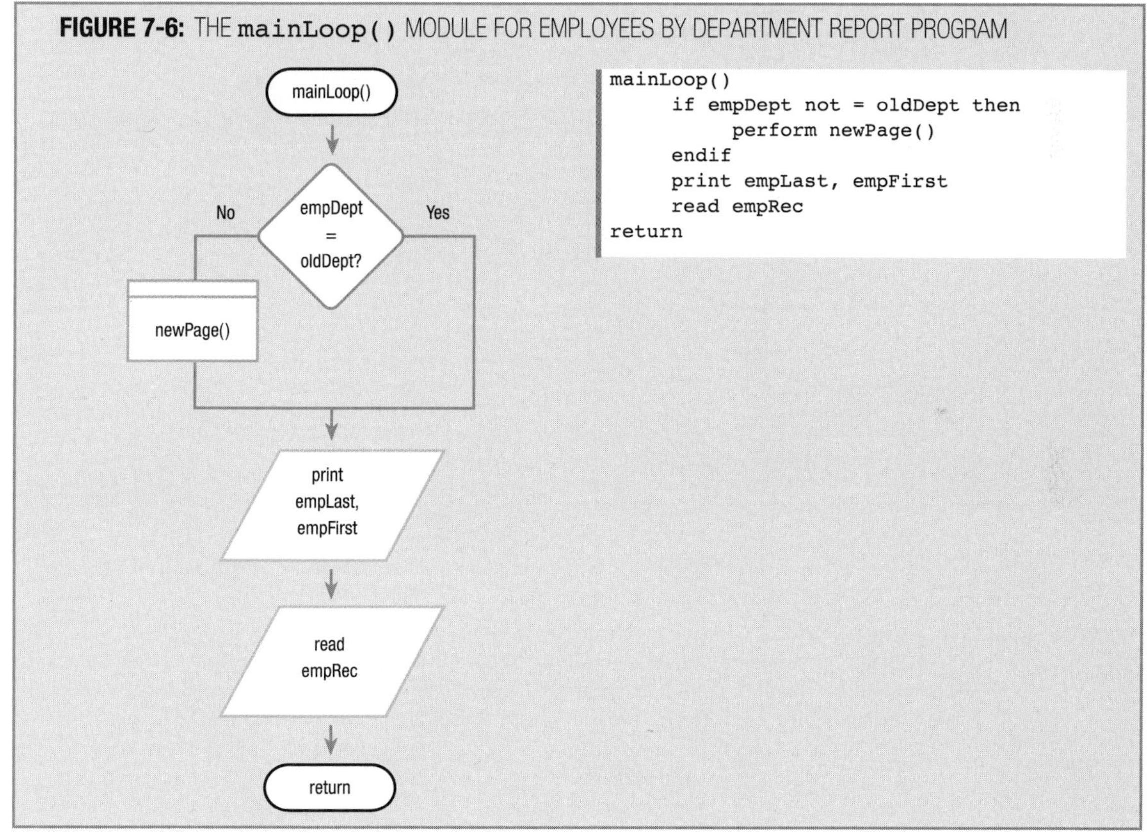


```
mainLoop()
     if empDept not = oldDept then
          perform newPage()
     endif
     print empLast, empFirst
     read empRec
return
```

**TIP** In the flowchart in Figure 7-6, you could change the decision to `empDept not = oldDept`. Then, the Yes branch of the decision structure would perform the `newPage()` module, and the No branch would be null. This format would more closely resemble the pseudocode in Figure 7-6, but the logic would be identical to the version shown here. In other words, you perform `newPage()` when `empDept = oldDept` is false or when `empDept not = oldDept` is true.

Eventually, you will read in an employee whose **empDept** is not the same as **oldDept**. That's when the control break routine, **newPage()**, executes. The **newPage()** module must perform two tasks:

- It must print headings at the top of a new page.
- It must update the control break field.

Figure 7-7 shows the **newPage()** module.

**FIGURE 7-7:** THE **newPage()** MODULE FOR EMPLOYEES BY DEPARTMENT REPORT PROGRAM

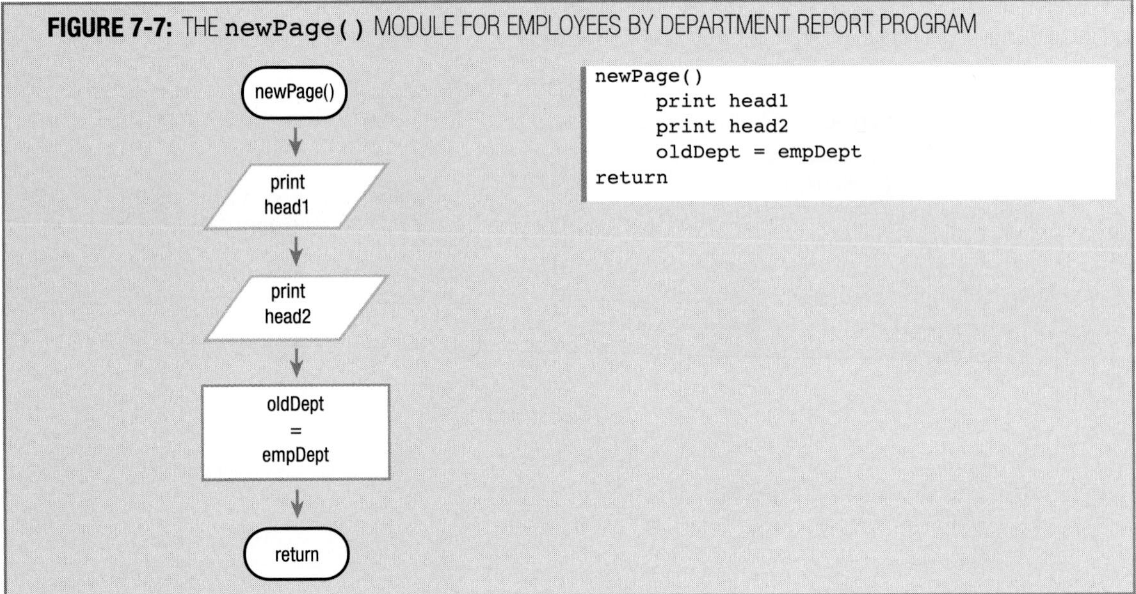


```
newPage()
     print head1
     print head2
     oldDept = empDept
return
```

**TIP** Notice that the steps in the newPage() module mimic steps in the housekeeping() module. You take advantage of this coincidence later in this chapter.

**TIP** In Chapter 4, you learned that specific programming languages each provide you with a means to physically advance printer paper to the top of a page. Usually, you insert a language-specific code just before the first character in the first heading that will appear on a page. For this book, if a sample report or print chart shows a heading printing at the top of the page, then you can assume that printing the heading causes the paper in the printer to advance to the top of a new page. The appropriate language-specific codes can be added when you code the program.

When you read an employee record in which **empDept** is not the same as **oldDept**, you cause a break in the normal flow of the program. The new employee record must "wait" while headings print and the control break field **oldDept** acquires a new value. After the **oldDept** field has been updated, and before the **mainLoop()** module ends, the waiting employee record prints on the new page. When you read the *next* employee record (and it is not **eof**), the **mainLoop()** module is reentered and the next employee's **empDept** field is compared to the updated **oldDept** field. If the new employee works in the same department as the one just preceding, then normal processing continues with the print-and-read statements.

The `newPage()` module in the employee report program performs two tasks required in all control break modules:

- It performs any necessary processing for the new group—in this case, it prints headings.
- It updates the control break field—in this case, the `oldDept` field.

**TIP** As an alternative to updating the control break field within the control break routine, you could set `oldDept` equal to `empDept` just before you read each record. However, if there are 200 employees in Department 55, then you set `oldDept` to the same value 200 times. It's more efficient to set `oldDept` to a different value only when there is a change in the value of the department.

The `finish()` module for the Employees by Department report program requires only that you close the files. See Figure 7-8.

**FIGURE 7-8:** THE `finish()` MODULE FOR EMPLOYEES BY DEPARTMENT REPORT PROGRAM

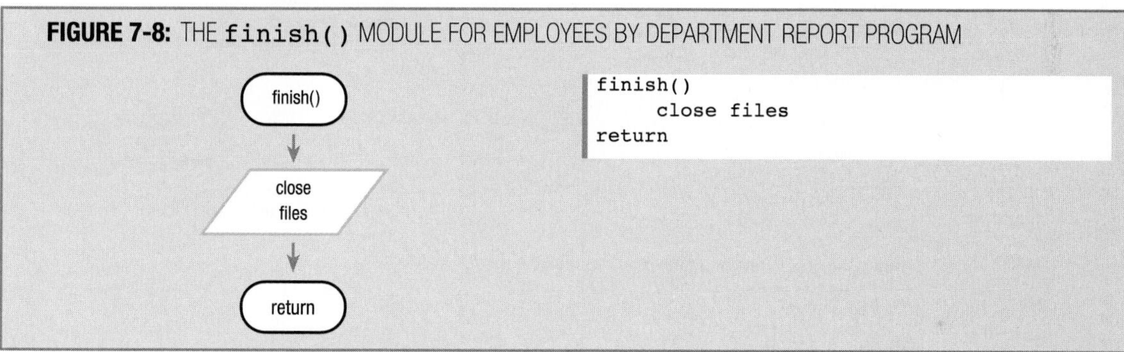


```
finish()
     close files
return
```

Notice that in the control break program described in Figures 7-4 through 7-8, the department numbers of employees in the input file do not have to follow each other incrementally. That is, the departments might be 1, 2, 3, and so on, but they also might be 1, 4, 12, 35, and so on. A control break occurs when there is a change in the control break field; the change does not necessarily have to be a numeric change of 1.

Figure 7-9 shows the entire Employees by Department control break program.

**FIGURE 7-9:** THE EMPLOYEES BY DEPARTMENT CONTROL BREAK PROGRAM

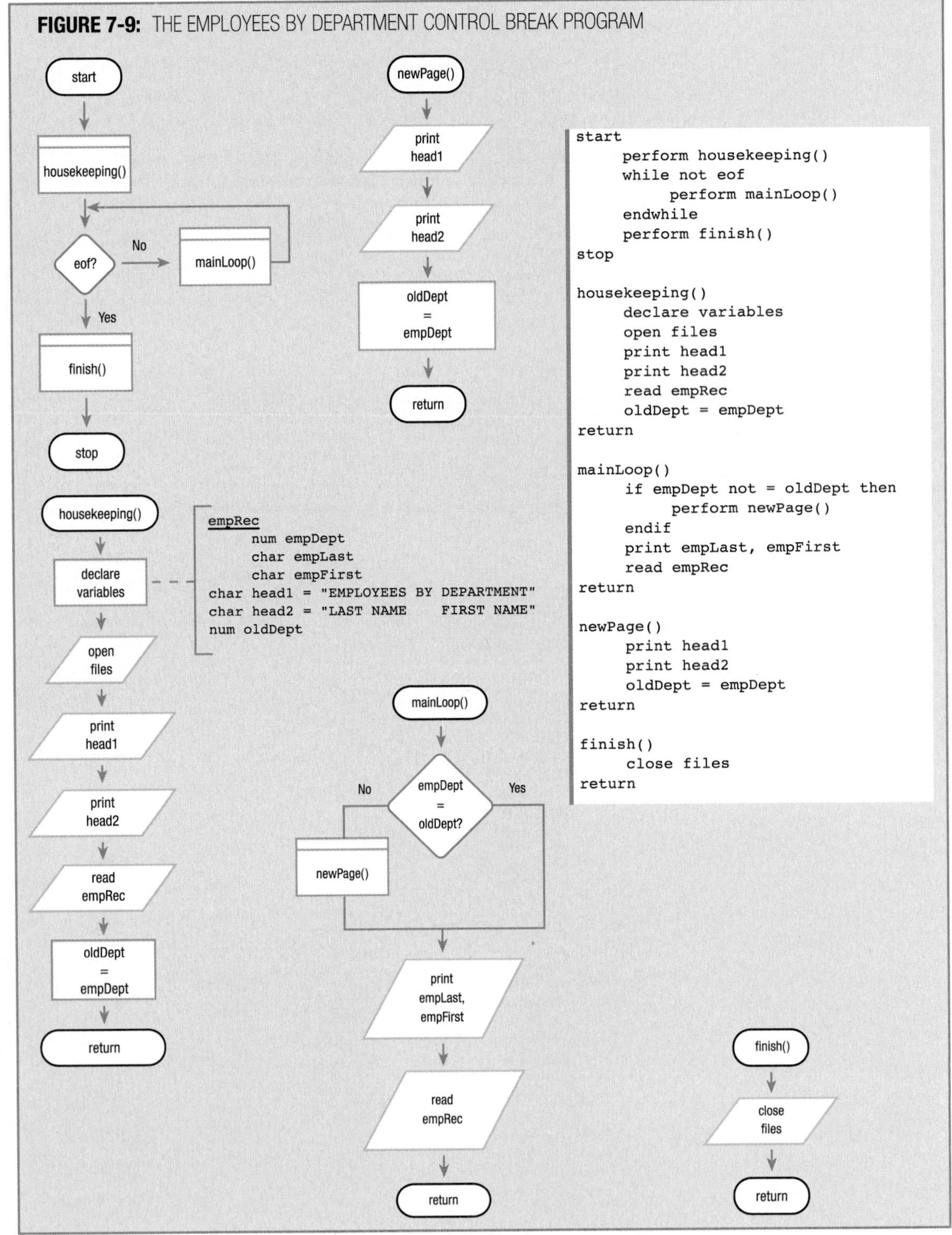


```
start
     perform housekeeping()
     while not eof
          perform mainLoop()
     endwhile
     perform finish()
stop

housekeeping()
     declare variables
     open files
     print head1
     print head2
     read empRec
     oldDept = empDept
return

mainLoop()
     if empDept not = oldDept then
          perform newPage()
     endif
     print empLast, empFirst
     read empRec
return

newPage()
     print head1
     print head2
     oldDept = empDept
return

finish()
     close files
return
```

## USING CONTROL DATA WITHIN A HEADING IN A CONTROL BREAK MODULE

In the Employees by Department report program example in Figure 7-9, the control break module printed constant headings at the top of each new page; in other words, each page heading was the same. However, sometimes you need to use control data within the heading. For example, consider the sample report shown in Figure 7-10.

**FIGURE 7-10:** SAMPLE REPORT FOR EMPLOYEES BY DEPARTMENT IN WHICH DEPARTMENT NUMBERS APPEAR IN THE HEADING

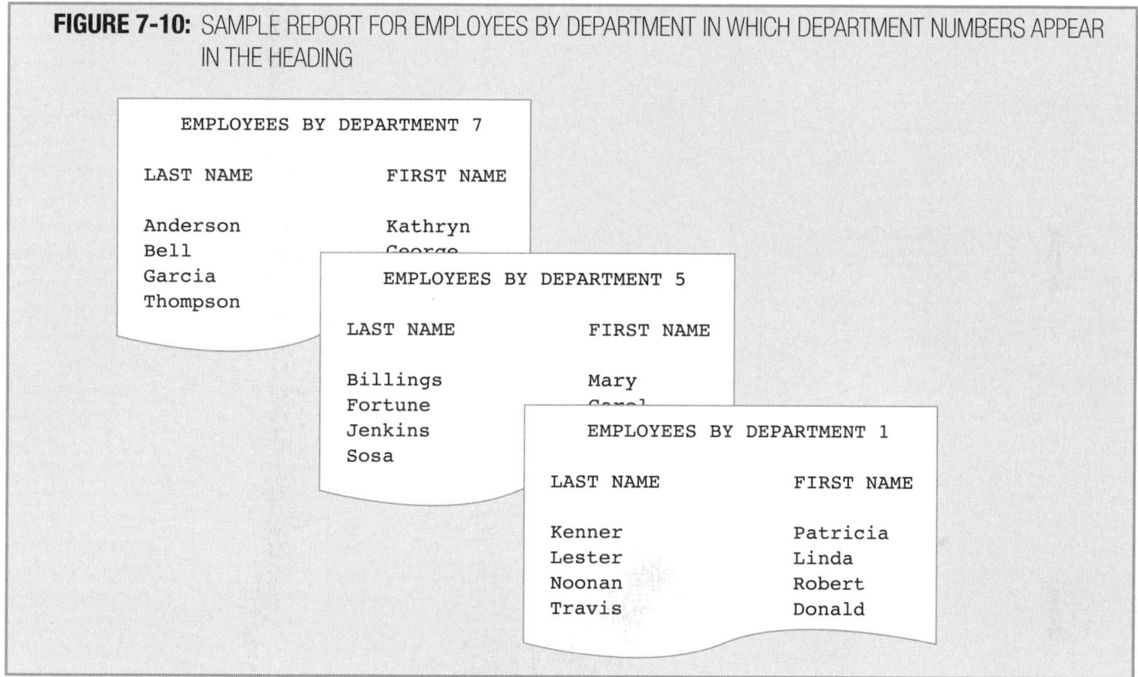


The difference between Figure 7-3 and Figure 7-10 lies in the heading. Figure 7-10 shows variable data in the heading—a different department number prints at the top of each page of employees. To create this kind of program, you must make two changes in the existing program. First, you modify the `newPage()` module, as shown in Figure 7-11. Instead of printing a fixed heading on each new page, you print a heading that contains two parts: a constant beginning ("EMPLOYEES FOR DEPARTMENT") and a variable ending (the department number for the employees who appear on the page). Notice that you use the `empDept` number that belongs to the employee record that is waiting to be printed while this control break module executes. Additionally, you must modify the `housekeeping()` module to ensure that the first heading on the report prints correctly. As Figure 7-11 shows, you must modify the `housekeeping()` module from Figure 7-5 so that you read the first `empRec` prior to printing the headings. The reason is that you must know the first employee's department number before you can print the heading for the top of the first page.

**FIGURE 7-11:** MODIFIED `newPage()` AND `housekeeping()` MODULES FOR EMPLOYEES BY DEPARTMENT REPORT THAT DISPLAYS THE DEPARTMENT NUMBER IN THE HEADING

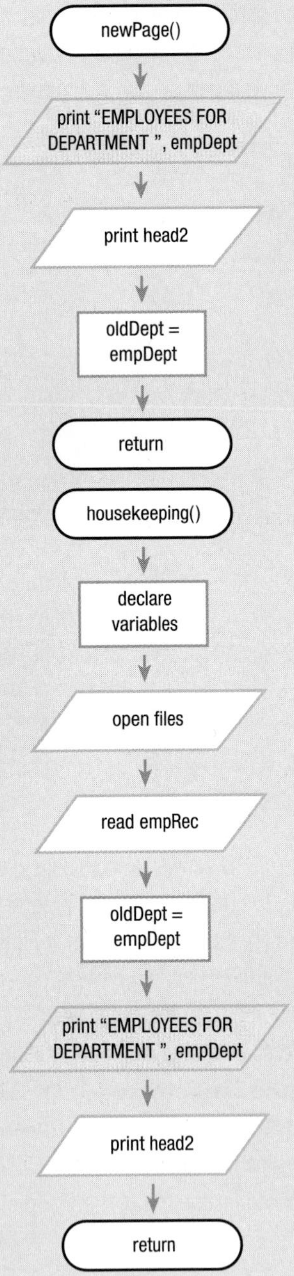

```
newPage()
     print "EMPLOYEES FOR
          DEPARTMENT ", empDept
     print head2
     oldDept = empDept
return
```

```
housekeeping()
     declare variables
     open files
     read empRec
     oldDept = empDept
     print "EMPLOYEES FOR
          DEPARTMENT ", empDept
     print head2
return
```

## USING CONTROL DATA WITHIN A FOOTER IN A CONTROL BREAK MODULE

In the previous section, you learned how to use control break data in a heading. Figure 7-12 shows a different report format. For this report, the department number prints *following* the employee list for the department. A message that prints at the end of a page or other section of a report is called a **footer**. Headings usually require information about the *next* record; footers usually require information about the *previous* record.

**FIGURE 7-12:** SAMPLE REPORT FOR EMPLOYEES BY DEPARTMENT IN WHICH DEPARTMENT NUMBERS APPEAR IN THE FOOTER

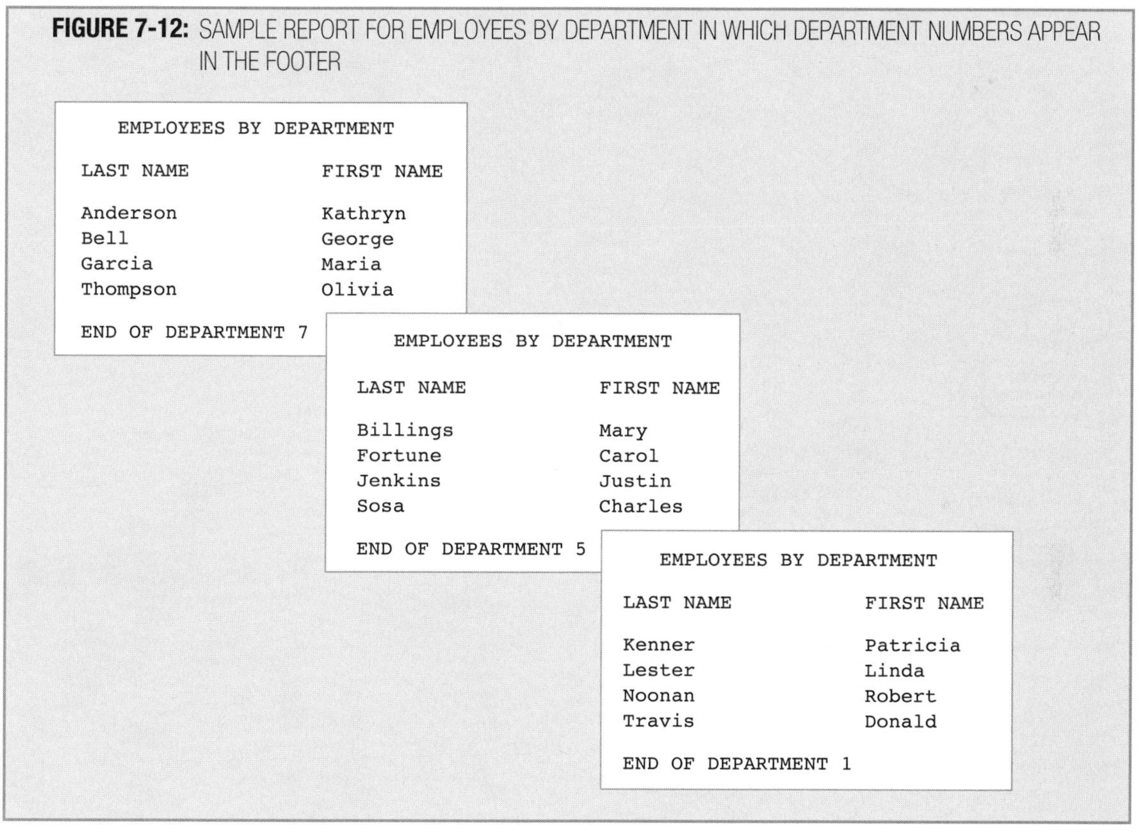

```
   EMPLOYEES BY DEPARTMENT

LAST NAME            FIRST NAME

Anderson             Kathryn
Bell                 George
Garcia               Maria
Thompson             Olivia

END OF DEPARTMENT 7
```

```
   EMPLOYEES BY DEPARTMENT

LAST NAME            FIRST NAME

Billings             Mary
Fortune              Carol
Jenkins              Justin
Sosa                 Charles

END OF DEPARTMENT 5
```

```
   EMPLOYEES BY DEPARTMENT

LAST NAME            FIRST NAME

Kenner               Patricia
Lester               Linda
Noonan               Robert
Travis               Donald

END OF DEPARTMENT 1
```

Figure 7-13 shows a program that prints a list of employees by department, including a footer that displays the department number at the end of each department's list. When you write a program that produces the report like the one shown in Figure 7-12, you continuously read records with `empLast`, `empFirst`, and `empDept` fields. Each time `empDept` does not equal `oldDept`, it means that you have reached a department break and that you should perform the `newPage()` module. The `newPage()` module has three tasks:

- It must print the footer for the previous department at the bottom of the employee list.
- It must print headings at the top of a new page.
- It must update the control break field.

**FIGURE 7-13:** PROGRAM THAT LISTS EMPLOYEES BY DEPARTMENT, INCLUDING DEPARTMENT NUMBER IN THE FOOTER

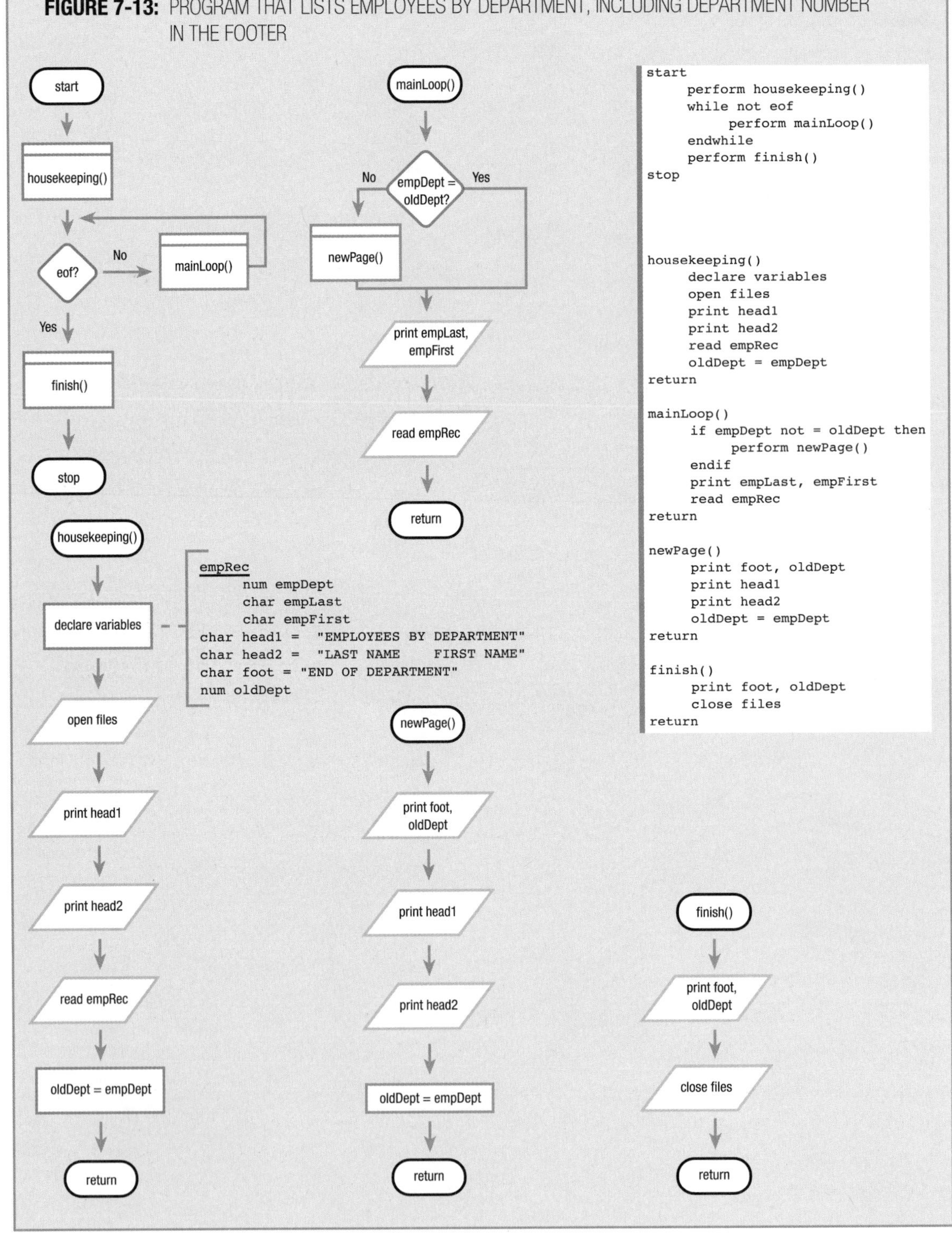


```
start
     perform housekeeping()
     while not eof
          perform mainLoop()
     endwhile
     perform finish()
stop

housekeeping()
     declare variables
     open files
     print head1
     print head2
     read empRec
     oldDept = empDept
return

mainLoop()
     if empDept not = oldDept then
          perform newPage()
     endif
     print empLast, empFirst
     read empRec
return

newPage()
     print foot, oldDept
     print head1
     print head2
     oldDept = empDept
return

finish()
     print foot, oldDept
     close files
return
```

When the `newPage()` module prints the footer at the bottom of the old page, you must use the `oldDept` number. For example, assume you have printed several employees from Department 12. When you read a record with an employee from Department 13 (or any other department), the first thing you must do is print "END OF DEPARTMENT 12". You print the correct department number by accessing the value of `oldDept`, not `empDept`. Then, you can print the other headings at the top of a new page and update `oldDept` to the current `empDept`, which in this example is 13.

The `newPage()` module in Figure 7-13 performs three tasks required in all control break routines: it processes the previous group, processes the new group, and updates the control break field.

When you printed the department number in the header in the example in the previous section, you needed a special step in the `housekeeping()` module. When you print the department number in the footer, the `finish()` module requires an extra step. Imagine that the last five records in the input file include two employees from Department 78, Amy and Bill, and three employees from Department 85, Carol, Don, and Ellen. The logical flow proceeds as follows:

1. After the first Department 78 employee (Amy) prints, you read the second Department 78 employee (Bill).
2. At the top of the `mainLoop()` module, Bill's department is compared to `oldDept`. The departments are the same, so the second Department 78 employee (Bill) is printed. Then, you read the first Department 85 employee (Carol).
3. At the top of `mainLoop()`, Carol's `empDept` and `oldDept` are different, so you perform the `newPage()` module while Carol's record waits in memory.
4. In the `newPage()` module, you print "END OF DEPARTMENT 78". Then, you print headings at the top of the next page. Finally, you set `oldDept` to 85, and then return to `mainLoop()`.
5. Back in `mainLoop()`, you print a line of data for the first Department 85 employee (Carol), whose record waited while `newPage()` executed. Then, you read the record for the second Department 85 employee (Don).
6. At the top of `mainLoop()`, you compare Don's department number to `oldDept`. The numbers are the same, so you print Don's employee data and read in the last Department 85 employee (Ellen).
7. At the top of `mainLoop()`, you determine that Ellen has the same department number, so you print Ellen's data and attempt to read from the input file, where you encounter `eof`.
8. The `eof` decision in the mainline logic sends you to the `finish()` module.

You have printed the last Department 85 employee (Ellen), but the department footer for Department 85 has not printed. That's because every time you attempt to read an input record, you don't know whether there will be more records. The mainline logic checks for the `eof` condition, but if it determines that it is `eof`, the logic does not flow back into the `mainLoop()` module, where the `newPage()` module can execute.

To print the footer for the last department, you must print a footer one last time within the `finish()` routine. The `finish()` module that is part of the complete program in Figure 7-13 illustrates this point. Taking this action is similar to printing the first heading in the `housekeeping()` module. The very first heading prints separately from all the others at the beginning; the very last footer must print separately from all the others at the end.

## PERFORMING CONTROL BREAKS WITH TOTALS

Suppose you run a bookstore, and one of the files you maintain is called BOOKFILE, which has one record for every book title that you carry. Each record has fields such as `bookTitle`, `bookAuthor`, `bookCategory` (fiction, reference, self-help, and so on), `bookPublisher`, and `bookPrice`, as shown in the file description in Figure 7-14.

**FIGURE 7-14:** BOOKFILE FILE DESCRIPTION

```
File name: BOOKFILE
Sorted by: Category
FIELD DESCRIPTION       DATA TYPE          COMMENTS
Title                   Character          30 characters
Author                  Character          15 characters
Category                Character          15 characters
Publisher               Character          15 characters
Price                   Numeric            2 decimals
```

Suppose you want to print a list of all the books that your store carries, with a total number of books at the bottom of the list, as shown in the sample report in Figure 7-15. You can use the logic shown in Figure 7-16. In the main loop module, named `bookListLoop()`, you print a book title, add 1 to `grandTotal`, and read the next record. At the end of the program, in the `closeDown()` module, you print `grandTotal` before you close the files. You can't print `grandTotal` any earlier in the program because the `grandTotal` value isn't complete until the last record has been read.

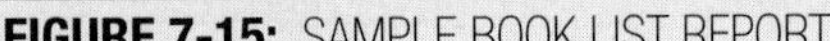

**FIGURE 7-15:** SAMPLE BOOK LIST REPORT

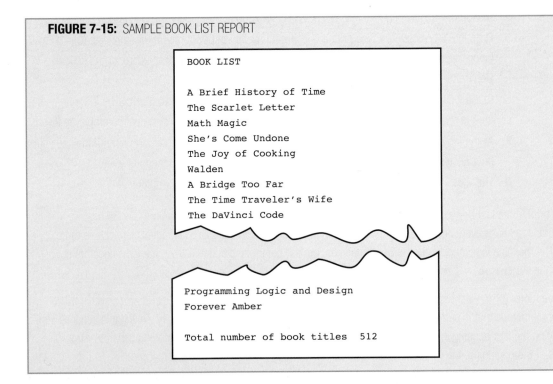

```
BOOK LIST

A Brief History of Time
The Scarlet Letter
Math Magic
She's Come Undone
The Joy of Cooking
Walden
A Bridge Too Far
The Time Traveler's Wife
The DaVinci Code

Programming Logic and Design
Forever Amber

Total number of book titles  512
```

**FIGURE 7-16:** FLOWCHART AND PSEUDOCODE FOR BOOKSTORE PROGRAM

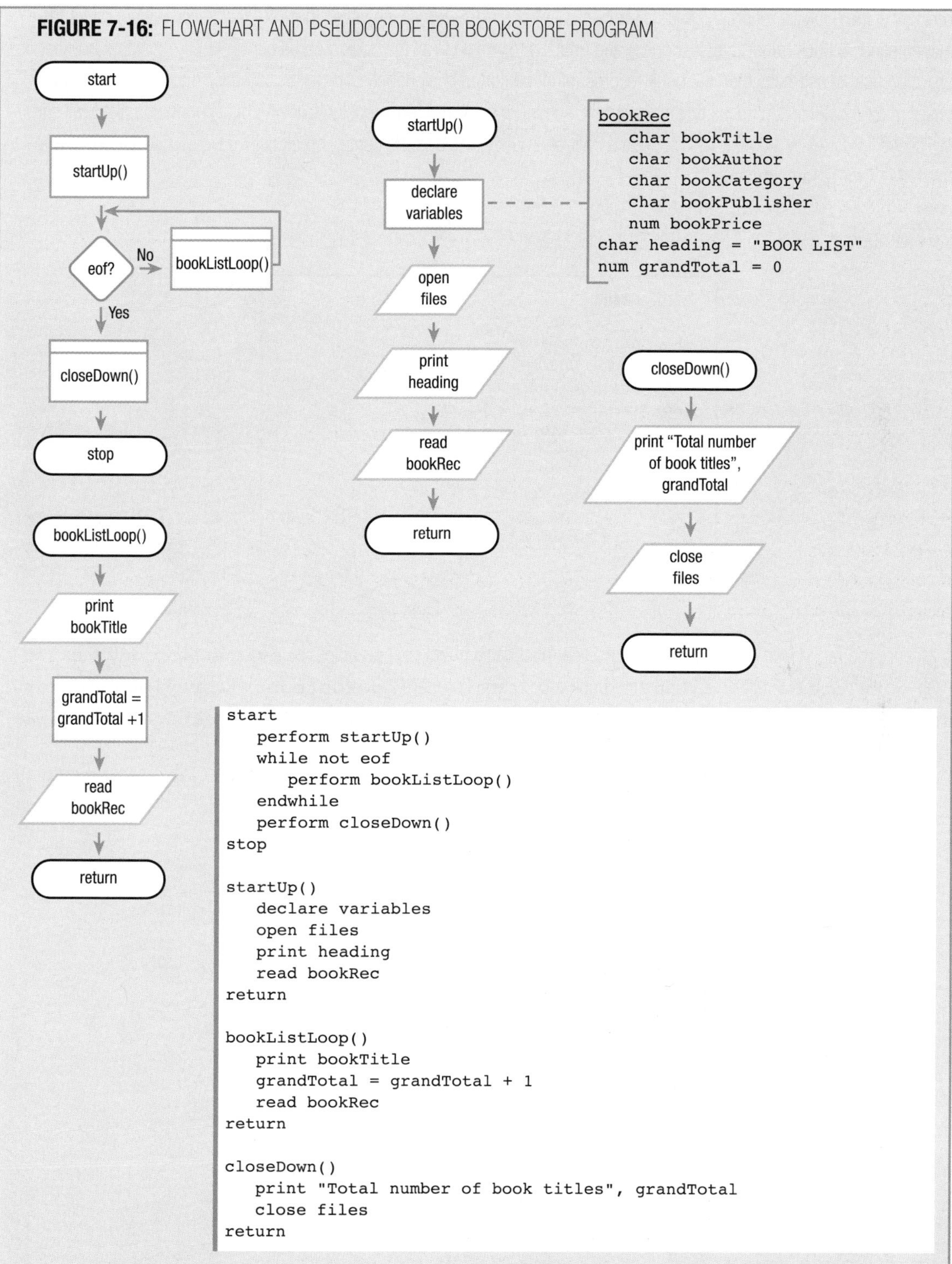


```
start
   perform startUp()
   while not eof
      perform bookListLoop()
   endwhile
   perform closeDown()
stop

startUp()
   declare variables
   open files
   print heading
   read bookRec
return

bookListLoop()
   print bookTitle
   grandTotal = grandTotal + 1
   read bookRec
return

closeDown()
   print "Total number of book titles", grandTotal
   close files
return
```

The logic of the book list report program is pretty straightforward. Suppose, however, that you decide you want a count for each category of book rather than just one grand total. For example, if all the book records contain a category that is either fiction, reference, or self-help, then the book records might be sorted in alphabetical order by category, and the output would consist of a list of all fiction books first, followed by a count; then all reference books, followed by a count; and finally all self-help books, followed by a count. The report is a control break report, and the control break field is `bookCategory`. See Figure 7-17 for a sample report.

**FIGURE 7-17:** SAMPLE REPORT LISTING BOOKS BY CATEGORY WITH CATEGORY COUNTS

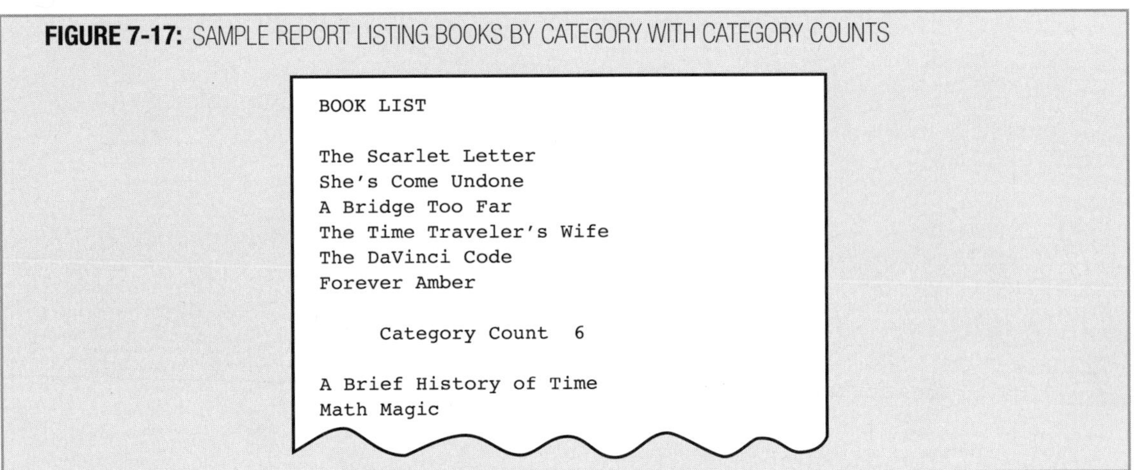

```
BOOK LIST

The Scarlet Letter
She's Come Undone
A Bridge Too Far
The Time Traveler's Wife
The DaVinci Code
Forever Amber

     Category Count  6

A Brief History of Time
Math Magic
```

To produce the report with subtotals by category, you must declare two new variables: `previousCategory` and `categoryTotal`. Every time you read a book record, you compare `bookCategory` to `previousCategory`; when there is a category change, you print the count of books for the previous category. The `categoryTotal` variable holds that count. See Figure 7-18.

**FIGURE 7-18:** FLOWCHART AND PSEUDOCODE FOR BOOKSTORE PROGRAM CONTAINING A COUNT AFTER EACH BOOK CATEGORY GROUP

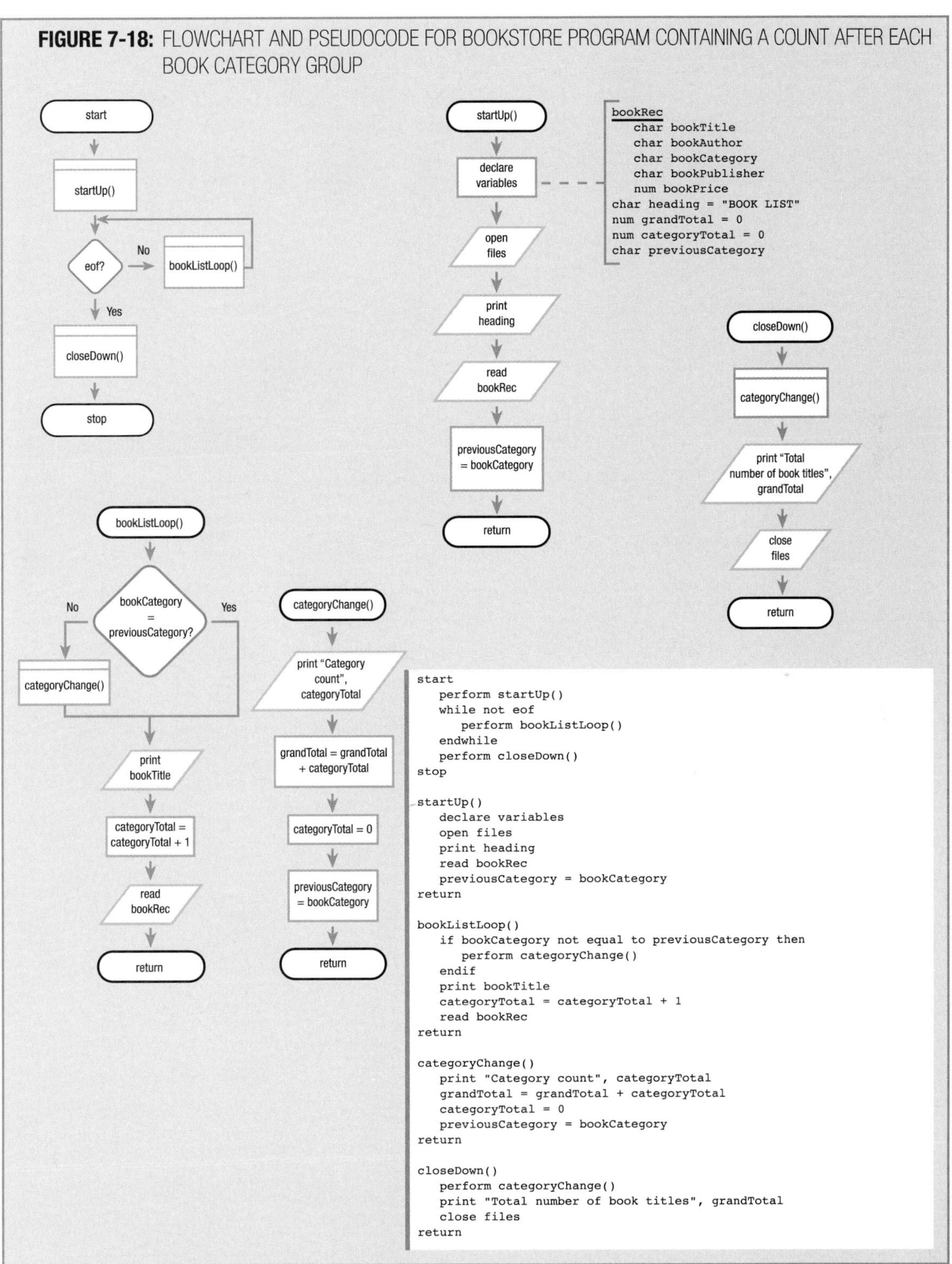


```
start
   perform startUp()
   while not eof
      perform bookListLoop()
   endwhile
   perform closeDown()
stop

startUp()
   declare variables
   open files
   print heading
   read bookRec
   previousCategory = bookCategory
return

bookListLoop()
   if bookCategory not equal to previousCategory then
      perform categoryChange()
   endif
   print bookTitle
   categoryTotal = categoryTotal + 1
   read bookRec
return

categoryChange()
   print "Category count", categoryTotal
   grandTotal = grandTotal + categoryTotal
   categoryTotal = 0
   previousCategory = bookCategory
return

closeDown()
   perform categoryChange()
   print "Total number of book titles", grandTotal
   close files
return
```

**TIP**

When you draw a flowchart, it usually is clearer to ask questions positively, as in "`bookCategory = previousCategory?`", and draw appropriate actions on the Yes or No side of the decision. In pseudocode, when action occurs only on the No side of a decision, it is usually clearer to ask negatively, as in "`bookCategory not equal to previousCategory?`" Figure 7-18 uses these tactics.

When you read the first record from the input file in the `startUp()` module of the program in Figure 7-18, you save the value of `bookCategory` in the `previousCategory` variable. Every time a record enters the `bookListLoop()` module, the program checks to see if the current record represents a new category of work, by comparing `bookCategory` to `previousCategory`. When you process the first record, the categories match, so the book title prints, the `categoryTotal` increases by 1, and you read the next record. If this next record's `bookCategory` value matches the `previousCategory` value, processing continues as usual: printing a line and adding 1 to `categoryTotal`.

At some point, `bookCategory` for an input record does not match `previousCategory`. At that point, you perform the `categoryChange()` module. Within the `categoryChange()` module, you print the count of the previous category of books. Then, you add `categoryTotal` to `grandTotal`. Adding a total to a higher-level total is called **rolling up the totals**.

You could write `bookListLoop()` so that as you process each book, you add 1 to `categoryTotal` and add 1 to `grandTotal`. Then, there would be no need to roll totals up in the `categoryChange()` module. If there are 120 fiction books, you add 1 to `categoryTotal` 120 times; you also would add 1 to `grandTotal` 120 times. This technique would yield correct results, but you can eliminate executing 119 addition instructions by waiting until you have accumulated all 120 category counts before adding the total figure to `grandTotal`.

This control break report containing totals performs the five tasks required in all control break routines that include totals:

- It performs any necessary processing for the previous group—in this case, it prints `categoryTotal`.
- It rolls up the current-level totals to the next higher level—in this case, it adds `categoryTotal` to `grandTotal`.
- It resets the current level's totals to zero—in this case, `categoryTotal` is set to zero.
- It performs any necessary processing for the new group—in this case, there is none.
- It updates the control break field—in this case, `previousCategory`.

The `closeDown()` routine for this type of program is more complicated than it might first appear. It seems as though you should print `grandTotal`, close the files, and return to the mainline logic. However, when you read the last record, the mainline `eof` decision sends the logical flow to the `closeDown()` routine. You have not printed the last `categoryTotal`, nor have you added the count for the last category to `grandTotal`. You must take care of both these tasks before printing `grandTotal`. You can perform these two tasks as separate steps in `closeDown()`, but it is often simplest just to remember to perform the control break routine `categoryChange()` one last time. The `categoryChange()` module already executes after every previous category completes—that is, every time you encounter a new category during the execution of the program. You also can execute this module after the final category completes, at the end of the file. Encountering the end of the file is really just another form of break; it signals that the last category has finally completed. The `categoryChange()` module prints the category total and rolls the totals up to the `grandTotal` level.

**TIP** When you call the `categoryChange()` module from within `closeDown()`, it performs a few tasks you don't need, such as setting the value of `previousCategory`. You have to weigh the convenience of calling the already-written `categoryChange()` module, and executing a few unneeded statements, against taking the time to write a new module that would execute only the statements that are absolutely necessary.

It is very important to note that this control break program works whether there are three categories of books or 300. Note further that it does not matter what the categories of books are. For example, the program never asks `bookCategory = "fiction"?`. Instead, the control of the program breaks when the category field *changes*, and it is in no way dependent on *what* that change is.

## PERFORMING MULTIPLE-LEVEL CONTROL BREAKS

Let's say your bookstore from the last example is so successful that you have a chain of them across the country. Every time a sale is made, you create a record with the fields `bookTitle`, `bookPrice`, `bookCity`, and `bookState`. You want a report that prints a summary of books sold in each city and each state, similar to the one shown in Figure 7-19. A report such as this one, which does not include any information about individual records, but instead includes only group totals, is a **summary report**.

This program contains a **multiple-level control break**—that is, the normal flow of control (reading records and counting book sales) breaks away to print totals in response to more than just one change in condition. In this report, a control break occurs in response to either (or both) of two conditions: when the value of the `bookCity` variable changes, as well as when the value of the `bookState` variable changes.

Just as the file you use to create a single-level control break report must be presorted, so must the input file you use to create a multiple-level control break report. The input file that you use for the book sales report must be sorted by `bookCity` *within* `bookState`. That is, all of one state's records—for example, all records from IA—come first; then all of the records from another state, such as IL, follow. Within any one state, all of one city's records come first; then all of the next city's records follow. For example, the input file that produces the report shown in Figure 7-19 contains 200 records for book sales in Ames, IA, followed by 814 records for book sales in Des Moines, IA. The basic processing entails reading a book sale record, adding 1 to a counter, and reading the next book sale record. At the end of any city's records, you print a total for that city; at the end of a state's records, you print a total for that state.

**FIGURE 7-19:** SAMPLE RUN OF BOOK SALES BY CITY AND STATE REPORT

```
BOOK SALES BY CITY AND STATE

Ames                                 200
Des Moines                           814
Iowa City                            291
    Total for IA                    1305
Chicago                             1093
Crystal Lake                         564
McHenry                              213
Springfield                          365
    Total for IL                    2235
Springfield                          289
Worcester                            100
    Total for MA                     389
    Grand Total                     3929
```

The **housekeeping()** module of the Book Sales by City and State report program looks similar to the **housekeeping()** module in the previous control break program, in which there was a single control break for change in category of book. In each program, you declare variables, open files, and read the first record. This time, however, there are multiple fields to save and compare to the old fields. Here, you declare two special variables, **prevCity** and **prevState**, as shown in Figure 7-20. In addition, the Book Sales report shows three kinds of totals, so you declare three new variables that will serve as holding places for the totals in the Book Sales report: **cityCounter**, **stateCounter**, and **grandTotal**, which are all initialized to zero.

**FIGURE 7-20:** FLOWCHART AND PSEUDOCODE FOR **housekeeping()** MODULE IN BOOK SALES BY CITY AND STATE REPORT PROGRAM

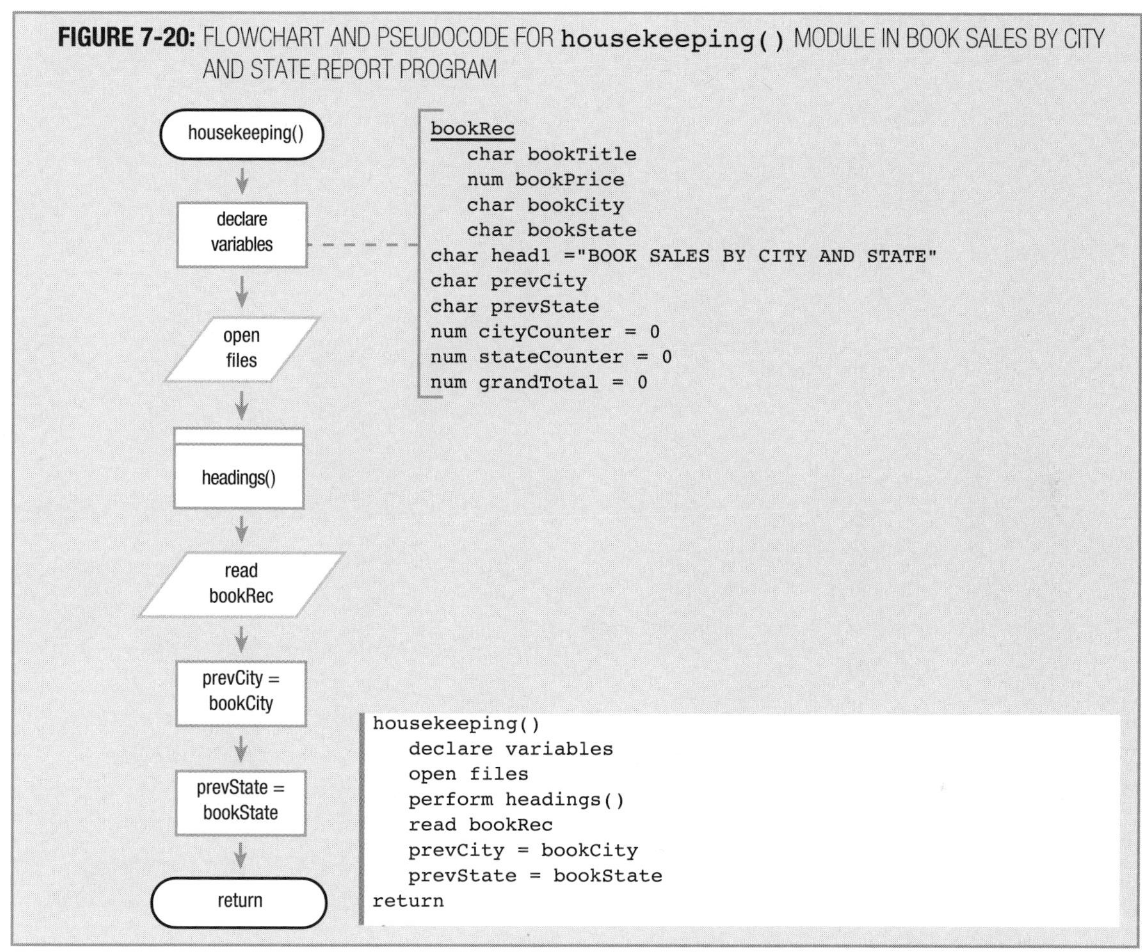


```
housekeeping()
   declare variables
   open files
   perform headings()
   read bookRec
   prevCity = bookCity
   prevState = bookState
return
```

This program prints both `bookState` and `bookCity` totals, so you need two control break modules, `cityBreak()` and `stateBreak()`. Every time there is a change in the `bookCity` field, the `cityBreak()` routine performs these standard control break tasks:

- It performs any necessary processing for the previous group—in this case, it prints totals for the previous city.
- It rolls up the current-level totals to the next higher level—in this case, it adds the city count to the state count.
- It resets the current level's totals to zero—in this case, it sets the city count to zero.
- It performs any necessary processing for the new group—in this case, there is none.
- It updates the control break field—in this case, it sets `prevCity` to `bookCity`.

Within the `stateBreak()` module, you must perform one new type of task, as well as the control break tasks you are familiar with. The new task is the first task: Within the `stateBreak()` module, you must first perform `cityBreak()` automatically (because if there is a change in the state, there must also be a change in the city). The `stateBreak()` module does the following:

- It processes the lower-level break—in this case, `cityBreak()`.
- It performs any necessary processing for the previous group—in this case, it prints totals for the previous state.
- It rolls up the current-level totals to the next higher level—in this case, it adds the state count to the grand total.
- It resets the current level's totals to zero—in this case, it sets the state count to zero.
- It performs any necessary processing for the new group—in this case, there is none.
- It updates the control break field—in this case, it sets `prevState` to `bookState`.

The `mainLoop()` module of this multiple-level control break program checks for any change in two different variables: `bookCity` and `bookState`. When `bookCity` changes, a city total is printed, and when `bookState` changes, a state total is printed. As you can see from the sample report in Figure 7-19, all city totals for each state print before the state total for the same state, so it might seem logical to check for a change in `bookCity` before checking for a change in `bookState`. However, the opposite is true. For the totals to be correct, you must check for any `bookState` change first. You do so because when `bookCity` changes, `bookState` also *might* be changing, but when `bookState` changes, it means `bookCity` *must* be changing.

Consider the sample input records shown in Figure 7-21, which are sorted by `bookCity` within `bookState`. When you get to the point in the program where you read the first Illinois record (*The Scarlet Letter*), "Iowa City" is the value stored in the field `prevCity`, and "IA" is the value stored in `prevState`. Because the values in the `bookCity` and `bookState` variables in the new record are both different from the `prevCity` and `prevState` fields, both a city and state total will print. However, consider the problem when you read the first record for Springfield, MA (*Walden*). At this point in the program, `prevState` is IL, but `prevCity` is the same as the current `bookCity`; both contain Springfield. If you check for a change in `bookCity`, you won't find one at all, and no city total will print, even though Springfield, MA, is definitely a different city from Springfield, IL.

**FIGURE 7-21:** SAMPLE DATA FOR BOOK SALES BY CITY AND STATE REPORT

| TITLE | PRICE | CITY | STATE |
|---|---|---|---|
| *A Brief History of Time* | 20.00 | Iowa City | IA |
| *The Scarlet Letter* | 15.99 | Chicago | IL |
| *Math Magic* | 4.95 | Chicago | IL |
| *She's Come Undone* | 12.00 | Springfield | IL |
| *The Joy of Cooking* | 2.50 | Springfield | IL |
| *Walden* | 9.95 | Springfield | MA |
| *A Bridge Too Far* | 3.50 | Springfield | MA |

Cities in different states can have the same name; if two cities with the same name follow each other in your control break program and you have written it to check for a change in city name first, the program will not recognize that you are working with a new city. Instead, you should always check for the major-level break first. If the records are sorted by `bookCity` within `bookState`, then a change in `bookState` causes a **major-level break**, and a change in `bookCity` causes a **minor-level break**. When the `bookState` value "MA" is not equal to the `prevState` value "IL", you force `cityBreak()`, printing a city total for Springfield, IL, before a state total for IL and before continuing with the Springfield, MA, record. You check for a change in `bookState` first, and if there is one, you perform `cityBreak()`. In other words, if there is a change in `bookState`, there is an implied change in `bookCity`, even if the cities happen to have the same name.

**TIP** If you needed totals to print by `bookCity` within a field defined as `bookCounty` within `bookState`, you could say you have minor-, intermediate-, and major-level breaks.

Figure 7-22 shows the `mainLoop()` module for the Book Sales by City and State report program. You check for a change in the `bookState` value. If there is no change, you check for a change in the `bookCity` value. If there is no change there either, you add 1 to the counter for the city and read the next record. When there is a change in the `bookCity` value, you print the city total and add the city total to the state total. When there is a change in the `bookState` value, you perform the break routine for the last city in the state, and then you print the state total and add it to the grand total.

**FIGURE 7-22:** FLOWCHART AND PSEUDOCODE FOR `mainLoop()` FOR BOOK SALES BY CITY AND STATE REPORT PROGRAM

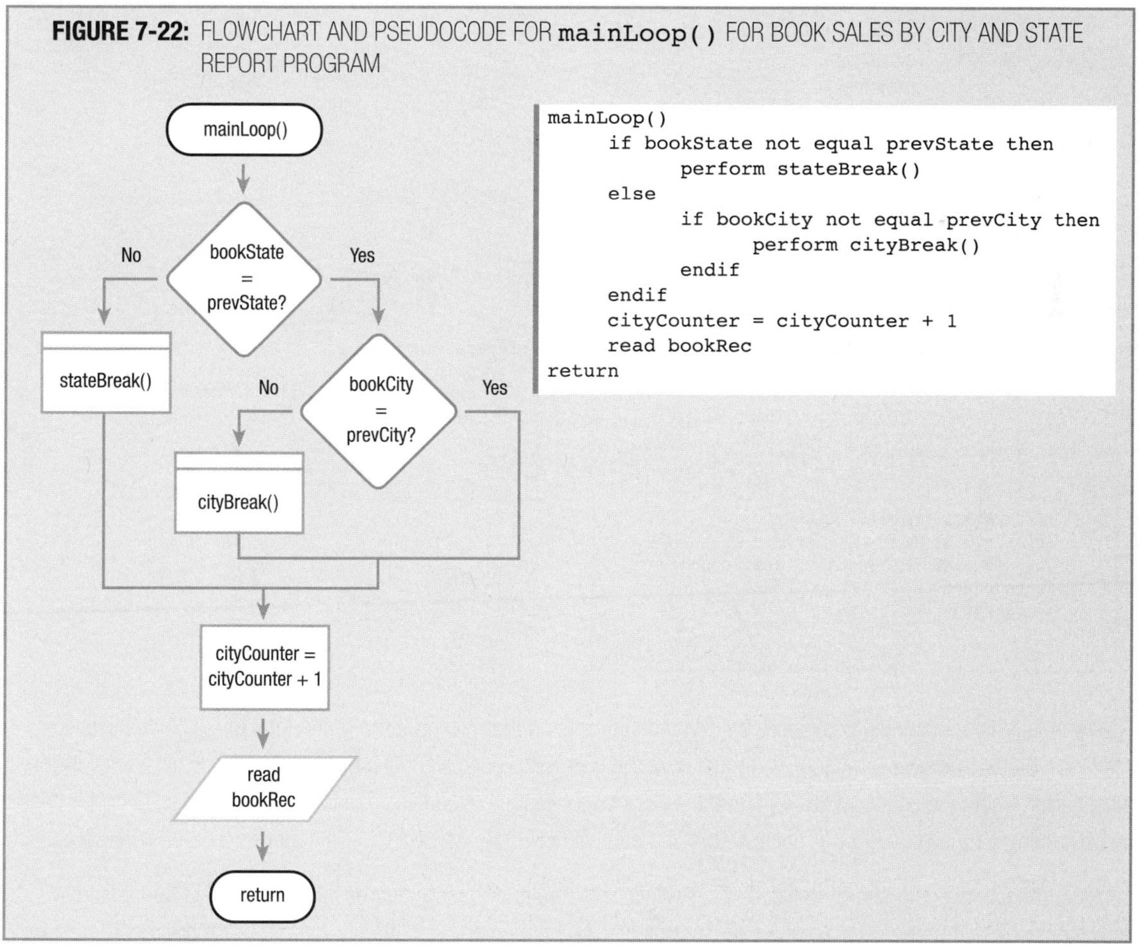


```
mainLoop()
     if bookState not equal prevState then
           perform stateBreak()
     else
           if bookCity not equal prevCity then
                 perform cityBreak()
           endif
     endif
     cityCounter = cityCounter + 1
     read bookRec
return
```

Figures 7-23 and 7-24 show the `stateBreak()` and `cityBreak()` modules. The two modules are very similar; the `stateBreak()` routine contains just one extra type of task. When there is a change in `bookState`, you perform `cityBreak()` automatically before you perform any of the other necessary steps to change states.

**FIGURE 7-23:** FLOWCHART AND PSEUDOCODE FOR `stateBreak()` MODULE

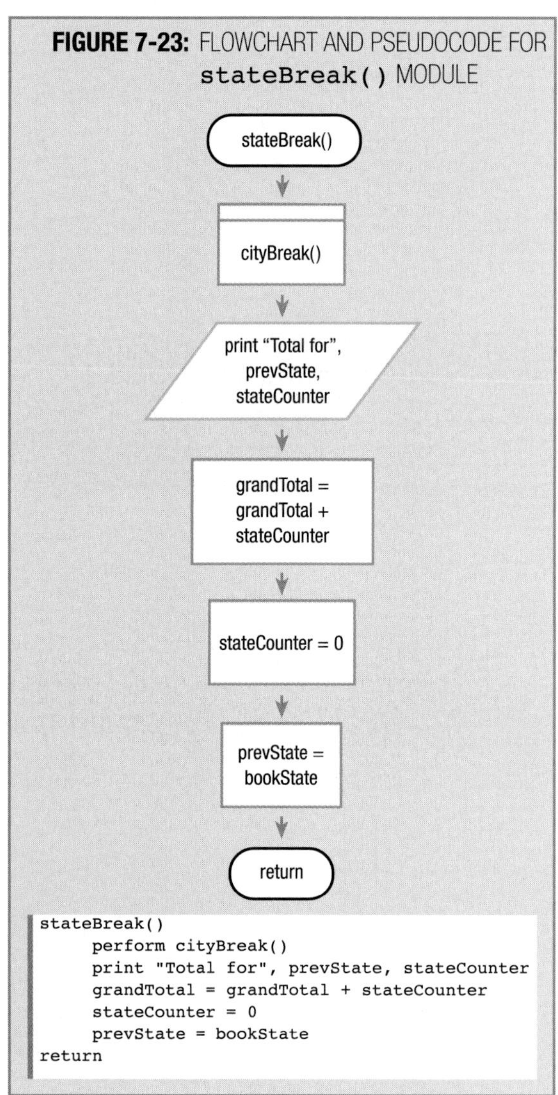


```
stateBreak()
     perform cityBreak()
     print "Total for", prevState, stateCounter
     grandTotal = grandTotal + stateCounter
     stateCounter = 0
     prevState = bookState
return
```

**FIGURE 7-24:** FLOWCHART AND PSEUDOCODE FOR `cityBreak()` MODULE

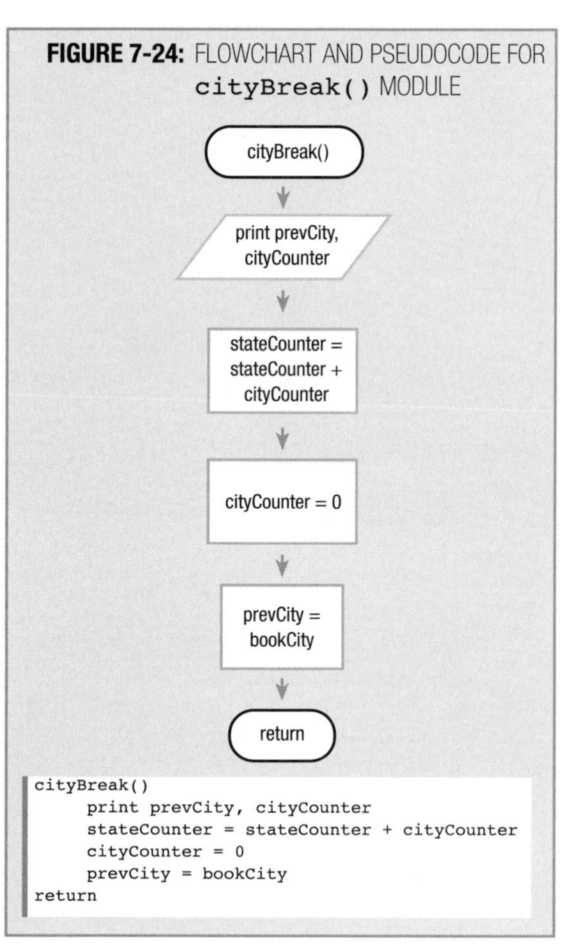


```
cityBreak()
     print prevCity, cityCounter
     stateCounter = stateCounter + cityCounter
     cityCounter = 0
     prevCity = bookCity
return
```

The sample report containing book sales by city and state shows that you print the grand total for all book sales, so within the `closeDown()` module, you must print the `grandTotal` variable. Before you can do so, however, you must perform both the `cityBreak()` and the `stateBreak()` modules one last time. You can accomplish this by performing `stateBreak()`, because the first step within `stateBreak()` is to perform `cityBreak()`.

Consider the sample data shown in Figure 7-21. While you continue to read records for books sold in Springfield, MA, you continue to add to the `cityCounter` for that city. At the moment you attempt to read one more record past the end of the file, you do not know whether there will be more records; therefore, you have not yet printed either the `cityCounter` for Springfield or the `stateCounter` for MA. In the `closeDown()` module, you perform `stateBreak()`, which immediately performs `cityBreak()`. Within `cityBreak()`, the count for Springfield prints and rolls up to the `stateCounter`. Then, after the logic transfers back to the `stateBreak()` module, the total for MA prints and rolls up to `grandTotal`. Finally, you can print `grandTotal`, as shown in Figure 7-25.

**FIGURE 7-25:** FLOWCHART AND PSEUDOCODE FOR `closeDown()` MODULE

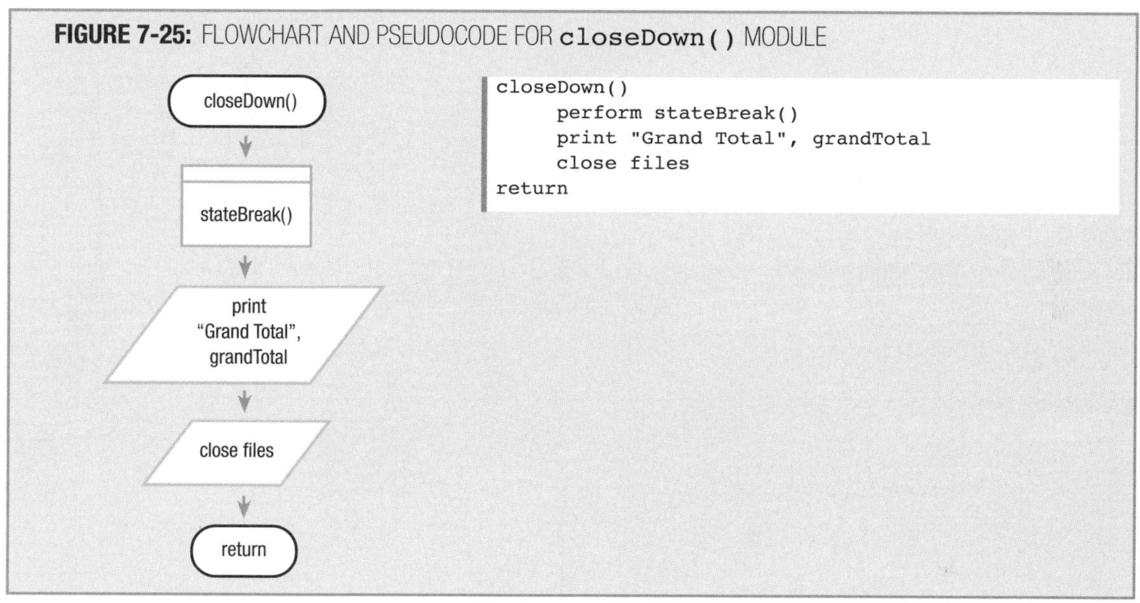


```
closeDown()
     perform stateBreak()
     print "Grand Total", grandTotal
     close files
return
```

Every time you write a program where you need control break routines, you should check whether you need to complete each of the following tasks within the modules:

- Performing the lower-level break, if any
- Performing any control break processing for the previous group
- Rolling up the current-level totals to the next higher level
- Resetting the current level's totals to zero
- Performing any control break processing for the new group
- Updating the control break field

## PERFORMING PAGE BREAKS

Many business programs use a form of control break logic to start a new page when a printed page fills up with output. In other words, you might want the change to a new page to be based on the number of lines already printed, rather than on the contents of an input field, such as department number. The logic in these programs involves counting the lines printed, pausing to print headings when the counter reaches some predetermined value, and then going on. This common business task is just another example of providing a break in the usual flow of control.

TIP Some programmers may prefer to reserve the term *control break* for situations in which the break is based on the contents of one of the fields in an input record, rather than on the contents of a work field such as a line counter.

Let's say you have a file called CUSTOMERFILE containing 1000 customers, with two character fields that you have decided to call `custLast` and `custFirst`. You want to print a list of these customers, 60 detail lines to a page. The mainline logic of the program is familiar (see Figure 7-26). The only new feature is a variable called a line counter. You will use a **line-counter** variable to keep track of the number of printed lines, so that you can break to a new page after printing 60 lines.

**FIGURE 7-26:** MAINLINE LOGIC OF CUSTOMER REPORT PROGRAM

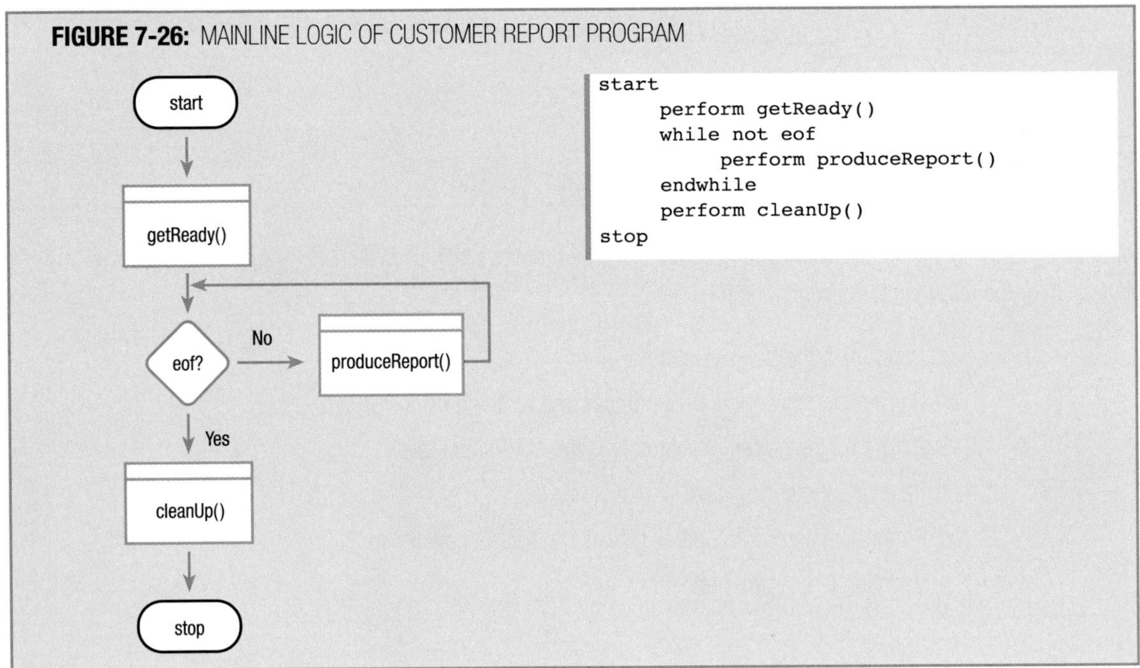


```
start
     perform getReady()
     while not eof
          perform produceReport()
     endwhile
     perform cleanUp()
stop
```

TIP You first learned about detail lines in Chapter 3. Detail lines contain individual record data, as opposed to summary lines, which typically contain counts, totals, or other group information culled from multiple records.

**TIP**

When creating a printed report, you need to clarify whether the user wants a specific number of *total* lines per page, including headings, or a specific number of *detail* lines per page following the headings. In other words, you must determine whether headings should "count" as part of the number of lines requested.

**TIP**

Although you might require any specific number of lines per page, this example uses 60 because it represents a commonly used limit. Printing is most legible with the least waste at about six lines per inch, so 60 lines fit comfortably on standard 11-inch paper.

Within the `getReady()` module (Figure 7-27), you declare the variables, open the files, print the headings, and read the first record. Within the `produceReport()` module (Figure 7-28), you compare `lineCounter` to 60. When you process the first record, `lineCounter` is 0, so you print the record, add 1 to `lineCounter`, and read the next record.

**FIGURE 7-27:** THE `getReady()` MODULE FOR CUSTOMER REPORT PROGRAM

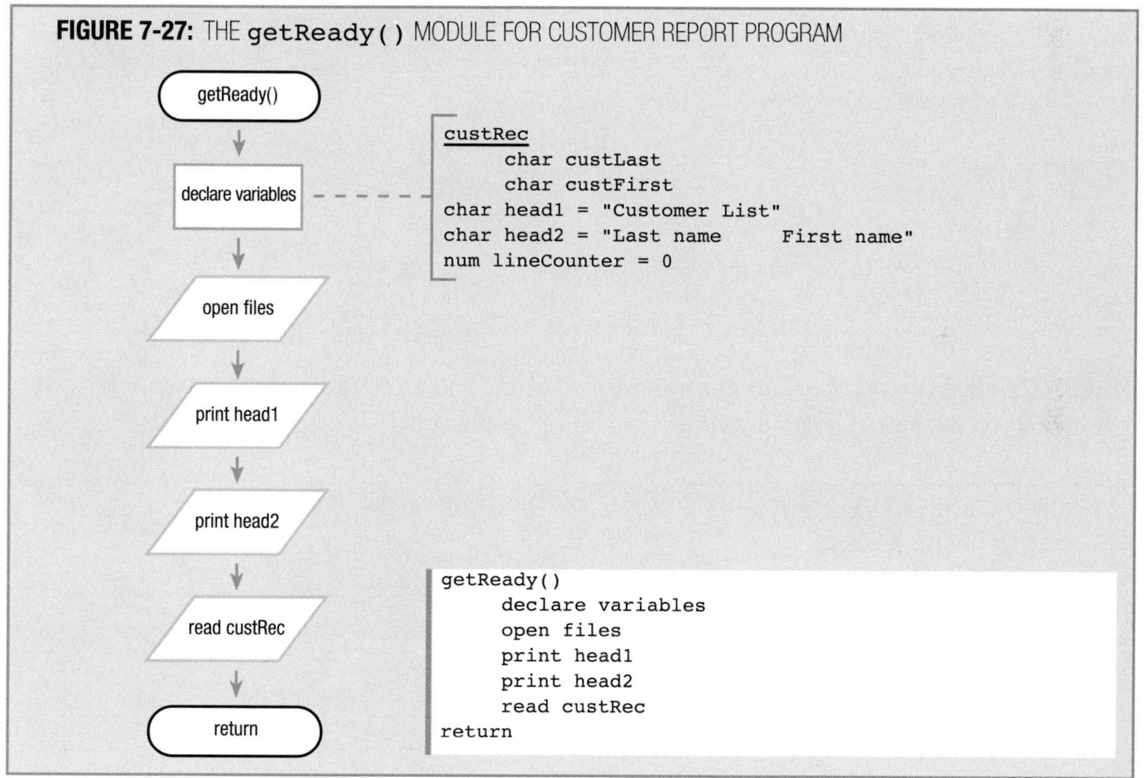
getReady()
declare variables
open files
print head1
print head2
read custRec
return
custRec
char custLast
char custFirst
char head1 = "Customer List"
char head2 = "Last name     First name"
num lineCounter = 0

```
getReady()
     declare variables
     open files
     print head1
     print head2
     read custRec
return
```

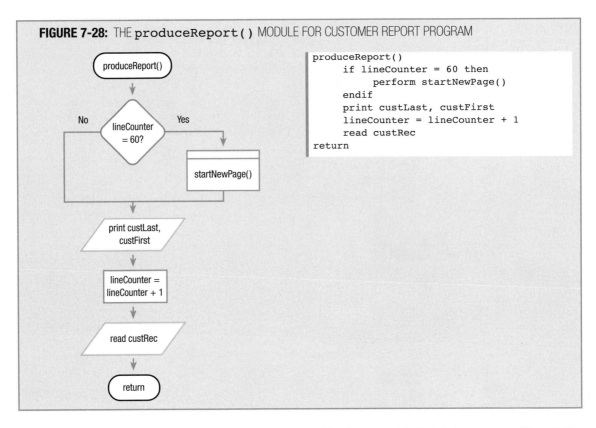

**FIGURE 7-28:** THE `produceReport()` MODULE FOR CUSTOMER REPORT PROGRAM

produceReport()
No
lineCounter = 60?
Yes
startNewPage()
print custLast, custFirst
lineCounter = lineCounter + 1
read custRec
return

```
produceReport()
     if lineCounter = 60 then
          perform startNewPage()
     endif
     print custLast, custFirst
     lineCounter = lineCounter + 1
     read custRec
return
```

In Figure 7-27, instead of printing **head1** and **head2**, you could perform a module that starts a new page. Figure 7-29 shows a `startNewPage()` module that the `getReady()` module could call.

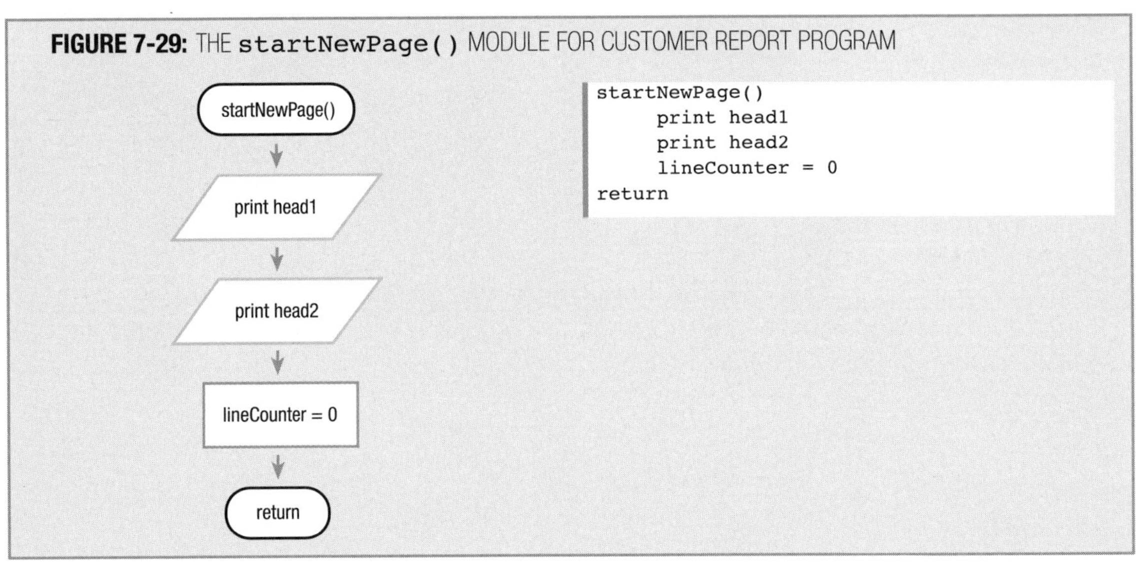


**FIGURE 7-29:** THE `startNewPage()` MODULE FOR CUSTOMER REPORT PROGRAM

```
startNewPage()
     print head1
     print head2
     lineCounter = 0
return
```

On every cycle through the produceReport() module, you check the line counter to see if it is 60 yet. When the first record is printed, lineCounter is 1. You read the second record, and if there is a second record (that is, if it is not eof), you return to the top of the produceReport() module. In that module, you compare lineCounter to 60, print another line, and add 1 to lineCounter, making it equal to 2.

After 60 records are read and printed, lineCounter holds a value of 60. When you read the 61st record (and if it is not eof), you enter the produceReport() module for the 61st time. The answer to the question lineCounter = 60? is Yes, and you break to perform the startNewPage() module. The startNewPage() module is a control break routine.

The startNewPage() module, shown in Figure 7-29, must print the headings that appear at the top of a new page, and it must set lineCounter back to zero. If you neglect to reset lineCounter, its value will increase with each successive record and never be equal to 60 again. When resetting lineCounter for a new page, you force execution of the startNewPage() module after 60 more records (120 total) print.

The startNewPage() module is simpler than many control break modules because no record counters or accumulators are being maintained. In fact, the startNewPage() module must perform only two of the tasks you have seen required by control break routines.

- It does not perform the lower-level break, because there is none.
- It does not perform any control break processing for the previous group, because there is none.
- It does not roll up the current-level totals to the next higher level, because there are no totals.
- It does not reset the current level's totals to zero, because there are no totals (other than lineCounter, which is the control break field).
- It does perform control break processing for the new group by printing headings at the top of the new page.
- It does update the control break field—the line counter.

You might want to employ one little trick to remove the statements that print the headings from the getReady() module. If you initialize lineCounter to 60 when defining the variables at the beginning of the program, on the first pass through produceReport(), you can "fool" the computer into printing the first set of headings automatically. When you initialize lineCounter to 60, you can remove the statements print head1 and print head2 from the getReady() module. With this change, when you enter the produceReport() module for the first time, lineCounter is already set to 60, and the startNewPage() module prints the headings and resets lineCounter to zero before processing the first record from the input file and starting to count the first page's detail lines. Figure 7-30 shows the entire program.

FIGURE 7-30: THE COMPLETE CUSTOMER REPORT PROGRAM

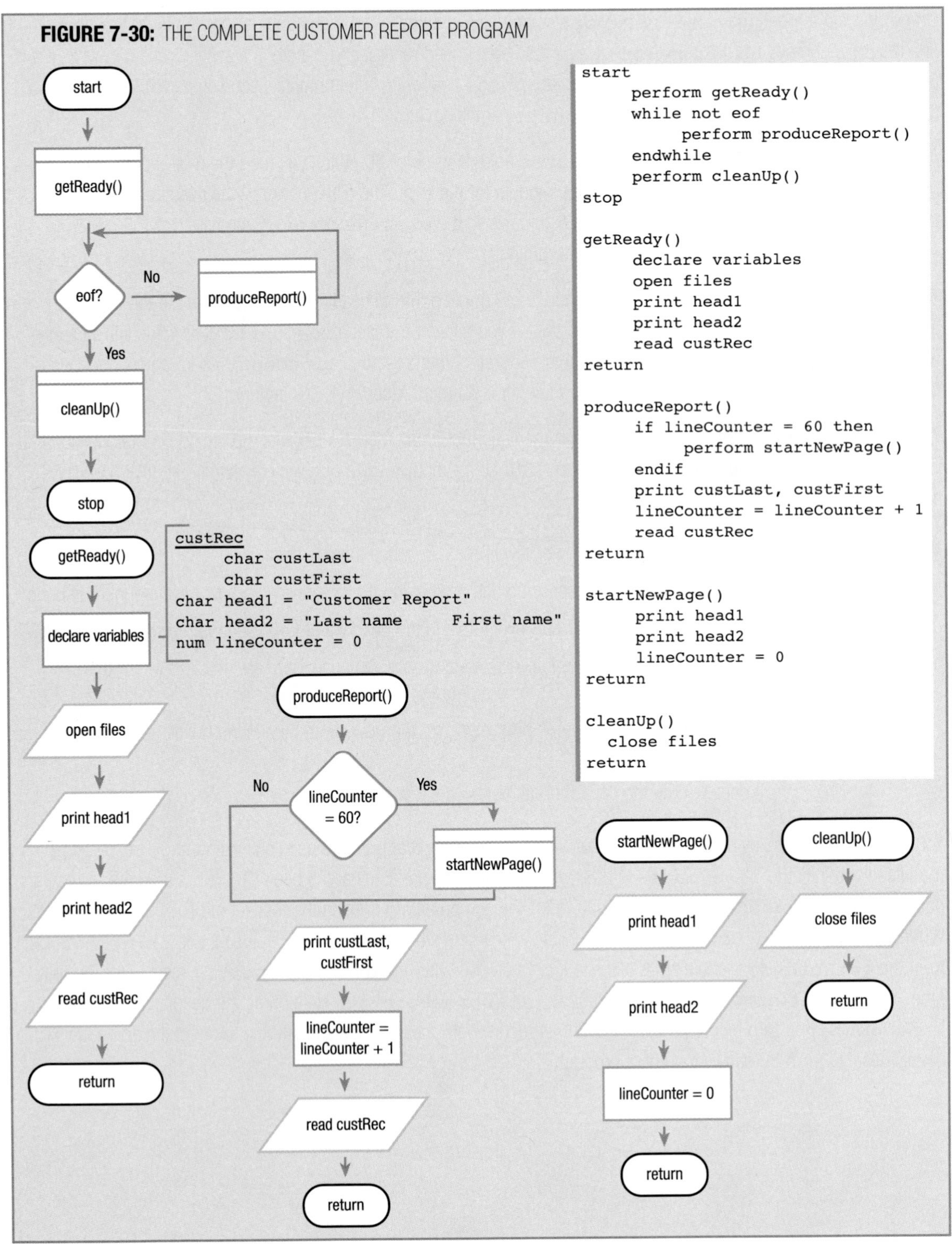


```
start
     perform getReady()
     while not eof
          perform produceReport()
     endwhile
     perform cleanUp()
stop

getReady()
     declare variables
     open files
     print head1
     print head2
     read custRec
return

produceReport()
     if lineCounter = 60 then
          perform startNewPage()
     endif
     print custLast, custFirst
     lineCounter = lineCounter + 1
     read custRec
return

startNewPage()
     print head1
     print head2
     lineCounter = 0
return

cleanUp()
  close files
return
```

TIP

In the program in Figure 7-30, you might prefer to create a constant named LINES_PER_PAGE and set it to be equal to 60. Then, in the `produceReport()` module, you would compare `lineCounter` to this constant. Doing this would provide you with two advantages. First, the meaning of LINES_PER_PAGE would be clearer than the number 60. Second, if you needed to change the number of lines per page, you could do so using the declaration list instead of searching through the program to find the reference.

As with control break report programs that break based on the contents of one of a record's fields, in any program that starts new pages based on a line count, you always must update the line-counting variable that causes the unusual action. Using page breaks or control breaks (or both) within reports adds a new degree of organization to your printed output and makes it easier for the user to interpret and use.

## CHAPTER SUMMARY

- A control break is a temporary detour in the logic of a program; programmers refer to a program as a control break program when a change in the value of a variable initiates special actions or causes special or unusual processing to occur. To generate a control break report, your input records must be organized in sorted order based on the field that will cause the breaks.
- You use a control break field to hold data from a previous record. You decide when to perform a control break routine by comparing the value in the control break field to the corresponding value in the current record. At minimum, the simplest control break routines perform necessary processing for the new group and update the control break field.
- Sometimes, you need to use control data within a control break module, such as in a heading that requires information about the next record, or in a footer that requires information about the previous record. The very first heading prints separately from all the others at the beginning; the very last footer must print separately from all the others at the end.
- A control break report contains and prints totals for the previous group, rolls up the current-level totals to the next higher level, resets the current level's totals to zero, performs any other needed control break processing, and updates the control break field.
- In a program containing a multiple-level control break, the normal flow of control breaks away for special processing in response to a change in more than one field. You should always test for a major-level break before a minor-level break, and include a call to the minor break routine within the major break module.
- Every time you write a program in which you need control break routines, you should check whether you need to perform each of the following tasks within the routines: any lower-level break, any control break processing for the previous group, rolling up the current-level totals to the next higher level, resetting the current level's totals to zero, any control break processing for the new group, and updating the control break field.
- To perform page breaks, you count the lines printed and pause to print headings when the counter reaches some predetermined value.

## KEY TERMS

A **control break** is a temporary detour in the logic of a program.

A **control break program** is one in which a change in the value of a variable initiates special actions or causes special or unusual processing to occur.

A **control break report** lists items in groups. Frequently, each group is followed by a subtotal.

Programs that **sort** records take records that are not in order and rearrange them to be in order based on some field.

A **single-level control break** is a break in the logic of a program based on the value of a single variable.

A **control break field** is a variable that holds the value that signals a break in a program.

A **footer** is a message that prints at the end of a page or other section of a report.

**Rolling up the totals** is the process of adding a total to a higher-level total.

A **summary report** is one that does not include any information about individual records, but instead includes only group totals.

A **multiple-level control break** is one in which the normal flow of control breaks away for special processing in response to a change in more than one field.

A **major-level break** is a break in the flow of logic that is caused by a change in the value of a higher-level field.

A **minor-level break** is a break in the flow of logic that is caused by a change in the value of a lower-level field.

A **line-counter** variable keeps track of the number of printed lines on a page.

## REVIEW QUESTIONS

**1. A control break occurs when a program ________.**

a. takes one of two alternate courses of action for every record
b. pauses to perform special processing based on the value of a field
c. ends prematurely, before all records have been processed
d. passes logical control to a module contained within another program

**2. Which of the following is an example of a control break report?**

a. a list of all employees in a company, with a message "Retain" or "Dismiss" following each employee record
b. a list of all students in a school, arranged in alphabetical order, with a total count at the end of the report
c. a list of all customers of a business in zip code order, with a count of the number of customers who reside in each zip code
d. a list of some of the patients of a medical clinic—those who have not seen a doctor for at least two years

**3. Placing records in sequential order based on the value in one of the fields is called ________.**

a. sorting
b. collating
c. merging
d. categorizing

**4. In a program with a single-level control break, ________.**

a. the input file must contain a variable that contains a single digit
b. the hierarchy chart must contain a single level below the main level
c. special processing occurs based on the value in a single field
d. the control break module must not contain any submodules

5. **A control break field __________.**
   a. always prints prior to any group of records on a control break report
   b. always prints after any group of records on a control break report
   c. never prints on a report
   d. causes special processing to occur

6. **The value stored in a control break field __________.**
   a. can be printed at the end of each group of records
   b. can be printed with each record
   c. both of these
   d. neither a nor b

7. **Within any control break module, you must __________.**
   a. declare a control break field
   b. set the control break field to zero
   c. print the control break field
   d. update the value in the control break field

8. **An insurance agency employs 10 agents and wants to print a report of claims based on the insurance agent who sold each policy. The agent's name should appear in a heading prior to the list of each agent's claims. In the housekeeping module for this program, you should __________.**
   a. read the first record before printing the first heading
   b. print the first heading before reading the first record
   c. read all the records that represent clients of the first agent before printing the heading
   d. print the first heading, but do not read the first record until the main loop

9. **In contrast to using control break data in a heading, when you use control break data in a footer, you usually need data from the __________ record in the input data file.**
   a. previous
   b. next
   c. first
   d. priming

10. **An automobile dealer wants a list of cars sold, grouped by model, with a total dollar amount sold at the end of each group. The program contains four modules, appropriately named `housekeeping()`, `mainLoop()`, `modelBreak()`, and `finish()`. The total for the last car model group should be printed in the __________.**
    a. `mainLoop()` module, after the last time the control break module is called
    b. `mainLoop()` module, as the last step in the module
    c. `modelBreak()` module when it is called from within the `mainLoop()` module
    d. `modelBreak()` module when it is called from within the `finish()` module

**11. The Hampton City Zoo has a file that contains information about each of the animals it houses. Each animal record contains such information as the animal's ID number, date acquired by the zoo, and species. The zoo wants to print a list of animals, grouped by species, with a count after each group. As an example, a typical summary line might be "Species: Giraffe Count: 7". Which of the following happens within the control break module that prints the count?**

a. The previous species count prints, and then the previous species field is updated.
b. The previous species field is updated, and then the previous species count prints.
c. Either of these will produce the desired results.
d. Neither a nor b will produce the desired results.

**12. Adding a total to a higher-level total is called ________ the totals.**

a. sliding
b. advancing
c. rolling up
d. replacing

**13. The Academic Dean of Creighton College wants a count of the number of students who have declared each of the college's 45 major courses of study, as well as a grand total count of students enrolled in the college. Individual student records contain each student's name, ID number, major, and other data, and are sorted in alphabetical order by major. A control break module executes when the program encounters a change in student major. Within this module, what must occur?**

a. The total count for the previous major prints.
b. The total count for the previous major prints, and the total count is added to the grand total.
c. The total count for the previous major prints, the total count for the major is added to the grand total, and the total count for the major is reset to zero.
d. The total count for the previous major prints, the total count for the major is added to the grand total, the total count for the major is reset to zero, and the grand total is reset to zero.

**14. In a control break program containing printed group totals and a grand total, the final module that executes must ________.**

a. print the group total for the last group
b. roll up the total for the last group
c. both of these
d. neither a nor b

**15. A summary report ________.**

a. contains detail lines
b. contains total lines
c. both of these
d. neither a nor b

**16. The Cityscape Real Estate Agency wants a list of all housing units sold last year, including a subtotal of sales that occurred each month. Within each month group, there are also subtotals of each type of property—single-family homes, condominiums, commercial properties, and so on. This report is a ________ control break report.**

a. single-level
b. multiple-level
c. semilevel
d. trilevel

**17. The Packerville Parks Commission has a file that contains picnic permit information for the coming season. They need a report that lists each day's picnic permit information, including permit number and name of permit holder, starting on a separate page each day of the picnic season. (Figure 7-31 shows a sample page of output for the Packerville Parks report.) Within each day's permits, they want subtotals that count permits in each of the city's 30 parks. The permit records have been sorted by park name within date. In the main loop of the report program, the first decision should check for a change in ________.**

**FIGURE 7-31:** SAMPLE PARKS REPORT

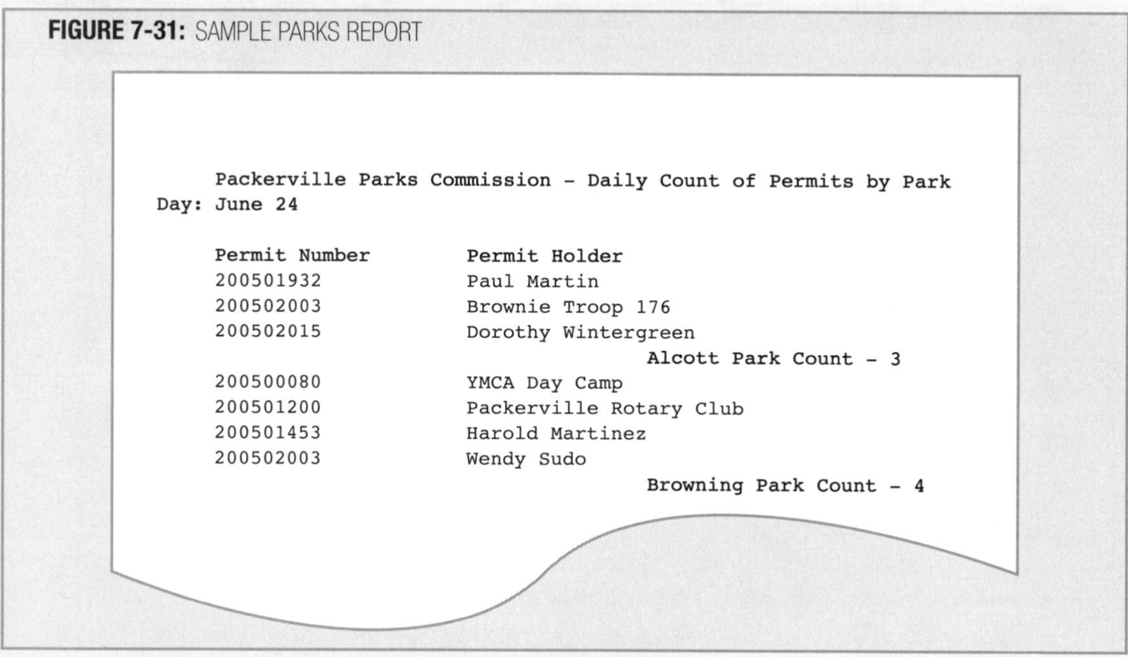

```
          Packerville Parks Commission - Daily Count of Permits by Park
     Day: June 24

          Permit Number          Permit Holder
          200501932              Paul Martin
          200502003              Brownie Troop 176
          200502015              Dorothy Wintergreen
                                                Alcott Park Count - 3
          200500080              YMCA Day Camp
          200501200              Packerville Rotary Club
          200501453              Harold Martinez
          200502003              Wendy Sudo
                                                Browning Park Count - 4
```

a. park name
b. date
c. permit number
d. any of these

**18. Which of the following is *not* a task you need to complete in any control break module that has multiple levels and totals at each level?**

a. Perform lower-level breaks.
b. Roll up the totals.
c. Update the control break field.
d. Reset the current-level totals to the previous-level totals.

**19. The election commission for the state of Illinois maintains a file that contains the name of each registered voter, the voter's county, and the voter's precinct within the county. The commission wants to produce a report that counts the voters in each precinct and county. The file should be sorted in ________.**

a. county order within precinct
b. last name order within precinct
c. last name order within county
d. precinct order within county

**20. A variable that determines when a new page should start based on the number of detail lines printed on a page is a ________.**

a. detail counter
b. line counter
c. page counter
d. break counter

## FIND THE BUGS

Each of the following pseudocode segments contains one or more bugs that you must find and correct.

1. **This application prints a student report for an elementary school. Students have been sorted by grade level. A new page is started for each grade level, and the numeric grade level prints as part of the heading of the page.**

```
start
     perform getReady()
     while not eof
          perform produceReport()
     endwhile
     perform finishUp()
stop

getReady()
     declare variables
         studentRec
             num studentID
             char name
             num gradeLevel
          char heading1 = "Student Report by Grade Level"
          char heading2 = "Students in Grade "
     open files
     print heading1
     print heading2, gradeLevel
     read studentRec
return

produceReport()
     if gradeLevel = holdGradeLevel then
         perform newGrade()
     endif
     print studentId, name
     read studentRec
return

newGrade()
     print heading1
     print heading2, holdGradeLevel
      holdGradeLevel = gradeLevel
return

finishUp()
     close files
return
```

2. **The Friendly Insurance Company makes a point to phone a birthday greeting to each of its clients on his or her birthday. The following program is intended to produce a report that lists the clients a salesperson should call each day for the coming year. Input records include the client's name and phone number as well as a numeric month and day. The records have been sorted by day within month, and each day's list appears on a new page. (It is very likely that some days of the year do not have a client birthday.) At the end of each page is a count of the number of calls that should be made that day. Two pages of a sample report are shown in Figure 7-32.**

**FIGURE 7-32:** SAMPLE REPORT

```
Calls to make on day 2
Of month 1

     Jeffrey Ed
     Martin Ric
     Brandy Ung
     George Wil

     Calls to m
```

```
Calls to make on day 1
Of month 1

     Enrique Nova        920-534-0912
     Barbara  Nuance     920-787-1290
     Allison Sellman     414-712-0019

     Calls to make today:  3
```

```
start
     perform prepare()
     while not eof
          perform produceReport()
     endwhile
     perform finish()
stop

prepare()
     declare variables
          appointmentRec
             char clientName
             char phoneNumber
             num month
             num day
          num oldMonth
          num oldDay
          char heading1 = "Calls to make on day "
          char heading2 = "of month "
          char footer = "Calls to make today: "
          num countAppointments
```

```
        open files
        read appointmentRec
        print head1, day
        print heading2, month
        month = oldMonth
        day = oldDay
return

produceReport()
        if day not = oldDay then
            perform newDay()
         else
                if month not = oldMonth
                    perform newMonth()
                endif
        endif
        print clientName, phoneNumber
        countAppointments = countAppointments + 1
return

newMonth()
        perform newDay()
        oldMonth = month
return

newDay()
       perform newMonth()
       print footer, countAppointments
       print heading1, day
       print heading1, month
       oldDay = day
return

finish()
        close files
return
```

## EXERCISES

1. **What fields might you want to use as the control break fields to produce a report that lists all inventory items in a grocery store? (For example, you might choose to group items by grocery store department.) Design a sample report.**

2. **What fields might you want to use as the control break fields to produce a report that lists all the people you know? (For example, you might choose to group friends by city of residence.) Design a sample report.**

3. **Cool's Department Store keeps a record of every sale in the following format:**

```
DEPARTMENT STORE SALES FILE DESCRIPTION
File name: DEPTSALES
Sorted by: Department
FIELD DESCRIPTION          DATA TYPE          COMMENTS
Transaction Number         Numeric            a 6-digit number
Amount                     Numeric            2 decimal places
Department                 Numeric            a 3-digit number
```

**Create the logic for a program that would print each transaction's details, with a total at the end of each department.**

a. Design the output for this program; create either sample output or a print chart.
b. Create the hierarchy chart.
c. Create the flowchart.
d. Create the pseudocode.

4. **A used-car dealer keeps track of sales in the following format:**

```
AUTO SALES FILE DESCRIPTION
File name: AUTO
Sorted by: Salesperson
FIELD DESCRIPTION        DATA TYPE        EXAMPLE
Salesperson              Character        Miller
Make of Car              Character        Ford
Vehicle Type             Character        Sedan
Sale Price               Numeric          0 decimal places; for example, 15000
```

**By the end of the week, a salesperson may have sold no cars, one car, or many cars. Create the logic of a program that would print one line for each salesperson, with that salesperson's total sales for the week and commission earned, which is 4 percent of the total sales.**

a. Design the output for this program; create either sample output or a print chart.
b. Create the hierarchy chart.
c. Create the flowchart.
d. Create the pseudocode.

5. **A community college maintains student records in the following format:**

```
STUDENT FILE DESCRIPTION
File name: STUDENTS
Sorted by: Hour of First Class
FIELD DESCRIPTION        DATA TYPE        EXAMPLE
Student Name             Character        Amy Lee
City                     Character        Woodstock
Hour of First Class      Numeric          08 for 8 a.m. or 14 for 2 p.m.
Phone Number             Numeric          8154379823
```

**The records have been sorted by hour of the day. The Hour of First Class is a two-digit number based on a 24-hour clock (for example, a 1 p.m. first class is recorded as 13).**

**Create a report that students can use to organize carpools. The report lists the names and phone numbers of students from the city of Huntley. Note that some students come from cities other than Huntley; these students should not be listed on the report.**

**Start a new page for each hour of the day, so that all students starting classes at the same hour are listed on the same page. Include the hour that each page represents in the heading for that page.**

a. Design the output for this program; create either sample output or a print chart.
b. Create the hierarchy chart.
c. Create the flowchart.
d. Create the pseudocode.

6. **The Stanton Insurance Agency needs a report summarizing the counts of life, health, and other types of insurance policies it sells. Input records contain policy number, name of insured, policy value, and type of policy, and have been sorted in alphabetical order by type of policy. At the end of the report, display a count of all the policies.**
   a. Design the output for this program; create either sample output or a print chart.
   b. Create the hierarchy chart.
   c. Create the flowchart.
   d. Create the pseudocode.

7. **If a university is organized into colleges (such as Liberal Arts), divisions (such as Languages), and departments (such as French), what would constitute the major, intermediate, and minor control breaks in a report that prints all classes offered by the university?**

8. **A zoo keeps track of the expense of feeding the animals it houses. Each record holds one animal's ID number, name, species (elephant, rhinoceros, tiger, lion, and so on), zoo residence (pachyderm house, large-cat house, and so on), and weekly food budget. The records take the following form:**

```
ANIMAL FEED RECORDS
File name: ANIMFOOD
Sorted by: Species within house
FIELD DESCRIPTION       DATA TYPE       EXAMPLE
Animal ID               Numeric         4116
Animal Name             Character       Elmo
Species                 Character       Elephant
House                   Character       Pachyderm
Weekly Food             Numeric         0 decimals, whole dollars; for example, 75
   Budget in Dollars
```

   **Design a report that lists each animal's ID, name, and budgeted food amount. At the end of each species group, print a total budget for the species. At the end of each house (for example, the species lion, tiger, and leopard are all in the large-cat house), print the house total. At the end of the report, print the grand total.**
   a. Design the output for this program; create either sample output or a print chart.
   b. Create the hierarchy chart.
   c. Create the flowchart.
   d. Create the pseudocode.

9. **A soft-drink manufacturer produces several flavors of drink—for example, cola, orange, and lemon. Additionally, each flavor has several versions, such as regular, diet, and caffeine-free. The manufacturer operates factories in several states.**

   **Assume you have input records that list version, flavor, yearly production in gallons, and state (for example: Regular Cola 5000 Kansas). The records have been sorted in alphabetical order by version within flavor within state. Design the report that lists each version and flavor, with minor total production figures for each flavor and major total production figures for each state.**

   a. Design the output for this program; create either sample output or a print chart.
   b. Create the hierarchy chart.
   c. Create the flowchart.
   d. Create the pseudocode.

10. **An art shop owner maintains records for each item in the shop, including the title of the work, the artist who made the item, the medium (for example, watercolor, oil, or clay), and the monetary value. The records are sorted by artist within medium. Design a report that lists all items in the store, with a minor total value following each artist's work, and a major total value following each medium. Allow only 40 detail lines per page.**

    a. Design the output for this program; create either sample output or a print chart.
    b. Create the hierarchy chart.
    c. Create the flowchart.
    d. Create the pseudocode.

## DETECTIVE WORK

1. **Control break reports are just one type of frequently printed business report. Has paper consumption increased or decreased since computers became common office tools? How soon do experts predict we will have the "paperless office"?**

## UP FOR DISCUSSION

1. Suppose your employer asks you to write a control break program that lists all the company's employees, their salaries, and their ages, with breaks at each department to list a count of employees in that department. You are provided with the personnel file to use as input. You decide to take the file home with you so you can work on creating the report over the weekend. Is this acceptable? What if the file contained only employees' names and departments, and not more sensitive data such as salaries and ages?

2. Suppose your supervisor asks you to create a report that lists all employees by department and includes a break after each department to display the highest-paid employee in that department. Suppose you also know that your employer will use this report to lay off the highest-paid employee in each department. Would you agree to write the program? Instead, what if the report's purpose was to list the worst performer in each department in terms of sales? What if the report grouped employees by gender? What if the report grouped employees by race?

3. Suppose your supervisor asks you to write a control break report that lists employees in groups by the dollar value of medical insurance claims they have in a year. You fear the employer will use the report to eliminate workers who are driving up the organization's medical insurance policy costs. Do you agree to write the report? What if you know for certain that the purpose of the report is to eliminate workers?

# 8 ARRAYS

## After studying Chapter 8, you should be able to:

- Understand how arrays are used
- Understand how arrays occupy computer memory
- Manipulate an array to replace nested decisions
- Declare and initialize an array
- Declare and initialize constant arrays
- Load array values from a file
- Search an array for an exact match
- Use parallel arrays
- Force subscripts to remain within array bounds
- Improve search efficiency by using an early exit
- Search an array for a range match

## UNDERSTANDING ARRAYS

An **array** is a series or list of variables in computer memory, all of which have the same name but are differentiated with special numbers called subscripts. A **subscript** is a number that indicates the position of a particular item within an array. Whenever you require multiple storage locations for objects, you are using a real-life counterpart of a programming array. For example, if you store important papers in a series of file folders and label each folder with a consecutive letter of the alphabet, then you are using the equivalent of an array. If you store mementos in a series of stacked shoeboxes, each labeled with a year, or if you sort mail into slots, each labeled with a name, then you are also using a real-life equivalent of a programming array.

TIP Besides the term "subscript," programmers also use the term "**index**" to refer to the number that indicates a position within an array.

When you look down the left side of a tax table to find your income level before looking to the right to find your income tax obligation, you are using an array. Similarly, if you look down the left side of a train schedule to find your station before looking to the right to find the train's arrival time, you also are using an array.

Each of these real-life arrays helps you organize real-life objects. You *could* store all your papers or mementos in one huge cardboard box, or find your tax rate or train's arrival time if both were printed randomly in one large book. However, using an organized storage and display system makes your life easier in each case. Using a programming array accomplishes the same results for your data.

TIP Some programmers refer to an array as a *table* or a *matrix*.

## HOW ARRAYS OCCUPY COMPUTER MEMORY

When you declare an array, you declare a programming structure that contains multiple variables. Each variable within an array has the same name and the same data type; each separate array variable is one **element** of the array. Each array element occupies an area in memory next to, or contiguous to, the others, as shown in Figure 8-1. You indicate the number of elements an array will hold—the **size of the array**—when you declare the array along with your other variables.

**FIGURE 8-1:** APPEARANCE OF A THREE-ELEMENT ARRAY AND A SINGLE VARIABLE IN COMPUTER MEMORY

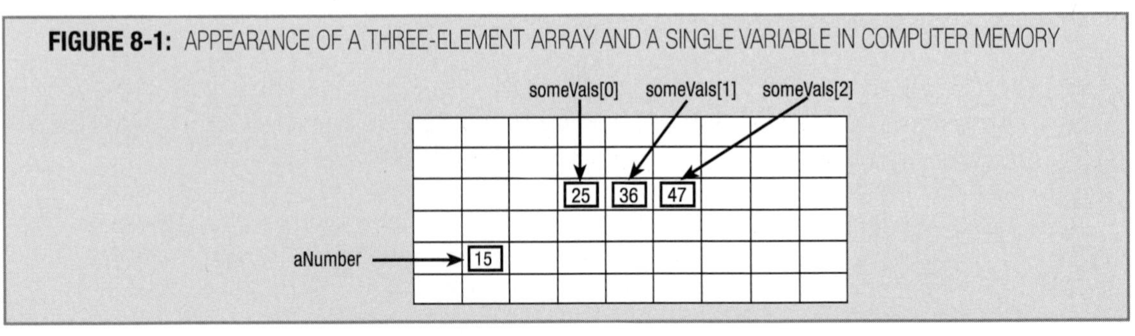

All array elements have the same group name, but each individual element also has a unique subscript indicating how far away it is from the first element. Therefore, any array's subscripts are always a sequence of integers, such as 0 through 5 or 0 through 10. Depending on the syntax rules of the programming language you use, you place the subscript within either parentheses or square brackets following the group name; when writing pseudocode or drawing a flowchart, you can use either form of notation. This text uses square brackets to hold array element subscripts so that you don't mistake array names for method names. For example, Figure 8-1 shows how a single variable and an array are stored in computer memory. The single variable named `aNumber` holds the value 15. The array named `someVals` contains three elements, so the elements are `someVals[0]`, `someVals[1]`, and `someVals[2]`. The value stored in `someVals[0]` is 25, `someVals[1]` holds 36, and `someVals[2]` holds 47. From the diagram in Figure 8-1, you can see that the memory location `someVals[0]` is zero elements away from the beginning of the array, the location of `someVals[1]` is one memory location away, and the location of `someVals[2]` is two elements away from the start of the array.

**TIP** In general, older programming languages such as COBOL and RPG use parentheses to hold their array subscripts. Newer languages such as C#, C++, and Java use square brackets.

**TIP** In many modern languages (for example, Java, Visual Basic .NET, C#, and C++), the first array element's subscript is 0; in others (for example, COBOL and RPG), it is 1. In Pascal, you can identify the starting number as any value you want. In languages in which the first subscript is 0, the subscript alone indicates the distance from the start of the array. In languages that use a starting subscript value other than 0, the compiler does the arithmetic for you to calculate the number of elements past the start of the array that you want to access. In all languages, however, the subscript values must be integers (whole numbers) and sequential.

Because the first element in an array in most programming languages is accessed using a subscript of value 0, the array is called a **zero-based array**. Because the lowest subscript you can use with an array is 0, the highest subscript you are allowed to use with an array is one less than the number of elements in the array. For example, an array with 10 elements uses subscripts 0 through 9, and an array with 200 elements uses subscripts 0 through 199. When you use arrays, you must always keep the limits of subscript values in mind.

**TIP** If you treat an array as though its lowest legal subscript is 1, when in fact it is 0, you will commit **off-by-one errors**. If you use an invalid subscript—for example, using a 10 in a 10-element array for which the subscripts should be 0 through 9—some language compilers will issue an error message and stop program execution, but others will allow you to make the mistake, resulting in incorrect output.

You are never required to use arrays within your programs, but learning to use arrays correctly can make many programming tasks far more efficient and professional. When you understand how to use arrays, you will be able to provide elegant solutions to problems that otherwise would require tedious programming steps.

**TIP** When you describe people or events as "elegant," you mean they possess a refined gracefulness. Similarly, programmers use the term "elegant" to describe programs that are well-designed and easy to understand and maintain.

## MANIPULATING AN ARRAY TO REPLACE NESTED DECISIONS

Consider a program that keeps statistics for requests about apartments in a large apartment complex. The developer wants to keep track of inquiries so that future building projects are more likely to satisfy customer needs. In particular, the developer wants to keep track of how many requests there are for studio, one-, two-, and three-bedroom apartments. Each time an apartment request is received, a clerk adds a record to a file in the format shown in Figure 8-2.

**FIGURE 8-2:** FILE DESCRIPTION FOR APARTMENT REQUEST RECORDS

```
APARTMENT INQUIRY FILE DESCRIPTION
File name: APTREQUESTS
FIELD DESCRIPTION      DATA TYPE    COMMENTS
Day of the month       Numeric      1 - 31, day request was made
Bedrooms requested     Numeric      0, 1, 2 or 3 for studio apartment
                                    or number of bedrooms
```

For example, if a call comes in on the third day of the month for a studio apartment, one record is created with a 3 in the date field and a 0 in the number of bedrooms field. If the next call is on the fourth day of the month for a three-bedroom apartment, a record with 4 and 3 is created. The contents of the data file appear as a series of numbers, as follows:

```
3 0
4 3
4 0
```

... and so on.

At the end of the month, after all the records have been collected, the file might contain hundreds of records, each holding a number that represents a date and another number (0, 1, 2, or 3) that represents the number of bedrooms the caller wanted. You want to write a program that summarizes the total number of each type of apartment requested during the month. A typical report appears in Figure 8-3.

**FIGURE 8-3:** TYPICAL APARTMENT REQUEST REPORT

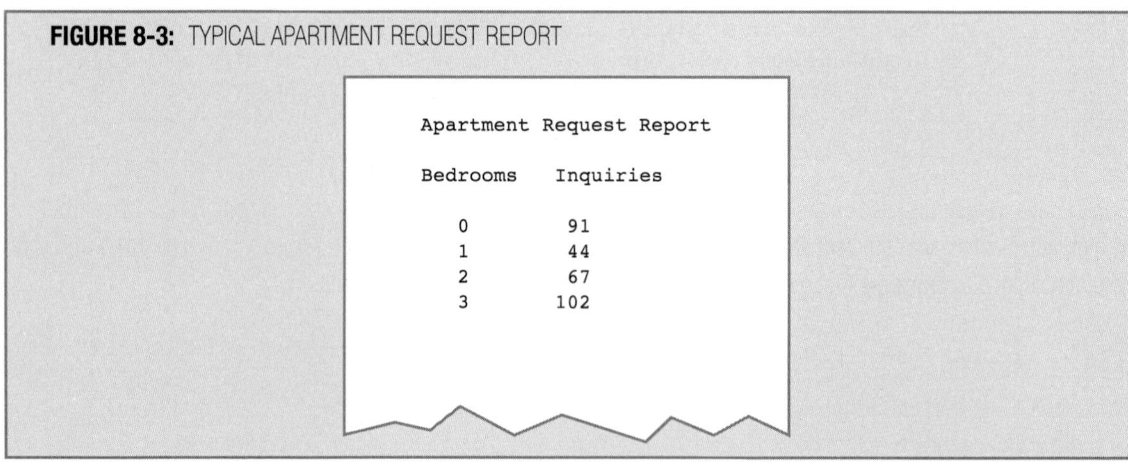

```
Apartment Request Report

Bedrooms   Inquiries

   0          91
   1          44
   2          67
   3         102
```

If all the records were sorted in order by the number of bedrooms requested, this report could be a control break report. You would simply read each record representing an inquiry on a studio apartment (zero bedrooms), counting the number of inquiries. When you read the first record requesting a different number of bedrooms, you would print the count for the previous apartment type, reset the count to zero, and update the control break field before continuing.

**TIP** You learned about control break logic in Chapter 7.

Assume, however, that the records have not been sorted by apartment type. Without using an array, could you write a program that would accumulate the four apartment-type totals? Of course you could. The program would have the same mainline logic as most of the other programs you have seen, as shown in Figure 8-4.

**FIGURE 8-4:** FLOWCHART AND PSEUDOCODE FOR MAINLINE LOGIC OF APARTMENT REQUEST REPORT PROGRAM

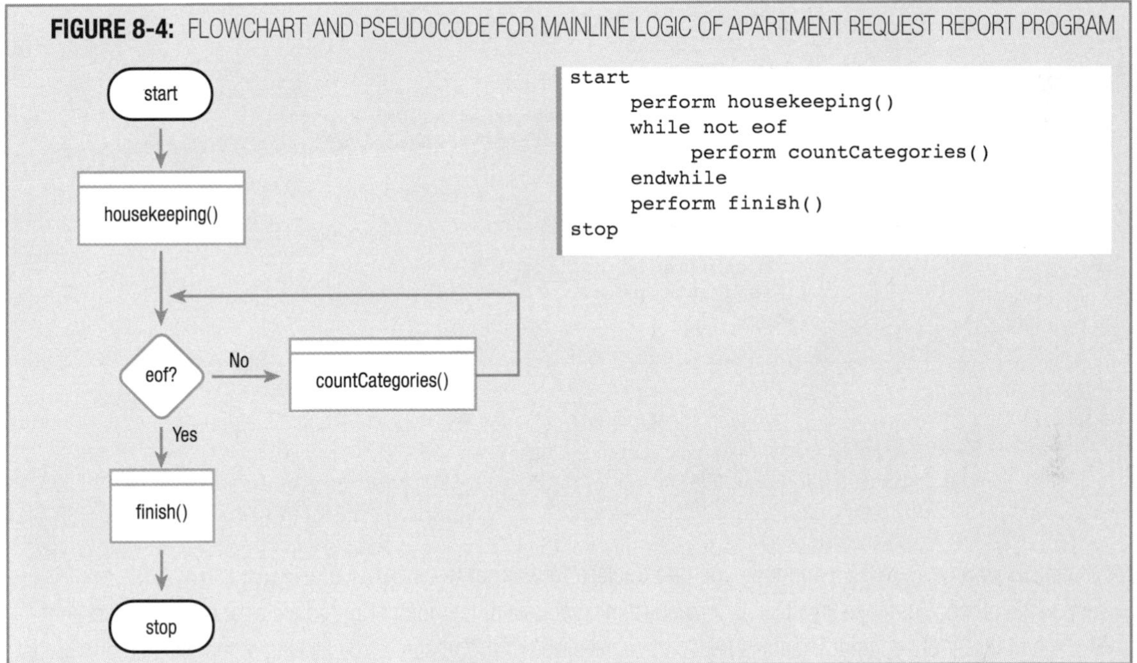


```
start
     perform housekeeping()
     while not eof
          perform countCategories()
     endwhile
     perform finish()
stop
```

**TIP** The program shown in Figures 8-4 through 8-7 accomplishes its purpose, but is cumbersome. Follow its logic here, so that you understand how the program works. Later in this chapter, you will see how to write the apartment request report program much more efficiently using arrays.

In the `housekeeping()` module of the apartment request report program (Figure 8-5), you declare variables including `day` and `bedrooms`. Then, you open the files and read the first record into memory. The headings *could* print in `housekeeping()` or—because no other printing takes place in this program until the `finish()` module—you can choose to wait and print the headings there.

**FIGURE 8-5:** THE `housekeeping()` MODULE FOR THE APARTMENT REQUEST PROGRAM WITHOUT AN ARRAY

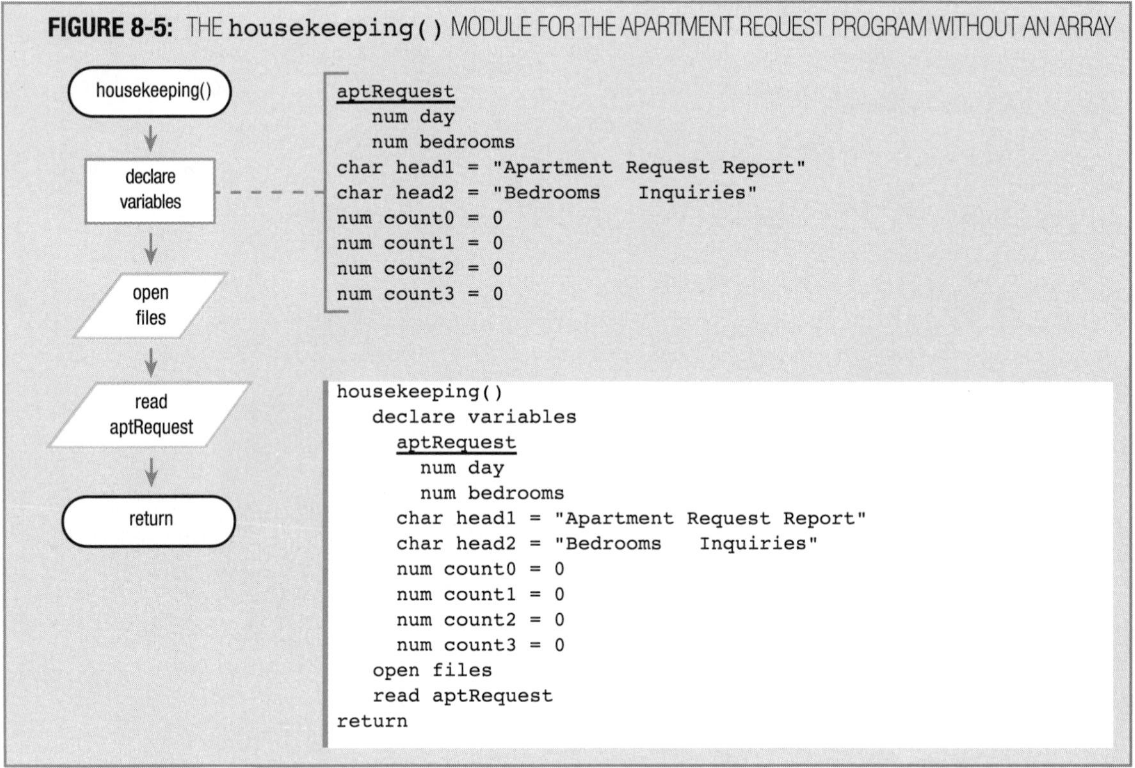


```
housekeeping()
   declare variables
     aptRequest
       num day
       num bedrooms
     char head1 = "Apartment Request Report"
     char head2 = "Bedrooms   Inquiries"
     num count0 = 0
     num count1 = 0
     num count2 = 0
     num count3 = 0
   open files
   read aptRequest
return
```

**TIP** In Figure 8-5, the variable list is identical for the flowchart and the pseudocode. It is included twice in this figure and in the next few for clarity because arrays are a new and complicated topic. In later examples in this book, the duplication of the variable list will be eliminated.

Within the `housekeeping()` module, you can declare four variables, `count0`, `count1`, `count2`, and `count3`; the purpose of these variables is to keep running counts of the number of requests for the four apartment types. Each of these four counter variables needs to be initialized to 0. You can tell by looking at the planned output that you need two heading lines, so `head1` is defined as "Apartment Request Report" and `head2` as "Bedrooms Inquiries".

Eventually, four summary lines will be printed in the report, each with a number of bedrooms and a count of inquiries for that apartment type. These lines cannot be printed until the `finish()` module, however, because you won't have a complete count of each apartment type's requests until all input records have been read.

The logic within the `countCategories()` module of the program requires adding a 1 to `count0`, `count1`, `count2`, or `count3`, depending on the `bedrooms` variable. After 1 has been added to one of the four counters, you read the next record, and if it is not `eof`, you repeat the decision-making and counting process. When all records have been read, you proceed to the `finish()` module, where you print the four summary lines with the counts for the four apartment types. See Figures 8-6 and 8-7.

**TIP** In the apartment request report program, assume that the input data has been previously edited to ensure that all apartment requests are for zero, one, two, or three bedrooms. In other words, there is no bad data. If this were not true, then the program would also need to include a step to check for incorrect data and take some appropriate action—perhaps ignoring it, or counting it in an error category.

**FIGURE 8-6:** THE `countCategories()` MODULE FOR THE APARTMENT REQUEST PROGRAM WITHOUT AN ARRAY

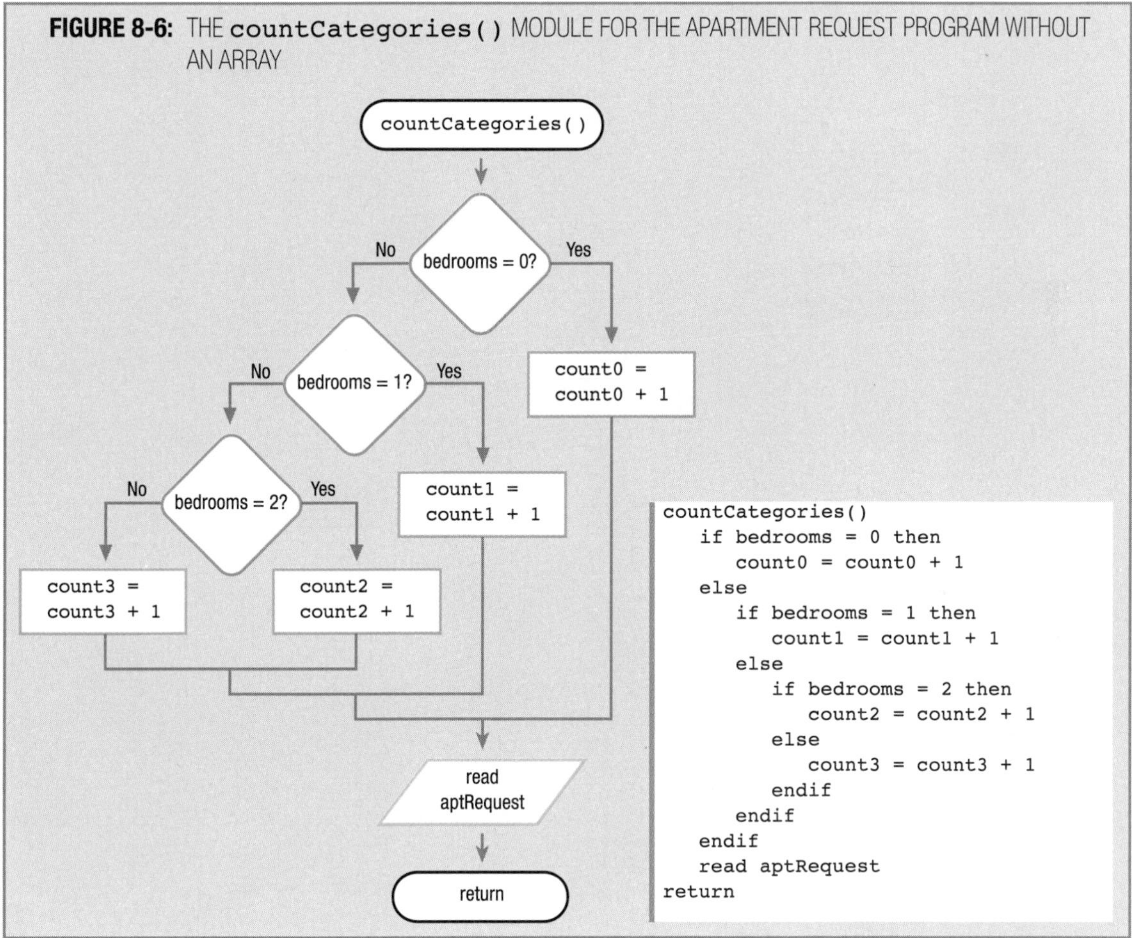


```
countCategories()
   if bedrooms = 0 then
      count0 = count0 + 1
   else
      if bedrooms = 1 then
         count1 = count1 + 1
      else
         if bedrooms = 2 then
            count2 = count2 + 1
         else
            count3 = count3 + 1
         endif
      endif
   endif
   read aptRequest
return
```

**FIGURE 8-7:** THE `finish()` MODULE FOR THE APARTMENT REQUEST PROGRAM WITHOUT AN ARRAY

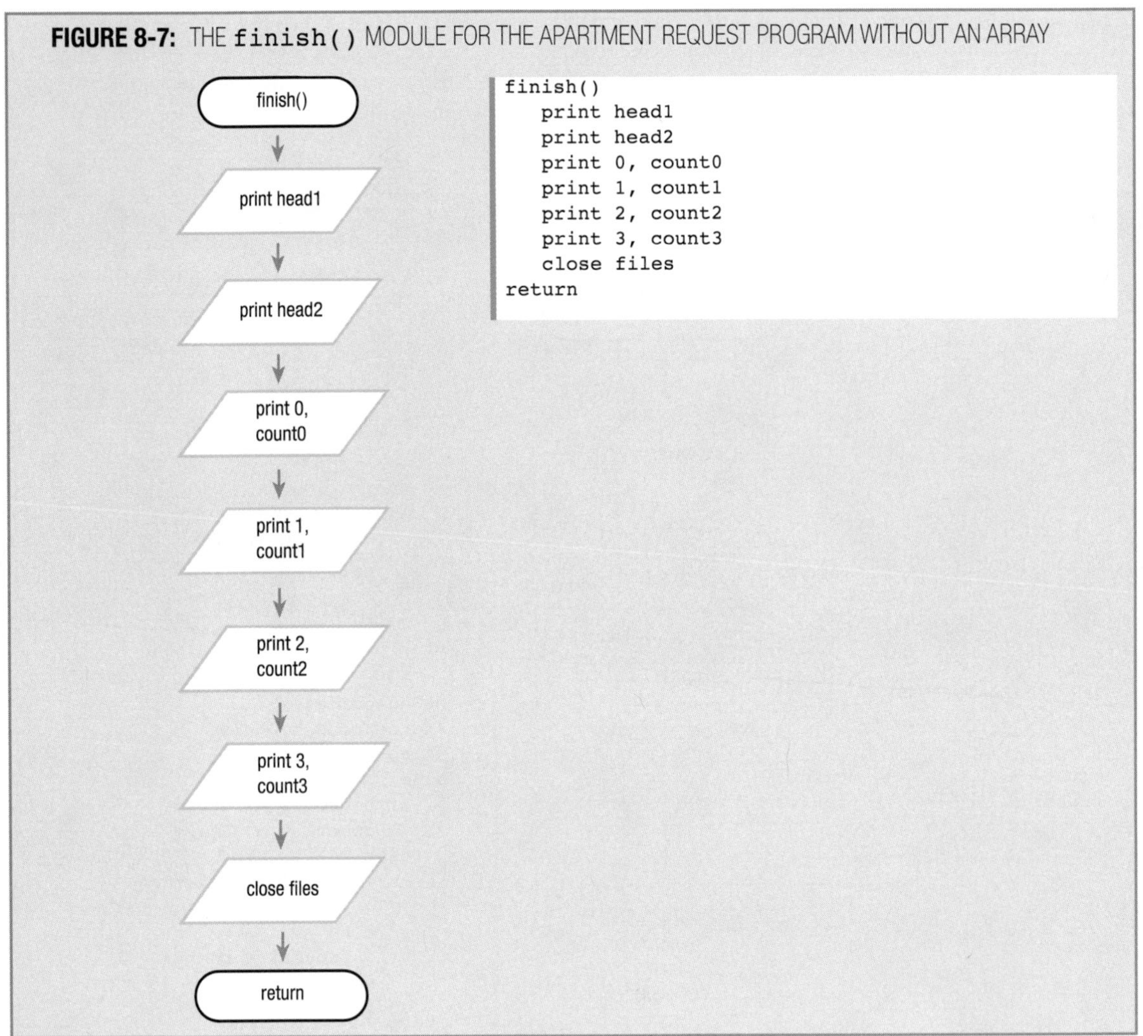


```
finish()
   print head1
   print head2
   print 0, count0
   print 1, count1
   print 2, count2
   print 3, count3
   close files
return
```

The apartment request report program works just fine, and there is absolutely nothing wrong with it logically; a decision is made for each of the first three types of apartments, defaulting to a three-bedroom apartment if the request is not for zero, one, or two bedrooms. But what if there were four types of apartments, or 12, or 30? With any of these scenarios, the basic logic of the program would remain the same; however, you would need to declare many additional counter variables. You also would need many additional decisions within the `countCategories()` module and many additional print statements within the `finish()` module to complete the processing.

Using an array provides an alternative approach to this programming problem, and greatly reduces the number of statements you need. When you declare an array, you provide a group name for a number of associated variables in memory. For example, the four apartment-type counters can be redefined as a single array named `count`. The individual elements become `count[0]`, `count[1]`, `count[2]`, and `count[3]`, as shown in the new `housekeeping()` module in Figure 8-8.

**FIGURE 8-8:** MODIFIED `housekeeping()` MODULE FOR APARTMENT REQUEST PROGRAM THAT DECLARES AN ARRAY TO COUNT REQUESTS

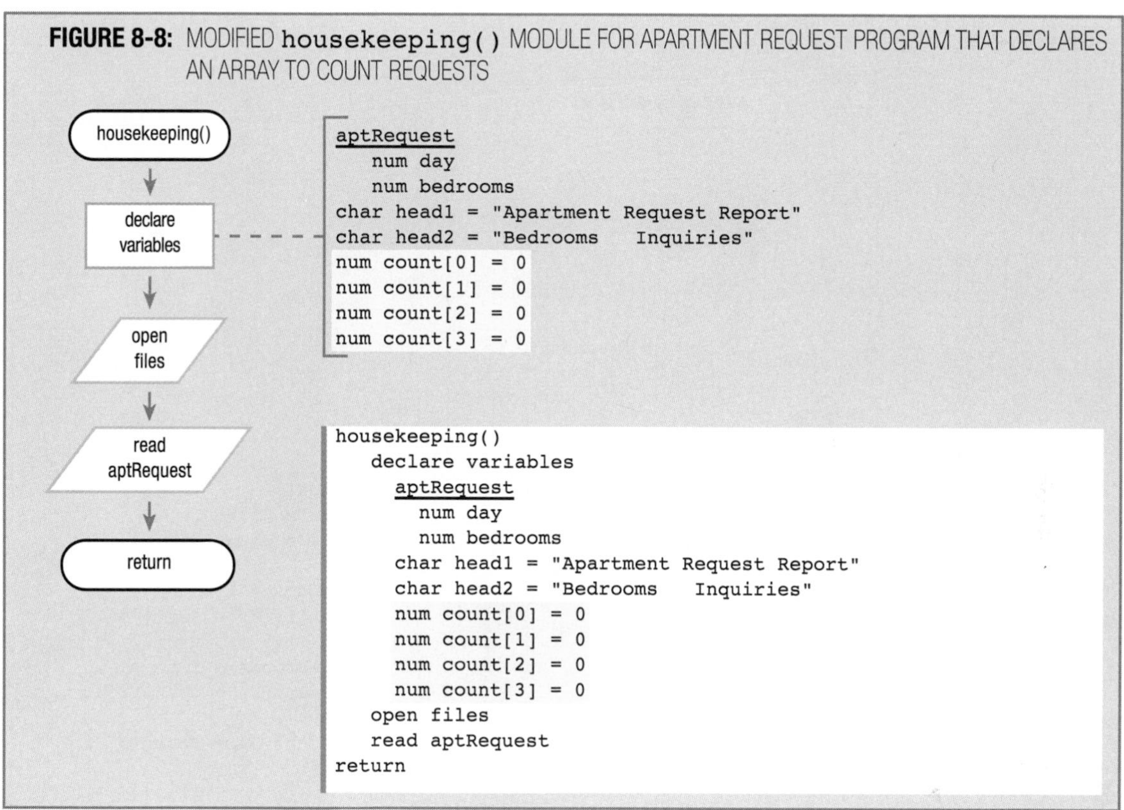


```
housekeeping()
   declare variables
     aptRequest
       num day
       num bedrooms
     char head1 = "Apartment Request Report"
     char head2 = "Bedrooms   Inquiries"
     num count[0] = 0
     num count[1] = 0
     num count[2] = 0
     num count[3] = 0
   open files
   read aptRequest
return
```

With the change to `housekeeping()` shown in Figure 8-8, the `countCategories()` module changes to the version shown in Figure 8-9.

**FIGURE 8-9:** MODIFIED `countCategories()` MODULE THAT USES `count` ARRAY

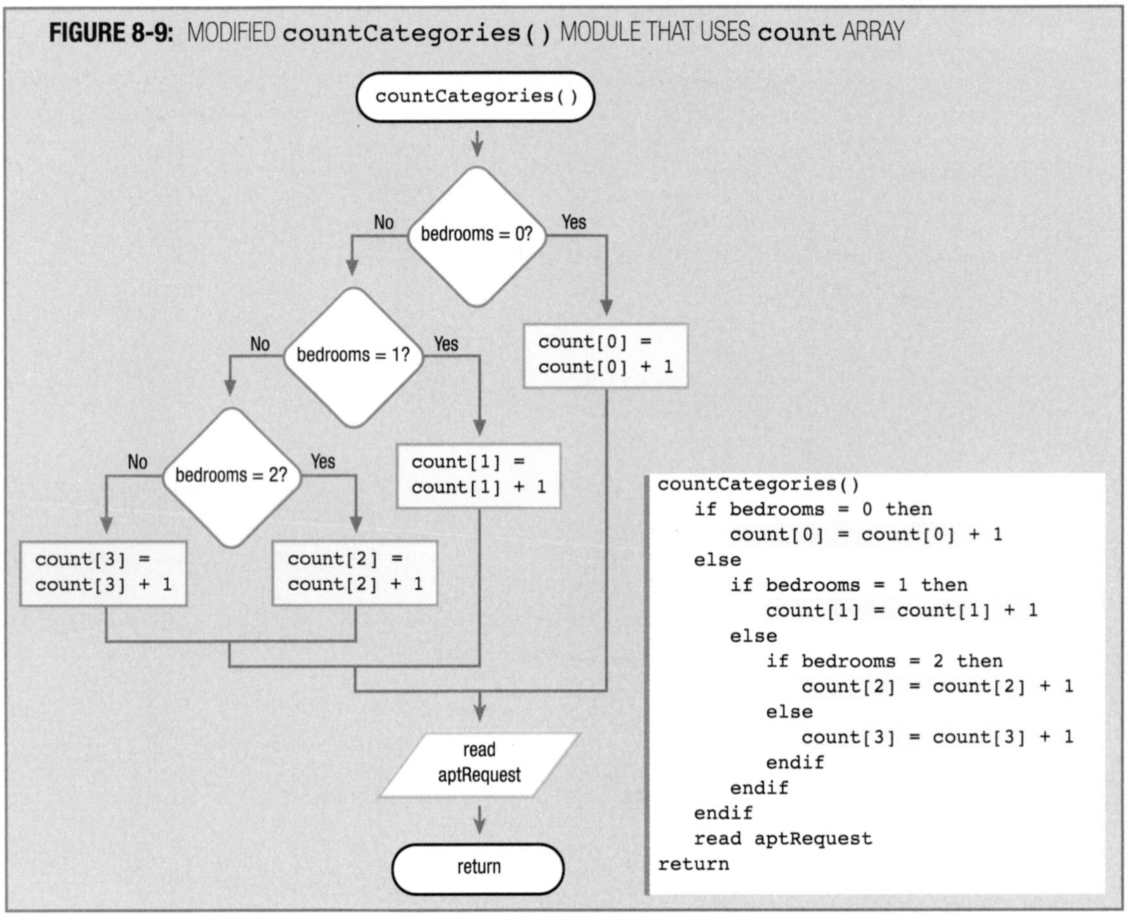


```
countCategories()
   if bedrooms = 0 then
      count[0] = count[0] + 1
   else
      if bedrooms = 1 then
         count[1] = count[1] + 1
      else
         if bedrooms = 2 then
            count[2] = count[2] + 1
         else
            count[3] = count[3] + 1
         endif
      endif
   endif
   read aptRequest
return
```

Figure 8-9 shows that when the **`bedrooms`** variable value is 0, one is added to **`count[0]`**; when the **`bedrooms`** value is 3, one is added to **`count[3]`**. In other words, one is added to one of the elements of the **`count`** array instead of to a single variable named **`count0`**, **`count1`**, **`count2`**, or **`count3`**. Is this a big improvement over the original? Of course it isn't. You still have not taken advantage of the benefits of using the array in this program.

The true benefit of using an array lies in your ability to use a variable as a subscript to the array, instead of using a constant such as 1 or 4. Notice in the **`countCategories()`** module in Figure 8-9 that within each decision, the value you are comparing to **`bedrooms`** and the constant you are using as a subscript in the resulting "Yes" process are always identical. That is, when the **`bedrooms`** value is 0, the subscript used to add 1 to the **`count`** array is 0; when the **`bedrooms`** value is 1, the subscript used for the **`count`** array is 1, and so on. Therefore, why not just use the value of **`bedrooms`** as a subscript? You can rewrite the **`countCategories()`** module as shown in Figure 8-10.

**FIGURE 8-10:** MODIFIED `countCategories()` MODULE USING THE VARIABLE `bedrooms` AS A SUBSCRIPT TO THE `count` ARRAY

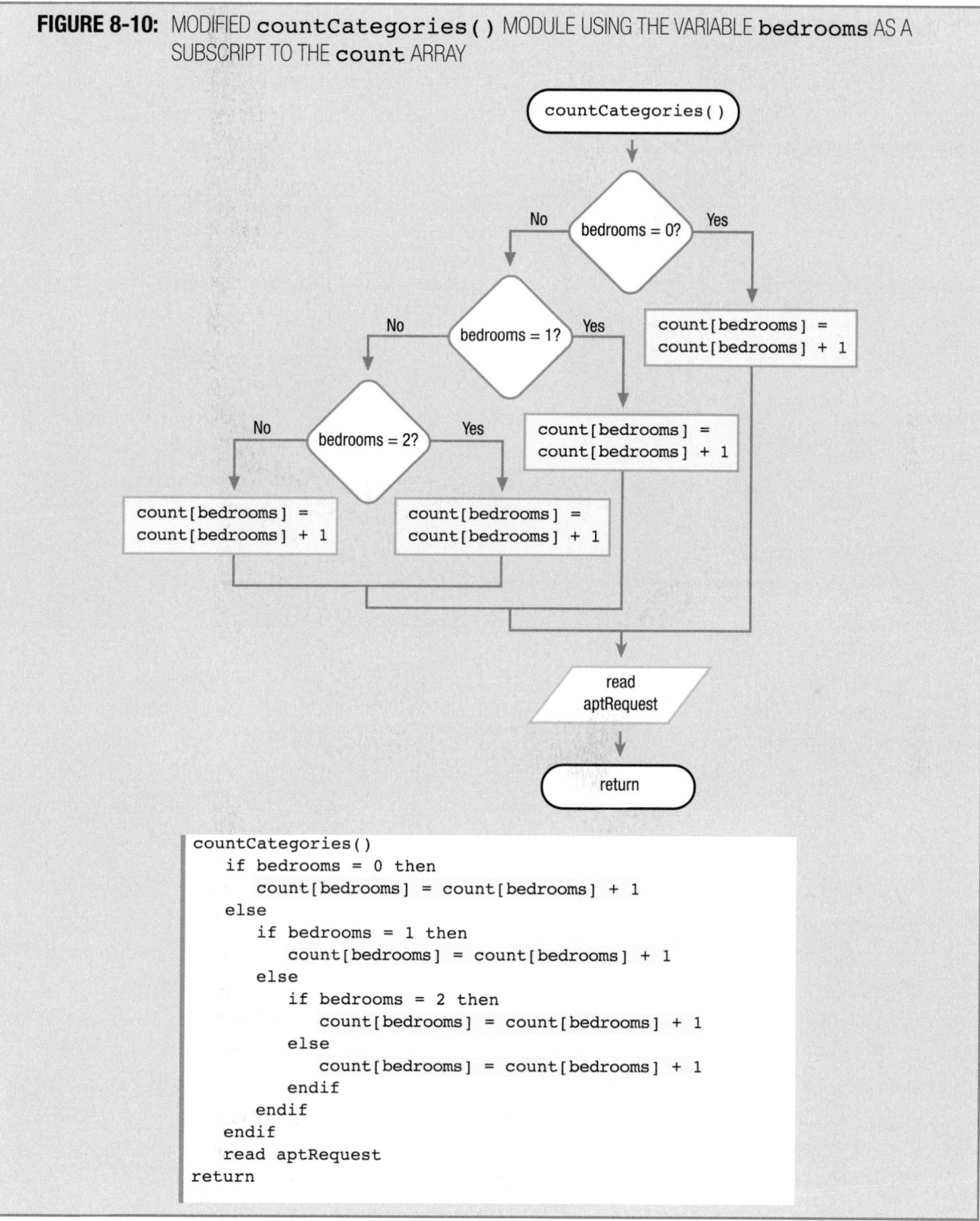


```
countCategories()
   if bedrooms = 0 then
      count[bedrooms] = count[bedrooms] + 1
   else
      if bedrooms = 1 then
         count[bedrooms] = count[bedrooms] + 1
      else
         if bedrooms = 2 then
            count[bedrooms] = count[bedrooms] + 1
         else
            count[bedrooms] = count[bedrooms] + 1
         endif
      endif
   endif
   read aptRequest
return
```

Of course, the code segment in Figure 8-10 looks no more efficient than the one in Figure 8-9. However, notice that in Figure 8-10 the process that occurs after each decision is exactly the same. In each case, no matter what the value of **bedrooms**, you always add one to **count[bedrooms]**. If you are always going to take the same action no matter what the answer to a question is, why ask the question? Instead, you can write the **countCategories()** module as shown in Figure 8-11.

**FIGURE 8-11:** MODIFIED **countCategories()** MODULE, ELIMINATING NESTED DECISIONS

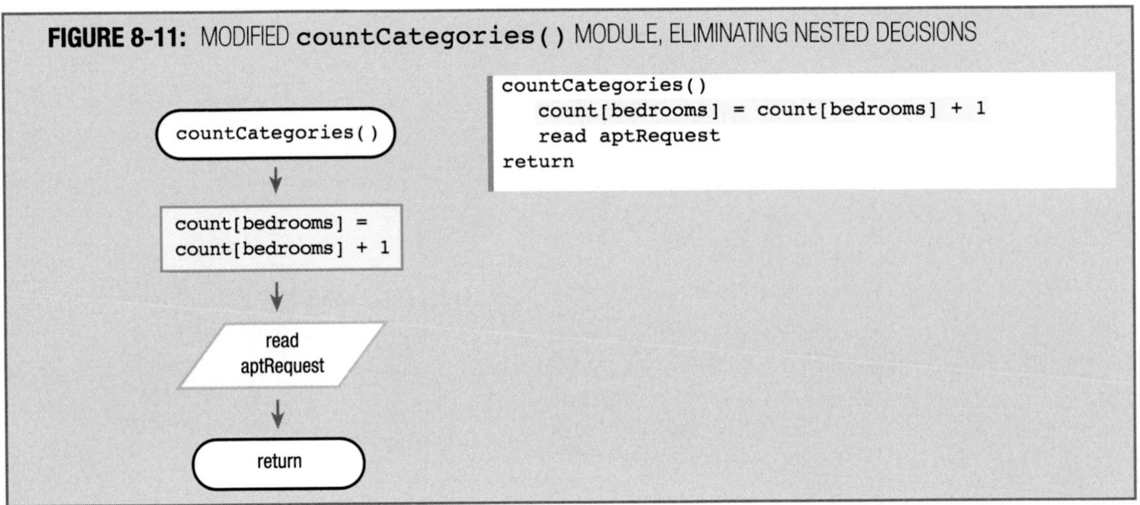


```
countCategories()
   count[bedrooms] = count[bedrooms] + 1
   read aptRequest
return
```

The two steps in Figure 8-11 represent the *entire* **countCategories()** module! When the value of **bedrooms** is 0, one is added to **count[0]**; when the value of **bedrooms** is 1, one is added to **count[1]**, and so on. *Now*, you have a big improvement to the previous **countCategories()** module from Figure 8-9. What's more, this **countCategories()** module does not change whether there are eight, 30, or any other number of types of apartment requests and **count** array elements, as long as the values in the **bedrooms** variable are numbered sequentially. To use more than four counters, you would declare additional **count** elements in the **housekeeping()** module, but the **countCategories()** logic would remain the same as it is in Figure 8-11.

The **finish()** module originally shown in Figure 8-7 can also be improved. Instead of four separate print statements, you can use a variable to control a printing loop, as shown in Figure 8-12. Because the **finish()** module follows the **eof** condition, all input records have been used, and the **bedrooms** variable is not currently holding any needed information. In **finish()**, you can set **bedrooms** to 0, and then print **bedrooms** and **count[bedrooms]**. Then add 1 to **bedrooms** and use the same set of instructions again. You can use **bedrooms** as a loop control variable to print the four individual **count** values. The improvement in this **finish()** module over the one shown in Figure 8-7 is not as dramatic as the improvement in the **countCategories()** module, but in a program with more **count** elements, the only change to the **finish()** module would be in the constant value you use to control the end of the loop. Twelve or 30 **count** values can print as easily as four if they are stored in an array.

**FIGURE 8-12:** MODIFIED **finish()** MODULE THAT USES AN ARRAY

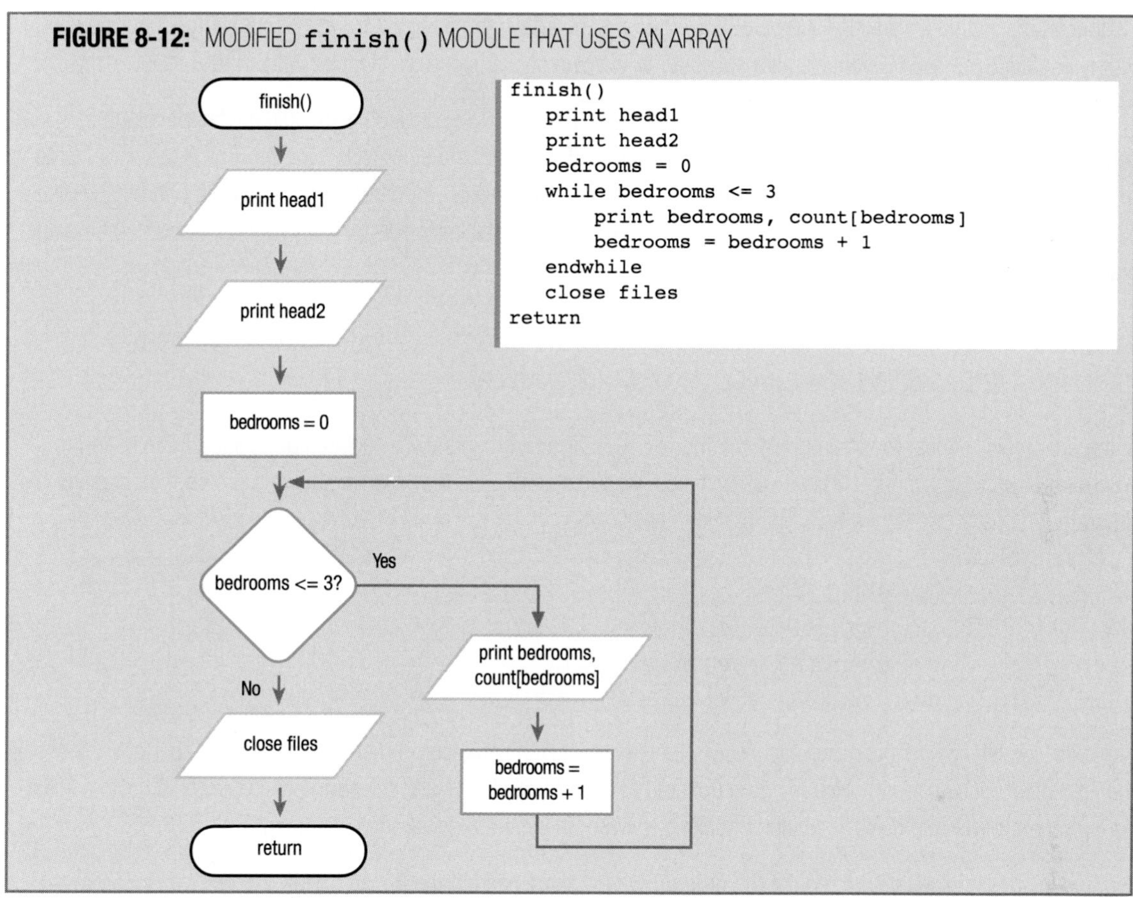


```
finish()
   print head1
   print head2
   bedrooms = 0
   while bedrooms <= 3
       print bedrooms, count[bedrooms]
       bedrooms = bedrooms + 1
   endwhile
   close files
return
```

**TIP**

In the `finish()` module in Figure 8-12, instead of reusing the `bedrooms` variable as a subscript, many programmers prefer to declare a separate numeric work variable to initialize to 0, use it as a subscript to the array while printing, and increment it during each cycle through the loop. Their reasoning is that `bedrooms` is part of the input record and should be used only to hold actual data being input—not used as a work variable in the program. Use this approach if it makes more sense to you. You might be required to use this technique if the input data is accessed from databases containing an input field that is no longer available after the input has reached the `eof` condition.

Within the **`finish()`** module in Figure 8-12, the **`bedrooms`** variable is handy to use as a subscript, but any variable could have been used as long as it was:

- Numeric with no decimal places
- Initialized to 0
- Incremented by 1 each time the logic passed through the loop

In other words, nothing is linking `bedrooms` to the `count` array per se; within the `finish()` module, you can simply use the `bedrooms` variable as a subscript to indicate each successive element within the `count` array.

The apartment request report program *worked* when the `countCategories()` module contained a long series of decisions and the `finish()` module contained a long series of print statements, but the program is easier to write when you employ arrays. Additionally, the program is more efficient, easier for other programmers to understand, and easier to maintain. Arrays are never mandatory, but often they can drastically cut down on your programming time and make a program easier to understand.

## ARRAY DECLARATION AND INITIALIZATION

In the apartment request report program, the four `count` array elements were declared and initialized to 0s in the `housekeeping()` module. The `count` values need to start at 0 so they can be added to during the course of the program. Originally (see Figure 8-8), you provided initialization in the `housekeeping()` module as:

```
num count[0] = 0
num count[1] = 0
num count[2] = 0
num count[3] = 0
```

Separately declaring and initializing each `count` element is acceptable only if there are a small number of `count`s. If the apartment request report program were updated to keep track of 30 types of apartments, you would have to initialize 30 separate `count` fields. It would be tedious to write 30 separate declaration statements.

Programming languages do not require the programmer to name each of the 30 `count`s: `count[0]`, `count[1]`, and so on. Instead, you can make a declaration such as one of those in Figure 8-13.

**FIGURE 8-13:** DECLARING A 30-ELEMENT ARRAY NAMED `count` IN SEVERAL COMMON LANGUAGES

| Declaration | Programming Language |
|---|---|
| `DIM COUNT(30)` | BASIC, Visual Basic |
| `int count[30];` | C#, C++ |
| `int[] count = new int[30];` | Java |
| `COUNT OCCURS 30 TIMES PICTURE 9999.` | COBOL |
| `array count [1..30] of integer;` | Pascal |

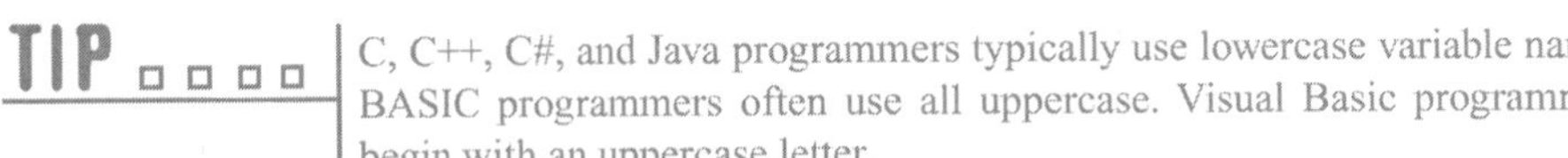

**TIP** C, C++, C#, and Java programmers typically use lowercase variable names. COBOL and BASIC programmers often use all uppercase. Visual Basic programmers are likely to begin with an uppercase letter.

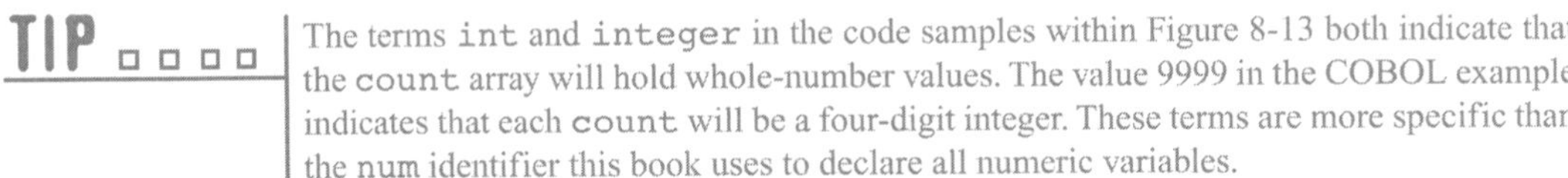

**TIP** The terms `int` and `integer` in the code samples within Figure 8-13 both indicate that the `count` array will hold whole-number values. The value 9999 in the COBOL example indicates that each `count` will be a four-digit integer. These terms are more specific than the num identifier this book uses to declare all numeric variables.

All the declarations in Figure 8-13 have two things in common: They name the `count` array and indicate that there will be 30 separate numeric elements. For flowcharting or pseudocode purposes, a statement such as `num count[30]` indicates the same thing.

Declaring a numeric array does not necessarily set its individual elements to 0 (although it does in some programming languages, such as BASIC, Visual Basic, and Java). Most programming languages allow the equivalent of `num count[30] all set to 0`; you should use a statement like this when you want to initialize an array in your flowcharts or pseudocode. Explicitly initializing all variables is a good programming practice; assuming anything about noninitialized variable values is a dangerous practice. Array elements are no exception to this rule.

Alternatively, to start all array elements with the same initial value, you can use an initialization loop within the `housekeeping()` module. An **initialization loop** is a loop structure that provides initial values for every element in any array. To create an initialization loop, you must use a numeric variable as a subscript. For example, if you declare a field named `sub`, and initialize `sub` to 0, then you can use a loop like the one shown in the `housekeeping()` module in Figure 8-14 to set all the array elements to 0. As the value of `sub` increases from 0 through 29, each corresponding `count` element is assigned 0.

**FIGURE 8-14:** A `housekeeping()` MODULE DEMONSTRATING ONE METHOD OF INITIALIZING ARRAY ELEMENTS

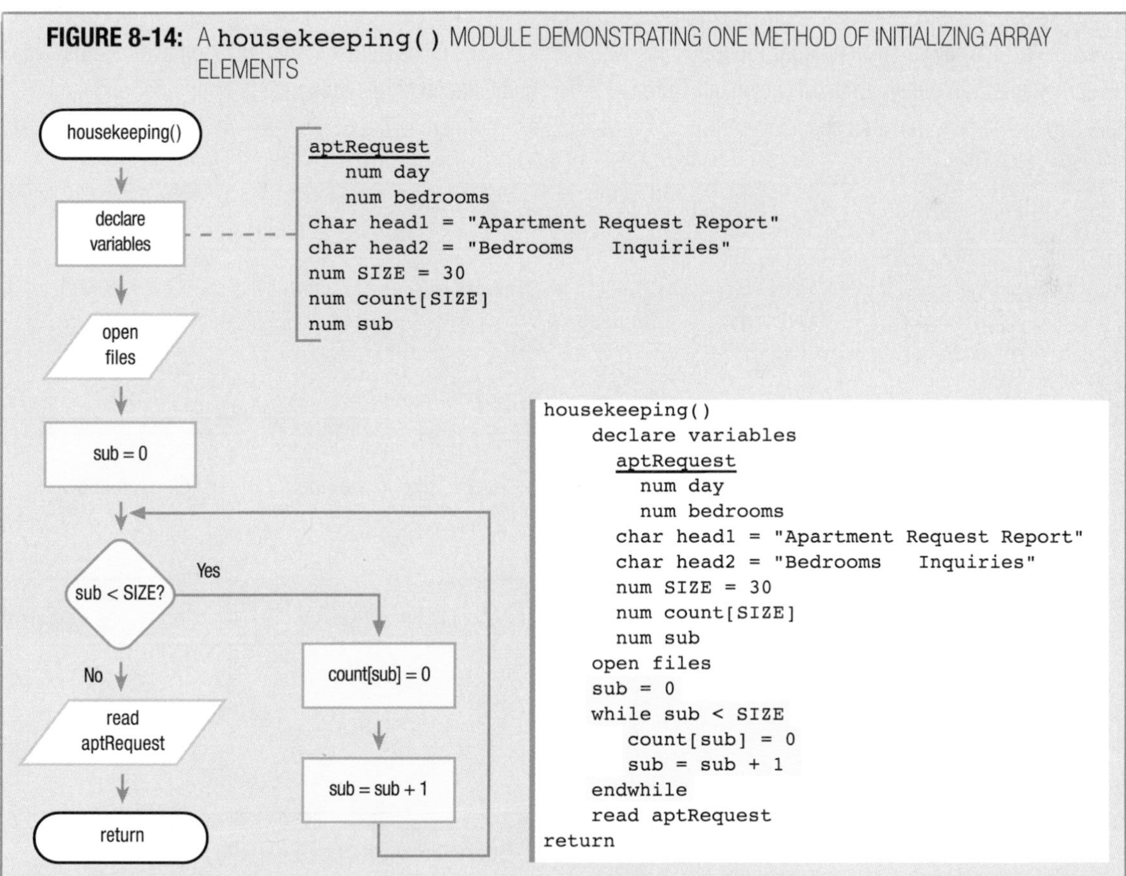


```
housekeeping()
    declare variables
      aptRequest
        num day
        num bedrooms
      char head1 = "Apartment Request Report"
      char head2 = "Bedrooms   Inquiries"
      num SIZE = 30
      num count[SIZE]
      num sub
    open files
    sub = 0
    while sub < SIZE
       count[sub] = 0
       sub = sub + 1
    endwhile
    read aptRequest
return
```

In Figure 8-14, a named constant SIZE is initialized to 30. This constant is then used in both the array declaration and the loop that controls how many elements are set to 0. Using a constant such as SIZE is a convenient way to make sure you access all the array elements. Additionally, if you want to alter the program to handle some other number of apartment types, the only change you need to make to the program is to provide a different value for the constant. You first learned about named constants in Chapter 4.

## DECLARING AND INITIALIZING CONSTANT ARRAYS

The array that you used to accumulate apartment-type requests in the previous section contained four variables whose values were altered during the execution of the program. The values in which you were most interested, the count of the number of requests for each type of apartment, were created during an actual run, or execution, of the program. In other words, if 1,000 prospective tenants are interested in studio apartments, you don't know that fact at the beginning of the program. Instead, that value is accumulated during the execution of the program and not known until the end.

Some arrays are not variable, but are meant to be constant. With some arrays, the final desired values are fixed at the beginning of the program.

For example, let's say you own an apartment building with five floors, including a basement, and you have records for all your tenants with the information shown in Figure 8-15. The combination of each tenant's floor number and apartment letter provides you with a specific apartment—for example, apartment 0D or 3B.

**FIGURE 8-15:** TENANT FILE DESCRIPTION

```
TENANT FILE DESCRIPTION
File name: TENANTS
FIELD DESCRIPTION      DATA TYPE    COMMENTS
Tenant name            Character    Full name, first and last
Floor number           Numeric      0 through 4 - 0 is basement
Apartment letter       Character    Single letter - A through F
```

Every month, you print a rent bill for each tenant. Your rent charges are based on the floor of the building, as shown in Figure 8-16.

**FIGURE 8-16:** RENTS BY FLOOR

```
Floor                   Rent in $
0 (the basement)           350
1                          400
2                          475
3                          600
4 (the penthouse)         1000
```

To create a computer program that prints each tenant's name and rent due, you could use five decisions concerning the floor number. However, it is more efficient to use an array to hold the five rent figures. The array's values are constant because you set them once at the beginning of the program, and they never change.

**TIP** Remember that another name for an array is a *table*. If you can use paper and pencil to list items like tenants' rent values in a table format, then using an array is an appropriate programming option.

**TIP** In most programming languages, you would include a modifier such as `const` or `final` in front of the array name to declare it to be truly constant, so that you could not alter any of its elements' values later in the program.

**TIP** Some programmers use the term "compile-time arrays" to refer to arrays that receive their usable values through initialization at the start of a program, whereas arrays that do not receive their ultimate values until the program is being used are run-time arrays.

The mainline logic for this program is shown in Figure 8-17. The housekeeping module is named `prep()`. When you declare variables within the `prep()` module, you create an array for the five rent figures and set `num rent[0] = 350`, `num rent[1] = 400`, and so on. The rent amounts are **hard coded** into the array; that is, they are explicitly assigned to the array elements. The `prep()` module is shown in Figure 8-18.

**TIP** The `prep()` module name was chosen as a change of pace from `housekeeping()`, which has been used in many examples in this book. Some programmers advocate being consistent in naming modules from program to program; others prefer varying names as long as the names are meaningful.

**FIGURE 8-17:** FLOWCHART AND PSEUDOCODE FOR MAINLINE LOGIC OF RENT PROGRAM

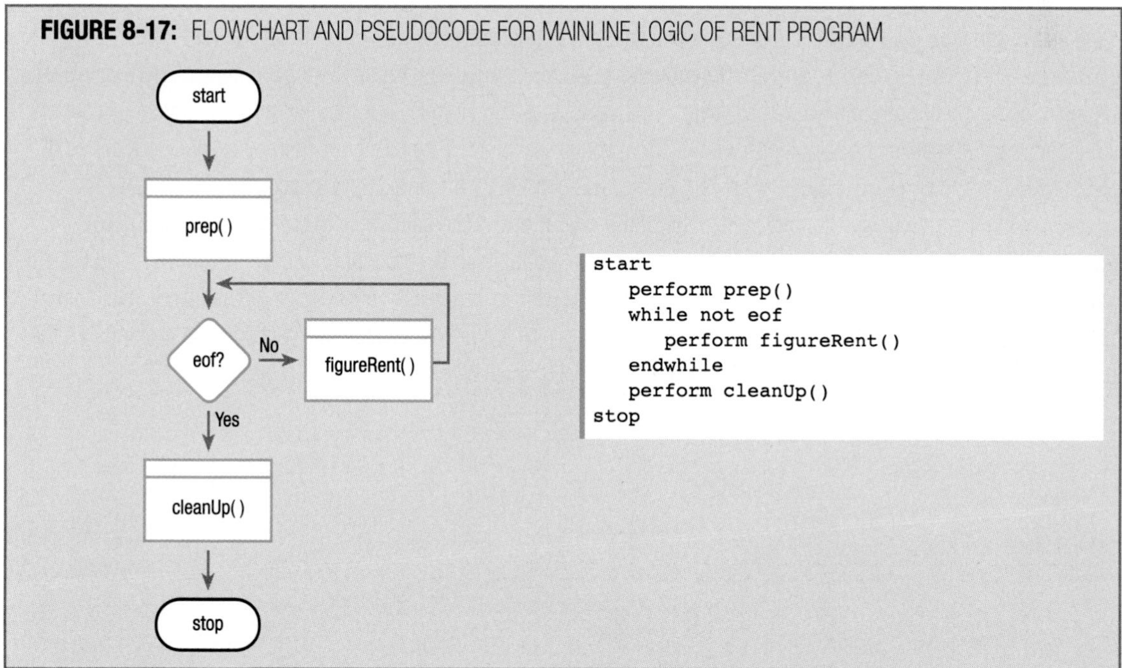


```
start
   perform prep()
   while not eof
      perform figureRent()
   endwhile
   perform cleanUp()
stop
```

**FIGURE 8-18:** FLOWCHART AND PSEUDOCODE FOR `prep()` MODULE OF RENT PROGRAM

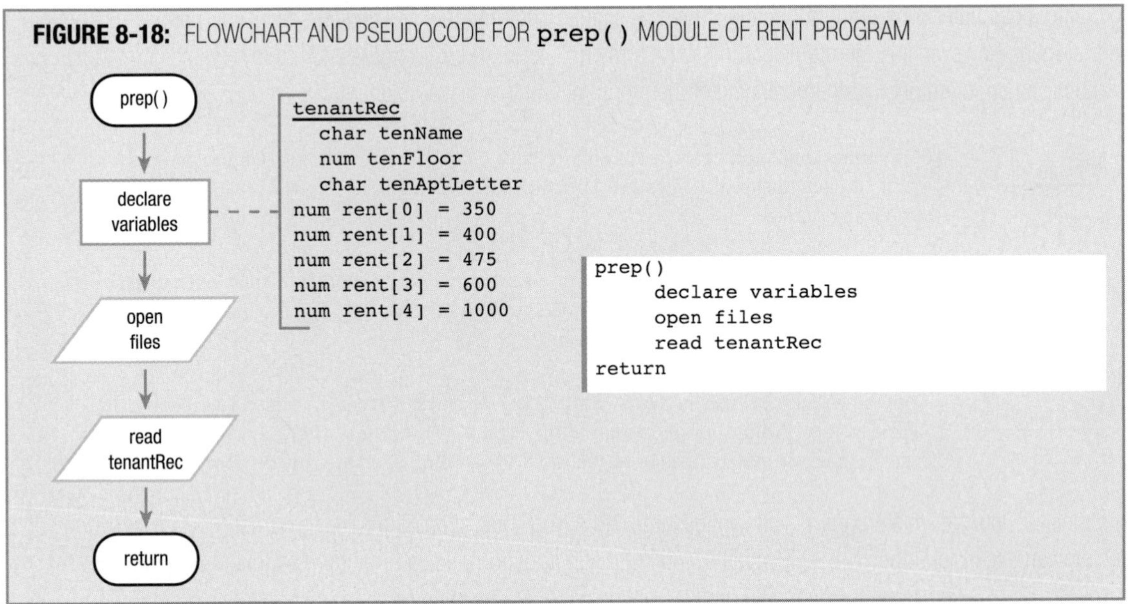


**TIP**

As an alternative to defining `rent[0]`, `rent[1]`, and so on, as in Figure 8-18, most programming languages allow a more concise version that takes the general form `num rent[5] = 350, 400, 475, 600, 1000`. When you use this form of array initialization, the first value you list is assigned to the first array element, and the subsequent values are assigned in order. Most programming languages allow you to assign fewer values than there are array elements declared, but none allow you to assign more values.

At the end of the `prep()` module, you read a first record into memory. The record contains a tenant name (`tenName`), floor (`tenFloor`), and apartment letter (`tenAptLetter`). When the logic enters `figureRent()` (the main loop), you can print three items: "Dear ", `tenName`, and ", Here is your monthly rent bill" (the quote begins with a comma that follows the recipient's name). Then, you must print the rent amount. Instead of making a series of selections such as `if tenFloor = 0 then print rent[0]` and `if tenFloor = 1 then print rent[1]`, you want to take advantage of the `rent` array. The solution is to create a `figureRent()` module that looks like Figure 8-19. You use the `tenFloor` variable as a subscript to access the correct `rent` array element. When deciding which variable to use as a subscript with an array, ask yourself, "Of all the values available in the array, what does the correct selection depend on?" When printing a `rent` value, the rent you use depends on the floor on which the tenant lives, so the correct action is `print rent[tenFloor]`.

FIGURE 8-19: FLOWCHART AND PSEUDOCODE FOR THE `figureRent()` MODULE OF THE RENT PROGRAM

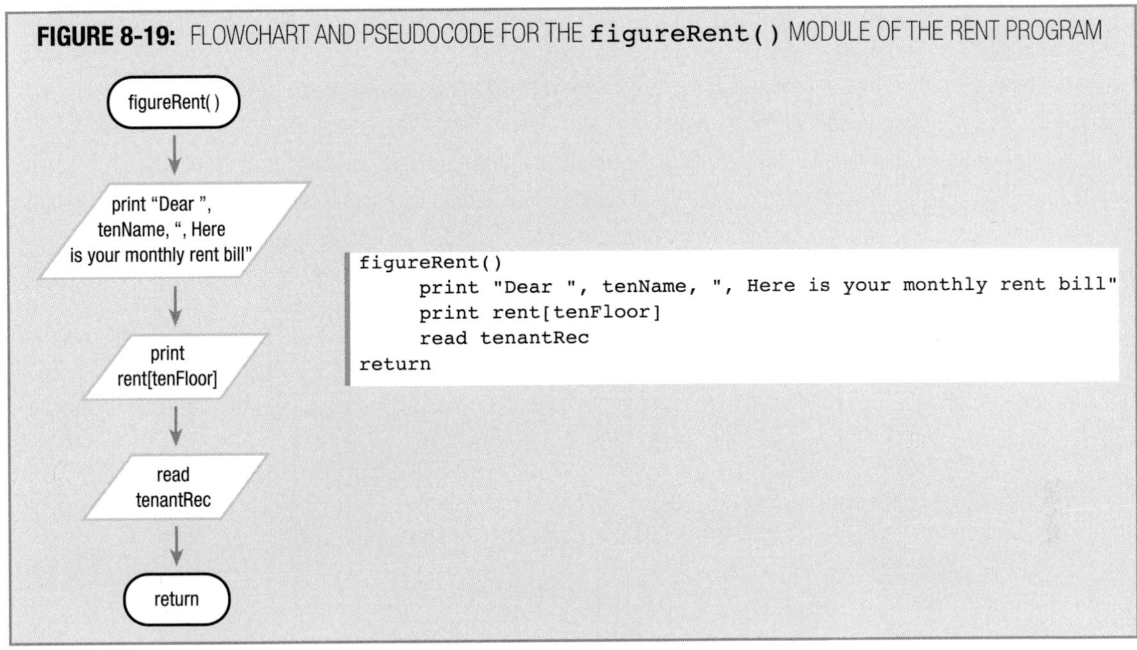


```
figureRent()
     print "Dear ", tenName, ", Here is your monthly rent bill"
     print rent[tenFloor]
     read tenantRec
return
```

**TIP** Every programming language provides ways to space your output for easy reading. For example, a common technique to separate "Dear" from the tenant's name is to include a space after the *r* in *Dear*, as in `print "Dear ", tenName.`

The `cleanUp()` module for this program is very simple—just close the files. See Figure 8-20.

FIGURE 8-20: THE `cleanUp()` MODULE FOR THE RENT PROGRAM

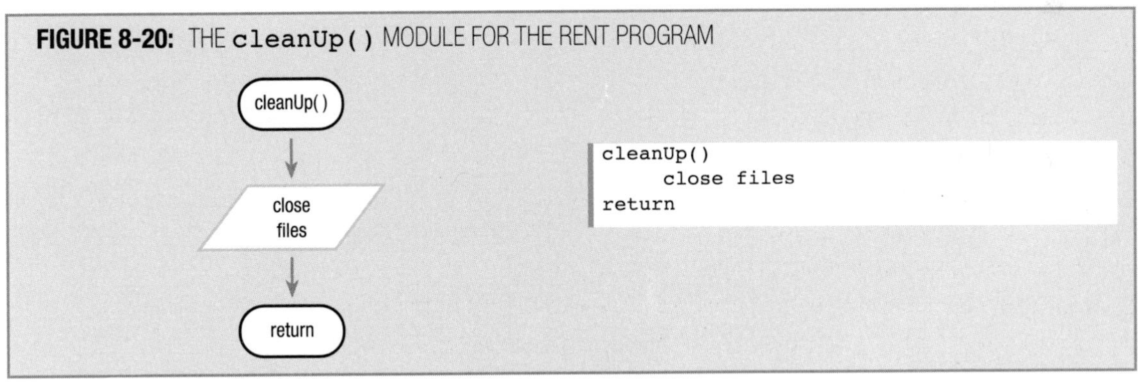


```
cleanUp()
     close files
return
```

Without a `rent` array, the `figureRent()` module would have to contain four decisions and five different resulting actions. With the `rent` array, there are no decisions. Each tenant's rent is simply based on the `rent` element that corresponds to the `tenFloor` variable because the floor number indicates the positional value of the corresponding rent. Arrays can really lighten the workload required to write a program.

## LOADING AN ARRAY FROM A FILE

Writing the rent program from the previous section requires you to set values for five **rent** array elements within the **prep()** module. If you write the rent program for a skyscraper, you may have to initialize 100 array elements. Additionally, when the building management changes the rent amounts, you must alter the array element values within the program to reflect the new rent charges. If the rent values change frequently, it is inconvenient to have hard-coded values in your program. Instead, you can write your program so that it loads the array rent amounts from a file. The array of rent values is an example of an array that gets its values during the execution of the program.

A file that contains all the rent amounts can be updated by apartment building management as frequently as needed. Suppose you periodically receive a file named RENTFILE that is created by the building management and always contains the current rent values. You can write the rent program so that it accepts all records from this input file within the **prep()** module. Figure 8-21 shows how this is accomplished.

**FIGURE 8-21:** FLOWCHART AND PSEUDOCODE FOR **prep()** MODULE THAT READS RENT VALUES FROM AN INPUT FILE

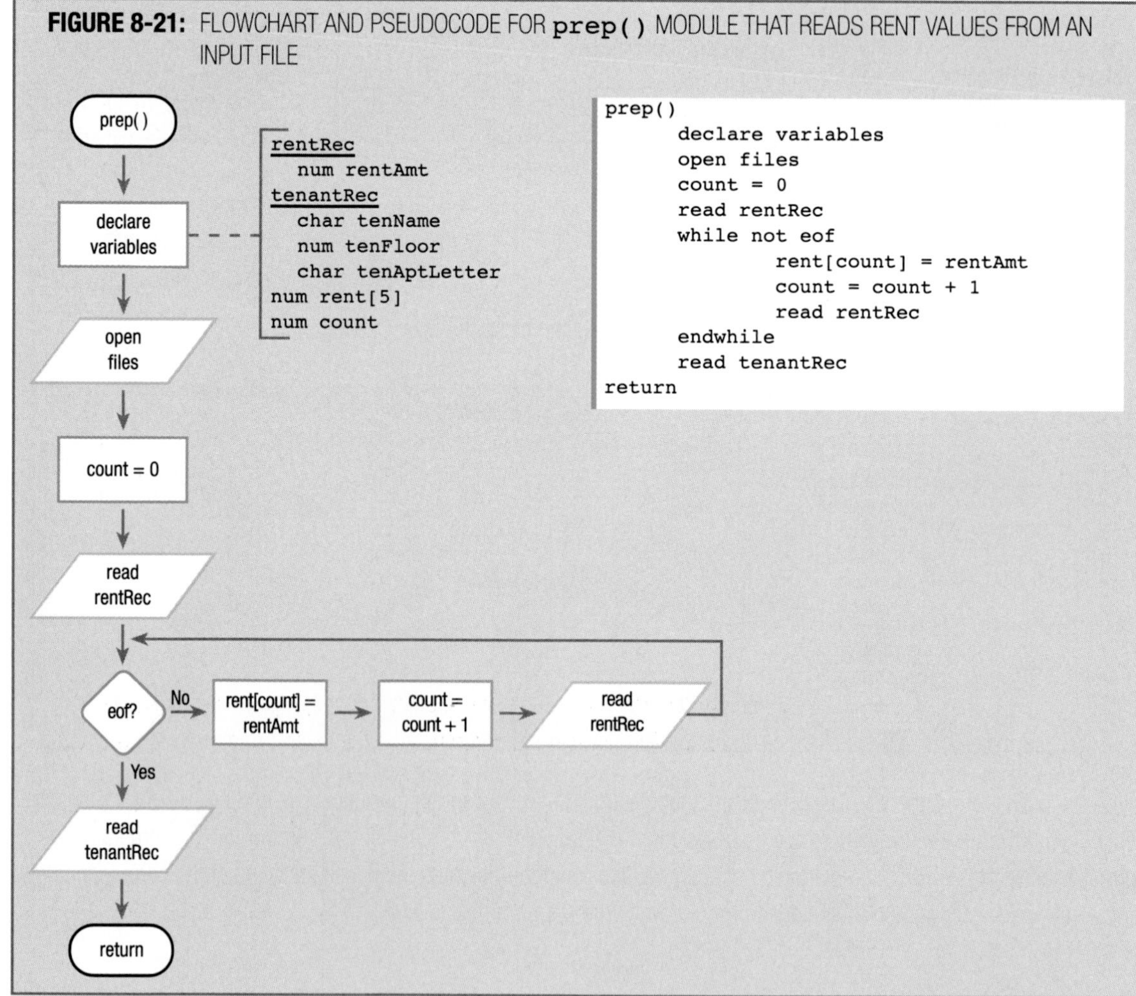


```
prep()
      declare variables
      open files
      count = 0
      read rentRec
      while not eof
              rent[count] = rentAmt
              count = count + 1
              read rentRec
      endwhile
      read tenantRec
return
```

In the `prep()` module in Figure 8-21, you set the variable `count` to 0 and read a `rentRec` record from RENTFILE. Each record in RENTFILE contains just one field—a numeric `rentAmt` value. For this program, assume that the rent records in RENTFILE are stored in order by floor. When you read the first `rentAmt`, you store it in the first element of the `rent` array. You increase the `count` to 1, read the second record, and, assuming it's not `eof`, you store the second rent in the second element of the `rent` array. After RENTFILE is exhausted and the `rent` array is filled with appropriate rent amounts for each floor, you begin to read the file containing the `tenantRec` records, and then the program proceeds as usual.

**TIP** You could choose to close RENTFILE at the end of the `prep()` module. Unlike the tenant file and the printer, it will not be used again in the program. Alternatively, you can wait and close all the files at the end of the program.

When you use this method—reading the rents from an input file instead of hard coding them into the program—clerical employees can update the `rentRec` values in RENTFILE. Your program takes care of loading the rents into the program array from the most recent copy of RENTFILE, ensuring that each rent is always accurate and up to date. Using this technique, you avoid the necessity of changing code within the program with each rent update.

**TIP** Another way to organize RENTFILE is to include two fields within each record—for example, `rentFloor` and `rentAmt`. Then, the records would not have to be read into your program in floor-number order. Instead, you could use the `rentFloor` variable as a subscript to indicate which position in the array to use to store the `rentAmt`.

**TIP** You might question how the program knows which file's `eof` condition is tested when a program uses two or more input files. In some programming languages, the `eof` condition is tested on the file most recently read. In many programming languages, you have to provide more specific information along with the `eof` question, perhaps `rentRec eof?` or `tenantRec eof?`

**TIP** The RENTFILE example assumes that management provides you with a file that contains no more records than the number of rents your program is prepared to hold. A more elegant program would check to make sure there are not too many rents. You will learn how to perform such checks later in this chapter.

## SEARCHING FOR AN EXACT MATCH IN AN ARRAY

In both the apartment request program and the rent program that you've seen in this chapter, the fields that the arrays depend on conveniently hold small whole numbers. The number of bedrooms available in apartments are zero through three, and the floors of the building are zero through four. Unfortunately, real life doesn't always happen in small integers. Sometimes, you don't have a variable that conveniently holds an array position; sometimes, you have to search through an array to find a value you need.

Consider a mail-order business in which orders come in with a customer name, address, item number ordered, and quantity ordered, as shown in Figure 8-22.

**FIGURE 8-22:** MAIL-ORDER CUSTOMER FILE DESCRIPTION

```
MAIL-ORDER CUSTOMER FILE DESCRIPTION
File name: CUSTREC
FIELD DESCRIPTION        DATA TYPE     COMMENTS
Customer name            Character
Address                  Character
Item number              Numeric       A 3-digit number
Quantity                 Numeric       A value from 1 through 99
```

The item numbers are three-digit numbers, but perhaps they are not consecutive 000 through 999. Instead, over the years, items have been deleted and new items have been added. For example, there might no longer be an item with number 005 or 129. Sometimes, there might be a hundred-number gap or more between items.

For example, let's say that this season you are down to the items shown in Figure 8-23. When a customer orders an item, you want to determine whether the order is for a valid item number. You could use a series of six decisions to determine whether the ordered item is valid; in turn, you would compare whether each customer's item number is equal to one of the six allowed values. However, a superior approach is to create an array that holds the list of valid item numbers. Then, you can search through the array for an exact match to the ordered item. If you search through the entire array without finding a match for the item the customer ordered, you can print an error message, such as "No such item."

Suppose you create an array with the six elements shown in Figure 8-24. If a customer orders item 307, a clerical worker can tell whether it is valid by looking down the list and verifying that 307 is a member of the list. In a similar fashion, you can use a loop to test each `validItem` against the ordered item number.

**FIGURE 8-23:** AVAILABLE ITEMS IN MAIL-ORDER COMPANY

```
ITEM NUMBER
106
108
307
405
457
688
```

**FIGURE 8-24:** ARRAY OF VALID ITEM NUMBERS

```
num validItem[0] = 106
num validItem[1] = 108
num validItem[2] = 307
num validItem[3] = 405
num validItem[4] = 457
num validItem[5] = 688
```

The technique for verifying that an item number exists involves setting a subscript to 0 so that you can start searching from the first array element, and initializing a flag variable to indicate that you have not yet determined whether the customer's order is valid. A **flag** is a variable that you set to indicate whether some event has occurred; frequently, it holds a True or False value. For example, you can set a character variable named `foundIt` to "N", indicating "No". Then you compare the customer's ordered item number to the first item in the array. If the customer-ordered item matches the first item in the array, you can set the flag variable to "Y", or any other value that is not "N". If the items do not match, you increase the subscript and continue to look down the list of numbers stored in the array. If you check all six valid item numbers and the customer item matches none of them, then the flag variable `foundIt` still holds the value "N". If the flag variable is "N" after you have looked through the entire list, you can issue an error message indicating that no match was ever found. Assuming you declare the customer item as `custItemNo` and the subscript as `x`, then Figure 8-25 shows a flowchart segment and the pseudocode that accomplishes the item verification.

**FIGURE 8-25:** FLOWCHART AND PSEUDOCODE SEGMENTS FOR FINDING AN EXACT MATCH TO A CUSTOMER ITEM NUMBER

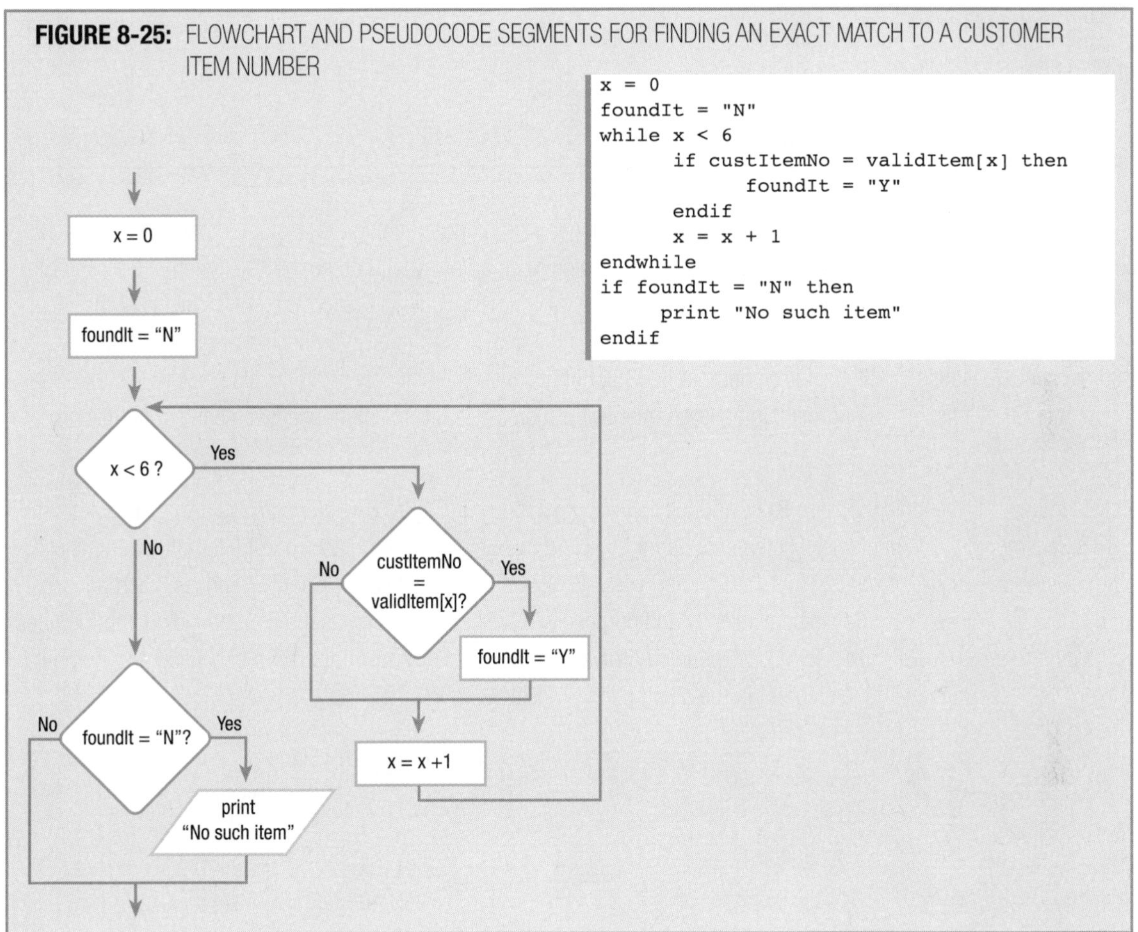


```
x = 0
foundIt = "N"
while x < 6
      if custItemNo = validItem[x] then
            foundIt = "Y"
      endif
      x = x + 1
endwhile
if foundIt = "N" then
     print "No such item"
endif
```

## USING PARALLEL ARRAYS

In a mail-order company, when you read a customer's order, you usually want to accomplish more than simply verifying that the item exists. You want to determine the price of the ordered item, multiply that price by the quantity ordered, and print a bill. Suppose you have prices for six available items, as shown in Figure 8-26.

**FIGURE 8-26:** AVAILABLE ITEMS WITH PRICES FOR MAIL-ORDER COMPANY

```
ITEM NUMBER          ITEM PRICE
106                   0.59
108                   0.99
307                   4.50
405                  15.99
457                  17.50
688                  39.00
```

You *could* write a program in which you read a customer order record and then use the customer's item number as a subscript to pull a price from an array. To use this method, you need an array with at least 689 elements. If a customer orders item 405, the price is found at `validItem[custItemNo]`, which is `validItem[405]`, or the 406th element of the array (because the 0th element is the first element of the array). Such an array would need 689 elements (because the highest item number is 688), but because you sell only six items, you would waste 683 of the memory positions. Instead of reserving a large quantity of memory that remains unused, you can set up this program to use two arrays.

Consider the mainline logic in Figure 8-27 and the `ready()` module in Figure 8-28. Two arrays are set up within the `ready()` module. One contains six elements named `validItem`; all six elements are valid item numbers. The other array also has six elements. These are named `validItemPrice`; all six elements are prices. Each price in this `validItemPrice` array is conveniently and purposely in the same position as the corresponding item number in the other `validItem` array. Two corresponding arrays such as these are **parallel arrays** because each element in one array is associated with the element in the same relative position in the other array.

**FIGURE 8-27:** MAINLINE LOGIC FOR THE PRICE PROGRAM

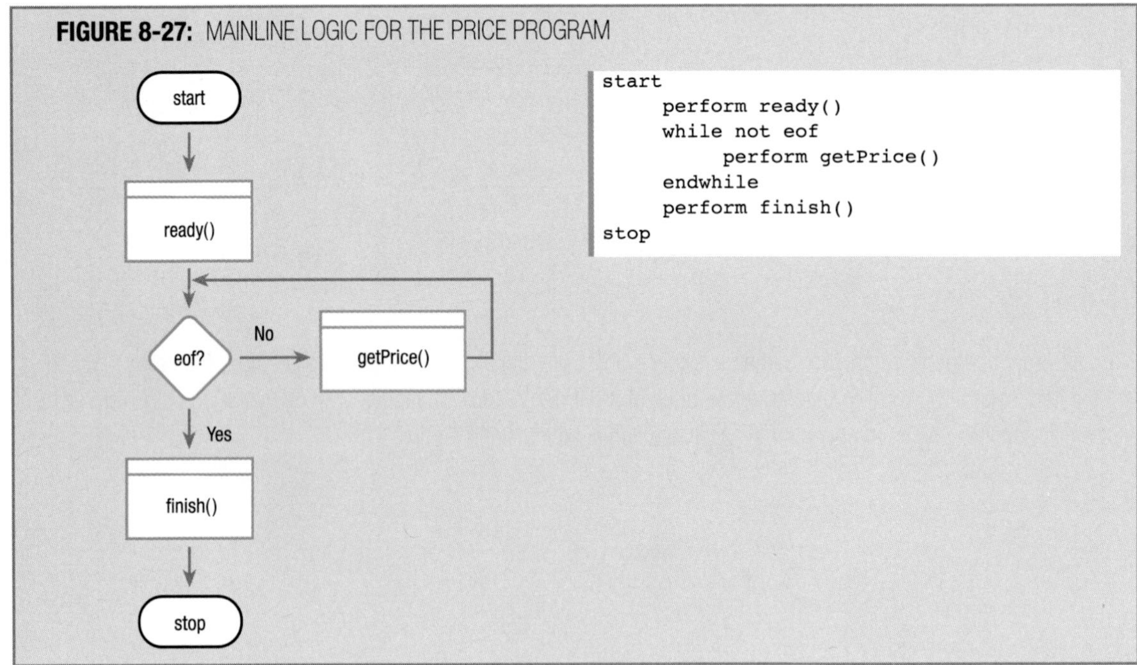


```
start
     perform ready()
     while not eof
          perform getPrice()
     endwhile
     perform finish()
stop
```

**FIGURE 8-28:** THE `ready()` MODULE FOR THE PRICE PROGRAM

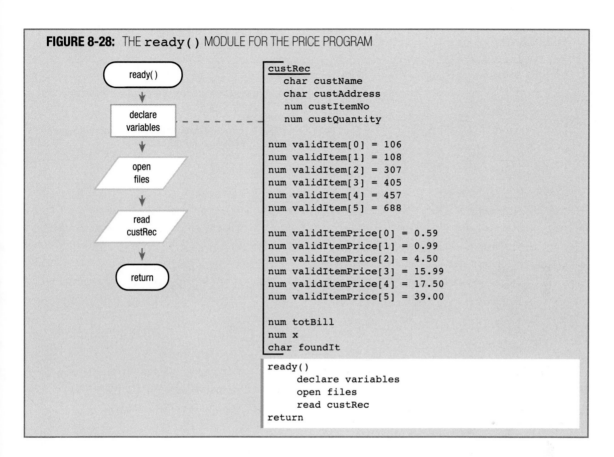

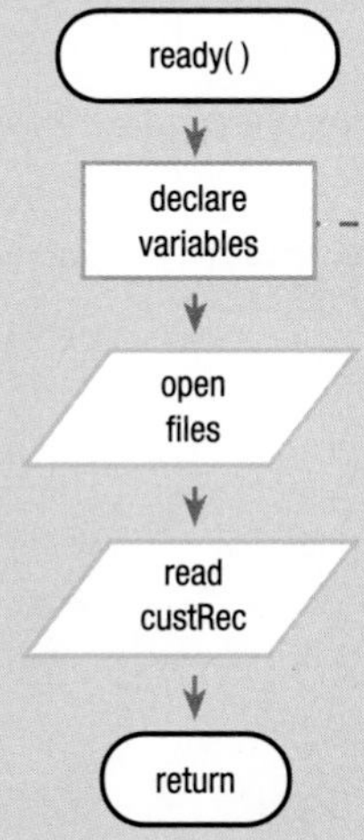

```
custRec
   char custName
   char custAddress
   num custItemNo
   num custQuantity

num validItem[0] = 106
num validItem[1] = 108
num validItem[2] = 307
num validItem[3] = 405
num validItem[4] = 457
num validItem[5] = 688

num validItemPrice[0] = 0.59
num validItemPrice[1] = 0.99
num validItemPrice[2] = 4.50
num validItemPrice[3] = 15.99
num validItemPrice[4] = 17.50
num validItemPrice[5] = 39.00

num totBill
num x
char foundIt
```

```
ready()
     declare variables
     open files
     read custRec
return
```

You can write the `getPrice()` module as shown in Figure 8-29. The general procedure is to read each item number, look through each of the `validItem` values separately, and when a match for the `custItemNo` variable on the input record is found, pull the corresponding parallel price out of the list of `validItemPrice` values.

FIGURE 8-29: THE `getPrice()` MODULE FOR THE PRICE PROGRAM

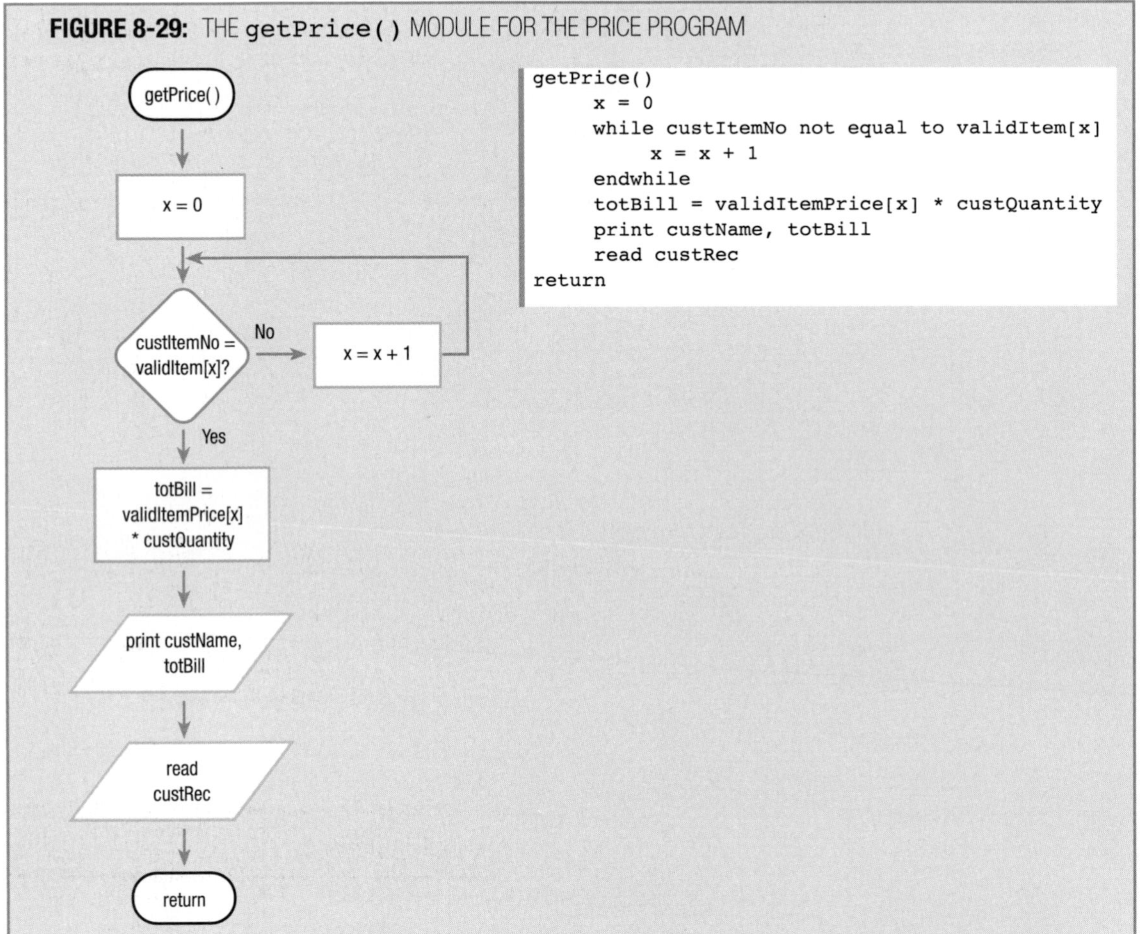


```
getPrice()
     x = 0
     while custItemNo not equal to validItem[x]
          x = x + 1
     endwhile
     totBill = validItemPrice[x] * custQuantity
     print custName, totBill
     read custRec
return
```

**TIP**

In this book, you have repeatedly seen the flowchart decision that asks the `eof` question phrased as a positive question ("`eof?`") so the program continues while the answer is No. You also have seen the pseudocode decision that asks the `eof` question in a negative form ("`while not eof`") so that the program continues while the condition is true. Figure 8-29 follows the same convention—the flowchart compares the customer item number to a valid item using a positive question so the loop continues while the answer is No, whereas the pseudocode asks if the customer item number is *not* equal to a valid item number, continuing while the answer is Yes. The logic is the same either way.

You must create a variable to use as a subscript for the arrays. If you name the subscript **`x`** (see the declaration of **`x`** in the variable list in Figure 8-28), then you can start by setting **`x`** equal to 0. Then, if **`custItemNo`** is the same as **`validItem[x]`**, you can use the corresponding price from the other table, **`validItemPrice[x]`**, to calculate the customer's bill.

**TIP** □□□□ Some programmers object to using a cryptic variable name such as `x` because it is not descriptive. These programmers would prefer a name such as `priceIndex`. Others approve of short names like `x` when the variable is used only in a limited area of a program, as it is used here, to step through an array. There are many style issues on which programmers disagree. As a programmer, it is your responsibility to find out what conventions are used among your peers in your organization.

Within the `getPrice()` module, the variable used as a subscript, `x`, is set to 0. If `custItemNo` is *not* the same as `validItem[x]`, then add 1 to `x`. Because `x` now holds the value 1, you next compare the customer's requested item number to `validItem[1]`. The value of `x` keeps increasing, and eventually a match between `custItemNo` and some `validItem[x]` should be found.

After you find a match for the `custItemNo` variable in the `validItem` array, you know that the price of that item is in the same position in the other array, `validItemPrice`. When `validItem[x]` is the correct item, `validItemPrice[x]` must be the correct price.

Suppose that a customer orders item 457, and walk through the flowchart yourself to see if you come up with the correct price.

## REMAINING WITHIN ARRAY BOUNDS

The `getPrice()` module in Figure 8-29 is not perfect. The logic makes one dangerous assumption: that every customer will order a valid item number. If a customer is looking at an old catalog and orders item 107, the program will never find a match. The value of `x` will just continue to increase until it reaches a value higher than the number of elements in the array. At that point, one of two things happens. When you use a subscript value that is higher than the number of elements in an array, some programming languages stop execution of the program and issue an error message. Other programming languages do not issue an error message but continue to search through computer memory beyond the end of the array. Either way, the program doesn't end elegantly. When you use a subscript that is not within the range of acceptable subscripts, your subscript is said to be **out of bounds**. Ordering a wrong item number is a frequent customer error; a good program should be able to handle the mistake and not allow the subscript to go out of bounds.

You can improve the price-finding program by adding a flag variable and a test to the `getPrice()` module. You can set the flag when you find a valid item in the `validItem` array, and after searching the array, check whether the flag has been altered. See Figure 8-30.

**FIGURE 8-30:** THE `getPrice()` MODULE USING THE `foundIt` FLAG



```
getPrice()
     foundIt = "No"
     x = 0
     while x < 6
          if custItemNo = validItem[x] then
               totBill = validItemPrice[x] * custQuantity
               print custName, totBill
               foundIt = "Yes"
               x = x + 1
          else
               x = x + 1
          endif
     endwhile
     if foundIt not equal to "Yes" then
         print "Error"
     endif
     read custRec
return
```

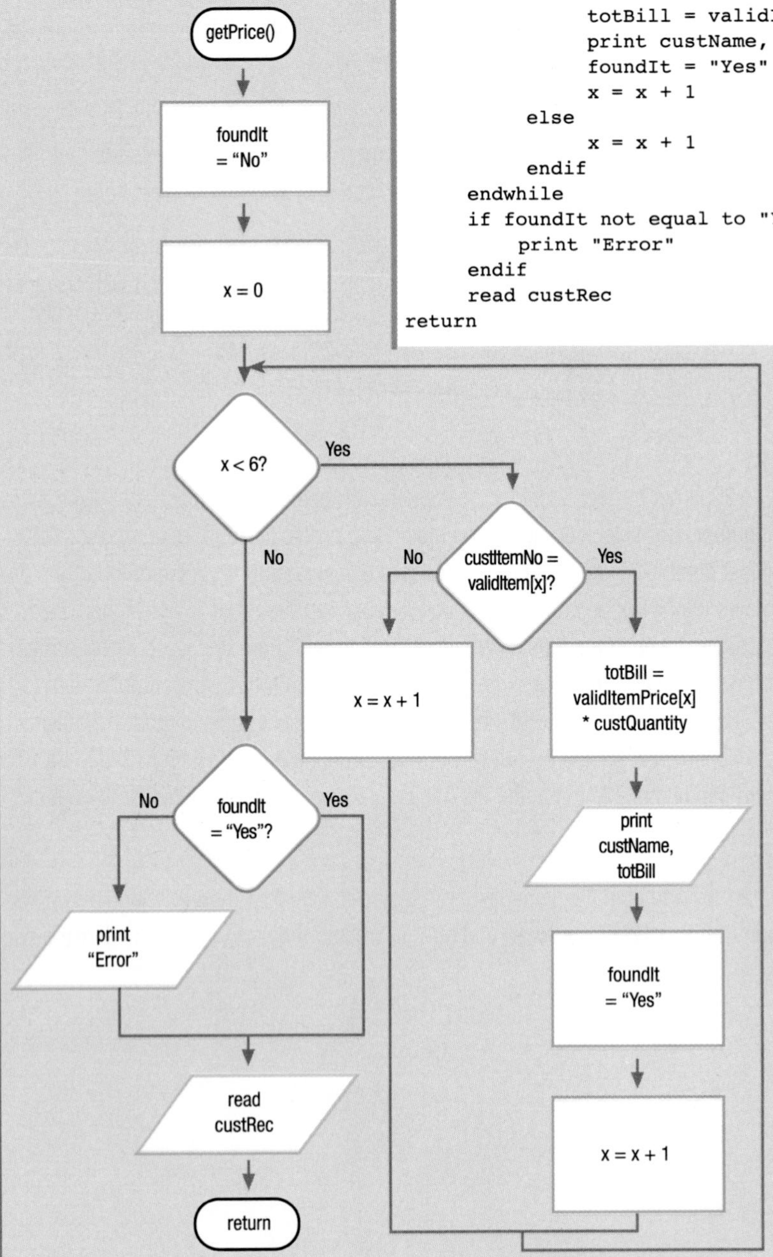

In the `ready()` module, you can declare a variable named `foundIt` that acts as a flag. When you enter the `getPrice()` module, you can set `foundIt` equal to "No". Then, after setting `x` to 0, check to see if `x` is still less than 6. If it is, compare `custItemNo` to `validItem[x]`. If they are equal, you know the position of the item's price, and you can use the price to print the customer's bill and set the `foundIt` flag to "Yes". If `custItemNo` is not equal to `validItem[x]`, you increase `x` by 1 and continue to search through the array. When `x` is 6, you shouldn't look through the array anymore; you've gone through all six legitimate items, and you've reached the end. The legitimate subscripts for a six-element array are 0 through 5; your subscript variable should not be used with the array when it reaches 6. If `foundIt` doesn't have a "Yes" in it at this point, it means you never found a match for the ordered item number; you never took the Yes path leading from the `custItemNo = validItem[x]?` question. If `foundIt` does not have "Yes" stored in it, you should print an error message; the customer has ordered a nonexistent item.

## IMPROVING SEARCH EFFICIENCY USING AN EARLY EXIT

The mail-order program is still a little inefficient. The problem is that if lots of customers order item 106 or 108, their price is found on the first or second pass through the loop. The program continues searching through the item array, however, until `x` reaches the value 6. One way to stop the search once the item has been found, and `foundIt` is set to "Yes", is to set `x` to 6 immediately. (Setting a variable to a specific value, particularly when the new value is an abrupt change, is also called **forcing** the variable to that value.) Then, when the program loops back to check whether `x` is still less than 6, the loop will be exited and the program won't bother checking any of the higher item numbers. Leaving a loop as soon as a match is found is called an **early exit**; it improves the program's efficiency. The larger the array, the more beneficial it becomes to exit the searching loop as soon as you find what you're looking for.

**TIP** Some programmers prefer to use a flag variable for early exits; others think it is fine to force a loop control variable to a value that stops loop execution if that is more convenient.

Figure 8-31 shows the final version of the price program. Notice the improvement to the `getPrice()` module. You search the `validItem` array, element by element. If an item number is not matched in a given location, the subscript is increased and the next location is checked. As soon as an item number is located in the array, you print a line, turn on the flag, and force the subscript to a high number (6) so the program will not check the item number array any further.

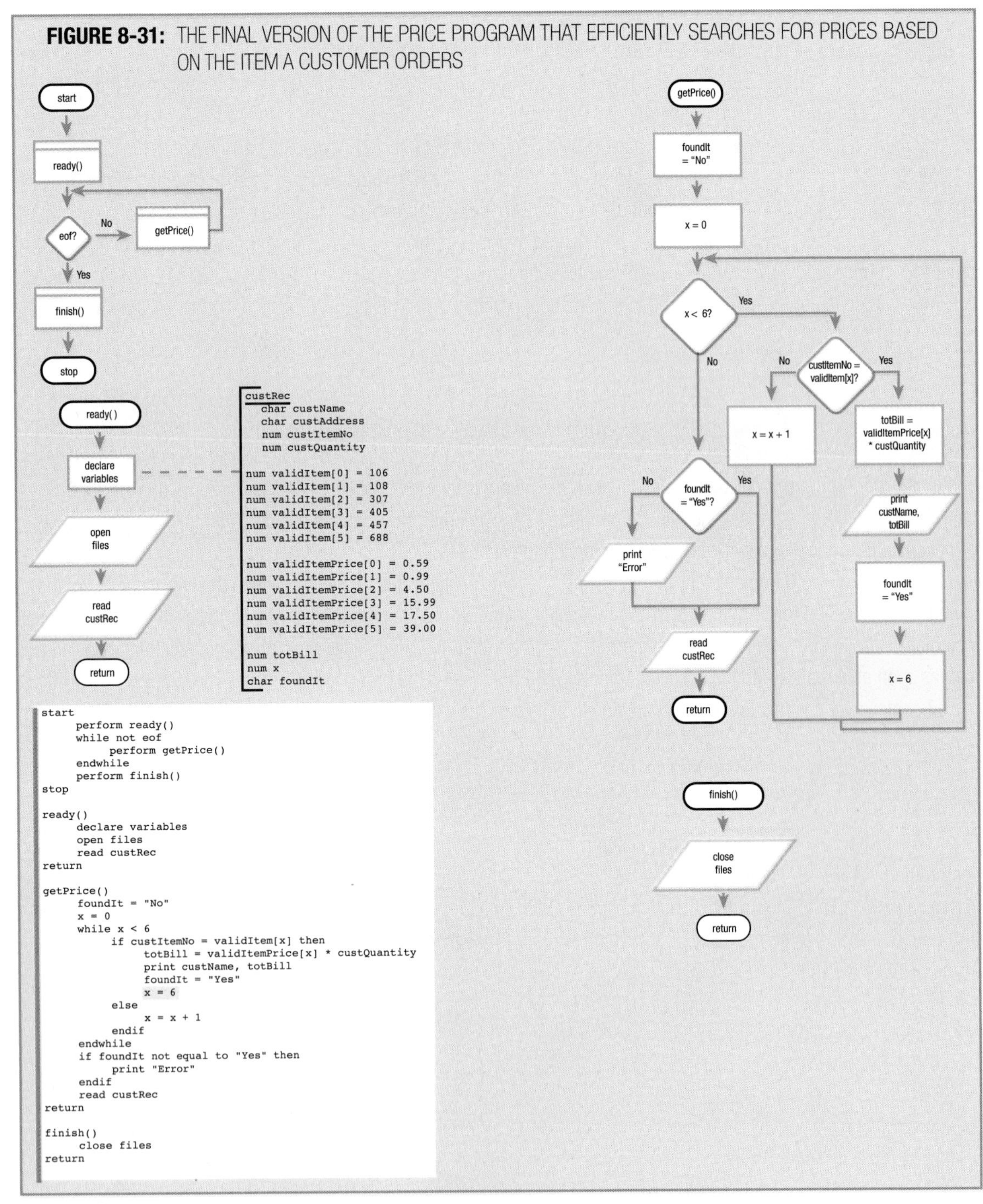
start
ready()
eof?
No
getPrice()
Yes
finish()
stop
ready()
declare variables
open files
read custRec
return
custRec
char custName
char custAddress
num custItemNo
num custQuantity
num validItem[0] = 106
num validItem[1] = 108
num validItem[2] = 307
num validItem[3] = 405
num validItem[4] = 457
num validItem[5] = 688
num validItemPrice[0] = 0.59
num validItemPrice[1] = 0.99
num validItemPrice[2] = 4.50
num validItemPrice[3] = 15.99
num validItemPrice[4] = 17.50
num validItemPrice[5] = 39.00
num totBill
num x
char foundIt
getPrice()
foundIt = "No"
x = 0
x < 6?
Yes
No
custItemNo = validItem[x]?
No
Yes
x = x + 1
totBill = validItemPrice[x] * custQuantity
print custName, totBill
foundIt = "Yes"
x = 6
foundIt = "Yes"?
No
Yes
print "Error"
read custRec
return
finish()
close files
return

**FIGURE 8-31:** THE FINAL VERSION OF THE PRICE PROGRAM THAT EFFICIENTLY SEARCHES FOR PRICES BASED ON THE ITEM A CUSTOMER ORDERS

```
start
     perform ready()
     while not eof
          perform getPrice()
     endwhile
     perform finish()
stop

ready()
     declare variables
     open files
     read custRec
return

getPrice()
     foundIt = "No"
     x = 0
     while x < 6
          if custItemNo = validItem[x] then
               totBill = validItemPrice[x] * custQuantity
               print custName, totBill
               foundIt = "Yes"
               x = 6
          else
               x = x + 1
          endif
     endwhile
     if foundIt not equal to "Yes" then
          print "Error"
     endif
     read custRec
return

finish()
     close files
return
```

**TIP** Notice that the price program is most efficient when the most frequently ordered items are stored at the beginning of the array. When you use this technique, only the seldom-ordered items require many cycles through the searching loop before finding a match.

**TIP** Remember that you can make programs that contain arrays more flexible by declaring a constant to hold the size of the array. Then, whenever you need to refer to the size of the array within the program—for example, when you loop through the array during a search operation—you can use the variable name instead of a hard-coded value like 6. If the program must be altered later to accommodate more or fewer array elements, you need to make only one change—you change the value of the array-size variable where it is declared.

## SEARCHING AN ARRAY FOR A RANGE MATCH

In the previous example, customer item numbers needed to exactly match item numbers stored in a table to determine the correct price of an item. Sometimes, however, instead of finding exact matches, programmers want to work with ranges of values in arrays. A **range of values** is any set of contiguous values, such as 1 through 5.

Recall the customer file description from earlier in this chapter, shown again in Figure 8-32. Suppose the company decides to offer quantity discounts, as shown in Figure 8-33.

**FIGURE 8-32:** MAIL-ORDER CUSTOMER FILE DESCRIPTION

```
MAIL-ORDER CUSTOMER FILE DESCRIPTION
File name: CUSTREC
FIELD DESCRIPTION      DATA TYPE    COMMENTS
Customer name          Character
Address                Character
Item number            Numeric      A 3-digit number
Quantity               Numeric      A value from 1 through 99
```

**FIGURE 8-33:** DISCOUNTS ON ORDERS BY QUANTITY

| Number of items ordered | Discount % |
|---|---|
| 1-9 | 0 |
| 10-24 | 10 |
| 25-48 | 15 |
| 49 or more | 25 |

You want to be able to read a record and determine a discount percentage based on the value in the quantity field. One ill-advised approach might be to set up an array with as many elements as any customer might ever order, and store the appropriate discount for each possible number, as shown in Figure 8-34.

**FIGURE 8-34:** USABLE—BUT INEFFICIENT—DISCOUNT ARRAY

```
num discount[0] = 0
num discount[1] = 0
num discount[2] = 0
.
.
num discount[9] = 0
num discount[10] = 10
.
.
num discount[48] = 15
num discount[49] = 25
num discount[50] = 25
.
.
```

This approach has three drawbacks:

- It requires a very large array that uses a lot of memory.
- You must store the same value repeatedly. For example, each of the first 10 elements receives the same value, 0, because if a customer orders from zero through nine items, there is no discount. Similarly, each of the next 15 elements receives the same value, 10.
- Where do you stop adding array elements? Is a customer order quantity of 75 items enough? What if a customer orders 100 or 1,000 items? No matter how many elements you place in the array, there's always a chance that a customer will order more.

A better approach is to create just four discount array elements, one for each of the possible discount rates, as shown in Figure 8-35.

**FIGURE 8-35:** SUPERIOR DISCOUNT ARRAY

```
num discount[0] = 0
num discount[1] = 10
num discount[2] = 15
num discount[3] = 25
```

With the new four-element `discount` array, you need a parallel array to search through, to find the appropriate level for the discount. At first, beginning programmers might consider creating an array named `discountRange` and testing whether the quantity ordered equals one of the four stored values. For example:

```
num discountRange[0] = 0 through 9
num discountRange[1] = 10 through 24
num discountRange[2] = 25 through 48
num discountRange[3] = 49 and higher
```

However, you cannot create an array like the previous one. Each element in any array is simply a single variable. Any variable can hold a value such as 6 or 12, but it can't hold every value 6 *through* 12. Similarly, the `discountRange[0]` variable can hold a 1, 2, 9, or any other single value, but it can't hold 0 *through* 9; there is no such numeric value.

One solution is to create an array that holds only the low-end value of each range, as Figure 8-36 shows.

**FIGURE 8-36:** THE `discountRange` ARRAY USING LOW END OF EACH DISCOUNT RANGE

```
num discountRange[0] = 0
num discountRange[1] = 10
num discountRange[2] = 25
num discountRange[3] = 49
```

Using such an array, you can compare each `custQuantity` value with each `discountRange` value in turn. You can start with the *last* range limit (`discountRange[3]`). If `custQuantity` is at least that value, 49, the customer gets the highest discount rate (`discount[3]`). If `custQuantity` is not at least `discountRange[3]`, then you check to see if it is at least `discountRange[2]`, or 25. If so, the customer receives `discount[2]`, and so on. If you declare a variable named `rate` to hold the correct discount rate, and another variable named `sub` to use as a subscript, then you can use the `determineDiscount()` module shown in Figure 8-37. This module uses a loop to find the appropriate discount rate for an order, then calculates and prints a customer bill.

**FIGURE 8-37:** FLOWCHART AND PSEUDOCODE FOR DISCOUNT DETERMINATION

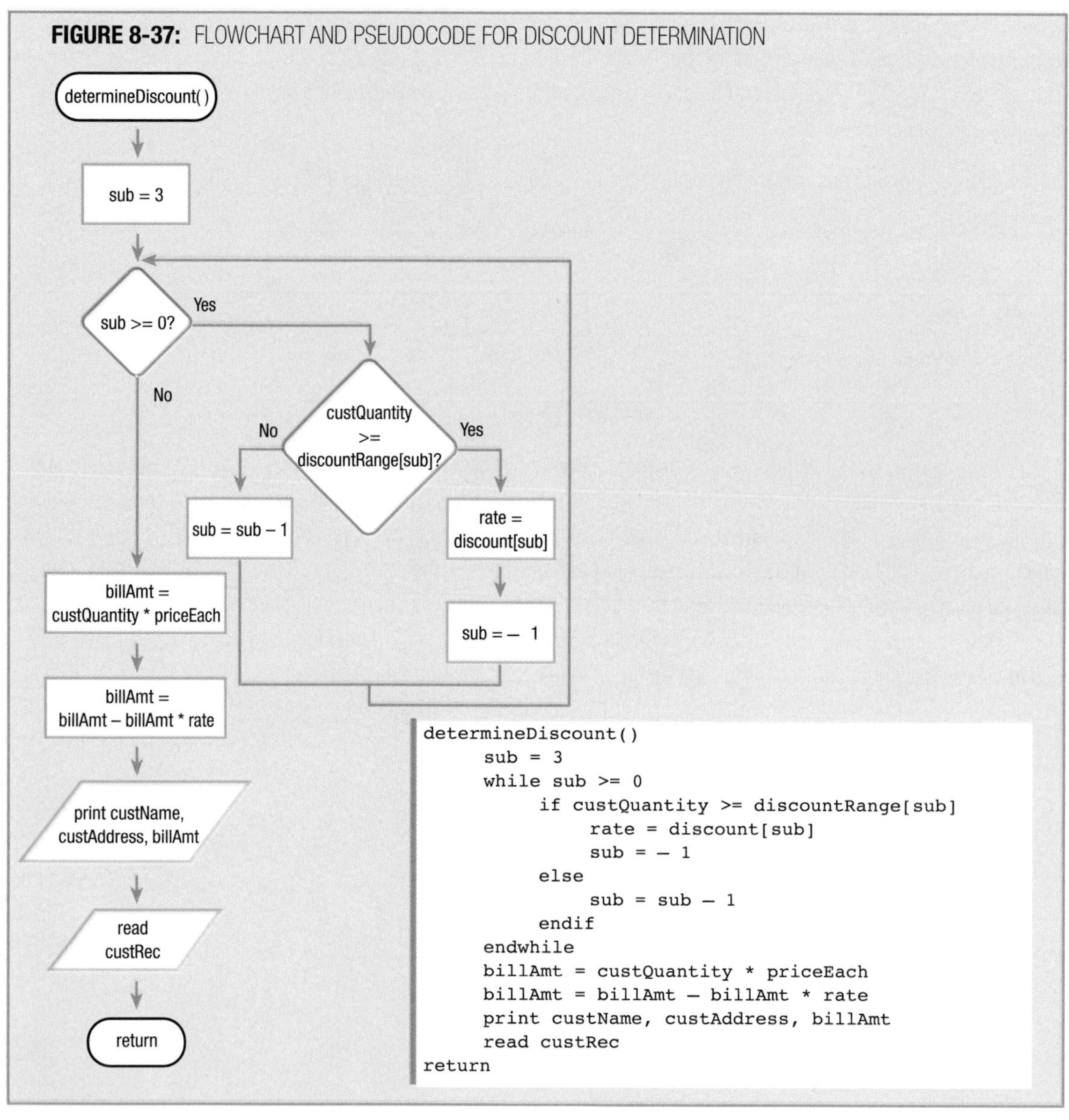


```
determineDiscount()
     sub = 3
     while sub >= 0
          if custQuantity >= discountRange[sub]
               rate = discount[sub]
               sub = – 1
          else
               sub = sub – 1
          endif
     endwhile
     billAmt = custQuantity * priceEach
     billAmt = billAmt – billAmt * rate
     print custName, custAddress, billAmt
     read custRec
return
```

**TIP** An alternative approach is to store the high end of every range in an array. Then, you start with the *lowest* element and check for values *less than or equal to* each array element value before using the appropriate discount in the parallel array.

When using an array to store range limits, you use a loop to make a series of comparisons that would otherwise require many separate decisions. Your program is written using fewer instructions than would be required if you did not use an array, and modifications to your program will be easier to make in the future.

## CHAPTER SUMMARY

- An array is a series or list of variables in computer memory, all of which have the same name but are differentiated with special numbers called subscripts.
- When you declare an array, you declare a programming structure that contains multiple elements, each of which has the same name and the same data type. Each array element has a unique integer subscript indicating how far away the individual element is from the first element.
- You often can use a variable as a subscript to an array, replacing multiple nested decisions.
- You can declare and initialize all of the elements in an array using a single statement that provides a type, a name, and a quantity of elements for the array. You also can initialize array values within an initialization loop.
- You can use a constant array when the final desired values are fixed at the beginning of the program.
- You can load an array from a file. This step is often performed in a program's housekeeping module.
- Searching through an array to find a value you need involves initializing a subscript, using a loop to test each array element, and setting a flag when a match is found.
- In parallel arrays, each element in one array is associated with the element in the same relative position in the other array.
- Your programs should ensure that subscript values do not go out of bounds—that is, take on a value out of the range of legal subscripts.
- When you need to compare a value to a range of values in an array, you can store either the low- or high-end value of each range for comparison.

## KEY TERMS

An **array** is a series or list of variables in computer memory, all of which have the same name but are differentiated with special numbers called subscripts.

A **subscript** is a number that indicates the position of a particular item within an array.

An **index** is a subscript.

Each separate array variable is one **element** of the array.

The **size of an array** is the number of elements it can hold.

In a **zero-based array**, the first element is accessed using a subscript of 0.

**Off-by-one errors** usually occur when you assume an array's first subscript is 1 but it actually is 0.

An **initialization loop** is a loop structure that provides initial values for every element in any array.

**Hard-coded** values are explicitly assigned.

A **flag** is a variable that you set to indicate whether some event has occurred.

**Parallel arrays** are two or more arrays in which each element in one array is associated with the element in the same relative position in the other array or arrays.

When you use a subscript that is not within the range of acceptable subscripts, your subscript is said to be **out of bounds**.

**Forcing** a variable to a value is assigning a specific value to it, particularly when the assignment causes a sudden change in value.

Leaving a loop as soon as a match is found is called an **early exit**.

A **range of values** is any set of contiguous values.

## REVIEW QUESTIONS

1. **A subscript is a(n) ________.**
   a. element in an array
   b. alternate name for an array
   c. number that indicates the position of a particular item within an array
   d. number that represents the highest value stored within an array

2. **Each variable in an array must have the same ________ as the others.**
   a. subscript
   b. data type
   c. value
   d. memory location

3. **Each variable in an array is called a(n) ________.**
   a. element
   b. subscript
   c. component
   d. data type

4. **The subscripts of any array are always ________.**
   a. characters
   b. fractions
   c. integers
   d. strings of characters

5. **Suppose you have an array named `number`, and two of its elements are `number[1]` and `number[4]`. You know that ________.**
   a. the two elements hold the same value
   b. the two elements are at the same memory location
   c. the array holds exactly four elements
   d. there are exactly two elements between those two elements

6. **Suppose you want to write a program that reads customer records and prints a summary of the number of customers who owe more than $1,000 each, in each of 12 sales regions. Customer fields include `name`, `zipCode`, `balanceDue`, and `regionNumber`. At some point during record processing, you would add 1 to an array element whose subscript would be represented by ________.**

   a. `name`
   b. `zipCode`
   c. `balanceDue`
   d. `regionNumber`

7. **Arrays are most useful when you use a ________ as a subscript.**

   a. numeric constant
   b. character
   c. variable
   d. file name

8. **Suppose you create a program with a seven-element array that contains the names of the days of the week. In the `housekeeping()` module, you display the day names using a subscript named `dayNum`. In the same program, you display the same array values again in the `finish()` module. In the `finish()` module, you ________ as a subscript to the array.**

   a. must use `dayNum`
   b. can use `dayNum`, but can also use another variable
   c. must not use `dayNum`
   d. must use a numeric constant

9. **Declaring a numeric array sets its individual elements' values to ________.**

   a. zero in every programming language
   b. zero in some programming languages
   c. consecutive digits in every programming language
   d. consecutive digits in some programming languages

10. **A ________ array is one in which the stored values are fixed permanently at the start of the program.**

    a. constant
    b. variable
    c. persistent
    d. continual

11. **When you create an array of values that you explicitly set upon creation, using numeric constants, the values are said to be ________.**

    a. postcoded
    b. precoded
    c. soft coded
    d. hard coded

12. **Many arrays contain values that change periodically. For example, a bank program that uses an array containing mortgage rates for various terms might change several times a day. The newest values are most likely ________.**
    a. typed into the program by a programmer who then recompiles the program before it is used
    b. calculated by the program, based on historical trends
    c. read into the program from a file that contains the current rates
    d. typed in by a clerk each time the program is executed for a customer

13. **A ________ is a variable that you set to indicate a True or False state.**
    a. subscript
    b. flag
    c. counter
    d. banner

14. **Two arrays in which each element in one array is associated with the element in the same relative position in the other array are ________ arrays.**
    a. cohesive
    b. perpendicular
    c. hidden
    d. parallel

15. **In most programming languages, the subscript used to access the last element in an array declared as `num values[12]` is ________.**
    a. 0
    b. 11
    c. 12
    d. 13

16. **In most programming languages, a subscript for a 10-element array is out of bounds when it ________.**
    a. is lower than 0
    b. is higher than 9
    c. both of these
    d. neither a nor b

17. **If you perform an early exit from a loop while searching through an array for a match, you ________.**
    a. quit searching as soon as you find a match
    b. quit searching before you find a match
    c. set a flag as soon as you find a match, but keep searching for additional matches
    d. repeat a search only if the first search was unsuccessful

**18. In programming terminology, the values 4 through 20 represent a(n) ________ of values.**

a. assortment
b. range
c. diversity
d. collection

**19. Each element in a five-element array can hold ________ value(s).**

a. one
b. five
c. at least five
d. an unlimited number of

**20. After the annual dog show in which the Barkley Dog Training Academy awards points to each participant, the Academy assigns a status to each dog based on the following criteria:**

| Points Earned | Level of Achievement |
|---|---|
| 0–5 | Good |
| 6–7 | Excellent |
| 8–9 | Superior |
| 10 | Unbelievable |

**The Academy needs a program that compares a dog's points earned with the grading scale, in order to award a certificate acknowledging the appropriate level of achievement. Of the following, which set of values would be most useful for the contents of an array used in the program?**

a. 0, 6, 9, 10
b. 5, 7, 8, 10
c. 5, 7, 9, 10
d. any of these

## FIND THE BUGS

Each of the following pseudocode segments contains one or more bugs that you must find and correct.

1. **This application prints a summary report for an aluminum can recycling drive at a high school. When a student brings in cans, a record is created that contains two fields—the student's year in school (1, 2, 3, or 4) and the number of cans submitted. Student records have not been sorted. The report lists each of the four classes and the total number of cans recycled for each class.**

```
start
     perform housekeeping()
     while not eof
          perform accumulateCans()
     endwhile
     perform finish()
stop

housekepping()
     declare variables
         studentRec
             num year
             num cans
         char heading1 = "Can Recycling Report"
         char heading2 = "Year         Cans"
         const num SIZE = 4
         num collected[SIZE] all set to 0
     open files
     read studentRec
return

accumulateCans()
     if year < 1 OR year >= SIZE then
           year = 0
     endif
     collected[SIZE] = collected[SIZE] + cans
     read studentRec
return


finish()
     print heading1
     print heading2
     year = 1
     while year < SIZE
          print year, collected[SIZE]
          year = year + 1
     endwhile
     close files
return
```

2. **This application prints a report card for each student at Pedagogic College. A record has been created for each student containing the student's name, address, and zip code, as well as a numeric average (from 0 through 100) for all the student's work for the semester. A report card is printed for each student containing the student's name, address, city, state, and zip code, as well as a letter grade based on the following scale:**

   **90–100 A**
   **80–89 B**
   **70–79 C**
   **60–69 D**
   **59 and below F**

   **The student's city and state are determined from the student's zip code. A file is read containing three fields—zip code, city, and state—for each of the 100 zip codes the college serves. For this program, assume that all the student averages have been verified to be between 0 and 100 inclusive and that all the zip codes have been verified as valid and stored in the zip code file.**

```
start
     perform housekeeping()
     while not eof
          perform produceGradeReport()
     endwhile
     perform finish()
stop

housekepping()
     declare variables
         studentRec
              char name
              char address
              num zipCode
              num average
         zipRec
              num zip
              char city
              char state
```

```
            const num ZIPSIZE = 100
            num storedZip[ZIPSIZE]
            char storedCity[ZIPSIZE]
            char storedState[SIZE]

            const num GRADESIZE = 5
            const num gradeLevel[1] = 80
            const num gradeLevel[2] = 70
            const num gradeLevel[3] = 60
            const num gradeLevel[4] = 0

            const char grade[0] = 'A'
            const char grade[1] = 'B'
            const char grade[2] = 'C'
            const char grade[3] = 'S'
            const char grade[4] = 'F'

           num zipCodeCount
           char zipFound
           num sub
       open files
       zipCodeCount = 0
       read zipRec
       while not eof
           zip = storedZip[x]
           storedCity[x] = city
           storedState[x] = state
           zipCodeCount = zipCodeCount + 1
          read zipRec
       endwhile
       read studentRec
   return
```

```
produceGradeReport()
     print "Grade Report"
     print name
     print address
     zipFound = "N"
     sub = 0
     while zipFound = "N"
          if zipCode = storedZip[ZIPCODESIZE]
               print storedCity[ZIPCODESIZE]
               print storedState[ZIPCODESIZE]
               print zipCode
               zipFound = "Y"
          endif
          sub = sub + 1
      endwhile
      sub = 0
      while sub < GRADESIZE
          if average >= gradeLevel[sub] then
              print grade[sub]
              sub = 0
          endif
      endwhile
      read studentRec
return

finish()
     close files
return
```

## EXERCISES

1. **The city of Cary is holding a special census. The census takers collect one record for each citizen, as follows:**

```
CENSUS FILE DESCRIPTION
File name: CENSUS
Not sorted
FIELD DESCRIPTION          DATA TYPE       EXAMPLE
Age                        Numeric         42
Gender                     Character       F
Marital Status             Character       M
Voting District            Numeric         18
```

**The voting district field contains a number from 1 through 22.**

**Design the logic of a program that would produce a count of the number of citizens residing in each of the 22 voting districts.**

a. Design the output for this program; create either sample output or a print chart.
b. Create the hierarchy chart.
c. Draw the flowchart.
d. Write the pseudocode.

2. **The Midville Park District maintains records containing information about players on its soccer teams. Each record contains a player's first name, last name, and team number. The teams are:**

```
Soccer Teams
TEAM NUMBER          TEAM NAME
1                    Goal Getters
2                    The Force
3                    Top Guns
4                    Shooting Stars
5                    Midfield Monsters
```

**Design the logic for a report that lists all players along with their team numbers and team names.**

a. Design the output for this program; create either sample output or a print chart.
b. Create the hierarchy chart.
c. Draw the flowchart.
d. Write the pseudocode.

3. **Create the logic for a program that produces a count of the number of players registered for each team listed in Exercise 2.**

a. Design the output for this program; create either sample output or a print chart.
b. Create the hierarchy chart.
c. Draw the flowchart.
d. Write the pseudocode.

4. **An elementary school contains 30 classrooms numbered 1 through 30. Each classroom can contain any number of students up to 35. Each student takes an achievement test at the end of the school year and receives a score from 0 through 100. One record is created for each student in the school; each record contains a student ID, classroom number, and score on the achievement test. Design the logic for a program that lists the total points scored for each of the 30 classroom groups.**
   a. Design the output for this program; create either sample output or a print chart.
   b. Create the hierarchy chart.
   c. Draw the flowchart.
   d. Write the pseudocode.

5. **Modify Exercise 4 so that each classroom's average of the test scores prints, rather than each classroom's total.**

6. **The school in Exercises 4 and 5 maintains a file containing the teacher's name for each classroom. Each record in this file contains a room number from 1 through 30, and the last name of the teacher. Modify Exercise 5 so that the correct teacher's name appears on the list with his or her class's average.**

7. **A fast-food restaurant sells the following products:**

```
Fast-Food Items
PRODUCT           PRICE
Cheeseburger      2.49
Pepsi             1.00
Chips              .59
```

   **Design the logic for a program that reads a record containing a customer number and item name, and then prints either the correct price or the message "Sorry, we do not carry that" as output.**
   a. Draw the flowchart.
   b. Write the pseudocode.

8. **Each week, the home office for a fast-food restaurant franchise distributes a file containing new prices for the items it carries. The file contains the item name and current price. Design the logic for a program that loads the current values into arrays. Then, the program reads a record containing a customer number and item name, and prints either the correct price or the message "Sorry, we do not carry that" as output.**
   a. Draw the flowchart.
   b. Write the pseudocode.

9. **The city of Redgranite is holding a special census. The census takers collect one record for each citizen as follows:**

```
CENSUS FILE DESCRIPTION
File name: CENSUS
Not sorted
FIELD DESCRIPTION        DATA TYPE          EXAMPLE
Age                      Numeric            42
Gender                   Character          F
Marital Status           Character          M
Voting District          Numeric            18
```

**Design the logic of a program that produces a count of the number of citizens in each of the following age groups: under 18, 18 through 30, 31 through 45, 46 through 64, and 65 and older.**

a. Design the output for this program; create either sample output or a print chart.
b. Create the hierarchy chart.
c. Draw the flowchart.
d. Write the pseudocode.

10. **A company desires a breakdown of payroll by department. Input records are as follows:**

```
PAYROLL FILE DESCRIPTION
File name: PAY
FIELD DESCRIPTION          DATA TYPE          EXAMPLE
Employee Last Name         Character          Dykeman
Employee First Name        Character          Ellen
Department                 Numeric            3
Hourly Salary              Numeric            18.50
Hours Worked               Numeric            40
```

**Input records are organized in alphabetical order by employee, *not* in department number order.**

**The output is a list of the seven departments in the company (numbered 1 through 7) and the total gross payroll (rate times hours) for each department.**

a. Design the output for this program; create either sample output or a print chart.
b. Create the hierarchy chart.
c. Draw the flowchart.
d. Write the pseudocode.

11. **Modify Exercise 10 so that the report lists department names as well as numbers. The department names are:**

```
Department Names and Numbers
DEPARTMENT NUMBER          DEPARTMENT NAME
1                          Personnel
2                          Marketing
3                          Manufacturing
4                          Computer Services
5                          Sales
6                          Accounting
7                          Shipping
```

12. **Modify the report created in Exercise 11 so that it prints a line of information for each employee before printing the department summary at the end of the report. Each detail line must contain the employee's name, department number, department name, hourly wage, hours worked, gross pay, and withholding tax.**

    **Withholding taxes are based on the following percentages of gross pay:**

```
Withholding Taxes
WEEKLY SALARY              WITHHOLDING %
0.00-200.00                10
200.01-350.00              14
350.01-500.00              18
500.01-up                  22
```

13. **The Perfect Party Catering Company keeps records concerning the events it caters as follows:**

```
EVENT FILE DESCRIPTION
File name: CATER
FIELD DESCRIPTION             DATA TYPE      EXAMPLE
Event Number                  Numeric        15621
Host Name                     Character      Profeta
Month                         Numeric        10
Day                           Numeric        15
Year                          Numeric        2007
Meal Selection                Numeric        4
Number of Guests              Numeric        150
```

**Additionally, a meal file contains the meal selection codes (such as 4), name of entree (such as "Roast beef"), and current price per guest (such as 19.50). Assume there are eight numbered meal records in the file.**

**Design the logic for a program that produces a report that lists each event number, host name, date, meal, guests, gross total price for the party, and price for the party after discount. Print the month *name*—for example, "October"—rather than "10". Print the meal selection—for example, "Roast beef"—rather than "4". The gross total price for the party is the price per guest for the meal times the number of guests. The final price includes a discount based on the following table:**

```
Discounts for Large Parties
NUMBER OF GUESTS          DISCOUNT
1-25                      $0
26-50                     $75
51-100                    $125
101-250                   $200
251 and over              $300
```

a. Design the output for this program; create either sample output or a print chart.
b. Create the hierarchy chart.
c. Draw the flowchart.
d. Write the pseudocode.

14. ***Daily Life Magazine* wants an analysis of the demographic characteristics of its readers. The Marketing Department has collected reader survey records in the following format:**

```
Magazine Reader FILE DESCRIPTION
File name: MAGREADERS
Not sorted
FIELD DESCRIPTION            DATA TYPE          EXAMPLE
Age                          Numeric            31
Gender                       Character          M
Marital Status               Character          S
Annual Income                Numeric            45000
```

a. Create the logic for a program that would produce a count of readers by age groups as follows: under 20, 20–29, 30–39, 40–49, and 50 and older.
b. Create the logic for a program that would produce a count of readers by gender within age group—that is, under 20 females, under 20 males, under 30 females, under 30 males, and so on.
c. Create the logic for a program that would produce a count of readers by income groups as follows: under $20,000, $20,000–$24,999, $25,000–$34,999, $35,000–$49,999, and $50,000 and up.

15. **Glen Ross Vacation Property Sales employs seven salespeople as follows:**

Salespeople

| ID NUMBER | NAME |
|---|---|
| 103 | Darwin |
| 104 | Kratz |
| 201 | Shulstad |
| 319 | Fortune |
| 367 | Wickert |
| 388 | Miller |
| 435 | Vick |

**When a salesperson makes a sale, a record is created including the date, time, and dollar amount of the sale, as follows: The time is expressed in hours and minutes, based on a 24-hour clock. The sale amount is expressed in whole dollars.**

SALE FIELD DESCRIPTION
File name: SALES

| FIELD DESCRIPTION | DATA TYPE | EXAMPLE |
|---|---|---|
| Salesperson | Numeric | 319 |
| Month | Numeric | 02 |
| Day | Numeric | 21 |
| Year | Numeric | 2008 |
| Time | Numeric | 1315 |
| Sale Amount | Numeric | 95900 |

**Salespeople earn a commission that differs for each sale, based on the following rate schedule:**

Commission Rates

| SALE AMOUNT | RATE |
|---|---|
| $0-$50,000 | .04 |
| $50,001-$125,000 | .05 |
| $125,001-$200,000 | .06 |
| $200,001 and up | .07 |

**Design the output and either the flowchart or pseudocode that produces each of the following reports:**

a. A report listing each salesperson number, name, total sales, and total commissions
b. A report listing each month of the year as both a number and a word (for example, "01 January"), and the total sales for the month for all salespeople
c. A report listing total sales as well as total commissions earned by all salespeople for each of the following time frames, based on hour of the day: 00–05, 06–12, 13–18, and 19–23

## DETECTIVE WORK

1. **Find at least five definitions of an array.**
2. **Using Help in Microsoft Excel or another spreadsheet program, discover how to use the** `vlookup()` **function. How is this function used?**
3. **What is a Fibonacci sequence? How do Fibonacci sequences apply to natural phenomena? Why do programmers use an array when working with this mathematical concept?**

## UP FOR DISCUSSION

1. **A train schedule is an everyday, real-life example of an array. Think of at least four more.**
2. **Every element in an array always has the same data type. Why is this necessary?**

# APPENDIX A

## SOLVING DIFFICULT STRUCTURING PROBLEMS

In Chapter 2, you learned that you can solve any logical problem using only the three standard structures—sequence, selection, and looping. Often it is a simple matter to modify an unstructured program to make it adhere to structured rules. Sometimes, however, it is a challenge to structure a more complicated program. Still, no matter how complicated, large, or poorly structured a problem is, the same tasks can *always* be accomplished in a structured manner.

Consider the flowchart segment in Figure A-1. Is it structured?

**FIGURE A-1:** UNSTRUCTURED FLOWCHART SEGMENT

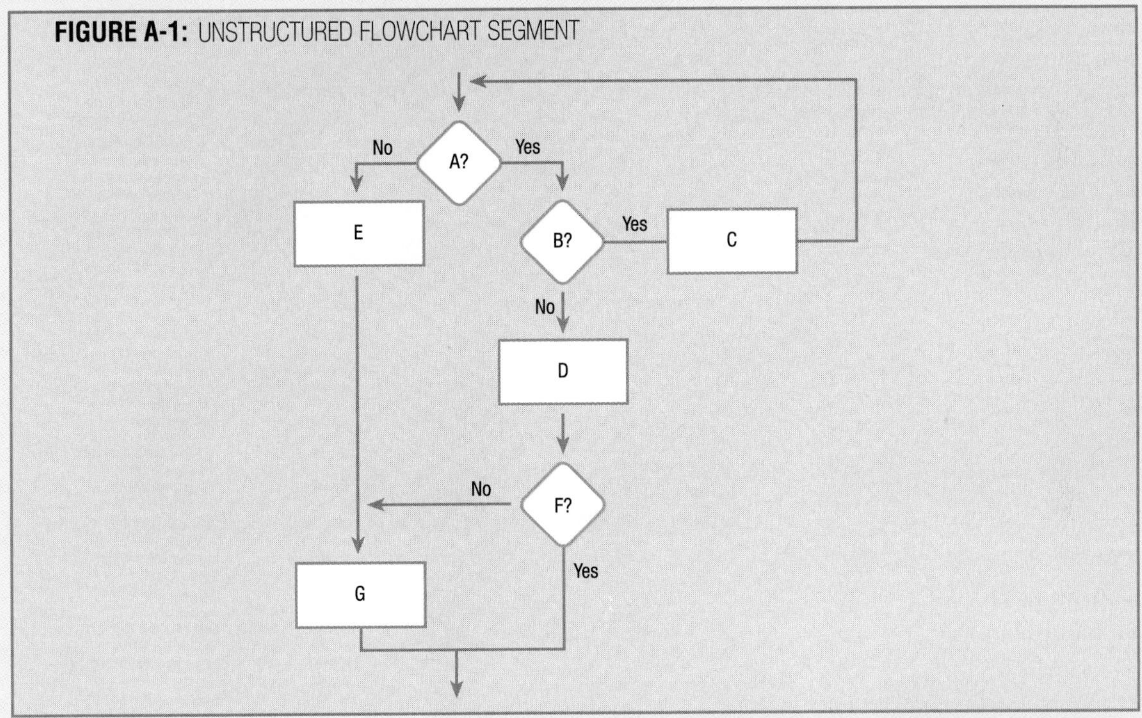


No, it's not. To straighten out the flowchart segment, making it structured, you can use the "spaghetti" method. Using this method, you untangle each path of the flowchart as if you were attempting to untangle strands of spaghetti in a bowl. The objective is to create a new flowchart segment that performs exactly the same tasks as the first, but using only the three structures—sequence, selection, and loop.

To begin to untangle the unstructured flowchart segment, you start at the beginning with the decision labeled A, shown in Figure A-2. This step must represent the beginning of either a selection or a loop, because a sequence would not contain a decision.

FIGURE A-2: STRUCTURING, STEP 1

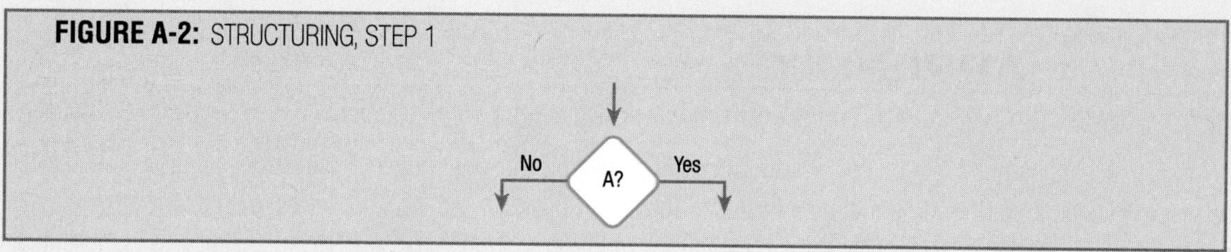


If you follow the logic on the No, or left, side of the question in the original flowchart, you can pull up on the left branch of the decision. You encounter process E, followed by G, followed by the end, as shown in Figure A-3. Compare the "No" actions after Decision A in the first flowchart (Figure A-1) with the actions after Decision A in Figure A-3; they are identical.

FIGURE A-3: STRUCTURING, STEP 2

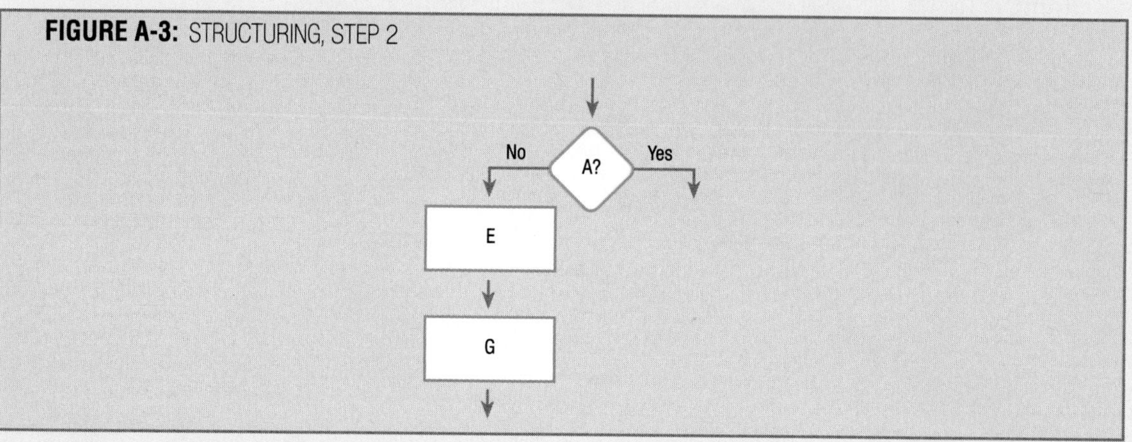


Now continue on the right, or Yes, side of Decision A in Figure A-1. When you follow the flowline, you encounter a decision symbol, labeled B. Pull on B's left side, and a process, D, comes up next. See Figure A-4.

FIGURE A-4: STRUCTURING, STEP 3

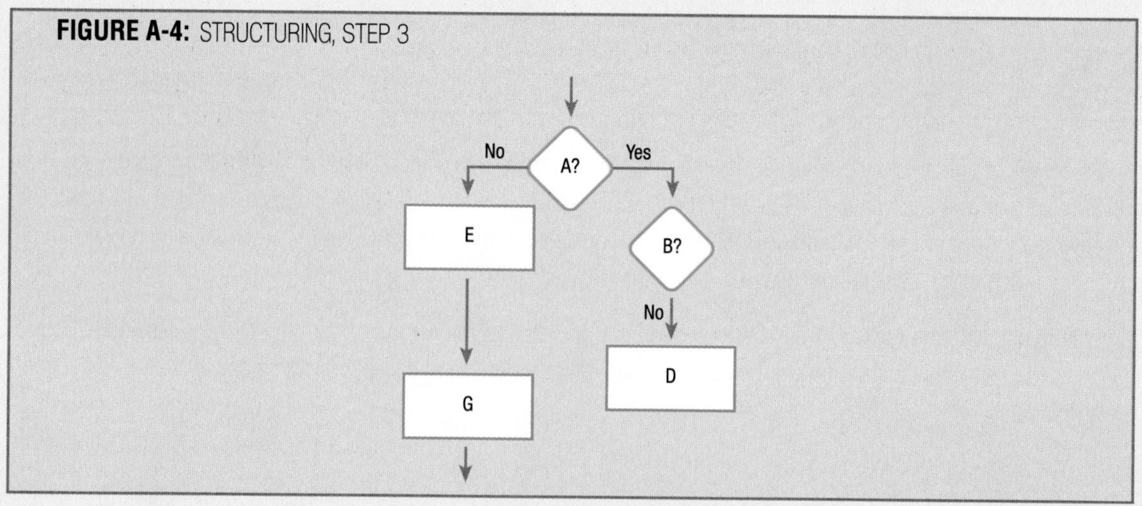

After Step D in the original diagram, a decision labeled F comes up. Pull on its left, or No, side and you get a process, G, and then the end. When you pull on F's right, or Yes, side in the original flowchart, you simply reach the end, as shown in Figure A-5. Notice in Figure A-5 that the G process now appears in two locations. When you improve unstructured flowcharts so that they become structured, you often must repeat steps. This eliminates crossed lines and difficult-to-follow spaghetti logic.

**FIGURE A-5:** STRUCTURING, STEP 4

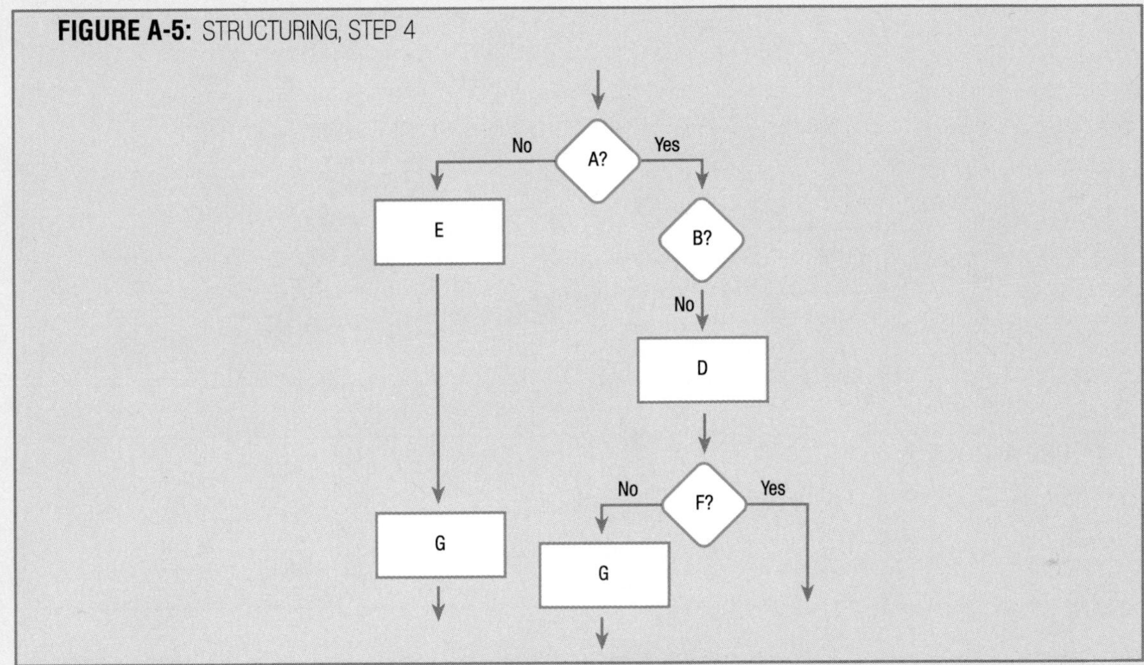


The biggest problem in structuring the original flowchart segment from Figure A-1 follows the right, or Yes, side of the B decision. When the answer to B is Yes, you encounter process C, as shown in both Figures A-1 and A-6. The structure that begins with Decision C looks like a loop because it doubles back, up to Decision A. However, the rules of a structured loop say that it must have the appearance shown in Figure A-7: a question, followed by a structure, returning right back to the question. In Figure A-1, if the path coming out of C returned right to B, there would be no problem; it would be a simple, structured loop. However, as it is, Question A must be repeated. The spaghetti technique says if things are tangled up, start repeating them. So repeat an A decision after C, as Figure A-6 shows.

FIGURE A-6: STRUCTURING, STEP 5

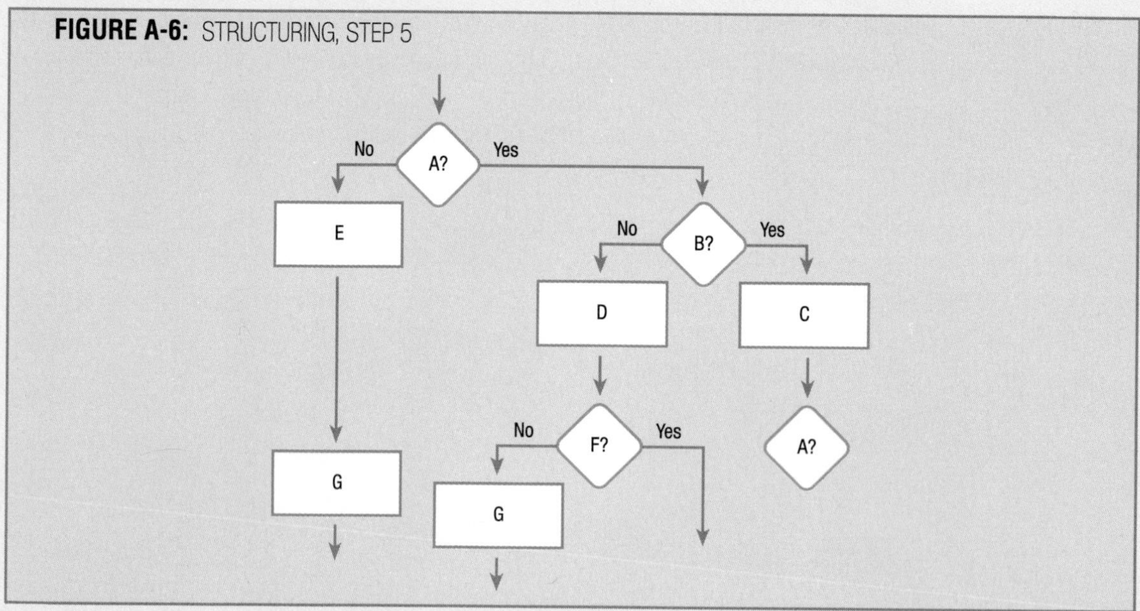


FIGURE A-7: A STRUCTURED LOOP

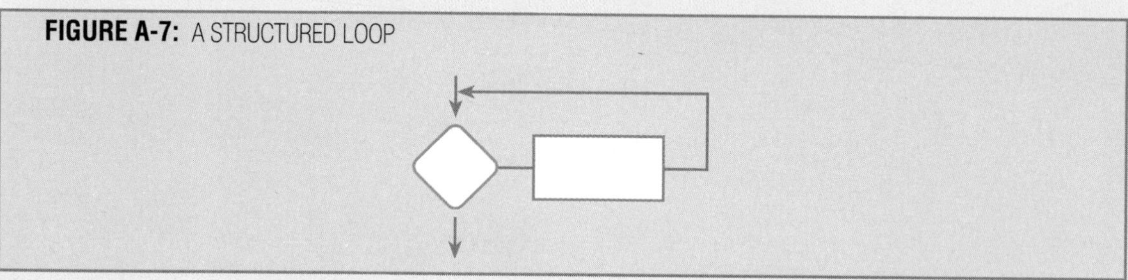

In the original flowchart segment in Figure A-1, when A is Yes, Question B always follows. So, in Figure A-8, after A is Yes, B is Yes, Step C executes, and A is asked again; when A is Yes, B repeats. In the original, when B is Yes, C executes, so in Figure A-8, on the right side of B, C repeats. After C, A occurs. On the right side of A, B occurs. On the right side of B, C occurs. After C, A should occur again, and so on. Soon you should realize that, in order to follow the steps in the same order as in the original flowchart segment, you will repeat these same steps forever. See Figure A-8.

**FIGURE A-8:** STRUCTURING, STEP 6, WHICH NEVER ENDS

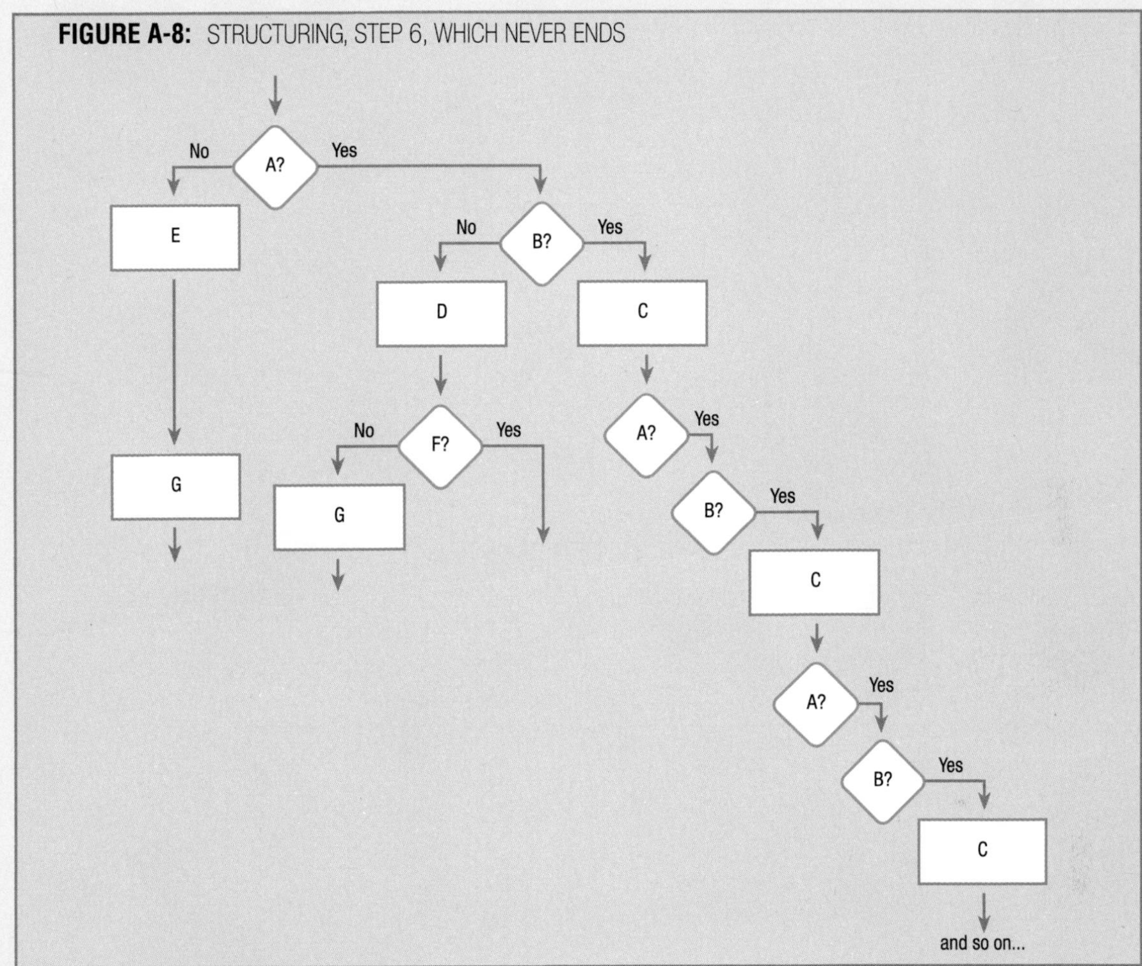


If you continue with Figure A-8, you will never be able to end; every C is always followed by another A, B, and C. Sometimes, in order to make a program segment structured, you have to add an extra flag variable to get out of an infinite mess. A flag is a variable that you set to indicate a true or false state. Typically, a variable is called a flag when its only purpose is to tell you whether some event has occurred. You can create a flag variable named `shouldRepeat` and set the value of `shouldRepeat` to "Yes" or "No," depending on whether it is appropriate to repeat Decision A. When A is No, the `shouldRepeat` flag should be set to "No" because, in this situation, you never want to repeat Question A again. See Figure A-9.

**FIGURE A-9:** ADDING A FLAG TO THE FLOWCHART

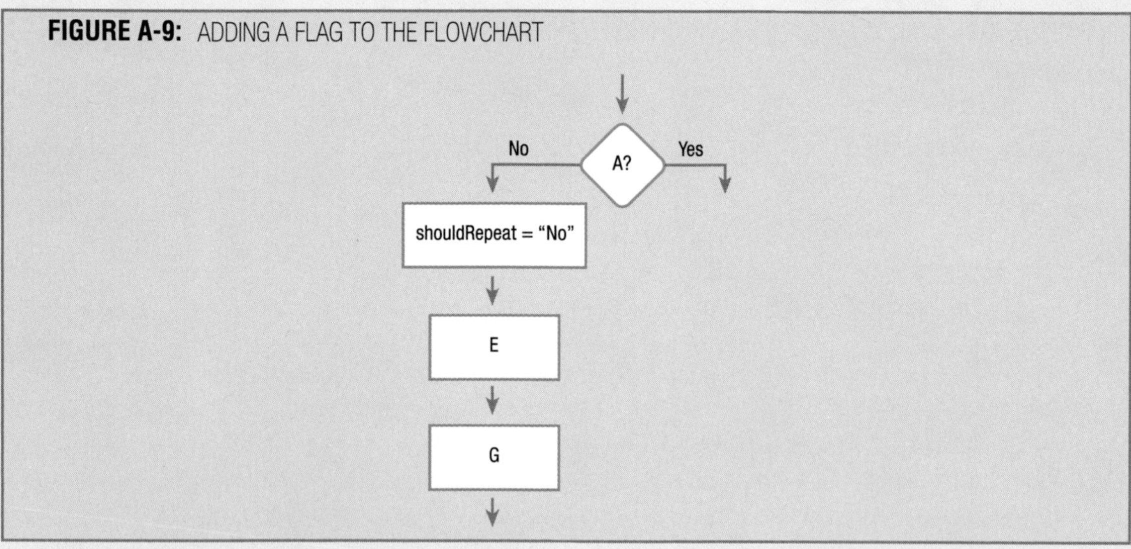


Similarly, after A is Yes, but when B is No, you never want to repeat Question A again, either. Figure A-10 shows that you set `shouldRepeat` to "No" when the answer to B is No. Then you continue with D and the F decision that executes G when F is No.

**FIGURE A-10:** ADDING A FLAG TO A SECOND PATH IN THE FLOWCHART

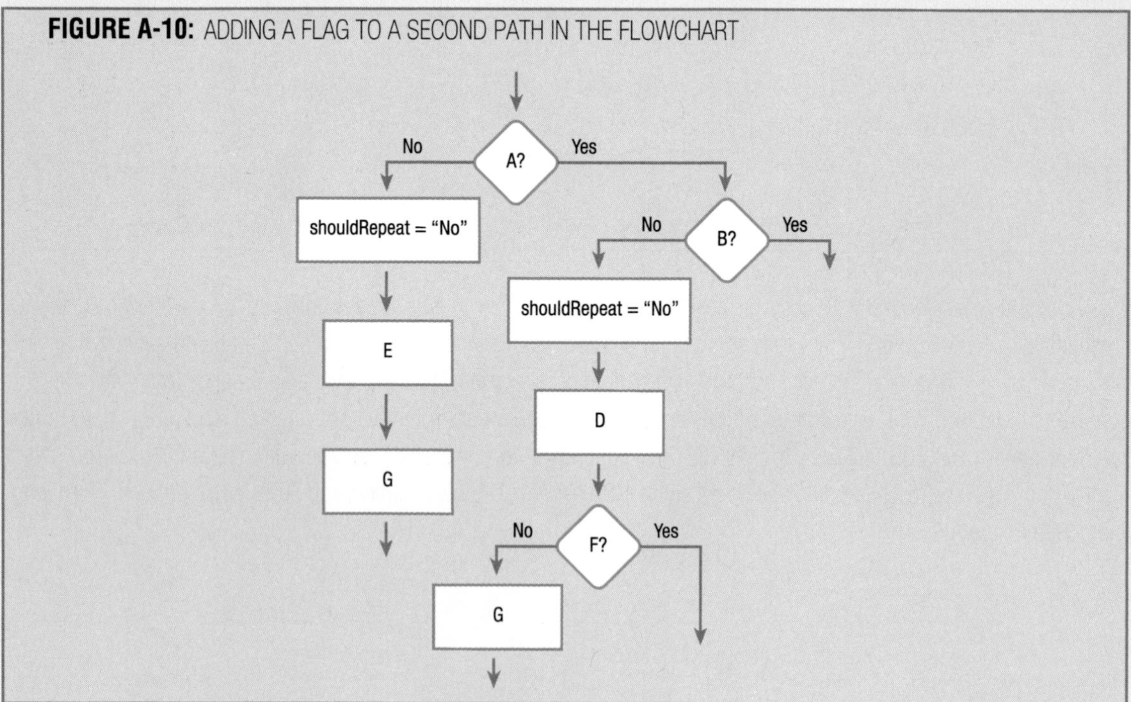


However, in the original flowchart segment in Figure A-1, when the B decision result is Yes, you *do* want to repeat A. So when B is Yes, perform the process for C and set the `shouldRepeat` flag equal to "Yes", as shown in Figure A-11.

**FIGURE A-11:** ADDING A FLAG TO A THIRD PATH IN THE FLOWCHART

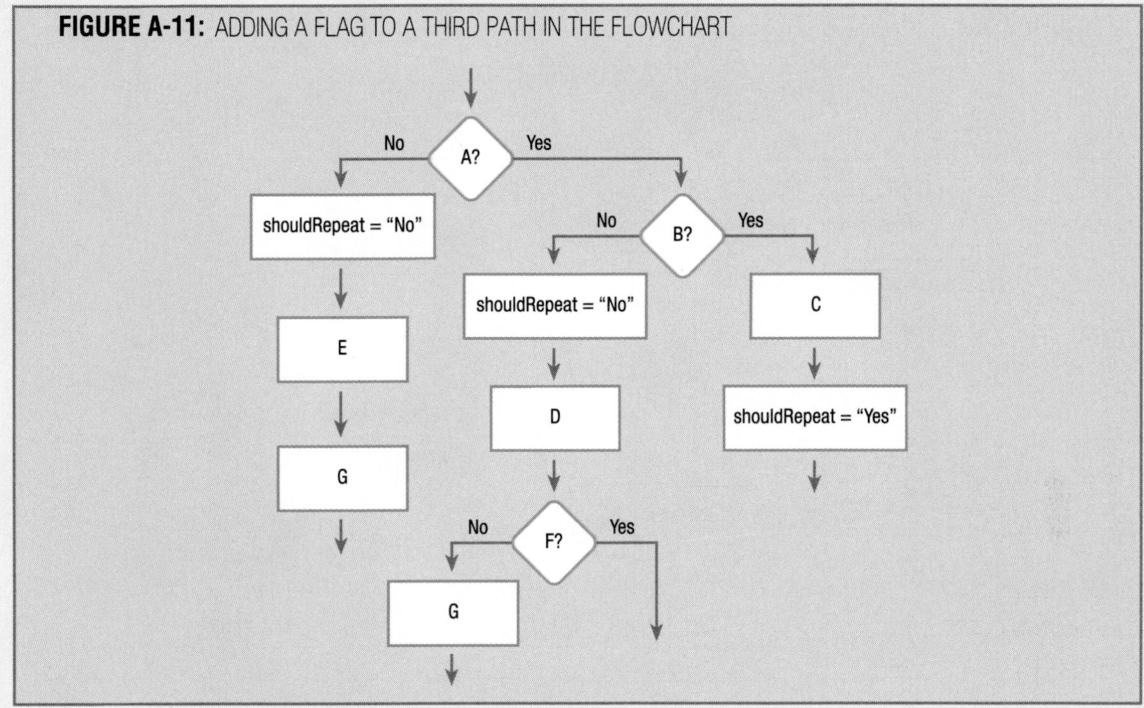


Now all paths of the flowchart can join together at the bottom with one final question: Is `shouldRepeat` equal to "Yes"? If it isn't, exit; but if it is, extend the flowline to go back to repeat Question A. See Figure A-12. Take a moment to verify that the steps that would execute following Figure A-12 are the same steps that would execute following Figure A-1.

- When A is No, E and G always execute.
- When A is Yes and B is No, D and decision F always execute.
- When A is Yes and B is Yes, C always executes and A repeats.

**TIP**

Figure A-12 contains three nested selection structures. In Figure A-12, notice how the F decision begins a complete selection structure whose Yes and No paths join together when the structure ends. This F selection structure is within one path of the B decision structure; the B decision begins a complete selection structure, the Yes and No paths of which join together at the bottom. Likewise, the B selection structure resides entirely within one path of the A selection structure.

**FIGURE A-12:** TYING UP THE LOOSE ENDS

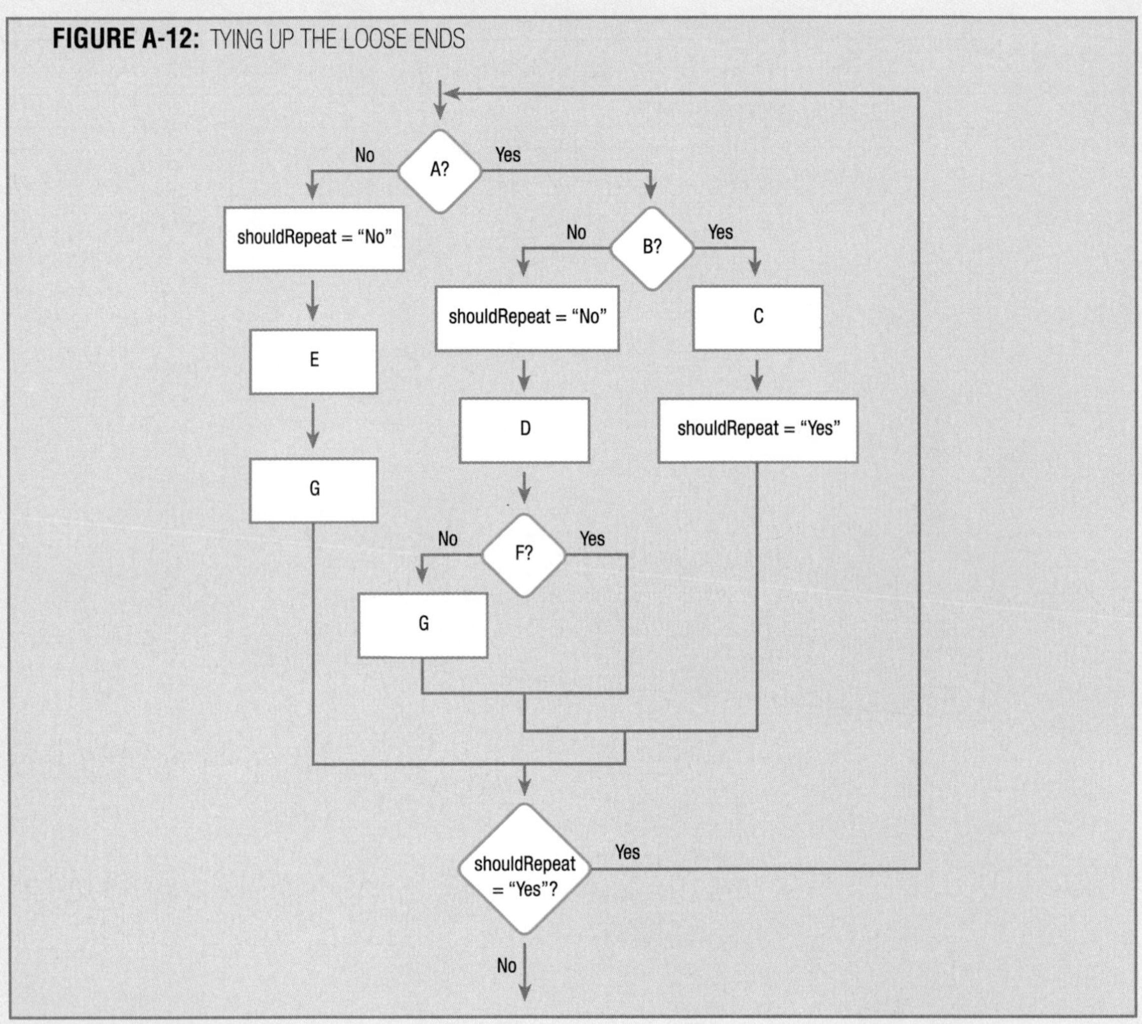


The flowchart segment in Figure A-12 performs identically to the original spaghetti version in Figure A-1. However, is this new flowchart segment structured? There are so many steps in the diagram, it is hard to tell. You may be able to see the structure more clearly if you create a module named `aThroughG()`. If you create the module shown in Figure A-13, then the original flowchart segment can be drawn as in Figure A-14.

**FIGURE A-13:** THE `aThroughG()` MODULE

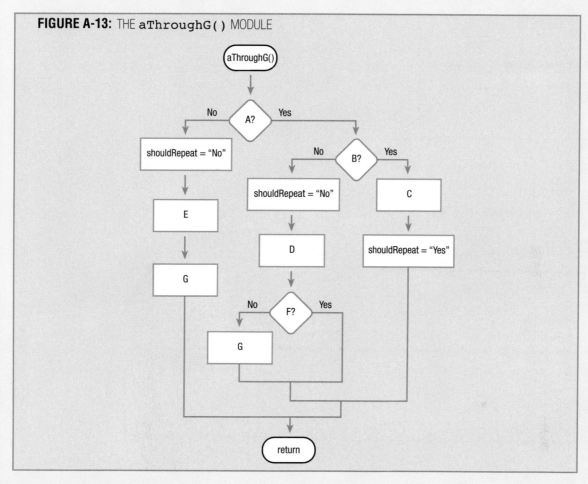

**FIGURE A-14:** LOGIC IN FIGURE A-12, SUBSTITUTING A MODULE FOR STEPS A THROUGH G

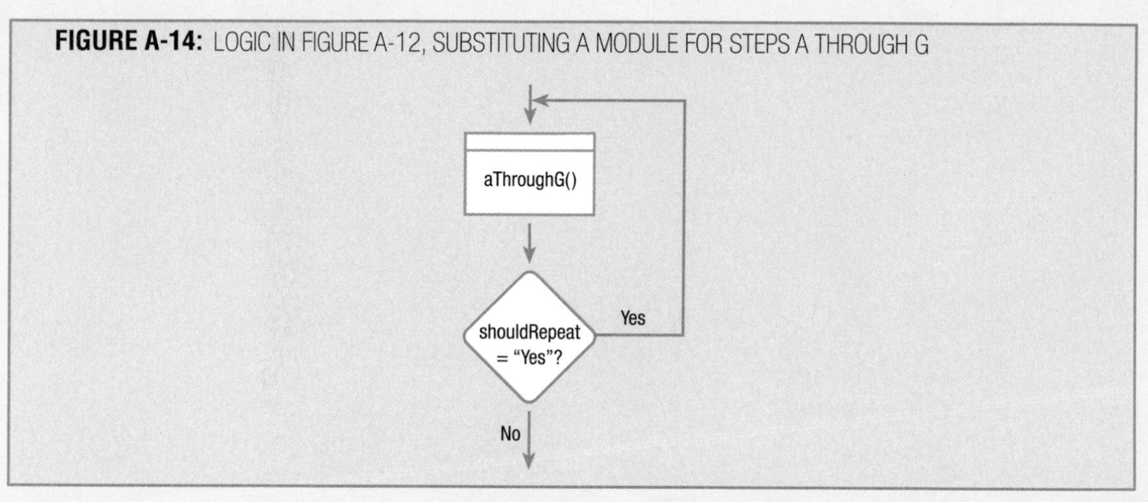

Now you can see that the completed flowchart segment in Figure A-14 is a `do until` loop. If you prefer to use a `while` loop, you can redraw Figure A-14 to perform a sequence followed by a `while` loop, as shown in Figure A-15.

**FIGURE A-15:** LOGIC IN FIGURE A-14, SUBSTITUTING A SEQUENCE AND `WHILE` LOOP FOR THE `DO UNTIL` LOOP

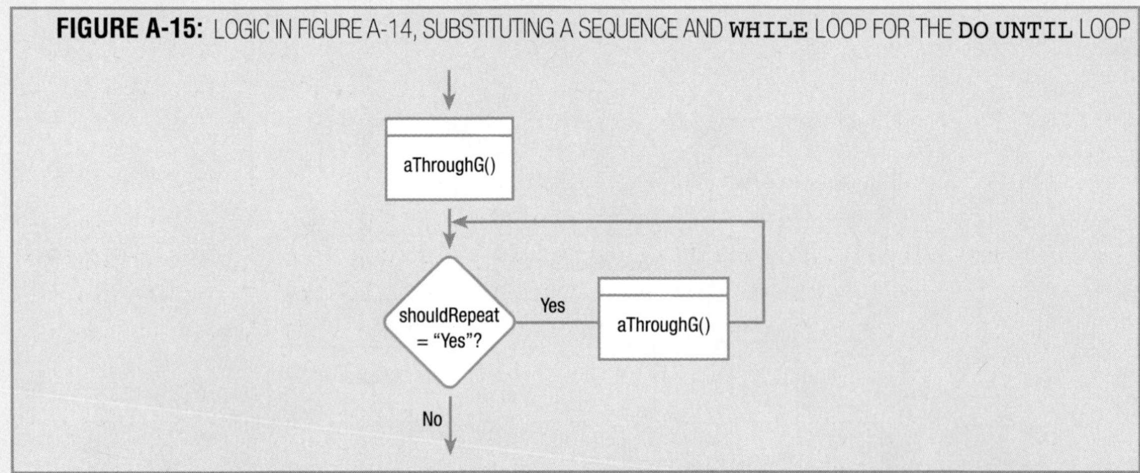


It has taken some effort, but any logical problem can be made to conform to structured rules. It may take extra steps, including repeating specific steps and using some flag variables, but every logical problem can be solved using the three structures: sequence, selection, and loop.

# APPENDIX B

## UNDERSTANDING NUMBERING SYSTEMS AND COMPUTER CODES

The numbering system with which you are most familiar is the decimal system—the system based on ten digits, 0 through 9. When you use the decimal system, there are no other symbols available; if you want to express a value larger than 9, you must resort to using multiple digits from the same pool of ten, placing them in columns.

When you use the decimal system, you analyze a multicolumn number by mentally assigning place values to each column. The value of the rightmost column is 1, the value of the next column to the left is 10, the next column is 100, and so on, multiplying the column value by 10 as you move to the left. There is no limit to the number of columns you can use; you simply keep adding columns to the left as you need to express higher values. For example, Figure B-1 shows how the value 305 is represented in the decimal system. You simply sum the value of the digit in each column after it has been multiplied by the value of its column.

**FIGURE B-1:** REPRESENTING 305 IN THE DECIMAL SYSTEM

| Column value: | 100 | 10 | 1 |
|---|---|---|---|
| Number: | 3 | 0 | 5 |
| Evaluation: | 3*100 | +0*10 | +5*1 |

The **binary numbering system** works in the same way as the decimal numbering system, except that it uses only two digits, 0 and 1. When you use the binary system, if you want to express a value greater than 1, you must resort to using multiple columns, because no single symbol is available that represents any value other than 0 or 1. However, instead of each new column to the left being 10 times greater than the previous column, when you use the binary system, each new column is only two times the value of the previous column. For example, Figure B-2 shows how the number 9 is represented in the binary system, and Figure B-3 shows how the value 305 is represented. Notice that in both figures that show binary numbers, as well as in the decimal system, it is perfectly acceptable—and often necessary—to write a number containing 0 as some of the digits. As with the decimal system, when you use the binary system, there is no limit to the number of columns you can use—you use as many as it takes to express a value.

**FIGURE B-2:** REPRESENTING 9 IN THE BINARY SYSTEM

| Column value: | 8 | 4 | 2 | 1 |
|---|---|---|---|---|
| Number: | 1 | 0 | 0 | 1 |

```
Conversion to decimal:  1*8 = 8
                       +0*4 = 0
                       +0*2 = 0
                       +1*1 = 1
                       ________
                Total:        9
```

**FIGURE B-3:** REPRESENTING 305 IN THE BINARY SYSTEM

| Column value: | 256 | 128 | 64 | 32 | 16 | 8 | 4 | 2 | 1 |
|---|---|---|---|---|---|---|---|---|---|
| Number: | 1 | 0 | 0 | 1 | 1 | 0 | 0 | 0 | 1 |

```
Conversion to decimal:          1*256 =  256
                              + 0*128 =    0
                              + 0* 64 =    0
                              + 1* 32 =   32
                              + 1* 16 =   16
                              + 0*  8 =    0
                              + 0*  4 =    0
                              + 0*  2 =    0
                              + 1*  1 =    1
                              _____________
                   Total:                305
```

**TIP** Mathematicians call decimal numbers **base 10 numbers** and binary numbers **base 2 numbers**.

Every computer stores every piece of data it ever uses as a set of 0s and 1s. Each 0 or 1 is known as a **bit**, which is short for **b**inary dig**it**. Every computer uses 0s and 1s because all values in a computer are stored as electronic signals that are either on or off. This two-state system is most easily represented using just two digits.

Every computer uses a set of binary digits to represent every character it can store. If computers used only one binary digit to represent characters, then only two different characters could be represented, because the single bit could be only 0 or 1. If they used only two digits, then only four characters could be represented—one that used each of the four codes 00, 01, 10, and 11, which in decimal values are 0, 1, 2, and 3, respectively. Many computers use sets of eight binary digits to represent each character they store, because using eight binary digits provides 256 different combinations. One combination can represent an "A", another a "B", still others "a" and "b", and so on. Two hundred fifty-six combinations are enough so that each capital letter, small letter, digit, and punctuation mark used in English has its own code; even a space has a code. For example, in some computers 01000001 represents the character "A". The binary number 01000001 has a decimal value of 65, but this numeric value is not important to ordinary computer users; it is simply a code that stands for "A". The code that uses 01000001 to mean "A" is the **American Standard Code for Information Interchange**, or **ASCII**.

**TIP** A set of eight bits is called a **byte**. Half a byte, or four bits, is a **nibble**.

The ASCII code is not the only computer code; it is typical, and is the one used in most personal computers. The **Extended Binary Coded Decimal Interchange Code**, or **EBCDIC**, is an eight-bit code that is used in IBM mainframe computers. In these computers, the principle is the same—every character is stored as a series of binary digits. The only difference is that the actual values used are different. For example, in EBCDIC, an "A" is 11000001, or 193. Another code used by languages such as Java and C# is Unicode; with this code, 16 bits are used to represent each character. The character "A" in Unicode has the same decimal value as the ASCII "A", 65, but it is stored as 0000000001000001. Using 16 bits provides many more possible combinations than using only eight—65,536 to be exact. With Unicode, not only are there enough available codes for all English letters and digits, but also for characters from many international alphabets.

Ordinary computer users seldom think about the numeric codes behind the letters, numbers, and punctuation marks they enter from their keyboards or see displayed on a monitor. However, they see the consequence of the values behind letters when they see data sorted in alphabetical order. When you sort a list of names, "Andrea" comes before "Brian," and "Caroline" comes after "Brian" because the numeric code for "A" is lower than the code for "B", and the numeric code for "C" is higher than the code for "B" no matter whether you are using ASCII, EBCDIC, or Unicode.

Table B-1 shows the decimal and binary values behind the most commonly used characters in the ASCII character set—the letters, numbers, and punctuation marks you can enter from your keyboard using a single key press.

**TIP** Most of the values not included in Table B-1 have a purpose. For example, the decimal value 7 represents a bell—a dinging sound your computer can make, often used to notify you of an error or some other unusual condition.

**TIP** Each binary number in Table B-1 is shown containing two sets of four digits; this convention makes the long eight-digit numbers easier to read.

**TABLE B-1:** DECIMAL AND BINARY VALUES FOR COMMON ASCII CHARACTERS

| Decimal number | Binary number | ASCII character | |
|---|---|---|---|
| 32 | 0010 0000 | | Space |
| 33 | 0010 0001 | ! | Exclamation point |
| 34 | 0010 0010 | " | Quotation mark, or double quote |
| 35 | 0010 0011 | # | Number sign, also called an octothorpe or a pound sign |
| 36 | 0010 0100 | $ | Dollar sign |
| 37 | 0010 0101 | % | Percent |
| 38 | 0010 0110 | & | Ampersand |
| 39 | 0010 0111 | ' | Apostrophe, single quote |
| 40 | 0010 1000 | ( | Left parenthesis |
| 41 | 0010 1001 | ) | Right parenthesis |
| 42 | 0010 1010 | * | Asterisk |
| 43 | 0010 1011 | + | Plus sign |
| 44 | 0010 1100 | , | Comma |
| 45 | 0010 1101 | - | Hyphen or minus sign |
| 46 | 0010 1110 | . | Period or decimal point |
| 47 | 0010 1111 | / | Slash or front slash |

**TABLE B-1:** DECIMAL AND BINARY VALUES FOR COMMON ASCII CHARACTERS (CONTINUED)

| Decimal number | Binary number | ASCII character | |
|---|---|---|---|
| 48 | 0011 0000 | 0 | |
| 49 | 0011 0001 | 1 | |
| 50 | 0011 0010 | 2 | |
| 51 | 0011 0011 | 3 | |
| 52 | 0011 0100 | 4 | |
| 53 | 0011 0101 | 5 | |
| 54 | 0011 0110 | 6 | |
| 55 | 0011 0111 | 7 | |
| 56 | 0011 1000 | 8 | |
| 57 | 0011 1001 | 9 | |
| 58 | 0011 1010 | : | Colon |
| 59 | 0011 1011 | ; | Semicolon |
| 60 | 0011 1100 | < | Less-than sign |
| 61 | 0011 1101 | = | Equal sign |
| 62 | 0011 1110 | > | Greater-than sign |
| 63 | 0011 1111 | ? | Question mark |
| 64 | 0100 0000 | @ | At sign |
| 65 | 0100 0001 | A | |
| 66 | 0100 0010 | B | |
| 67 | 0100 0011 | C | |
| 68 | 0100 0100 | D | |
| 69 | 0100 0101 | E | |
| 70 | 0100 0110 | F | |
| 71 | 0100 0111 | G | |
| 72 | 0100 1000 | H | |
| 73 | 0100 1001 | I | |
| 74 | 0100 1010 | J | |
| 75 | 0100 1011 | K | |
| 76 | 0100 1100 | L | |
| 77 | 0100 1101 | M | |
| 78 | 0100 1110 | N | |
| 79 | 0100 1111 | O | |

**TABLE B-1:** DECIMAL AND BINARY VALUES FOR COMMON ASCII CHARACTERS (CONTINUED)

| Decimal number | Binary number | ASCII character | |
|---|---|---|---|
| 80 | 0101 0000 | P | |
| 81 | 0101 0001 | Q | |
| 82 | 0101 0010 | R | |
| 83 | 0101 0011 | S | |
| 84 | 0101 0100 | T | |
| 85 | 0101 0101 | U | |
| 86 | 0101 0110 | V | |
| 87 | 0101 0111 | W | |
| 88 | 0101 1000 | X | |
| 89 | 0101 1001 | Y | |
| 90 | 0101 1010 | Z | |
| 91 | 0101 1011 | [ | Opening or left bracket |
| 92 | 0101 1100 | \ | Backslash |
| 93 | 0101 1101 | ] | Closing or right bracket |
| 94 | 0101 1110 | ^ | Caret |
| 95 | 0101 1111 | _ | Underline or underscore |
| 96 | 0110 0000 | ` | Grave accent |
| 97 | 0110 0001 | a | |
| 98 | 0110 0010 | b | |
| 99 | 0110 0011 | c | |
| 100 | 0110 0100 | d | |
| 101 | 0110 0101 | e | |
| 102 | 0110 0110 | f | |
| 103 | 0110 0111 | g | |
| 104 | 0110 1000 | h | |
| 105 | 0110 1001 | i | |
| 106 | 0110 1010 | j | |
| 107 | 0110 1011 | k | |
| 108 | 0110 1100 | l | |
| 109 | 0110 1101 | m | |
| 110 | 0110 1110 | n | |
| 111 | 0110 1111 | o | |

**TABLE B-1:** DECIMAL AND BINARY VALUES FOR COMMON ASCII CHARACTERS (CONTINUED)

| Decimal number | Binary number | ASCII character | |
|---|---|---|---|
| 112 | 0111 0000 | p | |
| 113 | 0111 0001 | q | |
| 114 | 0111 0010 | r | |
| 115 | 0111 0011 | s | |
| 116 | 0111 0100 | t | |
| 117 | 0111 0101 | u | |
| 118 | 0111 0110 | v | |
| 119 | 0111 0111 | w | |
| 120 | 0111 1000 | x | |
| 121 | 0111 1001 | y | |
| 122 | 0111 1010 | z | |
| 123 | 0111 1011 | { | Opening or left brace |
| 124 | 0111 1100 | \| | Vertical line or pipe |
| 125 | 0111 1101 | } | Closing or right brace |
| 126 | 0111 1110 | ~ | Tilde |

# APPENDIX C

## USING A LARGE DECISION TABLE

In Chapter 5, you learned to use a simple decision table, but real-life problems often require many decisions. A complicated decision process is represented in the following situation. Suppose your employer sends you a memo outlining a year-end bonus plan with complicated rules. Appendix C walks you through the process of solving this problem by using a large decision table.

```
To: Programming staff
From: The boss
I need a report listing every employee and the
bonus I plan to give him or her. Everybody gets
at least $100. All the employees in Department 2
get $200, unless they have more than 5 dependents.
Anybody with more than 5 dependents gets $1000
unless they're in Department 2. Nobody with an ID
number greater than 800 gets more than $100 even
if they're in Department 2 or have more than 5
dependents.
P.S. I need this by 5 o'clock.
```

Drawing the flowchart or writing the pseudocode for this task may seem daunting. You can use a decision table to help you manage all the decisions, and you can begin to create one by listing all the possible decisions you need to make to determine an employee's bonus. They are:

- `empDept = 2?`
- `empDepend > 5?`
- `empIdNum > 800?`

Next, determine how many possible Boolean value combinations exist for the conditions. In this case, there are eight possible combinations, shown in Figure C-1. An employee can be in Department 2, have over five dependents, and have an ID number greater than 800. Another employee can be in Department 2, have over five dependents, but have an ID number that is 800 or less. Because each condition has two outcomes and there are three conditions, there are 2 * 2 * 2 , or eight possibilities. Four conditions would produce 16 possible outcome combinations, five would produce 32, and so on.

**FIGURE C-1:** POSSIBLE OUTCOMES OF BONUS CONDITIONS

| Condition | Outcome | | | | | | | |
|---|---|---|---|---|---|---|---|---|
| empDept = 2 | T | T | T | T | F | F | F | F |
| empDepend > 5 | T | T | F | F | T | T | F | F |
| empIdNum > 800 | T | F | T | F | T | F | T | F |

**TIP**

In Figure C-1, notice how the pattern of Ts and Fs varies in each row. The bottom row contains one T and F, repeating four times, the second row contains two of each, repeating twice, and the top row contains four of each without repeating. If a fourth decision was required, you would place an identical grid of Ts and Fs to the right of this one, then add a new top row containing eight Ts (covering all eight columns you see currently) followed by eight Fs (covering the new copy of the grid to the right).

Next, list the possible outcome values for the bonus amounts. If you declare a numeric variable named `bonus` by placing the statement `num bonus` in your list of variables at the beginning of the program, then the possible outcomes can be expressed as:

- `bonus = 100`
- `bonus = 200`
- `bonus = 1000`

Finally, choose one required outcome for each possible combination of conditions. For example, the first possible outcome is a $100 bonus. As Figure C-2 shows, you place Xs in the `bonus = 100` row each time `empIdNum > 800` is true, no matter what other conditions exist, because the memo from the boss said, "Nobody with an ID number greater than 800 gets more than $100, even if they're in Department 2 or have more than 5 dependents."

**FIGURE C-2:** DECISION TABLE FOR BONUSES, PART 1

| Condition | Outcome | | | | | | | |
|---|---|---|---|---|---|---|---|---|
| empDept = 2 | T | T | T | T | F | F | F | F |
| empDepend > 5 | T | T | F | F | T | T | F | F |
| empIdNum > 800 | T | F | T | F | T | F | T | F |
| bonus = 100 | X | | X | | X | | X | |
| bonus = 200 | | | | | | | | |
| bonus = 1000 | | | | | | | | |

Next, place an X in the `bonus = 1000` row under all remaining columns (that is, those without a selected outcome) in which `empDepend > 5` is true *unless* the `empDept = 2` condition is true, because the memo stated, "Anybody with more than 5 dependents gets $1000 unless they're in Department 2." The first four columns of the decision table do not qualify, because the `empDept` value is 2; only the sixth column in Figure C-3 meets the criteria for the $1000 bonus.

**FIGURE C-3:** DECISION TABLE FOR BONUSES, PART 2

| Condition | Outcome | | | | | | | |
|---|---|---|---|---|---|---|---|---|
| empDept = 2 | T | T | T | T | F | F | F | F |
| empDepend > 5 | T | T | F | F | T | T | F | F |
| empIdNum > 800 | T | F | T | F | T | F | T | F |
| bonus = 100 | X | | X | | X | | X | |
| bonus = 200 | | | | | | | | |
| bonus = 1000 | | | | | | X | | |

Place Xs in the `bonus = 200` row for any remaining columns in which `empDept = 2` is true and `empDepend > 5` is false, because "All the employees in Department 2 get $200, unless they have more than 5 dependents." Column 4 in Figure C-4 satisfies these criteria.

**FIGURE C-4:** DECISION TABLE FOR BONUSES, PART 3

| Condition | Outcome | | | | | | | |
|---|---|---|---|---|---|---|---|---|
| empDept = 2 | T | T | T | T | F | F | F | F |
| empDepend > 5 | T | T | F | F | T | T | F | F |
| empIdNum > 800 | T | F | T | F | T | F | T | F |
| bonus = 100 | X | | X | | X | | X | |
| bonus = 200 | | | | X | | | | |
| bonus = 1000 | | | | | | X | | |

Finally, fill any unmarked columns with an X in the `bonus = 100` row because, according to the memo, "Everybody gets at least $100." The only columns remaining are the second column and the last column on the right. See Figure C-5.

**FIGURE C-5:** DECISION TABLE FOR BONUSES, PART 4

| Condition | Outcome | | | | | | | |
|---|---|---|---|---|---|---|---|---|
| empDept = 2 | T | T | T | T | F | F | F | F |
| empDepend > 5 | T | T | F | F | T | T | F | F |
| empIdNum > 800 | T | F | T | F | T | F | T | F |
| bonus = 100 | X | X | X | | X | | X | X |
| bonus = 200 | | | | X | | | | |
| bonus = 1000 | | | | | | X | | |

The decision table is complete. When you count the Xs, you'll find there are eight possible outcomes. Take a moment and confirm that each bonus is the appropriate value based on the specifications in the original memo from the boss. Now you can start to plan the logic. If you choose to use a flowchart, you start by drawing the path to the first outcome, which occurs when `empDept = 2`, `empDepend > 5`, and `empIdNum > 800` are all true, and which corresponds to the first column in the decision table. See Figure C-6.

**FIGURE C-6:** FLOWCHART AND PSEUDOCODE FOR BONUS DECISION, PART 1

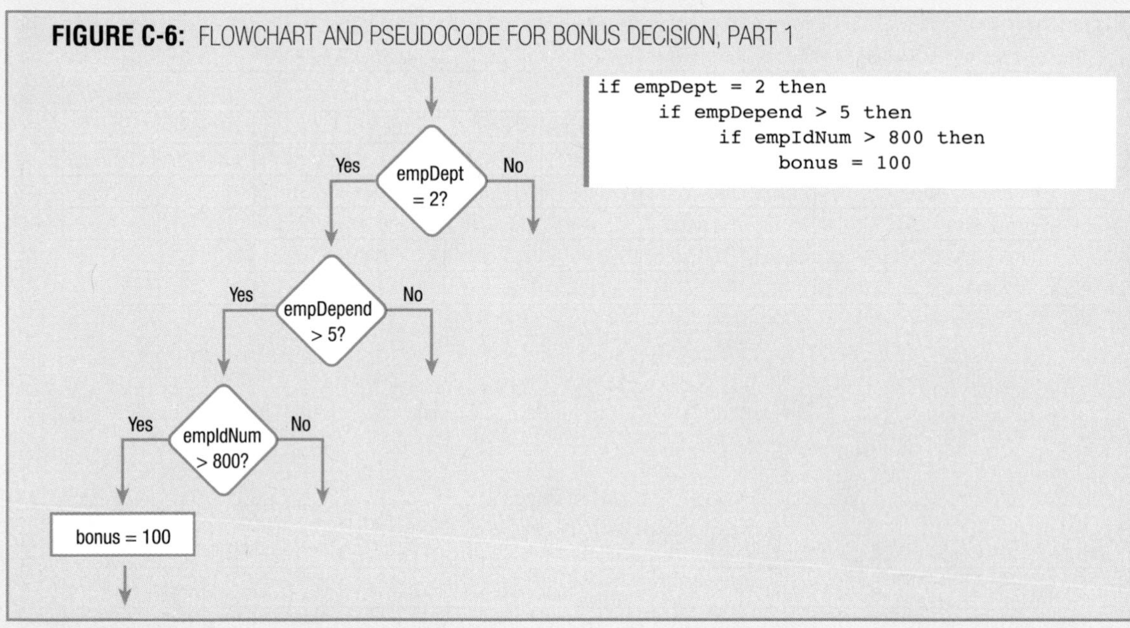


```
if empDept = 2 then
     if empDepend > 5 then
          if empIdNum > 800 then
               bonus = 100
```

To continue creating the diagram started in Figure C-6, add the "false" outcome to the `empIdNum > 800` decision; this corresponds to the second column in the decision table. When an employee's department is 2, dependents greater than 5, and ID number not greater than 800, the employee's bonus should be $100. See Figure C-7.

**FIGURE C-7:** FLOWCHART AND PSEUDOCODE FOR BONUS DECISION, PART 2

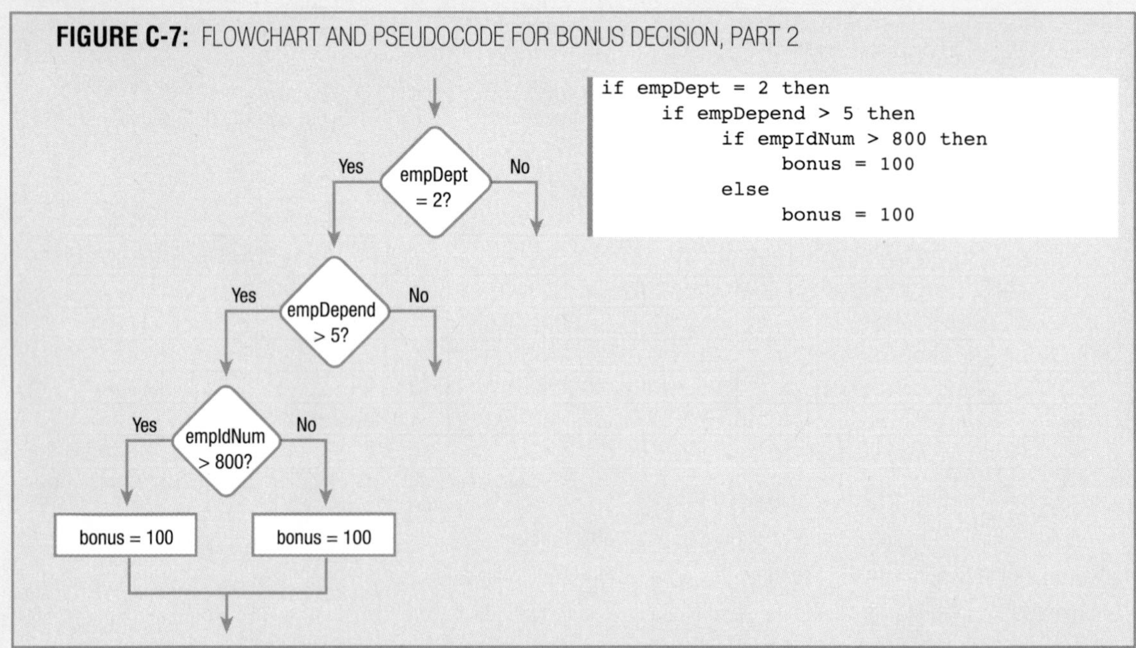


```
if empDept = 2 then
     if empDepend > 5 then
          if empIdNum > 800 then
               bonus = 100
          else
               bonus = 100
```

Continue the diagram in Figure C-7 by adding the "false" outcome when the `empDepend > 5` decision is No and the `empIdNum > 800` decision is Yes, which is represented by the third column in the decision table. In this case, the bonus is again $100. See Figure C-8.

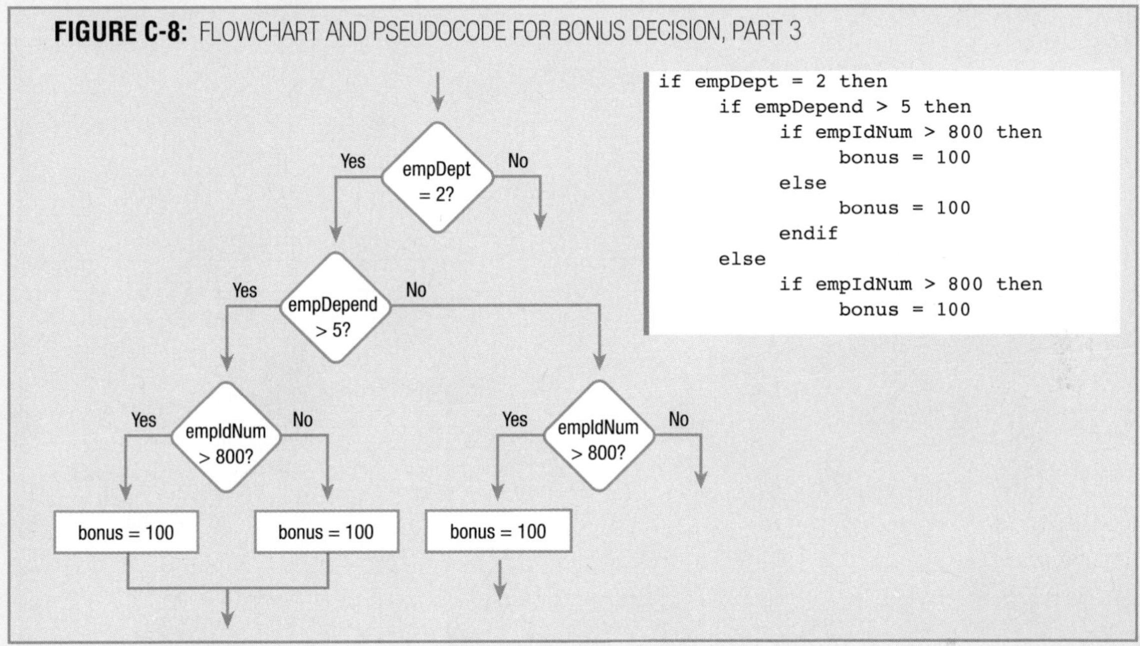


```
if empDept = 2 then
     if empDepend > 5 then
          if empIdNum > 800 then
               bonus = 100
          else
               bonus = 100
          endif
     else
          if empIdNum > 800 then
               bonus = 100
```

**FIGURE C-8:** FLOWCHART AND PSEUDOCODE FOR BONUS DECISION, PART 3

Continue adding decisions until you have drawn all eight possible outcomes, as shown in Figure C-9.

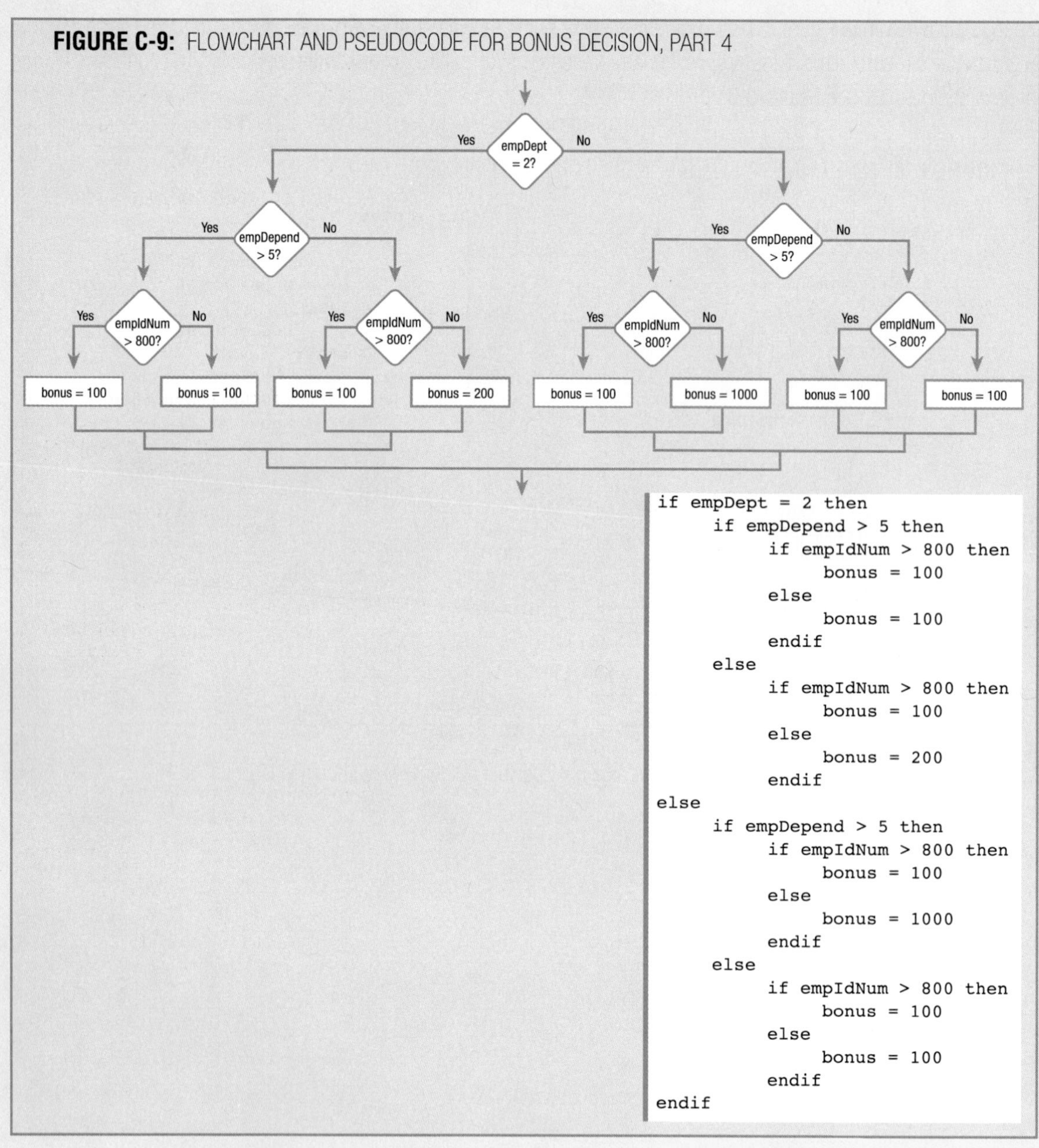


**FIGURE C-9:** FLOWCHART AND PSEUDOCODE FOR BONUS DECISION, PART 4

```
if empDept = 2 then
     if empDepend > 5 then
          if empIdNum > 800 then
               bonus = 100
          else
               bonus = 100
          endif
     else
          if empIdNum > 800 then
               bonus = 100
          else
               bonus = 200
          endif
else
     if empDepend > 5 then
          if empIdNum > 800 then
               bonus = 100
          else
               bonus = 1000
          endif
     else
          if empIdNum > 800 then
               bonus = 100
          else
               bonus = 100
          endif
endif
```

The logic shown in Figure C-9 correctly assigns a bonus to any employee, no matter what combination of characteristics the employee's record holds. However, you can eliminate many of the decisions shown in Figure C-9; you can eliminate any decision that doesn't make a difference. For example, if you look at the far left side of Figure C-9, you see that when `empDept` is 2 and `empDepend` is greater than 5, the outcome of `empIdNum > 800` does not matter; the `bonus` value is 100 either way. You might as well eliminate the selection. Similarly, on the far right, the `empIdNum` question makes no difference. Finally, many programmers prefer the True, or Yes, side of a flowchart decision always to appear on the right side. The result is Figure C-10.

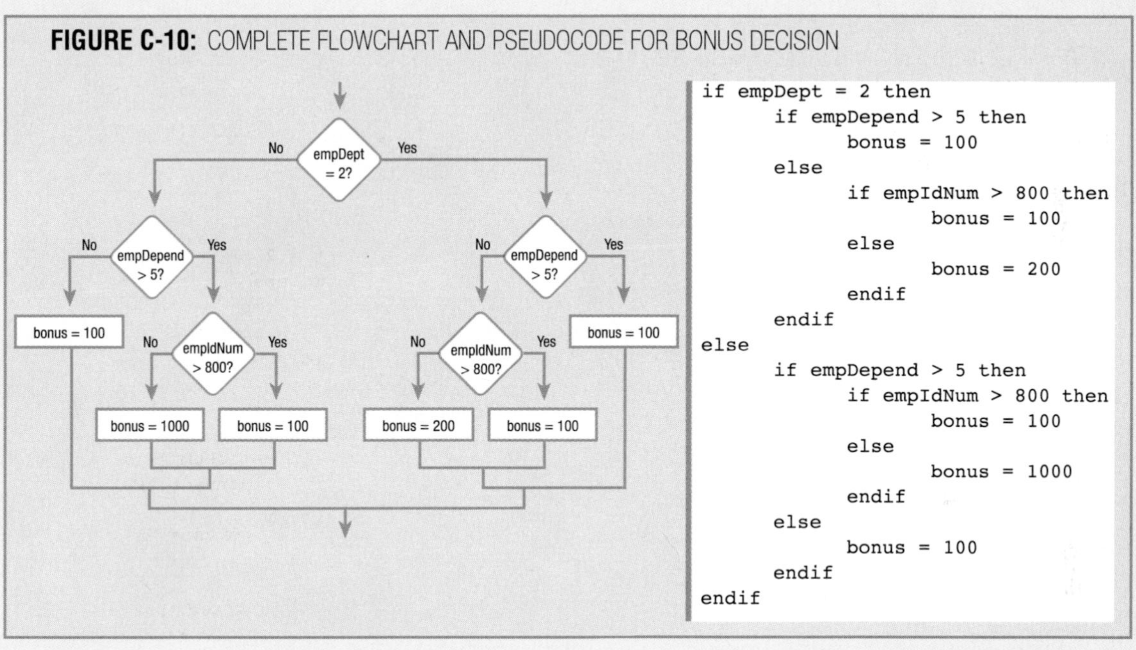


```
if empDept = 2 then
      if empDepend > 5 then
            bonus = 100
      else
            if empIdNum > 800 then
                  bonus = 100
            else
                  bonus = 200
            endif
      endif
else
      if empDepend > 5 then
            if empIdNum > 800 then
                  bonus = 100
            else
                  bonus = 1000
            endif
      else
            bonus = 100
      endif
endif
```

**FIGURE C-10:** COMPLETE FLOWCHART AND PSEUDOCODE FOR BONUS DECISION

# GLOSSARY

**abstraction**—The process of paying attention to important properties while ignoring nonessential details.

**accumulator**—A variable that you use to gather or accumulate values.

**algorithm**—The sequence of steps necessary to solve any problem.

**AND decision**—A decision in which two conditions must both be true for an action to take place.

**annotation symbol** or **annotation box**—A flowchart symbol that represents an attached box containing notes.

**arithmetic expression**—A statement, or part of a statement, that performs arithmetic and has a value.

**array**—A series or list of variables in computer memory, all of which have the same name but are differentiated with special numbers called subscripts.

**assignment operator**—The equal sign; it always requires the name of a memory location on its left side.

**assignment statement**—A programming statement that stores the result of any calculation performed on its right side to the named location on its left side.

**binary selection** or **binary decision**—A selection or decision structure that has an action associated with each of two possible outcomes. It is also called an if-then-else structure.

**block**—A group of statements that execute as a single unit.

**Boolean expression**—An expression that represents only one of two states, usually expressed as true or false.

**byte**—A unit of computer storage that can contain any of 256 combinations of 0s and 1s that often represent a character.

**calling module or calling program**—A module or program that calls a module.

**camel casing**—The format for naming variables in which multiple-word variable names are run together, and each new word within the variable name begins with an uppercase letter.

**cascading if statement**—A decision "inside of" another decision.

**case structure**—A structure that provides a convenient alternative to using a series of decisions when you must make choices based on the value stored in a single variable.

**central processing unit (CPU)**—The piece of hardware that processes data.

**character**—A letter, number, or special symbol such as "A", "7", and "$". *See also* data hierarchy.

**character constant**—In most programming languages, a character constant holds a single character. In this book, "character constant" is used synonymously with "string constant" to mean one or more characters enclosed within quotation marks. If a working program contains the statement `lastName = "Lincoln"`, then "Lincoln" is a character or string constant.

**character variable**—In most programming languages, a variable that holds a single character value. If a working program contains the statement `lastName = "Lincoln"`, then `lastName` is a character or string variable. In this book, "character variable" is used synonymously with "string variable" and "text variable".

**client**—A person who requests a program and who will actually use the output of a program. Also called a user.

**coding**—To write statements in a programming language.

**compiler**—Software that translates a high-level language into machine language and tells you if you have used a programming language incorrectly. Similar to an interpreter. However, a compiler translates all the statements in a program prior to executing any statements.

**connector**—A flowchart symbol used when limited page size forces you to continue the flowchart on the following page.

**control break**—A temporary detour in the logic of a program.

**control break field**—A variable that holds the value that signals a break in a program.

**control break program**—A program in which a change in the value of a variable initiates special actions or causes special or unusual processing to occur.

**control break report**—A report that lists items in groups. Frequently, each group is followed by a subtotal.

**conversion**—The entire set of actions an organization must take to switch over to using a new program or set of programs.

**counter**—Any numeric variable you use to count the number of times an event has occurred.

**data**—All the text, numbers, and other information that are processed by a computer.

**data dictionary**—A list of every variable name used in a program, along with its type, size, and description.

**data hierarchy**—The representation of the relationship of databases, files, records, fields, and characters.

**data type**—Describes the kind of values the variable can hold and the types of operations that can be performed with it.

**database**—A logical container that holds a group of files, often called tables, that together serve the information needs of an organization.

**dead path**—A logical path that can never be traveled. Also called an unreachable path.

**decision**—Testing a value.

**decision structure**—A programming structure in which you ask a question, and depending on the answer, you take one of two courses of action. Then, no matter which path you follow, you continue with the next task. Also called a selection structure.

**decision symbol**—A diamond shape that represents a decision in a flowchart.

**decision table**—A problem-analysis tool that consists of four parts: conditions, possible combinations of Boolean values for the conditions, possible actions based on the conditions, and the specific actions that correspond to each Boolean value of each condition.

**declaration**—A statement that names a variable and tells the computer which type of data to expect.

**declaring a variable**—To provide a name for the memory location where the computer will store the variable value and notifying the computer what type of data to expect. In contrast, when defining a variable, an initial value for the variable is also supplied.

**decrementing**—To decrease a variable, often by one.

**default value**—A value assigned after all test conditions are found to be false.

**defining a variable**—To provide a variable with a value, as well as a name and a type, when you create it. In contrast, when you are simply declaring a variable, the variable is not initialized.

**definite loop**—A loop for which you definitely know the repetition factor.

**delimiter**—A character that separates data items, such as a comma or space.

**desk-checking**—The process of walking through a program's logic on paper.

**detail line**—On a report, a line that contains data details. Most reports contain many detail lines.

**do until or do while loop**—A structure in which you ensure that a procedure executes at least once; then, depending on the answer to the controlling question, the loop may or may not execute additional times.

**documentation**—All of the supporting material that goes with a program.

**dual-alternative if**—A structure that defines one action to be taken when the tested condition is true and another action to be taken when it is false. Also called a dual-alternative selection or an if-then-else structure.

**dual-alternative selection**—A selection structure that has an action associated with each of two possible outcomes. Also called a dual-alternative if or an if-then-else structure.

**dummy value**—A preselected value that stops the execution of a program. *See also* sentinel value.

**early exit**—Leaving a loop before all scheduled repetitions—for example, as soon as a match is found.

**element**—Each separate variable in an array.

**else clause**—Part of a decision that holds the action or actions that execute only when the Boolean expression in the decision is false.

**end user**—A person who uses computer programs. Also called a user.

**end-of-job routine**—The steps you take at the end of the program to finish the application.

**eof**—An end-of-data file marker, short for "end of file."

**executing**—To have a computer use a written and compiled program. *See also* running.

**external program documentation**—The supporting paperwork that programmers develop before they write a program.

**external storage**—Persistent, relatively permanent storage outside the main memory of a computer, on a device such as a floppy disk, hard disk, or magnetic tape.

**field**—A single data item such as `lastName`, `streetAddress`, or `annualSalary`. *See also* data hierarchy.

**file**—A group of records that go together for some logical reason. *See also* data hierarchy.

**file description**—A document that describes the data contained in a file.

**flag**—A variable that you set to indicate whether some event has occurred.

**floating-point**—A value that is a fractional numeric variable and contains a decimal point.

**flowchart**—A pictorial representation of the logical steps it takes to solve a problem.

**flowline**—A line or arrow that connects the steps in a flowchart.

**footer**—A message that prints at the end of a page or other section of a report.

**footer line**—The end-of-job message line. Also called a footer.

**forcing**—Assigning a specific value to a variable, particularly when the assignment causes a sudden change in value.

**for statement**—A statement that is frequently used to code definite loops. Most often, it contains a loop control variable that it initializes, evaluates, and increments.

**function**—A small program unit. Functions are also called modules, subroutines, procedures, or methods.

**functional cohesion**—A quality of a module that determines the degree to which all the module statements contribute to the same task.

**functional decomposition**—The act of reducing a large program into more manageable modules.

**garbage**—The unknown value of an undefined variable.

**global variable**—A variable given a type and name once, and then used in all modules of the program.

**group name**—A name for a collection of associated variables.

**GUI**—Short for graphical user interface; an environment that uses screens to display program output. Users interact with GUI programs with a device like a mouse.

**hard copy**—A printed copy.

**hard-coded value**—A value that is explicitly assigned or used in a program.

**hardware**—The equipment of a computer system.

**heading line**—On a report, a line that contains the title and any column headings; usually appears only once per page.

**hierarchy chart**—A diagram that illustrates modules' relationships.

**high-level programming language**—A programming language that is English-like, as opposed to a low-level programming language.

**housekeeping**—A module that includes steps you must perform at the beginning of a program to get ready for the rest of the program.

**Hungarian notation**—A variable-naming convention in which a variable's data type or other information is stored as part of the name.

**identifier**—A variable name.

**if clause**—Part of a decision that holds the action that results when a Boolean expression in a decision is true.

**if-then**—Another name for a single-alternative selection structure.

**if-then-else**—Another name for a dual-alternative selection structure or dual-alternative `if` structure.

**implementation hiding**—Hiding the details of the way a program or module works.

**incrementing**—To add to a variable (often, to add 1).

**indefinite loop** or **indeterminate loop**—A loop for which you cannot predetermine the number of executions.

**index**—A subscript.

**infinite loop**—A loop that never stops executing; a repeating flow of logic without an ending.

**initialization loop**—A loop structure that provides initial values for every element in any array.

**initializing**—To provide a variable with a value when you create it, which is part of defining a variable.

**inner loop**—A loop that is contained within another loop. *See also* outer loop.

**input device**—A hardware device such as a keyboard or mouse; through these devices, data items enter the computer system.

**input symbol**—Represented as a parallelogram in flowcharts.

**integer**—A value that is a whole-number, numeric variable.

**interactive applications**—Applications in which the program interacts with a user who types data at a keyboard.

**internal program documentation**—The documentation within a program.

**internal storage**—Temporary storage within the computer; also called memory, main memory, primary memory, or random access memory.

**interpreter**—Software that translates a high-level language into machine language and tells you if you have used a programming language incorrectly. Similar to a compiler. However, an interpreter translates one statement at a time, executing each statement as soon as it is translated.

**iteration**—Repetition; another name for a loop structure. *See also* loop structure.

**line counter**—A variable that keeps track of the number of printed lines on a page.

**local variable**—A variable declared within the module that uses it.

**logic**—Instructions given to the computer in a specific sequence, without leaving any instructions out or adding extraneous instructions.

**logical AND operator**—A symbol that you use to combine decisions so that two (or more) conditions must be true for an action to occur.

**logical error**—An error that occurs when incorrect instructions are performed, or when instructions are performed in the wrong order.

**logical operator**—As the term is most often used, an operator that compares single bits. However, some programmers use the term synonymously with "relational comparison operator."

**logical OR operator**—A symbol that you use to combine decisions when any one can be true for an action to occur.

**loop**—A structure that repeats actions while some condition continues.

**loop body**—The set of statements that execute within a loop.

**loop control variable**—A variable that determines whether a loop will continue.

**loop structure**—A structure in which you continue to repeat actions based on the answer to a question.

**low-level detail**—A small, nonabstract step.

**low-level programming language**—A programming language not far removed from machine language, as opposed to a high-level programming language.

**lozenge**—A four-sided shape where the top and bottom sides are parallel straight lines and the left and right sides are convex curves; terminal symbols, or start/stop symbols, in flowcharts are lozenges.

**machine language**—A computer's on-off circuitry language; the low-level language made up of 1s and 0s that the computer understands.

**main loop**—The part of a program that contains the steps that are repeated for every record.

**main program**—The program that runs from start to stop and calls other modules.

**mainline logic**—The overall logic of the main program from beginning to end.

**major-level break**—A break caused by a change in the value of a higher-level field.

**method**—A small program unit. Methods are also called modules, subroutines, functions, or procedures.

**minor-level break**—A break caused by a change in the value of a lower-level field.

**mnemonic**—A memory device; variable identifiers act as mnemonics for hard-to-remember memory addresses.

**modularization**—The process of breaking a program into modules.

**module**—A small program unit. Programmers also refer to modules as subroutines, procedures, functions, or methods.

**multiple-level control break**—A break in which the normal flow of control breaks away for special processing in response to more than just one change in condition.

**named constant**—A constant that holds a value that never changes during the execution of a program.

**nested decision** or **nested if**—A decision "inside of" another decision.

**nesting**—To place a structure within another structure.

**nesting loop**—A loop within a loop.

**null case**—The branch of a decision in which no action is taken.

**numeric constant**—A specific numeric value.

**numeric variable**—A variable that holds numeric values.

**object-oriented programming**—A programming technique that focuses on objects, or "things," and describes their features, or attributes, and their behaviors.

**off-by-one errors**—Errors that usually occur when you assume an array's first subscript is 1 but it actually is 0.

**opening a file**—To tell the computer where the input is coming from, the name of the file (and possibly the folder), and preparing the file for reading.

**OR decision**—A decision that contains two (or more) decisions; if at least one condition is met, the resulting action takes place.

**out of bounds**—A subscript that is not within the range of acceptable subscripts.

**outer loop**—A loop that contains another loop. *See also* inner loop.

**output device**—A computer device such as a printer or monitor that lets people view, interpret, and work with information produced by a computer.

**output symbol**—Represented as a parallelogram in flowcharts.

**parallel arrays**—Two or more arrays in which each element in one array is associated with the element in the same relative position in the other array or arrays.

**posttest loop**—`Do while` and `do until` loops in which a condition is tested after the loop body has executed.

**precedence**—The quality of an operation that means it is evaluated before others.

**prefix**—A set of characters used at the beginning of related variable names.

**pretest loop**—A `while` loop in which a condition is tested before entering the loop even once.

**priming input** or **priming read**—The statement that reads the first input data record prior to starting a structured loop.

**print chart** or **print layout** or **printer spacing chart**—A tool for planning program output.

**procedural program**—A program in which one procedure follows another from the beginning until the end.

**procedural programming**—A programming technique that focuses on the procedures that programmers create.

**procedure**—A small program unit. Procedures are also called modules, subroutines, functions, or methods.

**processing**—To organize data items, check them for accuracy, or perform mathematical operations on them.

**processing symbol**—Represented as a rectangle in flowcharts.

**program comment**—A nonexecuting statement that programmers place within their code to explain program statements in English.

**program documentation**—The set of instructions that programmers use when they begin to plan the logic of a program.

**programming language**—A language such as Visual Basic, C#, C++, Java, or COBOL, used to write programs.

**prompt**—A message that appears on a monitor, asking the user for a response.

**pseudocode**—An English-like representation of the logical steps it takes to solve a problem.

**query**—A question that pulls related data items together from a database in a format that enhances efficient management decision making.

**range**—A series of values that encompasses every value between a high and low limit.

**range check**—A test that compares a variable to a series of values between limits.

**range of values**—A set of contiguous values.

**record**—A group of fields that go together for some logical reason. *See also* data hierarchy.

**relational comparison operator**—The symbol that expresses Boolean comparisons. Examples include =, >, <, >=, <=, and <>.

**reliability**—The feature of modular programs that assures you that a module has been tested and proven to function correctly.

**repetition**—Another name for a loop structure. *See also* loop structure.

**reusability**—The feature of modular programs that allows individual modules to be used in a variety of applications.

**rolling up the totals**—The process of adding a total to a higher-level total.

**running**—To have a computer use a written and compiled program. *See also* executing.

**saving**—To store a program on some nonvolatile medium.

**selection structure**—A programming structure in which you ask a question, and depending on the answer, you take one of two courses of action. Then, no matter which path you follow, you continue with the next task. Also called a decision structure.

**self-documenting program**—A program that describes itself to the reader through the use of comments and clear variable names.

**semantic error**—An error that occurs when a correct word is used in an incorrect context.

**sentinel value**—A limit, or ending value.

**sequence structure**—A programming structure in which you perform an action or task, and then you perform the next action in order. A sequence can contain any number of tasks, but there is no chance to branch off and skip any of the tasks.

**short-circuiting**—The compiler technique of not evaluating an expression when the outcome makes no difference.

**single-alternative if** or **single-alternative selection**—A selection structure where action is required for only one outcome of the question. You call this form of the selection structure an if-then, because no "else" action is necessary. *See also* unary selection.

**single-level control break**—A break in the logic of a program based on the value of a single variable.

**size (of an array)**—The number of elements it can hold.

**soft copy**—A screen copy.

**software**—Programs written by programmers that tell the computer what to do.

**sort**—To take records that are not in order and rearrange them to be in order based on some field.

**source code**—The readable statements of a program, written in a programming language.

**spaghetti code**—Snarled, unstructured program logic.

**stacking**—To attach structures end-to-end.

**standard input device**—The default device from which input comes, most often the keyboard.

**standard output device**—The default device to which output is sent, usually the monitor.

**string constant**—One or more characters enclosed within quotation marks. If a working program contains the statement `lastName = "Lincoln"`, then "Lincoln" is a character or string constant. In this book, "string constant" is used synonymously with "character constant."

**string variable**—A variable that holds character values. If a working program contains the statement `lastName = "Lincoln"`, then `lastName` is a character or string variable. In this book, "string variable" is used synonymously with "character variable" and "text variable."

**structure**—A basic unit of programming logic; each structure is a sequence, selection, or loop.

**submodule**—A module that is called by another module.

**subroutine**—A small program unit. Subroutines are also called modules, procedures, functions, or methods.

**subscript**—A number that indicates the position of a particular item within an array.

**summary line**—On a report, a line that contains end-of-report information. *See also* total line.

**summary report**—A report that does not include any information about individual records, but instead includes group totals and other statistics.

**syntax**—The rules of a language.

**syntax error**—An error in language or grammar.

**terminal symbol**—Represents the end of the flowchart; its shape is a lozenge. Also called a start/stop symbol.

**text variable**—A variable that holds character values. If a working program contains the statement `lastName = "Lincoln"`, then `lastName` is a text variable. *See also* string variable.

**total line**—On a report, a line that contains end-of-report information. *See also* summary line.

**trivial Boolean expression**—A Boolean expression that always evaluates to the same result.

**unary selection**—A selection structure where action is required for only one outcome of the question. You call this form of the selection structure an if-then, because no "else" action is necessary. *See also* single-alternative if or single-alternative selection.

**user**—A person who uses computer programs. Also called an end user.

**user documentation**—All the manuals or other instructional materials that nontechnical people use, as well as the operating instructions that computer operators and data-entry personnel need.

**variable**—A memory location whose contents can vary or differ over time.

**volatile**—The characteristic of internal memory, which loses its contents every time the computer loses power.

**while do loop**—A loop in which a process continues while some condition continues to be true. Also called a `while` loop.

**while statement**—A statement that can be used to code any loop.

**work field** or **work variable**—A variable you use to temporarily hold a calculation.

**zero-based array**—An array in which the first element is accessed using a subscript of 0.

# INDEX

## D

## J



## L



## M

## N



## O



## P

## T



## U



## V

## W